THE COGNITIVE-DEVELOPMENTAL PSYCHOLOGY OF JAMES MARK BALDWIN:

CURRENT THEORY AND RESEARCH IN GENETIC EPISTEMOLOGY

This Book Is the Second in the Series

PATH

PUBLICATIONS
FOR THE ADVANCEMENT
OF THEORY AND HISTORY
IN PSYCHOLOGY

Edited by David Bakan, *York University,*
John Broughton, *Teachers College, Columbia University,*
Howard E. Gruber, *Rutgers University,*
Miriam Lewin, *Manhattanville College,*
and Robert W. Rieber, *John Jay College, CUNY*

This is a series of volumes that display the following features:

▶ understanding of historical aspects of psychological theory and practice

▶ reflective examination of psychological theory

▶ awareness of the interconnections of psychology and other disciplines

▶ appreciation of the dialectical and philosophical nature of our subject matter

▶ frame of reference expressing a grasp of relationships between psychology and the political, economic and social problems of our times

Through PATH, we hope to publish works of a high scholarly quality that will avoid a narrow, empiricist approach to psychology. We favor books that avoid the traditions of alienation, anti-intellectualism, and obscurantism. We want to have a creative and productive influence on the future of psychological theory and research.

THE COGNITIVE–DEVELOPMENTAL PSYCHOLOGY OF JAMES MARK BALDWIN:

CURRENT THEORY AND RESEARCH IN GENETIC EPISTEMOLOGY

EDITED BY **JOHN M. BROUGHTON**
TEACHERS COLLEGE, COLUMBIA
UNIVERSITY
AND **D. JOHN FREEMAN-MOIR,**
CANTERBURY UNIVERSITY, NEW ZEALAND

ABLEX PUBLISHING CORPORATION
NORWOOD, NEW JERSEY   07648

Printed in the United States of America.

Library of Congress Cataloging in Publication Data
Main entry under title:

The Cognitive developmental psychology of James Mark
  Baldwin

  (Publications for the advancement of theory and
history in psychology); 2)
    Includes index.
    1. Cognition. 2. Genetic psychology. 3. Baldwin,
James Mark, 1861-1934. I. Broughton, John M.
II. Freeman-Moir, D. John. III. Series.
BF311.C5513   155   81-7885
ISBN 0-89391-043-0   AACR2

ABLEX Publishing Corporation
355 Chestnut Street
Norwood, New Jersey 07648

Dedication

For Doris and Ralph Broughton

and Joyce and Victor Moir

TABLE OF CONTENTS

ACKNOWLEDGMENTS TO PUBLISHERS

To A.M.S. Press (New York) for permission to quote Baldwin (1906) in Chapter 6, and Baldwin (1909) in Chapter 10.

To Augustus M. Kelley (Fairfield, N.J.) for permission to quote from Baldwin (1894) in Chapter 6.

To Paulist Press (Ramsey, N.J.) for permission to use figures and tables from Fowler (1977) in Chapter 10.

To Rand McNally (Chicago) for permission to quote Kohlberg (1969) in Chapter 9.

ACKNOWLEDGMENTS

The idea of this book was generated on a wet afternoon in 1975 at Peabody Terrace, Cambridge, Massachusetts, while we drank tea with Larry Kohlberg. He has certainly done as much as anyone to restore attention to Baldwin's work and to extend it in ways that Baldwin himself might have been quite sympathetic with. For his inspiration as a teacher, colleague, and friend, we offer our thanks.

We are most grateful to the following for the special assistance they have given in many different ways during the preparation of the book: David Bakan, Bart Berger, Renee Blumstein, James Fowler, Betty Freeman-Moir, Howard Gruber, the late Mary Howard, Joseph Lao, Benjamin Lee, Candice Leonard, Robert Rieber, Klaus Riegel, Rocky Schwarz, Jacques Vonèche, Sheldon White, Robert Wozniak, and Marta Zahaykevich.

John M. Broughton
D. John Freeman-Moir

BIOGRAPHICAL NOTES
ON CONTRIBUTORS

JOHN M. BROUGHTON is Associate Professor of Psychology and Education at Teachers College, Columbia University. English by birth, he was educated at Cambridge University and then at Harvard. He has also taught at Wayne State University in Detroit. His interests are in intellectual and personality development, political socialization, social theory, and the philosophy of the social sciences. He has published articles on perception, philosophical development, moral development, social cognition, the self, and ideology. He is involved in a longitudinal research study of adolescent and young adult ideology. He is currently completing a book of critical essays on Piaget and editing a collection of papers on developmental theory.

D. JOHN FREEMAN-MOIR is Lecturer in Education at the University of Canterbury in Christchurch, New Zealand. A New Zealander by birth, he was educated at Christchurch Teachers College, the University of Canterbury, and Harvard University. His basic concern is with the Marxist analysis of relationships between personality and social structure. His publications include articles on moral development, role-taking, and scientific thinking. He is currently doing research on school–work relationships in New Zealand.

HOWARD E. GRUBER is Professor of Psychology at the Institute for Cognitive Studies, Rutgers University, Newark. He was educated at Brooklyn College and has taught at the University of Colorado in Boulder, and at the Massachusetts Institute of Technology. His interests are in the case study method applied to evolving systems of thought in creative individual thinkers. He is the coauthor of *Darwin on Man* (1974), a National Book Award nomination. He is coeditor with J. Vonèche of *The Essential Piaget* (1977), and is currently working on a biography of Jean Piaget.

ROBERT H. WOZNIAK is McBride Lecturer in Education and Child Development, Bryn Mawr College. He was educated at the College of the Holy Cross and the University of Michigan. He has taught at the University of Minnesota, and Teachers College, Columbia University. His interests are in cognitive developmental psychology, cognition, perceptual processing, structuralism, Soviet psychology, and the history of psychology, and he has published widely in those areas.

J. JACQUES VONÈCHE is Professeur Ordinaire and holds the Chair in Child and Adolescent Psychology at the University of Geneva. Belgian by birth, he was educated at the University of Louvain and the University of Geneva. He has taught at Rutgers University, Newark, and at Clark University in Worcester, Massachusetts. His interests are in genetic epistemology, perception, hermeneutics, forms of literary expression, the history of the family, and educational reform. He is coeditor of *The Essential Piaget* (with H. Gruber, 1977), and of *Epistémologie Génétique et Équilibration* (with B. Inhelder and R. Garcia, 1977).

JEAN PIAGET, who died in 1980, was Director of the Centre International d'Epistémologie Génétique at the University of Geneva. Swiss by birth, he was educated at the University of Neuchâtel and later studied at the University of Zürich and the Alfred Binet Institute in Paris. He taught at the University of Neuchâtel and the Sorbonne. His interests were in genetic epistemology, biology, and logic, among other fields. During his lifetime, he published more than 50 books and monographs and literally hundreds of articles. His final publications in English include *The Development of Thought* (1977), *Behavior and Evolution* (1978), and *Intelligence and Adaptation* (1980).

DONALD T. CAMPBELL is New York State Board of Regents Albert Schweitzer Professor at Syracuse University. Previously, he was at Northwestern University. He is widely known for his work on social science research methodology (e.g., with J. C. Stanley, *Experimental and Quasi-Experimental Designs for Research* (1966)). He is a member of the National Academy of Sciences and Past President of the American Psychological Association.

BENJAMIN LEE is Research Director and Research Fellow at the Center for Psychosocial Studies, Chicago. He was educated at Johns Hopkins University and the University of Chicago. His interests are in semiotics, anthropology, literary criticism, and the social aspects of human development. He is coauthor of *The Development of Adaptive*

Intelligence (with Carol Feldman et al. 1974), editor of *Recent Approaches to the Self* (1982), and has also published on semiotics.

ERNEST WALLWORK is Associate Professor of Religious Ethics in the Department of Religious Studies, Yale University. He has also taught at Wellesley College and Union Theological Seminary. He is the author of *Durkheim: Morality and Milieu* (1972) and coauthor of *Critical Issues in Modern Religion* (1973).

MICHAEL PARSONS is Professor of Philosophy of Education at the University of Utah. English by birth, he was educated at Oxford University and the University of Illinois. His main interests are pragmatism, cognitive development (in general), aesthetic development (in particular), and teacher education. He has published a number of articles in these areas and has had a part in producing two books: *The Philosophy of Education: An Organization of Topics and Selected Sources* (1968) and *Philosophy of Education* (1974).

FOREWORD

Baldwin is not the only significant personage in history whose reputation has suffered a temporary eclipse. Piaget, after a meteoric rise, was all but forgotten for almost two decades. In my own otherwise excellent education there was hardly a whisper of his name. Then he was "rediscovered" in the mid-1950's, and his star rose again. Johann Sebastian Bach had to wait rather longer. For one hundred years after his death he was remembered only as a great instrumentalist, a master of the keyboard. His sons were esteemed as composers. Indeed Mozart said of Phillip Emanuel Bach, "He is the father, we are the children." But a century after Johann's death, lit up by the great enthusiasm of Mendelsohn, Schumann, and others, there was a great Bach revival which has not yet waned. Bach prepared the way for Bach prepared the way for Bach!

But why is there now a distinguished company busily rescuing Baldwin from oblivion? Unlike works of art, there is no urgent need to preserve the special aesthetic qualities of his compositions in the particular form Baldwin gave them. He wrote abstractly. Poetry is hard to translate and Swiss wine doesn't travel, but abstract ideas survive translation and paraphrasing, and manage transatlantic crossings very well. Why not simply exploit a few of Baldwin's main ideas, footnoting his name appropriately, and weave our own theoretical tapestry? Is this revival just an antiquarian exercise? If so, Baldwin is a poor subject: his works have not the patina of centuries.

I think there is a deeper reason. The present collaborative effort aims not only at a revival, but at seeing Baldwin *whole*. He struggled with the combined problems of growth and synthesis. This combination interests us today. Of course, there are many who do not see the need for it: in one widespread view of intellectual work, compartmentalized knowledge can grow without synthesis; when a particular task is presented, the requisite band of experts can assemble, not quite knowing how they came together; they can discharge their particular functions, carry out the task, then disband. No sense of self, no organic unity or continuity. But perfect know-how.

Baldwin's way was different. Going beyond pragmatism, he sought a larger vision. We, in our times, are embarking on a similar quest. The social disasters and intellectual disenchantments of the last 50 years reveal that we cannot rely on the blind operation of fragmented sciences to produce the *appropriate* growth of knowledge. We need to work harder and more wisely than ever to construct the necessary point of view, the necessary synthesis. Baldwin's effort toward system is for us a good point of departure. In contemporary life the cry is heard for "appropriate technology." We need also an appropriate epistemology.

It is interesting to compare Piaget and Baldwin in their attitudes toward truth. Neither was afraid of the word. Having grown up in an overly cynical and relativistic world, I find it cheering to know people who are comfortable with the idea of truth. Stirring. Piaget spoke of truth as a person forever fleeing from us, eluding our grasp—we approach it but never attain it. Baldwin's image is quite different. He spoke of truth as a psychological fact, something that could be ever-present in human experience. It occurs at the intersection of our way of thought with what we know of the world through acting in and upon it—the intercept of the domain of expectations or habits with the domain of fact. To be sure, such a truth can evolve, such a truth can never exhaust the riches of reality. Understood in this way, truth evolves without ever exhausting the riches of reality; but to say this is hardly to say that it is a meaningless idea. In Baldwin's view we are always constructing it and so we always clasp it. What an enviable frame of mind!

Although the present work is about one man, neither its authors nor its subject would subscribe to the Great Man Theory of History. Nor do I. But the Many Bricklayers Theory is not the only alternative. There are after all a few individuals who achieve greater vision, and if it is that vision we desire, we can try to stand where they stand, see with their eyes. Newton said, "If I have seen further it is because I stood on the shoulders of giants." Giants!

Darwin, Baldwin, and Piaget were men of larger vision, and although the differences among them are great, there is one line of thought that unites them, and that each advanced in his turn. I refer not merely to the evolutionary perspective which all three shared, but to a particular feature of it that is captured in the word *organism* if we read it the way Darwin wrote it, "organized beings."

Here is one of the supremely challenging questions: how do the manifold and seemingly piecemeal processes of evolution produce a series of organisms each of which is a *coherent* system? Similarly, how does the growing individual, ever-changing on many fronts, maintain his or her identity?

In the *Origin of Species* Darwin's main focus was on the way in which a set of small changes could permit an organism to evolve, to change in form and function so as to adapt and re-adapt to an ever-changing world. The theory of evolution through natural selection depends on the capacity of the organism to vary in a fragmentary way: change is not merely gradual; a host of separate characteristics vary and are selected *independently* of each other.[1]

At the same time, Darwin never lost sight of his aim to explain the occurrence of organized beings. In the *Origin of Species* he devoted a section to the "correlation of growth." Briefly, this meant that one change entails another, and a great part of evolutionary time and of the work of natural selection must go into the incessant re-harmonization of the organism. Any given evolutionary advance necessitates re-establishing the appropriate relationships of part with part. "Wholism" was certainly not Darwin's rallying cry, but he was aware of its demands and gave these matters much attention.

When Darwinian theory crossed the Atlantic, two quite different trends appeared: a synthetic approach, and an atomistic point of view that built on the piecemeal aspect of change in Darwin's theory. By and large the atomistic approach prevailed. Not only innovation but mass production was the next point on the social agenda. The technological-political means found for it was to destroy the organic character of work. The push for the division of labor and the transformation of workers into a collection of interchangeable parts was and still is mirrored in a persistent set of theoretical tendencies in psychology, notably the disparagement of the idea of the self and the neglect of the problem of internal organization.

This volume reveals how far Baldwin was from adopting this atomistic point of view. His ideas about organic selection, self, and reflectivity are fully presented and discussed. I would only re-iterate that, in enthusiastically supporting evolutionary theory, he transformed it. In Baldwin's view, each variation produced in the organism is not presented directly to the environment for the verdict of selection: first it goes through a complex process of internal or organic selection. On the psychological plane this is expressed in an image of humanity as a reflective species. Baldwin was not an early exponent of the model of divergent thinking—random variation

---

[1] A plausible account of the mechanism by which this might be accomplished did not become clear until the synthesis of Darwinism and Mendelism in the so-called "modern-synthesis" or neo-Darwinism.

followed by a separate process of selection. On the contrary, in his 1898 presidential address to the American Psychological Association, "On Selective Thinking," he ridiculed this scattershot image of thought ("scatterbrained" he called it) and spoke of human creativity as the product of purposeful, reflective thought.

It is true that Baldwin was hounded out of his job and country for an ostensibly personal incident. But it seems to me that he also found the European intellectual climate more congenial, and certainly, Europeans remained interested in him. In the 1909 Darwin Centennial, two speakers discussed Baldwin's principle of organic selection: August Weissman, the biologist, and C. Lloyd Morgan, the comparative psychologist.[2] More recently, the British biologist, Conrad Waddington has drawn upon and elaborated the idea. Baldwin and Waddington were each frequent visitors to Geneva. In his day, Baldwin was the friend and colleague of Edouard Claparède, who was to become Piaget's mentor; later, Waddington had the same collegial relationship with Piaget. In this volume the intellectual links among Baldwin, Waddington, and Piaget are examined.

How shall we think of all these personal and historical relationships? The point is certainly not that a new idea (e.g. organic selection) appears as a once-and-forever mutation, passed on from generation to generation of thinkers. Rather, each thinker has to reconstruct the idea for himself, and not as an isolated act but as part of a larger structure he is also constructing. In the process, he remakes his own environment, seeking out those thinkers, past and present, whose ideas have a structure similar to his own. Intellectual work, even when it seems at its loneliest, is a deeply collaborative process. But the social context of collaboration is in good measure constructed by the thinkers themselves. The web of past relationships presented in this volume, together with the new web now being spun in the making of it, are excellent examples of this world-making aspect of theoretical work.

One of the ideas that Baldwin pioneered was the constructive function of repetitive activity, for example in circular reactions with variations. It makes good sense to think that organic growth and change come about in this way. To be an organism, an organism must maintain its identity, its integrity. At the functional level, this means that it must do much the same today and tomorrow as yesterday. Small variations in this repetitive process make for change: "the assimilation of fortuitous events into strong structures," to borrow a phrase from Vonèche's chapter below.

---

[2] Weissman, Morgan, and a few others could rightly claim that they too had participated in the discovery of this principle, which is still known among geneticists as the "Baldwin effect."

We can apply these ideas to this volume. First, in the historical movement from Darwin to Baldwin to Piaget to the present, we do not see only variations in separate ideas, but in the structure as a whole—variations on a *vision*. Second, ideas and personages are not so much re-discovered as re-constructed. It is safe to say that the James Mark Baldwin of the present re-construction will prepare the way for some other events which will in turn provide a new platform for yet another re-construction.

As Parsons points out in his chapter below, in Baldwin's scheme "there were three major modes of experience: scientific, moral and aesthetic." For the most part the underlying epistemology of modern developmental psychology reflects a strong bias toward what is thought to be the scientific mode of experience: as a child's mind matures it resembles more and more the mind of a scientist.

Even research on moral development is only about moral judgment and to a small extent moral behavior. I doubt if the term "moral passion"—or any equivalent expression—occurs as often as once in one thousand pages of modern psychological discussion of moral development. Yet without passion the maintenance of morality is possible only in the palest human situations. To be morally present under difficult circumstances both requires and generates such passion.

Of course scientists are more than fact mongers, number crunchers and logic choppers. They do have great moral passions. They do devote great efforts to constructing world views of the kind Broughton discusses in this volume. And they do bring keen aesthetic sensibilities to bear on their scientific endeavours.[3] The narrow-gauge epistemology of contemporary psychology does justice neither to children nor to scientists.

The shape of Baldwin's intellectual growth was quite different from Piaget's or Darwin's. In Darwin's case, study of his early notebooks reveals that there was a protracted early struggle to develop a materialist philosophical platform for the evolutionary theory. This philosophical effort was neither the antecedent nor the consequent of the work in biological theory but contemporaneous with it. Each nourished the other. But when the theory of evolution was built, Darwin removed its philosophical scaffold and never published a word about it.[4]

In Piaget's case, study of his early published writing—almost juvenilia, now long forgotten and seemingly disconnected from his later logicising of human intelligence—a similar pattern appears.

---

[3] See *On Aesthetics in Science*, edited by Judith Wechsler, MIT Press, 1978.

[4] See Howard E. Gruber, *Darwin on Man: A Psychological Study of Scientific Creativity*, 2nd edition (University of Chicago Press, 1981).

Piaget, of course, always tried to be highly explicit about his episte-mological ideas and their relation to psychology. But at the start of his career there was another vector, moral passion. This was fully expressed in his prose poem, written in 1915 when he was 19: *La Mission de l'Idée*. In this long, idealistic *cri de coeur* Piaget espoused a Christian socialism and announced his faith in the eventual triumph of collective intelligence over egocentrism and greed. In this poetic setting, and in *Recherche (Quest)*, a philosophical novel he wrote in 1918, many of his more abstruse epistemological ideas found embry-onic expression. But as Piaget moved through his life, contending with a sceptical and positivist world, this grounding in moral passion became more and more concealed and perhaps somewhat desiccated.

Baldwin suffered no such progressive narrowing of his field of consciousness. Perhaps he was a system builder because he could not put social concerns, moral passion, and aesthetic experience to one side; perhaps he kept them in focus just because he was a system builder. Darwin and Piaget, for all their breadth of synthesis and their Herculean empirical works, were distinctly not system builders. Baldwin was, and this effort was his way of seeing humanity whole. Perhaps that is why we are remembering him today.

Howard E. Gruber
Institute for Cognitive Studies
Rutgers University

INTRODUCTION

In recent psychology, it has become customary to speak of two major paradigms, behaviorism and psychoanalysis, the "third force," humanistic psychology, and that child of the computer age, information-processing psychology. Yet in our contemporary discipline, there is a fifth force increasingly demanding recognition. This most recent contender for the title of "paradigm" is cognitive-developmental psychology.

Typically, this school of thought has been identified with a single author, Jean Piaget. Long considered merely a child psychologist (although he himself always denied it), Piaget now ranks with Freud as the most frequently cited person in the domain of the psychological sciences. As the validity and usefulness of his theorizing have been confirmed and its scope broadened by neo-Piagetians, Piaget's approach to mind has come to be seen less as a rather novel account of childhood and more as the basis of an alternative framework for psychology in general.

Piaget always preferred to describe himself as a genetic epistemologist, a specialist in combining biology and logic to generate fresh insight into the parallel growth of knowledge in cognitive development, the history of culture, and the evolution of the species. Increasingly, psychologists and other scholars in the social sciences and other disciplines find in Piagetian psychology a wedding of science to epistemology that challenges traditional concepts of the mind and traditional methods for studying it. This new paradigm, if we may call it that, restores the connection between science and theory of knowledge, a connection so willingly and deliberately dismantled by the last few generations of scientists.

As a paradigm becomes ascendant, its acceptance paradoxically renders conceivable its own obsolescence. So, while the Geneva School consolidates a position of new power and dominance, its opponents already foresee the end of a dynasty and scan the horizon for a new challenger. At the very time that genetic epistemology's impact is just beginning to be felt throughout the intellectual world, its claims are under the most intense attack within the narrower field of developmental psychology. There, it is "open season" on Piaget. His ideas are being taken most seriously and, at the same time, are being subjected to the most merciless scrutiny. Data, methods, concepts, theory, and metatheory are all equally grist for the critic's mill. Reactionary, revisionist, and radical alike look to form an uneasy alliance in opposition to Piagetian orthodoxy. What at first seemed so attractive about Piaget—the eclectic comprehensiveness of his approach—is now coming under the glare of the skeptical eye. Critics suspect that Piaget may have explained *too much*, so much that the heuristic value of his thinking has thereby been diminished. Piagetians, in turn, are closing ranks and engaging all the more energetically in the reinterpretation of texts, the creation of new distinctions, the broadening of applications, and the rebuffing of weak or misguided criticism. Other factions, neither pro- nor anti-Piaget, take a middle position and are exploring different post-Piagetian alternatives.

In the quest for truth, the opposition, defense, and nonaligned groups—all have reason to return to origins. How can Piaget be attacked, reinforced, or transformed more effectively by elucidating the roots of his ideas? How can an understanding of these foundations illuminate the real meaning and import of cognitive-developmental psychology? As the searchlight of inquiry now begins to turn back upon late nineteenth- and early twentieth-century psychology, an imposing figure can be dimly discerned in history's shadows. This mysterious individual developed a genetic epistemology nearly half a century before Piaget, brought into prominence the concepts of cognitive assimilation and accommodation, and proposed a progressive stage-by-stage intellectual development as a continuation and extension of principles of biological organization and adaptation. This important individual has occasioned the present volume. The shadowy figure who stands at the center of our concerns is James Mark Baldwin (1861–1934).

The first editor is fond of recounting a story from his own experience which illustrates Baldwin's reknown. As an undergraduate in England, he applied for a Kennedy fellowship to support a year's postgraduate study in social psychology at Harvard. The interview was an intimidating confrontation with twelve British notables, who were either scholars or nobility of repute. At a crucial point in the proceedings, one of the most eminent, Professor Sir Isaiah Berlin, leaned forward in his chair and asked with a kind but penetrating glance, "Are you aware of who founded the discipline of social psychology?" The accused, diminishing in size by every second, stammered an embarrassed admission of ignorance. The distinguished professor sat back in his chair, triumphantly answered himself, "William McDougall!" and rested his case.

As it turned out, a friend of the chagrined applicant, also pursuing an interest in social psychology, was the successful candidate in this competition. In a later comparing of notes, he divulged that in his interview the same professor had asked him the same question. The key to his success, he claimed, had been to outsmart his interrogator by responding "Floyd Allport, sir." Imagine the surprise of our editor several years later, after arriving on American shores under other auspices, when he discovered that both Allport and McDougall had been considerably antedated by a book entitled *Social and Ethical Interpretations in Mental Development: A Study in Social Psychology* (1898) by a certain James Mark Baldwin! For the first editor, therefore, there is a certain irony to the publication of the present volume. Doubtless, the eminent authority and the friend in question should each receive a review copy.

The professor and the friend are by no means the only culprits in this startling case of professional amnesia. Hardly anyone in any discipline seems aware of Baldwin's existence. Yet he was a man of great importance and influence in his day. In 1903, a survey of prominent psychologists by Cattell (1929) showed that his colleagues ranked Baldwin the fifth most eminent contributor to psychological research, ahead of such noteworthy competitors as Dewey and Titchener. Baldwin was also a founder and editor of the *Psychological Review*, editor of the *Psychological Bulletin*, and an early president of the American Psychological Association. It was Baldwin who, at the end of the last century, was able to summon the world's greatest minds in psychology and philosophy to a collective international task of unprecedented ambition and scope: the preparation of the four-volume *Dictionary of Philosophy and Psychology*.

Although it can justifiably be claimed that Baldwin was one of the founding fathers of social and developmental psychology and of sociology, his name is scarcely the household word one might expect. In a recent review of twelve introductory psychology textbooks, Mueller (1974) found not a single mention of Baldwin's name.

Mueller also analyzed the frequency of Baldwin citations in four major journals (two in psychology, two in sociology) and found that a total of 31 in the 1920s had sunk to a mere three in the 1960s. True, a few of the more historically minded contemporary psychologists, such as William Kessen, Sheldon White, Donald Campbell, and Howard Gardner, have tried to bring back our attention to the significance of Baldwin's work. Nevertheless, despite all of his accomplishments, Baldwin now almost completely escapes notice in the world of psychology. How could someone who played such a central role in the development of psychology as a discipline have faded so rapidly from the group memory?

As Mueller (1976) has pointed out, this amnesia can be attributed to a combination of factors. First, Baldwin bucked the positivist approach when in mid-career his thinking outstripped the available empirical tools, and he shifted his attention to the advance of theory rather than experimental fact. He also attempted to reinforce the relations between psychology and philosophy right at the point when G. S. Hall and others were vigorously "liberating" psychology from the authority of metaphysics and epistemology. In addition, he hardly fitted the other mold legitimate at the turn of the century: the applied scientist dedicated to the solution of concrete social problems, of immigration, urbanization, and industrialization (Cahan, 1978). Second, Baldwin failed to develop a cadre of students who would promote and develop his ideas. In this respect he was remarkably isolated. Third, like his colleague J. B. Watson, he suffered severe embarrassment when personal scandal forced him to resign from academic life in 1908 at the height of his prowess and move to Mexico and eventually to Paris.[1]

Despite his present lack of fame, Baldwin can justifiably be credited with constructing the first cognitive-developmental psychology. While the historical links between his theory and that of Piaget are clouded, as we shall see, Baldwin's ideas anticipate Piaget's to a remarkable degree (Cahan, 1978). Both approaches are undoubtedly rich and many-sided, and their differences as well as their similarities need to be taken into account in any truly comprehensive survey of developmental theory. Baldwin himself was highly complimentary in his one and only comment about Piaget, whose work he coupled

---

[1] The scandal erupted when Baldwin was discovered with black prostitutes in a Baltimore brothel. Baldwin convincingly protested that his visit had been the rèsult of a foolish practical joke (Mueller, 1974), but the scandal led someone to quip that his autobiography—originally called *Between Two Wars*—should be renamed "Between Two Whores." The scandal left a stigma on Baldwin's reputation that was never erased in American academic circles. Apparently the French laughed off the whole affair and warmly welcomed him to their country for the rest of his days.

with that of the Durkheim School as "the most promising" in the contemporary social sciences (Baldwin, 1930, p. 28). Nevertheless, Baldwin's ambition and scope do seem to exceed Piaget's. He lacks much of Piaget's precision and empirical flair, but there is something exhilarating about the grand scale of his total system. Many of the omissions or limitations of which Piagetian psychology is accused are not characteristic of Baldwinian psychology. This means that there are many problems of acute concern to Piagetians which could be helpfully illuminated by turning to Baldwin's theory.[2]

It was in this spirit of answering unanswered questions that we, the present editors, "discovered" Baldwin. Both of us had received a fairly traditional training in psychology. Both of us, in the later stages of this training, had begun to read Piaget extensively. Both of us arrived at Harvard around 1970, when genetic epistemology had already caught on there in a serious way. We became willing students of cognitive-developmentalism in the tradition of Piaget and Kohlberg. The latter had just published his influential state-of-the-art paper establishing the cognitive-developmental approach as a general paradigm of psychology (Kohlberg, 1969).

We retained a certain distance, however, a luxury which foreigners can perhaps afford. Therefore, we thrived on the lively critical exchanges within and outside the university. The growing popularity of Piaget seemed to be a source of considerable irritation to empiricists like Bruner and structuralists like Chomsky,[3] who in turn were hardly the closest of colleagues. The vital intellectual debate, combined with the climate of social change and political upheaval at that time, led us to deeper theoretical questioning of Piagetian ideas and eventually to a search for a more comprehensive synthesis. Independently of each other, we both chanced to settle upon Baldwin's theory, for reasons of its scope, its interdisciplinary quality, and its powerful amalgamation of cognitive development with social processes.

Since that time, we have had the good fortune to cross paths with a number of scholars from different fields who happened to share our concerns. This book is the outcome of that happy conver-

---

[2] This does not deny the many shortcomings of cognitive-developmental psychology, which are detailed in a number of recent analyses (Russell, 1978; Buck-Morss, 1975; Sullivan, 1978; Venn and Walkerdine, 1978; Freeman-Moir, 1978; Broughton, 1977, 1979a).

[3] In a recent conversation with Chomsky, Broughton was surprised to discover how far this structuralist linguist denied the validity of any aspect of Piaget's structuralist theory of cognitive development. In fact, Chomsky judges that the studies by Bever and others have provided a completely convincing empirical refutation of Piaget's claims, a judgment that has few adherents among developmental psychologists.

gence. It is, of course, no coincidence that all the contributors, whether philosophers or psychologists by trade, have combined in their studies interests in both philosophy *and* psychology. Nor is it happenstance that we have all pursued a historical orientation to those disciplines. After all, it was Baldwin who, with a particularly canny sense of the course of intellectual evolution, seized the historic moment in which philosophy and mental science achieved a new relationship.

Neither of the editors is, precisely speaking, a historian; hence this book is not strictly an annal in the history of psychology. Even if we were historians of psychology, we would not subscribe to the "great man" approach. We do not believe that developmental theory needs a pantheon for deceased heroes like the Baseball Hall of Fame. Nor do we take the necrophiliac's approach, which would lead to a post mortem on Baldwin's virtues and failures. We have no desire to pose as discoverers or promoters of a new unknown. There are enough stars in the firmament as it is. Baldwin is no savage waiting patiently in the jungle for anthropologists to capture and proudly bring home to the civilized world.

We are not suffering under the illusion that Baldwin is the Abraham of developmental psychology. The child development movement arose in America without any awareness of Baldwin's work (Broughton, 1979b). Even Piaget did not see any clear lines of influence running from Baldwin to himself, as he points out in this collection. In many ways Baldwin is noteworthy for his *lack* of long-term influence. This helped us to define our task. If Baldwin's work had been the exclusive formative power in the emergence of cognitive-developmental psychology, then his ideas would have already been transmitted to us more or less faithfully. Yet precisely the interruption of this transmission seems to have occurred. The odd term, like *circular reaction, assimilation,* or *deferred imitation* may have trickled down to the present, but the general gist of Baldwin's thinking is almost totally obscured. It would be tedious in the extreme for developmental psychologists to rediscover Baldwin's ideas one by one, as they researched specific problems in the field. The profession lends itself all too readily to fragmentation and packaging of part-ideas. Also, an unfortunate amount of kudos attaches to name-dropping, especially where the name has the half-familiar aura of a forgotten tribal totem.

To help forestall such fragmentary transmission and piecemeal reconstruction, we have tried to convey a holistic grasp of the man's theoretical vision. We have not tried to reconstruct his career. This has been ably done by Ronald Mueller (1974, 1976). (Although there is a rough correspondence between the order of chapters and the temporal sequence of phases in Baldwin's working life, historians will probably shudder at the lack of respect frequently shown here for historical rigor and specificity.) Nor have we endeavored to compile a systematic exegesis of Baldwin's concepts, a task skillfully completed by James Russell (1978, 1979). We have also steered clear of a bibliographic approach that proceeds systematically through each of his works. The several chapters here move in rather mysterious ways between and among different books in Baldwin's prolific *oeuvre*. Our watchword has been the splendid pronouncement of William James's:

> The whole Ph.D. industry of building up an author's meaning out of separate texts leads nowhere, unless you have first grasped his centre of vision, by an act of the imagination (1920, vol. 2, p. 355).

We hope at least to have initiated such an act of imagination.

This first part of the book comprises an assessment of Baldwin's intellectual biography and its place in the historical formation of psychology.

The second section deals with Baldwin's views on biology: on the understanding of evolution, and the evolution of understanding. Piaget's and Campbell's views are considered in relation to Baldwin's.

In the third section the focus shifts to Baldwin's psychology proper. Here we look at Baldwin's conception of the psychological function of mind and of intelligence as active, adaptive, and intersubjective. The relationship of his ideas to recent psychological and philosophical theory and research, including Piaget's, is outlined.

The fourth section looks at his genetic logic. In particular, this part focuses on his account of modes of scientific, philosophical, social, and moral thought. His account is related to empirically defined stage theories in modern cognitive-developmental psychology.

The fifth and final section treats the transcendent modes of consciousness—religion and art—as Baldwin conceives them in their genesis. Here, his speculative psychology is compared with modern cognitive-developmental theory and data on religious and aesthetic development.

These are some, but not all, of the intellectual domains touched by the synthetic mind of James Mark Baldwin. We have made a selection from his enormous repertoire, a deliberate choice intended to illuminate those parts of his work that are most fit to survive as the foundations for a cognitive-developmental psychology.

REFERENCES

Baldwin, J. M. In C. Murchison (Ed.), *The history of psychology in autobiography, vol. 1.* Worcester, Mass.: Clark Univ. Press, 1930; London, England: Oxford Univ. Press, 1930. (Reprinted by Russell & Russell, New York, 1961.)

Broughton, J. M. "Beyond formal operations": theoretical thought in adolescence. *Teachers College Record*, 1977, *71*, (9), 87–98.

Broughton, J. M. Structuralism and developmental psychology: without self, without history. In H. K. Betz (Ed.), *Recent approaches to the social sciences.* Winnipeg: Hignell Printing, 1979.(a)

Broughton, J. M. Child psychology in North America. Paper presented at the conference on Theological Anthropology of the Child, Celigny, Switzerland, 1979.(b)

Buck-Morss, S. Socio-economic bias in Piaget's theory and the cross-culture controversy. *Human Development*, 1975, *18*, 35–49.

Cahan, E. The comparative historical fates of James Mark Baldwin and Jean Piaget. Unpublished honors thesis, Radcliffe/Harvard Colleges, 1978.

Cattell, R. B. Psychology in America. *Science*, 1929, *70*, 335–347.

Freeman-Moir, D. J. Piaget and imagination: The limits of a perspective. Paper read at the annual conference of the New Zealand Psychological Society, Christchurch, 1978.

James, W. *The letters of William James* (Henry James, ed.). Boston: Atlantic Monthly Press, 1920.

Kohlberg, L. Stage and sequence: The cognitive-developmental approach to moralization. In D. Goslin (Ed.), *Handbook of socialization theory and research.* Chicago: Rand McNally, 1969.

Mueller, R. H. The American era of James Mark Baldwin (1893–1903). Unpublished doctoral dissertation, University of New Hampshire, 1974.

Mueller, R. H. A chapter in the history of the relationship between psychology and sociology in America: James Mark Baldwin. *Journal of the History of the Behavioral Sciences*, 1976, *12*, 240–253.

Russell, J. *The acquisition of knowledge.* New York: St. Martin's Press, 1978.

Russell, J. The status of genetic epistemology. *Journal of the Theory of Social Behaviour*, 1979, *9*, 14–26.

Schultz, D. P. *A history of modern psychology.* New York: Academic Press, 1960.

Sullivan, E. V. A study of Kohlberg's structural theory of moral development: A critique of liberal social science ideology. In P. Scharf (Ed.), *Readings in moral education.* Minneapolis, Minn.: Winston, 1978.

Venn, C., & Walkerdine, V. The acquisition and production of knowledge: Piaget's theory reconsidered. *Ideology and Consciousness*, 1978, *3*, 67–94.

PART I

INTELLECTUAL BIOGRAPHY AND THE HISTORY OF PSYCHOLOGY

Introduction

Despite the relative brevity of Baldwin's professional involvement in philosophy and psychology, he produced a substantial body of work: a score of books and 150 papers and articles. These are of special interest in understanding the roots of psychology, since Baldwin was a midwife at the birth of the discipline and one who took an active interest in every aspect of the infant's well-being. However, like most theorists who are both innovative and copiously productive, James Mark Baldwin presents any interested reader with a cognitive dilemma. His ideas are not at all easy to assimilate. Psychologists who refer to Baldwin tend to do so in a rather superficial fashion, showing little sign of having tried to understand the man's work. Various important things are vaguely attributed to Baldwin, for example, the concept of "adualism" in infancy, the theory of "symbolic interactionism," the first notion of "stages" in development, and so on. This, however, is a fetishization of Baldwin's

9

work. Rarely is any attempt made to fit these parts into a comprehensive, meaningful whole.

The sad truth is that Baldwin cannot be approached in a purely intellectual manner. He is the kind of thinker that one can come to know only motorically. That is, one must almost physically grapple with his work for a long time before one can begin to get a feel for it. One of the chief obstructions to a quick understanding is the sheer scale of Baldwin's enterprise. It was in the very nature of the task that he set himself to present the most comprehensive framework he could for a general psychology. To Baldwin, this meant embracing epistemology, philosophy of science, intellectual history, ethics, aesthetics, theoretical biology, anthropology, sociology of knowledge, the theory of meaning, and more besides. He passes with abandon from one discipline to another, eliding them with discomforting ease. If one finds Piaget interdisciplinary, one will find Baldwin transdisciplinary. Piaget appropriates only the selected parts of philosophy (logic and epistemology) which he finds adapted to his particular account of natural scientific knowledge. Baldwin, on the other hand, embraces *all* of philosophy and at a level where it is not yet separated from *all* of science. Figure 1 shows Baldwin's own vision of how his work stood in relation to, and synthesized, the various schools of scientific and philosophical thought, from their seventeenth century religious roots down to the pragmatic and rationalist paradigms of his own day.

What makes an understanding of Baldwin additionally difficult is that his thinking underwent severe changes. It is perhaps no coincidence that a man who formulated the earliest psychological conception of broad, systematically structured stages and qualitative sequences in intellectual evolution should exhibit in his own conceptual development breadth and systematic character of thought combined with dramatic transformations of its total structure. Although at any one time, Baldwin's thought appears comprehensive and virtually complete, at the next, it is reorganized into a qualitatively different whole.

It is this interplay of structure and transformation that Wozniak explicates in Chapter 1. Concentrating on the early period of Baldwin's intellectual development, Wozniak describes in detail the emergence of his interest in the relation of philosophy to science, of rationalism to empiricism, and of biology to psychology. These preoccupations defined a set of concerns that continued to be relevant to Baldwin's enterprise thereafter. As Wozniak carefully documents, however, Baldwin's personal paradigm underwent two major reformulations, graduating from mental philosophy and evolutionist psychology to the genetic epistemology for which he is best known.

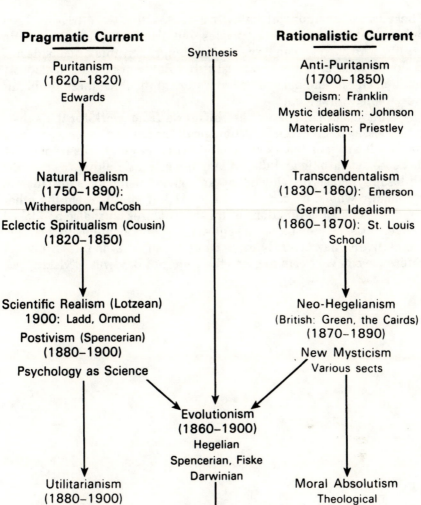

FIG. 1: The Development of Philosophical Thought in America (from Baldwin 1926)

These transformations of Baldwin's perspective were triggered not only by internal cognitive struggles, but also by key experiences in his life. The changes can be rendered comprehensible by considering both the general intellectual tasks that Baldwin so perspicaciously set himself and the particular environment in which these problems were being worked out.

This historical chapter establishes a framework for the subsequent essays. Like the psychological theory that emerged from Baldwin's arduous but exciting intellectual odyssey, this framework has both synchronic and diachronic dimensions. Baldwin's scientific philosophy must be viewed at any given point as a broad and systematic whole, a "cognitive structure," if you like. On the other hand, the changing functions of these structures must also be looked at over time, as they undergo sequential reorganizations that lead to qualitatively new worldviews. Only in such a double frame of reference can we begin to grasp the center of Baldwin's "vision."

1

METAPHYSICS AND SCIENCE, REASON AND REALITY: THE INTELLECTUAL ORIGINS OF GENETIC EPISTEMOLOGY

Robert Wozniak[1]
Bryn Mawr College

Among the participants in the late nineteenth century transformation of American psychology from faculty-oriented "intuitionalism" to the "new scientific experimentalism", there is hardly a more interesting figure than James Mark Baldwin.[2] Of those few individuals who constituted the first generation of American experimentalists, only Baldwin had deep intellectual roots in the "mental philosophy" tradition which had dominated American higher education during the nineteenth century.[3] At the same time, however, Baldwin was

---

[1] This essay was prepared while the author held a visiting appointment in the Psychology Department, Teachers College, Columbia University. For their critical commentary on an earlier draft, the author would like to express sincere appreciation to John Gach, Howard Gruber, Malcolm Kottler, Jonas Soltis, Sheldon White, William Woodward, and, especially, to this volume's first editor, without whose constant encouragement, this chapter would never have been written.

[2] Baldwin was born in Columbia, South Carolina, January 12, 1861. What little is known of his early life comes almost entirely from *Between Two Wars* (1926). These reminiscenses suggest an unexceptional childhood, suffused with the religious values typical of the time.

[3] Most first generation "experimentalists" in the United States were influenced by Wundt: Cattell, Scripture, Titchener and Münsterberg directly, Delabarre (under Münsterberg) and Bryan (under Külpe), indirectly. James had been trained in medicine and physiology. Hall, though taught by Hopkins at Williams, showed more the influence of Wundt and James. Jastrow and Sanford studied under Hall. Ladd and Dewey, though unquestionably well-grounded in the mental philosophy tradition, were not really "experimentalists."

also characteristically devoted, especially in his early years, to fostering the growth of laboratory experimentation.[4] As a consequence, many of the conceptual and methodological contradictions inherent in the conflict between philosophy and science which characterized the transformation of psychology can be found deeply embedded in the structure of Baldwin's thought. It was, in fact, toward a reconciliation of these contradictions that Baldwin explicitly oriented his primary theoretical work; and it was as a transformational figure, working toward a synthesis of philosophy with science in the study of the human mind, that Baldwin perceived himself (Baldwin, 1889a, pp. iii–v).

As might be expected of such a figure, Baldwin was himself the subject of a series of intellectual transformations. So great, in fact, are the differences in conceptual structure and content among his major books (compare 1889a, 1895a, and 1906-11), that one at first wonders if perhaps there might not have been three Baldwins at work: a mental philosopher (roughly to 1889), an evolutionary psychologist (approximately 1889–1903), and an evolutionary epistemologist (1903–1915). Yet it may be argued that these successive transformations in the structure of Baldwin's thought reflected the exercise of an invariant function[5], a consistent striving to resolve the contradictions inherent in the clash between the old psychology and the new, between philosophy and science, between internal description and external experimentation, between reason and material reality.

In order to lay the foundation for this assertion, this account will first focus on the formative period of Baldwin's intellectual career, that period extending roughly from 1881 to 1887 and eventuating in the production of a framework for his integrative mental philosophy. This will be followed by shorter sketches of the periods of transformation to evolutionary psychology and evolutionary epistemology, respectively. These sketches will be presented both to illustrate the functional continuity underlying these transformations and to indicate a direction for future, more detailed work on the latter part of Baldwin's intellectual career.

---

[4] Baldwin founded laboratories at Toronto and Princeton, reopened Hall's lapsed laboratory at Johns Hopkins, encouraged the publication of experimental research in the *Psychological Review* which he cofounded with Cattell, and used his influence to further the careers of "laboratory men" such as Kirschmann, Warren, Stratton, and Watson.

[5] For discussion of a model of intellectual development which views structural transformation as reflecting invariant function, see Piaget (1950).

Formative Period, 1881–1889

Princeton and McCosh, 1881–1884

In the fall of 1881, Baldwin entered Princeton's sophomore class, electing a course sequence which "turned out graduates nurtured mainly on linguistic study, philosophy and the rudiments of science" (Baldwin, 1926, p.19). Here, under the influence of the astronomer, Charles Young, and the geologist, W. B. Scott, Baldwin developed a lifelong respect for scientific method and for the place of scientific work in the university (Baldwin, 1926, p. 23). By his senior year, however, Baldwin had found himself increasingly attracted to philosophy, and, at Princeton in the early 1880s, "philosophy" was synonymous with the Scottish "intuitional realism" of President James McCosh (Baldwin, 1926, p. 31; see Ormond, 1903, for a brief but instructive biographical notice of McCosh). Of all the formative factors in Baldwin's intellectual development, none is of greater importance than that of McCosh. For this reason, it will be worthwhile to consider both the man and his thought at some length.

McCosh as a man of balance. Personally and professionally, McCosh was a man of balance, a man who avoided extremes in every form and who constantly sought truth in the middle road. Princeton philosophy professor, Alexander Ormond (1903), wrote shortly after the death of McCosh:

> As Philosopher and educator he combined in a remarkable degree progressiveness with true conservatism. He was an embodiment of the living spirit of his time, and yet tenacious in clinging to whatever had born the test of experience and proved itself permanently worthy. The factor of highest significance in his work is to be found, I think, in that strong and wise balance which he strove to maintain everywhere between opposite tendencies and in his firm belief that in such balance lies the secret of all true and healthy progress (p. 360).

That Baldwin was also deeply impressed by this characteristic is well reflected in his (1926) recollections of the "library meetings" which McCosh occasionally held in his home:

> The president in the chair held the balance firm between the two poles—Idealism and Materialism. "No," he would exclaim, pounding the table, "this table is real," in answer to all the subtleties of the Berkeleyan or Kantian analysis; or again, "the soul is real," against the refinements of pantheism on the one hand or the materialist deductions made from brain physiology or from Spencerian sensationalism, on the other (p. 20).

This tendency toward balance in McCosh was also manifest in another way. Although an ardent theist, he found no difficulty in remaining receptive to the new scientific conception of man which had begun to unfold in the latter half of the nineteenth century. As early as 1871, McCosh (1871) had declared himself open to a form of evolutionism and by 1881, within only seven years of its publication, McCosh had introduced Wundt's *Grundzüge der Physiologischen Psychologie* to Princeton (Baldwin, 1926, p. 21)[6]. Indeed, as Ormond (1903) has suggested:

> There is . . . an important respect in which much of McCosh's thinking was transitional in its character. The formative period of his own education fell at a time when there were many portents of a new order of conceptions that were, however, only foreshadowed in the thought of the time. Darwin's *Origin of the Species* and Spencer's *First Principles* belonged as yet to the secrets of the future. When the former appeared and revolutionized biology, and the latter heralded a corresponding change in the concepts of philosophy, McCosh was penetrating enough to see that the old truths could be adjusted to the new forms and he showed the largeness of his mind in the hospitable attitude he was able to take toward the new concepts that had invaded science and philosophy (p. 352).

McCosh and intuitional realism Philosophically, McCosh was the last of a long line of Scottish philosophers (McCosh, 1875) who had constructed a theistic epistemology on the twin pillars of intuitionalism and realism. By far the clearest statement of the "intuitional realist" position appears in McCosh's *Intuitions of the Mind* (1872).[7] First, intuitionalism is a form of nativism. Intuitions are aspects of the fundamental constitution of the human mind present in all men at birth. Second, although a nativism, intuitionalism is, for McCosh, definitely not an *a priorism*. This is true in both the methodological and epistemological senses in which the *a priori* may be taken. Methodologically, the intuitionalist inquiry into the nature and

---

[6] There is some confusion regarding both this date and the likelihood that Baldwin participated in the group which read the *Grundzüge* (Wundt, 1873–1874) at Princeton. Baldwin quotes a letter from H.F. Osborn, dated October, 1901, to the effect that during the winter, 1881–1882, McCosh talked "frequently about a course in physiological psychology . . . (and in) the following winter (1883–1884) we began this course." The following winter, of course, would have been 1882–1883, not 1883–1884, and in the highly structured course sequence at Princeton, Baldwin, then only a junior, would very likely have been unable to attend. The fact that Osborn, writing to Baldwin, provides details of the course which Baldwin might have been expected to know if he had been there also suggests that he did not attend.

[7] First published in 1860, *Intuitions of the Mind* (McCosh, 1872) appeared in its final form in a third revised edition in 1872. All citations are to this edition. That this represents the view McCosh still held in the early 1880s, when Baldwin attended Princeton, is evident from a comparison with McCosh (1880).

existence of native principles, "into the place which they hold in the constitution of the mind, into the laws by which they are guided, and the way in which they manifest themselves" (McCosh, 1872, p.2) proceeds not by *a priori* philosophical reasoning, but by induction from observed facts in self-consciousness. As McCosh (1872) puts it, "By introspection we may look on them (intuitions) in operation; by . . . analysis we may separate the essential peculiarity from the rough concrete presentations; and by generalization, we may rise to the law which they follow" (p.3). Intuitions, in other words, may be native, but inquiry into their nature requires a rigorous induction from introspected experience.

Similarly, the intuitional epistemology is opposed to the view that intuitions impose forms on things or give to the object what is not in the object. Rather, intuitions are simply the instruments by which we come to discover what is in the object. In the words of McCosh (1872):

> The mind, in looking at a material object, does not superinduce extension on it, but it observes that it is in space and must be in space. It does not carry with it a chain, wherewith to connect events . . . but it has a capacity to discover that events are so connected . . . to reflect (the object) as it is . . . The truth is perceived by the mind, not formed; it is cognized, not created . . . Our minds, in intuition, gaze directly on the object . . . as it were face to face, and with nothing coming between to aid the view on the one hand, or obstruct it on the other (p.17; pp.38–39).

It is in precisely this sense that intuitionalism is a natural realism.

Third, intuitionalism does not argue for the existence of either innate mental images or innate abstract or general concepts. We can imagine or recall external or internal experiences through images (or McCosh's preferred term, "phantasms") which reproduce past experience, but we are not born with a stock of such images ready to emerge. Similarly, although all cognitions[8] by the senses or by self-consciousness and all subsequent images are singular and concrete, the mind has the capacity to form abstract and general concepts. Concepts abstracted from concrete objects (e.g., "whiteness" from a white cloud) or generalized over single instances (e.g., the class of all men) are, like mental images, formed in experience. They are not innate.

Rejection of innate concepts, however, is not meant to imply that the process of concept formation itself is free from the regulation of innate principles, nor is it to suggest even that aspects of singular, concrete sense cognition which provide the experience from which

---

[8] Cognitions here has the sense of immediate, knowing contact.

concepts are formed are free from the regulation of such principles. On the contrary, intuitions regulate experience from birth. However, and this is a critical point, intuitions are always *of objects in experience*. Hence, intuitions require the presentation of appropriate objects in order to be called forth in appropriate mental action. It is through reflection on mental action elicited by objects in experience that abstract and general concepts are formed.

Finally, intuitionalism is not the view that native principles are, *as principles*, immediately available to consciousness. Rather, intuitive principles regulate cognitions, beliefs, and judgments by operating as native laws or rules of which we are not consciously aware. Consciousness has immediately before it only mental acts as regulated by the intuitive principles, and it is from a careful observation and analysis of these acts that accurate inductions concerning the principles can be formed.

Essentially, then, intuitionalism is the view that the human mind is constituted by innate rules or principles which regulate the original actions and primitive perceptions of the mind. These principles, intuitive principles, are the fundamental laws of thought. Intuitions are native tendencies to mental action, common to all men, and operating when appropriate objects are presented to call them forth. Although mental actions as regulated by the intuitive principles may be observed in conscious self-reflection, the intuitions themselves, as regulative, cannot. Furthermore, their operation depends only on the presentation of appropriate objects and not in any direct way on the will of the knower.

McCosh's influence on Baldwin. It is impossible to overestimate the extent to which Baldwin was influenced by McCosh, both as man and as thinker. McCosh was a man of balance; and as we shall see, much of Baldwin's work can and should be read as reflecting this same striving to maintain an integrative equilibrium between opposing tendencies. McCosh was transitional, willing to entertain the new ideas of evolution and of an experimental, physiological psychology, and it was through McCosh that Baldwin received his first introduction to both of these innovations. Finally, McCosh was, first and foremost, a theistic epistemologist, concerned to ground faith and morality on rational intuition, self-consciousness and natural realism. From McCosh, Baldwin adopted his unswerving commitment to reason, his belief in the existence of a separate and primary order of mental facts in consciousness, his realistic metaphysics, and his own concern with the psychological justification of morality.

Yet, if McCosh was transitional, his work was not. If he possessed sufficient breadth of intellect to allow the new conceptions to exist side by side with the old, he did not possess the ability to restructure the old to accommodate the new. As Ormond (1903), after discussing McCosh's positive inclination toward evolution, pointed out: "This attitude is all the more remarkable in view of the fact that he never became an evolutionist himself in his fundamental thought, and was never able to enter into and fully possess the new territory that had been opened up" (p. 352).

Much the same may be said of McCosh's relation to the new physiological psychology. Despite his interest in Wundt and his being among the first (McCosh, 1880) in the United States to call attention to both Carpenter's (1874) *Mental Physiology* and Ferrier's (1876) *Functions of the Brain*, McCosh was never really able to integrate the conceptions of the new psychology into his own natural realism. His was still the method of pure inductive introspection, the only method appropriate to the discovery of intuition in self-consciousness. The external experiment of the new psychology was foreign to his thinking. Just as McCosh never became an evolutionist, neither did he ever become a new psychologist. Philosophy, not science, provided him with his view of the human mind.

Perhaps for that reason, McCosh was able to rest content with a philosophical system which defined away that problem which constitutes the very heart of the relation of philosophy to science, the problem of the validation of knowledge, of the correspondence between reason and material reality. As McCosh well knew, any form of nativism can all too easily lead to a view of the external world as a mere projection of mind. From McCosh's (1872) point of view, the only means to avoiding this trap was adherence "to the natural doctrine . . . that the mind is so constituted as to know the object as it is, under the aspects in which it is presented to it" (p.18). Intuition and reality-in-itself, in other words, must exist in a kind of pre-established harmony, "a correspondence whereby the one knows and the other is known," (McCosh, 1872, p.17). For McCosh, this harmony is itself intuitive, a self-evident truth which must serve as a starting principle for inductive analysis.

The problem with this view, of course, is that it is fundamentally antiscientific. Knowledge is valid because knowledge is valid; and the ground on which philosophy meets science is abruptly ruled off limits. It is hardly any wonder, given this perspective, that McCosh could not adequately integrate the experimental method into his descriptive, introspectionist psychology and the new evolutionary, physiological science of man into his intuitional realist philosophy. His view of the relation of reason to reality precluded it.

Thereby hangs the central thread of James Mark Baldwin's intellectual development. Very early on, as we shall see, Baldwin conceived the task of effecting just what McCosh had been unable to accomplish. To achieve this, Baldwin had somehow to conserve what was to him self-evident in natural realism, i.e., its realism and its intuitional rationalism. Yet, at the same time, he had to restructure the conception, first to accommodate experimental science—to strike a balance in the best tradition of McCosh between internal and external method, between philosophy and science, and then to accommodate evolutionary science—to strike the more difficult balance between reason and material reality, between thought and things.

Leipzig and Berlin, Wundt and Spinoza, 1884–1885

Graduating from Princeton in the summer of 1884, Baldwin was awarded the Green Fellowship in Mental Science, the terms of which provided for a year's study in Germany (Baldwin, 1926, p.31). Although Baldwin had had some general introduction to the methods of Wundt, it is difficult to know whether he had yet become aware of the contradictions between the old psychology and the new. Be that as it may, his first semester in Germany, spent in Wundt's Leipzig laboratory, brought him face to face with the radical differences which existed between the methods of Leipzig and those of Princeton and served to give him a sense of both the spirit and the method of the new experimental science. He emerged, as he put it, "an enthusiast for the new psychology . . . (with) the full outfit of ideas—Fechner's and Weber's laws, the technique of reaction-time experiments, theories of mind and body, and cognate points of view as propounded by Lotze, Fechner and Wundt" (Baldwin, 1926, p.32).[9]

From Leipzig, Baldwin traveled to Berlin to attend Paulsen's seminar on Spinoza (see Paulsen, 1938, for general biographical information). Although he had often heard McCosh rail against "the great pantheist" and had, in fact, been attracted to Spinoza "by a natural curiosity . . . after hearing McCosh" (Baldwin, 1926, pp.19–20), Baldwin must have been rather surprised to find in Spinoza a powerful logical justification for what had been taken at Princeton to be a self-evident, intuitive maxim, that is, the pre-established coordination of the world of ideas with the world of extension, of reason

---

[9] It should be noted, however, that this statement is misleading on several counts. First, as will be discussed, there is reason to believe that Baldwin's real sense of the new psychology came more from a close reading of Ribot (1886) than it did from actual study with Wundt. Second, as Baldwin (1926, p. 35) himself points out, his introduction to Lotze was through a German student with whom he spent the summer of 1885, not through Wundt.

with material reality. What is more, Baldwin discovered that the powerful logical justification for this coordination proceeded directly from the pantheistic metaphysic against which McCosh had directed his most fervent criticism. For although Spinoza (1677) firmly maintained the qualitative and causal duality of spatiality and consciousness introduced by Descartes, he rejected the Cartesian view of extension and consciousness as attributes of two finite substances and argued instead that they could ultimately be attributes only of an infinite substance or deity. God is the universal essence or nature of all that which exists. The world of consciousness and the world of spatiality may be qualitatively and causally separate, but they are nonetheless only attributes of the same divine essence. The direct implication of this principle of unity of essence is that modes of consciousness and modes of extension are coordinated. They must correspond. Although modes of consciousness determine only other modes of consciousness and modes of extended motion only other modes of extended motion, the same divine essence forms the connections within both classes and everything which exists in consciousness as idea must also exist extended as actual, yet independent of any idea.

That Baldwin fully appreciated this coordinative epistemology of Spinoza is suggested by a paper, "Idealism in Spinoza" (Baldwin, 1889b.) which, though not published until 1889, appears to represent his work in Paulsen's seminar (Baldwin, 1926, p. 12).[10] "We would be justified," he notes, "in claiming for Spinoza a realistic theory of knowledge . . . Spinoza says distinctly (Eth., i., prop. 30), 'For the true idea must necessarily agree with its object—that is, . . . what is present in the understanding as the object of thought must necessarily exist in nature," (Baldwin, 1889b, p.75).

Lecturer in French and German, Princeton, 1885–1887

In the fall of 1885, Baldwin returned to Princeton as Instructor in French and German.[11] Although after a year in Germany, his German seems to have been reasonably adequate, it would appear that his French left something to be desired (Baldwin, 1926, pp. 36–37). Possibly, therefore, as a means to improving this ability and certainly as a means to extending his knowledge of philosophy and

---

[10] The delay in publication may have been occasioned by McCosh's objection to Baldwin's neo-Spinozan views. In this regard, it is interesting that Baldwin adopted a title for the paper, "Idealism in Spinoza," which belies the fact that the article is a thorough defense of Spinoza's realism.

[11] Baldwin also entered the Princeton Theological Seminary at this time but never completed the full course required for the ministry (Baldwin, 1926, p. 23).

psychology, Baldwin began to read extensively in the French literature. This resulted in his first psychological publication and in the beginning of an attraction to French thought which was to remain with him throughout his life.

Ribot and the new psychology in broad perspective. Baldwin's first psychological work was a translation from French to English of the second edition of Ribot's (1886) *German Psychology of Today.* Given Baldwin's relatively short stay in Leipzig and Wundt's tendency (Baldwin, 1930, p.2) when lecturing to omit mention of his immediate intellectual forebears, it seems very likely that Baldwin's first real perspective on the new psychology was actually gained from reading Ribot rather than from studying directly under Wundt (Compare Baldwin, 1887b with Ribot, 1886).

Ribot construes the growth of the new psychology in a post-Kantian mode. Kant, he points out, had ventured to predict that psychology would never be raised to the rank of an exact natural science. For this assertion, Kant gave two principal reasons (Ribot, 1886, p.43). First, mathematics is not applicable to internal phenomena because these phenomena are referred to one condition only, time. Second, internal phenomena are not accessible to experiment; that is, to observation made in circumstances that are determined, that are variable at will, and that are subject to the employment of measure.

Herbart, Ribot suggests, replied to Kant's first observation. Founding his psychology on a metaphysic which implies that sensations, perception, and feelings vary not only in time but in intensity, Herbart constructed a mathematized static and mechanic of mind. Fechner and Wundt replied to Kant's second observation. Drawing on the Herbartian notion of the threshold of consciousness as a means to establishing a fixed point on a scale of sensation determinately related to an excitation scale and employing the "just noticeable difference" to grade the scale, Fechner and Wundt succeeded in reasoning from the intensity of excitation to a measurement of the intensity of sensation.

This perspective on experimentation as proceeding from quantitative variation of the external to measurement of the internal provided Baldwin with a clear conception of the features distinguishing this method from the purely internal descriptive introspection of McCosh. What Baldwin still needed, however, was an understanding of how experimentation and descriptive introspection might be related in a way which conserved the latter. This understanding seems to have come through Baldwin's continued exploration of the French literature.

New French spiritualism and the integration of science and philosophy. As Baldwin's translation of Ribot was being published, he was already at work reviewing French philosophy in preparation for an article which he published in July, 1887 (Baldwin, 1887a). This review is notable for a number of things. First, Baldwin begins by establishing the roots of modern French spiritualism in Reid's refutation of Condillac. "Reid," as Baldwin rather gracelessly points out, "begat a son in his old age and called his name Maine de Biran ... Maine de Biran lived twenty years and begat Victor Cousin, and that Victor Cousin, being a mighty man and strong, is begetting every day" (1887a, p. 138).

Second, Baldwin (1887a) for the first time clearly articulates the general problem within which his own struggle to integrate experimentalism and intuitionalism must be conceived:

> The "new spiritualism" is the product of what has been called the nineteenth-century tendency—the tendency toward the reconciliation of philosophy and science ... (As) Vacherot, the historian of the "new spiritualism" (has asserted): "I do not believe that in the presence of these revelations (of science) it is possible to maintain the spiritualistic tradition entire. I am more and more convinced that the time has come to put science at the side of spiritualism, by the employment of its methods, its principles, and its incontestable conclusions. The old theology, which separates God from the world, has had its day, as the old psychology, which separates the soul from the body, and the old ontology, which separates spirit from matter." "Philosophy must bend to experience." "Spiritualism must submit to scientific methods." What could the positivist wish more? Where is metaphysic? If you mean the metaphysic of the noumenon, the metaphysic of the Unknowable, the Absolute, it is excluded ... By what law? By the law of experience. But if you mean the metaphysic of intuition, the ontology of introspection, I embrace it." "The true ontology is only a psychological revelation." This is the method, principle, and the conclusion of metaphysic and positive science confirms it. This brings us back to the Scottish psychology. (pp. 138–139)

Lastly, although the reconciliation of philosophy and science may indeed lead back to the Scottish psychology, for Baldwin it led back even further to Spinoza. Without naming him,[12] Baldwin (1887a) makes it quite clear that it is in the "great pantheist" for whom matter was spirit and spirit divine that a justification of the reconciliation of philosophy and science and of the coordination of reason and material reality may be found:

> As would be expected, this advance (of the new spiritualism) ... is repudiated by thinkers of the old school ... Ravaisson ... continues to maintain his "spiritualistic positivism," namely, that "the true substance of things is the activity of thought" ... He inverts the formula of the materialists and thinks he has escaped its implications. But matter

---

[12] Baldwin's reticence in this regard may again be presumed to reflect his respect for McCosh's views concerning Spinoza.

is spirit and spirit is divine, hence matter is divine, and we are as nearly materialists as spiritualists, because we are at once neither or both. (p. 139)

Postulates of a physiological psychology. Concurrent with the preparation of his review of the French philosophy, Baldwin was completing work on what is certainly the most important paper of his early period. This paper, "The postulates of a physiological psychology," also appeared in July, 1887 (Baldwin, 1887b). Its importance stems from the fact that, in it, Baldwin pulled together all of the diverse influences of his early years, the intuitionalism of McCosh, the metaphysics of Spinoza, the perspective on "experimentalism" of Ribot, and the rapprochement of philosophy and science in the French "new spiritualism" to construct a general framework for his own integrative mental philosophy.

Logically, Baldwin (1887b) had to begin with the metaphysic and the consequent justification of the coordinative epistemology.

To say that the soul is natural . . . is to say that nature is intelligent and that the laws of thought are the laws of things . . . if nature be natural it must be construed by mind. We know nature as we think it. Nature apart from thought would not be the nature that we know, since nature is realized thought . . . A thing is an object, and a thing which is not thought is . . . a thing with nothing objective about it—that is, no thing. And this is necessarily so from the nature of the perceptive process. Perception has both its objective and its subjective side; that is, perception without an object can not be perception, just as the object without perception cannot be an object. . . . (p. 428)

Having thus set out his metaphysic and epistemology, Baldwin (1887b) weds his philosophical stance to science:

For twenty centuries men have been reasoning from the ego-side of the equation of perception to the non-ego side, and the rich fruits of natural science are the consequence, while they have seldom thought to reason from the non-ego to the ego side, a process whose legitimacy stands or falls with its reverse. If you say I cannot reason from nature to mind, I reply that you cannot reason from mind to nature, since both rest upon the same perception. Why do I believe in external causation? Because I have a causal judgment, and perceive that it works in nature. So to the extent of causation I conclude that nature is realized thought. If there be subjective causation, nature could not have been constructed without objective causation, and if there be objective causation, the mind could not have been constructed without subjective causation; for the contrary in either case would invalidate perception. We must assume the validity of perception for all science. (p. 428)

For Baldwin (1887b), all science includes both the experimental psychology of Wundt and the inductive mental science of McCosh:

We may obtain psychic data from without as well as from within, for the without is as necessary to the within as the within is to the without

... Far from undermining the standpoint of the old psychology—that is, the inductive science of ... the Scottish school, this position tends to confirm it; for consciousness can never be escaped, and a groundwork of ascertained knowledge is necessary for scientific construction. The experimenter on association must know that there are ideas and that they are associated, and only a descriptive, that is, a subjective psychology can give these facts. (pp. 428–429)

What then of the new experimental physiological psychology? As experimental, it must stand or fall on whether "the mind (can) be subjected to experiment in analysis, synthesis and measure ... in duration or time ... (and) in quantity (Baldwin 1887b, p. 429). Following Ribot, Baldwin (1887b) notes that Kant had suggested that it could not; but that Herbart, in considering internal facts as forces subject to mathematization, and Wundt, "the most systematic, profound, and convincing defender of the theoretic position of the external experimentalists (p. 433), had proven Kant's judgment premature. "Evidently," Baldwin (1887b) concludes, "the most sensible ... method of procedure is to define psychology as the science of psychic phenomena, external and internal, and to consider the area of its domain the conscious wherever we find it" (p. 433).

As physiological, however, the "new" psychology deals with more than consciousness wherever we find it. What, then, is the status of the psychophysical connection, of the relation of mind to body? Baldwin's (1887b) answer is perfectly consistent with his metaphysic.

On our own definition of psychology as the science of the mind, as we know it, we must with Wundt admit a free intelligent actuality known in consciousness without material connection. Here is at once the necessity and justification of a higher science, inductive, internal, descriptive, analytic ... But it must be remembered that purely psychic phenomena are such only in consciousness, and not in fact, and by a necessary consequence the psychic laws of such phenomena are quite subjective, and can in no way supercede or contradict the psychophysical laws, which control all psychic phenomena in fact. Psychophysical laws ... must be recognized as in subconscious operation, even in the highest and most ideal processes of mind ... there is a necessary connection between mind and body. (p. 434)

The psychological laws of consciousness and the psychophysical laws of the relation between consciousness and the unconscious are coordinate, there is an invariable relation between mind and body.

This said, Baldwin (1887b) sums up his now well-developed integration of the old and the new psychology in the following postulates:

1. The naturalness of the psychic; psychology is a natural science.
2. The validity of the knowing process and the consequent reality of things; the function of experiment.

3. Uniformity of natural law in the domain of the psychophysical; the major premise and justification of induction.
4. Unity in the mental life; approach to the higher processes. (p. 439)

Diagrammatically, the integration of psychology can be viewed as in Figure 2 (Baldwin, 1887b, p. 439).

Based on the assumption of a neo-Spinozan metaphysic and its coordinative epistemology, Baldwin has succeeded in this paper where McCosh had not. Within one overall conception, Baldwin has integrated philosophy with science, the old psychology with the new, the descriptive with the experimental method, and the psychic with the psychophysical. The general plan of his mental philosophy is largely complete.

Professor of Philosophy, Lake Forest, 1887–1889

In 1887, Baldwin accepted the offer of a chair in philosophy at Lake Forest University (Baldwin, 1926, p. 40). At about this same time, at the request of McCosh, he was putting the finishing touches on a "refutation of materialism" presented as a thesis for the Princeton doctorate (Baldwin, 1926, p. 20). The degree was granted in 1888 and a portion of the thesis eventually published in 1890 (Baldwin, 1890a). By far the most time-consuming enterprise of the Lake Forest period, however, was the preparation of the first volume of the *Handbook of Psychology*, subtitled *Senses and Intellect* (1889a). First published in 1889 (revised in 1890), *Senses and Intellect* is a detailed elaboration of the ideas laid out in "The postulates of a physiological psychology," and it represents the most extensive statement of Baldwin's integrative mental philosophy.

With primary acknowledgment to McCosh, to Wundt, and to Élie Rabier,[13] a French philosopher writing from the standpoint of advanced spiritualism, Baldwin sets the tone of the work. Fundamentally, it is an integration of Wundt with McCosh through Rabier, empirical science with rational metaphysics through the coordinative

---

[13] Although little is known of Rabier, Baldwin identifies him (1887a, p. 142) as a member of the Lycée Charlemagne and the Superior Council of Public Instruction. Here, also, Baldwin describes Rabier's views as "attempts to reconcile empiricism and intellectualism in a doctrine which he denominates *intelligent empiricism*: knowledge is empirical, but internally empirical; it begins with experience, but with internal experience." "Certainly," Baldwin then suggests, "this is . . . only a *jeu de mots*, and we are glad to welcome M. Rabier as an intuitionist after all. His book, as a whole, is perhaps the finest résumé of the results of modern psychology of all schools that has yet been written." That Baldwin believed his own words is indicated by the fact that he modeled much of *Senses and Intellect* after Rabier's *Psychologie* (1888).

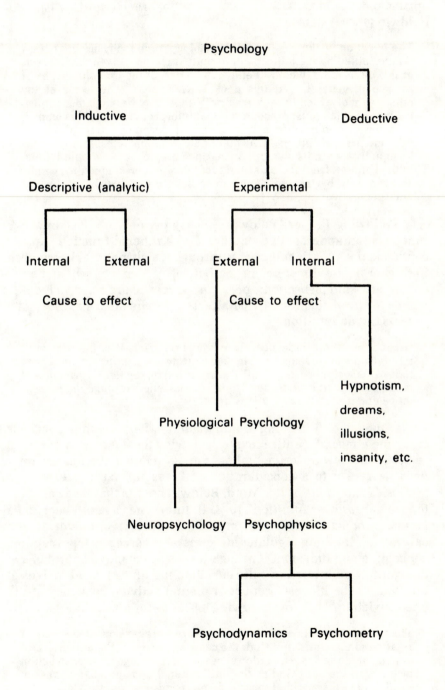

FIG. 2.   Baldwin's Integration of the old and new psychology

epistemology which Baldwin shared with French spiritualism. As Baldwin (1889a) states it:

> The question of the relation of psychology to metaphysics ... is now finally settled by the adjustment of mutual claims. It is in the interests of this adjustment, which I believe to be part of the true philosophy of science in general, that this book is written ... The terms of the adjustment of which I speak are briefly these: on the one hand, empirical investigation must precede rational interpretation, and this empirical investigation must be absolutely unhampered by fetters of dogmatism and preconception; on the other hand, rational interpretation must be equally free in its own province, since progress from the individual to the general, from the detached fact to its universal meaning, can be secured only by the judicious use of hypotheses, both metaphysical and speculative. (pp. iii–iv)

Following Rabier, Baldwin (1889a) divides intellect into two functions: an apperceptive function and a rational function. Apperception is the attentional process through which material is acquired for higher mental function, an *"activity of synthesis by which mental data of any kind (sensations, percepts, concepts) are constructed into higher forms of relation"* (p. 65). Reason, on the other hand, is not a process but an intuition:

> It conditions and underlies all mental processes. It is the nature of mind itself as it reveals itself in consciousness. Accordingly, by reason in its broadest sense, is meant: *The constitutive, regulative principle of mind, so far as it is apprehended in consciousness through the presentative and discursive operations.* (p. 312)

Under the general heading of apperception, Baldwin then proceeds to devote almost the entire text to reviewing the data and theoretical issues of the new experimental psychology. Only in the final chapter does he return to a consideration of "reason." With reference to McCosh's *Intuitions of the Mind*, Baldwin asserts that "we come ... to look at reason as *Intuition*" (p. 314). Intuition is a mental act and a mental product. Intuition is immediate, necessary, universal and categorical. Intuition regulates all forms of apperception: perception, conception and judgment. Through these apperceptive operations of thought turned inward in self-reflection, the human mind arrives at intuition as the highest product of mental activity, as general truth and conviction. Thus, for Baldwin (1889a) as for McCosh:

> The ultimate end of knowledge is the comprehension of the self in relation to the world and God: the comprehension of the universe as a system, of the self as realization of reason in its energetic reconstruction of the world, and of God as the final rational demand alike of reason itself, and of the world of its completed reconstruction. (p. 324)

Once again, it is evident that for Baldwin the integration of metaphysics and psychology is based on the pre-established coordination of reason and experience, reason in intuition and experience in apperception. This coordination, in turn, finds its metaphysical ground in God, a God of reason and a God of material reality.

Evolutionary Psychology, 1889–1903

Thus, by 1889, Baldwin had developed and consolidated what he conceived to be an adequate integration of the new psychology with the old based on a coordinative epistemology grounded in a neo-Spinozan metaphysic. Only a rejection of this epistemology could shake the foundation of this integration. Yet, between 1889 and 1892, just such a rejection occurred. When it did, the structure of Baldwin's conception was transformed from that of a mental philosophy to that of an evolutionary psychology. Then, around 1898, just as his evolutionary psychology was becoming fully consolidated, Baldwin once again entered a period of transition. Finding the available empirical methodologies inadequate to his theoretical concerns, he abandoned experimental psychology in a return to philosophical analysis, emerging from this transition with yet another radically altered conception, an evolutionary epistemology.

Both of these transformations in Baldwin's thinking were complex and multiply determined. An adequate historical account of this portion of his intellectual career is far beyond the scope of our discussion. However, as noted at the outset, there is reason to believe that these transformations, as radical as they were, were brought about in the exercise of the same general attempt to come to grips with the relation between reason and material reality which had motivated Baldwin's earlier construction of an integrative mental philosophy. In order to illustrate this functional continuity, a sketch of the remainder of Baldwin's active career will be presented. This sketch will conclude with a few brief critical comments preparatory to the chapters which follow in this volume.

Professor of Logic and Metaphysics, Toronto, 1889–1893

With the publication of *Senses and Intellect* in 1889, Baldwin assumed the Chair of Logic and Metaphysics at the University of Toronto. This move signaled the beginning of a second period of intense intellectual development, which culminated in the emergence of an evolutionary psychology.

Infant cognition and the development of reason. In the summer before the move, Baldwin's first child, Helen, was born. She was followed in 1891 by a second daughter, Elizabeth. With Helen's arrival, Baldwin initiated a series of observations of infancy and early childhood which he pursued, intermittently, over a period of four years (Baldwin, 1890b, 1890c, 1890d, 1891b, 1892a, 1892b, 1893). These observations led to a major revision in Baldwin's thinking. From his neo-Spinozan point of view, the laws of thought were conceived to exist in pre-established coordination with the laws of things. A thing which was not thought was, as Baldwin put it, "no thing" (Baldwin, 1887b, p. 428). Yet here, in the observation of his children, Baldwin was suddenly confronted with the extreme cognitive immaturity and rapid intellectual development of the human infant. Clearly, the laws of thought could not be conceived to be as fixed and immutable as the laws of things. Reason, Baldwin observed daily, is an evolving capacity of the human mind.

The primary implication of this observation must have struck Baldwin with some force. The coordination of reason and reality could not be pre-established. On the contrary, such a coordination is a hard-won ontogenetic achievement. Over the course of individual intellectual growth, reason becomes progressively more adequate to reality. The coordinative epistemology must be conceived within a developmental framework. Yet, if the fundamental insights of the intuitional philosophy were not to be sacrificed, this framework must be constructed without retreat to pure empiricism. Developing reason and a stable material reality must be integrated in such a way that neither reason nor reality was lost. Thought, it was true, could no longer be conceived to be regulated by fixed native principles; but such principles must control the direction of intellectual development toward a progressively more adequate conception of material reality as it is. Reason and reality could no longer be conceived to be in pre-established coordination, but this coordination, on which Baldwin had based his integration of metaphysics and science, must be the end-point toward which development is directed.

Having come to this realization, Baldwin faced the problem of finding a mechanism whereby the validity of such a developing coordination could be guaranteed. Although Baldwin was not yet fully aware of it, such a mechanism was already close at hand, in the theory of evolution. When Baldwin fastened on this theory, his conception of psychology was totally transformed.

Imitation and voluntary action. Concurrent with his infant observations, Baldwin was preparing an extension of his intellectual philosophy to problems of feeling, emotion, and voluntary action. In 1891, *Feeling and Will* (1891a) the second volume of the *Handbook of*

Psychology, appeared. Employing the formal characteristics of nervous integration as a model, Baldwin replaces the global concept of "apperception," around which *Senses and Intellect* had been organized, with a more differentiated view. Nervous integration, Baldwin notes, is "change in the direction . . . of simplicity, because it gives ease and rapidity to habitual movements; (and) of complexity, because it brings into play new elements which must be assimilated to the unity of the centre" (1891a, p. 24). Similarly, the psychological activity by which material is acquired for higher function can be conceived to involve both a consolidation of habit and an accommodation to new elements. "Habit," Baldwin suggests, issues "in established paths of least resistance" (1891a, p. 23) and is characterized, psychologically, by diffusion of attention and automatic action. Accommodation assimilates new elements in conformity to the demands of the environment and is characterized, psychologically, by concentration of attention and voluntary action.

At the same time, Baldwin was becoming increasingly impressed with the importance of imitation in the child's development, particularly with respect to the regulation of habit and accommodation in voluntary action. As he described it:

> In . . . a series of articles reporting observations on infants, published in part in the journal Science, 1890–1892 . . . I found it necessary constantly to enlarge my scope for the entertainment of a widened genetic view. This came to clearer consciousness in the treatment of the child's imitations, especially when I came to the relation of imitation to volition . . . The farther study of this subject brought what was to me such a revelation of the genetic function of imitation that I then determined . . . to work out a theory of mental development in the child, incorporating this new insight (Baldwin, 1895a, p. vii).

Professor of Psychology, Princeton: Period of Consolidation, 1893–1897

In 1893, Baldwin returned to his *alma mater* to occupy the Stuart Chair in Psychology (Baldwin, 1926, p. 53). Armed with a new appreciation for the genetic function of imitation, Baldwin organized his first graduate seminar at Princeton around the topic of mental development in the child (Baldwin, 1895a, p. vii). The outcome of this seminar was the conviction that "no consistent view of mental development in the individual could possibly be reached without a doctrine of the race development of consciousness" (Baldwin, 1895a, p. vii). With this broader issue in view, Baldwin (1895a) fell "to reading again the literature of biological evolution, with view to a possible synthesis of the current biological theory of organic adaptation with the doctrine of the infant's development" (p. vii).

Mental development in the child and the race. In December 1894, Baldwin completed the manuscript for *Mental Development* (which, though copyrighted in 1894, was first published in 1895). This work provided the purest extended statement of his evolutionary psychology. From the outset, Baldwin (1895a) makes it clear that he no longer subscribes to the mental philosophy view of mind:

> The older idea of the soul was of a fixed substance, with fixed attributes. Knowledge of the soul was immediate in consciousness, and adequate ... The mind was best understood where best or most fully manifested ... If the adult consciousness shows the presence of principles not observable in the child consciousness, we must suppose, nevertheless, that they are really present ... beyond the reach of our observation ... The genetic idea reverses all this. Instead of a fixed substance, we have the conception of a growing, developing activity. Functional psychology succeeds faculty psychology ... the adult consciousness must, if possible, be interpreted by principles present in the child consciousness (pp. 2–3).

Mind, Baldwin had now fully come to realize, is a developing function. What is more, if this development is to be guaranteed a validity with respect to material reality, mind must itself be conceived in terms of the broader phylogenetic history of the human species. This Baldwin (1895a) calls the question of *race experience*, the question of whether "what is present in the mind now, in the way of function, is due somehow to the past" (p. 27).

Adopting a modified "recapitulationism,"[14] Baldwin suggests that there is an analogy between individual and race growth. "We find more and more developed stages of conscious function in a series corresponding in the main with the stages of nervous growth in the animals; and then we find this growth paralleled in its great features in the mental development of the human infant" (Baldwin, 1895a, p. 15). Yet this parallelism is far from strict. In fact, necessary stages in the development of the ancestors in a phylogenetic series are often omitted in the descendants. These "organic 'short cuts' " (p. 20), as Baldwin calls them, suggest the possibility that adaptations achieved in the ontogenesis of single organisms may eventually find their way into the evolutionary progress of the species. The issue, as Baldwin sees it, is one of "whether the effects of habit, itself a phenomenon of development, would not be inherited, or selected, thus abbreviating the ontogenetic process" (p. 26). In order to explore this issue, Baldwin devotes the remainder of *Mental Development* to delineating a biological theory of individual intellectual growth or

---

[14] Baldwin's view of recapitulationism changed over successive editions of *Mental Development* as indicated by alteration of text and footnotes. The view described here is that of the first edition of 1895.

"adaptation" and to laying the groundwork for linking individual adaptation to the evolutionary history of the species.

In discussing individual intellectual adaptation, Baldwin starts from the principle that the natural tendency of the organism is to relate to objects by acting on them. "Every sensation or incoming process tends to bring about action or outgoing process (Baldwin, 1895a, p. 166). Baldwin terms this the law of dynamogenesis. Actions themselves, no matter how complex, are always of the character of an approach or a withdrawal, directed toward pleasurable and away from painful objects. In such action, two principles are operative, habit and accommodation. Habit provides for "the repetition of what is worth repeating." Accommodation "secures, progressively, further useful reactions, which at an earlier stage would have been impossible" (Baldwin, 1895a, p. 170).

The integration of habit and accommodation is achieved in imitative action in which "the stimulus starts a motor process which tends to reproduce the stimulus and, through it, the motor process again" in circular fashion (Baldwin, 1895a, p. 133). Imitative acts are never exact repetitions of one another. On the contrary, it is only through repetition with variation that the organism successfully secures and retains its vital stimulations. When successful, variations which bring about the pleasure or avoid the pain of maintaining contact with a stimulus are "selected so as to adapt the organism better and give it a life-history" (Baldwin, 1895a, p. 174). This process, which Baldwin terms *organic selection*,[15] is the natively given functional mechanism through which reason develops toward a more adequate apprehension of the world. The development of the coordination of reason with reality, in other words, is accounted for by organic selection.

What this principle cannot by itself explain, however, is the validity of the developing coordination. Why should the mechanism of organic selection lead to progressively more adequate knowledge when, like all rational principles, it is a natively given constitutive principle of human intellectual function? Although in 1894, Baldwin's answer to this question was less fully worked out than it would come to be, it is evident that he had already begun to see the direction which his argument would eventually take.

Having sketched out the theory of individual adaptation through

[15] The term organic selection first appears in *Mental Development* (p. 174) with reference to the ontogenetic mechanism described in the text. However, Baldwin later extended and then, ultimately, limited the term to the broader phylogenetic process which came to be known as the "Baldwin effect." For a helpful discussion of this issue, see Braestrup (1971).

organic selection, Baldwin lays the foundation for relating individual mental development to heredity. "No theory of development," he suggests, "is complete . . . which does not account for the transmission in some way, from one generation to another, of the gains of the earlier generations, turning individual gains into race gains" (Baldwin, 1895a, p. 204). From the neo-Darwinian point of view, natural selection, operating on congenital variation, is adequate to explain all progressive race gains. This view, Baldwin asserts, is compatible with his concept of organic selection. The ability to learn new actions, the processes of approach and withdrawal to pleasure and pain which underlie organic selection, may vary congenitally. If this is so, later acquisitions of individual organisms give evidence of additional variations from the earlier variations. As Baldwin (1895a) suggests, "it is only necessary to hold to a view by which variations are cumulative to secure the same results by natural selection as would have been secured by the inheritance of acquired characters from father to son" (p. 205).

The ontogenetic mechanism by which reason becomes more adequate to reality is, therefore, a mechanism which has been selected for in the evolutionary history of the species. Since the selection process is, by its nature, a process by which species function becomes increasingly more adequate to the structure of material reality, the mechanism underlying organic selection is guaranteed a certain validity. Grounded in the natural history of the species, the regulative principles governing the direction of intellectual development are just those which assure the survival of the species. A match between constitutional psychological endowment and the structure of material reality is thereby assured. In evolution, Baldwin has once again found the means to conserve that which seemed self-evident in the Scottish intuitionalism while remaining an active proponent of a scientific psychology.

Social and ethical interpretations and organic selection. By the time *Mental Development* was issued in 1895, Baldwin had already begun work on an extension of his developmental, evolutionary insight to the then neglected area of social psychology (Baldwin, 1895a, p. ix). As Baldwin described the situation, "we have no social psychology because we have had no doctrine of the *socius*. We have had theories of the *ego* and the *alter*; but that they did not reveal the *socius* is just their condemnation" (1895a, p. ix). Starting from the notion that the principle of circular reaction with selection is the "fundamental method of fruitful organic reaction to the environment of things and persons" (Baldwin, 1930, p. 4), Baldwin developed a theory of social adaptation to complement his theory of intellectual development. In 1897, he published his most thorough account of this theory in *Social and Ethical Interpretations in Mental Development.*

Briefly, it was Baldwin's view that "through conscious imitation and its variations and oppositions . . . through intercourse with others, thus established, . . . the individual self thought or *ego* is attained, along with its correlative term, the social fellow or *alter*, each using a common body of experiences and forming an identical social fellow or *socius* (Baldwin, 1897a, p. 5). From this view, as Baldwin summarized it himself, "the conclusion is drawn that the individual is a 'social outcome not a social unit' " (1930, p. 5).

As Baldwin was elaborating the social implications of his evolutionary concepts, he was also engaged in extending the very concepts being applied, particularly those involved in the principle of organic selection. Thus, in the period between 1896 and 1900, Baldwin published, among other papers, articles on "heredity and instinct," "consciousness and evolution," "physical and social heredity," "determinate evolution," and "isolation and selection" (Baldwin, 1896c, 1896d, 1896e, 1897b, 1898b). In 1902, these articles were pulled together, somewhat revised, and published as *Development and Evolution*, a book summarizing Baldwin's contributions to evolution theory.

As already indicated, Baldwin's primary interest lay in possible mechanisms mediating the influence of individual adaptations on the course of phylogenetic evolution. Neo-Darwinism, concerning itself with chance variations, left the seemingly directive or "determinative" course of evolution as, in Baldwin's words, "the point of greatest obscurity" (1930, p. 6). In the May–June, 1896, issue of the *American Naturalist*, Baldwin (1896a) announced the outcome of his thinking in this regard as an hypothesis for which he borrowed the term he had already introduced for individual adaptation, "organic selection." In its most developed form,[16] this was the hypothesis that:

> natural selection operating on "spontaneous variations" is sufficient alone to produce determinate evolution (without the inheritance of acquired adaptations or modifications), since—and this is the new point—in each generation variations in the direction of, or "coincident" with, the function to be developed will favor the organisms possessing them, and their descendants will profit by the accumulation of such variations. Thus the function will gradually come to perfection. In other words, the individual organism's accommodations, made through learning, effort, adaptation, etc., while not physically inherited, still act to supplement or screen the congenital endowment during its incom-

---

[16] This form resulted from Baldwin's interactions with Morgan, Osborn, and Poulton (Braestrup, 1971).

plete stages, and so give the species time to build up its variations in determinate lines (Baldwin, 1930, p. 7).

Professor of Psychology, Princeton: Period of Transition, 1897–1903

Paradoxically, just as Baldwin was producing his most important psychological work, providing in his evolutionary psychology perhaps the only justification for rationalism an experimentalist might hope to provide, he was beginning to abandon the field for philosophy. Between 1890 and 1897, in addition to his studies of infancy, Baldwin had published laboratory investigations of memory, size contrast, and reaction types (Baldwin, 1895b, 1895c, 1895d, 1896b). In 1897, however, experimental work virtually ceased. Baldwin entered still another period of intense intellectual development, a period of transformation away from experimental and toward philosophical psychology, yielding yet another radically restructured conception, an evolutionary epistemology.

Critique of experimental method. A number of factors contributed to Baldwin's intellectual growth during this period. One such factor was his growing awareness of the conflict between the methodological demands of his evolutionary views and the available empirical methods of experimental psychology. An evolutionary psychology required new methods. As Baldwin (1930) stated the problem:

> How can the development of the mental order of phenomena—or that of any other truly genetic order, involving progress—be fruitfully investigated? The . . . quantitative method, brought over into psychology from the exact sciences . . . must be discarded; for its ideal consisted in reducing the more complex to the more simple, the whole to its parts, the later-evolved to the earlier-existent, thus denying or eliminating just the factor which constituted or revealed what was truly genetic . . . A method is therefore called for which will take account of this something left "over and above" the quantitative, something which presents new phases as the genetic progression advances (pp. 7–8)

The difficulty which Baldwin faced in dealing with this problem was that he had no experimental method which satisfied this criterion. In his pursuit of a synthesis between mental philosophy and the new experimental psychology, he had gotten hold of an idea, in evolution theory, which transcended both. He had replaced intuitionalism with a biological theory of mind; but the empirical issues raised by his new theory could not be adequately addressed with the methods of psychophysics and reaction time. Baldwin's ideas, in other words, had far outstripped the available empirical methodology.

It is of small wonder, then, that Baldwin, having achieved the evolutionary insight, found little of relevance to his theoretical concerns in the experimentalism of the period. As he tells it:

> The experimental vein was worked, though with lessening interest, for the ten years of my stay at Princeton ... Already at Princeton the new interest in genetic psychology and general biology had become absorbing, and the meagerness of the results of the psychological laboratories (apart from direct work on sensation and movement) was becoming evident everywhere. I began to feel that there was truth in what James was already proclaiming as to the barrenness of the tables and curves coming from many laboratories (Baldwin, 1930, p. 4).

Nor is it surprising that as Baldwin's biological theory of mind led naturally to questions of the developing coordination of reason with reality as manifest in the changing relation of subject to object, self to other, logic to experience, and truth to value, he was led inevitably back to the only method of investigation open to him, the logical method of philosophical analysis.

Instrumental epistemology. A second factor contributing to Baldwin's intellectual growth during the period of transition was a general resurgence of interest in epistemological issues in American philosophy. As he described it:

> In the late nineties there was a return in America to problems of an epistemological character. It gave rise to a re-examination of the psychological bases of philosophy ... Truth, error, the method and validity of knowledge became topics of real vitality, and instrumental and pragmatic theories of many varieties saw the light. From the side of evolution theory, the futility of the older views, which made of thinking an absolute faculty and of truth a sort of psychograph of reality, was evident. The theory of adaptation saw in the rise of thinking a critical turn in the evolution of mind. Knowledge became a function of prime genetic significance, an instrument of supreme utility (Baldwin, 1930, p. 9).

In his presidential address to the December, 1897 meeting of the American Psychological Association, Baldwin (1898a) presented his first substantive contribution to the new discussions in epistemology. Arguing an interactive instrumentalism, Baldwin pointed out that thinking is both the means of adaptive action in the individual's environment of objects, persons, and beliefs and an instrument of the expansion and clarification of the social system of knowledge in science and culture. The validity of this knowledge is, of course, guaranteed by selection:

> The discovery of truth was recognized as being an adaptation to a given set of data, proceeding by a series of tentative selections from variations of imagery and fragments of hypothetical value ... Truth is what is selected under the control of the system of established thoughts and facts, and assimilated to the body of socially acquired knowledges and

beliefs. Truth thus becomes a tentative and slowly-expanding body of data, more or less adequately reflecting the stable whole of thought and action which is accepted as reality, and in turn enlarging and clarifying that whole (Baldwin, 1930, pp. 9–10).

As Baldwin (1930) later pointed out, this view, though compatible with the early versions of pragmatism, "stopped short . . . of the pure relativism and subjectivism of many pragmatic writers, inasmuch as it holds that . . . knowledge presupposes a dualism of controls: the agent, on the one hand, and the recognized world of truth and reality . . . on the other (p. 10).

Dictionary of philosophy and psychology The third, and perhaps the most important, factor in rekindling Baldwin's interest in philosophy and the emergence of his evolutionary epistemology was his activity as editor of the *Dictionary of Philosophy and Psychology* (1901–1902). As Baldwin (1930) described the rationale for the project:

> At an early day, I was impressed by the difficulty of profitable discussion in the newer branches of psychology, by reason of the paucity and ambiguity of the terms in use . . . there were many in America, among them notably C.S. Peirce, advocating his views in the New York *Nation*, who proposed to cut loose entirely from popular usage and coin a clear and consistent terminology for the mental and moral sciences as had been done for mathematics and symbolic logic. While not going the whole way with the latter, I was convinced that confusion lurked in most of the discussions of the day, from the lack of well-defined terms . . . As a step toward reform and common understanding in the matter, the project of . . . a dictionary or cyclopedia, took form . . . (p.26)

First formally announced at the end of 1896, the *Dictionary* had begun, by 1898, to usurp the majority of Baldwin's time as he dealt with the "complications . . . tribulations . . . (and) mountainous molehills" attending its preparation (Baldwin, 1926, p. 72). In the fall of 1899, Baldwin obtained leave from Princeton to travel to Oxford to supervise the *Dictionary*'s completion and by 1902, both volumes had been published.

It would be difficult to overestimate the impact of this activity on Baldwin's thinking. The plan of the *Dictionary* called for a collaborative effort on the part of many of the greatest minds of the day. James, Dewey, Peirce, Royce, G.E. Moore, Bosanquet, Cattell, Titchener, Münsterberg, Janet, Ladd-Franklin, Meyer, Stout, Giddings, and Poulton, among others, were involved in the project. The goal of the *Dictionary* was to provide a systematic definition for every major concept in philosophy and psychology. As the general editor of

---

[17] A third volume, containing Rand's "Bibliography of Philosophy and Psychology" was published in two parts in 1905.

this monumental compilation, Baldwin found himself perched atop a mountain of information relevant to practically every major issue in the philosophical domain. Every article was given Baldwin's personal attention, and Baldwin kept in constant communication with his various collaborators concerning issues raised by their contributions.

The effect of this extraordinary intellectual undertaking on the nature and direction of Baldwin's work was immediately apparent. His first deep appreciation of Hegel, an increasingly broad reference to the philosophical work of Lotze, an acquaintance with the thought of Meinong, and a deep interest in the nature and development of logic all date from the period immediately following the *Dictionary's* publication. After 1902, the content and method of Baldwin's work was almost entirely philosophical.

Evolutionary Epistemology, 1903–1912

Professor of Philosophy and Psychology, Johns Hopkins, 1903–1908

In 1903, Baldwin left his Princeton professorship of psychology for a position as a professor of philosophy and psychology at Johns Hopkins. This move and the attendant change in title closely reflected the redirection of Baldwin's interests. The new position afforded an opportunity to explore problems of epistemology free from the responsibility for the direct supervision of laboratory experimentation. As Baldwin (1926) describes the period: "The intellectual conditions at Baltimore were altogether favorable to work, and I began to put into shape the material which was to appear in the successive volumes of 'Genetic Logic' (pp. 122–123).

In 1906, the first volume of this massive and difficult work, *Thought and Things. A Study of the Development and Meaning of Thought. Or Genetic Logic*, was published (Baldwin 1906–1911). This was followed, in 1908 and 1911, by volumes 2 and 3 respectively and, in 1915, by a final volume separately titled *Genetic Theory of Reality* (Baldwin, 1915). In spite of the spacing of these publications (due partly to Baldwin's sudden resignation from Johns Hopkins in 1908 and the attendant disruption of his scholarly activities), it is clear from the preface to the first volume of the series that, by 1906, Baldwin already had his new conception fairly well worked out. In view of the separate appearance of volume 1, Baldwin (1906–1911) takes pains to spell out the general direction of the work as a whole, indicating "certain general results for the theory of knowledge . . . (in) advance. The genetic development of meanings, when carried through from the pre-logical into the logical and then through what I call the hyper-logical stages of mental development, shows us the growth and restatement of certain great Dualisms of 'Control': Mind and Body, Subject and Object, Reality and Appearance." (vol I, p. ix)

That Baldwin (1906–1911) is, as ever, struggling with the synthesis of reason and reality is evident as he continues:

> I find that these dualisms are of a certain first-hand and unreflective crudeness in the epochs before the rise of Judgment and Reflection, and that they cannot be finally resolved by the "practical" methods of that epoch, as is claimed by Instrumentalism or Pragmatism; that they are given refined and characteristic form when melted up and re-cast in the dualism of Reflection, that of Self and Not-self, or Subject and Object. Yet Thought as such, Reflection, cannot resolve its own Dualisms; Rationalism is as helpless before the final problem of the meaning of Reality as is the cruder Pragmatism. (vol I, pp. ix–x)

For Baldwin (1906–1911), the final synthesis is to be found:

> ... in a form of contemplation, Aesthetic in character ... (in which) the immediacy of experience constantly seeks to re-establish itself. In the highest form of such contemplation, a form which comes to itself as genuine and profound Aesthetic Experience, we find a synthesis of motives, a mode in which the strands of the earlier and diverging dualisms are merged and fused. In this experience of a fusion which is not a mixture, but which issues in a meaning of its own sort and kind, an experience whose essential character is just its unity of comprehension, consciousness has its completest and most direct and final apprehension of what reality is and means. (vol. I, p. x)

The telos of Baldwin's intellectual development—of the transformation from mental philosophy to evolutionary psychology and from evolutionary psychology to evolutionary epistemology—is again evident in the striving for an integrative balance between epistemological extremes. The oppositions of biology and culture, the individual and society, thought and action, and truth and value have their roots, one and all, in the developing coordination of reason and reality. This coordination, in its progressive elaboration, first generates and then overcomes the dichotomies between mind and body, subject and object, and reality and appearance, finding its final issue in aesthetic experience, in a *pancalism*. This realization was, in Baldwin's own estimation, one of his most important contributions to human thought (Baldwin, 1930, p.30).

Resignation and Removal to France and Mexico, 1908–1912

In 1908, at the peak of his career, recently elected to preside over the forthcoming International Congress of Psychology (Baldwin, 1926, p. 127), Baldwin was accused of an impropriety and asked to resign from Johns Hopkins (see the Titchener-Baldwin correspondence, Titchener Archives, Cornell Univ. Library). From 1908 to 1912 he divided his time between residence in Paris and visits to Mexico as a consultant on educational reform and as professor of philosophy and social science in the Escuela de Altos Estudios of the National University (Baldwin, 1926, p. 130). During this period he completed work on *Thought and Things* and published a number of smaller volumes.

Darwin and the Humanities appeared in 1909. Its source lay in an invited address delivered by Baldwin at the Darwin Anniversary Meeting of the American Philosophical Society (Baldwin, 1926, p. 149). Concentrating particularly on Darwin's " 'human' studies . . . in his 'Biographical Sketch of an Infant,' in his discussions in 'Descent of Man' of the origin of the moral sense, and in his views on instinct," Baldwin attempted to show how the theory of natural selection as applied in these areas could be extended through the application of his own principle of organic selection (Baldwin, 1926, p.149).

In 1911, *The Individual and Society*, a popular summary of the genetic logic in its relation to social problems and theory, appeared. Finally, in 1912, on his fourth and final visit to Mexico, Baldwin presented a series of lectures published as *History of Psychology. A Sketch and an Interpretation* (1913), in which he explores the notion of a "general serial correspondence" (Baldwin, 1913, p. 9) between the historical development of psychology and the intellectual development of the individual. Both developmental series, he suggests, reflect "the ways in which the human mind . . . (is) able at various epochs to apprehend or interpret itself" (Baldwin, 1913, p. 3).

Conclusion

1912 - 1934

From 1912 until his death, Baldwin lived in France, devoting much of his time, particularly during World War I, to strengthening Franco-American ties. An interesting account of these years appears in Baldwin's (1926) informal autobiography, *Between Two Wars (1861-1921)*. During this period as well, Baldwin was appointed a corresponding member of the Institut de France and came into contact with many of France's leading thinkers, especially Poincaré, Bergson, and Janet (Baldwin, 1926, p. 165, pp. 161-164). More importantly, it was also at this time that a previous acquaintanceship with Edouard Claparede developed into a warm friendship with Baldwin making periodic visits to Geneva (personal communication, Elizabeth Stimson Baldwin). In Geneva, Baldwin's views on mental development were being assimilated by the young Jean Piaget who was partially under the influence of Claparede.[18] In 1934, at the age of 73, Baldwin died in Paris.

Given this account, is it any wonder that when Baldwin left the American academic scene prematurely in 1908, he was, intellectually speaking, hardly missed? American psychology was already beginning to commit itself ever more deeply to experimental empiricism and Baldwin's concerns were not its concerns. Consequently, by 1929, Boring (1929), recounting the history of experimental psychology, dismissed Baldwin's intellectual (if not his administrative) achievements, noting simply that "Baldwin's felicitous literary style, surpassed only by James, gave a transient vitality to his ideas; but his effect was not permanent (p. 518)."

What Boring could not then know was that Baldwin's ideas had fallen on fertile ground, not in America, but in Geneva where he was read by Piaget, and in the Soviet Union where he was read and referenced by Vygotsky (1960). As Boring wrote, Piaget had already begun the momentous task of constructing a thorough-going genetic epistemology on a foundation which Baldwin had in part provided. Nor could Boring then have foreseen that American psychology, partly influenced by this same Piaget, would itself evolve to a point at which Baldwin's ideas would regain their lost vitality, not merely as one origin of an important intellectual movement, but, as is evident from this volume, as a continuing source of fresh insight into issues of fundamental contemporary importance.

In attempting to reconcile the nativistic rationalism of the Scottish philosophy with the empirical demands of a scientific psychology and in transcending experimentalism in the development of an evolutionary epistemology, Baldwin proposed a biosocial, genetic theory of intelligence, a theory of mind in the broadest sense, which was conceptually far ahead of its time. This theory contained within it, en germe, many of the most important concepts of the biological theory of intelligence and of the genetic epistemology which Piaget was to develop. More importantly, in his constant attempt to transcend the basic epistemological dualisms, Baldwin reached, in his most developed thought, a level of insight which is, in certain ways, still in advance of current conception. Baldwin realized, as Piaget apparently did not, that the formal logical thought of science, the reflective thought which maximizes the subject–object

---

[18] Piaget read Claparede's copy of the French edition of *Mental Development* (personal communication, Jacques Vonèche). As Piaget suggests in the interview published in this volume, Janet also piqued Piaget's interest in Baldwin. Furthermore, inasmuch as most of Baldwin's works appeared in French almost at the same time as they appeared in English and were well regarded in French intellectual circles, Piaget could hardly have avoided being exposed to Baldwin's ideas.

duality, objectifying reality at the expense of subjectivity, is not the pinnacle of human intellectual development. Whether it is in aesthetic experience and pancalism, as Baldwin thought, or through some other as yet uncharacterized means, the subject-object dualism is transcended in the most fully developed human understanding. Yet, our conception of the nature of this transcendent thought is today no more advanced than it was in July, 1911 when Baldwin completed the manuscript of the final volume of his "genetic logic".

REFERENCES

Baldwin, J. M. Contemporary philosophy in France. *New Princeton Review*, 1887, *3* (1), 137–144. (a)

Baldwin, J. M. The postulates of a physiological psychology. *Presbyterian Review*, 1887, *8* (31), 427–440. (b)

Baldwin, J. M. *Handbook of psychology: Senses and intellect.* New York: Holt, 1889. (a)

Baldwin, J. M. The idealism of Spinoza. *Presbyterian Review*, 1889, *10* (37), 65–76. (b)

Baldwin, J. M. Recent discussion in materialism. *The Presbyterian and Reformed Review*, 1890, *1* (3) 357–372. (a)

Baldwin, J. M. Origin of right or left-handedness. *Science,* 1890, *16* (404), 247–248. (b)

Baldwin, J. M. Right-handedness and effort. *Science*, 1890, *16* (408), 302–303. (c)

Baldwin, J. M. Infant psychology. *Science*, 1890, *16* (412), 351–353. (d)

Baldwin, J. M. *Handbook of psychology: Feeling and will.* New York: Holt, 1891 (a).

Baldwin, J. M. Suggestion in infancy. *Science*, 1891, *17* (421), 113–117. (b)

Baldwin J. M. Infants movements. *Science*, 1892, *19* (466), 15–16. (a)

Baldwin, J. M. The origin of volition in childhood. *Science*, 1892, *20* (511), 286–287. (b)

Baldwin J. M. Distance and color perception by infants. *Science*, 1893, *21* (534), 231–232.

Baldwin, J. M. *Mental development in the child and the race: Methods and processes.* New York: Macmillan, 1895. (a)

Baldwin, J. M. & Shaw, W. J. Types of reaction. *Psychological Review*, 1895, *2*, 259–273. (d)

Baldwin, J. M. & Shaw, W. J. Memory for square size. *Psychological Review*, 1895, *2*, 236–239. (b)

Baldwin, J. M. The effect of size-contrast upon judgments of position in the retinal field. *Psychological Review*, 1895, *2*, 244–259. (c)

Baldwin, J. M. A new factor in evolution. *American Naturalist*, 1896, *30*, 441–451, 536–554. (a)

Baldwin, J. M. The "type-theory" of reaction. *Mind*, 1896, *5*, 81–89. (b)

Baldwin, J. M. Heredity and instinct. *Science*, 1896, *3*, 438–441, 558–561. (c)

Baldwin, J. M. Consciousness and evolution. *Psychological Review*, 1896, *3*, 300–309. (d)

Baldwin, J. M. & Cope, E. D. Physical and social heredity. *American Naturalist*, 1896, *30*, 422–430. (e)

Baldwin, J. M. *Social and ethical interpretations in mental development. A study in social psychology.* New York: Macmillan, 1897. (a)

Baldwin, J. M. Determinate evolution. *Psychological Review*, 1897, *4*, 393–401. (b)

Baldwin, J. M. On selective thinking. *Psychological Review*, 1898, *5*, 1–25. (a)

Baldwin, J. M., Hutton, F. W., & Williams, H. S. Isolation and selection. *Science*, 1898, *7*, 570–571, 637–640. (b)

Baldwin, J. M,. (Ed.) *Dictionary of philosophy and psychology.* New York: Macmillan, 1901–1902. 2 Vol.

Baldwin, J. M. *Development and evolution. Including psychophysical evolution, evolution by orthoplasy, and the theory of genetic modes.* New York: Macmillan, 1902.

Baldwin, J. M. *Thought and things. A study of the development and meaning of thought. Or Genetic logic. I: Functional logic, or genetic theory of knowledge. II. Experimental logic, or genetic theory of thought. III. Interest and art. Being real logic. I: genetic epistemology.* New York: Macmillan, 1906–1911.

Baldwin, J. M. *Darwin and the humanities.* Baltimore, Md.: Review Pub., 1909.

Baldwin, J. M. *The Individual and society. or psychology and sociology.* Boston: Badger, 1911.

Baldwin, J. M. *History of psychology. A sketch and an interpretation.* London: Watts, 1913. 2 Vols.

Baldwin, J. M. *Genetic theory of reality. Being the outcome of genetic logic as issuing in the aesthetic theory of reality called pancalism.* New York: Putnam, 1915

Baldwin, J. M. *Between two wars (1861–1921). Being memories, opinions and letters received.* Boston: Stratford, 1926. 2 Vol.

Baldwin, J. M. James Mark Baldwin. In C. Murchison (Ed.), *A history of psychology in autobiography.* Worcester, Mass.: Clark Univ. Press, 1930.

Braestrup, F. W. The evolutionary significance of learning. *Videnskabelige Meddelelser Dansk Naturhistorisk Forening*, 1971, *134*, 89–102.

Boring, E. G. *A history of experimental psychology.* New York: Century, 1929.

Carpenter, W. B. *Principles of mental physiology, with their applications to the training and discipline of the mind, and the study of its morbid conditions.* London: King, 1874.

Ferrier, D. *The functions of the brain.* London: Smith, Elder & Co., 1876.

McCosh, J. Darwin's descent of man. *The Independent*, May 4, 1871.

McCosh, J. *The intuitions of the mind, inductively investigated.* New York: Carter, 1872 (3rd rev. edition).

McCosh, J. *The Scottish philosophy, biographical, expository, critical. from Hutcheson to Hamilton.* New York: Carter, 1875.

McCosh, J. *Notes on psychology. from lectures given by James McCosh.* Princeton, N. J.: Printed for private circulation, 1880.

Ormond, A. T. James McCosh as thinker and educator. *The Princeton Theological Review*, 1903, *1*, 337–361.

Piaget, J. *The psychology of intelligence.* (M. Peircy & D. E. Berlyne, trans.). New York: Harcourt, Brace, 1950.

Paulsen, F. *Friedrich Paulsen. An autobiography.* (T. Lenz, trans.) New York: Columbia Univ. Press, 1938.

Rabier, E. *Leçons de philosophie.* I. *Psychologie.* Paris: Hachette, 1888 (3rd edition).

Ribot, T. *German psychology of today. The empirical school.* (J. M. Baldwin, trans.). New York: Scribner's, 1886.

Spinoza, B. *Opera posthuma.* Amsterdam: J. Rieuwertsz, 1677.

Vygotsky, L. S. *Razvitie vysshikh psikhicheskikh funktsii* (Development of higher mental functions: From the unpublished works). Ed. by A. N. Leont'ev, A. R. Luria & B. M. Teplov. Moscow: Izd. APN RSFSR, 1960.

Wundt, W. *Grundzüge der physiologischen Psychologie.* Leipzig: Engelmann, 1873–1874.

PART II

BIOLOGY AND
KNOWLEDGE

Introduction

The impact of Darwinian theory on the origins of cognitive-developmental psychology has already been alluded to in the first section. Piaget's chapter in this section points to the special rapport between Baldwin and Darwin. Baldwin not only found the evolutionary perspective intellectually congenial in some general way, he took up and pursued quite specific questions in theoretical biology.

The following essays discuss Baldwin's biological interests and locate his work in relation to what has followed. In an area like biology it is no doubt surprising to find a turn-of-the-century amateur—for Baldwin claimed no biological expertise—still being listened to by general theorists of evolution. If anything, his biological reputation is firmer now than it was then.

A straightforward answer to this state of affairs is to be found in Baldwin's unerring sense for the central questions of evolutionary and developmental theory. To be more precise, he immediately saw the need to articulate the concepts of genesis and structure within a single explanatory framework.

Donald Campbell's essay introduces the full range of Baldwin's biological thought. One can see that Baldwin's general aim was to draw adaptation and evolution close together from the point of view of explanation. In fact, even more than that, Baldwin wanted to show that ontogenesis (developmental adaptation in the individual) and phylogenesis (evolutionary progression in the species) are causally related. For Baldwin this aim was tied to his other interests in analyzing mental processes and modes of consciousness, topics considered in subsequent chapters. Consequently, biology, psychology, and philosophy interpenetrated one another in Baldwin's thought, and from this amalgam, genetic epistemology emerged. The more biological aspects of the sequence are the focus of the essays in this section.

The general aim just noted actually issued in two more limited projects, as Campbell points out. These were the work on evolutionary epistemology and organic selection. The first of these projects concerned itself with showing that there is an evolutionary determination within the (ontogenetic) process of thought. The second project, by contrast, aimed to demonstrate that there is an ontogenetic-adaptive determination within the (phylogenetic) process of species evolution. This way of cutting up Baldwin's thought somewhat simplifies the issues involved, as the reader will see. Nevertheless, it serves, in the first instance, to point out the two principal aspects of Baldwin's thought taken up separately by John Freeman-Moir and Jacques Vonèche.

Before introducing these two essays it is worthwhile to take note of a theme which links them. The immediate context of Baldwin's theoretical biology was the pre-Mendelian debate between the Darwinians and Lamarckians. This debate is reflected as an interesting and productive tension in Baldwin's work. Indeed, to a degree remarkable for the day (since, at times, the debate was quite extreme), Baldwin preserved a balance between the two viewpoints. This was a kind of personal demonstration of cognitive equilibrium which his own psychological theory set out to explain.

The linkage Baldwin forged in his work at this point can be characterized by quoting a now-famous Piagetian maxim: "Genesis emanates from a structure and culminates in another structure, every structure has a genesis." In his interview here, Piaget again stresses the centrality of Baldwin's concept of genesis. Baldwin insisted time and again on the need to analyze genesis—evolution and adaptation— as the genesis of structures. In both his theory of organic selection and his theory of evolutionary epistemology, Baldwin demonstrated the connection between structural determinants and natural selection processes. This was Baldwin's major theoretical achievement in the area of biology.

Vonèche's essay shows how Baldwin attempted to solve the problem of structures within evolution. Baldwin's solution—the theory of organic selection or, more descriptively accurate, coincidental variation—consisted in showing how ontogenetic adaptations may serve to amplify innate variations and so maximize the selection of individuals showing useful structures.

This so-called Baldwin effect provides "a steady organizer behind the system of evolution." Later in this century, and long after Baldwin had finished with biology, this theory provided "a very good point of attack for those biologists who were dissatisfied with neo-Darwinism, since it is a process that simulates Lamarckism but actually consists in the replacement of modifications by imitations."

This is the kind of solution Piaget looked for since he was highly critical of two central neo-Darwinian tenets, that mutations are random and that the organism is essentially passive before the selective force of the environment. Thus, in Piaget's writing we find the Baldwinian theme that selection centers on "the assimilation of fortuitous events into strong structures," and Piaget here (Chap. 3) describes the role of Baldwin's theoretical biology in the recent development of his own. From Piaget's point of view it is perhaps more a matter of "convergence" than direct Baldwinian influence.

Vonèche argues that the range of the debate on evolution, originally billed as a title bout between Charles Darwin of England and Jean-Baptiste Lamarck of France, extends far beyond evolutionary biology to neurophysiology, psychology, linguistics, and even to the level of ideology. In this last extension, we get a sense of the outer limits of cognitive-developmental psychology as formulated by Baldwin, Piaget, and Kohlberg, matters of which it has not spoken or, more likely, cannot speak.

Within the realm of biology at least, Baldwin represents an attempt to break through what, in a beautiful metaphor, Vonèche calls "the frozen landscape" of our theories.

The problematic of structure and genesis is also the central issue of the essay by Freeman-Moir. Baldwin, however, is now seen from the viewpoint of a rather different tradition, one defined by the attempt to offer a toughminded Darwinian epistemology.

Interestingly, Baldwin's contribution here is again on the side of emphasizing structure and to that degree is Lamarckian in its intent. Baldwin wanted to keep clearly in view the structures, patterns, and complexities of thought. He emphasized, for example, that thinking shows certain trends and consistent directions. How could this be so and how could a natural selection theory explain these facts?

Freeman-Moir argues that Baldwin attended to one particular piece of this puzzle. When Baldwin's analysis is set alongside the work of James, Simmel, and Campbell, we find a concerted attack on a set of questions. How much progress has been made toward answering these questions is a matter for debate, but the right questions to ask seem to have been identified and clearly stated.

Among those contributors to the evolutionary epistemology discussed by Freeman-Moir we also find something like a division of labor, organized chronologically, with respect to the underlying problems. James and Simmel pay most attention to the variant-production and selectionist issues. Baldwin, as noted, wrestled with the constructionist features of thought. In the work of Campbell, though by admission and commission he is a strict neo-Darwinian, we find a careful analysis which attends to both aspects of the problem.

The biological thought of Baldwin is impressive not only when located within the contemporary milieu which gave rise to it, but also because it informed later thought and continues to do so. As Piaget points out, it is quite remarkable that Baldwin was able to be heard at all in the field of biology, since if biologists had known of his psychological preoccupations, they might well have dismissed him as a nonspecialist. Their inability to ignore his contribution is further testimony to the intellectual breadth and cogency of Baldwin's work.

2

EVOLUTION, DEVELOPMENT, AND THE GROWTH OF KNOWLEDGE[1]

J. Jacques Vonèche
University of Geneva

This chapter on Baldwin's biological ideas seeks (1) to retrace the reasons why the so-called Baldwin effect was repressed for more than 50 years and then revived by biologists; (2) to show the place of Baldwin's ideas on the theory of evolution in the general economy of his system; and (3) to present a theory of the growth of knowledge based on a combination of Piaget's and Kuhn's ideas on this topic.

Retracing the vicissitudes of the Baldwin effect constitutes the longest and most technical part of this essay. My position is that Baldwin's ideas about evolution were actively but not malignantly repressed when he advanced them because they did not fit the mainstream that opposed Lamarckism, a trend of ideas against which it had just won a battle by reviving Mendelism.

A philosopher and psychologist like Baldwin grew interested in discussing the theory of evolution because, in my view, he was preoccupied with genesis in its broadest sense. As other chapters illustrate, Baldwin meditated on genesis in a way both timely and original. His meditations were *coherent* with the general ideas of his time (Haeckel's recapitulation hypothesis still being very much alive rather than the exquisite cadaver that it now is), and yet *original* in the sense that he wanted to unify ontogeny and phylogeny through

[1] The writing of this essay would not have been possible without passionate discussions with the late Conrad Waddington, the late Jean Piaget, and above all, Marino Buscaglia, whose remarkable scholarship, large library of rare books in biology, sensitivity, and insight have helped me more than I could say here.

"orthoplasia." For him, individual and racial (today we would say species) variations were coinciding variations and not merely an embryological recapitulation. This difference between Baldwin and Haeckel shows how refined a thinker Baldwin was.

In studying the case of James Mark Baldwin with the sort of attention I learned from Howard E. Gruber, a goldsmith in these matters, I was forced to recognize that each scientific period has its own favorite prototype or paradigm, and that Baldwin fell victim to that sort of favoritism. But I wanted to go beyond the limits of Kuhn's structuralist explanation, which is totally relativist since it does not give the reasons for the occurrence of a change in paradigm. So I turned to Piaget for an explanation, and I tried to find out why a certain set of intellectual operations was explanatory at one time and not at another. This quest led me to formulate a functional law for the transformation of scientific theories.

Baldwin's Ideas about Evolutionary Theory

Besides neo-Darwinian or strictly selectionist theories and Lamarckian conceptions, there has been, in the history of the theories of evolution, a certain number of other theories which were not as extensive and as fundamental as these two typical conceptions. They did not play as considerable a role in the debate on the central question of biology and they could not be classified under either of these two main theories. Some were more or less external to them. Others tried to combine them. This was the case with Baldwin's theory of organic selection.

The idea of organic selection was formulated almost simultaneously (and with unimportant modifications) by Baldwin and Osborn in the United States and by the Welshman Lloyd Morgan in the United Kingdom. This gave rise to a debate about its ownership. For Welsh, Scottish, and English biologists, the idea was presented first by Lloyd Morgan and then by the two American authors. According to Sir Alistair Hardy in The Living Stream (1965, p. 164), James Mark Baldwin and Fairfield Osborn first spoke about it in a discussion following a lecture by Lloyd Morgan in 1896. The fact is that Baldwin's first mention of organic selection appeared in a 94-page article published in 1896, in the American Naturalist, whereas Lloyd Morgan's publication was dated 1897.

American biologists—Roe and Simpson (1958) were the first—have recently revived the name of Baldwin without mentioning Lloyd Morgan. The most indicative statement of the British position is that of Conrad Waddington (1969) who speaks of the Baldwin effect but thinks that its revival was "nothing more than a piece of American nationalism" (p. 336).

We shall discuss this point later. For the time being, let us say that Baldwin's theory represents an attempt to reconcile the predominant role of natural selection with the heredity of acquired character or, more accurately, to answer some of the most serious objections raised against natural selection by giving it, as an auxiliary, direct individual adaptation. This theory was diversely labeled at the time: *ontogenetic selection*, *orthoplasia*, *coincidental selection*, or theory of *coinciding variations* (this last being the most accurate denomination of the theory).

One of the main objections raised against the selectionist theory was that small variations, subliminal fluctuations, are not strong enough in the beginning to give rise to a worthwhile selective process. One had thus to explain why and how these early stages were conserved and transformed by heredity. It was already well known that throughout its existence every living being adapts constantly to its environment and in so doing acquires a certain number of useful structures. This is an *ontogenetic* form of adaptation, taking ontogenesis in its extensive meaning, the meaning retained by psychologists who apply it, generally speaking, to the entire life span and not only to the embryonic stages as biologists often do.

If the environmentally caused variations encounter corresponding innate variations in the organism, the effects of these two orders of variations are more likely to be manifested outwardly than if each of them existed alone. So it happens that a small inborn variation somehow gets amplified by an acquired variation which is grafted onto it, so that the combination of the two sorts of variations gives rise to natural selection. This last process preserves only the favored individuals (excluding the others) and so is an innate variation conserved and transmitted by heredity to the next generation, thanks to the usefulness of the acquired variation. Then things happen in the way described by Darwin in the case of innate useful variations: they accumulate by progressive additions and the character in question becomes more and more developed (Fig 1). Darwin himself mentioned certain characters which, without being useful by themselves, could take advantage of the usefulness of other characters correlative to them in order to survive. In Darwin's examples, the two characters were innate; here, the protective character is an acquired one. This difference should be noted.

According to Baldwin (but also for Osborn and Lloyd Morgan), this mechanism would solve the difficult problem of the beginnings of useful variations as well as the pending embarrassing question of the heredity of acquired character. This heredity would then be a

LAMARCKISM

Hierarchical scale of organisms
Environmental circumstances

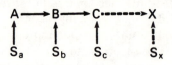

NEO-DARWINISM

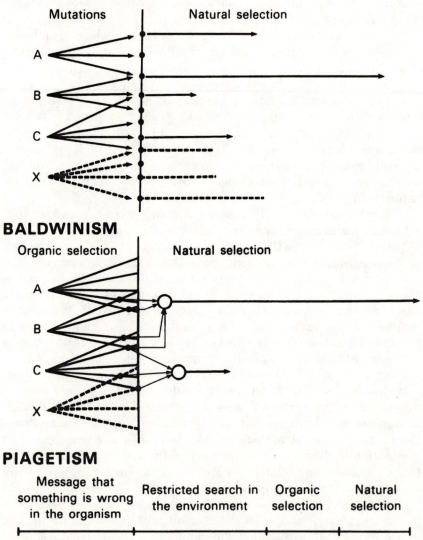

BALDWINISM

PIAGETISM

FIG. 1.   Diagrammatic representations of four approaches to evolution.

mere surface semblance, since what would be inherited would not be the visible somatic variation but the innate coinciding variation that was not apparent. Bit by bit, in the series of generations, this coincidence would become more complete because it would be advantageous, and natural selection would gradually eliminate those individuals that did not present the conjunction of the innate variation with the adaptive ones. In this process, what is transmitted by heredity is only germinal variations, which is perfectly orthodox. Since, however, these variations facilitate ontogenetic adaptation that will necessarily take place, it will seem, at the surface level, that this adaptation has been directly transmitted as Lamarck used to think.

Moreover, the theory of coinciding variations answers another objection against natural selection. This objection is based on the case of parallel adaptations, each of which, taken separately, is not of any use: for instance, the antlers of a stag which are not useful unless its neck and shoulder muscles are developed accordingly. This was one of Spencer's main arguments in his polemic against Weismann's theory of germinative heredity and in favor of the heredity of acquired characters. But, according to Baldwin, here again this heredity is only semblance. In fact, the development of well-grown antlers in some individuals is the result of an innate variation. Then, because of the extra load of these antlers, the muscles of the neck and shoulders of these animals were developed by adaptive ontogenetic variation, which turned the initially innate variation of the size of antlers into a very useful advantage. Conversely, an innate variation reinforcing the strength of neck and shoulder muscles, which would have disappeared in the absence of antlers, would be conserved and transmitted in the presence of antlers, since it would have a determinant role to play in the economy of the functioning organism of the animals concerned. Natural selection protects such a combination of variations, and they keep growing in parallel.

This simultaneous, accurate, and specific adaptation is difficult to explain in terms of natural selection alone. This is especially so in the case of complex instincts where the individual ontogenetic adaptation develops each one of the specific instincts which in isolation is of no use. But in the case of behavior, another circumstance increases the illusion of the heredity of acquired instincts: the rearing of the young by their parents. All the ontogenetic acquisitions of one generation are transmitted to the next one by imitation or socialization so that the new generation functions in the framework created by the previous one and imitates its example. This result of organic selection Baldwin calls *social heredity*.

The theory of organic selection explains especially well why variations can be canalized in one determined direction, generation after generation.[2] This determination lies, according to Baldwin, not in germinal variations, but, on the contrary, in the action upon them of acquired modifications. This feature of organic selection resembles orthogenesis, which starts, as does Osborn's theory, with germinal variations, but then assumes that they are directed toward a goal or *telos*. Baldwin, aware of the possible similarity between his theory and that of orthogenesis, speaks of *orthoplasia* for the sort of evolution that he has in mind.

In spite of its ingenuity, Baldwin's theory of organic selection or orthoplasia did not meet with success at the time of its presentation in 1896 and 1902.

The Repression of Baldwin's Concepts

The lack of interest in Baldwin's theory can be explained by many factors. First, a theory of compromise is bound either to become immediately successful because it allays the anxieties of most researchers in the field who are unsatisfied with one of the two competing theories, or to be neglected when its strength or caliber does not surpass that of the competing theories. This was clearly true of organic selection. Although it was intellectually satisfying, it lacked the breadth of either Darwinism or Lamarckism. It seemed too specific to many biologists, and it did not introduce a new factor into evolution.

In addition to this intrinsic defect, there also existed an unfavorable sociological environment. The thrust of scientific endeavor was still in Europe (more precisely, the United Kingdom and the German states). The United Kingdom was divided into two camps of evolutionists: those who, with Bateson as the prominent character, defended Mendelism, and those who gathered around Pearson and Wheldon to oppose Mendelism. Special journals were founded to publish the papers of each faction. The Mendelists had the *Reports of the Royal Society's Committee on Evolution* and the anti-Mendelists or biometrists the *Questions of the Day and of the Fray*.

The timing of Baldwin's papers was, to say the least, badly chosen for what he had to say: he was expressing in pre-Mendelian

---

[2] This vision neglects what is now known as *hot spots* in the genome, that is, such an increase in the rate of mutations that the regulation of the size of the antlers, for instance, is less and less adequate, giving rise to oversized antlers or monstrous variations in the muscular system of the neck.

terms a subtle question at the very moment of the rediscovery of Mendelian inheritance.

This moment deserves some attention, because it was epochal in the history of evolution theories. Before the rediscovery of Mendel's results, it was thought that inheritance involved some sort of blending of the constitutions of the two parents to produce the heredity of the offspring. After Darwin promulgated the idea of natural selection, F. Jenkins pointed out "very ferociously" (says Gruber, to whom I owe this information) that such a blending of constitutions would very rapidly reduce the hereditary constitution of all individuals to a uniform intermediary state on which natural selection could not work. For part of his life, Darwin was tempted to adopt the Lamarckian theory that new variations can be introduced by changes in the environment.

This problem was resolved by the rediscovery of Mendelian inheritance. By postulating that the hereditary characters are carried by discrete factors, so that factors from the two parents come together in the offspring but do not blend and resegregate again in the next generation, Mendel could explain in a very plausible way why variations do not disappear and why individuals do not become alike.

The main argument of the opponents of Mendelism was the existence of continuous variations in such characters as height and weight for which there was a large stock of statistics available (thanks, for instance, to compulsory military service in most European countries). The argument was thus largely mathematical. Biologically speaking, it was based upon the assumption that height or weight depends on one or a few Mendelian factors.

Udny Yule, a statistician well known to psychologists, showed, however, that if it is assumed that height and weight depend on a large number of factors, then the random distribution of these factors in a given population will be best represented by a continuous range of variations. But, since, like W. Bateson, he was a fellow of St. John's College, Cambridge, his paper was disregarded by the opposite group.

Moreover, we have evidence that Wilhelm Weinberg's contribution to population genetics was obviously known to, but not appreciated by, Karl Pearson (1910) who considered it clumsy and lacking in rigor. The significance of Weinberg's equilibrium rule to genetics does not need to be proved to a contemporary audience familiar with the presently known Hardy-Weinberg law of which Weinberg gave the first and most general formulation. Pearson missed the fundamental significance of Weinberg's work, because he concentrated on minor faults in mathematics instead of seeing that this work closed most of the gap between Mendelists and biometrists.

But Weinberg was only Weinberg, a simple medical practitioner with little or no mathematical training, who built no school around himself to develop his ideas and propagate them.

At this point, one should mention that Baldwin's book *Development and Evolution* was published in New York and London in 1902 the same year that Bateson's *Mendel's Principles of Heredity: A Defence* was published in London. One easily imagines that in such an atmosphere Baldwin's voice could not be heard. But then what prompted G. G. Simpson to revive it in 1952, 50 years after Baldwin's last publication on the topic? A very cryptic reply would be: the present difficulties of the strict neo-Darwinian theory of evolution.

The Return of J. M. Baldwin

In order to understand the theory of evolution today, it is necessary to retrace the penetration of Mendelism into Darwinism. In the aftermath of the Bateson-Wheldon battle, some biologists tried to demonstrate—*more mathematico*—that Mendelian factors could provide a satisfactory basis for natural selection.

J. B. S. Haldane and R. A. Fisher considered that, given a single recessive mutation in a randomly mating diploid population, the proportion of the varying types of individuals should come to a steady distribution which is in equilibrium[3] with selection pressure, unless the recessive mutation is at a disadvantage under natural selection; in that case, its frequency could be reduced by a factor which is simply linear for Haldane and exponential for Fisher (his famous "Malthusian factor").

This model simplifies reality in three ways. First, it supposes a state of nonequilibrium of the gene populations, but it does not say why these populations have departed from equilibrium. This is really a difficulty, because any population containing a number of different genes will normally settle down to an equilibrium after which the proportions of the various genes remain constant. Second, this model is formulated in such terms as to suppose very few varying genes. This again does not reflect the immense complexity of most genotypes in actual populations, as was discovered later. Third, the equations deal only with genotypes, whereas natural selection actually acts on phenotypes.

---

[3] This equilibrium should be related to population genetics, and the mere mention of Hardy-Weinberg's law suffices to show how crude Fisher's and Haldane's models were. This law states that, if reproduction is random, then there is no tendency for directional evolutionary change to occur. This statement is formulated mathematically in every elementary textbook on the subject.

Sewell Wright tried to solve the first two difficulties. From the beginning he considered (1) populations in which large numbers of genes were varying simultaneously, and (2) the fitness of whole complex genotypes instead of individual ones. Thus, the equilibrium of the populations was considered as metastable instead of stable, since his "fitness surfaces" represented various loci of best fit or points of temporary equilibrium for a given population which was never defined unidimensionally, but presented various surfaces of fitness. The question of the passage from one surface to the next was, however, left open, and C. Waddington attempted to answer it.

Waddington defined the problem in a way different from his predecessors. He regarded the genetic system as composed of the interaction of four different spaces: the genotype space, the epigenetic space, the phenotype space, and the fitness space. Why this multiplication of spaces? A very good reason commands such a complexity: the necessity to distinguish life from mere information, a preoccupation, by the way, that does not seem to be shared by most molecular biologists of the gene.

Let us suppose, for a moment, that genetic transmission is characterized only by the transmission from one generation to the next of mere information. In such a perspective, given a dislocation of one face of a crystal, it will be transmitted to the next layer of the crystal as it grows, in the very same way as the so-called natural slope of 45° is "transmitted" from one heap of sand to the next as more sand is poured upon the original heap. Let us suppose, in addition, that the natural slope is better adapted to a wider range of conditions (which it is, indeed). It will thus be favored over other sorts of slopes by natural selection.[4]

Are these sorts of transmissions and of natural selection interesting for understanding the evolution of living organisms? No, they are trivial. So purely genetic transmission of information is as fascinating as roll call in the army. What is appealing in life is that living things do something to their surroundings. So what is needed is transmissible *instructions* or programs or algorithms of behavior.

Biologically, this is solved by combining a very inert substance, DNA (which acts as a memory store) with protein enzymes, thus enabling DNA to be replicated and passed on to the next generation, as well as to be used to produce RNA corresponding to the information stored in the DNA; which, in turn, is used to program the synthesis of a corresponding protein. Thus, there is an inescapable

---

[4] Caudal regeneration in *Anurans* tadpoles follows the same principle: the new regenerated caudal segment is always perpendicular to the axis of the cut and then it later reverts to the normal position in the axis of the entire body.

difference between what is transmitted in the DNA, the genotype, and what is produced on the basis of DNA instructions, the phenotype.

Now, if we consider that human beings are made out of at least 1 million genes and that each gene conveys at least one instruction, the number of possible combinations becomes astronomical. If we want to represent that pictorially, we must rely on topological transformation called _sheaves_ in which each genotypic space is represented by one point, which considerably simplifies the handling of these spaces since from any particular genotype there eventually develops a corresponding phenotype, which could be located as a point within the multidimensional phenotype space. In between, the various genetic instructions interact with one other and with their surroundings during the development of the organism, leading Waddington to insert what he called the epigenetic space between the genotype and the phenotype spaces. However, during its development, the organism is also under the pressure of the surroundings in which some of the instructions given to the phenotype originate. As a result, the very same genotype can produce a number of phenotypes according to the characteristics of the environment of the developing organism.

Natural selection operates in a one-dimensional fitness space (i.e., on the number of offspring a phenotype leaves behind). Thus, there is a relation of indeterminancy between the fitness space and the multidimensional phenotype space, between this space and the epigenetic one, and between epigenesis and the genotype space. Moreover, because of their behavior, some phenotypes can influence the sort of environment they live in. An animal can move away from one environment—the sea, the woods, or the plain—and try another permanently or temporarily, as migrating species do. But there are aspects of the environment that are unrelated to the adaptive moves of the organism: geological revolutions, new predators, or new viruses.

The same is also true at the epigenetic level where the interactions among enzymes and the multisyntheses of these enzymes out of the same raw materials can lead to an extremely complex system of relations which is ordered in terms of stability. This stability is of a special kind since it is stability through change by keeping the proportions constant, thanks to appropriate feedback mechanisms. This is called homeorhesis, and it is a dynamic process of equilibrium.

In the epigenetic space, what seems important to stabilize is the time trajectory (for instance, the intrinsic time of pregnancy) so that each genotype can instruct the phenotype on which it acts to produce, thanks to a system of appropriate interacting differentiations, an organism with different and distinct organs out of what was, at an earlier stage, a single mass of undifferentiated tissue. This stabilized time trajectory Waddington calls chreod. The epigenetic space is characterized by a number of such chreods, each of which is defined by the instructions in the genotype which interact together to produce the organism under scrutiny.

How do these chreods come into being? Waddington's answer to this question is not very clear. On the one hand, he recognizes the influence of natural selection which has built up such genotypes as they operate harmoniously with one another to produce a canalization of the chreods sufficient to prevent the system from being thrown out of its trajectory. On the other hand, he seems to believe that the stability of the system is insured by its own mathematical properties, i.e., double randomness of initial conditions: interconnections and functions. We know that this last hypothesis has been recently confirmed by Japanese geneticists.

But if such a mathematical structure imposes an obligatory pathway on evolution, it also imposes an upper limit to the system, the so-called limit cycle in which the system has reached equilibrium and stops. This difficulty was clearly perceived by Waddington who remarked that as soon as an organism evolves, its very evolution changes all the environments of other organs with which it interacts, since the environment is made out of the interactions among organisms. This sort of chain effect will be exploited in two ways: (1) the production of new hereditary variations, and (2) the dispersion of organisms. Hereditary variations can happen in at least two different ways: (1) random mutation, and (2) recombination of existing genotypes. Random mutations are important only to replenish the stores of variations contained in the population which would eventually run out, if selection operated for a very long time. The role of genetic recombination is to produce an effective complex organ without having to wait for a mutation to "throw up" just the one gene that is needed, by simply selecting genes already present in low frequencies in a diploid population (i.e., a population with the normal number of chromosomes).

A third process helps an evolving population to find a way of meeting the demands of natural selection more directly than by merely waiting for an appropriate change in some nucleotide sequence to happen: stress adaptation in higher organisms. When repeated over generations and under the constant pressure of natural selection, this process produces a phenotypic alteration that modifies the corresponding chreod so that the existence of any environmental stress becomes unnecessary for the alteration to appear: thus, the phenotypic alteration has been assimilated by the genotype. This genetic assimilation process gives exactly the same effects as the Lamarckian inheritance of acquired characters, but it does not operate by any direct influence of the environment on the genetic constitution, but rather by a long-continued selection of appropriate responses[5] of organism to environmental pressures.

This rather lengthy description of Waddington's theory is necessary to understand why Baldwin's ideas were revived recently. But Waddington was not alone. Sir Alister Hardy developed a theory of behavior as selective force; there the important point is that, instead of passively responding to environmental stresses, the animal takes the initiative and develops a new habit which is then imitated by other animals. Here the case of the Japanese monkey who first rinsed her sweet potatoes in the sea comes to mind, as well as that of the blue tit that discovered how to pierce the cap of a milk-bottle left on the doorstep of a house in order to drink the milk, not to speak of the Galapagos finches of Darwinian memory. Furthermore, one behavioral change opens the way to others: overcoming fear of the sea and fishing for shrimps.

The Russian biologist Schmalhausen, in his book *Factors of Evolution* (1942), spoke of mutations as mere triggers for an infinitely more complex mechanism of adaptation. Let us take the case of an annual plant. It grows in the weather of one year but most of the selection on it is exerted during the next year when its seeds germinate in sometimes quite different conditions. The first part of this adaptation leads to the formation of a phenotype; the second aspect deals with natural selection, properly speaking. In such a picture, the genes are faced with two opposed strategies: either a maximization of structural stability through very strong homeorhesis or a maximization of flexibility. In nature, mice have selected the first strategy, whereas crustaceans have picked the other. Other species have used intermediate strategies. As one can easily see, this idea of a strategy of the genes anticipates Waddington's genetic assimilation involving selection, within a given population, of those genes which respond better to the environment.

In *Evolution, the Modern Synthesis* (1942), Sir Julian Huxley interpreted the Baldwin–Lloyd Morgan effect as a physiological adaptation to a stressful situation that persists and breeds in the given environment until a genetic mutation happens, bringing about the required phenotypic modifications. According to Huxley, the

---

[5] For a recent formulation of the mechanisms of environmental and phenotypical feedbacks on the genome, see Stroun, Anker, Maurice, and Gahan (1977).

concept of organic selection could be used in cases in which Weismann's distinction between variations due to modifications and those due to mutations is blurred. When, after a migration, animals of certain species have extended their habitat, this extension depends in the first instance on a noninherited modification of behavior. But, later, mutation and selection may step in to fix the change genetically. Thus, speciation or biological differentiation, in general, in its early stages appeared, for Huxley, to depend upon a form of organic selection. He gave examples of this process in apple flies (which were originally parasites of the hawthorn) and ermine moths. Another example is given by Harrison's experiment with Pontania (sawflies) which he transferred to new host-plants by means of their olfactory conditioning mechanisms. In the same way, it has been shown (Thorpe, 1930) that, although head lice are very different, morphologically speaking, from body lice, head lice can be transformed into the body-louse type by being kept on the body for four generations, exhibiting all the biological differences of the two types. The same seems to happen in the song of some birds (Heinroth, 1924–1926) which do not learn their song from their parents.

In sum, for Huxley, the Baldwin–Lloyd Morgan principle of organic selection is a special case of *subsidiary historical restriction*, that is, a mechanism making it easier for selection to act in certain ways than in others, while leaving the adaptive direction to be guided by selection.

This is very different from Osborn's *adaptive radiation* which consists of an extreme form of ecological divergence according to which, in each systematic groups of animals, numerous separate lines of descent run parallel far back into geological time before divergence from a common ancestor can be postulated.

The similarity between the Osborn effect and the Baldwin–Lloyd Morgan effect is very superficial indeed, since their only commensurability is that both postulate a number of gradual evolutionary trends, each tending to greater specialization. For the rest, they are quite different, since they are located at different levels of the theory of evolution. The Osborn effect attempts to deal with what Huxley calls the *groove effect* and Plate, orthoselection (i.e., the directional aspect of evolution). When evolution has begun in one direction, with the passage of time it becomes gradually harder to reverse this direction. This results in apparent orthogenesis, or goal-directed evolution, which is very different from subsidiary historical restriction which leaves the adaptive direction to natural selection. Only hasty historians of biology could confuse the two sorts of effects. This point will become important when Baldwin's biology is compared to Piaget's.

Mayr in his *Animal Species and Evolution* (1963) was also instrumental in the revival of the Baldwin effect. But since his interpretation is not basically different from Huxley's, we shall not dwell on it here.

The Baldwin effect was thus a very good point of departure for those biologists who were dissatisfied with neo-Darwinism, since it is a process that stimulates Lamarckism but actually consists in the replacement of modifications by mutations. This is an important point in order to understand the role of organic selection in the economy of the theory of evolution today.

The Difficulties of Neo-Darwinism

Opponents of Darwinism had made several points:

1. The separation of evolution from adaptation;
2. The occurrence of self-organization at all levels without the requirement of genetic control;
3. The distinction between analogies and homologies;
4. The emphasis upon the grammar of the genetic code versus the current emphasis upon its vocabulary;
5. The necessity, in order to avoid preformism, to admit the accumulation during evolution of the information carried by the genes;
6. Negentropy as a rule in living organisms.

The separation between the two concepts of evolution and adaptation is based on the following argument: evolution is a phenomenal fact proved by paleontology, but there is no reason to link it with adaptation which happens at any evolutionary level and which is proved by the permanence of all existing species. Organic selection allows for this separation in a very convenient way.

The occurrence of self-organization by organisms is not explained by the present theories of replication and protein synthesis. They lack an interpretation of the origin of the genetic text which is being replicated, translated, and expressed in functional proteins. They do not explain the relation between specific linear sequences of nucleic acid and proteins and any particular structural–functional property allegedly resulting from them. Once again, organic selection and *phenocopy* (or endogenous copy of a phenotype) would give a meaning to these observations.

That some organs are very similar in very different species pleads in favor of an inner necessity for these analogies (for instance, universal technological constraints on engineering). These constraints could be explained better by organic selection than by random genetic mutation plus natural selection.

The entire debate can be summarized by saying that the current theory of evolution lacks meaning or semantic grounding. We know much about the linear graph representing the spatial arrangement of the codons of messenger RNA, specifying the dictionary of the genetic code in different sequences of the same 20 amino acids, but very little about the algorithm for producing an organism. It should be understood here that such a linear reading is rather complex, since it is by no means continuous, as evidenced in "splicing" and "spacers," as well as in general by RNA processing, which all intervene in the determination of the translated products. Moreover, very little is known about the origin of new genes, except for rare cases of duplication. But it is assumed that such genes become available for new functions. A good example of this is given by the molecular evolution of neurohypophysial peptides.

In addition, to have a living system two conditions are required: a thermodynamically open system providing the energy necessary for the change of structure and an information-carrying system. One without the other is no life: a flame is an open system but it is not hereditary, morphogenetic, etc. The nucleic acid molecules are inert chemical substances, unless they are activated by an energizer coming from the thermodynamic side of the process. In the neo-Darwinist frame of reference postulating the generation of order out of random events, the problem is explaining how and why, in open systems which, in Prigogine's (1965) phrase, are "far from equilibrium," organic substances have formed. It seems then that some sort of prevital metabolism would be necessary to account for the emergence of such substances, unless one is willing to admit that metabolism (even reduced to catalyzers, cyclic processes, etc.) could act *in absentia.*

In conclusion, what was needed by embryology in the forties and fifties was a steady organizer behind the system of evolution. This organizer did not need to be outside the system. It could perfectly well have been immanent to the system. In such a global perspective, organic selection was an interesting theory because, without mentioning this organizer explicitly, it somehow was postulating it all along the way from early modifications to final "mutations." Without organizing forces, small modifications lasting a while would be pointless.

But we think that Baldwin's views are fundamentally misinterpreted, not only by Huxley who speaks of *mutations*—whereas Baldwin is anterior to the revival of Mendelism—but also in the writings of Simpson, Waddington, and even Hardy, as we shall now see by comparing Baldwin's biology to Piaget's.

Piaget's Organic Selection and Phenocopy

One of Piaget's most general aims has been a deeper understanding of the way in which knowledge processes are integral to, and yet an extension of, life processes. This general theme has been expressed in *Biology and Knowledge* (1971/1967). In good part, this work is an exposition of some of the complex analogies between organic functioning in general and cognition in particular, justified by the point that cognitive processes exploit the whole organism. But Piaget also wants to draw attention to crucial differences: the completeness, stability, and flexibility of the structures of intelligence, as well as the progressive dissociation of form and content.

In his essay on evolution, *Adaptation and Intelligence: Organic Selection and Phenocopy* (1980/1974), Piaget aims at three different targets: a critique of neo-Darwinism, a restatement of his own interactionist position, and a presentation of his hypothesis that changes in the gene complex can be viewed as an extension of the self-regulating activities of the organism.

Two key points in neo-Darwinism provoke Piaget's criticism: (1) the randomness of mutations, and (2) the passivity of the organism. In neo-Darwinism, the occurrence of a given mutation bears no relation to the adaptive needs of the organism, and moreover, it is the environment that responds to the mutation that has happened to the organism.

Piaget dislikes this picture of the organism as a sort of taxi-girl for genes and environment parties and he raises certain objections to it. First, he considers the sheer improbability of the evolution of complex organs or organisms on the basis of chance alone. He cites here the traditional example of the evolution of the human eye. Second, the gene complex is not sealed off from the rest of the body. Third, each individual gene is not simply sitting there waiting for a mutation to happen to it, or not, as chance decrees. It is interacting with other genes, influencing them, and being, in turn, influenced by them.

Piaget wants a model that presents the organism as perpetually active, choosing its environment and which mutations to try out, as his most recent book on this topic entitled *Behavior and Evolution* (1978) shows very clearly. The mutations that occur are in the first place part of the total process of organized self-regulation, and an internal process of "organic selection" plays a major role in determining which variants will be presented to the environment for further "natural" selection. Clearly, here is a strong influence of Baldwin's terminology and ideas, the central point being, for both authors, an insistence upon the assimilation of fortuitous events into strong structures. Hence, the role of anticipation in both theories. Anticipation is considered as a very general biological function in the sense that many structural changes occur in an organism that are not useful to it at the moment they occur, but will become useful later on. The development of anticipation, both phylogenetically and ontogenetically, must depend upon past experience stored in some sort of memory. Piaget's account of the series of feedbacks by which this is made possible is reminiscent of Waddington's genetic assimilation. Thus, there is a continuum from memory to anticipation, and a given scenario, once stored, can be run backward into memory or forward into anticipation.

This formulation seems clearly to have a ring of philosophical idealism in, at least, five ways:

1. The teleological note of autoregulation;
2. The assertion that cognitive processes are organs;
3. The claim of their universality and completeness;
4. The separation of form and content;
5. The ultimate claim that necessity has the advantage over chance, contrary to Democritus's contention that "all there is, is the fruit of chance and necessity."

But this is also somewhat similar to Baldwin's views on the question, although the place for chance was broader in Baldwin's theory than in Piaget's, as is especially clear in the phenocopy hypothesis, which restricts the locus of chance action. This hypothesis proposes that there are both exogenous and endogenous variations in phenotypes. Once the exogenous form is established, the organism *reinvents* it, that is, changes itself in such a manner that the same phenotypic result is now produced by endogenous means. This endogenous or genotypic form is in some sense a copy of the phenotype, hence *phenocopy*. This endogenous form is eventually substituted for the exogenous form.

How does this process come about? At each level, from gene complex to cognitive structures, the organism has a system for sensing that something is, or is not, working properly: hence, chance action in that locus. If not, a process of variation begins until a solution is found, resulting, usually, in reinvention and substitution leading toward a better equilibrium with the environment.

If the analogies with Baldwin's theory are striking, more striking still is the aloofness of Baldwin's and Piaget's ideas from not only current history but modern science in general.

Dominant Theory of Evolution

In biology, it is very clear that present biologists—and among them Waddington, especially—interpret genetic assimilation as a hereditary *fixation* by selection on phenotypes and not as a "reinvention" or reconstruction. This difference is of the utmost importance; and Piaget is well aware of it. In the case of fixation, any useful adaptation producing a stable phenotype, that is, re-forming itself at each new generation in the same environment but without genotypic fixation (small size, habit formation, language, etc.), should give rise to a hereditary fixation. This is clearly not the case, and a fixation model cannot explain this fact. On the contrary, the reconstruction model accounts for these variations in fixations, since, with it, variations happening in a stable milieu need not be inherited, since they are controlled easily enough by the chreodic process during epigenesis. Only those variations happening in unstable environments will be reconstructed endogenously, since they are no longer regulated by environmental pressures only but by a sort of balance sheet between the organism and the environment. The first sort of regulation is direct, the second involves a matching system, so that they depend on two different forms of causality: mechanical, or direct, and feedback (cybernetical) or circular, causality. In such a circular system of causality, regulator genes, from a certain threshold on, are kept informed of the imbalances in the relations between the organism and the environment, and the search mechanism begins. This heuristic process stops only when a new equilibrium level has been reached.

Such ideas run contrary to the contemporary mainstream of ideas in science. First, they have a very distinctly Lamarckian ring to the extent that they espouse Lamarck's basic principle of evolution. This principle is not the "inheritance of characteristics" (a gross oversimplification due to hasty readers of the neo-Darwinistic persuasion) but *the inherent tendency of living things toward greater complexity and perfection*, an idea shared by almost every scientist in the last century and by Teilhard de Chardin and I. Prigogine in this one. Today, after the experience of world wars, tortures, and dictatorships of all sorts, scientists are no longer so sure of the march toward complexity and perfection.

The present *thema*, in Holton's sense (the equivalent of Spitzer's *topos* in literary criticism), is selection, which is antinomic to that of reconstruction, as we shall now see. The strife between the two themata has lasted for more than a century. It started with the emblematic figures of the "selectionist-Darwin" and the "constructivist-Lamarck." It has extended to the question of antibodies where the opposition between Linus Pauling on the constructivist side and Joshua Lederberg on the selectionist side was an illustration of the same dilemma. For Pauling, antibodies were produced by the organism in a freewheeling manner without a definite structure. For Lederberg, the repertoire of highly specific antibodies was genetically determined prior to any contact with pathogenic invaders. The variety and the specificity (that is, the specific fixed structure) of antibodies antedated any experience. The role of experience was purely selective; it consisted of checking the right antibody among those stored in the organism—that is, the one with the right structure.

This intellectual phenomenon is now repeated in neurophysiology, psychology, and linguistics. A case in point is given by the work of Gerald Edelman (who was awarded the Nobel Prize for his researches on the structure of antibodies) and Vernon Mountcastle. Their theory of the basic processes of perception, memory, and learning is based on ideas similar to those of neurophysiologists, such as Rodolfo Llinas, philosophers, such as Jerry Fodor, psychologists, such as Thomas Bever, linguists, such as Noam Chomsky, and anthropologists, such as Dan Sperber. For them, living is a continuous exposure to the flux of sensations, perceptions, and experiences of all kinds which resembles the invasion of pathogenic agents. Experience consists in the fixation of selected concepts, mental structures, or operations that exist prior to any experience. Such mental structures have been refined and filtrated by centuries and centuries of evolution. In fact, for them, a newborn baby is not characterized by its learning possibilities but by the elimination of everything that is not immediately useful. For instance, the newborn can swim spontaneously at birth. After a few weeks of not using this skill, the baby ceases to swim spontaneously when placed in water. Thomas Bower (1974) has presented an entire developmental psychology based on such "revolutions."

For the selectionists, the mistake of Piaget and the constructivists who, as heirs to the Enlightenment, believe in the progressive enrichment of experience, is their benign neglect of the elimination of skills in development. Psychological and biological survival is, for the selectionists, linked to a process of immunization, that is, selection among the many and often useless skills stored in the organism.

In the same way as antibodies, concepts, logical operations, and linguistic structures, once selected, also fixate and precipitate external events, unprime their aggressive charge and their potential for invasion. They are the results of billions of neuronic connections that have been blocked together for ages and form well-established chreods in the organism. *Learning* is trimming down the inner tree of knowledge to the bare minimum that guarantees optimal survival.

Standing before this frozen landscape, one wonders how and when all that was frozen. On the question of time of fixation, the choice is simple: either it took place at the beginning, a solution which excludes evolution, or it happened at some point in history or prehistory, a solution bringing us back to our starting point: How did that happen?

Witnessing the success of such a logically weak theory, that, in addition, steals the workers from the product of their labor by hypostatizing into structures what has been lived through as a network of actions and taboos, struggles, and oppositions, one wonders whether this success is not due to sociological reasons only. I see here the communistic illusion, of an innate kernel, stable, eternal, and intangible, which organizes all its existing metamorphoses around itself in a preset plan. This sort of communism (which is best represented by Chomsky in linguistics) relays Saussure's ideas. It demonstrates scientists' incapacity to think linguistic practices otherwise than in the modality of mere execution, that is, under the negative form of a byproduct of the construction of systems of objective relations. The functional dimension, so important in Baldwin's and Piaget's thinking, is totally absent here. Instead, the realism of structures transforms the systems of relations into totalities already constituted *outside of the story of the subject and its environment.* This transformation excludes practical functions in favor of symbolic ones, which are detached from their practical content and homogenized into the "scientific" object which is "real" by opposition to the historical, actual, "accidental" object of everyday life. This parallels Saussure's distinction between *langue* (constructed object) and *parole* (preconstructed datum). In the case of antibodies, the role of organism is purely executive, since when facing bacterial aggression, it consists merely in selecting the one among the antibodies which has been preprogrammed to respond to this specific aggression and not in reinventing a response on the spot.

Is this not the mirror-image of a society divided into elites (constructed objects) and masses (preconstructed data) in which the former are the central, stable, and immutable kernel for the service of which the latter are made and thus cannot be given equal rights?

I do not think that this final question is out of place in a book devoted to the memory of a man who lost his job based on accusations of having fornicated with blacks. Life and science are closer than we think. Baldwin's lesson is that we should unmask the similarities between Waddington's various spaces (especially the distinction between phenotypes and genotypes) and Chomsky's deep and surface structures as stemming from the same sort of "communism", that is, giving the language of the intelligentsia for the language of all, making the children turn to its likeness, and *not* the other way around (Mark 10:15; Luke 18:17; Matthew 18:3), and giving an extreme example of selfrighteousness in human history.

Analysis of the Mechanisms of Scientific Growth

The repression and rediscovery of the Baldwin effect in biology is a good example of the way in which science operates. As Thomas Kuhn explained in *The Structure of Scientific Revolutions* (1962), each scientific domain, each scientific period has a favorite paradigm, a favorite style of research, and a favorite prototype explained by a favorite model or by a favorite metaphor. One could thus explain the oblivion and the success of Baldwin's ideas on evolution in Kuhnian terms: when neo-Darwinism was high, Baldwin was low; when neo-Darwinism was under criticism, Baldwin was raised again.

This view seems to reflect reality accurately. As seen earlier, Baldwin's theory of organic selection was untimely in at least two ways. First, it was expressed in pre-Mendelian terms at the very moment of the rediscovery of Mendel by de Vries, Correns, and Tschermak. Second, when Baldwin tried to bridge the gap between Darwinism and Lamarckism, the dominant figures in the field were interested in widening it as much as they could. There were several reasons for this strategy of conflict. First, the contrasting of viewpoints is a pedagogical device widely used to insure the penetration of one's own ideas in the field; it maximizes coverage in journals and debates. Second, Lamarckism was too reminiscent of ideas associated in many minds with religion, especially the idea that the organism became what it became because of its own active response to the immediate circumstances of life. This idea was the expression of the behavioristic educational dogma of the Jesuits ("Give me a child young enough," said Loyola, "and I will make out of it what I want"), and also was not far enough from divine design. Chance, as used in neo-Darwinism, sounded much more scientific an explanation to the positivistic minds of the time, since random processes seemed to them much more deprived of transcendental connotations than Lamarck's law of progress or Baldwin's orthoplasia or orthogenesis. They rather naively believed that neo-Darwinism did not imply a hidden hand behind the facts, whereas, with communism, neo-Darwinism was one of the various secularizations of Christian eschatology produced by the last century. Progress was somehow the replacement for the second coming of Christ, or *Parousia*, in a plot in which God the Father was recast as Mother Nature. As far as the argumentation by design was concerned, it had become, by a fatal irony, a vast conspiracy double-handedly led by chance and necessity to impose evolution or death.

The dictum that evolution was due to mutation (chance) followed by natural selection (necessity) contained also an implicit theory of the growth of knowledge according to a principle of cumulativity. The favorite model for the history of science became Mendeléev's table for the periodic ranking of chemical elements. New discoveries and new theories were supposed to come to occupy their respective cells on the systematic table in an unspecified order but in such a way as, in the end, to fill the entire table. The principle of indeterminacy (chance) accounted for the disorderly aspects of breakthroughs, whereas the principle of preadaptation (necessity) was the warrant that one and only one cell could be ready for the discovery. The metaphysics behind this model is Laplacean, since, as in Laplace's system, a superior being knowing the future could fill the entire table, for its constuction depends on an immanent law of history. The trouble with an immanent law of history is that it makes any progress impossible, since it denies the possibility of an external intangible criterion against which to measure progress. The absence of such an external standard has led to the well-known circularity: Who survives? The fittest. Who is the fittest? The surviving one.

Now, it has been said that this criticism missed the point of neo-Darwinism which was not selection but variation. This is factually false, since the belief that minute cumulative variations could not become true factors of evolution started the search for alternatives to neo-Darwinism. Five sorts of facts were considered as determinants in this process. No experimental mutation has ever presented an evolutive character. Bacteria which have been stable species for 150 million years present a rate of mutation billions of billions higher than mammals which have evolved considerably since their emergence. The evolution of complex organs, such as the human eye, requires simultaneous and coordinated mutations in series. Paleontology shows discontinuities in evolution which are not linked directly with external pressures such as climatic changes. There is a general acceleration of evolution toward the end: the branching tree of evolution started out at a rate of 1 billion years per branching and ended up with a branching-out rate of about 10 million years. Recent cancer research has cast some doubt upon the concept of superfecundity: the aggressively proliferating cancer cells should be winners in natural selection, since their net reproduction rate is far superior to that of noncancerous cells in the organism. To the historian of ideas that I am in this case, it is obvious that these facts carry very different weights in the controversy, in terms of both validity and importance.

In a different vein, the revival by Waddington of some old experiments by Piaget on the phenotypical adaptation of *Limnaea stagnales* to turbulent waters over generations has contributed to the rediscovery of Baldwin's biology. Under the action of water, the elongated shell of the *Limnaea* is modified into the more advantageous contracted shape, whereas the naturally contracted shape collected in the Alps bred in still waters for generations only sporadically returns to the elongated variety. According to Piaget, this phenotypical adaptation after few generations is anticipated by the genome and becomes genotypical by a copy of the phenotype, i.e., by phenocopy.

At the behavioral level, ethologists have shown that the selection of the fastest-running wolf in a pack of wolves was a figment of Darwin's imagination, because wolves hunt in groups in which each member has specific functions so that fast running becomes advantageous when it is not individual, contrary to the ideology of laissez-faire behind the struggle for life.

Conceptually, the explosion of cybernetics has shown the way to teleonomy rendering scientific a concept, teleology, which was considered as the worst heritage from Aristotle. The advances recently made in molecular biology have also contributed to a materially deeper understanding of hereditary transmission, further relegating chance as an explanatory concept.

This mere listing of factors determining a change in evolutionary theory obliges us to a reconsideration of Kuhn's ideas. It is not simply a question of mob psychology, as one can see. It is rather a matter of refutations and controversies. It is even more a matter of respecting a subtle blance between the ingredients of any theory: *successfulness* and *understanding*. A theory can be considered successful when its heuristic power is high: how many new facts does it produce, how great is its capacity to explain its refutations in the course of its growth? This is the performative aspect of a theory. This aspect is necessary, but not sufficient. It must be coupled with what I here call *understanding*, which is not only the heuristic power of a theory—which would not distinguish a theory from a research program—but that sort of creative shift that renders the theory both necessary and self-sufficient. It is the truly explanatory side of a theory.

Now, my claim here is that Darwin's prudential approach coupled with his preoccupation with factual evidence was bound to win over Lamarck's sweeping generalities and rather simple-minded mechanisms for the transmission of local adaptations. With Newton's concept of force, natural selection stands out in the great British (or Great-Britain) tradition of minimal theoretical commitment. It contrasts sharply with Lamarck's theoretical impulsivity. "In the crude English way," Darwin did not attempt to get into the inner mechanisms of evolution. He merely observed the external results of variations in a given organism regardless of their origin and assumed that these variations were simply filtered through by the organisms, thanks to natural selection. Lamarck, on the other hand, did not separate variations from assimilation nor assimilation from behavior and life in general, but made adaptation a goal-oriented behavior of each individual organism. By so doing, he entered the world of inner mechanisms.

Thus the passage from one theory to the other is not due to the discovery of anomalies suddenly resolved by young and rather ignorant scientists, but seems to depend upon a dialectical interface between successfulness and understanding. So I looked into Piaget's theory for help, since for Piaget, explaining something boils down to understanding it. Understanding means for Piaget assimilating— *more formale*—the object to be explained, or *explicandum*, to those aspects of human action that can be internalized into operations, namely the famed *schemata (schèmes)*. If explaining something means making it intelligible, it must mean that an explanation is an action by which the structure of the *explicandum* is made *similar* to, or *assimilated* by, the structures of intelligence, with the necessary consequence that a better explanation results in a cognitive change that is always an improvement, a progress, an advance over what was known before. This might apply to ontogenesis but certainly not to history, which is full of detours. Historians too often witness changes that are simply revolting.

How to combine the powers of Kuhn's historical model and Piaget's developmental one to account for scientific thinking's being characterized by both historical and developmental aspects? By supposing that a given set of intellectual operations serves intellectual assimilation better at one given moment and thus constitutes the paradigm or prototype for that moment. The succession of favorite models of explanation is made possible by the existence at any moment of a plurality of competing explanations. If we were to accept Piaget's model or Kuhn's model alone, any scientific progress would be insufficiently explained. Why? In Piaget's case, every change would be progressive, and in Kuhn's case, undecidable, because Piaget identifies change with progress and the illusion of progress with the reality of change. On the contrary, the combination of these inverted propositions leads us to consider explanation as a transformation that remains always partial and that will be followed by many other transformations. This combination restores to scientific discovery its dynamics as well as its relativism, which does not fit exactly the idea that an explanation is an assimilation to a given mental structure that could eventually be algebraically specified. That would still be too absolute an idea to be workable historically. Thus, it is the form in which mental structures are transformed into one another that will serve as a prototype for explanatory models and not one specific structure of intellectual transformation, regardless of which it might be and what its degree of equilibration.

At this point in my reasoning, genetic epistemologists incensed by my historicism could formulate a good objection: looking into history as you do for the secret of formative mechanisms requires at least the capacity to reconstruct the cognitive processes of prehistoric people and the stages of human formation in phylogenesis. This makes inescapable the solution of filling the gaps in one's own knowledge of this phylogenesis by means of an extrapolation from what is already known at the ontogenetic and embryological levels.

As the reader knows, this question is precisely the origin of all genetic epistemologies and especially Baldwin's and Piaget's. It accounts for the form of evolution theory that Baldwin proposed and that Piaget modified slightly. As Baldwin (1894) wrote in *Mental Evolution in the Child and in the Race:*

> We end up with the consideration that evolution from one generation to the next most probably took place under the joint action of natural selection and organic selection in such a way that the direction of racial variations coincided with that of individual adaptations. We arrive at an hypothesis unifying ontogeny with phylogeny in all animal series. All the influences helping animal adaptations and accommodations are combined in one resulting effect to give a determined orientation to the course of evolution. We call these *orienting* influences *orthoplasia.* (Chap. 7, Sect. 4)

This quotation shows the place of psychological research in the economy of Baldwin's genetic epistemology. Psychology should explain the role of individuals in evolution. *Individual accommodations* as Baldwin called them, were supposed to substitute momentarily "congenital variations" whenever these were either not adequate enough nor strong enough to be harmonized with the general evolution of the species. Baldwin conceived this distinction as an answer to an objection raised against natural selection when applied to complex entities, such as instincts, for instance. The complex correlations implied by instincts do not need to emerge all mounted in the hypothesis of organic selection, since the latter entails a period of individual and cumulative accommodations. Hence the central place of psychology which, as the study of behavior, is supposed to unfold the passage from one form of natural selection to another as well as to provide, thanks to ontogenetic observations, the missing links in phylogenesis. As Piaget used to say, the contemporary child is the real primitive man, since he is the adult of prehistoric ages. This is clearly a recapitulation hypothesis in spite of repeated disclaimers, and this hypothesis is logically necessary in the perspective of genetic epistemology; the point should be underscored.

On the contrary, my own point here, using the history of Baldwin's ideas in biology against Baldwin's ideas in epistemology, is that recapitulation theories are unnecessary hypotheses, because they confuse the issue of explaining the transformation of a theory of knowlege into another with that of establishing an absolute hierarchy of intellectual forms. The lesson I myself draw from the case-study method of approaching the psychology of thinking as initiated by H. E. Gruber is that there is no such rigid hierarchy in scientific thinking. In other words, I would like to do away with that sort of explanation that Marx used to call *reproduction processes*, because they are strictly endogenous models of change assuming that there is an immanent law to history, which is logically false and factually untrue. From a logical viewpoint, these models assume that predictions about the future states of the system under consideration are possible. But the condition *sine qua non* of predictions is a stationary reality forming a closed system, and something cannot be both stationary and historical. Factually, breakthroughs happen where they are not expected.

The repression of Baldwin's organic individual adaptation coincided with the rediscovery of Mendel's law with its dual effect upon Baldwin's ideas: they could be rapidly dismissed as pre-Mendelian and they overlooked the fact (so important to positivist minds inclined to dismiss everything like free will or design) that, thanks to Mendel, the locus of hereditary transmission was the gene sealed off from its environment, or genotypic space. Only after a long period during which animal organisms had been considered exclusively as mere vehicles for genes were other genetically important spaces discovered, namely, the epigenetic and phenotypic spaces. This discovery of new spaces was the work of more speculatively inclined embryologists who had grown interested in the Russian posterity of Lamarck (Schmalhausen and Michoorin) which had assimilated Darwin to different extents. Only then were they ready to read Cope, Osborn, Lloyd Morgan, and Baldwin with profit, because these authors had thought of the role of individual activity in a more refined way than Lamarck. For Lamarck, what the organism becomes is *in essence* independent of the environment because the general direction of its development is given in the law of progress; in *transitory details*, what it becomes is a direct reflection of its own active response to the immediate circumstances of life. By proposing the idea of an orthogenesis or orthoplasia giving a direction and developmental dimension to natural selection, these authors have made the law of progress logically necessary and its articulation with the transitory details of evolution more integrative of the general direction of evolution. But they also made development the mere reflection of phylogenesis by their adherence to this immanent law of progress. Such a methodological narcissism led them to overlook the logical difficulty that, in order to be, orthogenesis must be based upon a criterion transcending the system under scrutiny, which it contradicts with the very existence of an immanent law of progress. This contradiction could be removed only by accepting that the future acts upon the present, a solution ventured by Piaget and Inhelder when they state that *le futur oriente le présent*, a clearly eschatological statement indeed.

In conclusion, scientific growth is the result of this dual process of knowledge: performance, or successfulness, and understanding. Very early scientific developments tend to favor understanding over performance. Later on, the opposite takes place. Premature understanding serves generally the role of a reservoir of ideas and hypotheses for further understanding, when the very results of successfulness need to be tightened into a meaningful whole. By refraining from a complete explanation, Darwin was wiser than Lamarck who, by orienting the entire organism toward progress, paved the road to the relevance of individual behavior in evolution. More important still is the place of philosophy in scientific advances. Constantly underrated, it is constantly indicating the problem area (which tends all the more to be overlooked) that science has been building itself against philosophy, taking its own implicit philosophy for granted and troublefree, which it is not, as we have seen. Truth is a difficult person and scientists should be reminded that Salome took off seven veils before asking for John's head—a lesson in modesty indeed.

REFERENCES

Baldwin, J. M. A new factor in evolution. *American Naturalist*, 1896, *30*, 441–536.

Baldwin, J. M. *Development and evolution*. London: Macmillan, 1902.

Baldwin, J. M. *Mental development in the child and in the race*. New York: Macmillan, 1894.

Bateson, W. *Mendel's principles of heredity: a defence*. London: 1902.

Bertalanffy, L. von. *Problems of life*. New York: Harper, 1960. (Originally published 1949.)

Bever, T. G., Fodor, J. A., & Weksel, W. On the acquisition of syntax: a critique of contextual generalization. *Psychological Review*. 1965, *72*, 467–482.

Bower, T. G. R. *Development in infancy*. San Francisco: W. H. Freeman, 1974.

Darwin, C. *On the origin of species*. London: Murray, 1855.

Darwin, C. *The variation of animals and plants under domestication*. London: Murray, 1868.

Chomsky, N. *Aspects of the theory of syntax*. Cambridge, Mass.: M.I.T. Press, 1965.

Edelman, G., & Mountcastle, V. *The mindful brain*. Cambridge, Mass.: M.I.T. Press, 1978.

Fisher, R. A. The Fisher papers, (annotated by the author). Cambridge University, England (unpub. ms.).

Fisher, R. A. *The genetical theory of natural selection*. Oxford: Oxford, 1930.

Fodor, J. A. *Psychological explanation*. New York: Random House, 1960.

Gruber, H. *Darwin on man*. New York: E. P. Dutton, 1974.

Haldane, J. B. S. *The causes of evolution*. Ithaca, N.Y.: Cornell Univ. Press, 1966. (Originally published 1932.)

Hardy, A. *The living stream*. London: Collins, 1965.

Harrison, J. W. H. Experiments on the egg-laying habits of the sawfly. *Pontania Salicis Chr. Proceedings of the Royal Society*, 1927, *101*, 115.

Heinroth, O., & Heinroth, K. *Birds*. Ann Arbor, Mich.: Univ. of Michigan Press, 1958. (*Die Vögel Mitteleuropas*. Berlin, 1924–1926.)

Huxley, Sir Julian. *Evolution: the modern synthesis*. London: Allen & Unwin, 1974. (Originally published 1942.)

Kuhn, T. S. *The structure of scientific revolutions*. Chicago: University of Chicago Press, 1962.

Lamarck, J. P. *Philosophie zoologique*. Paris: Lubrecht & Cramer, 1960. (Originally published 1809.)

Lederberg. J. Humanics and genetic engineering. *Encyclopaedia Britannica 1970 Yearbook of Science and Technology*. Chicago: Encyclopaedia Britannica, 1970.

Mayr, E. *Animal species and evolution*. Cambridge, Mass.: Harvard Univ. Press, 1963.

Morgan, C. L. *Animal behavior*. Norwood N.J.: Johnson Reprint, 1970. (Originally published 1900.)

Morgan, C. L. On modification and variation. *Science*, 1897, *733*.

Osborn, H. F. The limits of organic selection. *American Naturalist*, 1897, *944*.

Pearson, K. In R. S. Moorhead & M. M. Kaplan (Eds.), *Mathematical challenges to the neo-Darwinian interpretation of evolution*. Philadelphia, Pa.: Wistar Institute Press, 1967.

Piaget, J. *Biology and knowledge*. Chicago: University of Chicago Press, 1971. (Originally published 1967.)

Piaget, J. *Behavior and evolution*. New York: Pantheon, 1978. (Originally published 1971.)

Piaget, J. *Adaptation and intelligence: Organic selection and phenocopy*. Chicago: University of Chicago Press, 1980. (Originally published 1974.)

Piaget, J. From noise to order: The psychological development of knowledge and phenocopy in biology. In H. Gruber & J. J. Vonèche (Eds.), *The essential *Piaget*. New York: Basic Books, 1977. (Reprinted, *Urban Review*, 1975, *8* (3), 209–218.)

Prigogine, I. Steady states and entropy production. *Physica.*, 1965, *31*, 719–724.

Roe, A., & Simpson, G. G. *Behavior & evolution*. New Haven, Conn.: Yale University Press, 1958.

Saussure, F. de. Cours de linguistique generale in *Fonds Ferdinand de Saussure*: Archives de la B. P. U. Geneve.

Schmalhausen, B. [*Factors of evolution*]. Moscow, 1942.

Simpson, G. G. *The major features of evolution*. New York: Columbia Univ. Press, 1953.

Spencer, H. *Principles of psychology*, vol. I. London: Williams & Norgate, 1870. (Originally published, 1855.)

Sperber, D. *Le structuralisme en anthropologie*. Paris: Presses Universitaires de France, 1971.

Stroun, M., Anker, P., Maurice, P., & Gahan, P. B. Circulating nucleic acids in higher organisms. *International Review of Cytology*, 1977, 54, 1–48.

Thorpe, W. H. Biological races in insects and allied groups. *Biological Review*, 1930, 5, 177.

Waddington, C. The theory of evolution today. In A. Koestler & J. R. Smythies (Eds.), *Beyond reductionism: New perspectives in the life sciences.* London: Hutchinson, 1969.

Weismann, A. *Aussere Einflüsse als Entwicklungsreize*. Jena, 1894.

Wheldon, W. F. R. A first study in natural selection in *Clausilia Laminata.* *Biometrika*, 1901, 1, 109.

Wright, S. Evolution in Mendelian populations. *Genetics*, 1931, 16.

Yule, G. U. Some statistics of evolution and geographical distribution in plants and animals. *New Phytologist*, 1902, 1, 193.

3

REFLECTIONS ON BALDWIN

Jean Piaget
(Centre Internationale d'Épistemologie
Génétique, University of Geneva)

An interview conducted in March 1979 by J. Jacques Vonèche
translated by Broughton and Vonèche, and introduced by Vonèche.

Introduction

There is always a risk in asking a man of Piaget's age and
importance for an interview on his memories. Piaget was well aware
of this risk; he had written that for years he had the most vivid
memory of his own kidnapping in Paris, a memory that happened to
be false, since it turned out to be a verbal excuse invented by Piaget's
nanny for coming home late with the baby. Awareness of this risk
explains to a certain extent Piaget's reluctance all through this
interview.

Another part of Piaget's rather guarded attitude was due to a
general feature of his personality: he was a man who inspired
admiration, devotion, love, even passion, but rarely confidence and
friendship. This was because of his immense sense of modesty.

Finally, there is most probably a contextual effect in this
attitude: the interview took place in Piaget's home, in his office
crowded with books and papers of all sorts *(un beau desordre est un
effet de l'art*, as they say in French) just an hour before dinner time.
As a matter of fact, the evening meal put an end to the interview with
the last pirouette: "Does Baldwin talk about genetic epistemology?"

allowing him the last word (and what a word, indeed) in this short skirmish.

The unprepared reader could gain the impression that Piaget did not want to recognize Baldwin's influence on his work. Such an impression should be quickly dispelled because in this interview Piaget tried to say two things at once. The first is that he had his own ideas long before knowing about Baldwin (a careful reading of *Recherche* as well as of Piaget's early biological papers, especially the one on Mendelian species published in Gruber and Vonèche, *The Essential Piaget*, could convince anyone of that). The other was his recognition of Baldwin's influence on him, as well as other influences that he had always dutifully spelled out: Bergson, Janet, Brunschvicg, and in Neuchâtel, Arnold Reymond, the logician and historian of Greek science, and the geologist (and philosopher of knowledge in his spare time), "the great Argand."

As evidence of this sentiment, one could limit oneself to the following passage, which Baldwin's biographer, Ronald Mueller (1976), quoted, from a letter that Piaget wrote to him in 1972:

> Unfortunately I did not know Baldwin personally, but his works had a great influence on me. Furthermore, Pierre Janet, whose courses I took in Paris, cited him constantly and had been equally very influenced by him . . . (p. 244)

There is no desire evident in Piaget to ignore his debt toward great predecessors. But in his reticence, one could read a certain position toward influences in knowledge which would be directly connected with his own version of genetic epistemology. Recognizing too readily the influence of somebody's thinking upon one's own epistemologically amounts to a sort of empiricism in which one believes that external ideas are more important than the men and women who conceive them. Moreover, it would mean that individual thinkers are shaped into ideas pretty much in the same way that Skinner shapes an animal into his box. In such a perspective, a person's thinking could be reduced to the sum of influences undergone by that person. Ideas would be external objective entities pretty much like the genes for the neo-Darwinists and the sociobiologists of the day. They would be the real and permanent agents of history using human minds as a means to travel from one generation to the next, thanks to the transitory blending of cultural intercourse, to separate again, to be reunited and reseparated, *ad infinitum*, according to the pulsations of evolution.

It is obvious that such an approach was foreign to Piaget. He believed strongly in *assimilation*. This means that he was convinced that the ideas of others became yours when they were truly digested or assimilated in the very same way, or to use one of his favorite images, that the cabbage became the rabbit once it was digested by the rabbit. Hence the pirouette on Baldwin's brand of genetic epistemology at the close of the interview.

What seemed much more important to him were the necessary convergences between his thoughts and those of others, such as Baldwin, on a certain number of themes and topics. These convergences he tended to call, in a mathematically somewhat emphatic language, *isomorphisms* or *partial isomorphisms*. Evidencing such partial isomorphisms between phylogeny and ontogeny, ontogeny and the history of science, or perception and intelligence, or even himself and Baldwin, restores the unity of knowledge and the unity between knowledge and adaptation—a unity indispensable to the existence of the very notion of equilibration, the focal concept of Piaget's theory. If there is such a thing as equilibration, then it should take the same form (in Greek: *iso-morphy*) under the same conditions everywhere. As one can see for oneself, there is a tremendous unity in Piaget's behavior, stretching from his *Introduction à l'épistémologie génétique* to a small talk between 6 and 7 P.M. with your author.

The Interview

What form did your contact with Baldwin take?

I never met James Mark Baldwin in person. By the time I was in Paris, he was already dead.[1] So I knew Baldwin, above all, through Pierre Janet. You see, I was suspicious of the fact that Janet (who never read anything) knew Baldwin thoroughly, and that surprised me. I asked him how that came about. Janet replied that, certainly, he had never read Baldwin, but that he had lunched with Baldwin every Monday for a year. Baldwin was in exile in Paris at that time. You know that Baldwin had been fired from Johns Hopkins University in Baltimore . . . So it was in this way that I knew Baldwin.

Afterward, I read *Les Interpretations Sociales et le Moi* (1907) [*Social and Ethical Interpretations*], *Le Developpement Mental chez l'Enfant* (1897) [Mental Development in the Child and the Race], and *La Logique Genetique* (1908) [*Thought and Things*, Vol. 1.] But when I got to pancalism, I stopped. What interested me in his work above all was the general genetic aspect.

You know that Janet constructed stages without ever having

---

[1] Here Piaget's report seems quite inaccurate. Baldwin died in 1934, long after Piaget's advent. Wozniak makes a relevant comment in footnote #18 of his chapter, above, p. 42 (Ed.)

looked at a child, entirely on the basis of observing cases of pathology. Ah yes, that's the way he was, Janet! (He laughs frankly.) One was very daring in those times, because everything still remained to be done.

What is, for you, the real contribution of Baldwin in science and epistemology?

The global idea of genesis. That's what's important to me.

Then what was his impact?

It seems that in the United States, one set oneself to reading Baldwin. In Europe, one didn't . . . except Janet, because he needed someone like Baldwin to confirm his own idea of stages drawn from pathology.

Nevertheless, in contrast with what you yourself have done, Baldwin speaks more of modes, than stages. By this I mean that your stages are hierarchically inclusive, and mutually exclusive, whereas Baldwin's were not, no?

All right, yes. That's where I differ, if you like.

In that case, can one really say that Baldwin exerted an influence on you?

I told you: the global idea of genesis.

But then the concepts that you use in common—like adualism, circular reaction, or assimilation and accommodation—are they simply convenient terms that you would have picked up from anyone, or is there something more?

It's a matter of convergences, of simple convergences of thinking. I was not influenced by the role of genetic logic in Baldwin's work, but it corresponded to what I was looking for at the time of my conversations with Janet. I came to know Janet rather late in my own mental evolution. I already had a certain number of facts and ideas at that moment. It happened that they converged with some of Baldwin's ideas. As for me, I had started from the facts in order to arrive there.

Because you think that Baldwin had no empirical basis?

On the contrary, I perpetually have the impression that Baldwin knew piles of facts, but he never cited any of them.

It seems that during your own development, your thoughts separated themselves from Baldwin's. In your first books, you seemed less

The same w/ Isaacs!

centered on formal logic and more on what Baldwin called real logic. You were more preoccupied with social dialectic, and with meaning in the sense of Peirce's semiotics. You were more interested in the continuity between biology and psychology—less in cybernetics then—as The Moral Judgment of the Child *shows. How do you account for that?*

I was not at all influenced by Baldwin in details. What appears to you to be an influence is nothing but a simple convergence. The *Moral Judgment of the Child* that you cite as an example is precisely a book that I wrote at the suggestion of the philosopher Reverdin, who was my colleague at the University of Geneva, and not on account of the influence of Baldwin.

Nevertheless, it is precisely in this book that there is a long discussion of Baldwin's point of view. . . .

Really? That's curious. I have no memory of that at all.

But at the moment when you were writing the Phenocopy (Biological Adaptation and the Psychology of Intelligence: Organic Selection and Phenocopy), *you found out about Baldwin's biology?*

Do you know that among biologists the fact that Baldwin was a psychologist is completely ignored? It is a point that I had to check out for myself. Biologists do not take psychologists seriously. If they had known that Baldwin was a psychologist, they wouldn't even have read him!

To get back to your question, at the time that I was preparing my book, I read an article which presented the ideas from an 1896 article of Baldwin's. That's what brought me back quite naturally to our author. The biologists believed that they had understood everything from the standpoint of Mendelism. But they read Mendel poorly. Pilet, who was a good theoretician at the same time as being a brilliant expert on the cell, told me that Mendel thought that an accumulation of phenotypes oriented in the same direction could lead to mutations, but nobody tells you that about Mendel. It is carefully forgotten.

I have never seen a domain as dogmatic as biology. When I went to America, the first or second time—in '29 or '36, I don't remember, anyway, at the time when one still went by boat—I made the voyage with a young biologist who told me, "There is some truth in Lamarck, but one cannot say so in public." It is because they lack the factual basis that the biologists do philosophy in this domain.

A striking difference between you and Baldwin, besides this need of yours for empirical verification, is the accent Baldwin places on the social dialectic instead of the relationship of the individual to the environment which characterizes your thought. How do you explain this?

Under the influence of Durkheim, which was after all immense in France, I wasted a fantastic amount of time trying to decide between the social and the individual. That lasted up until the moment I realized that cooperation could be spelled "co-", "operation." When the Durkheimians put the whole burden on society, they commit the incredible mistake of forgetting that, without the nervous system, nothing at all would happen. So, since Durkheim didn't dare to say that the nervous system was a social product, it was necessary to recognize its existence prior to society and social forces. Today, one can no longer imagine the power the Durkheimians had. Their imperialism was such that my friend, Leon Bopp, jokingly told me, "You'll see, next they are going to annex mineralogy!"

While we're on this topic, what relationship do you see between Baldwin and the major currents of the last two centuries?

I don't see him in relation to the neo-Kantians or the Hegelians. On the contrary, I see him in very great rapport with Darwin. He thought a lot about Darwinism and better than Dewey did, for example. That's what allowed him to derive the "Baldwin effect."[2]

What exactly was the precise significance of the Baldwin effect in your recent biological works?

Once again, there is a certain convergence here on the insufficiencies of neo-Darwinism. Waddington didn't attach much importance to Baldwin.

You're right. He considered the Baldwin effect only a product of American chauvinism. This is understandable since his theory of genetic assimilation has another line of descent: Schmalhausen and Soviet biology, don't you think?

Yes, that's right. At bottom, Waddington was more attached to neo-Darwinism than he appears to be. He said about Baldwin, with a certain contempt, that he was pre-Mendelian.

Don't you think that the definitive line of partition between Darwinians and Lamarckians passes through the epistemological choice-point between selectionism and constructivism?

Yes, without doubt. The biologists are wrong, taking chance for an explanation as Monod does.

---

[2] For an explication of the "Baldwin effect", see Vonèche's chapter, above (Ed.)

What are the most marked differences between your version of genetic epistemology and Baldwin's?

Ah, does Baldwin talk about genetic epistemology?

and Isaacs

REFERENCE

Mueller, R. H. A chapter in the history of the relationship between psychology and sociology in America: James Mark Baldwin. *Journal of the History of the Behavioral Sciences*, 1976, *12*, 240–253.

4

THE "BLIND-VARIATION-AND-SELECTIVE-RETENTION" THEME

Donald T. Campbell
Syracuse University

During my student years at the University of California, Berkeley, in 1937–41, I remember hearing of Baldwin only in sociology courses where his name was linked with that of George Horton Cooley as emphasizing the primacy of the social in the childhood development of the self. Karpf (1932, pp. 269–291), presenting the University of Chicago sociology department's view of the history of social psychology when that view dominated sociology everywhere, gives generous attention to Baldwin and is still well worth reading. She does not touch upon the terms and themes that Piaget has revived (e.g., *genetic epistemology, accommodation, assimilation*) nor the *Baldwin effect* that has kept his name alive in evolutionary biology (Baldwin, 1902, to be touched upon briefly later) nor the theme of this essay. The books she cites actually contain most of these themes, too, although she fails to cite *Thought and Things* (1906–11), where the Piagetian themes are most explicitly elaborated. (She uses mainly *Mental Development in the Child and the Race,* 1900; *Social and Ethical Interpretations in Mental Development: A Study of Social Psychology,* 1897; *The Individual and Society,* 1911; and *History of Psychology,* 1913.) That Baldwin could contribute effectively to such a diverse set of intellectual trends, all related to a unified point of view of his own, demonstrates his greatness. In our reevaluation of the intellectual heroes of psychology's history, he deserves to be placed on a par with William James, in the brilliance of his theoretical contributions as seen from our day even if not in his historical influence. His name is still alive in philosophy, too, not yet because they recognize his brilliant contributions to epistemology, but rather for his *Dictionary of Philosophy* (1901–1905) a monumental example of highly intelligent industriousness, recently reprinted, still used, and not yet made obsolete by any superior successor.

The central contribution of Darwin to the thought both of his day and ours lies in the concept of natural selection as it relates to the puzzle of explaining teleological achievement without recourse to teleological causation. For those of my generation, the extension of the abstract algorithm underlying it to a wide variety of adaptive achievements was stimulated by cybernetics. Ashby's *Design for a Brain* (1951) makes explicit use of analogies between variation and selective retention processes in learning, thought, and biological evolution. Pringle's (1951) influential essay flags the extended model in his title, "On the Parallel between Evolution and Learning." An enthusiasm for this insight has been a unifying theme for many of my own papers (1956a, 1956b, 1959, 1960, 1965, 1974a, 1974b). Beginning in 1959, I cite Baldwin in passing as an early exponent of these ideas. As I have increasingly sampled his work, I have come to realize that he anticipated my insights and those of Karl Popper, etc., on almost all details, including my emphasis on vicarious blind-variation-and-selection processes which do make human actions and overtly expressed hypotheses so intelligently purposive and creative. This dogma can be expressed succinctly as follows:

1. A blind-variation-and-selective-retention process is fundamental to all inductive achievements, to all genuine increases in knowledge, to all increases in fit of system to environment.
2. The many processes which shortcut a more full blind-variation-and-selective-retention process are in themselves inductive achievements, containing wisdom about the environment achieved originally by blind variation and selective retention.
3. In addition, such shortcut processes contain in their own operation a blind-variation-and-selective-retention process at some level, substituting for overt locomotor exploration or the life-and-death winnowing of organic evolution (Campbell, 1960, p. 380).

Baldwin was a militant non-Darwinian, accepting August Weismann's purification of Darwin's paradigm, eliminating the Lamarckianism which Darwin tolerated. He was creative in this venture, emphasizing rather than denying the creative, purposive, emergent organization produced in the course of evolution, while vigorously eschewing vitalistic or teleological explanation or unexplained intuitive foresight.

The best brief introduction to Baldwin's thought on these issues is his relatively unknown *Darwin and the Humanities* (1909). Except for outmoded uses of some words (*positivist, instrumentalist,* and *humanities,*) it is easily readable as a modern contribution (quite in contrast with his obscure *Thought and Things*). This was a Darwinian centennial book (100 years after Darwin's birth) and seizes upon what we today find most valuable in Darwin's thought. This is quite in contrast with Dewey's banal *The Influence of Darwin on Philosophy* (1910), in which the natural selection concept is totally neglected; Darwinism is used instead to refer to the evolutionary continuity between man and animals, a belief which Darwin shared with predecessors such as Buffon and Lamarck, and which Darwin merely popularized. Boring (1950), in reviewing Darwin's influence on psychology, similarly omits the natural selection theme and its analogues.

Within *humanities*, Baldwin includes psychology, social sciences, ethics, logic, philosophy, and religion, with a chapter for each. From Baldwin's (1909) introduction and summaries come the following illustrative emphases.

> Many things seem to be covered from this point of view as from no other. My favorite doctrines, and those in which my larger books have been in some measure original, seem now, when woven together, to have been consciously inspired by the theory of Natural Selection: I need only mention 'Organic Selection,' 'Functional Selection,' 'Social Heredity,' 'Selective Thinking,' 'Experimental Logic,' thoroughgoing 'Naturalism of Method,' etc. Such views as these all illustrate or extend the principle of selection as Darwin conceived it—that is, the principle of survival from varied cases—as over against any vitalistic or formal principle. Wherever I have found it necessary to go beyond the 'Selection' principle, thus defined, it has been by interpretations, such as that of the theory of 'Genetic Modes,' which do not controvert or deny the universality of this principle, but explicitly recognize and utilize it. I am not a *philosophical* Dualist or Positivist; but *in the domain of science* I accept both these points of view. And I further hold that our philosophy must preserve and utilize the great results of scientific thought without subtracting one jot or tittle from their full and legitimate force. So, to make this confession complete—as far as may be without abusing the liberty allowed in a Preface—I must admit that the result of my labors for twenty-five years, the net result, that is, of my scientific work until now, is a contribution, whatever it may turn out to be worth, to the theory of Darwinism in the sciences of life and mind. I call it a 'confession,' but 'claim' would be a better word; for who would not consider it an honor to be allowed to 'claim' that he had done something to carry Darwin's great and illuminating conception into those fields of more general philosophical interest, in which in the end its value for human thought must be estimated?.... Natural selection is in principle the universal law of genetic organization and progress in nature—human nature no less than physical nature. (pp. viii–ix)

> Summing up our conclusions so far with reference to Darwinism in Psychology we may say:
> (1) The individual's learning processes are by a method of

functional 'trial and error' which illustrates 'natural' in the form of 'functional selection.'

(2) Such acquisitions, taken jointly with his endowment, give him the chance of survival through 'natural,' in the form of 'organic selection.'

(3) By his learning, he brings himself into the traditions of his group, thus coming into possession of his social heritage, which is the means of his individual survival in the processes of 'social and group selection.'

(4) Thus preserved the individual's endowment or physical heredity is, through variation, directed in intelligent and gregarious lines through 'natural' as 'organic selection.'

(5) Individuals become congenitally either more gregarious or more intelligent for the maintenance of the group life, according as the greater utility attaches to one or the other in the continued operation of these modes of selection.

It is thus that a Darwinian foundation is laid for the more complex sciences which deal with the development of the individual in psychological and social ways.

The further development of the social sciences requires the detailed working out of the methods of individual accommodation or learning. This requirement is reflected in the recent striking advances made in Genetic Psychology, which has two great branches: Comparative and Social Psychology. In both of these—that is, in Genetic Psychology as a whole—important principles have been found at work which afford further illustrations of the vitality of the Darwinian theory.

Play. In the play function recent writers, especially K. Groos, have discovered one of the instruments of the highest utility in the learning process. It is believed to be a function by which immature and undeveloped tendencies and endowments are practised, in conditions which escape the actual struggle and stress of life, and so give the 'trial and error' method its full opportunity. Animals play in the line of their later activities, and so make themselves proficient for the serious struggle for existence. Both the personal and the gregarious impulses are thus brought to perfection behind the screen of play. Play is a generalized native impulse toward the exercise of specific and useful activities. It is itself a functional character which has arisen by the selection, among the individuals of a very great number of animal forms, of variations toward the early and artificial use of their growing powers. It is a natural and powerful tendency in vigorous and growing young; in fact, it is an impulse of extraordinary strength and persistence, and of corresponding utility.

On the psychological side, a corresponding advance has been made in the interpretation of the state of 'make-believe,' which accompanies and excites to the indulgence of play. Make-believe is found in animals of many orders and is strikingly developed in the child. It leads to a sort of sustained imagination of situations, treated as if real—a playful 'dramatization'—in which the most important principles of individual and social life are tentatively and experimentally illustrated. Play thus becomes a most important sphere of practice, not only on the side of the physical powers, but also in intellectual, social, and moral lines.

Moreover, once learned, this method of experimentation by imaginative make-believe is extended, as the individual's powers mature, to the more theoretical and voluntary functions. Recent work in logic and aesthetics has shown that the instrumental or hypothetical characters of knowledge—seen in experimental science—and the characters of detachment and 'semblance' in art, have their roots in this sort of imaginative forecasting of what may be or might be true.

Imitation. The impulse to imitate is the companion to that of play. It is the same sort of tendency in type—a native generalized activity. It is a sort of social counterpart to the play tendency; for by playing in imitative ways young animals are brought into fruitful and useful coöperation. The correlation actually holds between them, indeed; animal and human plays are both imitative and social. Among the animals, both impuses seem to be largely restricted to the activities which are to come into play in adult life. With advance in the scale of life, however, and especially in the anthropoidal and human forms, both become more plastic and more intelligent, thus allowing them wider application to all the processes of learning. In the development of the human individual, these two functions, imitation and play, become the principle [sic] instruments used by nature for the development of the individual's native powers, and for leading him into the mass of culture called 'social tradition.' This latter province of imitation is taken up again below. The actual mechanism of both impulses illustrates throughout the Darwinian principle of selection by trial and error.

Origin of the Faculties. Genetic psychology also teaches that in the foregoing principles we have in outline an account of the origin of the mental faculties as illustrated in the series of minds from lower animals up to man. Before man, we find the sort of 'profiting by experience' which comes with learning through trial and error, and the conservation in great habits of the accommodations thus secured. A habit is simply a tendency to do again what has once been done, whenever the slightest suggestion appears of the original conditions of action. This suggestion may come through a renewal of the actual conditions, or simply through memory—whether this be a mere residual or trace of the original function, or an actual revived image. The imaging faculty finds here its *raison d'etre* and utility: it enables the animal to utilize his earlier experiences in conditions remote in time and place from the original situation.

A further step is taken when images are used experimentally or instrumentally for purposes of adjustment by trial and error, a process for which the play function affords excellent opportunity. The child playfully imagines all sorts of situations, and experiments upon them with direct utility to himself and his group.

Finally, in the operations of thought, involving adjustment to the common or 'general' aspects of things, this process of trial-and-error becomes the conscious and explicit method of progress in knowledge and conduct. Among the animals, the best authorities find this shown in a rudimentary way in the case of the higher anthropoids, which are able, on occasion, to readjust a habitual way of action to a somewhat changed situation. This has been called 'practical judgment'; it is no doubt a preliminary stage in the development of theoretical judgment which uses 'general' ideas. Thus interpreted, the operations of thought or 'reason' are shown to be evolved from simple processes of accommodation which rest upon trial and error and habit. The 'general' idea is a general way of acting upon a mass of details, recognized as requiring the same sort of treatment.

The highest functions of thought are thus to be looked upon as experimental; they never entirely lose that reference to actual situations which shows their origin in the genetic processes mentioned. (pp. 32–37)

Scientific method becomes, when the full implications of the matter are thought out, the exhaustive epistemological method; that is, we must hold that there is no method of reaching results to be called truths which is not found, when genetically considered, to go back to the fundamental processes of experimentation. There is no royal road to truth; no golden rule of revelation or inspiration by which the philosopher can deduce the 'universe and the contents thereof.' The ambitious *Naturphilosophie* of the last century remained barren and speculative until, through the development of experimental and evolutionary science, it became *Naturwissenschaft*.

But what shall we say of the principles of knowledge itself? Are there no final *a priori* and absolute tests of truth such as we are accustomed to find in 'identity,' 'consistency,' and 'sufficient reason'? Are there no constructive categories which do not themselves owe their establishment to experiment?

As for the categories—here again instrumentalism has its adequate reply; and its reply is strictly Darwinian. These, too, it claims, the categories, are principles which have been selected from numberless possible variations of thought in the course of racial evolution. They represent selections, adjustments to the natural situations which have confronted the mind. They are rules of systematization found useful for thought and experience, for individual knowledge and practice, and for common social belief in the vast stretches of history. The mind has built up a structure, as the body has; and by a similar method: that of tentative and experimental functional adjustment, followed up by the coincident variations of mental structure fixed by selection.

It is here that Herbert Spencer's most valuable intuition appears—a conception to be placed beside that of Darwin. The weak point in Spencer's harness, however, was his resort to Lamarckian inheritance for the fixing of the rib-structures of mind. But for the theory of knowledge, the result is the same. The most absolute and universal-seeming principles of knowledge, viewed racially, are 'practical postulates' which have been woven into human thought as presuppositions of consistent and trustworthy experience. They were 'original ideas' at some time, found to be useful for the organization of knowledge and for the conduct of life; and, now, by processes of reflective abstraction, they are set up as schemes or forms divorced from the concrete contents which alone gave them their justification and value, and called 'the categories.'

All knowledge, all thought, must conform to the law of consistency because this has become the fixed rule of safe and profitable experience (pp. 69–70).

In this summary, the *selection theory* or trial-and-error component in imitation is not well spelled out, but as Baldwin makes explicit elsewhere (e.g., 1906, vol. 1, p. 169), even in imitations there is no direct transfer of knowledge or behavior patterns from the model to the imitator. Instead, the child acquires in memory a criterion image, which it learns to match by a trial and error of its own actions. Recent studies of the learning of bird song (e.g., Hinde, 1969) document such a process.

In his chapter on psychology (1909, pp. 9–23), he presents in some 15 pages a summary of the evolutionary puzzle of instinct and the solution proposed by him and independently by several others-called by him *organic selection* and now known to evolutionary biologists as the *Baldwin effect*. This important concept overlaps almost completely with one of Waddington's major modern contributions to evolutionary theory and is treated in considerable detail in Piaget's (1978) book. It deserves mention here as an illustration of the creativity with which Baldwin operated within the neo-Darwinian antiteleological, antivitalistic explanatory framework. I find it most convenient to quote from my own (1974a) summary of it, which differs considerably from Piaget's:

> . . . the evolutionary discreteness of the two processes (habit and instinct) is not as clear as implied nor should instinct necessarily be regarded as more primitive than habit. Complex adaptive instincts typically involve multiple movements and must inevitably involve a multiplicity of mutations at least as great in number as the obvious movement segments. Furthermore, it is typical that the fragmentary movement segments, or the effects of single component mutations, would represent no adaptive gain at all apart from the remainder of the total sequence. The joint likelihood of the simultaneous occurrence of the adaptive form of the many mutations involved is so infinitesimal that the blind-mutation-and-selective-retention model seems inadequate. This argument was used effectively by both Lamarckians and those arguing for an intelligently guided evolution or creation. Baldwin, Morgan, Osborn, and Poulton (Baldwin, 1902) believing that natural selection was the adequate and only mechanism, proposed that for such instincts, learned adaptive patterns, recurrently discovered in similar form within a species by trial-and-error learning, preceded the instincts. The adaptive pattern being thus piloted by learning, any mutations that accelerated the learning, made it more certain to occur, or predisposed the animal to certain component responses, would be adaptive and selected no matter which component responses, or in what order affected. The habit thus provided a selective template around which the instinctive components could be assembled. (Stating it in other terms, learned habits make a new ecological niche available

which niche then selects instinct components.) It is furthermore typical of such instincts that they involve learned components, as of nest and raw material location, etc.

This can be conceived as an evolution of increasingly specific selection-criteria, which at each level select or terminate visual search and trial-and-error learning. In what we call learning, these are very general drive states and reinforcing conditions. In the service of these general reinforcers, specific objects and situations become learned goals and subgoals, learned selectors of more specific responses. (Even for drives and reinforcers, of course, the environment's selective relevance is represented indirectly, as in the pleasurableness of sweet foods, the vicariousness of which is shown by an animal's willingness to learn for the reward of nonnutritive saccharine.) In the habit-to-instinct evolution, the once-learned goals and subgoals become innate at a more and more specific response-fragment level. For such an evolutionary development to take place, very stable environments over long evolutionary periods are required. (pp. 425–426)

One of the most profound contemporary influences of evolutionary theory on epistemology lies in the reinterpretation of the *a priori* categories of perception and thought (the Kantian categories, etc.) as products of biological and social evolution. Popper, Quine, Sellars, Toulmin, and Shimony are just a few of the eminent contemporary philosophers who have found this an important insight (Campbell, 1974a). Baldwin (1902) had the same reconceptualization in a well-developed form by the turn of the century, or earlier:

As Kant claimed, knowledge is a process of categorizing, and to know a thing is to say that it illustrates or stimulates, or functions as, a category. But a category is a mental habit; that is all a category can be allowed to be—a habit broadly defined as a disposition, whether congenital or acquired, to act upon or to treat, items of any sort in certain general ways. These habits or categories arise either from actual accommodations with "functional" or some other form of utility selection, or by natural endowment secured by selection from variations. (p. 309)

In general, evolutionary epistemologies from Simmel (1895) and James (1880) on have been tempted by a positivism, conventionalism, or pragmatism that rejects the distinction between useful beliefs and the reality to which they refer, that denies any distinction between useful and true beliefs. This is in spite of the clear-cut distinction between organismic form and environmental characteristics which is essential in evolutionary theory, and which entails a parallel distinction between organismic behavior patterns and environment, and organismic cognitive maps, beliefs, etc., and environment. In this perspective it greatly increases my respect for Baldwin to find him making such a clear distinction between his instrumentalism and James's and Dewey's pragmatism. (In current terms, his *instrumentalism* seems to me an experimental, evolutionary version of *critical realism*. In today's usage, the word instrumentalism would not be distinguished from pragmatism as an epistemological position.)

So far we may recognize the two great conquests of the instrumental or experimental logic. It holds that *all truth is confirmed hypothesis*, and that *"reason" is truth woven into mental structure.* These two great formulations are handed over to philosophy. Both are Darwinian. The first cites the selection of ideas for their utility in personal and social development; the second cites the 'coincident' racial selection that fixes them in the constitution of the mind.

But a more radical point of view is possible. What is now known as Pragmatism proceeds out from this point. It is pertinent to notice it here, for it offers a link of transition to the philosophical views with which we must briefly concern ourselves.

Pragmatism turns instrumentalism into a system of metaphysics. It claims that apart from its tentative instrumental value, its value as guide to life, its value as measured by utility, seen in the consequences of its following out, truth has no further meaning. Not only is all truth selected for its utility, but apart from its utility *it is not truth.* There is no reality then to which truth is still true, whether humanly discovered or not; on the contrary, reality is only the content of the system of beliefs found useful as a guide to life.

I wish to point out that, in such a conclusion, not only is the experimental conception left behind, but the advantages of the Darwinian principle of adjustment to actual situations, physical and social, is lost; and if so interpreted, instrumentalism defeats itself. This clearly appears when we analyze a situation involving trial and error. Trial implies a problematical and alternative result: either the success of the assumption put to trial or its failure. When we ask why this is so, we hit upon the presence of some "controlling" condition or circumstance in the situation—some stable physical or social fact—whose character renders the hypothesis or suggested solution either adequate or vain, as the case may be. The instrumental idea or thought, then, has its merit in enabling us to find out or locate facts and conditions which are to be allowed for thereafter. These constitute a *control upon knowledge and action*, a system of "things." Now we may, indeed, say that nothing of what we think can be considered real except what has been experimentally discovered; but we cannot go on to say that it is the discovery that makes it real. For if that were true, what account could we give of this painstaking and often most laborious process of gradual correction and proof?—what account, that is, of the "control" exercised upon knowledge and action by facts or things?

I know there are ways of replying to this criticism—ways of reducing the environment and its controlling facts to the level of postulates of earlier personal or racial experience. But while not finding these replies sufficient, I may simply say—confining the discussion to the Darwinian text—that the method of selection by trial and error requires that relative stability, fixity and permanence be discovered in the "control" conditions in the environment, since the genesis of truth lies in the checking off of hypotheses under this more stable control. The truth of a thought may be discovered through its successful working; but we have to consider also the failures, the errors, and indeed the whole situation in which truth and error are alike possible.

Such analysis supports instrumentalism, but it does not support pragmatism. I may "bring about" reality perhaps, without this external control, by "willing to believe" in something for which I have no proof or reason, in cases in which the sort of event willed—as, for example, some one else's conduct—may be conditioned upon my act of will. But nature does not take to suggestions so kindly. The will of a general may stimulate his troops and so bring to him the victory he believes in; but such an act of the general's will cannot replenish the short supply of powder or shells, on which the issue of the battle perhaps more fundamentally depends. (Baldwin, 1909, pp. 70–73)

I cannot claim to be a Baldwin scholar nor to have read more than one fourth of his currently relevant writings, but it is clear that I join others—such as Piaget, Russell (1978), and my editors and co-contributors to this book—in regarding Baldwin as the greatest pioneer in psychology and philosophy, now the subjects of my most central concern. We regret, for the sake of the advancement of our own fields, that he has been so long neglected, and we hope that this neglect will be soon generally corrected.

REFERENCES

Ashby, W. R. *Design for a brain*. New York: Wiley, 1952.

Baldwin, J. M. *Social and ethical interpretations in mental development*. New York: Macmillan, 1897.

Baldwin, J. M. *Mental development in the child and the race*. New York: Macmillan, 1900.

Baldwin, J. M. *Dictionary of philosophy and psychology* (3 vols.). New York: Macmillan, 1901–1905. (Reissued, Gloucester, Mass.: Peter Smith, 1960.)

Baldwin, J. M. *Development and evolution*. New York: Macmillan, 1902.

Baldwin, J. M. *Thought & things or genetic logic*. Vol. I. *Functional logic*; Vol. II. *Experimental logic*; Vol. III. *Real logic, interest & art*. New York: Macmillan, 1906–1911. (Reprinted, New York: Arno Press, 1975.)

Baldwin, J. M. *Darwin and the humanities*. Baltimore, Md: Review Publishing, 1909.

Baldwin, J. M. *History of psychology*. New York: Putnam, 1913.

Boring, E. G. The influence of evolutionary thought upon American psychological thought. In S. Persons (Ed.), *Evolutionary thought in America*. New Haven: Yale Univ. Press, 1950.

Campbell, D. T. Adaptive behavior from random response. *Behavioral Science*, 1956, *1*, 105–110. (a)

Campbell, D. T. Perception as substitute trial and error. *Psychological Review*, 1956, *63*, 330–342. (b)

Campbell, D. T. Methodological suggestions from a comparative psychology of knowledge processes. *Inquiry*, 1959, 152–182.

Campbell, D. T. Blind variation and selective survival as a general strategy in knowledge processes. In M. C. Yovits & S. H. Cameron (Eds.) *Self-organizing systems*. Oxford: Pergamon Press, 1960.

Campbell, D. T. Blind variation and selective retention in creative thought as in other knowledge processes. *Psychological Review*, 1960, *67*, 380–400.

Campbell, D. T. Evolutionary epistemology. In P. A. Schilpp (Ed.), *The philosophy of Karl R. Popper. The library of living philosophers* (Vol. 14, I & II). LaSalle, Ill.: Open Court Publ., 1974. (a)

Campbell, D. T. Unjustified variation and selective retention in scientific discovery. In T. Dobzhansky & F. J. Ayala (Eds.), *Studies in the philosophy of biology*. London: Macmillan, 1974. (b)

Dewey, J. *The influence of Darwin on philosophy*. New York: Henry Holt, 1910.

Hinde, R. A. (Ed.). *Bird vocalizations*. Cambridge: Cambridge Univ. Press, 1969.

James, W. Great men, great thoughts and the environment. *Atlantic Monthly*, 1880. *46*, 441–459.

Karpf, F. B. *American social psychology: Its origins, development, and European background*. New York: McGraw-Hill, 1932.

Piaget, J. *Behavior and evolution*. New York: Pantheon, 1978.

Pringle, J. W. S. On the parallel between learning and evolution. *Behaviour*, 1951, *3*, 175–215.

Russell, J. *The acquisition of knowledge*. New York: St. Martin's Press, 1978.

Simmel, G. On a relationship between the theory of selection and epistemology. June 1968 (Mimeo) 1–14. (I. L. Jerison, trans.). (Originally published June 1968, *Archiv für Systematische Philosophie*, 1895, *1*, 34–45.)

5

EVOLUTIONARY EPISTEMOLOGY

D. J. Freeman-Moir
University of Canterbury

This chapter considers three aspects in the history of evolutionary epistemology most relevant to Baldwin's own contribution to the area: (1) the evolutionary epistemologies of James and Simmel to which Baldwin reacted, at least briefly; (2) Baldwin's natural-selection model of thinking; (3) the more recent and detailed evolutionary epistemology of Campbell which starts out from these nineteenth-century pioneers.

Baldwin's Contemporaries

In 1880 Huxley confidently announced: "The struggle for existence holds as much in the intellectual as in the physical world. A theory is a species of thinking, and its right to exist is coextensive with its power of resisting extinction by its rivals" (Huxley, 1881, p. 312). In fact Huxley did nothing more to show how his "tooth and claw" interpretation of evolution as "the struggle for existence" could clarify the issue.

In the same year William James made one of the most impressive contributions to evolutionary epistemology. In his essay, "Great Men, Great Thoughts and the Environment," James argued in detail for a direct parallel between the "mental growth of the race" and the Darwinian conception of evolution—the first such argument of its kind. Starting out with the person who is distinguished by some quality, James draws a fundamental distinction between two classes of causation, those causes which originally produce the distinctive quality and those which maintain it. For explanation, these two "cycles of causation" are regarded as independent and to see this, as James (1880) rightly pointed out, was the crucial insight underlying the Darwinian theory.

> Separating the causes of production under the title of "tendencies to spontaneous variation," and relegating them to a physiological cycle which he forthwith agreed to ignore altogether, he continued his attention to the causes of preservation, and under the names of natural selection and sexual selection studied them exclusively as functions of the cycle of the environment. (pp. 443–444)

In light of Campbell's later discussions, James quite successfully conceptualizes the appropriate grounds for defining variations as "random" or "spontaneous." According to James (1880) the causes of variation "are molecular and invisible; inaccessible, therefore to direct observation of any kind (p. 444)."

James got closer to defining the meaning of random by postulating that these causes of variation are independent of the environment or the processes of selection. Selection, then, cannot be a direct determinant in this cycle of causation. From the point of view of selection mechanisms, the variations are spontaneous, random, or blind.

Despite obvious, even glaring, gaps in the explanation, James's position was uncompromisingly Darwinian. This can be seen from his application of the natural selection model to the mind's motivational or affective dispositions, the more subjective "personal tone of each mind," and to the Kantian a-priori synthetic categories of knowledge. Campbell has made exactly the same point in the second of his three postulates on evolutionary epistemology (see Chap. 4).

The naturalistic reinterpretation of the Kantian a priori is one of the more significant aspects of modern epistemology. According to Kant, the categories of space and time are given a priori to experience. Although agreeing with Hume that all our knowledge begins in experience, Kant disagreed that knowledge is based wholly on experience. Kant (1929) begins with the hypothesis that "it may well be that even our empirical knowledge is made of what we receive through impressions and of what our own faculty of knowledge (sensible impressions serving merely as the occasion) supplies from itself" (pp. 41–42). In fact, Kant was arguing for a new concept of experience on the grounds that our "sense impressions, in order to be sense impressions at all, must be subject to certain conditions" (Hartnack, 1967, p. 10).

James accepts the Kantian claim that without prior categories of reason, ordinary experience, much less scientific experience, would be utterly impossible. But the idea that these categories have an a-priori validity is at odds with an evolutionary explanation of the mind. James wanted nothing less than a fully scientific explanation for the possibility and evolution of science.

While disagreeing with Kant's philosophical explanation of experience, James (1890) also denied that the form of knowledge— our "organic mental structure" as he termed it—is simply a passive duplicate of the world as Spencer's so-called universal law maintained.

The notion of the outer world inevitably building up a sort of mental duplicate of itself if we only give it time, is so easy and natural in its vagueness that one hardly knows how to start to criticize it. One thing, however, is obvious, namely that the manner in which we *now become acquainted with complex objects need not in the least resemble the manner in which the original elements of our consciousness grew up.* Now it is true, a new sort of animal need only be present to me, to impress its image permanently on my mind; but this is because I am already in possession of categories for knowing each and all of its several attributes, and of a memory for retracing the order of their conjunction. I now have preformed categories for all possible objects. The objects need only awaken these from their slumber. But it is a very different matter to account for the categories themselves. I think we must admit that the origin of the various elementary feelings is a recondite history, even after some sort of neural tissue is there for the outer world to begin its work on. The mere existence of things to be known is even now not, as a rule, sufficient to bring about a knowledge of them. Our abstract and general discoveries usually come to us as lucky fancies; and it is only *après coup* that we find that they correspond to some reality. What immediately produced them were previous thoughts, with which, and with the brain-processes of which, that reality had naught to do. (Vol. II, p. 630 ff.)

With these considerations in mind, James was ready to introduce his Darwinian explanation of the Kantian categories.

'Why may it not have been so of the original elements of consciousness, sensation, time, space resemblance, difference, and other relations? Why may they not have come into being by the back-door method, by such physical processes as lie more in the sphere of morphological accident, of inward summation of effects, than in that of the "sensible presence" of objects? Why may they not, in short, be pure *idiosyncrasies*, spontaneous variations, fitted by good luck (those of them which have survived) to take cognizance of objects (that is, to steer us in our active dealings with them), without being in any intelligible sense immediate derivations from them? I think we shall find this view gain more and more plausibility as we proceed. (James, II. pp. 630–631)

According to this theory, internal processes, not environmental stimuli, are the proximate causes of an a-priori mental structure. In particular, James applied this explanation to the mental categories of time, space, and cause, to theory construction in natural science, to mathematical and logical relations, to aesthetic and moral principles, and even to instincts.

The themes and problems outlined by James have remained central to all subsequent discussions in evolutionary epistemology—the role of chance in thought, a nonteleological explanation of the scientific imagination, and an objectivist conception of science as leading toward, rather than following from, epistemological certainty.

The scientist or naturalistic epistemologist does not set out by first establishing the validity or possibility of knowledge. There are no irreducible elements of sense data so long sought for by those in the empiricist tradition, no subjectively guaranteed certainty following from the Cartesian *cogito*, no Kantian transcendental deduction of an epistemological a priori to be handed over to the Newtons of this world. All we have, as James so clearly saw, are the bits and pieces of ordinary experience, scientific knowledge, and a method of procedure by which hypotheses are tested against evidence.

I turn now to Simmel, better known as a theoretical sociologist, who, like James, also produced an evolutionary epistemology with which Baldwin was familiar. In a short, rather opaque essay *On a Relationship between Theory of Selection and Epistemology* Simmel (1895) cut through the illusion of knowledge as grounded in absolute or a-priori truth. Once again Kant's theory is the subject of criticism. Simmel proceeds by linking cognition and its products to a principle of utility.

For Simmel, knowledge "has its origins in the practical needs for preserving life and providing for it." The effect of this move is immediately to relativize across the entire range of systems concerned with making (adaptive) responses to the environment.

> The sensory concepts with which animals respond to the influences of their environment must be different from ours in many ways. . . . The reason for such differences cannot be anything other than the fact that various animals find different kinds of sensory apparatus the most useful and the most appropriate to their living conditions. It is then inevitable that quite different world-views evolve from such different raw materials. . . . A true concept for an animal is that which makes him believe in a way most fitting its circumstances since it was the demand for such behavior that formed the organs that govern its knowing in the first place. (Simmel, 1895, p. 8)

In the kind of relativization advanced here by Simmel, we have the hypothesis which underlies, for example, Campbell's recent suggestions for a comparative psychology of knowledge processes. This is done by extending the concept of knowledge. Simmel rejects the idea of an absolutely guaranteed truth, but he does not reject the central aim of all epistemology—to show how knowledge is objective.

In Simmel's language, *objectivity* is the "assurance that practice based on thought will not collide with the harsh actuality of things and thus become subject to a painful adjustment (Simmel, 1895, p. 2). The problem is finding some way of relating cognition which is always in the service of practical need (i.e., subjective utility) to the structure of an objectively knowable world (i.e., external reality).

Simmel (1895) regarded it as an error to think that this project could be realized by postulating "some independent truth in order for the outcome of an action to be evaluated" (p. 4). This error assumes, as it were, that the cause and effect of thought—belief or knowledge and its referent—are isomorphic. If not then, according to this view, cognition could lead to any conceivable result including delusions. But knowledge is corrigible and it is a common psychological fact that the knower can be mistaken. Any epistemology must recognize this possibility. Kant's great error, as Popper has shown, and Simmel recognized, was to "prove" too much. "In trying to show how knowledge is possible, he proposed a theory which had the unavoidable consequence that our quest for knowledge must necessarily succeed, which is clearly mistaken" (Popper, 1963, p. 48).

Starting out from the principle of utility, Simmel (1895) defined *truth* as the "quality of concepts which makes them the cause of most beneficial action" (p. 3). The only evidence for the truth of our concepts is, in fact, the benefit derived from actions which are based on them. This is similar to James's criterion. "Nature turns out to act as if they (the concepts) *were* of the kind assumed." Simmel's (1895) Darwinism is unqualified.

> There is no theoretically valid "truth" on which we can base appropriate actions. Rather we call those concepts true which have proved to motivate expedient and life-promoting actions. . . . Truth no longer means that the nature of concepts is established in accordance with theoretical criteria. Rather, it is those concepts which, from among innumerable emerging ideas, have subsequently proved useful that have been preserved as significant by means of natural selection. (p. 3)

Although postulating a necessary dualism of thought and reality without which objectivity would not be possible, Simmel proposes a resolution in terms of actions which lead to conceptualization. Knowledge is arrived at by no other method: "the forms of thought which create the world as concept are determined by the practical effects and counter-effects fashioned by our mental constitution—nothing other than the body—according to evolutionary needs" (Simmel, 1895, p. 14).

James and Simmel represent two vigorous attempts to naturalize epistemology by turning it into a science, a perspective now commonplace among philosophers and psychologists. Baldwin was one of the next advocates of a Darwinian epistemology and within the entire tradition, prior to Campbell and Popper, perhaps the most prominent.

Baldwin's Evolutionary Epistemology

From Huxley through James and Simmel to Baldwin we can see increasingly more attention being paid to the internal dynamics of the evolutionary process. James's distinction between the causal cycles of variation and selection left open further questions about the range of variation, the mechanisms of selection, and the meaning of truth. The core of Baldwin's theory consists of answers to these questions.

"By selective thinking I understand *the determination of the stream of thought* considered as having a trend or direction of movement, both in the individual mental history and also in the development of mind and knowledge in the world" (Baldwin, 1898, p.1). No one doubts that there are consistent themes and developments in thought. Baldwin, for example, mentions the consistency shown in empirical knowledge, logicomathematical propositions, aesthetic and ethical thought. The problem, obviously, is accounting for the trend or direction of thought—that is, for its evolution. Baldwin approached this problem from the standpoint of a functional psychology designed to analyze the processes presumed to underlie the stream of thought. For Baldwin the central question was,—"How does the mind invent anything new?"

Baldwin observed that cognitive development depends on more than the simple enlargement of experience. Clearly, it is not sufficient to have repetitions of former experiences; there must be variation. Working against this, however, is the retention of previously selected variations through the operation of memory. Selective retention is, of course, a necessary assumption but it operates as a conservative force in human cognition and evolution generally. For example, cognitive caution in the generation and testing of counterintuitive hypotheses is well known. The negative relationship between variation and selective retention has also been noted by Campbell who proposes a minimax principle of operation.

The source of variation then might be the imagination, "a theatre in which seeming novelties of various sorts are constantly disporting themselves (p. 3)." The passive imagination—daydreams, dreams, fancy—results in "scattered products" at all levels of cognition. Baldwin then asks whether the development of knowledge can be accounted for by "accidental but happy hits in these overproduced *disjecta membra?*"

Although Baldwin ascribes this view to James and Simmel, neither thinker speculated about the immediate source or range of variation. For James, *accidental, random, spontaneous,* and *lucky* referred only to the fact that variations are independent of selection. Indeed, in a crude approximation to Baldwin's argument James, (1880) noted that each mind has its determinate direction which makes it "more alive to certain classes of experience than others, more attentive to certain impressions, more open to certain reasons" (p. 444). But these, too, are the result of prior selections, and in turn, they impose restraints on the range of variation. Baldwin's analysis served to clarify and advance this key insight without which a plausible evolutionary epistemology would be impossible.

Baldwin (1898) countered what might be called the theory of *weird-and-wonderful variations* with two objections: (1) dream-states do not lead to knowledge; and (2) we do not simply scatter our thought about in random trials.

> On the contrary, we succeed in thinking well by thinking hard; we get the valuable thought-variations by concentrating attention upon the body of related knowledge which we already have: we discover new relations among the data of experience by running over and over the links and couplings of the apperceptive systems with which our minds are already filled; and our best preparation for effective progress in this line or in that comes by occupying our minds with all the riches of the world's information just upon the specific topics of our interest. (p.4)

Like every other scientific epistemologist Baldwin rejects the teleological theory that the mind thinks "its own true thoughts" since it is governed by an inner principle of truth; "this theory, it is plain is analogous to the theory of vitalism, with a self-directing impulse, in biology." The Kantian theory takes another criticism for "the question to which the *a priori* theory gives no answer is . . . even given the "categories" what sorts of experience fit the categories, and how is the fitting done" (Baldwin, 1898, p. 4).

Rejecting both the idea of "mere stray products of fancy" and a theory which locates the explanation of knowledge outside experience, Baldwin (1898) proposes the following answer: "The thought-variations by the supply of which selective thinking proceeds occur in the processes at the level of organization which the system in question has already reached—a level which is thus the platform for further determinations in the same system" (p. 5). He illustrates this hypothesis by noting that the child and the adult test experience in radically dissimilar ways. "The child thinks the moon is made of green cheese, that birds grow on the limbs of trees," and so on—at which conceits the adult smiles. Baldwin (1898) continues: "The difference is that at the child's level of what we go on to call 'systematic determination,' these (i.e. re the moon and birds) are variations of possible value; he has yet to test them; but to the man they are not on the level or platform which his selective thinking has reached" (pp. 5-6).

Whereas the scientist proceeds in a systematic fashion, the young child does not have the requisite cognitive structure to make a similar attack on experimental problems. The scientist's systematic procedure is not just the consequence of possessing a qualitatively superior cognitive structure, it is also a matter of having a further-ranging knowledge base than the child.

The problem now arose for Baldwin to define more closely what was meant by the "level or organization in thought or the platform." He comments:

> It is just of the nature of knowledge to be an organization, a structure, a system. There is no such thing as mere "acquaintance with" anything; there is always—to abuse James' antithesis—more or less "knowledge-about." And the growth of thought is the enlargement of the "knowledge-about" by the union of partial with partial "knowledge-about" in a constantly wider and fuller system of thoughts. Selective thinking is the gradual enlargement of the system, a heaping-up of structure. If this be true, a little reflection convinces us that variations in the items of material merely, in the stones of the structure, in the brute experiences of sense or memory, cannot be fruitful or the reverse of the system. It is variation only *in the organization* which can be that. It is the readjustments, the modifications or variations in the "knowledge-about," which constitute the gain or loss to thought (Baldwin, 1898, p. 7).

Baldwin is maintaining that a thought-variation, to be counted as a variation at all, must have some connection—whatever that means—with the already existing system. Experience which is merely repetitive or which does "not fit into co-ordinations of knowledge which are ours" will not bring about any readjustment in our arrangements of knowledge.

This view of the psychology of knowledge envisages an intimate connection between the present structure of knowledge and the generated variations. It is this intimacy which lends meaning to Baldwin's particular claims, already considered, that variations cannot emerge from a *disjecta membra* of imagination. Without something approximating to a structure—whether we call it a rudimentary theory, expectation, hypothesis, or habit does not matter much; experience would be meaningless for the organism.

Accepting Baldwin's general principle that there are internal or structural limits on the overall range of variations in no way limits which variations will occur or how. Even so, it is a notoriously difficult task to specify with any precision what "the level of organization" in cognitive structure actually is. There is, nevertheless, a note of caution evident in Baldwin at this point since maybe variations do occur which lie beyond the current level of organization. Campbell (1974b), for example, has noted the possibility of quantum indeterminacy effects in the generation of thought variations.

We return now to consider what Baldwin thought he was ruling out from his explanation—unruly imagination and randomly scattered thought trials. Both objections need to be considered. There are reasonable construals of "imagination" and "random thought trials" which make both of these potential sources of thought variations.

As to the first objection, there is solid evidence that dream processes and unconscious thought are productive of possible theories and problem solutions. To take two famous cases, Kekulé and Poincaré both attributed fundamental scientific discoveries to what Jung appropriately termed "sudden pictorial revelations from the unconscious."

Baldwin found himself disagreeing with a concept of imagination which he regarded as altogether too spare in what it connoted. Hence, Baldwin's first objection amounts to disagreeing with the theory that discovery is a *creatio ex nihilo* on the grounds that out of nothing, nothing comes. In asserting as he did that discovery and the growth of knowledge is an integrated, systematic process, Baldwin comes close to the denial of the value of imagination altogether. When Baldwin (1897) claims that the elements within thought can be interpreted as the result of prior selections all the way back to the first hypothesis, he is inviting the analyst "to look in all cases of imagination for elements of construction themselves more or less familiar beforehand to the thought of the person who makes the invention" (p.101).

Baldwin's second objection asserts "we do not scatter our thoughts as widely as possible in order to increase the chances of getting a true one; on the contrary, we call the man who produces the most thought variations a 'scatter-brain,' and expect nothing inventive from him" (Baldwin, 1898, p. 4).

Having settled on the mind's organization of knowledge as the central issue, Baldwin turned to the problem of teasing out the dynamics involved—how certain variations are selected. So far as empirical knowledge is concerned—for example, the construction of scientific theories—the general function of selection is optimizing explanations which "reflect for our practical purposes, the actual state of things existing in the world." Baldwin postulates two selection mechanisms.

The first test—habit—requires that a new experience fit into the

already existing structure. It is "a testing of the general character of
a new experience as calling out the acquired motor habits of the
organism." If this did not occur, then either the event would not be
an experience for the organism in question or else it would be a gross
accident, not a variation "to be selected for the upbuilding and
enriching of the system." There is a logical point embedded here as
well, for the criterion "calling out the acquired motor habits"
amounts to a definition within the theory of what is minimally
necessary for there to be anything called *experience* at all. Baldwin
(1898) summarizes what Piaget calls the *assimilatory* side of knowledge: "In order to be really the thought-variations which selective
thinking requires, all new items must, in the first place, secure and
hold the attention; which means that they must enter, however
vaguely, into the complex of earlier knowledge, in order that the
habitual motor reflex may be called out" (p. 13).

Baldwin makes the interesting point that this test of assimilation
to habit transfers part of the selection process from the environment
to the organism and constitutes a "sort of intra-organic selection," an
explicit reference to the intraselection theory of Weismann, a contemporary exponent of neo-Darwinian evolution. Intraorganic selection is an important concept and reappears in part as the internal
selectors of Whyte (1965) which in turn have been divided into
structural and vicarious selectors by Campbell (1974b).

According to Whyte, internal selection is the selection of mutants at the molecular, chromosomal, and cellular levels, in accordance with their compatibility with the internal coordination of the
organism. At the level of psychological processes, the test of assimilation to habit is precisely a selection in terms of internal coordination.

Baldwin's reinterpretation of the Kantian categories can be
understood from this point of view; they are a set of internal
selectors. As early as 1891 Baldwin suggested that space, for example,
"is built up from tentative experiences of objects," although his
attempts to explain this psychologically were only approximate (see
Chapter 6). As Campbell notes in Chap. 4, Baldwin interpreted
cognitive categories as mental habits, whether innate or acquired.
Consistent with a Darwinian epistemology "these habits or categories
arise either from actual accommodations with 'functional' or some
other form of utility selection, or by natural endowment secured by
selection from variations" (Baldwin, 1902, p. 309).

The second selector of variation is "a testing of the special
concrete character of the experience, as fitted to the environment
. . . to bring about a new determination in the system in which it goes"
(Baldwin, 1898, p. 10). The organization of what is known has to be

accommodated to the world. This selector also serves to make a logical claim, for without something called correspondence between the idea and the fact there could be nothing which constitutes objectivity or provides a basis for it.

There is first "the direct necessity of accommodation and recognition which the physical enforces upon us." An object at a distance in the dust may be taken as a tree stump, a man, or an animal. A closer inspection shows it to be, beyond a doubt, a tree stump. The social context is the second accommodatory force. Considered as a "system of organized truth" the environment of selection is social:

> The environment of thought can only be thoughts; only processes of thought can influence thoughts and be influenced by them. The sources from which spring items in the world of thought are ordinarily centres of thought—minds either one's own or someone's else. So the environment must be persons about the thinker. (Baldwin, 1898, p. 18.)

Baldwin (1898) describes the significance of the social environment for the growth of knowledge in the individual this way:

> But then—and this is a vital fact in the growth of the individual—this selection by a social criterion *becomes personal to the learner through his renewed action.* The selected functions, with their knowledge contents, *are added to the organization within, so that the "systematic determination" of the future is influenced by the assimilation of each new selected element.* Thus the inner attitude which the individual brings to his experience undergoes gradual determination by the continued selective action of the social environment. He himself comes more and more to reflect the social judgment in his own systematic determination of knowledge; and there arises within himself a criterion of a private sort which is in essential harmony with the social demand, because genetically considered it reflects it. The individual becomes a law unto him, exercises his private judgment, fights his own battles for truth, shows the virtue of independence and the vice of obstinacy. But he has learned to do it by the selective control of his social environment, and in his judgment he has just a sense of this social outcome. (p. 19–20)

With respect to the functions of habit and accommodation this is as far as Baldwin manages to penetrate. Baldwin made no studies at different stages in the developmental sequence of the sort made by Piaget and he made no studies in the history of science. However, he did make the important point (emphasized in Chap. 6) that the two aspects of selection are linked together.

> The tests of habit, the intra-organic tests, represent an organization or systematic determination of the things guaranteed by the tests of fact; and, on the other hand, things which are not assimilable to the life of habit can not come to be established as intelligible facts. The great difference between the two tests is that the habit is less exacting; for

after a datum has passed the gauntlet of habit—or several alternative data have together passed it—it still competes for survival in the domain of fact. (Baldwin, 1898, p. 11)

As Campbell has indicated (See Chap. 4) Baldwin was not tempted to adopt a pragmatist view of truth of the kind which attracted James and Simmel. On this Baldwin (1898) is very clear.

What, then, do we, finally mean by *truth* in the sphere of external knowledge? This, I think: a truth in nature is just something selected by the test of fact (after having passed the gauntlet of habit, of course), and then so passed back into the domain of habit that it forms part of that organization which shows the systematic determination of the thinker. What the word "truth" adds to the word "fact" is only that a truth is a presentative datum of the intra-organic system which has stood the test of fact *and can stand it again*. A truth is an item of content which is expected, when ensuing in movement, to work under the exactions of fact. We speak of a correspondence between the idea and the fact as constituting truth; and so it does. But we should see that a truth is not selected because it is true; *it is true because it has been selected*, and that in both of two ways: first, by fulfilling habit, and second, on recreating fact. There is no question of truth until both these selective functions have been operative. (p. 11)

I want to make just two remarks about this concept of truth. First, Baldwin's view is *objectivist*. That is, truth is a criterion which is external to the observer, and in this sense, truth is not relative. Either there is a correspondence between the idea and the fact, as Baldwin says, or there is not. The notion of correspondence here is clearly normative, not psychological. The proposition (i.e., the equivalent to Baldwin's "idea") that "the maple tree outside my window has its new leaves on" is true if and only if, as a matter of fact, spring leaves have appeared on the maple tree in question. Second, Baldwin's analysis also takes into account the subjective side of knowledge. What is judged to be true is the property of a particular thinker, although it is not true on that account. For this reason, Baldwin rejected as too crude James's (1907) view of truth that: "Any idea upon which we can ride, so to speak, any idea will carry us prosperously from any one part of our experience to any other part, linking things satisfactorily, working securely, simplifying, saving labor; it is true for just so much, true in so far forth, true instrumentally" (p. 58). Alternatively, Baldwin might say that we take as true any idea which carries us along, although in the end the truth of an idea depends on the more stringent test of accommodation.

It might be objected that my interpretation seriously misrepresents Baldwin's concept of truth. This objection would argue that Baldwin's account is confused as to whether the analysis should be philosophical or psychological. I think the distinction between truth, as an absolute, and what we take to be true provides a way of handling this difficulty. The standard against which we judge the results of epistemic activity is absolute and in Baldwin's case it is the "correspondence between the idea and the fact." Psychologically, it seems that we never reach the truth. What we take to be the truth in most areas of our experience turns out to be nothing more than an approximation. But we do not thereby give up the criterion of truth and opt for relativism. Instead, we reject as false that which we formerly took to be true.

Baldwin's analysis focuses primarily on the what-we-take-to-be-true side of the distinction. He tells us, in short, that what we take to be true is a function of habit and accommodation. But the notion of taking something to be true makes sense only if it is linked to an objective criterion of truth; that is why I said Baldwin's account is objectivist at its center. In development, therefore, mind works it way up through a series of tentative correspondences, a process which Baldwin envisages in the following manner:

> Our question may be put in the familiar terms of an analogous biological problem, if we ask: when a particular truth has been shown by selection to be such, *why was it found fit to survive?*
>
> In answer to this question we may say at once, concerning knowledge of the external world, that the motor accommodations by which the selective process proceeds are, by the conditions of the environment, *of necessity made in this direction or that.* The reason a given movement is fit is because it actually reports fact. The dictum of the environment is: accommodate to x y z or die in the attempt! The facts are there; nature is what it is; the adjustments are such just because they are fit to report a state of facts. The environment in which the accommodations take place, and to which they constitute adjustments, is the control factor, and its facts constitute the only reason that the selections are what they are. The criterion here, therefore, is simply the adaptive aspect of the movement, as reporting fact. It can be determined in each case only after the event; that is, after the selection has taken place.
>
> But even in this lower sphere, where the exigencies of the physical environment are the control-factor in the selective process, we find the further result that the preservation of the fact selected depends upon its having already been assimilated to the organized habits of the individual. As knowledge it becomes part of a system; it is added to the platform from which subsequent selections are made; and it thus carries forward the 'systematic determination' of thought. In this way *the organism gradually reproduces in its own platform of determination the very criteria of selection at first enforced only by the environment.* (Baldwin, 1898, pp. 16–17)

Campbell's Evolutionary Epistemology

Among biologists, most accept the neo-Darwinian or synthetic theory. In the view of one of its distinguished advocates (Dobzhansky,

1974), it provides a satisfactory explanatory framework for evolution. Campbell has gone even further and, with Popper, claims the random-variation-plus-selective-retention model as the all-purpose nonteleological explanation of adaptation—from crystal formation to the fit between scientific theories and the world they claim to describe.

Campbell does not think that evolutionary theory, more especially as it is applied to knowledge processes, is without problems nor that we have achieved a complete, even reasonably partial, understanding of the mechanisms underlying the production of variations and selective retention. Nor, any more than Baldwin, does he deny the important facts emphasized by the vitalists—that thought is structured, directional, and purposeful, that it has a design, and even that it displays emergent levels of organization, "but while we must join them in admitting that natural selection and its analogues produce only puny, tedious and improbable explanations, we judge these to be the only ones available . . . there are, at present at least, no rival explanatory theories" (Campbell, 1974b, p. 142).

In continuing the tradition of evolutionary epistemology already outlined, Campbell has made two principal contributions: clarifying the notion of randomness first introduced by James and, second, developing an insight by Baldwin into a hierarchy of knowledge processes. We shall consider these topics in turn.

"Blind," "unjustified," or "random" variation (at various times Campbell has used all three qualifiers) on which selective elimination operates is a key feature of any evolutionary theory. Critics have argued over this claim, and, as Campbell recognizes, the claim provides the major stumbling block to accepting the theory. The same, of course, has been true within evolutionary biology itself as the debates between Darwinians and Lamarckians have demonstrated.

Monod (1971) identifies the probable reason for opposition to the concept of chance. Stating his case somewhat extremely, as Dobzhansky (1974) notes, Monod argues

> Pure chance, absolutely free but blind, lies at the very root of the stupendous edifice of evolution . . . it is the sole conceivable hypothesis . . . There is no scientific concept, in any of the sciences, more destructive of anthropocentrism than this one, and no other so arouses an instinctive protest from the intensely teleonomic creatures that we are. (pp. 112–113)

Simpson (1967) has pointed out that evolution is not invariably accompanied by progress nor even that progress is an essential feature though evolution has certainly resulted in progress. Dobzhansky (1974) reminds us that "from the fact that evolution exhibits a direction or a trend, it does not follow that evolution is being directed by some outside agency, or that it has been programmed beforehand" (p. 311). In the domains of cognitive psychology and epistemology the same problems must be confronted. How, indeed, are we to square the creative structural complexities of knowledge—the *lines of consistent determined thought*, as Baldwin termed them—with an explanation which rests on the concept of chance?

We have seen that James began his discussion by focusing on the question of variations due to chance and thus independent of the selection process. Campbell has tried further to specify what is meant by *chance*. To speak simply of variation, (whether one substitutes chance, random, or some other term), is to invite various interpretations and hence criticisms. Indeed, considerable misunderstanding has resulted from critics using multiple meanings all of which are neither necessary nor intended by the Darwinian epistemologist. Certain common connotations of "chance" are rejected by Campbell as irrelevant to an evolutionary theory.

For the psychologist trained in statistical theory, *equiprobability* is the most obvious meaning of randomness. The standard example is the fair coin where the probability of an H or T is .5. This notion, however, has nothing to do with randomness in evolutionary variations. Gene mutants, for example, are not equiprobable; indeed, lethal mutants are more probable than others. Furthermore, there can be a structural selection of mutation sequences. The same lack of equiprobability can be seen on the level of behavior. For example, the behavior of the cats in Thorndike's puzzle boxes did not display equiprobable response emission. Nor does the behavior of any human in a problem situation display equiprobability owing, of course, to innate biases, learned preferences, and habits. "Equiprobability is both descriptively wrong and analytically nonessential. But variability reaching into responses beyond the already adaptive is essential" (Campbell, 1974b, p. 148).

Another connotation of randomness is *unrestrained variability*—recall Monod's phrase, "pure chance, absolutely free." This, however, is too extreme since, as a matter of fact, there are always limits on the range of variation. This, it is important to point out, in no way falsifies the Darwinian position. Evolutionary theory assumes only the possibility of variations in combination with selection and not a virtually unlimited range of variations. The retention of past variants places limits on subsequent variation. There is, then, a kind of essential conservatism in evolution. There are also obvious stuctural limits on variation "both of physical impossibility and viability."

Statistical independence between successive variations is also not regarded by Campbell as an essential feature of randomness, though it might be a convenience. The usual example is the circular sweep scanning of a radar antenna. Certainly there is a gain in employing a regular sweep, though the same result can be gained from a set of purely random emissions.

Campbell identifies two features essential to an appropriate concept of randomness. The first is that variations display a relative independence, "relative to the eventual fit or structured order that is to be explained." This requirement is a reworking of James's criterion of independence between cycles of causation.

The problem must be raised of the often observed correlations between variations, for example, behavioral responses and the structure of the environment. But on this, like James and Baldwin, Campbell remains a consistent Darwinian. "For this adaptive bias in variations is itself an evidence of fit needing explaining. And the only available explanation (other than preordained harmony) is through some past variation and selective retention process" (Campbell, 1974b, p. 150).

A second feature of randomness regarded as essential is the notion that successive variations (trials) are not corrections of earlier ones. Variations which seem to operate as adjustments "must be operating a substitute process carrying on the blind search at another level, feedback circuits selecting "partially" adequate variations, providing information to the effect that 'you're getting warm.' "

Using these two criteria—relative independence and noncorrective succession—Campbell defends a Darwinian epistemology. A substantial part of his reply to critics, as we shall see, has been just that they operate with illegitimate or irrelevant concepts of "random."

Campbell's second contribution takes off from a suggestion by *Darwin and the Humanites* (1909) that variation plus natural selection might account for the actual origin of "faculties." In the material Campbell quotes (Chap. 4), Baldwin outlines a sequence of knowledge (adaptations) which runs from simple action patterns (habits) to abstract thought. Baldwin (1902) goes on to provide the evolutionary analysis of this hierarchy.

> As to the actual origin of the different typical "faculties" of the older psychologists—perception, memory, imagination, thought—we may look upon them as progressive variations in mental endowment, each having its utility, and each in turn fixed by selection. There is no difficulty in establishing the enormous utility of each of these faculties ... we may suppose residual processes left by actual experiences serving in their day until established by variation in the form of memory. The experimental use of memory images, with corresponding success and utility, would, be followed in time, by further variations,

giving imagination and thought. The series of functions of trial and error, each in turn projecting its tentative schemes of knowledge, would run ahead and be followed by "coincident" variations, which would then remain fixed as a permanent part of the mental endowment. The process of evolution of psychic function, then, in its great morphological stages, shows the same method—that of natural and organic selection— found operative in organic evolution generally. (pp. 37-38)

This conjecture brings the multiple levels of cognition together with their individual operations under the single principle of variation plus selection. The breadth of Baldwin's claims is reflected in Campbell's three postulates which define an all-encompassing evolutionary theory. It is not difficult to grasp the intellectual motivation behind this move, for with it the facts emphasized by those skeptical of extreme neo-Darwinism (pattern, structure, organization) are admitted; each level of operation "is itself a discovery produced by natural selection, and containing partial or general knowledge about the nature of the world" (Campbell, 1974b, p. 147).

Campbell first tested the theoretical possibilities of this general theory of evolution by applying it to perception. Consider a situation in which responses are goal oriented (e.g., walking along a crowded sidewalk avoiding other people, dogs, and obstacles, or assembling the parts of a mechanism by picking them out of a box). The most obvious feature of such responses is their ordered quality; a smooth patterned sequentiality which seems far removed from what might be expected from a Darwinian trial-and-error process. Campbell (1956) hypothesizes that perception "must serve this function of trial-and-error exploration, substituting for the motor trial and error found in the blind object-consistent response" (p. 335).

The antennae of insects and echo location in bats seem to fit this model quite easily, but what of the more problematic case of vision? Even eye movements, though complex, are highly systematic and far from random. So even if vision—following Campbell's second postulate—is the result of selections made from prior variations, it does not seem to be characterized by blind variation and selection in its own operation—following Campbell's third postulate. If this is so, then the universal applicability of the random-variation-plus-selection model is unrealizable. Campbell's (1956) solution is to draw an analogy between vision and the radar beam:

The radar beam presents in its ever-repeated scanning sweeps multiple alternative loci for reflection ... The rods and cones of a fixed-focus eye can be regarded as the simultaneous presentation of a myriad of alternative loci for possible excitation, blindly available in that their location or availability does not anticipate the location of objects, except as this glance has been preceded by other glances and other sources of information. We could build a radar device in this manner, so that instead of one scanning beam of varying direction, it had a million simultaneously operating beam emitters and receivers, all of fixed aim. (p. 336)

Campbell proposes that knowledge processes at all levels of phylogenetic evolution and ontogenetic development can be analyzed in a similar way. Toward this end, he has described a hierarchy of knowledge processes in which each step in the hierarchy represents an evolutionary achievement and a system for obtaining knowledge. The levels in the hierarchy are only partially discrete, and lower ones are not abandoned to higher levels. These levels cannot, therefore, be treated as a set of evolutionary stages, though clearly they show a marked correlation with evolution. Table 1 presents a summary of Campbell's hierarchy.

Campbell's picture of epistemological evolution agrees with Popper's thesis that what results from the selection process is a series of plastic controls. Each of these hierarchical steps serves in turn as a variant-producing and selector system. What is required, however, is a detailed analysis of each step in the hierarchy and more particularly the last—for the particular interest of evolutionary epistemology lies, as I have already indicated, in explaining the fit between scientific theory and the world. I want to turn finally to consider the main objection brought against a Darwinian approach to knowledge, if not Campbell's particular version of it.

Whyte (1965) has made a suggestion which might help us to understand what lies behind the debate over Darwinian evolutionary epistemology. According to Whyte, nineteenth-century scientific thought was heavily influenced by the concept of kinetic atomism— the idea that material particles move about at random. The twentieth century by comparison is more influenced by the concept of structure and stability. Admittedly, the contrast is an oversimplification but the two themes—random atomism and structural stability—point to the deep-seated problem which Campbell's evolutionary epistemology is trying to resolve.

On the one hand, Campbell is impressed by the structure of thought (i.e., theoretical achievements) and the systematic character of thought processes, as evidenced in the powerful heuristics which can guide human problem solving. On the other hand, Campbell is equally impressed that knowledge processes are often uncertain, tentative, and random and that knowledge itself is corrigible. There is no direct route to knowledge which, once located, provides certain results thereafter. To pretend otherwise is to fall into the trap of espousing a simple-minded teleology or a priorism. Evolutionary epistemology attempts to explain the structural stability of knowledge as an achievement over randomness.

TABLE 1
Campbell's Hierarchy of Knowledge Processes

Level	Description
0. Genetic adaptation	Genetic mutation and selective survival (e.g., bisexuality, heterozygosity)
1. Nonmnenomic problem solving	Blind variation of locomotor activity (e.g., Jenning's paramecium, Ashby's homeostat)
2. Vicarious locomotor devices	Substitution for spatial exploration (e.g., ship's radar, echo location in bats, lateral-line organ in fish)
3/4. Habit, instinct (hierarchical separation imposible here)	Visual diagnosis of reidentifiable objects (e.g., reflex patterns in human infants)
5. Visually supported thought	Insightful problem solving (e.g., Köhler's monkey, instrumental actions in human infants)
6. Mnemonically supported thought	Environment being searched is represented in memory of "knowledge" structure (e.g. Poincaré's mathematical unconscious)
7. Socially vicarious exploration; observational learning and imitation.	Action by one member of a group substitutes for actions by individuals (e.g., trial and error by scouts in groups of migratory animals or humans, imitation in the child).
8. Language (overlapping levels 6 and 7)	The outcome of exploration is presented without illustrative locomotion or the environment being present (e.g., language in bees and humans)
9. Cultural cumulation	Social borrowings (e.g., technology, institutional structures)
10. Science	Systematically controlled testing of conjectures (e.g., scientific experiment)

In his references to "molecular instability" and "random flashes in the brain," James displays a characteristic orientation; indeed the metaphor of kinetic atomism is peculiarly appropriate to his entire psychology. Baldwin, however, places the emphasis on assimilation to habit and accommodatory correlation with the real world. His phrase describing thought as a "consistent line of development" points to a fascination with structure. Nothing, for example, seems more remote from the Jamesian stream of consciousness than the reversible logico-mathematical operations of Piagetian structuralism.

Campbell has repeatedly emphasized that random variation

and selective retention are equally necessary and sufficient for defining the evolutionary scheme. He studiously avoids placing the emphasis on one aspect rather than another as James and Baldwin tended to do. Not surprisingly, he remains unimpressed by any criticism which tends to overlook the significance of either criterion.

The prevailing criticism of Darwinian epistemology centers in one way or another on the degree of "permitted" randomness. A number of critics have thought that evolutionary theory, or the trial-and-error approach to thought, permits no restraint whatsoever on the range of mutants or variations. As Campbell dryly puts it, "some critics write as though advocates of random mutation believed that the mutations from an octopus could include a giraffe."

One version of this criticism attempts to turn the theory into an absurdity. Newell, Shaw, and Simon pointed out that the spaces of all real problems is very large indeed—perhaps of the order of 10^{120} for the set of realizable combinations. For example, take the problem of moving from a present situation on a chessboard to checkmate; although the number of possible moves is discouragingly large, we continue to play and conclude games. The reason for this seems obvious. In the face of real problems we do not seem to proceed by a trial-and-error method. Instead, we employ various heuristic procedures. All this has suggested to some critics that problem-solving thought is intrinsically "insightful" and not to be explained by reference to trial and error or blind variation and selection.

The well-known example, cited by Campbell, is the logic theorist (LT) of Newell, Shaw, and Simon (1958) which employs systematic search procedures (heuristics) to discover proofs for theorems in symbolic logic. The success of the LT depends on choosing not blindly but in terms of the structure of a problem.

Consider the case of proving a theorem by substitution. The extreme case of trial and error would be to generate expressions in a way that is independent of the theorem to be proved until a logically identical pairing occurs. Discovery could be made more efficient by using in the substitution only variables which appear in the original theorem. Additional heuristic principles can be used which would reduce still further the number of trials required.

Clearly the LT proceeds in a meaningful or structured way. By implication so does the human problem solver. Newell, Shaw, and Simon (1958) conclude

> Trial-and-error attempts take place in some "space" of possible solutions. To approach a problem "meaningfully" is to have a strategy that either permits the search to be limited to a smaller subspace, or generates elements of the space in an order that makes probable the discovery of one of the solutions early in the process. (p. 152)

This recognition of meaningful problem solving is not at odds with a Darwinian explanation just because it assumes the existence and current operation of an heuristic principle. These principles are evolutionary discoveries and hence the result of prior trial-and-error procedures. Furthermore, as we have just seen, the heuristic operates by a trial-and-error procedure.

Heuristics at whatever level in the hierarchy of knowledge processes serve to reduce the number of variations explored and so make the problem-space more manageable. For most psychologists, perhaps, it is this capability, however conceptualized, which is definitive of intelligence and which needs to be understood. Given this research goal some commentators find Campbell's (1960) position somewhat diversionary:

> [Minsky asks:] "I would really like to know if you believe you are saying something constructive rather than anarchistic?... What is the constructive purpose in emphasizing the role of trial-and-error which is what we are trying to get rid of?"
> [Sewell comments:] "The interesting question, which is why I find myself not emphasizing the blind variation aspect of it [Neither does Campbell, *Ed.*]—the interesting question is, how do you get from a big space to a little space?" (Discussion response)

Campbell admits that trial and error may be a trivial truism for those intent on analyzing the structure of various heuristics. But Campbell is attending to the problem of knowledge on a different level. His evolutionary epistemology is offered as a general explanation for the existence of various knowledge processes. The products which result from these knowledge processes, when they operate as selector systems, can, of course, be approached in relative independence from the general picture mapped out by Campbell.

Another version of the criticism I have been considering is made by systems theorists who want to emphasize the internal regularities of evolution. Bertalanffy (1967) is well known for his charge that Darwinian theory is insufficient:

> Selection, i.e., favored survival of "better" precursors of life, already presupposes self-maintaining, complex, open systems which may compete; therefore selection cannot account for the origin of such systems.... Structure and formation of physical entities at any level—atoms, molecules, high molecular compounds, crystals, nucleic acids, etc.—follow laws which are progressively revealed by the respective branches of science. Beyond this level, we are asked to believe, there are no "laws of nature" any more, but only chance events in the way of "errors" appearing in the genetic code, and "opportunism" of evolution, "outer-directed" by environment.... There is good reason to believe that the code does have organisational and regulative properties, not well known at present, but indicating that not all mutations are

equiprobable.... These aspects deserve emphasis and investigation equal to those given to undirected mutation and selection. Evolution then appears essentially co-determined by "internal factors" ..., or "inner-directed." (pp. 82–87)

Why can't systems be accounted for by prior selections? Does evolutionary theory really require a concept of mutant equiprobability or "pure" chance? Our previous discussion has already answered these questions and shown, by implication, how badly mistaken Bertalanffy's view of evolution is.

Biological and epistemological systems are structured wholes. Yet like Bertalanffy, Blachowicz (1971) thinks that this proposition is the undoing of Campbell's evolutionary epistemology: "The stabilizing reaction of a system to its environmental disturbances will effect some compensatory change in the internal structure of the system. This change in the system will subsequently affect the manner in which it will experience future disturbances" (p. 193). The "input structure" has been altered and will operate as an *a priori* restriction on the range of variations in the next generation. Blachowicz rightly concludes that the evolution of systems does not result from the play of pure chance but entails something like the processes of internal selection already referred to.

Blachowicz (1971) allows, indeed thinks likely, that science arose in the first instance through the operation of chance, but that subsequently variations became restrained in range. "The primary source of new theoretical knowledge, at this stage of development, is found, not in the mechanisms of chance constellations of data or imaginative guesswork, but rather in the articulation of the existing theoretical structure" (p. 195).

But once again these considerations miss the point by failing to understand the essential features of evolutionary theory. Biological evolution (as Dobzhansky, 1974, has shown) and epistemological evolution equally do not require a concept of pure chance, as Blachowicz implies. Campbell rejects the view that chance entails unrestricted variation at each selection point. Furthermore, the internal selectors are perfectly consistent with an unqualified Darwinian epistemology since they are explained by reference to selection from previous variations. In each case the criticisms of Bertalanffy and Blachowicz wrongly emphasize variation to the exclusion of selection mechanisms. Variation and selective retention are equally part of the total evolutionary process.

Blachowicz treats imaginative guesswork and theory articulation as disjunctive without seeing that the latter must surely involve something like the former. Numerous case studies in science have established this point. Einstein, for example, spoke of wild speculations and guesses. Feynman, referring to the origin of Einstein's general theory of relativity, suggests the importance of guesswork in theory construction when he says "I still can't see how he thought of it." Such examples could be multiplied.

The point against Blachowicz's view of scientific creativity is much the same as the point already made about the role of heuristics. Given a theory—the equivalent here of heuristic restriction on a problem-space—the only way of proceeding is by trial and error; conjecture and guess are submitted to test. Indeed, if it is to preserve any explanatory significance, it is difficult to see what else theoretical articulation in this context could mean. On this problem Baldwin's analysis of the thought platform is vastly more sophisticated than that of Blachowicz.

Evolutionary epistemology does not reduce thought to mere or absolute chance, and to think so is to miss the crucial insight implied by recognizing the distinction between variations, whatever their cause, and selection. The crucial insight—which James spotted long ago—is that variations are blind, or random, relative to the sequence of selection.

The distinction, as drawn, between the two cycles of causation—variation and selection—is a methodological stance against pseudo explanations which allow the possibility of "direct" knowledge. Such explanations slide over the phenomenon requiring explanation by making the fallibility of knowledge the exception rather than the rule. The first major achievement of evolutionary epistemology was to show the possibility of treating knowledge scientifically.

Beyond this, evolutionary epistemology provides an overarching explanatory scheme. Each step in the hierarchy of knowledge is an inductive achievement which must be accounted for. To date, however, the explanatory detail is lacking. In 1880, James admitted that the underlying causes of thought variation lie beyond observation. A century later we seem, in this respect, to be little further advanced.

The rich introspective evidence of Poincaré (1913) and others suggests that variation is largely unconscious and this, of course, puts the theory beyond direct test. Campbell (1974b), for instance, concludes that "general acceptance cannot come until we have a detailed neurological model for the processes James refers to in such phrases as 'because the instability of the brain is such as to tip and upset itself,' etc." (p. 161)

There is, perhaps, a gentle irony in the return of our discussion of evolutionary epistemology to its starting point and the very problems mapped out by James. Interestingly, this also underscores the difficulty of achieving even partial knowledge. Against what seems to be an ever-present wall of ignorance, our only weapon is the blind generation and testing of further hypotheses.

REFERENCES

Baldwin, J. M. *Social and ethical interpretations in mental development.* New York: Macmillan, 1897.

Baldwin, J. M. On selective thinking. *Psychological Review,* 1898, *5,* 1–25.

Baldwin, J. M. *Development and evolution.* New York: Macmillan, 1902.

Baldwin, J. M. *Darwin and the humanities.* Baltimore, Md.: Review Publ., 1909.

Bertalanffy, L. *Robots, men and minds.* New York: Braziller, 1967.

Blachowicz, J. A. Systems theory and evolutionary models of the development of science. *Philosophy of Science,* 1971, *38* 178–199.

Campbell, D. T. Perception as substitute trial and error. *Psychological Review,* 1956, *63,* 330–342.

Campbell, D. T. Blind variation and selective retention in creative thought as in other knowledge processes. *Psychological Review* 1960, *67,* 380–400. (a)

Campbell, D. T. Blind variation and selective survival as a general strategy in knowledge processes. In M. C. Yovits & S. H. Cameron (Eds.) *Self-organizing systems.* Oxford: Pergamon Press, 1960.

Campbell, D. T. Evolutionary epistemology. In P. A. Schilpp (Ed.), *The Philosophy of Karl Popper* (2 Vols.). La Salle, Ill.: Open Court Publishing, 1974(a), 2:413–463. (a)

Campbell, D. T. Unjustified variation and selective retention in scientific discovery. In T. Dobzhansky & E. J. Ayala (Eds.), *Studies in the philosophy of biology.* London: Macmillan, 1974. (b)

Dobzhansky, T. Chance and creativity in evolution. In T. Dobzhansky & E. J. Ayala (Eds.), *Studies in the philosophy of biology.* London: Macmillan, 1974.

Hartnack, J. *Kant's theory of knowledge.* (M.H. Hartshorne, trans.). New York: Harcourt, Brace, & World, 1967.

Huxley, T. H. *Science and culture.* London: Macmillan, 1881.

James, W. Great men, great thoughts and the environment. *Atlantic Monthly,* 1880, *46,* 441–459.

James, W. *Principles of psychology* (Vol. 2). New York: Henry Holt, 1890.

James, W. *Pragmatism.* New York: Longmans & Green, 1907.

Kant, I. *Critique of pure reason.* (N.K. Smith, trans.). London: Macmillan, 1929.

Monod, J. *Chance and necessity.* New York: Knopf, 1971.

Newell, A., Shaw, J. C., & Simon, H. A. Elements of a theory of human problem solving. *Psychological Review,* 1958, *65,* 151–166.

Poincaré, H. *The foundations of science.* New York: Science Press, 1913.

Popper, K. *Conjectures and refutations.* New York: Harper & Row, 1963.

Simmel, G. On a relationship between the theory of selection and epistemology. June 1968 (Mimeo) 1–14. (I. L. Jerison, trans.). (Originally published June 1968, *Archiv für Systematische Philosophie,* 1895, *1,* 34–45.)

Simpson, G. G. *Biology and man.* New York: Harcourt, Brace & World, 1967.

Whyte, L. L. *Internal factors in evolution.* New York: Braziller, 1965.

PART III

THE STRUCTURE OF INTELLIGENCE

Introduction

The psychology of Baldwin can be seen as an attempt to explain how the relationship between mind and the world develops. This he formulated at the biological and psychological levels as the problem between thought and things. How does an individual come to make novel adjustments? How can new habits of a useful kind get formed? How does the mind grow? How are new experiences organized? How is knowledge structured? Baldwin centered his psychological epistemology around these questions. Indeed, the initial aim was to work out an adequate general framework within which such questions could be formulated and explored.

The two essays in this section focus on this aspect of Baldwin's work by showing how he placed the analysis of mental development within a determinedly psychological perspective. We have already seen Baldwin the biological constructionist at work. In this section Baldwin the psychological constructionist comes more clearly into view.

John Freeman-Moir focuses on Baldwin's attempt to adduce a general theory of intelligence around the acquisition of instrumental action. Benjamin Lee takes up Baldwin's intensionalist position and

123

shows how it supported a view of the mind as interactive and inferential.

Readers of Piaget's work on the sensorimotor period will be familiar with his two-pronged attack on the development of intelligence. On the one hand, Piaget used his biological model of adaptation to describe the modes of instrumental actions, what Piaget calls the "first truly intelligent acts." On the other hand he has shown that these actions form the basis of a relationship between thought and reality. Instrumental or purposive actions allow the child to construct an objective view of the world in terms of the categories of space, time, causality, and object permanence. In retrospect it has become obvious just how efficient was this way of approaching the development of intelligence. In essence it entailed treating the mind as both process and product. Furthermore, the assumptions, by being simple, guaranteed a relatively elegant theory. These assumptions consisted of postulating a set of reflexes—sucking, looking, hearing, grasping—and a model for describing their environmental adaptation (i.e., the processes of assimilation and accommodation) and internal structuration (i.e., the processes of organization).

In Baldwin's work we can see a brilliant first attempt to analyze the problem of intelligence by means of precisely a similar two-pronged approach. In his essay, Freeman-Moir shows the Baldwinian origins of this theoretical strategy.

Not surprisingly, the construction of the theory provides an illustration of the phenomenon that the theory is trying to understand—the growth of thought. There is, then, a double fascination in watching Baldwin craft his viewpoint out of the psychology available to him. Overall, the process is a creative one, for no simple conjunction of Kant, Hegel, Darwin, Bain, and Spencer, if any such strange creature could be imagined, would produce the Baldwinian theory. More than anything else, it is probably on account of his sources that Baldwin's writing will seem unfamiliar and somewhat inaccessible to the modern psychology student. This holds true even after the Kantian flavor of Piaget has become *passé*.

Freeman-Moir concludes by suggesting that there may be something to Baldwin's Hegelian ambitions after all, though these are furthest removed from current psychological practice. The ambition, in brief, is to formulate more general theories. Increasingly, the fragmentation and specialization of psychological research makes such formulation both less probable and more urgent.

Baldwin's psychology asks us to consider again the scope and possible unity of human experience based, in the last instance, on a principle of biological operation. Since Baldwin, Piaget has also worked in the same direction, though less ambitiously, by making logico-mathematical operations the core of human thought. This sort of claim strikes many, perhaps most, psychologists as implausible in the extreme. Nevertheless, cognitive-developmentalists have pinned their theories to this thesis. True or false, the original problem, of the unity of experience, remains.

In his essay, Benjamin Lee interprets Baldwin from the perspective of some recent work in analytic philosophy which places emphasis on the conceptual connections among knowledge, belief, action, and inference. Lee's central point is that Baldwin, unlike Piaget, assumed the intentional quality of mind across the entire span of its development. This led Baldwin to place relatively greater emphasis than Piaget has done on the place of social interaction in mental life. In addition, Baldwin placed a concept of self at the center of his scheme as the intentionalist structure around which all mental states are organized and oriented.

An apparently obvious feature of mental states—belief, thought, judgment, wish, imagination, and so on—is that they point to objects which may or may not exist in fact. Without this reference to an object it is impossible to imagine what sense could be made of any psychological state. The connection say between emotion and object (e.g., I am angry with Tom) is intrinsic. This is so because emotion depends on a relationship between a person's view and an object. In fact, the object is constituted by the view, where "view" might be suggested more fully if it is treated as synonymous with terms like *belief, judgment, evaluation, apprehension,* etc.

The concept of *intentionality*—that psychological states point to objects—has been used, since Brentano, both in analytic philosophy and phenomenology as part of a general attempt to drive a wedge between mental and physical phenomena. The latter are not, or need not be, characterized in this way. Lee begins his essay by showing how philosophers have advanced intentionality. According to Lee, "every intentional object is what the representation contained in an intentional state is a representation of."[1]

---

[1] "Intentionality" in Brentano's sense (derived from the Scholastic *intentio*) should not be confused with "intentionality" in the more colloquial sense that we owe to Bentham, who took the term to mean "an action possessing intention." Bentham's sense implies deliberately purposive activity, such as goal-directed behaviour. Unfortunately, confusion of the two senses is bound to arise when discussion focuses upon the representation of goals. Thus goal-directed behavior (intentional in Bentham's sense) must be admitted as involving mental states that have goals as their intentional objects (intentional in Brentano's sense)!

Both these terms should be differentiated from "intensionality." "Intension"

Lee argues that social science methodology must be so formulated as to preserve these intentionalist features. For example, this would entail seeing humans as basing their actions upon "inferences they make in the light of their beliefs and desires." Intentions, therefore, are central to psychological analysis, and for this reason, Lee provides a careful analysis of the place of goals, functions, and inferences in teleological explanations. Development can then be seen in terms of how the child comes to understand and utilize particular patterns of inference from representations of intentional objects or goals. This is the core of Lee's interpretation of Baldwin's theories of epistemological development, meaning, and the development of self. Human development, it is concluded, is dependent on the ability to represent oneself and others as agents able to modify behavior in terms of inferential feedbacks from representations.

The structure of intelligence—the relationship of thought to the physical world, to oneself and other persons and reflexively, of thought to itself—lies at the center of psychology. In his analysis of this problem we find Baldwin at his most assured. The result, he believed, would be a framework for a complete genetic epistemology.

One can only speculate to what extent his concern with intentionality represents a potential within his thinking for a genetic phenomenology as well.

---

refers to the qualities or properties making up a concept, in contrast to the "extension" of that concept, which consists of the things properly falling under it. The adjective "extensional" refers to notions or points of view which tend to confine attention to truth values of propositions, whereas "intensional" has to do with the meanings constituting the propositions themselves.

A related meaning of "intensional" is the one employed below in Lee's chapter. He speaks of "intensional contexts", which are those contexts where there is a failure of referential substitutability. These have also been termed "opaque" or "oblique" contexts. Intentional state verbs such as believing, intending and desiring (sometimes termed "propositional attitudes") have this property of referential non-substitutability (see p. 172). However, intensional contexts also include modal contexts such as expressed by notions of possibility and necessity. Thus the problem of intentionality is, at least logically, a subset of the problems raised by intensionality.

It is not just a coincidence that neither the intention nor the intension of "intention" is always clear, which will probably leave most readers in tension. This effect is, of course, entirely unintentional.

6

THE ORIGIN OF INTELLIGENCE

D. J. Freeman-Moir
University of Canterbury

Introduction: The Idea of a Cognitive Psychology

One way to grasp the nature of mind, Baldwin maintained, is through a study of its genesis, a view which many philosophers regard as off key at best, downright fallacious at worst. Nevertheless, although distinguishing between formal epistemology and psychology, Baldwin would argue that both disciplines should come together in the investigation of mind. This is, of course, the core notion of genetic epistemology, the discipline now most closely associated with Piaget.

For Baldwin, the problem confronted by psychology is quite general. As his first statement on the theory of intelligence puts it, "the great question, which is writ above all natural history records, is—when put in the phraseology of imitation, what is the final World-copy, and how did it get set? (Baldwin, 1894, p. 488)." The language is outmoded but the question stands out clearly enough. How do we come by the view of reality we, in fact, have?

How we come to view reality is the kind of question which Hegel, for example, tackled in his *Phenomenology of Mind*, an important antecedent to later genetic epistemologies, especially Baldwin's. What definitely separates Baldwin from Hegel is the Darwinian revolution. It seemed obvious to Baldwin that knowledge must be based on a biological interaction between organism and world—the whole process of ontogenesis starting from phylogenetically endowed reflexes.

Baldwin's psychology is remarkable less for what it told us about the child's mind than for the conceptual framework it offered those studying mental development. Piaget, who has given us a richly detailed picture of cognitive development, is the notable example here. Piaget's attempt to work out a biology of knowledge—from *The Origin of Intelligence in the Child* (1936) to *Biology and Knowledge* (1971)—represents a brilliant realization of much that is contained in Baldwin's psychology.

For psychology, the evolutionary theory had spelled the end of the idea that "the soul was of a fixed substance, with fixed attributes. The genetic idea reverses all this. Instead of a fixed substance, we have the conception of a growing, developing activity" (Baldwin, 1894, p. 2). Psychology had to rethink its program; in the face of this challenge from biology, a number of psychologists felt the impulse to work out a new descriptive epistemology.

Of course, British empiricism had taken a genetic view of knowledge, mind being built up associatively from simple ideas or impressions. By the end of the nineteenth century, however, the doctrines of associationism were beginning to be severely questioned by psychologists (Baldwin, 1889-91, 1:136, James, 1890, I, p. 224; II, p. 688). Baldwin proposed to solve the problem genetically. He wanted to discover how psychological processes cut into the relatively undifferentiated form of primitive experience and to show that the resultant forms of differentiation could be ordered into a developmental sequence.

Like the better-known functionalists, James and Dewey, Baldwin shifted the focus of analysis from entities or faculties to actions and processes. Mind is no longer a mysterious entity which governs the organism; consciousness becomes the *structure* of the interrelationship between organism and environment. This relationship is called *psychophysical* because it represents a *level* of organization distinguishable from mere matter and other kinds and levels of organization. A brain, for example, is not a psychophysical system but just a blob of tissue. *In situ*, however, the brain is part of an integrated system, crucial in the level and kind of organized system involved. Baldwin regarded the child as a complex psychophysical system which develops through interaction with its environment. How, then, did Baldwin arrive at this solution?

Darwin, Bain and Spencer

Baldwin (1894) said that he wrote *Mental Development* because "I found it necessary constantly to enlarge my scope for the entertainment of a widened genetic view" (p. viii). Darwin's theory of evolution was the reason. Baldwin envisaged being able to provide "a possible synthesis of the current biological theory of organic adaptation with the doctrine of the infant's development" (p. vii).

He noted first that Darwin gave only a rough account of the variations on which natural selection operates. Because variations are more than a theoretical assumption in evolutionary theory, some explanation of their existence and development is required. In Baldwin's (1894) view the evolutionary biologist "must recognize all the processes of the development of the individual in order to define the variations which rendered these results possible in the life of the individual" (p. 206).

In general terms the evolutionary theory reset the problem of biological development in functional terms. For psychologists it provided an exemplar of methodology and theory which *ceteris paribus* was taken to apply to psychological development. Baldwin certainly adopted this view.

The central Darwinian question was this: how have a number of species become adapted? Darwin answered by saying that from a range of chance variations some are selected naturally. Those variations which fit the environment survive, the rest are extinguished. Even the most dramatic of evolutionary achievements—eye and brain—were encompassed by the theory, as Darwin made clear: "although the belief that an organ so perfect as the eye could have been formed by natural selection, is more than enough to stagger anyone; yet in the case of any organ, if we know of a long series of gradations in complexity. . . . there is no logical impossibility in the acquirement of any conceivable degree of perfection through selection" (Darwin, 1968, p. 231).

Now for Baldwin's puzzle about adaptation in the individual organism: how can certain reactions of one organism be selected? Put another way, how does an organism acquire an adaptive movement? Baldwin's application of the evolutionary point of view was achieved by something like a trial-and-error process. Interestingly, he recorded his first tentative solution. As an approximation to the final answer it involved trying to fit the special biological theory directly on to the psychological problem.

Baldwin asks us to consider "the state of an organism at any given moment with its readiness to act in an appropriate fashion" (Baldwin, 1894, p. 171). A formal statement of this proposal will help to bring out its main features. At a given time, T_1, an organism, O, is in state, S_1^o such that it is ready to act appropriately by doing, A_1. The judgment that A_1 is indeed appropriate can be made only relative to O and the environment, E, which will also be in a given state, S_1^e. Any response which leads to a mismatch between O and E will be said to be inappropriate. The whole formula can now be abbreviated to

$$T_1 : O(S_i^o) \cdot E(S_i^e) \underline{\hspace{5cm}} A_1,$$

which reads: at a given time when the organism and the environment are in given states an appropriately adaptive response will occur.

How does the organism achieve a match between S_i^o and S_i^e for the first time? Baldwin rejected the answers of special creation, because that gives up the idea of development altogether, heredity, because it does not say how the ancestral forms achieved S_i^e and therefore A_1, and consciousness, because it assumes that A_1 has already occurred since one can be conscious only of that which, in some sense, has already been experienced.

Baldwin's first answer was to postulate a set of "organisms capable of reacting to stimulations by random diffused movement." These random movements will bring the organisms into contact with stimuli which will be variously beneficial or injurious. If the beneficial stimuli recur more frequently to some organisms than others, then those organisms will be selected out and the others will die. This solution "*amounts to the same thing* as if organisms of neutral character had learned, each for itself, to react to certain beneficial stimuli only" (Baldwin, 1894, p. 171). The organisms can be said to be adapted, but it is nothing in the organisms which has adapted. At any moment these lucky organisms may be killed off by random fluctuations in either their own state or in that of the environment.

Baldwin (1894) added a further element to the argument. "Among the variations in organic forms, it is easy to see that some of them might react in a way to keep in contact with the stimulus, to lay hold on it, and so keep on reacting to it again and again" (p. 171). The situation can be pictured by extending the original schema as follows:

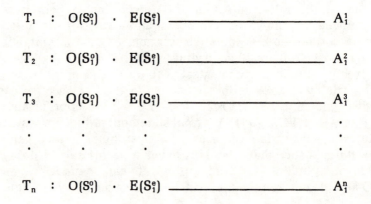

$$T_1 \; : \; O(S_i^o) \; \cdot \; E(S_i^e) \underline{\hspace{5cm}} A_i^1$$

$$T_2 \; : \; O(S_i^o) \; \cdot \; E(S_i^e) \underline{\hspace{5cm}} A_i^2$$

$$T_3 \; : \; O(S_i^o) \; \cdot \; E(S_i^e) \underline{\hspace{5cm}} A_i^3$$

$$\vdots \qquad \vdots \qquad \vdots \qquad\qquad\qquad \vdots$$

$$T_n \; : \; O(S_i^o) \; \cdot \; E(S_i^e) \underline{\hspace{5cm}} A_i^n$$

The maxim of this organism is: I am as I have always been or nearly so, and things in the world are as they have always been or nearly so—therefore, I shall act as I have always acted before. The act, A_1, is a definite hypothesis with which the organism works. In this sense, the organism which repeats its act represents a definite advance over one which continues to act randomly. Should, however, S^o or S^e change, then the organism's hypothesis of A_1 may well prove lethal, for the criteria of appropriateness will also have changed. If the organism is to survive, then adjustments in its behavior will be required.

Baldwin's first answer to the question of how organisms adapt actually transformed the question into one about how there are adapted organisms. But the ontogenetic questions were left untouched by this line of attack, although, as we have just seen, not left entirely out of sight. Indeed, after this brief excursion Baldwin was even more convinced of the necessity for an ontogenetic theory of adaptation. The idea of organisms repeating acts in order to retain stimulation was to become an important feature of the final theory. To it was added the idea of organismic adjustment.

> We are, accordingly, left to the view that the new stimulations wrought by changes in the environment, themselves modify the reactions of an organism in such a way that these modified reactions serve to hold or repeat the new stimulations as far as they are good, and further, negatively, in such a way that the former reactions become under the new conditions less useful or positively damaging. (Baldwin, 1894, p. 175)

Baldwin saw that a narrow application of Darwin's theory would not suffice as an explanation of developmental phenomena in individual organisms. Generalizing, he argued

> There is a process by which the theatre of the application of natural selection is transferred from the outside relations of the organism, its relations to its environment, to the inside relations of the organism. It takes the form of the *functional adjustment of the life processes to variations in its own motor responses*, so that beneficial reactions are selected from the entire mass of responses (Baldwin, 1894, p. 176)

Darwin was one major impetus behind the work of Baldwin. The other was the Spencer-Bain theory of action—as Baldwin termed it. An abbreviated account of the psychologies of Bain and Spencer will be given sufficient only to set the context of Baldwin's critique.

Bain (1894) introduced the notion of spontaneous activity into British empiricism which, from Locke to James Mill, had viewed the organism as typically passive before the world, a mere recipient of stimulation. Without postulating activity, Bain thought it impossible to account for the growth of will. But activity alone is still insufficient to explain intentional action which involves much more than mere spontaneity. Somehow, the organization of actions or their patterning into sequences where means are adjusted to ends must be accounted for. Bain's answer was to join feeling and activity. Actions accompanied by pleasure will tend to be maintained, and with a few repetitions, habits will form. Now the child is not born with anything like intentional action at its command.

According to Bain, involuntary reflex motions shade into voluntary actions by "insensible degrees" through a process of trial-and-error learning. For Bain, then, the mind develops as a consequence of the child's *acting* and *feeling*. With his emphasis on action Bain came very close to rejecting the empiricist tradition altogether—something Baldwin was happy to do.

Spencer (1901), by comparison, gave a purely physiological account of action. Organisms with sufficiently complex nervous systems were thought to be endowed with "a certain diffused discharge to the muscles at large." This was the equivalent of Bain's *spontaneous activity*. Spencer then presented his case using the following hypothetical situation. An organism, in moving its head to seize prey, continually fails. Suppose that a nervous discharge to the musculature, correlated with the approximate actions of the head, causes a forward motion of the body, and success; pleasure will result. Spencer (1901) argued that the

> lines of nervous communication through which the diffused discharge happened in this case to pass, have opened a new way to certain wide channels of escape.... On recurrence of the circumstances, these muscular movements that were followed by success are likely to be repeated; what was at first an accidental combination of motion will now be a combination having considerable probability. (I, 544)

Spencer believed, therefore, that the first chance reaction of the body is neurologically associated with both the complex of visual impressions, or stimuli, inducing the approximate head movements and the response itself. Like Baldwin, Spencer (1901) emphasized the importance of repetition: "Every repetition of it [the successful movement] will make still more permeable the new channels, and increase the probability of subsequent repetitions; until at length the nervous connection becomes organized" (p. 545). Spencer too stressed the repetition of movement as the key to psychological organization.

Baldwin's Critique

Baldwin's critique of Bain and Spencer is the negative side of his work. In it we find him moving toward a new explanation of human action and its development. Seeing what Baldwin rejects in empiricism and why (and Piaget's more recent rejection has been offered on exactly the same grounds) will help us to understand more precisely just what his own theory is committed to.

Baldwin agreed with only the most general characterization of the Spencer-Bain theory—that there must be a source of movements from which selections can be made and some way of making and fixing them. He thought the Spencer-Bain theory false in its details. More particularly, he pointed out that it depended on assuming the highly improbable—a constant environment. It also assumed a consciousness endowed with pleasure and pain, which seemed irrelevant to Baldwin.

If the connection between pleasure and movement is an associative one, then a feeling of pleasure or a movement alone should be sufficient to call up the other, assuming, of course, that the two are empirically distinct. In other words, there need be no reference to the demands of the environment in which the movements occur and to which they are judged to be adaptive. If this feeling:movement connection is given major emphasis, then the relationship between organism and environment, the reason for offering a theory in the first place, is quickly overlooked. Without such external reference it becomes necessary to postulate a constant environment in order to explain how the organism succeeds at all.

The significance of an organism's movement can only be determined if reference is made to the environmental context. Of themselves movements are neither adaptive nor nonadaptive. The same movement may be adaptive on one occasion, lethal on another, and this fact is quite independent of whether movements have particular feelings connected with them.

An internal causal link between feeling and movement could be a necessary and sufficient explanation of adaptive movement only under the assumption of a constant environment. This would be the only way to insure that a given movement was never nonadaptive. In a changing environment, the probability of chance adaptations (i.e., chance connections between feeling and movement) surviving would be zero or close to zero. Sooner or later an organism's formerly adaptive actions would prove nonadaptive.

Although acknowledging that chance adaptive movements may lead to a repetition of response and a maintenance of pleasure, Baldwin asked, "What is the reason that the movements which are accidentally more adaptive than others, give pleasure?" He replied: "The only answer evidently is, that the pleasure is not in the movement in itself but in what the movement gets for the organism . . . those movements only are adaptive which secure a new element of sense process, such as light, chemical action, food stimulus, etc., in addition to the ordinary advantage of movement itself which all movements qua movements have in common" (Baldwin, 1894, p. 189). Baldwin concluded that the Spencer-Bain theory failed to recognize this fact because it concentrated on the feelings derived from movements and not on what the movements brought to the organism.

Bain's error, of placing too much weight on the associative bond between feeling and movement, was a subtle one. It was not so much that he misdescribed the relevant events as he misinterpreted them. One example of his method, in which he discusses how the child learns to direct its head to the light, brings out the nature of his error. At first the child's head movements are spontaneous or random. The feelings of light brought on by the movements are agreeable and stimulate a repetition of the movement. Bain (1872) concluded: ". . . the pleasure grows to be associated with these movements; where-upon, when this feeling is present to the mind as a wish, it prompts the requisite exertions. Thus it is that a child learns to search out a light in a room in order to enjoy the maximum of the illumination (pp. 410–411). There can be no objection in principle to the claim that feelings of light are agreeable to young infants. But Bain mistakenly supposed this factor to be the central aspect of the phenomenon. The feeling:movement link had come to be treated as a necessary and sufficient explanation of adaptive action.

Baldwin also saw that the Spencer-Bain theory was ambiguous as to what must be understood by a consciousness endowed with pleasure and pain. The hedonic principle, that pleasure and pain are associated with movement, was a theoretical red herring. We have noted that it is the connection between movements and the stimulations they gain that Baldwin chose to treat as necessary. According to the Spencer-Bain theory, feelings are the cause of motoric effects. Baldwin (1894) charged this assumption with irrelevancy and so cut the Gordian knot of hedonic empiricism.

> If it is the organism's stimulations, such as food supply, contact with the oxygen of the air, equilibrium under the action of gravity, etc.—if it is such things which give the organic bases of pleasure—then these it is which serve to bring about the motor excess discharge which produces the abundance and variety of movements necessary to selection (p. 190).

But this leads to a conclusion which was quite different from what might be expected on the basis of the Spencer-Bain theory: "we do not need the first accidentally adaptive *movement* to give pleasure, and through pleasure so to secure the excess discharge" (Baldwin, 1894, p. 190).

The Spencer-Bain theory was, then, unable to explain how the organism responds to the world as it is; "it . . . gives no criterion as to what kind of movements it is desirable the organism should get into the habit of performing" (Baldwin, 1894, p. 215).

This was a telling objection. If the organism has no special preferences, then there is no logical reason why one movement rather than another (or any movement at all, for that matter), should lead to pleasure. From this it follows that no link between pleasure and action could ever be formed, in which case the Spencer–Bain theory is vacuous.

As the result of his attack on empiricist psychology, Baldwin adopted a very different concept of the organism. "We reach in fact . . . a new construction in which our organism begins with a susceptibility to certain organic stimulations, such as food, oxygen, etc. (Baldwin, 1894, p. 191). A Baldwinian organism cannot be neutral with respect to the world, as the Bain and Spencer organisms were. Its anatomy, physiology, and behavior already announce certain tendencies, "hypotheses," "beliefs," and "theories" about the world.

Early Cognitive Development

The Concepts of Habit and Accommodation

"Habit expresses the tendency of the organism to secure and to retain its vital stimulations" (Baldwin, 1894, p. 216). This is the first tenet of Baldwin's theory of development.

Habit is intimately connected with another fundamental process: *accommodation*. How can any element in the environment be the cause of central processes and further movements in the infant? Baldwin could find only one answer: the infant must be accommodated to those elements. Mental development was to be understood as the product of interactions between these two processes.

Baldwin agreed in part with James that habit is conservative, that it "keeps us all within the bounds of ordinance." He referred to the smoothing of the nervous system through habit and to the structuring of movements to the point where they can be described as automatic, reflexive, or instinctual. According to James our ordinary training should attempt to "make automatic and habitual, as early as possible, as many useful actions as we can." If the daily tedium can be handed over to the "effortless custody of automatism" then mind will be free to do its own "proper work." Habit, according to James, is an important part of education because it allows the mind to be creative in an unencumbered way.

Baldwin's concept of habit is more complex than James's; in the very exercise of habit he found the possibility of development. In Baldwin's view, excessive emphasis on the conservative features of habit distracts attention from the fact that organisms do develop and change. This must mean that habits are broken, amended, and replaced. Pure habit would suffice only in an unchanging environment. In a changing environment pure habit would result in rigid behavior and maladjustment. Baldwin (1894) likened the child fixed by habit to a "self-repeating mechanical device (say a swinging pendulum), which never gets exhausted nor grows" (p. 270).

Baldwin argued (as Popper has since) that repetitions are, in fact, never exact, nor habits pure. Because they are only more or less similar they give rise to new movements and sources of stimulation. In turn these new stimulations lead to further adaptations—"to movements which are an evident improvement upon those which the organism has formerly accomplished." (Baldwin, 1894, p. 167).

In Baldwin's theory, habit is the cause of change and not merely a process or state which allows the organism to run free. Baldwin's organism is, therefore, a creature of habit but not because, to use James's famous words, "the character has set like plaster and will never soften again." Habit, in a pure sense, simply defines what stimuli the organism will most likely show a preference for, all things being equal. This view—that habit is marked by a predilection for certain stimuli rather than by the mindless repetition of movement—was an important innovation in psychology.

But all things are not equal. Movements run into all kinds of obstacles in the environment which make modifications (i.e., accommodations) necessary. Modulations in the organism's internal state are a further source of variations in movements which, in turn, lead to new sources of stimulation and, therefore, to new habits. The process is an endless one:

$$\text{habit}_1 = \text{accommodation}_1 \xrightarrow{\text{assimilation}} \text{habit}_2 = \text{accommodation}_2 \xrightarrow{\text{assimilation}} \text{etc.}$$

The child begins with some initial habit (i.e., a "preference," "tendency," or "point of view") which at the same time describes an initial accommodation (i.e., the object of "preference," "tendency," or "point of view"). At birth the child's habits or reflexes are connected to food supply, oxygen, light, contact, etc. The child has a system accommodated or receptive to these elements. The world, in a manner of speaking, begins in the mouth and expands through the exercise of sucking. In the process of maintaining these early objects of accommodation, new stimulations and movements occur.

Habit holds on to stimulation in that, Baldwin found an explanation for why the child attempts to improve on previous movements. Certain stimulations are necessary to life, so the child must retain them; the more efficiently they are retained, the easier life becomes.

Baldwin emphasized the relative instability of habit by referring to "accommodation running ahead of habit," thus causing the disintegration of old habits. But the two sides of action work together. "Continued accommodation is possible only because the other principle, 'habit,' all the time conserves the past and gives *points d'appui* in solidified structure for new accommodations" (Baldwin, 1894, p. 479). Or again,

> The environment being a changing one, every structure, with its function, represents a habit which is being constantly modified by the law of accommodation. But these modifications themselves . . . provide again for their own habituation; so there is a constant erosion and constant accretion, to the net attainment of the organism. (Baldwin, 1894, p. 481)

Baldwin thought that the habit:accommodation process was best covered by the term *imitation*, a not altogether happy choice, as Baldwin readily acknowledged. He rejected "adaptation" as too general, "repetition" as too narrow, and "habit" as obviously insufficient. "If any one will suggest a more happy term for the reaction *which is at once a new adaptation to any sort of stimulation and the beginning of a habit or tendency to get that sort of stimulation again,* I shall hail it gladly (Baldwin, 1894, p. 279). Unfortunately, imitation is rather narrow, too; it suggests mere copying, although that is not what Baldwin had in mind. Elsewhere, in speaking of the relationship between imitation and the representative arts, Baldwin (1894) has this to say about the concept of imitation:

> The imitative arts are those in which the content is imitatively derived in both a narrower and a broader sense, according to the meaning given to the term "imitation." In the narrower sense, imitation means a conscious copying of a model or "copy" externally set up; in the broader sense, it means the achievement of results modelled after a "copy," whether or not that copy is external to the mind. In this latter case, all forms of "self-imitation"—from auto-suggestion to the shaping of a psychical process upon self-erected models, standards or ideals— are included in the one term "imitation." There are facts and considerations which indicate that art is imitative in both these senses. (pp. 308–309)

As it is well known, Piaget has chosen *adaptation* as the most suitable term and defines it as an equilibrium between assimilation and accommodation. Although Baldwin did not sort out his definitions quite so precisely as Piaget has done, he did lay the necessary conceptual groundwork, as the following passage demonstrates.

The principle of assimilation, made much of in recent discussions, clearly illustrates not only that a copy-image may be so strong and habitual in consciousness as to assimilate new experiences to its form and colour, but also that this assimilation is the very mode and method of the mind's digestion of what it feeds upon. Consciousness constantly tends to neglect the unfit, the *mal apropos*, the incongruous, and to show itself receptive to that which in any way conforms to its present stock. A child after learning to draw a full face—circle with spots for the two eyes, nose, and mouth, and projections on the sides for ears— will persist, when copying a face in profile, in drawing its circle, with two eyes, and two ears, and fail to see its error, although only one ear is visible and no eyes. My child H. having been told that her shadow was herself, called all shadows "little Henen" (little Helen). The external pattern is assimilated to the memory copy, or to the word or other symbol which comes to stand for it. The child has a motor reaction for imitating the latter; why should not that answer for the other as well? As everybody admits, in one way or another, such assimilation is at the bottom of recognition, and of illusions which are but mistaken recognitions.

Let us look at each of these facts—assimilation and recognition— more closely, from the genetic point of view.

In what has been said of the principle of association, we find ground for the production of its particular forms to the one law of *assimilation*.

In assimilation—and in the "apperception" of the Herbartians— we have the general statement of all the forms, nets, modes of grouping, which old elements of mental content bring to impose upon the new. In the light of their motor effects, we are able to construe all these elements of content under the general principle of habit, and say that the assimilation of any one element to another, or the assimilation of any two or more such elements to a third, is due to the unifying of their motor discharges in the single larger discharge which stands for the apperceived result. The old discharge may itself be modified—it cannot remain exactly as it was when it stood for a less complex content. So this larger discharge represents the habit of the organism in as far as both the earlier tendencies to discharge belonging to these elements of content are represented in it; but it also represents accommodation— i.e., if the assimilation, apperception, synthesis, is smoothly accomplished—since it stands for a richer objective content. (Baldwin, 1894, pp. 308–309)

I turn now to consider in more detail Baldwin's analysis of the habit:accommodation process. Baldwin started with *simple imitation* which he identified as a primitive developmental approximation to persistent imitation, the basis of intentional action.

Simple Imitation

Simple imitation occurs when a response is made but no attempt is made to compare it with the copy. The child does not try to improve by making a second response or if a second response occurs it will be a simple repetition of the first. "This is ... a case of simple sensorimotor suggestion, and is peculiar psychologically only because of the more or less remote approximation the reaction has to the movement which the child copies" (Baldwin, 1894, p. 132). In simple imitation the child has no end in sight, and no conscious control is exercised over the imitatory movements—a situation pictured by Baldwin in Fig. 1.

Unconscious imitation, like the two cases just mentioned, lacks intentionality as well. We sometimes imitate the mannerisms and actions of others we especially admire. But this is blind imitation and for Baldwin not centrally relevant to an understanding of human behavior.

Baldwin insisted that in imitation "there is in all ... instances some kind of constructive idea, a 'copy,' in more or less conscious clearness which calls the action out, and which it is the business of

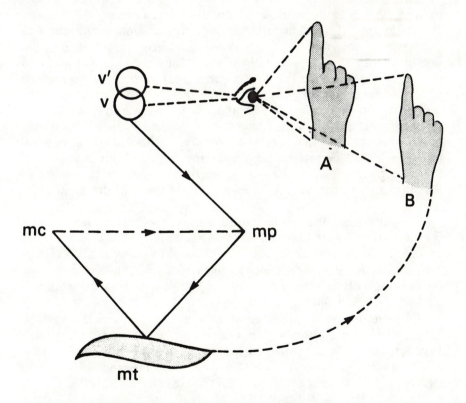

FIG 1.   Simple Imitation. v,v' = Visual seat; mp = Motor seat; mt = Muscle moved; mc = Muscle-sense seat; A = "Copy" imitated; B = Imitation made. The two processes (v and v') flow together in the old channel v, mp, fixed by association, and the reaction is repeated without change or effort (from Baldwin, 1894, p. 356).

the imitator to reinstate or bring about somehow for himself (Baldwin, 1894, p. 267). Baldwin thought the barest element of imitation was to be found in the general organic tendency to act so as to retain life sustaining stimulations. This *organic imitation*, as Baldwin called it, does not, however, involve the elements of conscious control implied by imitation proper. The earliest forms of imitation are "lower down than the conscious picturing of copies . . . in the sense of not involving . . . a conscious sensory or intellectual suggesting stimulus, with the possibility of its revival in memory" (Baldwin, 1894, p. 351). Baldwin is postulating a simple organic system set up to accept certain stimulations; it constantly reaches out after them and in the process tends to achieve a level of biological efficiency, through successive approximations, and this we call *adaptation*. This process is the prototype of consciously controlled activity which aims to bring about certain ends. Thus, according to Baldwin the characteristically human behavior of *acting* so as to achieve *ends* has its biological roots in the tendency to *respond* so as to retain *stimulation*.

Baldwin referred to this biological foundation of imitation as *subcortical* because it represents the initial accommodations of the organism "made independently of conscious reception of stimulations and adaptation to them" (Baldwin, 1894, p. 351). The conscious control of response depends on the growth of memory so that present and past movements can be compared. Baldwin believed that the circular reaction—the tendency of the organism to repeat its movements—was the physical basis of memory. Without offering a neurophysiological explanation of the circular reaction, Baldwin supposed that repetitions lead to the development of the nervous centers so that they can reinstate movements in the absence of direct stimulation.

At this point the human mind comes to achieve a measure of freedom from the dictates of biological necessity: "Man then becomes an agent. He reflects upon both the old and the new and his choice represents the best adjustment into which all the elements and tendencies within him may fall for future reaction or conduct" (Baldwin, 1894, p. 301).

To summarize: organic imitations—the circular reactions which retain vital stimulations—give rise to the memory function; this function serves to keep before the organism what it is after and it allows each approximation or attempt to be compared with a copy; assuming that discrepancies are psychologically distasteful, the organism is intrinsically motivated to try again. In this manner Baldwin hoped to explain the origins of intentional action.

In this model an approximate action occasions the stimulus to further action. The stimuli at the beginning of the ontogenetic sequence are only stimuli because they fall within an organism's range of action. They are reached out for by a tendency-ridden organism. Thus, it is the act which constitutes the stimulus and not the other way round.

This conception of action, which Baldwin first subscribed to in *Feeling and Will* (1891), regards the stimulus and movement as being a single sensorimotor coordination. For this reason it is to be distinguished from the reflex arc concept. At times Baldwin did treat the stimulus, central processes, and movements in the circular reaction as "distinct psychical existences." Indeed, the processes as pictured in Fig. 1 and 3 tend to suggest sequences of "disjointed parts", a vestige of the motor square (Fig. 2) on which they are based.

As is well known, Dewey exposed the kind of error inherent in this motor square in his 1896 analysis of the reflex arc concept.

> Let us take, for example, the familiar child-candle instance. The ordinary interpretation would say the sensation of light is a stimulus to the grasping as a response, the burn resulting is a stimulus to withdrawing the hand as response and so on. There is, of course, no doubt that it is a rough practical way of representing the process. But when we ask for its psychological adequacy, the case is quite different. Upon analysis, we find that we begin not with a sensory stimulus, but with a sensorimotor co-ordination, the optical-ocular, and that in a certain

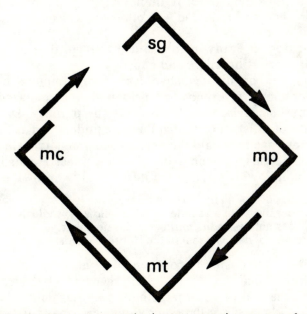

FIG 2. The motor square. sg = suggestion (sensory process); mp = seat of motor process; mt = movement of muscle; mc = consciousness of movement (kinaesthetic process) (from Baldwin, 1894, p. 109).

sense it is the movement which is primary, and the sensation which is secondary, the movement of the body, head and eye muscles determining the quality of what is experienced. In other words, the real beginning is with the act of seeing; it is looking, and not a sensation of light. The sensory quale gives the value of the act, just as the movement furnishes its mechanism and control, but both sensation and movement lie inside, not outside the act. . . . What we have is a circuit; not an arc or broken segment of a circle. This circuit is more truly termed organic than reflex, because the motor response determines the stimulus, just as truly as sensory stimulus determines movement. Indeed, the movement is only for the sake of determining the stimulus, of fixing what kind of a stimulus it is, of interpreting it. (pp. 358–359)

In a footnote Dewey acknowledges Baldwin's contribution to the solution of the problem posed by the disjointed psychology of the reflex arc. Despite later terminological slips, Baldwin's postulation of the circular reaction in 1891 was a significant anticipation of Dewey's conceptual clarification.

Persistent Imitation and Intentional Action

It is impossible to conceive a rational human action apart from intention because action is based on the continual consideration of means and ends. Baldwin realized that any theory of human development would be deficient if it did not explain "the performance of actions foreseen and intended"; in other words, some account must be given of volition.

According to Baldwin the concept of volition entails three criteria; desire, deliberation, and effort.

Desire can be distinguished from mere impulse because it makes intentional "reference to a presentation or pictured object." Impulse, by comparison, lacks direction or purpose. Desires also signal a lack of satisfaction which Baldwin understood as the thwarting of motor reaction. Baldwin focused on realistic desires where appropriate actions, if taken, will attain the object. He distinguished between the following instances of desire (Baldwin, 1894, p. 369):

1. J. M. B. does desire an increase in salary.
2. J. M. B. does desire to associate with his fellow psychologists.
3. J. M. B. does not desire the millions of his neighbor.
4. J. M. B. does not desire a seat in the House of Lords.

For Baldwin, desire is conceptually linked to a judgment of attainability. Hence, points 1 and 2 are cases of desire because Baldwin judges that he can reach them, whereas points 3 and 4 are unattainable—"my sense that such things are unattainable inhibits all active attitude." The third and fourth instances might be referred to as *wishful* or *mistaken* desires. Of course, the degree of attainability will vary from instance to instance, a complication which leads to the next criterion.

The various features of the desired object or action must "become clearly pictured, coordinated in the attention, and estimated, as to relative suitableness for execution" (Baldwin, 1894, p. 372). It is unclear what deliberation could be beyond what is already involved in a complete analysis of desire. If *to desire* X means to lack an attainable object considered as valuable then one must, in whatever sense, have attended to the object. It is just this attention which Baldwin makes the desideratum of deliberation.

Effort is the final criterion of volition. It is the action taken to achieve the object of deliberate desire.

At this point in Baldwin's analysis the inappropriateness of the term *imitation* as a label for what he is talking about becomes more obvious. Baldwin (1894) speaks of imitating either something external (e.g., movements, noises) or something internal (e.g., an object of memory, imagination, or thought) (p. 367). But if, for example, I have a tree in my mind's eye, even a particular kind of tree, is my subsequent drawing an imitation of the imagined object? This surely sounds absurd. Certainly, the imagined tree may operate as a kind of standard against which I may judge my effort; declaring, perhaps, "that's not what I had in mind at all." I start, again and again, fail, and if I care enough, I shall start yet again. And so, my drawing gradually approximates to an end. This simple account suggests what lies behind Baldwin's concept of volition. The whole process may be further complicated because the desired end changes during the so-called successive approximations; indeed one may begin with no very clearly defined end in mind at all. In young children, at least, this is the more usual case.

Baldwin did not discuss these complications or the differences between the imitation of internal as opposed to external ends. His paradigm is the relatively simple case of a copy or standard set up at the beginning of a series of successive approximations. At each attempt, the discrepancy between it and the copy acts as the stimulus to further attempts. Baldwin added to his diagram of simple imitation to show how this process operates (Fig. 3).

A comparison between the event imitated and the imitation is made possible "on the mental side, when the two presentations are held together in the attention, so that together they represent one intended movement or mental end; and on the physical side, when the two processes started respectively by the 'copy' [the event imitated] and the reactive result [the imitation] are co-ordinated together in a common motor discharge (cc, mp' in Fig. 3) (Baldwin, 1894, p. 376). When identity between copy and result occurs, the

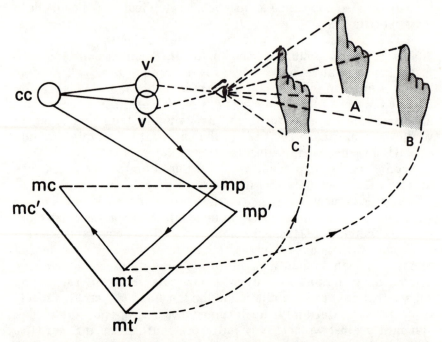

FIG 3.   Persistent imitation with effort. C = Successful imitation; cc = Co-ordinating centre, either local or purely functional. Other letters same as in Fig. 2, with the added circuit cc, mp', mt', mc'. The processes at v and v' do not flow together in the old channel v, mp, but are co-ordinated at cc in a new reaction mp', mt', which includes all the elements of the 'copy' (A) and more. The useless elements then fall away because they are useless and the successful effort is established (from Baldwin, 1894, p. 358).

sense of dissatisfaction disappears and "the reaction tends to become simple as habit" (Baldwin, 1894, p. 377).

Persistent imitation goes a step beyond the simple achievements of organic imitation, for with the development of central processes, the child can deliberately alter movements in an experimental way. In organic imitation new stimulations occur as variations in the simple circular reactions of movements designed to retain vital stimulation.

> But persistent imitation—how different! The same reaction is not repeated. He [the child] is no longer delighted with his circular activity. He detects differences between what he sees or hears and what he produces by hand or tongue, and finds there differences unpleasant to him. Then he makes effort to reduce the differences by altering his movements, and what is most remarkable, he succeeds in doing so. (Baldwin, 1894, p. 158)

Baldwin reports observations of H. trying to put an eraser on the end of a pencil. The point about her efforts was that she gradually approximated to an end; the whole series was a very clear case of persistent imitation. With this example Baldwin passes final comment on the Spencer–Bain theory.

> The complex "copy" of persistent imitation is necessary . . . as a stimulus to the tentative voluntary use of the muscles. The theory that all voluntary movements are led up to by spontaneous reactions which result in pleasure or pain, and then get repeated only because of their hedonic result, will not hold water for an instant in the presence of the phenomena of imitation. Suppose H. endeavouring in the crudest fashion to put a rubber on the end of a pencil after seeing me do it. What a chaos of ineffective movements! But after repeated efforts she gets nearer and nearer it, till at last, with daily object lessons from me, she accomplishes it. . . . If it [imitation] is due to the fact simply that movement gives pleasure, why does she not turn to other movements? Why persist in this one failure-bringing thing? Suppose there had been no impulse to do what she saw me do, no motor force in the simple idea of the rubber on the pencil, no instinct to imitate; what happy combination of Bain's spontaneous and accidental movements would have produced this result. . . . In cases of persistent imitation there is more than association as such. . . . For this reason . . . I believe that in persistent imitation we have the skeleton-process of volition; meaning that at this stage consciousness is not held down in its motor outcome strictly to motor reactions held in memory, but issues as a new and more adaptive co-ordination of them. (Baldwin, 1894, pp. 381–382)

Persistent imitation marks the beginnings of truly intelligent behavior. It releases the child from reflexive patterns of response by allowing behavior to be guided by goals; this advance in development confronts the child for the first time with the demands of evaluation.

In a brief criticism of the pencil example, Miller and Dollard (1941) make this comment; "what is not explained here is how the child strikes the right response, and how it is connected to the preceding stimulus" (p. 299). The answer to this criticism is that the child does not strike the right response—at least initially. The perceived discrepancy between the response and the original stimulus becomes the stimulus or signal for further action. So, the connection between the penultimate response, which defines the final discrepancy, and the final and correct response is nothing more than the relationship between an approximation to success and the achievement of success. The connection with the prior stimulus seems obvious enough if it is allowed that the child uses its head. It may require an extensive description of mental events, in whatever language, to set out all this, but the basis answer is surely not the mystery Miller and Dollard think it is; human beings perceive discrepancies between their responses and those "things" which serve as standards and as a consequence they act so as to make success more probable.

Baldwin's analysis of persistent imitation provides a model of intentional action. Once described, the rest of mental development could be explained in terms of the continued operation of the process. Of its significance for individual development and as a phylogenetic achievement Baldwin drew this conclusion.

> In volition, therefore, we find the point of meeting of the two principles, Habit and Accommodation, and their common function. It is through volition that the levelling effects of habit are counteracted in the higher orders of life, since it brings possibilities of adjustment to absent and distant conditions, and so wages conflict with the dictates of present sensation. Yet it is through volition on the other hand, that new habits are formed. Only by the continued inhibitions and controls of volition is a new action which is still hard to perform preserved amid the pressing urgencies of what is old and easy. So volition ministers to both kinds of development and sums them up; and so justifies both its survival and its splendid eminence among all the survivals in the mental series. (Baldwin, 1894, p. 386)

Baldwin was pleased with one immediate consequence of his theory: it allowed nature to move smoothly. The alternative, accepted by other theorists, of assuming quantum leaps in development seemed, to Baldwin, unwarranted by the facts and theoretically unnecessary.

Preyer and Sully for example, were both interested in the phenomenon of imitation. Preyer concluded that "the first imitations about the fourth month are the first distinct, represented, and willed movements" (Baldwin, 1894, p. 391). No explanation for this abrupt appearance of voluntary activity is ventured by Preyer: "this magnificent appearance of discontinuity . . . is the point of greatest difficulty," comments Baldwin (1894, p. 392).

By a judicious choice of quotations Baldwin shows that Sully tries to have it both ways. First, imitation is an acquired function associated with voluntary activity, then only a mechanical process with no conscious purpose, then the agent of desire, and finally instinctive. Baldwin charges this hodge-podge description as "typical of the uncertainty which seems to shield itself behind eclecticism."

Tarde (1903), too, who based a whole social psychology on the function of imitation, treated it as an instinct. Baldwin was unsatisfied, "for one of the great problems of the theory of development is to account for instincts of all kinds."

Baldwin saw that each of these theorists was caught by the problem of discontinuity. Either volition is "explained" by reading it into the infant's earliest actions or else it is identified as a sudden acquisition. Either way intentional action is left unaccounted for. In the first case, the facts do not warrant the ascription of intention; in the second case, no attempt is made to show how intention develops

from more primitive structures through a series of functional transformations. Baldwin solved this problem by studying the development of imitation "from the simple vital processes of an organism
through the occurrence, among 'spontaneous life variations' of crea-
tures whose vital discharges are movements of the 'circular' type,
which tend directly to secure the repetition or maintenance of certain
good stimuli" (Baldwin, 1894, p. 283).

Baldwin took the view that organic stimulation shades into
persistent imitation or volition. A single process—the habituation
and accommodation of movement—achieves this result by gradual
means. In this way Baldwin accounted for a distinct form of behavior—volition—without being forced to make its prototypes voluntary
as well or itself absolutely novel and, therefore, without a genesis.

Baldwin and Piaget

I have argued that Baldwin's main achievement was to replace
the empty doctrines of empiricism with the habit-assimilation-accom-
modation model. This replacement, we have seen, consisted of much
more than a simple exchange of terms and a rearrangement of old
concepts; it was, in fact, a shift to a new perspective.

Baldwin's break with the past was radical in the sense that he
rejected a whole conception of what it is to do psychology—a view
which continues to persist in the various guises of behaviorism. This
misguided view holds that psychological theory can build up a picture
of the mind by using nothing more than elementary units like S–R;
one is reminded of Hull's illusory belief that psychology could rely
entirely on "colorless movements." The idea was, of course, that
these units or "brute data" would be the guarantee of objectivity
against the dangers of subjective interpretation. The appeal of this
method no doubt lay in its austerity and its promise to put psychology
among the natural sciences.

The data relied on by Bain and Spencer—movements and
feelings—were offered as objective in just the sense I have referred
to. Later empiricists, notably Watson and subsequent behaviorists,
got rid of anything so inconveniently subjective as feelings but the
basic intentions of the program remained unchanged. But then,
internal adjustments are not the stuff of which paradigm changes are
made.

All this Baldwin toppled over. For him the psychologist should
ask two questions of any behavior: "What did the infant do, and what
did his doing that mean?" The aim, Baldwin stated, was to get at the

versus the mind itself

"mental condition" which lies behind movements. Actions are made intelligible by being subsumed under the concept of mind, and, in particular, the notion of intention. Piaget adopted the same general aim in his psychology.

Baldwin and Piaget are little interested in behavior per se, and both would reject as a serious conceptual blunder the definition of psychology as the science of behavior. It is, instead, the science of the mind. Our behavior—that is, the motions of our bodies—is merely indicative of the minds we have. Both theorists start their analyses at the level of interpreted action. *Meanings*, not movements, are the data of psychology. How are meanings to be accounted for?

Baldwin holds, it will be recalled, that actions, and what actions bring to the child, are assimilated to an already existing habit structure. The process of assimilation assigns meaning to experience. Thus, new experiences do not merely connect up (i.e., associate) with old experiences, but become part of what already exists and consequently change it. The connections are internal to experience itself, rather than external, as is the case for the laws of association; this is why Baldwin speaks of old content being "modified" or "readjusted," rather than merely being added to. Baldwin rightly concluded that he was "giving new meaning to the principle of association."

Piaget has also delineated a wider perspective for understanding action and thought. He indicates his disagreement with empiricism by substituting $S \rightleftarrows R$ or $S \rightarrow A \rightarrow R$ (where A stands for assimilation into a schema) for the classical $S \rule{1cm}{0.4pt} R$. These substitutions change, in effect, the meanings of S and R; they are no longer simple givens which link together in linear sequence. The new analysis works in terms of a dialectical relationship between action and schema. It is the action which determines the content of the schema and simultaneously the schema which sets limits on response. The important point, as Dewey indicated long ago, is to take the terms *stimulus* and *response* together (or, better, as a single unit) and not as single elements.

Piaget set out the implications of this conceptual clarification in many places—indeed, his whole theory rests on it. By way of illustration, consider his comments on the candle example which Baldwin had also discussed. Like Baldwin, Piaget wants to show that it is the meaning of the situation rather than the movements employed in the situation which are crucial.

When the hand is retracted when confronted by fire or the foot is raised at the step of a staircase, the precision of the sensorimotor accommodations which constitute these behavior patterns depends entirely on the meaning which the subject attributes to the flame or to the staircase. It is this active relationship between the subject and the objects that are charged with meanings which creates the association and not the association which creates this relationship. (Piaget, 1953, p. 131)

Like Baldwin, Piaget holds that "intelligence presupposes intention." Thus, the main requirement for a developmental theory is to show how we come by actions which are governed by intentions. The explanation of intention raises the problem of developmental continuity, a problem for which Baldwin considered he had a solution. The problem is this. The successive levels of mind, when characterized as relatively autonomous structures, appear, as Piaget notes, to be developmentally discontinuous. More particularly, the level of intentional action and representative thought is sharply distinct, structurally speaking, from reflexive sensorimotor action. How then, are we to account for characteristically human action? We already know the answer Baldwin gave to this problem: a continuous process. Half a century later we find Piaget echoing Baldwin's approach exactly: "When we studied the beginnings of intelligence we were forced to go as far as the reflex. . . . In the same way, if we call the act by which a model is reproduced imitation, we again find ourselves obliged to trace step by step . . . all the behaviors which may achieve this result." Here Piaget criticizes Wallon who had maintained that imitation does not occur before 18 months of age. Piaget admits that this hypothesis acknowledges the evident discontinuity of mental development. Nevertheless, it begs the question of development by assuming an "absolute opposition" between levels; "the fact remains," Piaget claims, "that in spite of the relative discontinuity of the structures, there is a certain functional continuity, each structure preparing for its successors while utilizing its predecessors (Piaget, 1951, pp. 6–7). Piaget's answer is, then, identical in form to Baldwin's.

I want to return now to the notion of intention. Recall that Baldwin's analysis was in terms of desire, deliberation, and effort. Piaget, too, has considered the conceptual problems. He first rejects the idea that intention is restricted to those with the capacity for linguistic representation (i.e., there would be no intention prior to the development of language) or that it is present in what he calls any consciousness of meaning (i.e., there would be no time when we did not possess intentions—young babies have no intentions). Piaget adopts a more functional approach by pointing to features of an act which warrant the ascription of intentional. It is a set of intermediaries which give the appearance of intentions. Because some actions have to be set up as means, Piaget argues that intentions must be characterized by a consciousness of desire and a sense that the action pattern as a whole has a direction—that is, a goal. Because of this last feature, intentional actions introduce the child to relationships of value—actions as means and actions as goals (i.e., ideals).

Piaget also suggests that the development of intentional action leads to the differentiation of assimilation and accommodation. Schemata become more flexible—"capable of various involvements"—and from the point of view of accommodation, "by clasping more tightly the external universe," the child will refine its understanding of space-time relationships which thus far have been embedded in general organic functioning. Indeed, for the first time assimilation and accommodation come together as dialectical partners which thus leads to the development of true intelligence rather than the exercise of reflexive schemata. This is the same insight as Baldwin's—that in volition "we find the meeting of the two principles, Habit and Accommodation."

Piaget is ready to admit that in practice the division between preintentional and intentional actions is artificial—that there is an unbroken transition between Stage Two (i.e., first acquired adaptations) and Stage Three (i.e., secondary circular reactions) of sensorimotor intelligence. But this does not mean that distinguishing reflexive and intentional action is unimportant (it very obviously is important), or that it is impossible to distinguish in practice between the two kinds of actions (we can and do so distinguish all the time). The problem is a relative one. At points in the developmental sequence where new structures are emerging we will have a set of blurred cases which do not fall clearly on either side of a criterion line. In the particular example we are discussing, the transitional cases are categorized as such only because of the distinction we have already drawn. For both Baldwin and Piaget this kind of conceptual work goes hand in hand with the task of interpreting evidence—indeed, without it there would be no such thing as evidence.

In all this I do not want to deny that Piaget's account goes beyond that provided by Baldwin; it does. A detailed picture of the origins of mind is simply missing in Baldwin's work. What we have is a promising theoretical model, but little flesh was put on the skeleton. That was a task for a more empirically minded psychologist like Piaget. Despite Piaget's outstanding success in detailing the course of sensorimotor intelligence many of the questions which Baldwin's speculations suggested remain as questions for Piaget. Let me list some of the more important ones:

> What range of accommodations will be assimilated to the habit structure (schemes)?
>
> Of a range of potential assimilations how can we account for the one which is actually made?
>
> What is the most adequate way to describe cognitive structures?
>
> What are the rules of transformation and in Baldwin's terms, how can we explain "solidification in the habit structure"?

What degree of transformation is possible and under what conditions?

These are the kinds of questions which cognitive-developmental psychology must now answer, but only because the work of Baldwin and Piaget has made it possible to ask them.

The Construction of Reality in the Child

From Action to Reality

We have seen that Baldwin started out with the problem of understanding the relationship between mind and the world. His analysis showed that mind does not stand over against the world by treating it as mere object. On the contrary, it is regarded as a process of exchange or, better, a construction in which a subject builds up a picture of the world in which it lives. This is not, however, an invitation to psychological subjectivity, for the world does not simply confirm the child's construction or view. Accommodations are as essential as assimilations to the mind's activity even though the latter may predominate for a time—as is the case in fantasy and play.

After working out the habit–assimilation–accommodation model of action Baldwin turned back, in *Thought and Things*, to reconsider his original question: what view of reality do we have at different stages? Or put more simply, what understanding of the world results from our experience of it?

Indeed, in *Mental Development* (1894) Baldwin had claimed that "we ought now to find the further development of consciousness an illustration of the same processes" (p. 291). In that work we find Baldwin commenting on such topics as memory, association, imagination, judgment, classification, and emotion. Baldwin tried to show how each of these phenomena resulted from a dialectic of habit and accommodation. For example, he interprets the judgment of identity as the tendency "to act in one way upon a variety of experiences," and thus it is the logical expression of habit. Conversely, the principle of sufficient reason is an instance of accommodation: "anything in the child's experience which tends to modify the course of habitual reactions in a way which it must accept, endorse, believe." Although these formulas were little more than vague hints of how consciousness might be analyzed Baldwin's theoretical insight was, once again, incisive

> I have argued . . . that a conflict between the established, the habitual, the taken for granted, on the one hand, and the new, raw, and violent, on the other hand, is necessary to excite doubt, which is the preliminary

to belief. And belief follows only when a kind of assimilation or reconciliation takes place. But this assimilation of the new, the doubtful, to the old, the established, is done by the union of the potencies for action, in a common plan of action. Belief arises in the child in the readjustment or accommodation of himself actively to new elements of reality. (Baldwin, 1894, p. 323)

In *Thought and Things* Baldwin argues that mind proceeds through the following sequence: prelogical → quasilogical → logical → hyperlogical. Each level has its own characteristic structures and processes which, taken as a whole, define modes of experiencing the world. Baldwin attempted in particular to map out the transitions of experience within each level. Thus, in the prelogical stage the mind shifts from memory objects to fanciful objects to play objects and finally to what Baldwin termed *substantive* objects. These labels are not very helpful but, to reiterate a point, they are supposed to capture the central features of *how*, or in what manner, we experience the world.

In what follows I want to focus on the prelogical and quasilogical levels of cognition, for it is the shift from sensory to substantive objects which is intimately associated with the development of intentional action, the problem we have been discussing thus far.

Sense Objects

Baldwin assumed that the human mind—even in its most primitive form—has the capacity to construct some kinds of objects no matter now ephemeral they might be. The child is born with the elements of cognition: "It is just this way of doing—this singling out of an element from among the contents of consciousness, and holding it up as having a sort of self-integrity and unit-quality for our personal ends—that is the function of cognition" (Baldwin, 1906, p. 41).

For Baldwin, however, this assumption was more than the theoretical convenience it might appear to be. In the analysis of action, as we saw, Baldwin advanced reasons for rejecting chance behavior as the starting point of volition. "All is neutral so long as nothing touches upon his appetites, instincts, native propensities, and organic susceptibilities. But as soon as something does so touch him, there is then a change; some element of experience at once stands out from the neutral panoramic movement, and is found to be fulfilling, stimulating, embodying, and determining of his interest" (Baldwin, 1906, p. 46). Without the necessary propensities and susceptibilities an organism could not be affected at all. There could be, therefore, no so-called state of pure experience as the starting point to cognitive development. If the canvas of experience is absolutely pure, whatever that means, then no further development in experience would be possible—unless one postulates some inner principle of development. But this is precisely what Baldwin rejected in the Hegelian theory, he was looking for a "natural genesis." In many other respects Baldwin's theory is reminiscent of Hegel's system, a connection Baldwin was more than willing to acknowledge.

The problem with assuming something like pure experience is illustrated by a passage from James, which Baldwin quotes.

> "Pure experience" is the name which I give to the original flux of life before reflection has categorized it . . . pure in the literal sense of a *that* which is not yet any definite *what*, tho' ready to be all sorts of whats; full both of oneness and of manyness, but in respects that don't appear; changing throughout, yet so confusedly that its phases interpenetrate; and no points, either of distinction or of identity, can be caught. Pure experience in this state is but another name for feeling or sensation. But the flux of it no sooner comes than it tends to fill itself with emphases, and these to become identified and fixed and abstracted; so that experience now flows as if shot through with adjectives and nouns and prepositions and conjunctions. . . . Prepositions, copulas, and conjunctions, "is," "isn't," "then," "before," "in," "on," "beside," "between," "next," "like," "unlike," "as," "but," flower out of the stream of pure existence, the stream of concretes or the sensational stream, as naturally as nouns and adjectives do, and they melt into it again as fluidly when we apply them to the new portion of the stream. . . . Is purity only a relative term, meaning the proportional amount of sensation which it still embodies. (James, 1905, p. 29)

This vivid description leaves the problem of development quite intractable. How does the "flux" begin? Rather unhelpfully, James can declare only that emphases do tend to come.

Interest is the term Baldwin gave to the innate tendency of an organism to reach out after objects in the world; it indicates "a certain direction in the course of experience." Baldwin suggested that interests can be looked at in two quite different ways. We can concentrate on the terminus of interest, that is, on "the sort of object or meaning which is the natural fulfilment of the interest." Alternatively, a functional or process view of interest is possible, by teasing out the "progressive selection, arrangement, and control of the contents of consciousness." The processes which make these selections possible are habit and accommodation; an object may already fall within the habitual system or be new and require motoric accommodation on the part of the child.

Here we can see a direct parallel between the two levels of Baldwin's theory—that of action and that of consciousness. Within consciousness there are two kinds of possible objects: the familiar (i.e., habitual) and the novel (i.e., those to which the child must accommodate). Baldwin did not think that the objects of consciousness could be divided easily into two groups—one group familiar and the other novel—any more than actions can be divided into those which are habitual and those which are accommodatory.

In Baldwin's terminology a familiar object is said to be *complicated* or *integrated* because it is already part of the texture or context of consciousness. A large part of Baldwin's enterprise was concerned with showing how, and in what sequence, the process of complication proceeds.

One possibility is that objects become attached through a process which is primarily affective. The appetitive and impulsive reactions become the criterion of selection and determine the mind's objects. Baldwin was unimpressed with the hedonic theory of motor development and he was equally critical of a hedonic theory of consciousness.

According to such a theory, an object stimulates the active processes of mind which is in turn disposed to select that object and assimilate it. This theory of objects stresses the processes by which mind assimilates them. On its own it leads to a form of subjectivism, for mind will be open only to objects which it alone desires. Even if affective and conative dispositions partially explain the fact of assimilation, they cannot be the whole story; "if such were indeed the case, there would be no possibility of experiences of unfulfilled and dissatisfied conation" (Baldwin, 1906, p. 49). As a matter of fact, mind is invariably confronted by that which is unsatifying and feels the absence of the satisfying.

At the very earliest stage of consciousness mind has no way of combating the unsatisfying or the absence of the satisfying. The world is simply there. Mind has no means of escape. With the development of memory as the next stage, mind begins to find a way of backing off from the world of hard fact.

The unwelcome presence of the unsatisfying or the conflicting provides the counterexample against which the strong case of the conative theory cannot be advanced. Just for this reason the object is an *object-something to object to or avoid*.

> In the case . . . of an unwelcome presence the opposition and conflict of conative with presentative or sensational processes testifies to the impossibility of accounting for the object entirely in terms of the dispositions which contribute to determine it. The very marks which make an experience an object may be those which excite an attitude of revolt or rejection and lead to disorganization of the presented context. (Baldwin, 1906, p. 50)

Here Baldwin is asserting that, although the determination of an object always involves active processes, these psychological processes do not alone constitute the object. In some cases the active processes may be exceedingly minimal, requiring nothing more than the orientation of the sense organs (e.g., following a moving ball through a series of spatial positions). Baldwin argued that it would be absurd to say that the ball as an object of perception was determined by eye movements, although it could not be an object without those movements.

From these considerations Baldwin came to draw a sharp distinction between *the interest and the datum*. Relatively unfamiliar objects stimulate "a throng of affective–conative elements, a mass of kinaesthetic stuff, arising as if to give it a context." But again Baldwin insisted that it is the object itself which determines its meaning. The sight enters as a visual sensation, the sound, as an auditory sensation. Each object in the world, Baldwin said, makes its own "stark and brutal demand." This distinction between the datum and the interest is a difficult one to understand, as we shall see.

Baldwin summarized the relationship between thought and things at the level of sensation this way.

> There are indeed wide variations here and exceptional cases—cases of extremely strong suggestion and of actual illusion—but the regular case is that of a *visual object determined through visual sensation, an auditory object through auditory sensation, a taste object through taste sensation*, etc., each enmeshed so far as may be a context of ready-made and familiar complication.
>
> If we were writing out an exhaustive psychology of developed sense-objects called percepts, many additional things should, of course, be said. But our problem is the restricted one of determination, that is, of finding what the character of the percept as being this or that, and not another, consists in. And we find that, whether the moment of psychic drift, dispositional tendency, conative urgency, may set in this direction or in that, the resulting object is after all moored to a peg, held to a sense-process and term, *because of which the object is this and no other*. Give the calf rope—let this rope comprise strands of memory, association, selective interest, social suggestion, and other directive psychic motives—yet when all its coils have been unwound, the calf must feel the final tug and hold-up of attachment to this central sense-peg. The control is from the stimulating, intruding novel something that effects a new equilibrium and contributes elements to the enlarging context. When this is not so—when the dispositional or interest factor fairly prevails—then we have a new departure and a dawning dualism, which is matter of later study. The objects which do detach themselves, the calves that do break the rope, congregate in a sphere—that of images and fancies—which have other control and other determination than those of objects of sense. (Baldwin, 1906, p. 52)

The interaction of primitive interest and datum gives rise to a very simple system of sensory experience. The original panorama has begun to take on stresses here and there. Each object has a context made up of its own sensations, actions, and other objects. It is from this that memory carries the development of mind a step further.

Memory Objects

One very important distinction begins to crystallize in this stage—that between persons and things. The basis of the distinction Baldwin thought was "the essentially capricious behaviour of persons, and the difficulty of reducing them to the type of the regular series to which the dead things of the environment lend themselves." Now Baldwin is not suggesting here that the prelogical mind makes this distinction. The point is rather that, as a matter of fact, the person is "the source of novel, very interesting, very vital and pungent experiences" (Baldwin, 1906, p. 56). This distinction becomes increasingly heightened during the next stages of development. Baldwin's social psychology (discussed by Kohlberg in Chap. 9) is, in fact, part of his more general cognitive psychology and not easily to be separated from it.

The elaboration of memory marks the transition away from a consciousness which is tied to objects of sense, although Baldwin's account of this is sketchy at best. His attention is concentrated on explicating the developmental significance of memory. Of this Baldwin (1906) wrote:

> So far as the child does question memory and resolve to test it, he shows that he has become aware of the great chasm or cleft in his experience, which is now only beginning to open up—that between the system of his images and the world of sense objects existing apart from them. This—*the great inner-outer dualism*—is now indeed fast upon him, but the function of memory does not involve it ... memory indicates the first departure of the cognitive construction from its immediate touch with the external things of sense. (p. 52)

The objects of memory are quite similar to sense objects in two respects. According to Baldwin sense objects are said to be *whole*. By this Baldwin meant that they cannot be reduced to a series of conjoined impressions. For example, one has the whole sensation of a tree and not of many simple sensations added together. Memory objects are said to have this same characteristic. The object of the tree in memory has its own separable identity as an organized whole, and Baldwin referred to this identity as *representation*. Objects of sense are also stubborn, they cannot be escaped or got around. In memory the stubbornness of fact is referred to as *conversion*, indicating, presumably, that memory must bear some degree of fidelity to what is remembered.

How, then, do memory objects differ from sense objects? Baldwin maintains that they represent sense objects, at least in principle. Negatively, memory lacks whatever it is that makes an object of sense so "direct, stark, compelling." Nevertheless, memory objects differ only by degree from those of sense.

For the reason just given, memory is not fanciful. So long as it is treated as a memory it must fit the actual event remembered through the process of conversion. "This reconversion does not indeed take place in the memory function, and yet it is part of the representing function that it should be possible" (Baldwin, 1906, p. 67). Very clearly, this is a logical requirement without which the concept of memory could have no meaning.

In the sensory mode, mind has little control over experience, appetites run off in a regular way and objects come and go. By contrast, memory objects involve a measure of control on the part of the subject, although this is extremely limited at first. Baldwin suggested that control—the idea that there must be a fit between memory and fact—"arises from frequent experiences of actually faithful memories, terminating in the facts and things for which their contexts fit them" (Baldwin, 1906, p. 68).

Baldwin recognized that memory is more than a simple representation of sense experience. Memory is not a "purely photographic rendering of the data." This is "due to some variation in emphasis or urgency in the determining conditions . . . there is a shading of this in most cases of memory; the sense of possible variations in the result, if the test of conversion were actually made" (Baldwin, 1906, p. 68).

Although the first memory objects involve no major distinctions (e.g., inner–outer) they do signal some advance beyond the immediate controlled-by-the-world sense objects. Memory objects are, therefore, distinguishable in their own right although they are indirectly controlled by the requirement of convertibility. Because of this, memory images are tied to the external world although different from that world as projected in sense objects.

This achievement—the detachment of the memory object from sense objects—determines the direction of further development. Not only is the actual presence of sense objects lost but sooner or later so is the demand for convertibility; consciousness begins the construction of fanciful objects. Genetically, the actual presence of sense objects gives way to the indirect presence of memory objects, which in turn gives way to the objects of fancy. It should be noted that each stage represents a new complication in the structure of consciousness and not the loss of what has already been achieved; the child who has developed the memory function still has sense objects. Each stage represents a further layer of consciousness. At the same time each stage occasions the internal reorganization of consciousness as well.

Fanciful Objects

The progression beyond the stage of memory is made possible in the first instance through the failure of memory processes to "reinstate valid sense experience." Memory also breaks down because of the demands of new experience which "constantly taxes the powers of assimilation." Baldwin also noted that the affective side of consciousness—conation, desire, interest—modifies memory by disrupting it.

Thus, consciousness comes to distinguish, in a crude way, between those aspects of experience which are inner (e.g., images) and those aspects which are outer (e.g., sense objects). It is the content of consciousness, not the processes involved, which distinguishes fanciful images from memory objects. The processes are the same in both cases; it is the result of conversion and not the process of conversion which separates memory from fancy. Memories are tied to sense objects whereas images are not. One can, after all, remember a dream or a wish. In this latter case it is the persistence of experience rather than of objects which is occurring. For the most part, however, memory in Baldwin's theory refers only to the memory of physical objects.

Baldwin regarded dreams as clear examples of fanciful objects. "As a fact, the dream does conflict both with the regular constructions of memory, and also with the constructions present to sense" (Baldwin, 1906, p. 87). Baldwin was undoubtedly right in this although he underestimated the subtleties involved in learning to distinguish dreams from other events, mental or physical. Although it is obvious to an adult observer that dreams as data are different from other data, the child is unaware of this at first. Kohlberg has shown that the concept of the dream develops gradually from an initial differentiation between unreal-symbolic events and real events. Next, the child distinguishes unreal internal events which are private to the self from unreal events like pictures and films. Finally, the distiction is made between internal mental events and external physical events. Nevertheless, Baldwin did conclude that faulty memory as well as dreams lead the child to recognize that he possesses an inner world which is to be distinguished from the outer world. For this reason Baldwin well understood the significance of the dream in the child's developing epistemological framework. He did, however, tend to think of the dream as an easily understood phenomenon for the child.

The child's imitations of others also assist in the construction of an inner–outer distinction. Through imitation the child "comes to feel how the other feels." But these feelings, arising from the imitated act, are not attached to a specific sense object although the memory of imitation is. I recall copying an act but not of sensing the other person's feelings.

A further feature of imitation makes it important in the development of an inner–outer distinction: imitation involves a measure of conscious selection and control. "The object, even when successfully but imitatively reinstated, is not really a present persisting sense object. The process gives a result psychically detached from the persisting thing of the world" (Baldwin, 1906, p. 88). This harks back to the case of remembered dreams and wishes which are equally as detached from the sense world.

Baldwin thought of inner and outer as mutually exclusive. A psychic event is either one or the other, it cannot be both. The line between the two falls between memory (which can be converted and hence is external) and the pseudo–memories which remain detached from sense.

Baldwin describes the fanciful object this way:

> It is a bare creature of detachment and seemingly accidental occurrence. . . . There is . . . no apparent external control of fancy. There is also no inner control, even indirect, no sense of conversion-at-will into anything more real than itself . . . its creatures are bizarre, disconnected, fragmentary, temporary—they are merely a fleeting stream of inner happenings. (Baldwin, 1906, p. 90)

In commenting on the interpretation of dreams, I noted that Baldwin tends to overestimate the cognitive capacities of the emerging quasilogical mind. But, as we have seen, the child only gradually comes to realize that the dream conflicts with memory and physical events. Baldwin tends to grant too much rationality to the developing mind in the fanciful stage.

In classifying the objects of fancy Baldwin speaks of their being *detached*, i.e., not yet fully assimilated. He then decides that these objects are so aloof that "the conative dispositions and interests are not carried out, nor, in any great degree, implicated by them" (Baldwin, 1906, p. 90). In assuming that the objects of fancy are relatively independent of the real world, Baldwin mistakenly supposed that they are independent of our interests altogether. But surely certain of our interests give rise to such objects in the first place. They cannot be as detached as Baldwin maintains, for then they could not be objects at all. In this, Baldwin's insight is much less keen than that of Freud who saw that mind is riddled with all kinds of unconscious interests. Baldwin's theory of mind is, perhaps, too restrained, too intellectualist to grasp the full measure of human cognition and in particular the less than rational impulses which underlie it at times. I think the same kind of restraint is to be found in Piaget's conception of cognitive psychology.

The general point I have been making can be underscored with a conclusion Baldwin draws about fanciful objects. He notes that: "We smile at the pranks of our fancy, and decline to be in any way responsible for its doings" (Baldwin, 1906, p. 90). We smile, to be sure, but it is something we have learned to do. The quasilogical mind, caught as it is by its own lack of independent judgment, is simply not in a position to smirk: the pranks of fancy are serious affairs and it is only by degrees that we escape from them, and then, perhaps, not entirely. This is something Baldwin did not sufficiently understand.

For Baldwin, the objects of fancy are marked by a lack of convertibility to the external world and by a lack of persistence. Enough has been said about the first point. As to the second, memory guarantees the persisting quality of objects which is fundamental in our transactions with the world; "an object which is once recognized or identified as the same cannot be simply the momentarily past or the momentarily present, but must be *the continuous between the past and the present*" (Baldwin, 1906, p. 92). But fanciful objects are purely inner—they have no attachment to persisting physical objects and so the operation of conversion cannot operate. Baldwin concluded that it is "not the inner objects which persist but the inner world itself." Mind thereby arrives at its first major structure—*the inner:outer dualism*, as Baldwin terms it.

Baldwin uses the concept of dualism to indicate that consciousness is taking on a given structure. It is not something that the quasilogical mind can be self-reflectively aware of, but it is the structure which is assumed to account for epistemological activity at this level and in terms of which the child assigns meaning to the world. The inner:outer dualism, "the starting point for further great dualisms," is an extremely unstable system. The instability centers on the placement of the body which seems to hover uneasily between the inner and the outer.

The boundary of the outer is the body. Testing the validity of memory, for example, is achieved by the efforts and explorations which bring about the "contact of the body with things." But the body is also an inner phenomenon—at least it is the seat of what is inner. From the beginning, and prior to the rise of the inner:outer dualism, the body is the source of all kinds of events which do not have an obvious reference to external objects and perhaps they have no reference at all; these are the "pains, pleasures, strains, efforts, dispositional gropings, urgent emotional cravings and rebellions."

But they are not entirely internal. As part of a total psychophysical system they are connected with the environment in which the system operates. They are, therefore, indirectly affected by external or outer events. They can be controlled somewhat by the actions of the organism as, for example, when a painful area is stroked to soothe the pain. Then, of course, the body seems to be the location of fanciful images which are the exemplars of inner phenomena. Finally, the imitative actions of the child are closely tied to the arousal of inner states. Through the imitation of others "the whole inner meaning to the person imitated, comes to himself." This is the key insight of Baldwin's social psychology.

The body is not, however, merely the repository of inner events, nor is it an inert physical object. It is an agency of action and it operates on the world through "actual trial, selection, elimination and reduction." It is in this sense that the body is both inner and outer. As Baldwin says, "the body is frequently caught *in flagrante delictu*, having intercourse with impersonal nature, while still posing as a virgin personal centre" (Baldwin, 1906, p. 98). Slowly, consciousness begins to recognize that "body" has two distinct parts, one inner, the other outer.

The inner:outer dualism represents, then, a first attempt to structure the world of objects. Although it is a confused system it does at least recognize, if only in an imperceptible fashion, that the objects of thought are not all of a piece.

Because of its inherent confusions Baldwin emphasized that the inner:outer dualism is far removed from the subject:object dualism of logical thought. At best, the child at this stage can distinguish between a vague subjective realm and a persisting external world. In mature thought all objects are inner and "some of them carry besides the coefficient of externality." In the quasilogical mind the classification of objects is like this:

```
                          objects
                             |
        ┌────────────────────┴────────────────────┐
  those without direct                       those with external
  external reference                             reference
    (i.e., fancy)                            (i.e., memory, sense)
```

As [sic] matter of fact, the inner as subjective attains considerable development, as relative to the external or physical, before the latter goes far toward becoming the reflectively objective. It appears that a *certain development of the subjective whereby the content of the inner itself becomes capable of determination as object or psychic content* is a necessary condition of the rise of the psychic dualism of subject and object. (Baldwin, 1906, p. 95)

So far we have traced out the first three levels of consciousness.

Each level might be thought of as a scheme in terms of which the child constructs an understanding of the world. In all this the child is an actor and not merely a passive receiver of inputs. The sensory scheme becomes complicated as memory develops which, in turn, leads to the possibility of fanciful objects and with them the first dualism of consciousness.

Play Objects and a Digression on Meaning

Play is the next stage of development. Taken as a whole, it culminates in a measure of control over the objects of fancy and begins the work of connecting them with sense objects. The play situation is constructed out of the content of real life. For example, the child may play at being an astronaut, doctor, firefighter, builder, etc. Most significantly, the details of the play activity are "worked out with more or less fidelity to the real or possible." For this reason the uncontrolled freedom of fancy objects is no longer a dominant force: a measure of control has been introduced. "The player as much as says to himself, this is real, or would be, but for the fact that I know that it is not; it stands for reality in so far as I choose to let stand—by not altering or abolishing it" (Baldwin, 1906, p. 111). The objects of play give the semblance of the real world while not simply being memories of it. The play world is, therefore, on the inner side of the inner:outer dualism. The real world remains as a kind of background against which play operates. "Consciousness, even while busy with the play objects, casts sly glances behind the scenes, making sure that its firm footing in reality is not lost. There is a sort of oscillation between the real and the semblant object, taking place in the psychic sphere, giving an emphasized sense of the inner:outer contrast" (Baldwin, 1906, p. 111).

Play introduces the child to a new sense of personal agency. Aware of the made-up character of the play the child knows that it can continue at the activity without having to subject the results to the demands of immediate test. Baldwin captures the character of play as "the selective or experimental determination of objects, situations, and the like, under the reservation, consciously faced and allowed, that it is only for personal and temporary purposes" (Baldwin, 1906, p. 114).

Baldwin offers two considerations in support of this view. First, the real world does intrude into play on occasions and makes it impossible. Second, play has all the appearances of an activity which protects itself from intrusion; children are obviously absorbed by the fantasies they construct. Play is a fragile affair: "both the inner freedom and the outer semblance must be retained; the latter gives consistency, pattern, dramatic quality, all that is meant by 'semblance'; the former gives control, selective character, essential inwardness" (Baldwin, 1906, p. 111).

Baldwin regarded play as the prelude to genuine experimentation. Imagination is the source of ideas which must be tested against the objective facts of the real world; the play object is experimental in so far as it can be said to stand for certain prospective solutions. It does not, however, demand solutions; the stage of play is not fully experimental because external control is not reinstated. The demands of "practical need" budge consciousness away from the comforts of play toward genuine experimentation.

Play, Baldwin argues, introduces the problem of meaning. *Meaning* "is the passage from the bare recognition of each item presented as being just what it is, to its treatment as being in some sense not what it is, but what it may become or be used as, that psychic meanings as such arise" (Baldwin, 1906, p. 130).

Substantive Objects

Consciousness attempts to split the outer term or 'body' into two and so distinguish between inner content and outer material bodies. According to Baldwin (1906):

> The subjective psychic life, now a more or less self-controlled subjective mass of data, is free from the outer persistence co-efficient. Over against it, the externally controlled objects ... fulfil the persistence guaranteed ... by the conversion co-efficient of memory.... The substantive mode is but the knitting together of the essential factors of the advancing dualism of controls—one control resident in the subject or self now found detached from any particular body, and the other resident in the context which is or means such bodies. (p. 210)

This rather opaque language comes down to a rather simple suggestion. Some aspects of body are treated as inner or mental while others are regarded as definitely outer or physical. It is not a classification of objects which can work since the original ambiguity of body remains. This mind:body dualism, therefore, represents only a slight advance over the inner:outer dualism.

At this level the child's understanding of the world begins to become genuinely experimental. As the outgrowth of playful experimentation with objects, the instrumental schema—which mediates recognitive meanings—reaches out after a generalized appreciation of objects. Till now the child has acted in a piecemeal fashion with respect to objects. The instrumental schema is "a device of a pragmatic sort to aid reconstruction, induce accommodation and relieve embarrassment.... The schema is a meaning ... sometimes called 'vague general'—i.e., the merely large, undifferentiated, and habitual . . . it is as if general in reference to the cases with which it urges consciousness to cope" (Baldwin, 1906, p. 215).

The implication of this statement seems to be that it is only in the mind:body or substantive mode that the child first begins to act "with a sense of the general." If this is so then Baldwin has contradicted himself, for everywhere else he claims quite the opposite; habitual or "general" actions are the *terminus a quo* of development. It is unlikely that Baldwin would have committed such a crude error. Instead, Baldwin is saying that in the substantive mode the child comes to the task of generalizing in a self-conscious way. The "sense of the general" becomes an intentionally directed instrument. The child begins to apply provisional schemes to events in experience—asking all the time "is it this or that?" In each instance a decision must be made as to whether the event is included within the scheme or excluded from it.

The substantive mode with its mind:body dualism is a temporary arrangement, "for the attempt to treat the private body as exclusively body and in no sense mind does not succeed . . . it is through the essential usableness and utility of the muscular and other mechanisms of adaptation, manipulation, etc., . . . that the substantive mind member of the dualism exists (Baldwin, 1906, p. 253). This double placement of the body is also the basis of the self's understanding of the other person; the other's body is not a mere "thing." Furthermore, mind cannot be treated as a separable entity because it "is in all experience given . . . in the dispositional processes," and these are located in the body.

Following the quasilogical stage Baldwin proceeds to a long discussion of scientific (logical) and aesthetic (hyperlogical) thought. But all that goes well beyond the confines of this discussion. It is important to note, however, that Baldwin saw these higher forms of thought as being firmly based on the use of ends-means schemas, the basic achievement of the quasilogical stage. For Baldwin then, explaining the development of consciousness amounts to showing the principles in terms of which the child classifies or demarcates experience as a whole. We have seen how the primitive consciousness is confronted with a range of objects immediately present or present to memory through recall. In Baldwin's view, the world has at least some form for the infant. Without this form the child could notice nothing and react to nothing and hence further development would be quite impossible. In a very different context (the development of perspectivism in art) Gombrich (1960) has drawn the same conclusion.

Without some starting point, some initial schema, we could never get hold of the flux of experience. Paradoxically, it has turned out that it matters relatively little what these first categories are. We can always adjust them according to need. Indeed, if the schema remains loose and flexible, such initial vagueness may prove not a hindrance but a help. An entirely fluid system would no longer serve its purpose; it could not register facts because it would lack pigeonholes. But how we arrange the first filing system is not very relevant. (p. 323)

Sooner or later the infant finds that the world is not as it first seemed. The category system provided by sense and memory begins to break down. What is taken for a memory, for example, may turn out on test to be a fiction. The structure of consciousness is forced to change and the child finds itself with a division being forced into experience between the inner and the outer. Given this complication the child requires some method of testing experience; play is the first step toward meeting this requirement. But in the process the child finds itself on both sides of the line. Consciousness adjusts its structure once more by distinguishing now between mind and body. But, more importantly, the child achieves an experimental approach to the world, characterized by the intentional use of conceptual schemes which are modified in the light of conflicting experiences.

Baldwin's theory of consciousness is not the product of direct observation, nor could it ever be. It is an abstract and largely interpretative attempt to take consciousness whole, and at the same time to place it in a developmental framework. The construction of cognitive structures for the control of experience is the central theme of the early stages we have been considering, as of the logical and hyperlogical stages which follow. These stages emerge out of the interaction of dispositional interest and resistant experience. The paradox of development lies in the impossibility of knowing the world apart from our interest in it and the futility of trying to know it without regard for the kind of world it actually is. Gradually the child comes to regulate his interests (i.e., hypotheses) by reference to the data of experience. This is possible because the child learns to recognize the sources and kinds of experience. Such, for Baldwin, is the meaning of the inner:outer and mind:body dualisms.

Conclusion

In the remainder of this discussion, I want to stand back from the details we have so far been considering in order to get a sense of the general context into which Baldwin fits his analyses of intentional action and the child's construction of reality. Perhaps the best way to do this is to see how Baldwin and Piaget differ in their respective theoretical objectives.

The differences between Baldwin and Piaget center mainly, I think, on the scope they assign to their respective theories. Baldwin aims to analyze all experience and this gives his work a decidedly Hegelian sweep. This rather vast ambition is missing from Piaget's theory which, for the most part, confines itself to explaining the development of logico-mathematical thought. Piaget evidently thinks that there is plenty to do here without running off in other directions.

In retrospect, the theories of the development of consciousness proposed by Hegel and his followers, in particular Baldwin and the English philosopher Collingwood, may seem overly ambitious. Trying to fit the forms of experience (e.g., aesthetic, religious, logical, and scientific) into a single scheme appears to destroy their autonomy. Except for the form of experience designated as the endpoint, all other forms are treated as mere transition stages. For this reason the structure of different kinds of experience may well be misunderstood. As a consequence our understanding of different kinds of development may be obscured in a radical way. In any event, without the details of how various forms of experience develop, we are hardly in a position to fit them into an overall pattern, developmental, historical, or otherwise.

Despite the rather cold reception given to Hegel and Collingwood these days, the pursuit of general theories of development is not, in principle, a worthless enterprise. The only dangers are prematurity and a prejudicial forcing of the data to a prefixed scheme; there is, after all, no reason to suppose that the result will be a Hegelian type developmental sequence.

Suppose, however, that we start out with a Hegelian hypothesis. Now I do not want to imply that knowing all about the development of say X, Y, and Z will show us exactly what larger sequence they fit into (e.g., X → Z → Y). But these preliminary analyses will be necessary for out of them we will, in part, derive a set of endpoints, X, Y, and Z, the articulation of which a larger pattern depends on.

Although these Hegelian-like speculations may very well seem misplaced in twentieth-century cognitive psychology the fundamental issue that they raise cannot be overlooked. Baldwin's ambitious program, within which Piaget's research into logico-mathematical thought might be said to fit, calls attention to a question which needs to be asked. What relationships hold between the various forms of experience and what does psychology have to say about these relationships? A general theory of the development of mind should aim to answer this question. Baldwin, like Hegel and Collingwood, has offered a conjecture and a challenge. Even so, we have hardly the beginnings of an answer.

So then, consideration of Baldwin's theory has brought us to a frontier, from which further explorations can be launched. Perhaps, for example, it is here that we will find a synthesis of the two great traditions of cognitive-developmental psychology and psychoanalysis, both of which cut across many of the forms of experience we have already mentioned—or have the potential to do so. Bringing together the explanation of reason and passion in a single theory would be a happy result taking us one step further toward the general psychology sought by Baldwin, and, more recently, advocated by Piaget.

REFERENCES

Bain, A. *The Sense and the intellect*, 3rd ed. New York: Appleton, 1872, 4th ed., 1894.

Baldwin, J. M. *Handbook of psychology*, Vol. 1 : *Senses and the intellect*. Vol. 2 : *Feeling and will*. New York: Holt, 1889–1891.

Baldwin, J. M. *Mental development in the child and the race : Methods and processes*. New York: Macmillan. 1894.

Baldwin, J. M. *Thought and things*. Vol. 1 : *Functional logic*. London: Swan Sonnenschein, 1906.

Baldwin, J. M. *History of psychology: A sketch and an interpretation*, 2 Vols. New York: Putnam, 1913.

Baldwin, J. M. *Between two wars*, 2 Vols. Boston: Stratford Co., 1926.

Darwin, C. *The Origin of species*. Harmondsworth, Middlesex: Penguin, 1968.

Dewey, J. The reflex arc concept in psychology. *Psychological Review*, 1896, 3, 357–370.

Gombrich, E. H. *Art and illusion*. Princeton, N.J. : Princeton Univ. Press, 1960.

Hegel, G.W.F. *The Phenomenology of mind* (J. B. Baillie, trans.) London: Macmillan, 1970.

James, W. The thing and its relations. *The Journal of Philosophy, Psychology and Scientific Methods*, 1905, 2, 29–40.

Miller, N. E., & Dollard, J. *Social learning and imitation*. New Haven: Yale Univ. Press, 1941.

Mink, L. O. *Mind, history and dialectic : The philosophy of R. G. Collingwood*. Bloomington, Ind. : Indiana Univ. Press, 1969.

Piaget, J. *Play, dreams and imitation in childhood* (G. Gattegno & F. M. Hodgson, trans.). London: Routledge & Kegan Paul, 1951.

Piaget, J. *The origin of intelligence in the child*. (M. Cook, trans.). London: Routledge & Kegan Paul, 1953 (originally 1936).

Piaget, J. *Biology and knowledge*. (B. Marsh, trans.) Edinburgh: Edinburgh Univ. Press, 1971.

Piaget, J. *Genetic epistemology* (E. Duckworth, trans.). New York: Norton, 1971.

Preyer, W. *Mind of the child* (H. W. Brown, trans.). 2 Vols. New York: D. Appleton, 1888–1889.

Romanes, G. J. *Mental evolution in man*. London: Routledge & Kegan Paul, 1888.

Spencer, H. *The Principles of psychology*, 2 Vols. New York: Appleton, 1901.

Sully, J. *The Human mind*, 2 Vols. New York: Appleton, 1892.

Tarde, G. *The laws of imitation* (E. C. Parsons, trans.). New York: Holt, 1903.

7

COGNITIVE DEVELOPMENT AND THE SELF

Benjamin Lee
Center for Psychosocial Studies,
Chicago

Introduction

At the turn of the century, James Mark Baldwin began to create a complete functionalist account of the development of thought whose theoretical premises Piaget would later incorporate into his own pioneering work. Baldwin's mature work, like that of his colleague and friend Charles Sanders Peirce, has been relatively neglected. Although Peirce has recently enjoyed a belated rediscovery by those interested in "semiotics," Baldwin's work is still unappreciated. Part of the reason for this neglect is the difficulty and inaccessibility of Baldwin's work, but the main reason is that his theory of cognitive development went against the grain of the behaviorism which dominated American social science shortly after Baldwin's departure from the United States for France.

The goal of *Thought and Things* (1906, 1911; reprinted in 1975) is to provide a genetic and functionalist theory of the relationship between thought and inference, where inference does not consist of the laws of thought that characterize formal, deductive reasoning, but is rather the process by which thought develops and is modified. Baldwin (1906) explicitly distinguishes this process from the sort of deductive reasoning that logicians study.

For this reason I shall call the formal logical inquiry the "Logician's Logic"; it is certainly not the psychologist's logic—that is, not the science of the actual thought process as the psychologist finds it—nor is

the ϕes epistemology

it the logic of the knower himself in his processes of acquiring and utilizing knowledge. (p. 6)

Thought or cognition is minimally the "being aware of an object" (Baldwin, 1906, p. 39), and as children develop, what they can become aware of changes and becomes more abstract. For Baldwin, these more abstract and complicated levels of representation develop through the child's interaction with other agents who help to shape not only the content of the child's thought, but also its very form. Social interaction forms the basis for the child's ability to represent others as agents who are the loci of such mental states as belief, desire, and feeling. This interest in studying how the child is able to form representations of others as possessing mental states led Baldwin to formulate an integrated theory of the development of the self, aesthetics, ethics, and logic.

Baldwin's interest in the social construction of intentionality leads to some interesting and important differences between his work and that of Piaget. Both writers find behaviorism incompatible with their theoretical outlooks and share emphases on structural stages, on equilibration as the mechanism through which thought and knowledge develop, and on the attainment of abstract thought through the internalization of action. However, Baldwin's concern with the problems of intentionality and agency (as compared with Piaget's focus on logical structures) led him to investigate the development of meaning and the self, especially as these relate to the child's ability to formulate more and more abstract ends or goals. One of Piaget's major theses is that thought develops through the progressive internalization of action. His work on the sensorimotor period is a careful analysis of how the development of the child's "conceptions" of objects, space, time, and causality rest upon changes in its ability to coordinate various means–end relations (the last stage of the sensorimotor period he calls *the invention of new means through mental combination*). However, Piaget does not try to show how higher levels of cognitive development might also be dependent upon the child's ability to represent various means and ends of its own. Since the development of language and social relationships is dependent upon the child's ability to represent others as agents, it is not surprising that Piaget's work in these areas has been controversial and probably inadequate.

Most of Piaget's later work concentrates on developing formal models of the child's thought which are usually based upon its interactions with physical objects. These formal models have been either classical extensional logics (such as the propositional calculus for the level of "formal operations") or modifications thereof (the system of "groupings" for concrete operations). An immediate problem that arises with such models is whether or not they can also be extended to representations of the intentional states of others. Recent work in analytic philosophy on the logical nature of intentional state verbs suggests that they have very different properties from terms used to designate physical objects and these differences seem to be insurmountable with classical logical techniques. If these results are correct, then much of Piaget's project would seem to be inapplicable to social and linguistic development which seems to depend heavily upon the ability to represent others as agents with beliefs, desires, and intentions.

The first section of this chapter discusses some of the logical issues involved in the analysis of intentionality. Baldwin felt that representations of agents required seeing them as centers of control. Control is the "checking, limiting, or regulation" of the process of inference and was not reducible to the principles of formal logic. These control principles are actually those that underlie the notion of goal-directedness and self-correction. Goal-directed systems differ from physical objects in that they are sensitive to their interactive contexts and are able to transform some aspect of the environment in accordance with some end of the system. In order to represent something as goal directed, it is thus necessary to represent a context-sensitive transformative relationship between means and end. Much of Baldwin's theory of cognitive development attempts to show how such representations develop, and his various levels of cognition are different levels of representation of the control relationships present in all inference.

The second part of this discussion describes Baldwin's theory of cognitive development as presented in Volume 1 of *Thought and Things*. Correlations are drawn between some of Baldwin's theoretical points and Piaget's research on the child's development of means–end relations during the sensorimotor period. Piaget's interest in this progression seems to end with the early preoperational period, and Baldwin's theory takes off at the point at which Piaget stops.

The third and final section shows how Baldwin's theory of the development of intentionality allows him to create a theory of idealization and the self which is congruent with recent cognitive-developmental and psychoanalytic work. According to Baldwin, idealization is a special type of end which a person uses to give meaning to and guide his actions. He views this process as developing out of the *semblant*, or play aspect, of cognition, and, like Vygotsky, he views play and creativity as the leading edge of cognitive and emotional development. Idealization becomes the process by which people construct ends which they know are not real, but nevertheless use to give coherence to their actions. For Baldwin, idealization becomes a representational analog to the very self-correcting nature of inference itself. If Baldwin's ideas about idealization are correct, then it is not surprising that both cognitive-developmental psychologists and pyschoanalysts have found idealization to be critical in the development of the self.

Theoretical Issues

Intension, Extension, and Representation

A longstanding debate exists about the proper form of explanations in natural and social science: are natural science modes of explanation and description developed through research upon physical objects applicable to the study of human action where the "objects" seem to have properties different from those studied in the natural sciences? Are there logical problems in attributing intentional states to agents, and do these make a difference in explanatory form? If it is necessary to attribute mental states to agents, are there further problems in attributing to agents representations of the intentionality of other agents?

These questions are crucial to a proper understanding of Baldwin's work. Baldwin's "genetic" logic can be interpreted as trying to give an account of how people form representations of intentionality. However, in order to understand some of the issues involved in constructing such a theory, it is necessary to look at the distinction between intension and extension.[1]

This distinction, first noticed by Frege (1892) in his work on sense (or intension) and reference, deals with certain problems of logical identity and substitution. Extensional contexts are those in which terms that refer to the same object(s) may be substituted for one another without changing the truth value of the overall expression. For example, if "Venus" is the name of the second planet from the sun, and the second planet from the sun is also 60 million miles away from the sun, then the term "Venus" can be substituted for the term "second planet from the sun" in the sentence, "the second planet from the sun is 60 million miles from the sun," without changing the truth value of that sentence.

This is not true for contexts introduced by such intentional verbs as believe, think, intend, or desire. These verbs introduce intensional contexts in which the substitution of terms that stand for identical objects may lead to a change in truth value of the overall expression.

---

[1] See the footnote concerning "intention" and "intension" above on p. 214

For example, while the sentence "John believes that Venus is 60 million miles from the sun" may be true, the sentence "John believes that the second planet from the sun is 60 million miles from the sun" could be false, if John does not believe that Venus is the second planet from the sun.

The critical difference between extensional and intensional sentences and contexts is that with *extensional sentences*, language seems to be used to talk about the referents of expressions and not the senses or the ways in which expressions present their referents. Therefore, the substitution of coreferential terms does not affect the truth value of the sentence.

With *intensional sentences*, one has to distinguish between talking about the senses of expressions, the way they represent their referents, and talking about the referents themselves. Intensional contexts introduce a distinction between a representation and what it represents—between a representation and its representational object (where *object* means any sort of phenomenon). The failure of substitutability in the example hinges upon whether the expressions in the sentences are interpreted as referring to the objects or referents of John's representations or the representations themselves. Although the expressions "Venus" and "the second planet from the sun" both have the same referent or representational object, they differ in the way they represent that object.

In natural science, it does not seem necessary to attribute such representations to physical objects in order to explain their behavior. However, the explanation of human action seems to require the attribution to agents of representations which have an irreducible *intentionality* and *intensionality* to them. If human beings can represent the intentionality of others and attribute to others mental states, this requires that they be able to represent others as making the distinction between representation and representational object. A critical problem that arises: how do human beings become able to represent the distinction between extension and intension?

In his later work, Piaget seems to take the position that the structures internalized through interaction with physical objects contain formal properties which are extendable to the development of social relations and intentionality. However, all his logics are extensional—they all depend upon the intersubstitutability of coreferential or identical terms, and since there is still no successful extensional treatment of intentionality, the possibility of such an extension remains only a dubious hypothesis.

Baldwin took a different tack than that adopted by Piaget. As pointed out earlier, Baldwin did not believe that cognitive development followed the principles of a logician's logic; indeed, his account in Vol. 1 of *Thought and Things* seems to suggest that early cognitive development rests upon the child's ability to represent increasingly complicated means–end relationships. Formal logic develops out of this progression.

Baldwin's account develops the means–end progression that Piaget analyzes in his work on the sensorimotor period. Piaget's interest in this progression seems to end with the beginning of the preoperational period; the child is able to represent the distinction between means and end, but the analysis is not continued to see when the child represents others as making similar distinctions. When Piaget discusses role-taking, he describes it as formally equivalent to the type of reversibility that the child acquires in his interactions with physical objects. Baldwin reverses these priorities; the processes that govern the child's acquisition of formal structures develop out of his representation of goal directedness. The move is from intension to extension, not vice versa.

Functions, Goals, and Teleology

Baldwin's theory is an account of how what Baldwin calls *mental objects* develop. For Baldwin (1906), a mental object is "whatever it is possible to take interest in, whatever it is possible to describe, whatever it is possible in anyway to apprehend or think about, to remember, recognize, forget, consciously identify, anticipate, intend, or mean" (p. 41). Baldwin calls that which controls the construction and development of mental objects at any particular moment the *interest* of that moment. The interest guides and arranges mental contents "toward a better realization of that which more or less adequately fulfills the interest" (Baldwin, 1906, p. 42). He then specifically links this process with the problem of teleology.

> In the higher modes of consciousness, there is what we call "voluntary" direction of thought to an end, as seen in voluntary control of conduct, deliberate reflection upon a problem, etc.; but the same characters attach to the development of interests in those cases in which such a deliberate purpose is absent. The bee, for example, has a psychic interest in building his hive, and the dog in chasing a bird, no less than the man in marrying a wife. (Baldwin, 1906, p. 42)

In his discussion of the *terminus* and *plan of development* of an interest, Baldwin (1906) comes close to formulating a goal directed theory of inference.

> By the "terminus" of the interest what is meant is the sort of object or meaning which is the natural fulfillment of the interest. It is a "terminus," because by the establishing of such an object the interest reaches its satisfaction and completion. By "the plan of development"

cf. R.B. Perry & Tolman

of the interest is meant the progressive selection, arrangement, and control of the contents in consciousness, whereby in time the required object is successfully attained. (p. 43)

Although Baldwin never explicitly brings together the problems of goal directedness, teleology, and functional explanations, recent work in philosophy has shown that they are related concepts.

Teleological explanations formulate the cause or presence of some phenomenon in terms of some end or state of affairs to which the phenomenon is directed. A paradigmatic form for such statements is "A exists in order to do B," e.g., the heart exists to pump blood, he robbed the bank in order to get enough money to pay for his tuition. Goal ascriptions also state some end or outcome toward which certain behaviors of a system or its parts are directed, while function ascriptions typically state what are some of the effects of a given item or its behavior on a given system. Such statements can become teleological explanations of that behavior if it can be shown that the behavior occurred because of its effect upon the system.

All three types of accounts can be combined in the case of goal-directed system. Goal-directed systems depend upon the establishment of feedback relations between some internal state of the system, its "end" or "goal setting," and the effects that system's interactions have upon the environment. A feedback system is any system whose present state can be affected by the effects of past interactions the system has had with the environment and whose future interactions can also be affected by these effects (Woodfield, 1976). Previous outputs from the system bring about changes in the environment which affect later inputs, and these present inputs affect future outputs or interactions of the system. There are thus two causal chains operating to control the system's interactions. The first operates through the environment—a given output of the system changes the environment in a way that influences later inputs into the system. The second chain which runs through the system is from these inputs to the outputs that the system produces. These outputs, by influencing the environment, can bring about changes in the inputs. The first chain is controlled by the system's "sensor" which is sensitive to environmental changes, and the second chain is controlled by an "effector" which produces the outputs given certain inputs. In between these portions of the system there must be an internal link (the goal setting) that maps variables measured by the sensor with variables of the effector, bringing together two causal chains which would otherwise be independent. The internal link creates a reciprocal causal chain between sensor and effector.

A room thermostat is a simple example of a negative feedback, goal-directed system. Air temperatures cause a bimetallic strip to expand or contract, turning on or off some electrical power source for the room heating system. The desired temperature is adjusted by means of a dial which determines the point of contact between the bimetallic strip and the electrical system. The dial provides the link between the sensor and the effector, determining the internal state that constitutes the goal setting of the system. For example, a thermostat has the goal of keeping the room at 70° when the internal state of the system is such that the contact between the bimetallic strip and the electrical contact breaks at 70°. Systems such as thermostats demonstrate both plasticity and persistence with regard to the behaviors they will use to reach their goals. For example, a thermostat will achieve its goal under a variety of temperature conditions and will persist in modifying the temperature until the goal setting is reached.

In the case of a goal-directed system, it is possible to say that the function of the means chosen, the behavioral output controlled by the system, is its effect in attaining the goal setting or end of the system. However, it is probably not until a system can learn from the effects of its interaction with its environment that one can say that the means or behavior existed because it had that effect. In the thermostat example, if the outputs were not believed to have some of the effects that they did, the inventor would not have created the link between sensor, effector, and goal setting that governs the behavior of the thermostat. A thermostat can neither learn nor make inferences that can modify its goal setting, although it can behave in a way that brings about the desired temperature.

Much of the behavior of many animals and humans can be explained by the agent desiring a certain state of affairs which constitutes its goal setting or end and believing that a particular action will bring about that goal. Such behavior is feedback controlled; the actions are based upon perceptions (the sensor) of the environment and the behavior is modified according to the believed consequences of those actions in reaching the desired end (the effector chain). The representations that constitute the organism's beliefs, desires, and perceptions are the products of inferences that the organism makes which are influenced by all its learned experience which, in turn, is based upon its previous inferences and interactions. Unlike the thermostat and other simple feedback systems, the sensor, effector, and internal links are representations which are created by inferences the organism makes in accordance with its total world view.

Teleological explanations of actions use sentences which refer to representations. These representations are contained in such intentional states as belief, desire, and intention, which are attributed to the agent and which are necessary components in the explanation of his behavior. The intension–extension distinction is present in the very definition of a goal-directed system. The extension is the class of behaviors controlled by the goal setting or end. The intension is the property shared by all those behaviors; in the case of the thermostat, the intension is the goal setting of maintaining the room temperature at 70°. Of course, the thermostat is not aware of the distinction; however, when the child is able to represent means and end as separate and then coordinate them, which Piaget indicates occurs around the age of 9 months, it shows an incipient awareness of this distinction.

Baldwin's concepts of the terminus and plan of development of interest link his analysis of the development of thought with these issues of teleology, functional explanation, and goal directedness. The function of a thought or representation is the role it plays in fulfilling the terminus of the interest. The terminus controls the plan of development of thought. The relationship between terminus and the "mental objects" whose development it controls is that of end to means. More abstract levels of thought develop through the process of representing different levels of this control relation. If means and end in a goal-directed system stand in the relation of extension and intension, then the representation of this relationship forms the foundation for a theory about the representatiion of intentionality. It is not by accident that Baldwin insisted that the representation of intentionality is a critical factor for any complete functional and genetic account of thought. Such representations put in representational form the very functions and structures that underlie all inference.

Inference

It is useful to distinguish between two types of inference or reasoning. Theoretical reasoning or inductive inference is the process by which we modify our representations in the light of both representations not explained by other inferences (sense data), and those representations based on other inferences. Practical reasoning, or practical inference, is the process of modifying plans and intentions, in the light of the way things are represented to be, so as to achieve one's goals (Harman, 1973 p. 45).

Inference is very much like a negative feedback process which works with representations and whose starting point and conclusion are total explanatory accounts and whose standard (or goal) is the logical coherence of the resulting view. As Harman (1973) puts it,

Inductive inference is a way of modifying what we believe by addition or substraction of beliefs. Our "premises" are all our antecedent beliefs; our conclusion is our total resulting view. Our conclusion is not a single explanatory statement, but a more or less complete explanatory account. Induction is an attempt to increase the explanatory coherence of our view, making it more complete, less ad hoc, more plausible. At the same time we are conservative. We seek to minimize change. We attempt to make the least change in our view that will maximize coherence. (p. 159)

Inference, however, should not be confused with logic. Logic is concerned with the soundness and unsoundness of arguments. An argument consists of various statements, a set of which are called its "*premises*," from which another statement (the *conclusion*) is claimed to follow. The premises entail the conclusion. From a logically contradictory premise, any conclusion can be deduced. It does not follow from this result that if someone discovers that his beliefs are inconsistent, that he should infer anything or everything he can think of. Perhaps he should modify his premises by giving up or adding some beliefs. If inference is the process by which one modifies one's representations so as to increase explanatory coherence, then rules of logical implication are relevant to inference insofar as they increase such coherence. Harman (1973) puts the point in the following way:

It is true that reasons can often be stated in the form of a deductive argument. But that does not mean that inference or reasoning is an argument. It means that deductive arguments have something to do with explanatory coherence. An argument is not an inference, but it may be part of a conclusion. When, as we say, someone reasons P,Q,R; so S, it is not just that he believes P,Q, and R, and comes as a result to believe S. He comes to believe S, because P,Q, and R. (p. 162)

Practical inference is the process by which a person modifies his goals, plans, and intentions in order to achieve his desires. Such reasoning has a theoretical component insofar as it depends on how the person represents his world to be. However, the criterion of coherence for practical reasoning is not explanatory coherence, with its strictures of simplicity and elegance among competing explanations. Rather, its criterion would seem to involve some sort of efficiency or least-effort principle: choose the ends and means that will allow the greatest chance for success given the interactive situation. Furthermore, the inferences involved in creating a goal or end seem not to involve a comparison with other goals or ends (except at the most abstract levels), but rather the creation of some goal or end that is most coherent with one's emotions and overall affective state. Although such emotional states may have a representational component, they themselves are not representations, so part of the criterion for practical coherence will involve factors which are not the same as those for theoretical reasoning whose criteria for coherence work on competing explanatory representations. Baldwin (1911) sums up the the differences between theoretical and practical reasoning by saying that the latter lacks the principle of the excluded middle and the sort of universality attaching to logical deduction that theoretical reasoning has. These are implied in theoretical reasoning as reasoning to the best explanatory account given one's total view.

> If we would answer this question to any profit, we should recall, in the first place, the nature of theoretical implication. The presence of logical contradiction is essential to it; and it is by such contradiction, with its mutual exclusion of classes, that the deductive system takes the place of mere inductive identities and classifications. . . . This process, found to be essential to formal inference, is not present, in any strict sense, in the affective life. Affective negation. . .proceeds not by limitation, as between two mutually exclusive classes, but by rejection and privation under the progress of a positive motive; not by contradiction, but relative inclusion in a dominant interest. It is the play of interest that determines the whole of the affective content, over against all else. There is no determination of a limited non-B class, which taken with the B class, exhausts the sphere of a determinate sort of control or existence. (p. 119)

Rescher (1978), in a discussion of Peirce's contention that scientific reasoning leads inevitably to truth, shows that Pierce's theory of inference relates several levels of self-correcting processes.

> If a productive process P is composed of several constituent subprocesses P_1, P_2, etc., then the idea of self-corrective monitoring of performance can be construed in two ways.
> 1. Distributively. Each cognitive process P_i monitors its own performance: for every P_i belonging to P, P_i monitors the performance of itself.
> 2. Collectively. Some one (or conceivably, several of the process) P_i monitors the performance of P as a whole, and this unit is in turn self-corrective on its own account; the overall performance of P is thus monitored by certain of its constituent components, which are themselves self-monitoring. (p. 6)

This account contains three levels of goal-directed, self-correcting systems. The first level consists of those cognitive processes which monitor their own performance. Since this is part of the definition of being goal-directed, all goal-directed systems possess this level of self-correction, although many such systems such as thermostats cannot learn what interactions are successful in achieving their goals (in what contexts self-correction is successful or not). The second level consists of a subprocess which monitors the performance of P as a whole. This type of cognitive process is a subprocess which must be able to represent the overall process and the effect interactions have on the overall process. If the overall process is goal directed, then this subprocess must be able to represent the overall goal of the process and the effect of the interactive means on reaching that goal. In short, such a second-order process must be able to represent means and end, which is equivalent to being able to represent a first order system which consists of a means–end pair. Finally, the third level of self-correction is when a second level self-correcting process is able to take itself as a representational object. Since the second-level process already self-corrects its representations of the goals of the overall process and ongoing interactions, these third level processes must be able to represent and examine the representational accuracy (in terms of their truth conditions) and would be the foundation for hypothetical deductive thought in the propositional mode.

Peirce's levels of inference allow the construction of at least three levels of representations. Baldwin's *prelogical*, *quasilogical*, and *logical* periods correspond to those levels of Peirce's theory. As will be shown later, each of Baldwin's stages differs from the previous levels in that they take as their intentional objects the representations of the previous stages, thus creating a developmental hierarchy of cognitive levels. In Baldwin's *prelogical* phase, the child's representations are of the physical aspects of objects and events, and the child has no awareness of the distinction between representation and representational object; although the child's behavior is self-correcting, it does not have any cognitive awareness of means and end as separate. During the *quasilogical* period, the child begins to develop representations which separate intension from extension, representation from representational object, and means from ends. This would correspond to the development of the second level of self-correction that Peirce proposes, a level which can take as its intentional objects the procedures of the lower level, and which therefore must have some way of representing those lower-level procedures. In Baldwin's *logical* level, these second-order representations are made the representational objects of third-order procedures. Thus procedures investigate and act upon the representational properties of second-order representations, treating them as representations, as ideas. For Baldwin, the cognitive "subject" is no longer identified with any kind of means-end representation, but with the self-correcting process itself. Thus Baldwin's theory can be viewed as providing a developmental foundation for Peirce's theory of inference.

Baldwin

Baldwin's (1906) definition of cognition is intensionalist. *Cognition* is " 'the being aware of an object' which is to be understood as not simply being affected by contact with an object, but experience which includes in itself 'the being aware' as well as the being affected (p. 39)." Anything that the mind is attentively directed to is a mental object, an object of cognition or thought. Such a definition would include as potential objects of thought not only physical objects, but also other thoughts. In his discussion of the difference between content and object, Baldwin makes the same distinction discussed earlier between representations not caused by inference (what Baldwin calls content and Harman calls sense data), and representations produced by inferences. According to Baldwin (1906) only the latter would be *mental objects.*

> Content is the mere stuff or matter presented to consciousness, considered as stripped of the special meanings and modifications peculiar to the psychic process going on. The content "this bird" for example, is that visual presentation common to your perception and mine, given and so far stable, whatever further meanings we, the perceivers, may give to it. In the modes before reflection it is "content of presentation or apprehension, as distinct from object. "Object" *includes the meaning and intent taken with the content.* (p. 40, my emphasis)

A *mental object* is thus what Peirce would call a sign, something which stands for or represents something for someone in some respect. A mental object has a meaning and intent that go beyond the sense data or mere content of the thought.

Starting from this definition of cognition, Baldwin's project is to investigate both the conditions determining the construction of mental objects at any given stage of mental development and also what properties these mental objects have. Baldwin calls the "checking, limiting, or regulation" of this constructive process control. The construction of an intentional state by an organism is controlled both by its total cognitive and emotional state at the moment of interaction and the nature of the object represented (the intentional or representational object). The construction of different intentional states is controlled by different factors, and a control *coefficient* is a "sign, mark, or toning of any kind which makes a given content or mental object in a given sense, meaning, or for a given purpose, distinctive" (Baldwin, 1906, p. 58). Control coefficients signal differences in the construction of the relations between a representation and what it represents. A representation whose intentional object is a physical object will have different control coefficients than a representation whose representational or intentional object is another mental state. Baldwin distinguishes different levels of cognition by the different types of control they possess. More abstract levels of thought differentiate and integrate the control coefficients of less abstract levels. In the first volume of *Thought and Things,* he describes the stages of cognitive development up to the point of reflective thought, or what he calls the *subject-object* dualism. Later volumes describe even more abstract levels of thought, but in each case the more abstract modes differentiate among and reintegrate at a new level of organization the control coefficients of the less abstract modes.

Volume 1 of *Thought and Things* describe the development of two modes of thought, the prelogical and quasilogical, as the construction of a sequence of progressively more complicated and abstract mental objects. The *prelogical stage* consists of two types of mental objects, sense and memory, with the latter developing out of the former. This stage probably corresponds with the sequence Piaget outlines in his work on the sensorimotor period. During the *quasilogical period*, which probably corresponds to Piaget's preoperational period and the early part of concrete operations, the child constructs "fancy" objects, "play" objects, "experimental" objects, and then learns the dualism of mind vs. body and finally that of subject vs. object. The construction of representations at each of these levels is controlled by the properties of their representational objects, the types of things that are represented. More abstract levels of representation take as their intentional object the properties of the representations of lower levels, thus creating a developmental hierarchy of mental objects with each successive level embedding the previous one.

Prelogical period. In the prelogical period, the first representations (sense objects in Baldwin's terminology) are controlled by the physical properties of the objects or actions they represent as mediated by sense data. These sense objects correspond to Piaget's sensorimotor schemas whose construction and behavior are completely controlled by the physical properties of the ongoing interaction. A child at this level of development might recognize something as "graspable" or "suckable," but there is no need to attribute to it any symbolic order intervening between it and the world or any sophisticated differentiation between means and end. The properties of the sense datum become the limiting control coefficients for the construction of representations in the sense mode.

For Baldwin, the development of memory is the critical ingredient in the child's development of some sort of cognitive awareness of the distinction between representation and representational object, intension and extension. Memory objects (representations in the memory mode) have two properties which distinguish them from other representations. First, memories are representational: they are of something. Second, memories are convertible into what they represent. Part of the representing function of memory is that a memory claims to be reconvertible into what it represents. For example, a hope does not claim to be immediately reconvertible into that which is hoped for. In the case of a memory of a sense object, the representational aspect of the memory lacks the constraints upon its construction that its intentional object, the sense object, has. Memories lack the "direct, stark, compelling, and limiting character" of the coefficients of control of representations in the sense mode, and are thus potentially "liftable" from the context of the original sense data. A further contrast between memory and sense objects is that the sense coefficient no longer directly controls the construction of a memory object as is the case with sense objects, but mediately or indirectly through the requirement that the memory be reconvertible into the sense coefficient which is attached to physical objects outside the train of memory itself.

In Piaget's work, the first clear cut example of a child's behavior being controlled by a memory object occurs during the fourth period of the sensorimotor period when the child is able to distinguish means from end, which enables it to see some ongoing activity as a sign of a future state of affairs. Piaget's example is of a child crying when it sees its mother put on a coat, an action recognized as a sign of her impending departure; the child remembers that such actions by the mother mean that she is leaving. The separation of means from ends that is the hallmark of this period in Piaget's work depends upon the development of memory. In order to represent something as a means for some future end, the child must remember what the means is for.

The combination of representational and convertible properties to form a memory distinguish it from other types of mental objects. Sense objects have control coefficients characterized by "separableness, wholeness, stubbornness, and uncontrollableness," which are the properties of the physical objects they represent. The coefficients of *separableness* and *wholeness* of sense objects develop into the actual removal from the sense context characteristic of the representational aspect of memories. The coefficients of *stubborness* and *uncontrollableness* of the sense mode develop into the properties of persistence and continuity upon which the mediational properties of memory depend. In the case of sense objects, the representational aspects and the intentional object (the physical object as mediated by the sense data representations) are not distinguished by separate control coefficients. The memory mode differentiates among these coefficients, some of which apply to the representational aspects of memory, others to its convertibility. A memory is thus a representation which differentiates among the control coefficients of the sense mode and reintegrates them at a new level. A memory is also the first type of representation that distinguishes through this separation of control coefficients between a representation and its representational object.

The development of memory places the child at the verge of the development of what Piaget calls the *symbolic function* and what Baldwin calls the *quasilogical period*. At this point, the child distinguishes between signified and signifier, between thought and action, and begins to construct an inner representational world separate from the representations he has of the outer world.

Inner–outer dualism. Baldwin theorizes that the critical element that allows these further developments to be possible is the child's becoming aware of and differentiating among the control coefficients of memory. In the memory mode of the prelogical period, the attributes of memory objects are the same as those of sense objects, differing only in the substitution of mediate control for the immediate foreign control of representations in the sense mode. In the quasilogical period, representations lose both their sense coefficients and their conversion character. The representational aspects are "lifted" or freed from their claim of a direct tie to physical reality, as is the case for a prelogical memory object. Baldwin says that this later mode develops through the failure of some memories to be convertible into the sense objects they claim to represent. The child learns to distinguish those cases in which a memory object determines a valid sense object and is thus convertible into what it remembers, and those cases where the memory fails of conversion (for example, if the child thinks that the mother putting on her coat is a sign of her leaving, and then discovers that it is mistaken). These later types of representations Baldwin calls *fancy objects*, and they are marked by their failure of convertibility into sense objects. When the child has learned to distinguish between memory objects and fancy objects, it has learned that representatives can either be outer (convertible into sense reality) or inner (and lacking such outer convertibility). Baldwin calls this point in the child's cognitive development the beginning of the inner–outer *dualism*, and it corresponds with the start of the symbolic function in Piaget's developmental scheme. The classic Piagetian example is when Lucienne tries to remove a chain from inside a matchbox whose slit has been left slightly open. At first she fails, but then Piaget observes that she seems to stop and think about what to do and then mimics the widening of the slit by opening her mouth, a kind of iconic representation of the means.

> Soon after this phase of plastic reflection, Lucienne unhesitatingly puts her finger in the slit and, instead of trying as before to reach the chain, she pulls so as to enlarge the opening. She succeeds and grasps the chain. (1936, pp. 337–338)

If we take a means–end point of view and examine Lucienne's case closely, we see that her opening her mouth stands for, or represents, the class of possible behaviors that will enlarge the slit and enable her to fulfill her goal of reaching the chain. Having thought out the solution to her problem, she then enacts it through a particular token movement of her hand. Lucienne's behavior also presupposes that she has some representation of the goal setting which guides her thinking. She thinks of, and creates, her particular representation in order to solve the problem of how to get the chain. Piaget argues that she is thinking over various solutions in her head and that she finally hits upon one that she recognizes as solving the problem, implying that her symbolic thought is being monitored or corrected by her representation of her goal. However, what gets explicitly represented by her opening her mouth is not the overall goal setting, but rather a class of behaviors (those actions that will widen the opening) which will solve the problem. Piaget's account of Lucienne's behavior thus involves a self-correcting relation between two representations—one of the goal setting (getting the chain) which monitors the other (iconic) representation of a class of behaviors which will produce a particular token action (the class of behaviors being those which widen the opening, the token being Lucienne's actual token action).

If we compare Lucienne's action with the behavior of a simple goal-directed system such as a thermostat, it seems necessary to attribute to her a self-correcting relation between her representation of the end or goal setting, and a representation of a class of means. A thermostat might have some representation of the temperature of the room which *constitutes* its goal setting (usually a gap in a bimetallic strip) and which controls its behavior via some negative feedback process; but it is not necessary to attribute to it any representation of its goal setting or of the means. Piaget's description of Lucienne's behavior implies that Lucienne was thinking of different possible solutions to the problem of getting the chain, and then that she hit upon one that seemed correct, and she chose to act upon it. It does not seem necessary to attribute to the thermostat any capacity to choose among possibilities. In the case of the thermostat, the total goal-directed system consists of the self-correcting relation between the goal setting and the behavior it controls, but only we as observers can represent that behavior as leading up to the goal setting. The thermostat enacts or embodies the relation between means and end, without being aware of either means or end or the relation between them. The point is similar to Piaget's contention that children's earliest actions embody properties of a mathematical group without their being able to represent actions as having those properties. Most of Piaget's work on the sensorimotor period is to show how the child's thought develops from an early period where the behavior is much like that of a thermostat (the first sensorimotor period of reflex behavior), to this later point where it can internally represent both means and end, and use these representations to foresee possible consequences of its actions before it acts.

Piaget (1962) then describes how more complex activities, such as symbolic play, develop out of the child's ability to internally represent actions. For example, in the case of deferred imitation, the child chooses some representation of someone else's behavior, and uses that representation to control its own behavior. A famous example is of Jacqueline, who imitates a temper tantrum thrown by a young boy a day earlier. One of the major differences between Lucienne's behavior and later symbolic activity is that the controlling representation becomes further and further removed in time and space from the ongoing activity of the child.

At no point in his later work does Piaget show how more abstract levels of thought might develop out of ever more complicated representations of means–end relations. We have seen that in Lucienne's case, the child has a representation of the end and a representation of the means which is an internalized imitation of the extensional portion of some action. The next stage might be when the child is able to monitor a representation of a means–end pair used as an end with another representation of a means–end pair used as a means. In Lucienne's case, she coordinates a representation of a means with a representation of an end; in this later development, the child coordinates or monitors a representation of a means and end with another means and end. The child self-corrects representations of two self-correcting mechanisms, using one as means and the other as end. Piaget describes similar coordinations among schemas during the fourth period of the sensorimotor period when the child coordinates two hitherto independent schemas into one totality, using one as means and the other as end. At the end of the sensorimotor period, it can represent internally before it acts what it can only enact during the fourth period. By parity of argument, at this later stage the child can represent as a new type of end what was previously a separate means-and-end representation, and represent as means what were earlier separate means and ends. This would allow children to represent as part of their definition of the interactive situation that both they and others were agents, that is, goal-directed systems who do things in order to achieve desired effects.

Baldwin and Piaget both agree that the child's discovery and use of symbols is the foundation for future cognitive development. However, Piaget does not discuss how later stages of cognitive development might depend upon increasingly complicated representations of ends. Even in his discussion of Lucienne, the representation of the end is presupposed, rather than explicitly analyzed. If such basic concepts as agency, the self, and meaning all depend upon an intensional component derived from the goal directed nature of action, it is not surprising that Piaget's later work neglected these domains or tried to reduce their properties to those that objects possess. Baldwin, however, took the intensional as his starting point; his stages of cognitive development depend upon a subtle interplay between representation and representational object, intension and extension, inner and outer. The inner world of representation is contrasted with the outer world of sense, and only gradually does the inner develop into a locus of control over and against the outer. When the child is able to represent the inner as having its own control and thus separate from the outer, he has begun to develop the mind–body dualism which later on, through a further development of the relation between representation and representational object, will lead to the subject–object dualism. The self is also a product of this developmental path. "The self function is in its essence a control function. It arises by the substitution of inner for outer coefficients, in a partial way, which reinstates on a higher plane a form of joint or mediate control (Baldwin, 1906, p. 117)."

By the end of the sensorimotor period, the child is able to represent both means and end, as the example of Lucienne shows. Like Piaget, Baldwin emphasizes that imitation is a critical factor in the child's development at this stage because it sharpens the inner-outer distinction. Unlike Piaget, however, Baldwin (1906) sees imitation as a crucial factor in the child's self and social development.

> The very important fact of imitation, used by others as well as by the present writer in connection with the development of the consciousness of self in its social relations, again illustrates this fundamental motive in the development of fancy objects. The child imitates the act of another, and in so doing what he had only observed, comes to feel how the other feels . He thus learns to distinguish the arena of his direct feeling (the inner) from the larger range of presentative experience (the outer) from which this feeling was and may still be absent. (p. 87)

When Lucienne opens her mouth in imitation of the opening of the matchbox, her imitation is linked both to the inner and the outer. It is outer because it is an imitation of something external, the matchbox opening. It is inner because the imitation is part of the means used by her internal goal setting of obtaining the hidden chain: however, this inner goal setting is also of something external, the hidden chain.

Baldwin argues that the inner–outer dualism is further developed when children recall their imitative behavior. When the child remembers its imitative act, the actual behavior or thing imitated (as mediated by sense objects) would be the goal of its memory conversion, but because the imitative representation is only a copy of what it represents, not the actual thing or behavior, the child can only recapture the "inner" imitation. If Lucienne were to try to remember her total act of imitating the matchbox opening, she could capture and repeat her imitation of the matchbox by opening her mouth, but the original representational object of that imitation would no longer be present unless the matchbox happens to be lying around. Successive experiences of this kind harden the inner–outer distinction. Each experience emphasizes the reconvertibility of the signifier, the interiorized imitation and its mediating qualities, as contrasted to the nonreconvertibility of the representational object of the imitation, the original signified, or outer. A good example of a child being aware of the representational nature of imitation (as contrasted with the behavior imitated) is when Jacqueline sees another child in a playpen throw a temper tantrum and then imitates the tantrum the next day when in her own playpen. Then when she sees him again, she reimitates his behavior, laughing all the while (Piaget, 1962, p. 63).

Semblant progression. With the development of the inner–outer distinction and its recall through memory, the child now enters Baldwin's *quasilogical* period, or what Piaget calls *preoperational* thought. According to Baldwin, at the beginning of this period the child constructs semblant mental objects. These are representations which are given a semblance of reality coefficients that would control them if they were real. The most graphic examples of such behavior are children's symbolic play behaviors, when they pretend or make believe that something is real or that something stands for something else ("I'll be daddy, you be mommy," "This stick is a horse and I'm riding on it"). Baldwin points out that play objects are imitative and made up out of material drawn from real life, but the memories which make up play are treated as representations which do not have to be directly convertible into legitimate sense reality. The child chooses to play at being a fireman, doctor, or nurse; it knows the stick is not a horse, but treats it as if it were. Its behavior presupposes the previous inner–outer distinction of the fancy object; it chooses an inner representation derived by imitation, and realizing that it is a copy of reality, alters it to control its behavior. The imitation, previously a means at the service of an inner end but controlled by outer reality, now becomes an end in itself, no longer controlled by the outer, but instead controlling it.

> The entire determination of the play object—and of all semblant objects—is in the inner, as contrasted with the outer sphere. It presupposes, therefore, the antecedent development of the fancy object as such. It is accordingly a new modal determination, continuing the earlier progression. The reinstatement of the object imitatively is an "inner" imitation. The selection of the object for play is a "personal" selection, although in its context true to a possible or actual copy. The reconstruction of the real world, taking place earlier indeed in memory, and used for practical purposes in the pursuit of real interests, now

becomes a construction to be distinguished as within the inner world, and as such to be brought into contrast with those objects, perhaps the same ones, which have their existence in the outer world. Not only is the child using his imagination, but he is also aware that the construction is imaginative. (Baldwin, 1906, p. 112)

For Baldwin, the development of the semblant function in play forms the basis for not only the dualism of mind and body and self and not self, but also truth and falsity and the aesthetic mode of thought. The major development is that children are able to represent their actions as standing for something which they are aware is not real, but rather a make-believe, counterfactual semblance of reality. A comparison of Lucienne's and Jacqueline's actions with those of a child stomping its feet while imagining it is riding a horse highlights some of the major shifts in the child's cognitive development that the full utilization of the semblant function allows. When Lucienne imitates the matchbox opening, the representation (her mouth opening as a sign of some inner mental representation) and its representational object (the matchbox) are copresent, and the representation of the means is a direct copy of its object. When Jacqueline stomps her feet in a deferred imitation of the boy's temper tantrum, the representation and its representational object are no longer copresent, but her behavior still seems to be a direct copy of the original behavior. However, when she sees him again and then laughingly re-imitates his behavior, her laughter seems to indicate that she is aware that her behavior is only an imitation, a playful copy of the boy's movements. In the case of symbolic play where the child uses something to stand for something else, (such as when it stomps on the ground imagining it is riding a horse), its behavior is no longer an imitation of reality but a modification of it. The means it uses are no longer behavioral copies, as in Jacqueline's case, but an alteration of reality for the purpose of play. The child's behavior includes within the behavior itself signs of sembling, while Jacqueline's behavior does not. The representation of means is now freed from direct control by sense and memory objects; representations now signal counterfactual possibilities, and the link between perception and action is broken. Representations of the outer are now seen as controlled by and standing for inner control. Vygotsky (1978), whose analysis of play remarkably coincides with Baldwin's, says that

Play gives a child a new form of desires. It teaches him to desire by relating his desires to a fictitious "I," to his role in the game and its rule. In this way a child's greatest achievements are possible in play, achievements which tomorrow will become his basic level of real action and morality. (p. 100)

The semblant progression is furthered by the development of experimental objects. These mental objects develop after the child has made the inner-outer distinction and sees certain representations as outer, under foreign control, and others as inner, lacking such control. There is a group of representations which, although they claim to hold in the real world and be convertible into sense objects, have not yet been tested. In the semblant mode these mental objects are of inner meaning only until they are tested and then found to be also outer. An experimental object is a representation "which claims the value attaching to a memory object, while apprehended under the determination, so far forth, only of an image object (Baldwin, 1906, p. 118)." Play objects are experimental to some degree because they stand for some other state of affairs, but the actual testing or conversion process is never carried out. The experimental mode carries out the implied convertibility of play objects, testing what is seen as possibility against the reality it purports to represent.

The easiest way to summarize the whole train of cognitive development up to this point in Baldwin's scheme is that there has been a development from external, unmediated control to internal, mediated control. At first, the child only has sense objects whose control coefficients are completely determined by the physical characteristics of their representational objects. Control is completely external, and there is no awareness of the inner at all as being attached to any sort of cognitive representation. Prelogical memory objects are still controlled by the physical properties of those sense objects into which they purport to be convertible. Only with the failure of some mental objects to be convertible into sense reality does the child become aware of some level of the inner (fancy objects), but these are still defined in terms of the failure of certain representations to be convertible into sense objects. The inner is still not seen as separate from the outer and also possibly determining the outer. Lucienne's and Jacqueline's representations of means and ends are internally mediated copies of external objects or behavior. The inner representations that are their goal settings are constrained by external control, by their convertibility into sense objects. Lucienne seeks to get the chain, Jacqueline to reenact the boy's behavior. With the development of symbolic play, the representations that make up the child's goal setting begin to be controlled by inner interests. The controlling representations are no longer merely copies or imitations of sense reality, but transformations of these representations controlled by inner psychic processes.

Mind-body dualism. The hardening up of the inner-outer dualism through the development of play and experimental objects leads up to the mind-body dualism. According to Baldwin, the mind-body dualism arises through the child's differentiation between the way inner and outer mental objects persist. For example, if a child remembers its experiments with semblant objects, it will discover that inner and outer representations differ with respect to the type of control they possess. Outer mental objects all share the quality of external persistence, of control by something external. Inner objects are characterized by a sameness of inner control.

> The two persistences, looked at from this point of view, are correlative though not equivalent meanings. They represent the hardening dualism of controls. The external content, and with it the recognitive context of every sort, persists as "the same" in the sense that a form of control not subjective is recurrently and convertibly at work in it. Over against this inner life persists as "the same," not in the objective context which it holds, but in the control which this context embodies and is employed to fulfill. External persistence is a meaning of discontinuous function, remoteness, and recurrence; inner persistence is a meaning of continuous function, intimate ownership, and immediate presence. (Baldwin, 1906, p. 209)

With the recall of imitated behavior, the child begins to separate representations which are controlled by something external (the memory of the sense object which is the representational object of the imitation), and those with the mark of inner control. When the child recalls an imitative act, it must remember two representations and the relationship between them. The first representation is that of the representational object of the imitation, the second the imitative copy of the sense object itself. The former is represented as under foreign, external control; the latter is a representation claiming convertibility into its representational object, but subject to inner, mediate control. Furthermore, when children imitate the behavior of someone else, they discover that in the other person whom they perceived as merely outer before the imitation, there is a whole range of psychic events, some of which they themselves might have previously felt. At the same time, by the act of imitation they take over into the inner a body of data about actions and sensations which before imitating were thought by them to be merely outer, external, and not personal. Through repeated instances of this sort, the inner develops as "a more or less self-controlled mass of data . . . free from the outer persistence co-efficient (Baldwin, 1906, p. 210)." Control is now found to reside in two areas. One sort of control is located in mental objects which are controlled by the self and detached from any particular body, and the other in mental objects which are or stand for such bodies.

At this point in the child's cognitive development, the child is aware that the inner is a goal-directed, transformational, and controlling sphere of mental activity in its own right, separate from the control of the outer. Mind, or the psychic, becomes subjective when the child realizes that inner representations persist through control coefficients that are different from those of outer representations. In the experimental objects of the semblant mode, there is a sense in which the outer control is to be tested, while the inner control is already present in the mental object chosen to be tested. In the mind-body dualism, these two control coefficients are separated completely, inner control and choice being the coefficient of mind, outer control and resistance being the coefficients of body.

Subject-object dualism. According to Baldwin, the great dualism of mind and body that develops at the end of the substantive progression leads to certain problems for the child in interpreting his own body. The mind–body dualism separates the child's representations of mind and body into two exclusive categories of representations, each with its own control coefficient, which leads the child to classify its own body as exclusively "body" and in no sense "mind." However, two types of experiences tend to undermine the rigidity of this classification. First, it is through the child's muscular and emotional activity that it develops the experience of effort and volition which provide the ground for all activity controlled by the mind vis-à-vis the outer world, and these sensations are never completely separated from the mind. Second, the child views others as having inner processes which are "carried" with them, cooccurrent with their physical bodies. Through the combination of both these types of experiences, the child begins to realize that the mind is attached to the body through the experience of effort which brings outer meaning into the inner and also inner meaning out to the body. The body becomes a mediator between both internal and external processes, a locus of interaction which is both inner and outer. When the child applies these discoveries about its own cognitive processes to others (through the process Baldwin calls ejection), it realizes that its apprehension of the inner control processes of its own body is a common meaning with others. Both self and other are aware that each perceives its own body and that of the other as the locus of both inner and outer control.

This representation of the nature of the personal body is an "embarrassment" because the body has become a nexus between two types of representation, mind and body, which are under different types of control and thus viewed as separate and exclusive. The solution to the problem is to differentiate the control and representational aspects. What mind and body share in the substantive progression is that both are representations, content for thought, mental objects; what differentiates them is their different control coefficients. The body consists of those representations under external, outer control. The mind is externally determined to the extent it is located in a particular body, and it is not controlled by coefficients of exernal or extrapsychic control, but instead has a mark of agency and subjectivity. The inner has an objective, representational aspect, and is also a mode of control and organization, not representational, but transformational. This control factor is also tied up with the body through feelings of volition and effort, further complicating the mind-body dualism. The conflict is resolved when mind as objectively determined, as representational content, passes over into the total system of objectively determined content which will include all representations, all mental "objects." Mind and body are both treated as representations, as ideas. The subjective becomes all those unrepresentable factors of control which regulate and limit the organization of any kind of objective, representational content, and thereby escapes determination by that content. The subject–object dualism is completed when the separation of control and representation hardens, with all the "objective" coming under the control of the judging subject.

> It is of the essence of the achievement of this mode in which the new dualism of reflection is present, that all objects and meanings, which before belonged in especially distinguished worlds or spheres or classes—being "inner" or "outer," "extra-psychic" or "subjective," "recognitive" or "selective",—which represent dualisms of essential significance in the development of mental life as a whole, that all of these now become once for all part of a life of experience or of ideas which is now content of reflection. Everything thinkable or meanable, dreamable or semblable, real or unreal, now takes its place in the great system of thought-contents—everything except that one thing, the subject, which by just the movement which makes the entire world of such contents possible, holds its own presence and act in the shadow of a final reserve. (Baldwin, 1906, p. 252).

The subject becomes a pool of inner control, relating *ideas* of mind and body which are its objects.

Baldwin's sequence of developmental stages of cognition corresponds very nicely with the levels of goal-directed or self-correcting mechanisms outlined earlier. A goal-directed system has some internal goal setting or end which controls a range of behavior through a feedback process. The means are the system's interaction point with the environment. They face the outer, and produce changes in the environment so as to achieve some state of affairs congruent with the inner goal setting. All the distinctions that Baldwin draws upon to establish his developmental progression (inner, outer, transformational control) are present in rudimentary form in a goal-directed system. Baldwin's task can be interpreted as analyzing how the child gradually is able to represent these distinctions.

During Baldwin's prelogical period and Piaget's early sensori-motor stages, the child, though goal directed, has now awareness of means and end as separate and combinable. Its behavior is much like that of an antiaircraft gun programmed to follow and hit a target, or a computer that can play chess. Although to an outside observer the child does appear to do things in order to reach some end, the child does not cognitively differentiate between means (outer) and end (inner). However, by the fourth stage of Piaget's sensorimotor period, because of the development of what Baldwin calls *memory objects*, the child begins to distinguish between means and end, using a given schema as a means to reach an end connected with some other schema.

With the representation of means as separable, children enter Baldwin's quasilogical period. However, during the early part of this period, both means and ends are representations of external sense objects. The representations that constitute the inner goal settings or ends are still of external, outer reality (such as Lucienne wanting to get the watch chain). Only with the development of semblant mental objects (as in symbolic play) do the controlling inner representations begin to take on control coefficients which are no longer of external reality, but transformations of the outer, an example being the alteration of an imitative copy of sense objects for the purpose of play. The representations that constitute ends or goal settings are now seen as having a different type of control coefficient than those associated with the means. *Mind* becomes the class of all inner representations marked off as having inner, subjective control as compared with *body*, which consists of all those representations of bodies subject to outer, external, and nonsubjective control. In a goal-directed system established by negative feedback, means and end also have different control coefficients. The end acts upon the means, modifying them so as to reach the goal setting, whereas the means acts upon the environment transforming it in accordance with the goal setting. If a system can learn from the effects of its interactions with the environment, then the means (or body in many cases) acts as a mediator between both inner and outer. The means produces effects upon the environment, and in turn the success or failure of these interactions can change the inner goal setting. At this point in the Baldwin progression, children are able to represent means and end as separate, with the inner goal representations having the mark of agency and transformative power, while representing the body as a means subject to external control. The child also learns that its personal body is in an anomalous position with regard to the mind–body dualism, and that "the experience of effort . . . brings meaning inward into the mind, as it is also that experience that carries inner meaning outward into the body (Baldwin, 1906, p. 254)." The two types of control connected by a feedback process in a goal-directed system are thus separated, with one type associated with the mind and the other with the body.

In the mind–body dualism, mind and body are two classes or representations differentiated by different control coefficients. In the subject–object dualism, the control coefficients separated by the mind–body dualism are differentiated from their representational contents, mind and body, and reintegrated to form a reflective, judgmental self or subject. Both mind and body becomes ideas to a subject in which the previously separated control coefficients are united. The self or reflective subject now becomes a mediating locus of control. It no longer possesses any representational qualities, but rather acts upon representations of both mind and body which it distinguishes from its own control function. In the goal-directed model outlined, the self is now located in the self-correcting feedback process itself, uniting the two previously separated modes of control. This process controls both representations of mind and of body, treating them as ideas, as "mental objects" standing for or representing other mental objects or ideas.

Baldwin on the development of social meaning. Baldwin's developmental sequence depends heavily upon social interaction. It is through conscious imitation that children are able to develop some awareness of their own inners, and it is through realizing that others see their bodies as loci of both inner and outer control that children are forced from the mind–body dualism to that of subject and object.

When children are able to represent the intentionality of others, they become able to represent the social nature of that intentionality. Baldwin constructs a theory of social meaning based upon the levels of shared knowledge or belief that people have of each other's intentionality. In order to do this, he distinguishes between the knowledge or awareness that a subject has of his own psychological processes (*psychic* meaning) and the knowledge an outside observer might have of those processes (*psychological* or *objective* meaning). Baldwin then presents a series of levels of common meaning in which the higher levels of psychic meaning take as their intentional objects previous levels of psychological meaning.

For example, if Tom and Mike both believe that P, but do not know that the other believes that P, they each have a "simple" object or meaning. To an outside observer, they have an *aggregate* meaning: they both believe that P. When either one of them realizes that they both believe that P, then that person is psychically aware of the *psychological* aggregate meaning and has what Baldwin calls a *syndoxic* meaning, or common meaning in common. He believes they share a mutual belief. If one now imagines a situation where an observer is aware that both Tom and Mike are aware that they share a mutual belief, this observer would have an aggregate of syndoxic meaning, or as Baldwin calls it, a *con-aggregate* meaning. If this level of con-aggregate meaning were to become psychically real, the subject would have a *social* meaning, a knowledge of a con-aggregate meaning as common. This would occur, if Tom believed both that he and Mike believed that P, and also that each knew that the other knew that they both believed that P. An example might be deliberately telling a lie, knowing that the other person would know that you were doing so. Baldwin's last stage of common meaning is the case of an outside observer watching a group of people whose knowledge consisted of *social* meanings. This level of *public* meaning is a *social* meaning taken as common. There is a potentially infinite hierarchy of levels of mutual belief, but undoubtedly these levels become increasingly psychically unreal.

Baldwin's progression of levels is actually a hierarchy of levels of role-taking. At the level of *simple meaning*, the children have their own point of view, but do not realize that it can be shared by others. At the *syndoxic level*, they realize that their beliefs can be shared with others, that others can think the same things they do. Finally, at the level of *social meaning*, a person realizes that the other can think the same thing about one's self that one's self is thinking about the other, and that there is a potentially infinite regression of levels of role-taking. Kohlberg (1969) and Loevinger (1976) have placed a heavy emphasis on the development of role-taking skills as a necessary component in moral and ego development, and others such as a Flavell (1968) have argued that these skills also underlie linguistic development.

The key concept in Baldwin's theory of social meaning is that of levels of common meaning which presuppose that the child is able to represent the intentionality of others. His work also suggests that not only does the development of thought depend upon the representation of intentionality, but that the representation of intentionality is not sufficient to capture the social nature of inference. What people represent as being transformed in social interactions is not only the intentions and thought of others, but an emergent social definition of the situation (the common meaning) which cannot be reduced to the intentionality of any one agent. The development of the syndoxic level of common meaning is just as critical for the development of thought as the representation of intentionality and opens the way for a truly social theory of thought and inference.

The Self and Its Development

The development of the self has both cognitive and emotional aspects. Baldwin and Kohlberg have proposed that the cognitive aspects of self-development emerge out of social interaction through the child's imitation of and eventual identification with its role models. The basic motivation for such learning is cognitive effectancy which is another way of stating that inference is the process by which representations are changed so as to maximize cognitive coherence and explanatory power. In their view, the development of the child's ability to form ideals (representations which both guide and give meaning to its activities) plays a critical role in the child's self development.

Psychoanalytical theories have focused on the development of the child's emotional structure, and, at first glance, seem incompatible with the cognitive-developmental position. Recently, however, Heinz Kohut (1977) developed a psychoanalytically based theory of the child's emotional development in which the development of the child's self out of social interaction is a crucial component. Underlying this convergence of cognitive and psychoanalytical theories of the self is the thesis that the self emerges out of social interaction through the process of mutual interpretation between child and model. In order to explore the implications of this convergence, this section will discuss some of the conceptual relations between representations, emotions, the self, and a theory of developmental levels. The Baldwin–Kohlberg approach will then be analyzed, with special consideration of their views on identification and idealization which provide the link to the discussion of Kohut's theory of the self. Finally, mutual interpretation is introduced as the process which allows the integration of both approaches to form a unified theory of the cognitive and emotional development of the self.

Kenny (1963), for example, has pointed out that an emotion is a complex state of an organism consisting of certain thoughts and desires, accompanied by certain physiological sensations and symptoms. For example, if someone is afraid, he usually believes that something is threatening him and wants to escape the threat, perhaps with an accompanying pit-of-the-stomach sensation. If the requisite circle of thoughts, desires, and sensation is lacking, it becomes impossible to attribute a particular emotion to a person. If it is known that an animal believes it is threatened, it will be unclear whether it is afraid or angry unless it can also be determined whether it wants to escape the threat or attack the threatening object. The mere fact of something occurring in the world will not produce an emotional response without the mediation of some thought or belief. Your snubbing me at a party will not make me angry, unless I think that I have been snubbed.

Since every thought is the product of an inference from a person's total view, every emotion will have an inferential component. Since our emotions are produced by the inferences we make, then how we think can influence how we feel. I am angry because I think you have forgotten the appointment we made; I discover that I have misread my calendar and instantly my anger vanishes. My thoughts (which are based upon the inferences I have made) have changed my emotions and the way I feel.

If emotions involve beliefs and desires, then it is possible to attribute higher order emotions to organisms which possess higher-level intentional states. Human beings can become angry not only at what they infer are physical threats, but also at what they represent others as thinking about them, or even at someone's violation of a moral standard regardless of their intentions. Certain emotions, such as guilt or resentment, require higher levels of representational ability as part of their basic definition. With guilt, it seems necessary for the person who feels guilty that he be able to represent himself as violating some standard and blaming or condemning himself for that transgression. With resentment, it is possible to resent a person no matter what he does or what his intentions are. With the advent of second-order and higher representations, children become able to represent themselves and others as having certain beliefs and desires, as goal-directed systems which exist independently of their actions and representations and are separate centers of initiative. At the same time, certain aspects of the child's linguistic and communicative ability arise out of this underlying cognitive ability. Before the age of three or four, by adult standards the child's linguistic structure is still fairly primitive and many of its utterances do not show any ability to change its speech according to how it thinks others will interpret that speech (Halliday, 1975). As children become able to represent others as agents who base their behavior upon their own interpretations, their linguistic structures gradually enter the adult system. Since language is a social phenomenon based upon a mutual interpretative coordination problem between speaker and hearer, it is not surprising that some psychoanalysts have used the patient's linguistic reconstructions of early childhood events as the basis for much of their craft and have considered disorders which arise before the onset of second-order representations and the concomitant language skills as unanalyzable.

Although emotions have a representational component and thus can be influenced by changes in cognitive development, they are not reducible to those representations. Emotions may also involve feelings associated with the representations which make up their cognitive component. At the same time that children learn the cognitive structure of their world through their interactions with the world and others—where, when, and how to use certain goal directed procedures—they also learn through social interaction which feelings accompany the use of those procedures. For example, a young child learning how to put a puzzle together with his mother will have certain emotional responses to the task at hand. The mother will respond to these emotions in certain ways which may ease or aggravate the tensions and anxieties the child might feel while learning the cognitive procedures necessary to carry out the task. Later on, the child may be able to make the same puzzle by itself, without the aid of its mother, becoming self-regulated in its behavior. Besides having learned what to do from its mother, it has also learned from its mother's reactions to it, what to feel in such situations.

Emotions are the link between our desires, feelings, and representations of the world. They constitute our subjectivity and form a connection between theoretical reasoning which is concerned with how to represent the world (i.e., threatening in the case of fear), and practical reasoning which is concerned with what to intend (i.e., to flee or not to flee). Considerations of representational coherence are relevant to both theoretical and practical reasoning, and since emotions have a representational component, that component develops in accordance with the principles that underlie representational coherence such as consistency, simplicity, and explanatory power. Emotions involve inferences that constitute a person's sense of self as an agent, and function so as to maximize coherence among those representations. At the level of prelogical emotions, a goal to which the effect of maximizing coherence may contribute is that of self-survival. Fear functions so as to concentrate attention on a threat in the environment and prepare the appropriate flight response. The coherence in the self that is maximized by fleeing is probably to minimize the disruptive physiological sensations caused by the fear response. The sense of self at this first level of emotional development may consist only of the various sensations accompanying the representations produced by the fear provoking situation. The internal representations that constitute the goal are probably biologically based and developed through evolution.

At higher levels of representational ability, people may maximize the coherence between their representations of their interactions with others, how others think about them, and such coherence may function so as to maximize their self-esteem. For example, contempt maximizes a person's self-esteem by representing its object as inferior or subhuman (not an agent at all). More abstract representations are not produced by biological evolution, but are the product of higher-level social coordination problems.

Both cognitive developmental and psychoanalytical approaches have dealt with the problems of the self and social interaction. The former have concentrated on the cognitive aspects of self development, the latter on its emotional side. Baldwin, like some modern psychoanalytical thinkers such as Kohut (1977), insists that the child's self-concept develops out of social interaction and is directly correlated with the development of its conceptions of others, particularly of their goals and ideals. Young children first imitate the novel and interesting behavior of others, learning to transform that behavior into something they can do themselves. In so doing, they create and experience the feelings that accompany the imitated behavior. When they see others perform similar actions, they then "eject" these feelings and the accompanying intentional states upon the other, reading into the other via this "emphatic transference" what they themselves feel. Gradually, the child begins to be able to have second-order representations of how others think and feel in certain situations. At the same time, the child begins to realize that its physicialistic representations are confirmable not only through "primary conversion" or verification via immediate sense experience, but also through information supplied by others (Baldwin's *secondary conversion*). The child begins to go to others to confirm its own representations and behavior. Since others are the source of much that is interesting for it, it turns to them for confirmation of its imitative behavior. Gradually, this process of using significant others to confirm its own behavior becomes one of identification with and dependence upon the model. At first it merely imitates the behavior of others. As its cognitive ability increases, it then begins to imitate behaviors which it interprets as being relevant to the goals and thoughts of others, at the same time being dependent upon them for defining what is correct or incorrect (which procedures and activities are applicable in which situations).

Baldwin stresses that the child's self is dependent upon the development of its ideals. The child's ideals indicate to it which of its activities and representations of itself are peculiarly important and whose impact extends beyond its short-term goals. Ideals form the link between the child's activities and its future, giving it a representation of itself which remains constant across its development. Many of the rebuffs and frustrations the child suffers seem to have little long-term deleterious effect on its self-development because they do not affect its ideals. Attack the child's ideals or anything related to them, and it will react as if it were threatened. For example, a child might not care whether or not it was good at mathematics, but be very concerned abouts its ability to play baseball because its ideal for itself is to become a great baseball player like Mickey Mantle.

For Baldwin, *idealization* is a development out of the process of inference itself, "a reflection of the selective and prospective nature of the psychic process" (1906, p. 238). Theoretical reasoning is the process by which representations are changed in accordance with the goal of maximizing explanatory coherence, coherence among other representations of the ongoing situation. Learning implies that there is some standard which determines accuracy and error. If goal-directedness and feedback form the basis for cognitive development then idealization is a direct outgrowth of these processes, an attempt to put into representational form the processes of thought itself.

Idealization is a turning in of the process of inference upon itself, an attempt to create some representation toward which our actions strive, an ultimate telos which makes all of our activities meaningful and significant insofar as they are related to that goal which constitutes the ideal. Idealization unites both theoretical and practical reasoning, determining actions which make sense both emotionally and cognitively. With regard to theoretical reasoning, ideals are representations which function so as to maximize coherence among other representations of ourselves and our actions, and since idealization is the process by which such a representation is created, it is a representational analog to the process of theoretical reasoning itself. At the same time, idealization is an outgrowth of the semblant function of thought, and thus intimately tied to feelings of agency, emotions, and the inner itself. Like in play, the representations that make up our ideals are not real, but rather take reality as a given (the child plays at being a doctor, nurse, etc.) and adapt and modify it for personal ends. Ideals provide emotional coherence in the same way play does by allowing the child to inject an aura of counterfactuality into what it does, thus allowing it to give its actions further meaning by expanding their cognitive and emotional possibilities. Idealization is a development of inner representations which ultimately give both cognitive and emotional meaning to our actions, making these actions "stand for" something more than themselves. Baldwin (1906) states:

> It is characteristic of the organization of psychic stuff as such, to be progressive and selective; to aim at something no less than to recognize something; and these are the characters of the sort of meaning we call ideal. It is progressively embodied, but never completed, in the meaning already fulfilled. It selects and intends a fuller realization than that already accomplished. It sets up ends for attainment which are defined only so far as they embody insight beyond the present fact. (p. 237)

The ideals which guide the child's behavior change with its level of cognitive development. During the quasilogical period, the child at first merely imitates the behavior of interesting others. With the development of play and conscious imitation, it begins to incorporate not only the behavior of others, but also the feelings that accompany such behavior into its repertoire. By the end of this period, it imitates others' behaviors not just because the extensional portions are novel or interesting, but because such behaviors are interesting and novel marks of intentionality, of the inner. It sees its behaviors as interesting and competent insofar as they approach the goals and standards of the model. By the end of the quasilogical period, the child may interpret its parents' behavior as obeying some "external" rule or ideal. This would require seeing the rule or ideal as stable and controlling the goal directed behavior of the parents, as a coordination point among many inners which determine outer behaviors. When the child is able to represent the model as having its own ideals, separate from the child's, it can begin to choose to identify with an ideal model's ideals, and make judgments about its own and others' actions as standing for, or representing, the sort of goals that an ideal model might have, or as symbolic embodiments of some virtue or moral principle. These ideals begin to develop during Baldwin's logical mode of thought, and form the foundation for future moral judgments. At each level of development, the child's ideals make certain of its activities and abilities more important to it than others, establishing the bonds of coherence for the development of the self at each level.

Baldwin's theory of the development of the self contrasts interestingly with Piaget's theory of the development of imitation. In *Play, Dreams, and Imitation* (1962), Piaget presents a series of developmental stages for play and imitation which correspond to the sequence of sensorimotor stages outlined in his *Origins of Intelligence* (1936). For Piaget, imitation is an integral part of the development of the child's representational ability. In his model of cognition, thought develops through the child's ability to represent actions. This ability is tied to the process of equilibration, which is a balance between assimilation and accommodation. Assimilation takes place when the organism's representations function as the independent variable and the object or action to be represented functions as the dependent variable. Properties of the representational object are changed and modified so as to fit previous representations. Accommodation takes place when the organism's representations are modified in accordance with properties of the representational object. In accommodation, the organism's representations are the dependent variable. Adaptation occurs through a coordinated balancing between the assimilation of features of external reality to the organism's representations and the accommodation of these representations to features of external reality. This is a process which is similar to Harman's analysis of inference as reasoning to the best explanation consistent with one's total view of the world. Imitation is a process in which accommodation prevails because the child is trying to mold its behavior in accordance with features of the behavior of the model. Imitation is thus dependent upon the cognitive level of the representations that make up the child's world view. Piaget traces how changes in the child's cognitive development in the sensorimotor period change what it imitates. In the earliest forms of imitation, the child reproduces behaviors which are already part of its repertoire and are perceptually present to it. Only at the end of the sensorimotor period can the child imitate behaviors that are not part of its repertoire or reproduce behaviors of an absent model. Kohlberg (1969) points out that both Piaget and Baldwin are proposing cognitive effectance as the underlying motivation for the development of imitation.

> The assumption that the motivation of imitative behavior is best explained by effectance theory, then, is the assertion that the primary conditions which arouse imitation are a moderate degree of mismatch between the child's behavior structure and the behavior of the model (or later between the behavior structure of the child and the structure of the situation as this mismatch may be reduced by imitating the model), and the conditions which terminate it as a better state of match, balance, or "mastery" between the child's behavior and the model's (or between the child's behavior and the situation). (p. 434)

Children will imitate behaviors which are consistent with their world views, yet different enough to be novel and interesting. They thereby create representations of action which maximize explanatory power and yet are also consistent with his total world view.

Although Baldwin and Piaget share a competency model of cognition, Piaget's discussion of the developmental stages of imitation ends with the close of the sensorimotor period when the child can imitate the interesting and novel behavior of absent agents. Baldwin's theory of imitation begins at the transition point between the end of the sensorimotor period and the development of second-order representations. As children move up into Baldwin's quasilogical period, they imitate the behavior of others because they identify with the goals and later the ideals of their models. They begin to imitate the behavior of others because they are interesting and consistent with their second-order representations. Kohlberg (1969) extends Baldwin's theory of imitation into a complete developmental theory of identification which consists of:

> (1) tendencies to imitate the parent or other model; (2) emotional dependency and attachment to the parent; (3) tendency to conform to the parent's normative expectations; (4) perceived similarity to the

parent; (5) idealization of the parent or of his competence and virtue; (6) vicarious self-esteem derived from the parent's competence or status; (7) ability to derive self-esteem from the parent's approval and so to forego other sources of prestige or competence, with associated security of self-esteem, moderate level of aspiration, etc. (p. 426).

This process begins roughly at the age of four and extends almost until adolescence and is directly correlated with the development of second-order representations which allow the child to represent others as having beliefs, desires, and emotions. It imitates the behavior of others insofar as they are congruent with the goals and ideals of the models with whom it identifies.

Kohlberg also points out that the cognitive-developmental theory of identification and self-development differs from anaclitic theory in which (1) parental nurturance (and nurturance withdrawal) causes (2) identification, which leads to (3) the internalization of parental moral expectations and ideals. Instead, the cognitive-developmental progression is that the child's intrinsic competency motivation leads to its (1) imitation of the interesting model, which causes (2) its dependence on the model for definitions and competent behavior; leading to (3) attachment and dependence on the model. He then uses this model for the development of identification to criticize both psychoanalytic and social-learning theory approaches to moral and psychosexual development, showing that they presuppose a cognitive-developmental approach. In summarizing a great deal of research on sex-role development and moral reasoning, he concludes:

> There is little reason to support the Freudian view that father-identification is the result of anxiety based defensive inhibition of sexual or other impulses. While father-identification does relate to moral attitudes and adjustment, these relationships seem more interpretable as linked aspects in the development of positive identifications with normative social roles, than as aspects of either "superego formation" or "sex-role identification." (Kohlberg, 1966, p. 143)

Instead, Kohlberg proposes that the child develops a cognitive sex-role typing at around the age of two (several years before the Oedipal period) as indicated by the child's choosing sex-appropriate toys. Given this early sex typing, a boy will begin to imitate and then identify with his father along a gradient of perceived similarity between himself and his father. As this developmental process accelerates, it gradually begins to imitate and identify with its father's moral values and ideals.

Psychoanalysts might reply to Kohlberg's critique that even if he is correct about the development of the child's *conceptions* of self and other via imitation, what they are interested in is how the child *feels* about itself and others. Given that the child represents itself and others as such and such, the analyst would focus on how and why the child feels the way it does in that situation.

Cognitive-developmental theory has contributed little to the study of affect, and thus the two theories seem to be independent of each other. The cognitive developmental research seems to be focusing on factors irrelevant to the analyst. However, as pointed out earlier, there are developmental changes in emotional structure based on representational level: someone can become angry at what he thinks others think about him. A given interaction may be interpreted as threatening because it undermines an ideal one has identified with and is thus a threat to one's self whose coherency depends on the ideal. Recently, Heinz Kohut has developed a psychoanalytically based theory of the self which is similar to that of Baldwin-Kohlberg in emphasizing the relation between idealization and how the child's emotional structure is formed by social interaction. The affective structure of the self consists of an emotional "tension arc" between one's idealized goals and one's ambitions, between how one feels about one's activities and talent as they relate to one's ideals. The nuclear self emerges between the ages of two and four, just at the point when the child begins forming second-order representations. At this point, the affective structure of its nuclear ambitions develops through the empathic mirroring of its parents, and during late childhood (ages 4–6), nuclear idealized goal-structures develop. The quality of the emotional gradient between nuclear ideals and ambitions depends upon the empathic responses on the part of the parent to the child, which, in turn, is based on the parent's interpretation of the child and what that interpretation means to the parent. It is only when the cohesion of the self is threatened by nonempathic responses of the parents (or any figure the child has identified with) that the child turns to the various erogenous zones for self satisfaction and compensation for the lack of empathic support.

> It is the self of the child that, in consequence of the severely disturbed empathic responses of the parents, has not been securely established, and it is this enfeebled and fragmentation-prone self that . . . runs defensively toward pleasure aims through the stimulation of erogenic zones, and then, secondarily, brings about the oral (and anal) drive orientation and ego's enslavement to the drive aims correlated to the stimulated body zones. . . . From the beginning, the drive experience is subordinated to the child's experience of the relation between the self and the self-objects . . . (This) changes our evaluation of the significance of the libido theory on all levels of psychological development in childhood. (Kohut, 1977, p. 74)

If the healthy, self-assertive behavior of the child is not empathically responded to by other agents whom it looks up to, it may regress to controlling various erogenous zones for pleasure for itself. Some aspects of this psychoanalytic critique of classical drive theory are surprisingly similar to Kohlberg's (1969) conclusions that

> Freud's reasoning (1938) that pathological feelings of being blamed by others (paranoia) and of self-blame (depression) require a notion of fixed self-blaming structure, somewhat ego-alien but at the same time internalized within the psyche and based on identification, still seems convincing. Self-criticism and self-punishment by definition require identification in the broad sense of taking the role of the other, and severe forms of self-punishment and self-blame must be modeled in some sense on parental reactions in young childhood since the parent is ordinarily the only agent who engages in intensive punishment and blaming activities. (p. 472)

For Kohut, the key mechanisms in the child's development are the interpretations and interactions between the child and those other objects which are experienced as part of its self ("self-objects") such as its parents.

> I suggest that we undertake the examination of the question of the existence of a rudimentary self in earliest infancy from a perhaps surprising starting point, namely by stressing that the human environment reacts to even the smallest baby as if it had already formed such a self ... The crucial question concerns, of course, the point in time when, within the matrix of mutual empathy between the infant and his self object, the baby's innate potentialities and the self-object's expectations with regard to the baby converge. Is it permissable to consider this juncture the point of origin of the infant's primal, rudimentary self?
> ... (The infant) is, from the beginning, fused via mutual empathy with an environment that does experience him as already possessing a self—an environment that not only anticipates the later self-awareness of the child, but already, by the very form and content of its expectations, begins to channel it into specific directions ... The nuclear self, in particular, is not formed via conscious encouragement and praise and via conscious discouragement and rebuke, but by the deeply anchored responsiveness of the self-objects, which, in the last analysis, is a function of the self-objects' own nuclear selves. (Kohut, 1977, p. 99–100)

This is also the key point of the Baldwin–Kohlberg analysis. The self emerges out of social interaction. In their interactions with their child, parents are constantly interpreting the child's goal-directed behavior in terms of the ideals they have for the child. By empathically or nonempathically responding to the child, they segment, create, and indicate which of the child's activities mean more emotionally and are important for the child's development of its own nuclear self. Through their interpretation of it and what it means to them in terms of their aspirations for it (interpretations which depend on their own nuclear selves), they establish the child's nuclear ambitions and goals and its feelings toward having those ambitions and ideals. Between the ages of 2 and 4, the child is also learning the second-order aspects of these abilities and ideals. Since it is at this point that the child begins to represent others as agents, it is not surprising that this time is developmentally critical both cognitively and emotionally. The child imitates the behavior of interesting others. Those others will in turn interpret and respond to its behavior, giving it not only the feedback necessary to establish and confirm its cognitive strategies, but also, by the emotional quality of their interactions, determining how it feels about how it represents itself and others. As the identificatory process begins, it will internalize the cognitive structure of significant others, and its feelings about others will develop through their reactions to it. As its representational abilities develop, it will identify not only with the behavior of its models, but also their goals, ideals, thoughts, etc. Two possible scenarios disruptive to the child's self-development and thus relevant to psychopathology come to mind.

In the first one, the child proudly performs some piece of behavior for the model's approval which the model finds unacceptable and instead of supporting the child's healthy self-assertiveness, responds inappropriately, undoing the child's originally healthy emotion. An example might be a child presenting a fecal gift to its parents for their approval and their immediately interpreting and responding to the behavior as if it were deliberately done to upset them. The other, possibly more damaging situation might be when the child imitates and presents for the model's approval, behaviors of the model which the model finds unacceptable in itself.

If the self emerges out of social interaction through the interpretive mechanism just outlined, then meaning and interpretation become the key to the development of the self, as Baldwin pointed out over fifty years ago. Both the child's representations and its feeling about itself and others emerge out of this interpretive matrix. The child strives for the sort of representational coherence described by Harman, seeking a maximum of explanatory power and simplicity consistent with previous representations. The principles underlying such coherency are probably very close to those underlying Piaget's equilibration model. In both cases there is a fine balance struck between previous thoughts and the new experiences which must be integrated. However, since the basic cognitive categories develop out of the interpretive situation, they will be derived from the child's ability to represent others as agents not just from the object interaction situations Piaget focuses upon. Furthermore, the *cognitive* aspects of the development of the child's self are dependent upon a special category of its agent-representations, namely its ideals, and these develop through the imitation-identification process outlined earlier.

Besides its cognitive coherence, a child's emotional coherence, the way it feels about itself and others, also develops out of the interpretive situation between parent and child. At the same time as it learns to represent the world and others in increasingly complicated ways structured by social interaction, its feelings toward the world and others are also developing, perhaps along the self-ambition-ideal gradient Kohut describes. If the parents' responses to the child (which are based upon their interpretations of it) are phase-inappropriate, the child's emotional coherence will be threatened and possibly fragmented.

The premise that the self develops out of the interpretive situation allows an integration between psychological and cultural theories of meaning. If the parents' interpretations of their child's behavior are based on inferences consistent with their total world view, then the total cultural order (where culture is considered to be a set of meanings which constitute a person's world view) is present in the parent-child situation. If the child's self develops through the imitation-identification-idealization process outlined, then it is the parents' interpretations which not only create the child's goal-directed representations, but also create the child's self by establishing the cognitive and emotional links between those representations and his nuclear self. The parents interpret some of the child's interactions as relevant to the aspirations they have for it, and by picking these out through their empathic reactions to it, they establish the emotional connections between its nuclear ambitions and ideals, tapping into the very goal-directed nature of the inferential process itself. It is their interpretations, derived from their cultural world view which segments out, selects, and creates which of the child's activities are relevant to what later will become its own ideals. Interpretation and the push for coherence, both cognitive and emotional, establish the link between activity and ideal, action and self, not drive reduction. Fixation on bodily functions occurs only in the face of nonempathic response to the self, a regression to the control and possession of part of the self rather than the whole, to individualized pathological gratification.

The later volumes of *Thought and Things* treat the development of formal logical thinking, aesthetics, and ethics. In all these domains, idealization plays a critical role; since idealization is part of the process of inference itself and all these domains have an inferential component, Baldwin uses it to link cognitive and emotional development with aesthetic and moral development. These other volumes suggest the possibility of an integrated study of man rather than the separation of perspectives characteristic of much present research. As Baldwin emphasized many years ago, such an integrated study of man is only possible if the theoretical apparatus starts with the nature of inference itself and proceeds to study how psychological development is dependent on the ability to represent others as agents able to modify their behavior in terms of their own goals, ideals, and interpretations. To focus only on extensionality is to eliminate the possibility of an integrative apprach, to mistake the dead, outer skin for the living, inner subject.

REFERENCES

Baldwin, J. M. *Thought and things (Vol. 1)*. New York: MacMillan, 1906. Reprint, New York: Arno, 1975.

Baldwin, J. M. *Thought and things (Vol. 3)*. New York: MacMillan, 1911. Reprint, New York: Arno Press, 1975.

Carnap, R. *Meaning and necessity*. Chicago: Univ. of Chicago Press, 1956.

Colby, A. & Kohlberg, L. The relationship between logical and moral development. Unpublished paper, 1977.

Davidson, D. Agency. In R. Binkley, R. Bronaugh, A. Marras (Eds.). *Agent, action, and reason*. Toronto: Univ. of Toronto Press, 1971.

Flavell, J. *The developmental psychology of Jean Piaget*. Princeton: Van Nostrand, 1963.

Flavell, J., Botkin, P. T., Fry, C. L., Wright, J. W., & Jarvis, P. E. *The development of role-taking and communication skills in children*. New York: Wiley, 1968.

Frege, G. Uber Sinn und Bedeutung, 1892. In *Philosophical writings of Gottlob Frege*, (P. Geach and M. Black, trans. & ed.). London: Oxford Univ. Press, 1960.

Friedman, M. Explanation and scientific understanding. *The Journal of Philosophy, 71*, 1974, 1.

Furth, H. *Piaget and knowledge*. Englewood Cliffs H. J. : Prentice Hall, 1969. (second edition: University of Chicago Press, 1981).

Ginsburg, H. & Opper, Sylvia. *Piaget's theory of intellectual development: An introduction*. Englewood Cliffs, N.J.: Prentice Hall, 1969.

Halliday, M. *Learning how to mean*. London: Edward Arnold, 1975.

Harman, G. *Thought*. Princeton: Princeton Univ. Press, 1973.

Kenny, A. *Action, emotion, and will*. London: Routledge & Kegan Paul, 1963.

Kohlberg, L. A cognitive-developmental analysis of children's sex-role concepts and attitudes. In E. Maccoby (Ed.). The Development of Sex Differences. Stanford: Stanford Univ. Press, 1966.

Kohlberg, L. Stage and sequence: The cognitive-developmental approach to socialization. In D. A. Goslin (Ed.), *Handbook of socialization theory and research*. Chicago: Rand McNally, 1969.

Kohut, H. *The restoration of the self*. New York: International Universities Press, 1977.

Lewis, D. *Convention*. Cambridge, Mass.: Harvard Univ. Press, 1969.

Loevinger, J. *Ego development*. San Francisco: Jossey-Bass, 1976.

Piaget, J. *Origins of intelligence in children*. New York: Norton, 1952 (originally 1936).

Piaget, J. *The construction of reality in the child*. New York: Basic Books, 1954.

Piaget, J. *Play, dreams, and imitation*. New York: Norton, 1962.

Piaget, J. *Psychology of intelligence*. Totowa, N.J.: Littlefield & Adams, 1966.

Piaget, J. *Genetic epistemology*. New York: Columbia Univ. Press, 1970.

Piaget, J. *Structuralism*. New York: Harper & Row, 1970.

Rescher, N. *Peirce's philosophy of science*. Notre Dame, Ind.: Univ. of Notre Dame Press, 1978.

Searle, J. What is an international state? *Mind* 1979, No. 349.

Shatz, M. & Gelman, R. The development of communication skills: Modifications in the speech of young children as a function of listener. *Monographs of the Society for Research in Child Development*, 1973. 152, 38, no. 5.

Sinclair, H. Note On Piaget and dialectics. *Human Development*, 21, 211–213.

Vygotsky, L. *Mind in society*. Cambridge, Mass.: Harvard Univ. Press, 1978.

Woodfield, A. *Teleology*. Cambridge, Mass.: Cambridge Univ. Press, 1976.

PART IV

THE DEVELOPMENT OF THEORETICAL AND PRACTICAL REASON

Introduction

A major part of Baldwin's *oeuvre* was his construction of a genetic version of Kantian rationalism. Kant had distinguished pure (theoretical) and practical reason *(Vernunft)* from empirical intelligence or understanding (*Verstand*). The significance of this distinction has recently been pointed out in an important work by the late Hannah Arendt (1977, Vol. 1). Reason involves "principles known variously as categories, laws of thought, a priori principles etc." (Baldwin, 1930, p. 21). Intelligence, or intellect, designates reasoning, knowing, or "cognition" as we would currently call it. The aim of cognition is truth, whereas the aim of reason is meaning.

Baldwin followed Hegel in assuming that the metaphor of genesis not only could, but must, be transferred to the realm of reason and intellect. This meant that both the *a priori*, formal aspects of the mind and its knowledge had to be interpreted in terms of a developmental process. Like Hegel, Baldwin arrived at a grand scheme depicting the emergence of rationality as a stage-by-stage progress. Like Hegel, Baldwin proposed that this progressive movement took place through a self–other dialectic. Unlike Hegel, Baldwin cast his whole scheme in the Darwinian mould, arguing that the mind—even in its *a priori* forms of thought—could be "looked upon as variations empirically hit upon and fixed by selection" (Baldwin, 1930, p. 21). Thus both the progressive developmental movement and the self-other dialectic that was its vehicle were removed from the metaphysical sphere that Hegel had placed them in and transported to the empirical plane. Mental development was to be studied in terms of natural modes of psychic functioning as they became adaptively organized. What Baldwin called his *psychogenetic* inquiry complemented in a consistent manner Darwin's *biogenetic* approach to the phylogeny of mind, which was taken up by empirical psychology at the end of the nineteenth century.

Baldwin presented his psychogenetic analysis in terms of a general progression of levels of consciousness. As in Hegel, these were constructed and described in such a way that they combined the ontogeny of the individual with the history of philosophy (the intellectual development of the race, if you like). In addition, the levels of consciousness could be read as a phenomenology: an analysis of the layers of prereflective and reflective experience compounded in any activity of the mature mind. Like phenomenologists, Baldwin appealed for evidence to our common experience and our reflective knowledge about that experience, rather than to experimental or observational studies. Unlike most phenomenologists, Baldwin was not adverse to experimental psychology. Far from it: he had in fact founded one of the first laboratories of experimental psychology in the British Commonwealth, in Toronto in 1900. Rather, he appealed to the "empirical" data of our own consciousness because of the way in which he construed the psychogenetic method itself:

> Its problem is that of tracing out by the observation of the processes actually going on the essential stages of mental development of the normal human minds taken singly or in groups—the reconstruction of the essential experience by which each individual mind lives, together with its fellows, through its life history from infancy to maturity. This takes us into a research which is mainly subjective, since it must be controlled at every stage by direct individual or social experience. (Baldwin, 1930, p. 11)

The phenomenological implications of Baldwin's theory and method have not been taken up in any subsequent psychological writings. However, the stage-by-stage account and the self–other dialectic have formed the basis of two major social science traditions in American academe. The structural transformations represented by Baldwin's stages are now familiar to us through cognitive-developmental psychology (Piaget, Kohlberg, et al.), while the dialectic of self and other inspired the tradition of symbolic interactionism in sociology and social psychology (Becker, 1968).

The developmental stage theory can be divided into two parts. First, there is the development of theoretical reason and scientific intelligence, primarily dealt with by Baldwin in his (1906) *Thought and Things (Vol. 1)*. Second, there is the development of practical reason and the active, rather than cognitive, life of the mind. This is dealt with in *Social and Ethical Interpretations* (1897). an earlier work which treats morality in combination with religious consciousness. The first named work, while functionally oriented, is the clearest presentation of the stage theory, while the second best explicates the dialectic of self and other.

Both these books, now rightly considered classics, remained works of speculative pshychology for half a century and more. While some influence on Piaget is suspected (see the interview in Chap. 3), there was no explicit incorporation of Baldwin's ideas into an empirical psychology until Lawrence Kohlberg's (1958) pioneering dissertation. Kohlberg not only borrowed from Baldwin's ideas, but made an important contribution in amalgamating the two aspects of his thinking that we have just mentioned. Educated at Chicago, Kohlberg was naturally influenced by the heritage of Dewey and Mead. However, as he points out in his chapter, a chance encounter with the much less known writings of Baldwin led him eventually to feel much closer to him than to the Chicago School. Kohlberg's work is strongly in the symbolic interactionist tradition which, broadly construed, embraces Baldwin, Mead, Dewey, and Cooley. From this school of thought, Kohlberg derives his central theoretical concept of *role-taking* which, he argues, is the basis of morality *qua* justice. With the concept of role-taking, Kohlberg was able to "psychologize" formalist ethics in the Kantian tradition, interpreting justice as an "ideal role-taking structure" (cf. Rawls, 1971).

Where Kohlberg departs from (or creates his own version of) symbolic interactionism is in emphasizing the cognitive and "monological" aspects of role-taking. Whereas in Baldwin and Mead role-taking and imitation are functionally defined as processes of self-other dialogue, Kohlberg focuses on the cognitive-structural representation of role-taking in the judgments of individuals. Influenced by the monological structuralism of Piaget and employing Piaget's interview methodology, Kohlberg arrived at a six-stage theory of the development of individual moral cognition. Strangely enough, Baldwin had anticipated such a six-stage scheme of intrapsychic structures. In Chapter 7, Benjamin Lee describes this little-known segment of Baldwin's writing (see also Broughton, 1974, chap. 5). Kohlberg appears to have been unaware of this more monological and structural account, or at least he could not have been very affected by it. At any rate, however, Kohlberg's stages were attained, they bore a considerable resemblance to the steps in the evolution of moral consciousness described by Baldwin.

A generation later, John Broughton took up another side of the task of relating Baldwin's theory to empirical psychology. Influenced by both Piaget and Kohlberg, as well as by some empirical studies by William Perry (1968), he undertook an interview study somewhat parallel to Kohlberg's, although less inclusive in scope. The focus of this study was theoretical reason: the categories and structural relations of concepts underlying naive metaphysical and epistemological beliefs. Thus Broughton was more influenced by *Thought and Things* (especially Volume 1) than by *Social and Ethical Interpretations*, and there is no explicit debt to symbolic interactionist concepts in his developmental scheme.

In his chapter, Broughton lays out in detail the framework of Baldwin's *genetic logic*, pointing out that this was not a stage theory in the modern sense of the term. While Piaget can be considered a functionalist psychologist in many ways (Broughton, 1979), he is much more a structuralist than is Baldwin. Because Baldwin is equally concerned with the possible historical and phenomenological interpretations of his levels of consciousness, he does not describe them as stage-by-stage transformations of the structure of intelligence. He prefers instead to emphasize the functional role of each new level as it interacts with and restructures previous modes of experience. His theory is also far wider in scope than Piaget's, bearing upon sense, meaning, aesthesis, sociality, religion etc., rather than just the purely structural features of scientific knowing.

Nevertheless, the Piagetian and Baldwinian projects have many features in common. The levels of consciousness are like Piagetian structural stages in that they are both created and destroyed by contradictions that they embody. In the sphere of theoretical reason, these contradictory organizations take the form of *dualisms* in consciousness, one dualism at each level in Baldwin's scheme. Development is motivated by inconsistencies arising when the attempt to impose these dualistic frameworks upon experience falls short of complete success. Starting from an adualistic consciousness, the mind moves progressively through an inner-outer dualism, a mind-body dualism, and a subject-object dualism, before reaching the *telos* or endpoint of the theoretic interest, the final mode of immediate aesthetic experience in which all dualisms are reconciled.

Broughton describes an empirical interview study which found, in the material of reflective discourse between interviewer and subject, corroboration of the sequence of dualisms proposed by Baldwin. Broughton offers this description in the context of an "ego-developmental" theory of his own. This set of developmental levels of the self draws out and elaborates some parts of Baldwin's original theory. Broughton's findings indicate the validity of the opinion often voiced in contemporary cognitive-developmental psychology that Piaget's theory "gave up too early." It is becoming increasingly clear that there is intellectual development in various domains "beyond formal operations" (Broughton, 1977).

Kohlberg's chapter presents some original scholarship concerning Baldwin's moral philosophy and its relation to traditions in ethics and social theory. This scholarly work was initiated by Kohlberg as a graduate student 25 years ago. This is the first publication of the important conceptual and philosophical insights that set the scene for his own theoretical and empirical work in moral development. This is of particular interest at a time when Kohlberg's own research has moved away from philosophic concerns toward two other activities; the completion of his psychometric instrument (Kohlberg, 1978a; Kohlberg et al., 1978), and the significant 'social engineering' experiments in education and prison reform (Kohlberg, 1978b; Kohlberg et al., 1975).

Kohlberg gives a thorough account of Baldwin's approach to the sequential development of practical reason (value and obligation, the good and the ought).[1] He shows how this domain of *active* reason, comprising the norms and imperatives of conduct, evolves through a sequence of levels parallel to those in the domain of theoretical reason.[2] This sequence starts from an adualistic state, and proceeds via instrumental morality to an ideal ethical stage. Progress through these levels entails transformations in the objects of affective interest, advancing from identification with personal images to an eventual valuing of abstract principles. As Habermas (1975) has remarked, this process of universalization of norms and identifications could be

---

[1] Note that Baldwin, unlike Kant, Kohlberg, and Rawls, subordinates justice and duty to the *good*. Technically speaking, then, his ethical theory is a teleological rather than a deontological one, although his teleology is by no means utilitarian. (For a lucid treatment of these different approaches to moral theory, see Boyd, 1977).

[2] For Baldwin, as for Kant, there is a certain priority of practical reason over its theoretical equivalent. This is somewhat paradoxical in the case of Kant, who initiates his critiques by starting with the cognitive rather than the moral subject (Broughton, 1980). Baldwin's opus is less contradictory in that he has always clearly stated that the thinking individual is socially formed and is really an abstraction from the intersubjective context.

compared in many ways (although Kohlberg does not do so) with the sequence described in Parsons's structural functionalist theory (Parsons & Bales, 1955).

Kohlberg's own research has illuminated and made concrete the speculative scheme which Baldwin presented in *Social and Ethical Interpretations* and in *Thought & Things (Vol. 3)*. This research with adolescents has led Kohlberg to define three basic levels of moral reasoning: preconventional, conventional, and postconventional, corresponding in many respects to Baldwin's levels of value and obligation. The latter levels are partially paralleled by the better known moral stages of Piaget (1932), which were actually formulated in explicit contrast to Baldwin's theory (Piaget, 1932, pp. 386-395). However, Kohlberg argues, it is Baldwin's stages rather than Piaget's that fit the facts. Elsewhere, Kohlberg (1958) demonstrates that Piaget's account of moral development does not meet the criteria for a structural stage theory anyway.

In addition, there are specific important features of moral development captured by Baldwin's scheme but not by Piaget's. Baldwin, for example, is able to account for the emergence and transformation of sentiments of "respect" (see Wallwork's Chapt. 10), whereas Piaget is not. Baldwin shows how duty in the sense of truly ethical obligation cannot arise until an ideal moral self has been formulated, a stage not present in Piaget's account. Piaget sees the sense of duty arising at an earlier point, and so does not continue research beyond adolescence, where he feels that moral judgment is already "autonomous."

Baldwin's account also extends beyond Piaget's in delineating the noncognitive side of moral development: "affective role-taking" and the "conflict of wills." For Baldwin, the determinant of moral action is a *self*, implying the centrality of will. For Baldwin, this self is shared, it is a *socius*. This means that experience is social from the start. This self is *bipolar*, revolving around a self–other axis. Thus, Baldwin proposes a qualitatively different notion of reciprocity from that outlined by Piaget. The latter sees moral development as involving decreasing egocentrism, and thereby depicts progress as movement away from the self rather than toward it (Broughton, 1980).

Kohlberg moves on to show how Baldwin's account of the development of the ideal self (also described in Wallwork's chapter) has implications for the broad spectrum of social development in general, and not only for the moral domain. Baldwin's theory helps make sense of empirical findings on human social bonds in general, including such key processes as attachment and identification, which involve various kinds of sharing between self and other. Baldwin's goal was a genetic account comprehending everything mental, and so leads us away from the professionalized fragmentation of psychology and back towards a synthetic developmental theory encompassing the whole of social development, as well as the growth of logical, scientific and philosophical concepts.

REFERENCES

Arendt, H. *The life of the mind* (Vol. 1). New York: Harcourt Brace & Jovanovich, 1977.

Baldwin, J. M. *Social and ethical interpretations in mental development.* New York: Macmillan, 1897.

Baldwin, J. M. *Thought and things* (Vol. 1). London: Swan Sonnenschein, 1906.

Baldwin, J. M. *Thought and things* (Vol. 3). London: Swan Sonnenschein, 1911.

Baldwin, J.M. James Mark Baldwin. In C. Murchison (Ed.), *The history of psychology in autobiography.* New York: Russell & Russell, 1930.

Becker, F. *The structure of evil.* New York: Free Press, 1968.

Boyd, D. The moralberry pie: some basic concepts. *Theory into Practice,* 1977, *16,* 67–72.

Broughton, J. M. The development of natural epistemology in the years 10–26. Unpublished doctoral dissertation, Harvard University, 1974.

Broughton, J. M. 'Beyond formal operations': theoretical thought in adolescence. *Teachers College Record,* 1977, *79,* 1, 87–98.

Broughton, J. M. Developmental structuralism: Without self, without history. In H. K. Betz (Ed.), *Recent approaches to the social sciences.* Winnipeg: Hignell, 1979.

Broughton, J. M. Piaget's structural developmental psychology, Parts I–V. *Human Development,* 1981, *24.*

Broughton, J. M. Psychology and the history of the self: from substance to function. In R. W. Rieber & K. Salzinger (Eds.), *The roots of American psychology.* New York: Academic Press (1980).

Habermas, J. Moral development and ego identity, *Telos,* 1975, *24,* 41–55.

Kohlberg, L. The development of modes of moral thinking and choice. Unpublished doctoral dissertation, University of Chicago, 1958.

Kohlberg, L. The meaning and measurement of moral development. Paper presented at the annual meeting of the American Psychological Association, Toronto, August 1978. (a)

Kohlberg, L. Reconsiderations on the relation between developmental theory and educational practice. Paper presented at the University of Minnesota, April, 1978. (b)

Kohlberg, L., Scharf, P., & Hickey, J., The 'just community' approach to corrections: the Niantic experiment. In L. Kohlberg (Ed.), *Collected papers on moral development and moral education* (Vol. 2). Cambridge: Center for Moral Education, Harvard University, 1975.

Kohlberg, L., Colby, A., Gibbs, J., & Speicher-Dubin, S. Standard form scoring manual for moral judgment. Cambridge: Center for Moral Education, Harvard University, 1978.

Parsons, T., & Bales, R. F., *Family socialization and interaction process.* Glencoe, Ill.: Free Press, 1955.

Perry, W. *Intellectual and ethical development in the college years.* New York: Holt, Rinehart & Winston, 1968.

Piaget, J. *The moral judgement of the child.* New York: Free Press, 1965 (1932).

Rawls, J., *A theory of justice,* Cambridge, Mass.: Harvard Univ. Press, 1971.

8

GENETIC LOGIC AND THE DEVELOPMENTAL PSYCHOLOGY OF PHILOSOPHICAL CONCEPTS

John M. Broughton
Teachers' College, Columbia University

Modern psychology involves a series of assumptions about knowledge that Baldwin did not accept: (1) that scientific and philosophical thinking are academic activities confined to their respective professions; (2) that philosophical thought is speculative and has no place in a scientific psychology; (3) that knowledge is essentially pragmatic, serving to reach goals, solve problems, and generally make itself useful; and (4) that knowing is therefore an activity which has no place for reflection. In contrast to these positivistic preconceptions, Baldwin argued forcibly that all knowledge has a theoretical interest based in reflection, that all individuals in the full course of development come to reason scientifically *and* philosophically, that these two types of reflective knowing are necessarily intertwined, that they grow out of developmentally lower levels of common sense knowledge, and that any psychology has to account for the emergence of such reflective forms of knowledge if it is to achieve scientific objectivity.

When Baldwin's position is taken seriously, a significant empirical task comes to the fore: the mapping of the developmental emergence of naive "theorizing," whether it be reflective scientific or philosophical knowledge. Elsewhere (Broughton, 1980), I have called this the developmental psychology of world views. Baldwin's "genetic logic" provides a useful framework for directing such an inquiry.

In this chapter, an exploratory study will be described which was conducted within that framework. The results of that research will then be used to give some empirical content to Baldwin's scheme of development. The aim is to shed some light on the relevance that Baldwin's theory still has for modern psychology, and the contribution which psychology can make in turn to interpreting and validating Baldwin's claims. As we shall see, the interpenetration of philosophical and empirical projects raises some important and knotty problems for a theory of intellectual development.

Baldwin's "Genetic Logic"

Baldwin conceived of "Logic" in its traditional, broad sense, including all aspects of the structure and function of knowledge. Its various components and their relations (Table 1) are expounded in detail in a four-volume series (Baldwin, 1906, 1908, 1911, and 1915). The grand developmental scheme of nine logical modes which he presents is summarized in Table 2. This table draws out from Baldwin's oeuvre, and particularly from his 'functional logic,' those developmental levels which have to do specifically with the theoretical interest of scientific and philosophical thought, rather than social, moral, religious, or aesthetic consciousness.

The logical level of consciousness proper, where thought is mediated by rational judgment, is attained only gradually via prelogical and quasilogical levels. As the developing individual passes through these levels, he or she encounters a sequence of cognitive dualisms (as we have already seen in the second half of Chap. 6, and the middle section of Chap. 7). The resolution of each dualism eventuates in a qualitatively reorganized theoretical world view. In each new world view, concepts of self, mind, body, reality, and truth are reworked in relationship to one another.

Development starts from an original state of adualism, or self-world fusion. From here, attempts to consistently relate sense, memory, and imagination gradually lead to the initial separation of two realms. One realm is that of real happenings which are marked by their persistent relation to external sense. Any impression of such events can, at least in principle, be traced back to some sensory object, a process Baldwin calls primary conversion. Such happenings are separated cognitively from those events which cannot be objectified and found to persist in that manner, a vague realm housing feelings, images, dreams, and errors of memory. This provides the basis for the first rough division of experience into interior and exterior poles. Baldwin calls this phase the inner-outer dualism. This rending of the psychic texture in twain is potentiated by the agency

TABLE 1
General scheme of organization of Baldwin's "Genetic Logic," as presented in his five-volume series (1906–1915)

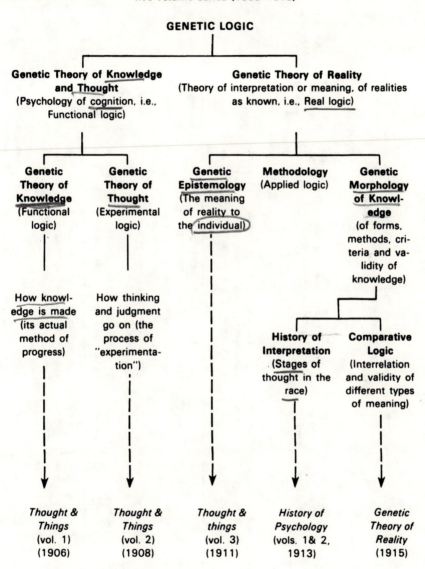

Table 2
Baldwin's Genetic Analysis of Consciousnss in its Passage Towards and Eventual Transcendence of Mind/Body Dualism

Logical Mode	Psychic Objects	Dualism (forms of persistence)	Dialectic (to be mediated)	Psychic Organization and Kinds of Existence Experienced	Conflict or Disequilibrium (which "embarrasses" the current psychic organisation, leading to further genetic advance)	Common Meaning	Corresponding Histori-cal Stage
A. PRE-LOGICAL	1. SENSE	*"Adualistic"* (animistic)	Figure & ground	Presentation and its reality not distinguished. Only an incipient perception of persons as different from things. Reality presumed.	Nonvoluntary (experience under external control)		Projective
	2. MEMORY (representation)	Present vs. Persisting	Person & thing	*Factual* (persistent) memories of perception, always "convertible" into the represented sense object, i.e. the original object of sense can always be restored to immediate perception (at least in principle).	Inconsistency between sense and memory.	Psychic	
B. QUASI-LOGICAL	3. FANCY	*Inner* vs. *Outer* (personal vs. impersonal)	Fancy & reality	The first notion of mind. Non-factual images (lacking persistence), as well as convertible representations. Since the inner is entirely confined to fleeting imaginary objects, the only persistence it has is insofar as the inner *world* continues to exist, as ground to the figure. Subjectively determined actions of imitation and play articulate the segre-	By "introjection," the inner psychic is found to include outer; by "ejection" the outer is found to include the inner. (a) More conscious control: objective fact can be distinguished from subjective fancy by testing memories through	Anomic	Subjective

gation of inner and outer worlds. Imitation separates inner psychic state from external manifestation, and tests the image so formed by exemplifying it. Embarrassments of the paradoxical body are thus "solved" by split into inner and outer moieties. Through imitation, inner feelings of the private body are seen to be part of a collective subjective shared with others, no longer inaccessible simply because not immediately given to the senses. Similarly, the outer takes on the character of a shared objective realm. The self is found to be imitated by others too, leading to a reciprocal effect. The other, previously outer, now becomes inner as well.

Playful experimentation connects fancy objects with potential objects of sense, introducing a degree of control into the subjective realm, and a degree of reconciliation between sense and memory.

the body, to see if they represent something separate from the body. *But the body is not only outer, public and impersonal; it is also inner, private, and personal.*

(b) Convertible memory is *outer*, as is its object, although clearly it has psychic characteristics in common with pseudo-memory (fancy).

	Syndoxic	Ejective

4. PLAY

Semblance & memory | Objects of play as a "semblance" of the real world are distinguished from memories of it (imagination vs. image). This ambiguous sembling is a kind of pre-experimental activity which assumes reality rather than presuming it, and provides the basis for *possible* or *probable* existence (knowledge as imaginative and schematic).

Doubt, residing in mere possibility, conflicts with a passionate will-to-believe (as in superstition).

Different customs and habits conflict.

Con-aggregate	Objective
	Immature dualism

Table 2 (continued)

Baldwin's Genetic Analysis of Consciousness in its Passage Towards and Eventual Transcendence of Mind/Body Dualism

Stage	Dimension	Sub-label	Description	Detail	Level	Dualism type
5. SUBSTANTIVE	*Mind* vs. *Body*	Existent & nonexistent	The inner, detached as a general class from specific bodies, now hardens into a substance. Mind, which combines all selves. Reality as common to different selves assumes a persistence and unity of its own through processes of "social conversion" or corroboration. The private body is included wholly in Body (outer physical substance). Mind and Body form a pair of contrasting substances, true general classes subsuming particular minds and bodies. "Experimental thought," prepared in the play mode, becomes possible because there are now clear answers: the child can now ask schematic questions re experienced objects and get an answer one way or other, in terms of either Mind or Body kinds of existence (inner or outer substance).	Conflict between inner/outer and Mind/Body dualism. a) As previously, the private body *has characteristics of Mind*. b) Mind, in both action and sense perception, *works only through the private body*, and is dependent upon its spatio-temporal location. c) Self understands and imitates the other through the body, but as something which is *more than just a thing*. d) The Mind qualities of the other are given to the self through the other's *bodily dispositions*. Also, Mind *qua* self is *unique*, not general.	Social	Psycho-physical dualism
6. CONTENT (reality)	*Self* vs. *Not-self*	Knower & known	The self is differentiated as unique, not general, realm of mind. Content of both	The public nature of meaning conflicts with	Public	Reflective Dualism

				Synnomic	Logical
C. LOGICAL	7. JUDGED THOUGHT (scientific & theoretical objects)	*Truth vs. falsity*	inner and outer spheres is included as ideas in the category of "experience," as object of thought to the reflections of a subject-self. This self is not the content of present experience, but is the organisation, direction and control of experience. Subjective interest separable from objective datum. The subject is not a free and spontaneous creativity, but is constrained by the systematic nature of the whole datum of experience. Within experience, relational meanings form dualities of general/particular, universal/singular etc. Mind and Body become contrasting *ideas*, symbols or predicates, which are also objective, because they *mean* things (experiences mean existences). This means that there is existence without reality. Multiple existences acknowledged, not just two.	the individualism of knowers. Experience threatens to be purely subjective.	
		Reason & reality	Self is not an individual knower, but becomes a generic reflective function, dealing critically with ideas and realities, in order to establish a set of perfectly general common meanings fit for all. Experimental thought becomes logical as social corroboration is internalised. Judgments relate ideas to facts, revising, redistributing and furthering meanings through rational, prescriptive and synthetic judgments.	The "I" is inaccessible to scientific or theoretical thought. Judgment is abstract. No experience is complete in itself. The particular and immediate, and the appreciative, imaginary and selective aspects of experience are subordinated.	

Table 2 (continued)

Baldwin's Genetic Analysis of Consciousnss in its Passage Towards and Eventual Transcendence of Mind/Body Dualism

	Good vs. Bad	Fact & value	Development of the *ideal* (interest) aspect of experience, in *practical* reason.	Actual and ideal establish a tension.	Synnomic
D. EXTRA-LOGICAL					
8. MORAL					
E. HYPER-LOGICAL	"Pancalistic" (synthesizes all dualisms)	All previous dialectics mediated	The self reads itself into experience, interpreting the generality of cognition through the singularity of sentiment. The immediacy of feeling is restored, and the personal and concrete enter back into the scientific and theoretical, so that experience attains an aesthetic unity and becomes complete in itself, while the real undergoes an expansion beyond the logical or scientific. There is a complete reconciliation of the dichotomies: actual/ideal, knowledge/value, objectivity/intimacy, and producer/spectator.		Pantelic
9. AESTHETIC					

(N.B. Each successive level represents a new "layer" of consciousness, added on to previous layers and to be integrated with them to a greater or lesser extent in experience). This schematic summary was prepared from Baldwin's various works (1902,1903,1904,1905a, 1906, 1908, 1911, 1913, 1915), with much help from Freeman-Moir's (1975) analysis.

of imitative "introjection" and "ejection" (described in Chaps. 9 and 10).

As Freeman-Moir explains in detail in Chap. 6, it is the paradoxical status of the body, experienced as both inner and outer, that compromises any clear distinction, making the dualism an unstable one. Instead of allowing the body this ambiguous meaning, consciousness moves to a further differentiation, with the particular aid of processes of imitation. This new distinction is made possible by the emergence of experimentation in play, from which a generalization of meanings derives. Consciousness now differentiates the body along with the rest of reality into two entirely general classes of existence: Mind and Body. Each of these becomes a substance, and a center of control—subjective and objective, respectively. This then is the period of "substantive dualism." While Baldwin names the two substances *Mind* and *Body* to remind us of their origins in the self-conception of the individual person, he means *mental* and *material*. Imitation and acts of social corroboration (what Baldwin terms *secondary conversion*) lead to the discovery that the same inner content can attach to two different bodies. Thus the inner can be detached from any specific body and hardened into a general class of persisting mental substance which combines all selves. Correspondingly, experience of outer reality which is common to different selves (what Baldwin calls *syndoxic* knowledge) assumes a persistence and unity of its own as the general class of material substance. The ambiguity of the body is resolved, as in Descartes' philosophy (M. Bakan, 1980), by passing the private characteristics of the personal body over to the objective side. Thus sensorimotor affect in general becomes a part of the mechanical organization of the Material world. Whatever aspects of the privately experienced body cannot be so handled retreat into the subjective pole of the Mental. Thus, while specified parts of the body are objectified as material, residual parts of inner body still have to be sorted into the subjective class, where they coalesce with the active motoric characteristics of mental process. Thus what had been a vague paradox is deepened and made more specific as an embarrassing contradiction, precipitating a cluster of related inconsistencies (see Table 2.).

Among these inconsistencies is the intuition that selves possess unique qualities which cannot be accounted for by merging them in a purely general class of Mind. Partial relief from these pressing problems within consciousness is gained by a differentiation of the Self as a unique, not general, realm of mind. In this new differentiation of consciousness, called the *reflective dualism*, Self is contrasted with a sphere of Experience, within which both Mind and Body lose their status as inner and outer substances, and become objects or contents of thought itself (hence, this is termed the *Content stage*—Table 2). Thus, mind and body are now different meanings that experiences can have to the experiencing self. It is in the Self and in Experience that the *controls* (see Chaps. 6 & 7) exist, not in some substance or other. The substantive dualism is not supplanted by the subject–object or reflective dualism. It is reinterpreted within it, as is apparent when the corresponding phase in the history of philosophy is considered:

> The terms of distinction between mind and body being now understood . . . speculation takes the form of an interpretation of this dualism itself. If we look upon the earlier thought as being a spontaneous or direct consideration of nature and man, we may look upon the latter as being a reflection upon the result of this former thinking. . . . These questions as now formulated show later thought to be an interpretation of dualism, as the earlier was an interpretation of the world issuing in dualism. (Baldwin, 1913, vol. 1, 95ff.)

At this point, where the reflective interpretive capacities of the individual emerge in all their splendor, reality threatens to be absorbed into the subjective realm. What can possibly constrain this emergent self from simply selecting or inventing an illusory experience according to its own whims and desires? It is the constraint imposed by the rest of experience, in all its various modes, says Baldwin, which leads to the differentiation of rational from irrational in the subjective sphere.

In his account of this next phase (the logical mode), Baldwin becomes something of a realist, arguing that experience can only be organized at all if it is constantly referred back to its original and correct sphere of existence in reality by acts of judgment. Why exactly fact exerts such a persuasive control is never quite made clear. Neither is it clear that the reflective content stage is really separable from the period of factual judgment, the logical stage proper. Whether these are two steps or just one, it is clear that in passing beyond the substantive dualism into a dualism of subject and object, the self becomes truly reflective, and that the distinction of rational reflection from irrational makes possible reasoned and objective thought about ideas or meanings. Reason interrelates these objects of thought, works them through, and assesses and reassesses their validity in relation to each other and to facts.

> By judging, the subject takes the objective point of view; he is now not simply a knower, he is perforce a critic, an epistemologist, a reasoner about ideas and realities. (Baldwin, 1906, p. 266)

The *social* aspect of logical or scientific judgment inheres in the fact that reason operates according to certain norms which are prescriptive, meaning that they are binding on all people. These norms are not just customs or widespread habits acceptable to the majority. That kind of lower-level common (or syndoxic) meaning is a much earlier acquisition, appearing in the quasilogical mode (Table 2). Rather, reason has the special command over us that it does in the logical mode precisely because the norms of thought guiding it are the most correct that we so far know. When one judges therefore, one makes more than a personal preference, and one states more than a shared meaning. One makes a generally valid assertion of fact, in the awareness of a whole context (such as the way that the knowledge was acquired—the methodological strictures bearing on it). In so doing, one makes a judgment fit (potentially, or ideally) for all others—one expresses what Baldwin calls *synnomic* meaning.[1]

Synnomicity of judgment is the ultimate criterion of the good in the *moral* sphere as well, where judgment concerns *values* rather than facts. That strand of genetic logic is pursued fully in Kohlberg's chapter, showing how Kohlberg's Stage 6 of moral judgment, like Rawls's "original position," is the stage of truly synnomic moral thought. Nevertheless, these heights of theoretical and practical reason are not the end of the road for Baldwin's genetic logic. Genetic logic is more than "logic" alone, precisely because the latter can only deal with mediated experience: the general and abstract character of ideas. Such a cognitive organization leaves what Baldwin calls certain "embarrassments," chief among which is the fact that, unlike the "me," the "I" is *singular* and *immediate* and therefore cannot be expressed within a logic of the purely general and mediated. For Baldwin, this implies that there must be a further mode of knowing, the *hyperlogical*, in which such embarrassments are overcome in a more comprehensive synthesis. Fortunately for us, this visionary part of the genetic logic is dealt with in Chapters 10 and 11.

Empirical Study: Conceptualization, Design, and Method

Baldwin considered his sequence of modes "empirically" derived because they were explained in terms of more or less familiar aspects and levels of our ordinary experience, in conjunction with principles of selection analogous to those of Darwinian biological science (see Chapter 5). He neither attempted nor anticipated confirmation through any empirical psychological research.

---

[1] In his day, this was far from an unusual way of talking about knowledge. The 'Pragmatist' philosopher C.S. Peirce proposed a similar, social or procedural model of logical and scientific truth (Habermas, 1971).

Perceiving Baldwin's genetic logic as simply a speculative and unconfirmed theory of psychological development desperately in need of some content that was empirical in the narrower, modern sense of the term, I set about applying Piagetian methodology to the validation of Baldwin's ideas. In the early 1970s, certain trends in developmental psychology made this seem a logical step. Attention had been drawn back to Piaget's early work on children's beliefs about the world by Kohlberg (1963) and others. In these early studies of thought, names and dreams, Piaget had dealt with the emergence of concepts of the inner, mental life, and of the relation of thought to things. Kohlberg (1966; see Chap. 9 in this volume) had followed Piaget in trying to show that children's struggle to understand the epistemological status of dreams was central to their gradual differentiation of unreal from real, inner from outer, and eventually mental from physical. In later work (Kohlberg & Gilligan, 1971), the epistemological interpretation of adolescence by Inhelder and Piaget (1958) was extended into a general speculative account of the emergence of subjectivity as the mark of chldhood's end. Meanwhile, Perry (1968) had anticipated the expansion of interest in development after childhood by constructing a stage theory of epistemological development in the college years.

Borrowing rather eclectically from Piaget, Kohlberg, and Perry, as well as Baldwin, and stimulated concretely by my experiences of trying to teach Piagetian epistemology to undergraduates, I sketched out some hypothetical a priori stages of what I then called 'natural epistemology' (Broughton 1974). Some informal pilot interviews led me to believe that Baldwin was right; there appeared to be a complex, natural evolution of concepts of self, mind, body, reality, and truth, all interlinked in a network of mutually implicative beliefs.

Using Baldwin's five volumes and the pilot data, an extensive semistructured questionnaire was developed (available upon request). The questions required subjects to demonstrate, define, and reflect on their intuitive understanding within a variety of philosophical categories: self–world, mental–material, person–thing, reality–appearance, knower–known, subjective–objective, fact–theory, truth–illusion, thought–feeling, and so on. Strictly speaking, these were as often metaphysical categories as epistemological ones, and so with this realization, the more apt and inclusive term 'natural philosophy' will be used henceforth (meaning "theoretical reason" in the sense employed by Husserl, 1978, pp. 1–3).

Questions were direct, and pitched at a philosophical level (e.g., "What is the self?"). Subjects' responses were probed with further inquiries in order to identify the grounds of their judgments and to clarify ambiguous statements. This is essentially Piaget's method of *critical exploration* (Piaget, 1929, pp. 1–31; Inhelder, Sinclair & Bovet, 1974, pp. 18–24). If someone replied, "The self is you," as one 10-year-old did, the interviewer then asked, "What do you mean by 'you'?" These probe questions were administered systematically, in the interests of obtaining as much comparability between interviews as possible.

Interviewees were 36 male and female subjects, ages 10, 14, 18, 22, and 26. The lower limit chosen was late childhood because it was felt that the work of Piaget and Kohlberg described above had already dealt with epistemological development at more primitive levels. The subjects were predominantly middle-class, suburban residents of Boston and were of mixed ethnicity and religion. Up to age 18, they were typical students, of a little above-average intelligence. The 22- and 26-year-olds were, respectively, undergraduates and postgraduates. These subjects were included as a way of potentially sampling higher levels of natural epistemology. Although most of these older individuals were involved in academically related pursuits, a selection was deliberately made from a wide range of disciplines to diminish the chances that any particular intellectual convictions would be dominant. This and other facets of the methodological strategy employed in this study reflect the techniques and precautions appropriate for generating "grounded theory," codified in Glaser and Straus (1967). It was not the study's aim to test specific hypotheses, to assess the influence of demographic variables, to look for sex differences, or to construct a measurement instrument. The purpose was to ground an initial theoretical scheme defining and mapping out a coherent domain of developmental phenomena.

In addition to the natural philosophy interview, subjects were administered traditional Piaget and Kohlberg measures of logical and moral thought. The assumption was that if Baldwin were correct about genetic logic, it should be possible to identify qualitative strata of development spreading across logical, epistemological, and moral domains. The instruments developed by Piaget and Kohlberg seemed most appropriate for testing this possibility, since both were grounded in cognitive-developmental theories which owed a lot to, and seemed quite compatible with, Baldwin's account of genetic logic. Both instruments had the added advantage that the theories they derived from had received independent empirical support (Inhelder & Piaget, 1958; Kohlberg, 1971).

Results: Levels of Philosophic Reason

Transcripts of the 36 interviews were checked against the initial scheme of speculative levels that had been roughly based on a reading of Baldwin. To no one's surprise, the fit between a priori speculations and actual empirical interview material was quite unsatisfactory (Broughton, 1974, App. F). The next step was the construction of a "second generation" developmental scheme. This was derived directly from an analysis of the 36 transcripts. It consisted of a set of "ideal types," designed to blend theoretical categories with recurrent interview content in the way described originally by Max Weber. The ideal types were generated through a complex procedure of interpretation, cross-comparison and abstraction, which aimed at identifying the grounds most generally given by subjects for their judgments.[2]

The types have been expounded directly elsewhere (Broughton, 1978a, 1980), where the reader will find that only parts of the scheme overlap with Baldwin's genetic logic. The express purpose here is to accentuate those areas of overlap and point to potential analogies between the types of natural philosophy and modes of genetic logic. To enhance comparability with Baldwin's developmental scheme, as well as to improve scope and clarity, some interviews will be called on which were ancillary to the main study. They will be used particularly with respect to the ages below 10, which so far have only been informally sampled. Here, the child studies of my coworkers Cross (1975) and Schecter (1979) have been invaluable sources of supplementary case material.[3] As will be apparent, the best and most extensive data were obtained in the midadolescent to young-adult range, and as a result more space is devoted to a consideration of those interviews. At present, the age range of youth is the "fovea" of the research, while earlier and later ages are still only glimpsed in "peripheral vision."

One can perhaps summarize the general drift of philosophical development as pivoting around the period of adolescence, where the "great philosophic dualisms" arise (Table 3). In this epoch, the dialectical categories just mentioned become sets of polarized opposites: mind *versus* matter, reality *versus* appearance, self *versus* world, etc. In childhood, there is little of this dualizing; children are predualistic. In adulthood, there are efforts to develop the dualisms self-consciously, and (in some cases) to attempt one kind of reconciliation or another. Monistic *and* more sophisticated solutions appear.

---

[2] This procedure for generating ideal types is best understood and learned by perusing some good exemplars of its use: see Piaget (1929), Furth (1976), Schecter (1979). On ideal types in general, see Broughton & Zahaykevich (1980).

[3] I would like to acknowledge here as well the resources, both material and psychological, made available by Jim Fowler, whose support during a difficult period in my research was invaluable.

Level One: "Objective"

Baldwin drew analogies between the initial phase of cognitive development and the orientation of the pre-Socratic Greeks. Theirs was primarily an "ontological" frame of reference, in which *reality* [4] had an absolute, external quality. In the child, this is manifest in failure to make any metaphysical distinction between inner and outer, accompanied by a corresponding epistemological assumption of "automatic knowledge." Subjective appearance is always taken as the real. Thus, dreams must have objective reality, as this five-year-old boy seems to believe:

A.H. (5.4, M)   Where could a dream be? Are dreams outside? I DON'T KNOW. Are they ever in your room? YEAH. When? NIGHT. Let's say you're dreaming about a teddy-bear. Would I be able to see it if I were standing right by your bed? YEAH. What if I was standing by your door? NO. Why? BECAUSE YOU'RE TOO FAR AWAY. If I were by the bed could I touch the teddy-bear? YEAH.

The phenomenal is the real; conversely, mental processes have no existence independent from that of their external referents:

A.H. (5.4, M)   Are thoughts real? YEAH. Why? I DON'T KNOW. Is a thought about a bed real? YEAH. Why? I DON'T KNOW. Is a thought about a giant real? NO. How come? BECAUSE A GIANT ISN'T REAL.

The real–unreal opposition does not mark a distinction of inner and outer. It can therefore only be erected as a boundary *within* the objective world. The ontological dimension chosen is typically that of life, so that real v. unreal is superimposed upon alive v. inanimate.

S.T. (6.0, F)   Is God real? NO. No? HE'S DEAD. He's dead? HIS SPIRIT IS REAL.

A.H. (5.4, M)   Give me a list of things that are real. BEARS. How come? BECAUSE THEY CAN WALK AND MOVE. What else? PERSONS. Why? BECAUSE THEY CAN WALK AND MOVE TOO. What's not real? GIANTS. Why? THEY CAN'T WALK, AND THEY CAN'T MOVE. What else isn't real? GLASSES AREN'T, GLASSES YOU DRINK OUT OF. Why not? BECAUSE THEY CAN'T WALK OR MOVE EITHER . . . How about a car? YES. Why? BECAUSE IT CAN MOVE.

---

[4] The words *reality, truth, knowledge, self* and *mind-body* are italicized repeatedly at each level to help the readers in organizing the material and locating sections of particular interest to them.

Table 3

Levels of Natural Philosophy across Four Major Categories

Level	Self—World	Mental—Material	Reality—Appearance	Knower—Known
1. Objective (age 4–7)	*Presumptive:* Self-evident, bodily self. Not differentiated from reflexive "itself."	*Adualist:* Gross head/body distinction. Visible and invisible not differentiated. Mind and body mutually permeable.	*Objective:* Reality presumed. Simple and immediate existence of external things. Real undifferentiated from nonartificial. Reality confounded with life.	*Dogmatic:* Thought and its objects undifferentiated. Direct, automatic knowing. Single extrinsic truth, known and handed down by authority.
2. Individual (age 8–12)	*Individual:* Self is specific person, me or you. Perceiving, acting person. Source or agent.	*Organic:* Mind differentiated from body as brainlike organ controlling rest of body. Discrete nonvisible mental contents.	*Naive realist:* Certainty of reality directly sensed. Appearance is the way something "looks" and this *is* reality. Real differentiated from imaginary as persistent.	*Empirical:* Thought/object differentiation. Experience directly caused by object. Truth is absolute fact, is opposed to lie, and is individually apprehended and asserted.
3. Divided (age 12+)	*Divided:* Self is mind (mental self) more than body (physical self). Unique subjective traits, opinions, beliefs, or values. Authentic inner self differentiated from false outer appearance (social personality or role self).	*Immature dualist:* Abstract mental differentiated from concrete physical as a fluid and invisible medium. Mental and physical as overlapping classes.	*Realist:* Appearance generally realistic, but mind may add personal distortion (opinion or value). Mental is belief rather than reality.	*Social:* Concrete facts known by individuals. Truth as interpersonal demonstration and plausibility (overlap). Nascent skepticism.
4. Dualist (age 18+)	*Substantial:* Self as system: soul, intellect, logic, identity, or "cogito" (self-control). Self has mental and physical attributes. Self-concept, or "me," rather than "I." Generalized self or perspective.	*Cartesian:* Dualism between objective mechanistic system of scientific cause/effect, and subjective or spiritual world of belief, purpose, and reason. Unconscious differentiated from conscious.	*Dualist:* Reality assumed. Noumenon differentiated from phenomenon. Substantial reality is lawlike system generating appearances (data).	*Positivist:* Knowledge is inductive generalization of observation-constructive copy of world. Truth, which subordinates reality, is replicable and is achieved through social-conventional testing of models. Impartial "generalized other" defines objective standpoint.

5. Subjective (age 20+)	*Experiential*: Self as undetermined. Flux of experience, or process of self-realization. Self-objectification illegitimate. Breakdown of substantial soul or identity. Everything has self, and so experiences.	*Reductionist*: Monistic materialism, with mind as epiphenomenon, and/or monistic spiritualism where consciousness dominates matter.	*Subjectivist*: All reality phenomenal, equated with "reality-forme." Full mechanistic determinism at level of data. Subjective automatically excludes objective.	*Relativist*: All knowledge is subjective and particular. Generalizations or shared ideas are arbitrary conventions. Opposition to objectification. Skepticism or solipsism. Intuitionism: true is instinctive or natural.
6. Rational (age 25+)	*Epistemological*: Self as transcendental ego, or function of universal self-consciousness. Self-conceiver or subject-self differentiated from empirical or object-self.	*Parallelist*: Functional "mental" and "physical." Psychology vs. physiology, as ideational systems of explanatory constructs. Related to logical meanings such as form/content.	*Perspectivist*: Reality presupposed. Reality defined by coherence and utility of system within which it is interpreted.	*Methodological*: Objective relativism. Knowledge and truth defined by paradigmatic assumptions, e.g., idealist, materialist, etc. Logical level distinguished from empirical.
7. Critical (age 30+)	*Historical*: Subjectivity can be individual subject (e.g., class subject), transforming natural/social reality. Individual subjectivity does not exist in a dualism with objects of knowledge.	*Interpenetrative*: Mind and matter are differentiated from culture and nature. These penetrate each other and can be transformed into each other through life: human activity. Form and content are historically related.	*Materialist*: Reality is never "given," either as fact or as presupposition. At both levels, the dialectic of appearance is dynamically mediated by human interest and action.	*Social*: Knowledge as active. social transformation of reality through man-made. historical categories. Interest can promote truth or conceal it through ideological formations. Logical and empirical dialectically related.

Does your dog think? YEAH. How can you tell he thinks? BECAUSE HE'S REAL. Why is he real? BECAUSE HE MOVES.

J.V.(5.9, M)   Why are people, trees, tables real? BECAUSE THEY LIVE. What doesn't live? THE DEVIL. How do you know? HE'S NOT ALIVE. NO, HE'S NOT REAL. What else isn't alive? GHOSTS. Is this box alive? NO. Why not? DOESN'T HAVE ANYTHING TO MOVE WITH.

As Schecter (1979) has found, not alive is a diffuse category, which the young child confounds with immobile or dead, with not human, with nonconscious, and with imaginary or fake. All of these fall under the rubic not real, leading to a kind of family resemblance between static objects, immobile people, corpses, things without names, images, plastic imitations, monsters, and thoughts about monsters. What Baldwin called the as-if or semblant mode (see Chaps. 7 and 11) therefore enjoys a certain scope and fluidity, so much so that it permeates the apprehension of the real. This observation implies that there is a cognitive order prior to systematic classification, one which does not yet comprehend the constant, regular and law-abiding in the world. In the context of such a conceptual framework, the interpenetration of cognition and fantasy, and the mythopoetic quality of child consciousness, become more understandable. As Baldwin (1915, pp. 75–76) points out, and Schecter empirically corroborates, these children are not properly called animistic. Rather than projecting animate qualities into inanimate objects, it is more the case that such category boundaries as that between living and nonliving things have yet to be established. We have, therefore, something akin to Baldwin's adualistic mode of consciousness, one in which mind, matter, life and reality are yet to be segregated.

The epistemological corollary of this metaphysical undifferentiation is a naively realistic understanding of knowledge. As in the ancient Greeks, there really is no epistemology, things being simply apprehended "as they are." Affectively, there is what Baldwin calls a direct reality feeling (1905b, p. 249); conatively, reality is "presumed" as obvious (1915, p. 419). One is reminded of Hegel's first stage of sense-certainty. There is a failure to realize any problematic aspect to realness. Any question about how one comes to know something is automatically answered in terms of the simple fact of that thing's existence, which is the obvious terminus of such questioning:

S.T. (6.0, F)   How do you know that chair over there is really there? CAUSE IT'S SITTING THERE. How do you know it's sitting there? I DON'T KNOW.

The only other possible way to understand questions about reality is to see them as questions of origin: how something came to be there:

> A.H. (5.4, M) How do you know that chest is really over there? THEY PUT IT THERE. How do you know that house is over there? THAT'S WHERE THEY BUILT IT.

Agencies human or divine may be invoked:

> J.V. (5.9, M) What is your mind? YOUR MIND IS YOUR HEAD ISN'T IT? Is the mind real? YEAH. Why? I DON'T KNOW. (Pause) GOD CREATED IT.

Truth is not distinguished from reality, so authority figures are invoked in this definition, much as they are implicated in the existence of things.

> I.M. (6.0, M) Can you see a society? YEAH, I CAN SEE THE WHITE PEOPLE. How do you know it's real? BE-CAUSE GOD TOLD ME. Say God hadn't told you. NO, BUT IT'S STILL A SOCIETY. Why? BECAUSE MY MUMMY TOLD ME. How did she know? BE-CAUSE GOD TOLD HER.

The absolute unitary quality of reality and truth, and the concomitant objectification of thoughts and dreams, excludes any concept of someone having their own subjective experience. Conse-quently, there is no need for the level one child to conceptualize a subjective principle or organ of mind. Mind and matter are not so much fused as they are undifferentiated. In this relatively primitive world view, the functional equivalent of mind is life. "Almost every living thing has a mind," says a 6-year-old girl, R.F. "Everything that moves or walks" has a mind, says a 5-year-old boy, J.V. As we have seen, life is external, visible "liveliness" or activity. However, this life is in the body. So much so that without a mind, says 4 year-old S.S., "You'd run around in a circle." These children understand that there is something called thinking, but they do not see it as essential to all activity. Also, thoughts are not confined to a specific delimited organ. I.M., 6, says mind "flows through the body like two ghosts flying." When asked if your thoughts can be in your body, he replied, "Yes, the blood takes them."

Bodily thought, and its connection to activity, is paralleled by an undifferentiated bodily self. Dead people and even objects, therefore, may be said to have a self. This primitive selfhood, like the presump-tion of a self-evident reality, is obvious, the terms self and itself being roughly equivalent. Such a self knows itself automatically and immediately. "I just feel it," says I.M., who later goes on to explain how you know yourself just by being and doing. Knowing, being and doing are all confounded, as Schecter (1979) has implied in showing the relative fusion of *life* and *consciousness* concepts at ages 5–7.

Level Two: "Individual"

This level could also be called *naive subjective* in its orientation. The basic distinctions between thought and its referents and between phenomenal and real are crystallized for the first time. The differentiation of *real* from unreal, which at Level One was seen as a division within the external, objective world, is now given its first subjective tinge, by connecting it to a distinction between inner and outer. This is a very inchoate segregation of subjective from objective, however. While the notion that reality is immediately present is now transcended, it is improved upon only slightly. It is replaced with what we usually think of as *naive realism.* In other words, while reality remains constant, unitary and absolute in character, it undergoes a partial sensory mediation in its passage from outer to inner. The notion of a someone sensing something is introduced into the consideration of how we know. It is no longer totally nonsensical to ask how we know something exists. The reality-feeling presumed at Level One enters explicitly into justifications of our intuitive apprehension.

> L.B. (9.11, F)   YOU'D KNOW IF YOU WERE IMAGINING A TABLE. YOU JUST FEEL THAT IT ISN'T THERE. YOU'D HAVE SOME IMAGINARY SENSE THAT YOU'RE FEELING IT. A SORT OF TINGLY FEELING INSIDE TELLS YOU THAT YOU'RE REALLY TOUCHING IT OR NOT REALLY TOUCHING IT.

This change reflects Piaget's and Schecter's finding that concepts of conscious sentience emerge during the later phase of childhood. In one of his more precocious moments, a bright 6-year-old in transit from Level One to Level Two exemplifies this.

> I.M. (6.0, M)   How do you know there is a real world? BECAUSE THE HOUSES LOOK REAL. What makes them look real? THEY *ARE* REAL. THEY FEEL REAL. I FEEL THEM. IT FEELS KIND OF CEMENTY AND WOODISH.

"To be is to be seen," believes the Level-Two thinker, for whom reality is real to a perceiving organism. To quote Hegel (1967), regarding his second (or "perception) stage:

> In this as in the preceding section, apprehension is effected under conditions of sense. But whereas in the preceding type of consciousness the universality which knowledge implies and requires no sooner appeared than it melted away, here in Perception we start from a

certain stability in the manner of apprehension, and a certain constancy in the content apprehended. (p. 161)

Phenomenal is distinguished from real (see I.M. above), and yet it is naively realistic: it directly tells us about the real. The houses look real because they are real. It could not be otherwise, since there is as yet no notion that sense is subjective. It still simply registers what is there. There is an objective, enduring quality to real materials, corresponding to the duration and constancy of this passive sensing.

Now that things are real because they look or feel real to me, *real* is spontaneously contrasted with nonexistent, rather than with "phony" or "fake." Imagination is understood to exist, as L.B. witnesses above. However, it does not usually interfere, because if you imagine that "hard," then "you know when you're imagining," as another 10-year-old put it. "You can't imagine something that isn't there," said the same boy, revealing the limits to mental creativity. You just see "what is there" (what is persistent). Things look different from reality because of "mistakes," or "if you're far-sighted," but these are not major interferences in the realistic experience either, because they are avoidable.

Truth has a parallel status. It is known by "going and looking for yourself," "finding out yourself" (phrases used by two 10-year-olds). These children stress the active resort to sensory evidence that Baldwin calls *primary conversion* of the idea or claim in question. Another person may mediate reality, only if direct individual confrontation with the potential object of sense is not possible. However, the other may mediate it falsely by lying. You can only know the other is not lying because "he doesn't laugh," or "is willing to bet on it," a criterion that is clearly subjective, embroiled as it is with the inner conviction experienced by the other. In involving this subjective side, the child reveals the incompleteness of differentiation between different kinds of interest: theoretical, practical, and aesthetic. The notion of the *real* is still caught up with the realm of value and taste, while remaining at the individual and personal level:

G.S. (9.4, M)   What is a fact? IF I SAY "TRY HAMBURGERS," AND YOU SAY "THEY'RE GOOD," THEN THAT'S A FACT.

While knowledge and truth are connected with individuals, the question of differences in what people hold to be true or real is not spontaneously reflected on by any of the 10-year-old subjects. This finding is corroborated by Schecter's research, in which opinion differences were not spontaneously conceptualized until ages 12-14. This is so despite the fact that we know from Selman's (1974) work that from age 6, children are aware of the existence of such differences, in a nonreflective or prereflective way. Where the possibility of conflicting interpretations is explicitly raised by the interviewer, Level-Two thinkers tend simply to affirm truth, with a dogmatic, individual attitude to *knowledge:*

> K.W. (9.5, M)   WE KNOW WHO'S RIGHT . . . YOU JUST DO. OUR BRAIN TELLS US. Which person do we believe? ME. Why? BECAUSE THAT'S THE WAY IT IS.

So far, the constellation of empirical features of Level-Two thought suggests that there can be a naive kind of subjectivity which is not yet relativistic in the sense of admitting a different point of view on reality for each individual. If this could be substantiated, it would comprise a departure from Piaget's (1929) and Selman's (1974) conclusion that early subjectivism and relativism (or perspectivism) are inevitably tied together in the genetic process.

The partial quality of the nascent subjective is again visible in the Level-Two concepts of *mind and body.* While there is not yet a division of reality into mental and physical, the child starts to use the word *mind* spontaneously, as referring to part of the body which is distinguished within the head as a brainlike organ. It is "a lot smarter than the other parts of your body," said C.S. (10.2, M). There appear to be two alternative ways to "organify" mind: (a) by positing it as a separate organ with an integrity of its own, or (b) by denying the distinction and identifying mind with brain:

> (a) L.B. (9.11, F)   MIND AND BRAIN ARE LIKE TOGETHER IN THE SAME PLACE. THEY LIKE WORK TOGETHER . . . Could a brain surgeon see the brain? HE COULD SEE THE BRAIN. NOT THE MIND I DON'T THINK. I DON'T KNOW. LIKE I GUESS YOU COULD SEE THE MIND. What would it look like? OH, MESSED UP AND CURLED TOGETHER WITH THE BRAIN. The mind is harder to see? YEAH, BECAUSE THE BRAIN'S BIGGER. How small is the mind? IT'S GOT TO BE SMALL ENOUGH TO FIT IN YOUR HEAD, SO IT WOULD PROBABLY BE 3 OR 4 INCHES.

> (b) J.W. (10.0, F)   What is the mind? THE BRAIN. The same thing? YEAH. Is it different from the brain at all? I DON'T THINK SO. Why are there two words then? SO PEOPLE CAN USE TWO DIFFERENT WORDS. SO IF THEY DON'T UNDERSTAND THE OTHER WORD, THEY CAN TALK ABOUT THE OTHER WORD.

Paralleling the increased separation of inner and outer, there is some incipient differentiation of function between mind and brain. Paradoxically, this division of labor seems to apply even in individuals who equate mind with brain. While mind and brain share thinking and deciding, there is a tendency to see mind as imagining and dreaming, and brain as having a more executive function (Table 4).[5]

In passing to Level Two, the diffuse mental-bodily vitality of Level One becomes differentiated into a hierarchical relationship. The mind–brain controls the initiation and restriction of the body's activity, in a simple master–slave relationship.

G.S. (9.4, M)   BUT YOUR BRAIN JUST TELLS YOU TO. JUST LIKE PINOCCHIO AND JIMINY CRICKET . . . LIKE IF THE MIND DIDN'T CONTROL THE SELF, YOU WOULD JUMP RIGHT OUT THE WINDOW ANY DAY . . . THE MIND CONTROLS YOU, TELLS YOU NOT TO JUMP OUT THE WINDOW.

As Table 4 suggests, there arises at Level Two a primitive notion of mental contents (thoughts, images) distinct from their objects, and from their container. They are restricted to the mind or brain, and cannot "flow through the body." They are invisible things—discrete, and not yet seen in terms of a process. They are nonvisible, "not solid," rather than immaterial. Yet this does not prevent them from being real. When asked about the reality of thought, for example, G.S. echoes the sentiment mentioned above with respect to imagination:

But is that thought real? YES, YOU'RE REALLY THINKING ABOUT IT. BECAUSE YOU CAN SORT OF HEAR YOURSELF THINK IT. YOU CAN'T BE THINKING AND NOT KNOW, LIKE. YOU CAN'T REALLY HEAR YOURSELF. YOU JUST KNOW.

The initial, partial differentiation of mind from body and thought from thing helps in discriminating persons from objects, and in the definition of a *self*. The concept of self is inchoate, as we would expect given the limited subjectivity already noted. The self is the individual source or agent. When asked what changes about him, K.W. (9.5, M) replies:

MY ATTITUDES TOWARD PEOPLE, AND TOWARD THE WAY I THINK. Is that part of you? YEAH, BECAUSE THE WAY I ACT IS WHAT I DO, AND WHAT I DO IS PART OF ME BECAUSE IT'S ME DOING IT.

---

[5] Elsewhere (Broughton, 1980) I have suggested that the conceptual differentiation of mental and physical work implicit in the mind-brain dichotomy may be closely linked to the development of sex-role concepts such as "mother's work" vs. "father's work."

Table 4
Level Two Emerging Conceptions of Division of Labor in Brain and Mind Function

Subject (age, Sex)	Mind	Brain	Relation
Females (ordered by age)			
M.F. (7.2, F)	Dreams	Thinks	Mind "spells" brain (i.e., *can* think).
E.W. (8.0, F)	Pictures what someone tells you.	Thinks things out (e.g., math).	Mind knows you're going to do something and sends message to tell you to do it.
C.K. (9.4, F) (unclear if she thinks they're synonymous)	Imagines, pictures things. Very powerful, smart.	Thinks. Tells body what to do.	
K.Y. (9.9, F)	Imagines, "says" things.	Thinks. Doesn't think. Repeats things.	Brain "smarter", and tells mind everything (e.g., gives it answers).
L.B. (9.11, F)	Thinks & feels	Works (thinks too). Memory. Figures out math. Tells you to do things.	Brain "shares" things with mind.
A.M. (10.0, F)	Thinks.	Controls your muscles. Thinks.	
N.G. (12.0, F)	A feeling. Contains ideas. What you know.	Where you get knowledge (on how to do things). Tells body to do them.	Brain causes your ideas to go to mind. Then gets ideas from mind and tells body to do them.
Males (ordered by age)			
D. E. (8.0, M)	Dreams. Daydreams.	Has and sends messages (to body), tells it what to do.	Brain thinks things up and sends them to mind, and mind does or doesn't do them.
K.W. (9.5, M)	Imagines, dreams. Knows. Tells (e.g., right vs. wrong).	Power source. Figures out. Helps decide (whether or not to do something). Tells you where to go.	Brain figures what the mind figures. Brain helps mind figure out. (Brain gives mind what is figured out, and changes it if necessary?) Mind may imagine what to do, brain tells you how to do it.

Table 4 (continued)
Level Two Emerging Conceptions of Division of Labor in Brain and Mind Function

P.S. (9.7, M)	Thinks. Transmits messages. Makes decisions.	Makes body move. Helps body (e.g., sets pulse). Makes you think.	
M.W. (10.0, M)	Knows, pictures things, imagines what someone tells you to imagine.	Helps you think (e.g., math).	Mind knows you're going to do something, and sends message to brain, which sends message to tell you to do it.
M.U. (10.0, M)	Tells you how to think, feel. Tells you to like people.	Makes you react. Tells you how to move and where to go.	
C.S. (10.2, M)	Feels and sees. Thinks. Has knowledge. Responds to things. Controls you (keeps you sane).	Makes you think. Makes you move. Takes things in.	Mind helps brain (which helps body).
J.L. (12.0, M)	Thinks, decides, judges. Visualizes.	Remembers. Thinks? Visualizes.	
P.R. (12.0, M)	Remembers. Sees and knows people. Pieces things together.	Controls things, e.g., moves arm.	

When asked what the self is, his reply discloses how near in meaning self is to individual person:

> THE PERSON WHO IS SAYING IT. IT MEANS HIM AND IT DOESN'T MEAN ANYBODY ELSE.

As me rather than you, the self or person is closely related to his name, as C.S. (10.2, M) reveals:

> What about your self, what is it? MY SELF IS C., A PERSON WHO WAS BORN ON THE PLANET EARTH.

However, he goes on to show how this individual achieves a degree of free will, self-awareness, and subjective uniqueness:

> I AM ONE OF A KIND. What does that mean? THERE COULD BE A PERSON WHO LOOKS LIKE ME OR TALKS LIKE ME, BUT NO ONE WHO HAS EVERY SINGLE DETAIL I HAVE. NEVER A PERSON WHO THINKS EXACTLY LIKE ME. Why not? BECAUSE WHEN ONE PERSON TALKS, THE OTHER WOULD TALK AT THE SAME TIME, AND THEY'D NEVER BE ABLE TO EXCHANGE SENTENCES.

Even though it was found that these 10-year-olds had reached the level of formal operational thought, self-consciousness as such is not yet articulated reflectively by them. Reflectivity is confined to a sense of "me," the way I look or sound (C.S.), what I think, and what I do (K.W.). These are qualities with persistence, but they are not yet conceptualized as traits. Personality is not differentiated from self, and the usage of both terms is close to that of *person*. There is, however, the added advantage over level one that this person has a vague interiority, one which is intuitively and immediately known by self:

> A PERSONALITY, IT'S REALLY SORT OF WHAT YOU ARE ... A PERSONALITY'S SORT OF IN-SIDE YOU, AND YOU KNOW THAT YOU'RE A CERTAIN PERSON.

Level Three: "Divided"

The first adolescent level resembles a transitional state between Baldwin's *inner-outer* dualism and the *substantive dualism* proper. At times it seems to reflect characteristics of the former, while at other points it corresponds more to the latter. In one work dealing with stages of thought in the race, Baldwin (1913) depicts such an interstitial phase, which he aptly calls *immature dualism*. Many features of Level Three qualify it to fall under such a rubric. It is at this level that consciousness first clearly dualizes appearance and reality, knower and known, mental and material, self and world, but each distinction involves a separation of meanings that remains incomplete.

In a sense, the categories of *reality* and *mind-body* converge. For the first time, reality can take two forms, mental and physical. Despite the fact that the world in which children move is saturated with the dualistic world view of adults, terms like *mental* and *physical* are hardly ever employed before early adolescence. This finding is corroborated again by Schecter (1979), who found that mental and physical are first distinguished explicitly (e.g., in the domain of metaphors) in early adolescence. According to her, this is the same time that consciousness as such becomes a clear concept, and the mental comes to be the defining criterion in concepts of life.

At Level Two, the mind-body problem was construed as exactly that: a relation between an individual mind and an individual body. Level Three is capable of advancing beyond such individualistic metaphysics, interpreting the issue as one of the mental characteristics of minds and the physical characteristics of bodies, where mental and physical are qualities shared by individuals. These subjects fall short of a Cartesian dualism. Mental and physical are not quite substances, but are more like classes of things, used to account for the makeup of persons relative to things.

C.G. (13.5, M)   What is the self? I THINK IT MEANS NOT JUST THE PERSON, BUT THE INSIDE OF THE PERSON. EACH PERSON IS THE SELF, DIFFERENT FROM ANOTHER PERSON. BECAUSE EACH PERSON IS DIFFERENT IN THE WAY THEIR MIND WORKS. Can you tell me how a person's mind works? IT IS NOT PHYSICAL. IT IS AN EMOTIONAL OR MENTAL THING LIKE THAT.

J.F. (13.11, M)   YOUR MIND IS WHAT YOU DO IN YOUR BRAIN, LIKE YOUR MIND, YOU THINK. THE BRAIN IS THE MATTER ITSELF. THE MIND IS MORE THE ENERGY THING. YOU CAN'T SEE ENERGY, BUT YOU CAN SEE MATTER. ENERGY IS IN MATTER, BUT MATTER ISN'T IN ENERGY ... How is the energy in the matter? THE ENERGY IS WHAT MAKES IT WORK, RIGHT? GASOLINE MAKES A CAR ENGINE WORK. But gasoline is matter! RIGHT. BUT PUT THE TWO MATTERS TO-GETHER CREATES ENERGY.

There is a noticeable difficulty in separating mental and physical here. The more J.F. tries, e.g., through concrete analogy, to make a distinction, the more it seems to collapse again. For both J.F. and C.G., mind is still conceptualized as quasimaterial, its only status acquired negatively in terms of what solid material quality it does not have. For C.G., *mental* is a vaguely defined personal *interior*, equated with *the way the mind works*. Yet surely there is a physical interior, too?

Since mental and physical still overlap in this way, their relationship is difficult to specify. In the absence of any more differentiated conception., it tends to be personified as a kind of dependence or obligation:

C.H. (13.8, F)   (THE MIND) HAS A RESPONSIBILITY, IT HAS TO—WITHOUT THE MIND, THERE WOULDN'T BE ANYTHING HERE ... IT STAYS AS LONG AS IT'S SUPPOSED TO.

The combination of slippage and dependence provides a fertile ground for mystical views of astral projection, reincarnation, trans-migration, etc., as Baldwin's own writings (1913, 1915) point out in locating a historical phase of immature dualism in the time of the Scholastic philosophers prior to Descartes.

While mind overlaps with body, it is no longer thought of as part of the body. It *is* the brain, but not in J.W.'s sense at Level Two where, inexplicably, two words had to be coined for the same organ. Mind's identity with brain is of a new and further differentiated variety:

C.H. (13.8, F)   THE BRAIN IS THE PART OF ME WHERE THE MIND IS. MIND IS PART OF THE BRAIN, *IS* THE BRAIN. I DON'T KNOW IF YOU COULD CUT IT OUT. MAYBE THE MIND ISN'T THE INSTINC- TIVE THINGS. I WOULD CONSIDER IT THE WHOLE BRAIN . . . I HAVE NEVER THOUGHT OF THE MIND AS A SOLID THING. I THINK OF IT AS LIKE A COVER ROUND THE BRAIN, TAKING OUT MESSAGES AND STUFF. YOU CAN'T SAY "THERE IS THE MIND," BECAUSE IT IS THE WHOLE BRAIN. It isn't solid? NO. SPIRITUAL MAYBE? THAT MEANS NOT SOLID, NOT A GAS, NOT SOMETHING YOU CAN GRAB. IT'S NOT THERE! WELL, IT IS NOT *BODILY* THERE. YOU COULDN'T PROVE IT EITHER, BECAUSE IT IS NOT THERE. YOU COULD NOT PROVE THAT WE HAVE A SPIRIT. YOU COULD NOT DO TESTS ON IT OR ANYTHING, BECAUSE IT ISN'T PHYS- ICALLY THERE. BECAUSE ALL OUR TESTS ARE MADE TO TEST SOMETHING SOLID . . . MAYBE THE MIND IS SOMETHING YOU *CAN* HOLD ON TO. WE HAVE TO SAY IT IS SOMETHING.

This new mind is "the whole brain." It is an invisible faculty, meaning a presence or activity that the whole brain is engaged in:

A.B. (14.1, M)   How do you know you have a mind? DID WE CLARIFY THE MIND IS THE SAME THING AS THE BRAIN? I MEAN THE BRAIN IS AN ACTUAL THING, BUT THE MIND IS WHAT GOES ON IN THE BRAIN . . . THE MIND IS WHAT THE BRAIN DOES.

Schecter (1979) has pointed out that in early adolescence, it is the *volitional* aspects of mind as choosing and intending that define consciousness, and indirectly life itself. Remember, C.H. was quick to exclude "the instinctive things" from the mental sphere. "And like voluntary control of the body, the mind controls everything the body does," says her classmate. Two further peers expand on this: "We can make our own judgments, and do what we feel is right"; "it (the mind) decides between alternative ways of doing it, on the basis of their consequences." Mind is a kind of will, consciously mulling over ideas, opinions, and feelings in the process of making practical decisions about the value of different action possibilities.

Qua will, and *contra* instinct, the mental is essentially a princi- ple of variety, uniqueness, and freedom, while the involuntary physical is automatic, unchanging, and determined. This vision of mind implicit in C.G.'s statement above, is replicated in the following:

S.R. (14.0)   What is the self? THE INNER SIDE, THE MIND
MOSTLY. HOW THE MIND WORKS. BECAUSE
YOUR BODY IS YOUR OUTSIDE, BUT YOUR
SELF IS MORE YOUR MIND .., IT'S JUST YOUR
MIND—THE WAY YOUR THOUGHTS GO. THERE
ARE PHYSICAL THINGS THAT EVERYBODY
HAS, AND THEY ARE STILL A PART OF YOU,
BUT A MORE MINOR PART.

What is unique to the inner is its style. Now that mental has been
clearly distinguished as invisible, it makes sense to talk about its
dispositional qualities. Baldwin (1906) talked about the emergence of
such *transitive meanings* pertaining to relations between states
during his period of the inner–outer dualism. This peculiar transitive
or stylistic quality of each mind is erected into the first real concept
of *self*, somewhat separate from and superior to the body. Moreover,
to be a self, it must stand apart from other sources of automatic and
unchanging action. For adolescents, the most salient source of this
kind is the peer group.

M.C. (18.4, F)   What is the self? BEING YOURSELF, ACTING
NATURAL ... NOT PHONY ... THE SELF IS
SOMETHING YOU WANT PEOPLE TO SEE. IT'S
NATURAL IN ONE WAY AND PHONY IN AN-
OTHER. I MEAN I THINK EVERYBODY IS
REALLY PHONY, BUT YOU'RE TRYING TO ACT
NATURAL. THE MIND ... IS WHAT YOU REALLY
THINK INSIDE OF YOU ... AND SOMETIMES
YOU'RE SCARED TO SAY. AND THE SELF IS
SOMETHING YOU KIND OF LIKE IMITATE. LIKE
IF YOU HAVE AN IDEAL, YOU IMITATE THAT,
YOU BASE YOUR IDEAS AROUND IT. I THINK
LIKE EVERYBODY HAS THE IDOL THEY LOOK
UP TO, AND IN A WAY THEY MIGHT NOT BE
INTENDING TO DO IT, BUT THEY DO, LIKE
IMITATE THEM IN SOME WAY. THAT'S PART OF
THE SELF ... THE MIND HAS ITS OWN WAY OF
THINKING ... THE SELF IS SOMETHING LIKE
IMITATING, BUT YOU'RE TRYING TO BE YOUR-
SELF.

If the self does not stand out from the crowd, it becomes part of a
body of people, where it is no more than a copy or fake, a self-for-
others which is reduced to a not-self. The metaphysical form of the
self is like that description of schizoid alienation presented in
Winnicott (1965), Gabel (1975), and Laing (1960). This *divided self* has
a real inner core, masked, protected and stifled by an outer social
role-self, an appearance or affected "personality" put on for the
benefit of others (Broughton, 1981; Kohlberg & Gilligan, 1971).
Two kinds of self-consciousness are here juxtaposed without

being integrated. There is immediate, intuitive awareness of "the real me" which constantly makes itself different, and relational or interpersonal awareness of self disguising itself to the other by taking its role, making itself the same as the other. The adolescent is thus caught between individuation and merging. While there is no problem knowing one's inner being, knowing another's is impossible:

> J.M. (16.0, F)   Can you ever know what someone is like on the inside? NO, NOT COMPLETELY . . . WE HAVE NO WAY OF JUDGING ON THE INSIDE . . . SO THE ONLY THING WE HAVE TO GO BY IS WHAT'S ON THE OUTSIDE, WHICH IS THE PERSONALITY.

It is their prerogative to know themselves. "Your mind is something very secret," said M.L. (17.6, F), "you mostly keep it to yourself. You don't want to go out and tell everybody what you think. That is why you are a separate person, different." Thus the prerogative is at the same time a metaphysical fact and a voluntary psychological strategy. It is made possible by the combined fact that (a) mind and body are only loosely tied, and (b) the self-determining self has complete control over the determined body. The consequence of this double whammy is that observation of someone's external bodily appearance does not give away their innermost mental reality.

As regards knowing the other (person), the Level-Three thinker is totally skeptical. Skepticism could presumably invade *knowledge* of the world in general now. In fact, this does not seem always to be the case. These young adolescents still believe in a naive empiricism: that on the whole our faculties give us a realistic impression of the world. However, under certain conditions, it is found that whereas Level Two innovated the possibility of sensory fallibility, Level Three has created the conditions for a more threatening fallibility of the mind. Because of the subjective and voluntary nature of mind, it can bias perception selectively. Others can question your perception of things. So truth, like the role-self, and in some ways like the relationship between mind and body, has to become "interpersonal."

> C.H. (13.8, F)   THEY COULD SAY "YOUR MIND IS MESSED UP," "YOUR MIND IS TRICKING YOU." . . . YOU HAVE TO—YOU NEED AN OPINION. YOU NEED THE SUPPORT OF SOMEONE SAYING "THAT'S GOOD."

Objectivity can now become social and corroborative, but note how little it has escaped the subjective sphere. Truth is a matter of plausibility or acceptance, of reassurance from one doubting individual to another. The values, preferences, and biases of the self can still invade the real, so that knower and known are no more a truly complete dualism than mental and physical.

To conclude, Level Three moves beyond the naive individualism and naive realism of Level Two. Individualism and realism do not disappear, however. The individual self is set in relation to other individuals. Ontologically, this compromises the individual's inner being, but epistemologically it offsets the fallibility of knowledge that results from the emergence of an augmented subjectivity, the newly powerful and creative mental control. The sameness of the inner object found in *secondary conversion* is the basis of the oneness of the physical object. Secondary conversion assures that something is fact, stripped of any supplementary opinion added by an individual self. So as the meaning of selfhood develops as mutual implication of selves, so also emerge the things in common that are not selves, much as Baldwin describes in the transition from his inner–outer dualism to the mind–body dualism proper.

Level Four: "Dualist"

Among our late adolescent and young adult subjects, further levels of development in natural philosophy appear. The first of these, Level Four, corresponds with Baldwin's "substantive dualism." Like the previous *immature* dualism, this adult level is based on a convergence of the categories of *reality* and *mind–body*. Level Four differs from Level Three in that it views reality as comprising two totally different, and mutually exclusive types of existence, Mind substance and Body substance (i.e., Matter).

The latter is more fully articulated than at the previous level, having an internal structure conceived in terms of lawful scientific mechanism. V. F. (26, F), for example, said, "I believe in action/reaction. Something happened, something caused it. And that is a whole world view." Said rather differently:

E.L. (22, F) CERTAIN CHEMICALS ALWAYS IN THE SAME PROPORTIONS DO THE SAME THING. AND YOU KNOW THAT'S SO, AND THERE'S JUST NO WAY TO REFUTE IT. THAT IS SOMEHOW A PHYSICAL TRUTH I GUESS. A CHEMICAL PHYSICAL TRUTH.

We are bound by such lawfulness:

K.X. (20, M) ONLY WHEN PEOPLE UNDERSTAND THE LAWS ARE THEY ABLE TO MAKE THEIR BEHAVIOR CONFORM WITH THE LAWS, AND THEREBY CONTROL THOSE LAWS.

Although there is not yet a reflective conception of law per se, there is a lawful quality to the physicochemical world, which is ordered positivistically in a series of discrete antecedent and consequent units, and which is discussed in a language of force. *Knowledge* is control of the empirical regularities. The mental world on the other hand is contrasted as "nonscientific" flux, unregulated by law, because it is beyond the senses.

Meeting in the person, mental and physical are related as the "ghost" to the "machine" (cf. Ryle, 1949). Meeting in the process of knowing, they strive to achieve a correspondence, which has been rendered impossible. This is so because the realism that remained at Level Three has now been rejected in favor of extending level three's skeptical aspect. The result of this is the creation of an absolute dualism of noumenon and phenomenon (essence and appearance). *Minds* construct the best copy or model they can of the physical and social world, *truth* reflecting the degree of match (empirically tested through prediction and control). Empiricism remains, but realism is seriously altered.

A systematic connection between the two halves of reality is sought within Level Four. However, this is hampered by the mutual exclusion of Mind and Body. As Baldwin (1913) points out, whereas the problem for immature dualists was one of *segregating* mind and body, the problem for substantive dualists is one of *reconciling* them. The realm of the mental remains puzzling:

V.F. (26, F)   THERE IS SOMETHING THAT GOES ON IN YOUR MIND THAT IS REAL, AT THE BASIC LEVEL OF ELECTRON FLOWS, SOMETHING THAT IS HAPPENING AND IS REAL. NOW I DON'T KNOW HOW TO TRACE FROM AN ELECTRON FLOW TO AN IDEA IN MY MIND. THE CONCLUSION IS THAT THE ONE IS THE CAUSE OF THE OTHER, AND THEREFORE I THINK IT IS REAL . . . THE ELECTRON THING IS REAL. IT IS MEASURABLE, AND IT IS A REACTION, A THING. I BELIEVE IF I CAN DO CALCULUS IN MY MIND, THAT IT IS ASSOCIATED, IT IS A REACTION TO THAT ELECTRON FLOW, AND THEREFORE IT IS REAL. IT IS A BELIEF. I BELIEVE IT, BUT I CAN'T PROVE IT . . . MAYBE THE MIND IS PART OF THE BRAIN WE DON'T UNDERSTAND.

Elsewhere she distinguishes from the "physical reality of the self," the "metaphysical" of "intellectual reality." Here is another example where, in the process of describing thoughts, someone finds that the intellect resists physical interpretations:

M.L. (22, F)   THERE ARE CHEMICAL THINGS. AND A MENTAL THING TOO, WHICH IS THE ACTUAL PICKING OVER OF THE THOUGHT, THE MEMORY. THE DISSECTIONS AND PUTTING BACK TOGETHER AGAIN. THE IDEA OF THOUGHTS IS MORE ROMANTIC THAN JUST CHEMICALS.

Because *knowledge* is reluctantly admitted to be a scientific form of understanding, *mind* retains a mysterious, spiritual quality. It is almost a "religious" realm housing the unknown. However, unlike Level Three, Level Four does construe the mental as something qualitatively quite different. It is a reality in itself, requiring a separate kind of explanation

W.W. (22, M)   FROM MY POINT OF VIEW, THE BRAIN IS THE PHYSICAL MACHINE THAT MAKES THE MIND GO. IF YOU BELIEVE IN LIFE AFTER DEATH, IF YOU BELIEVE IN A SOUL, THEN THE BRAIN IS KIND OF LIKE A PHYSICAL EXPLANATION TO SATISFY PEOPLE ABOUT THE DEFINITION OF THE MIND. AND THE MIND IS SOMETHING ABOVE THAT. I DON'T KNOW IF I BELIEVE THAT . . . NO ONE QUITE UNDERSTANDS HOW IT WORKS. I DON'T THINK WE'LL EVER FIND OUT. IT'S SOMETHING TO DO WITH ELECTRIC CHARGES IN THE BRAIN. IT'S INCOMPREHENSIBLE TO ME THAT ELECTRIC CHARGES COULD DO THAT, BUT IT SEEMS MORE LOGICAL THAN THE MIND JUST BEING BECAUSE GOD MADE IT SO. The mind is electricity? IT'S SOMETHING BEYOND THAT . . . IT'S FAR BEYOND ELECTRICITY . . . THEY ARE JUST SUCH OPPOSITE THINGS: ELECTRONS ON THE ONE SIDE, AND MENTAL IMAGES ON THE OTHER. NO ONE KNOWS HOW THEY'RE JOINED. THERE ARE SCIENTIFIC EXPLANATIONS FOR IT, MECHANICAL EXPLANATIONS. THEY CAN TELL YOU HOW IT HAPPENS BUT NOT WHY.

W.W. goes on to explore the epistemological consequences of this.

What would be "why"? I CAN'T EXPLAIN WHY I SEE THE LAMP HERE. THAT LAMP, THE LIGHT RAYS HIT MY EYE. THAT'S THE EXPLANATION, BUT—I'M TALKING ABOUT THE TRANSFER OF PHYSICAL PROPERTIES TO THE MENTAL PROPERTIES. HOW THE PHYSICAL PRESENCE OF THE LAMP IS TRANSMITTED TO YOUR MIND. THAT GETS BACK TO CODING. A MAN IS SCARED OF THE THOUGHT OF THE LION, NOT THE LION . . . YOU DON'T ACTUALLY SEE THE LAMP, YOU SEE THE IMAGE OR THE THOUGHT

> OF THE LAMP. How come you don't see the lamp?
> IT'S WHAT IT'S CALLED. THE LAMP'S KIND OF
> IN YOUR HEAD NOW. THE LAMP'S CODED ON
> TO YOUR BRAIN AND YOU SEE IT.

W.W.'s sharp dualizing results in a "copy theory of knowledge." Noumenon and phenomenon are parted, and it seems that never the twain shall meet. He goes on to characterize the noumenal reality, but finds a certain relative subjectivity, which drives him finally to a conventional definition of truth:

> THE CHAIR SHOULD EXIST INDEPENDENTLY
> OF PEOPLE SEEING IT ... IF I GO OUT OF THE
> ROOM, THAT CHAIR'S STILL "APPEARING" TO
> BE THERE, EVEN THOUGH I WOULD NEVER
> SEE IT ... IT IS ALL A PERSON'S PERCEPTION.
> THAT CHAIR IS A CHAIR. IF IT APPEARED DIF-
> FERENT TO SOMEONE ELSE, THEN IT WOULD
> BE A DISTORTION IN HIS PERCEPTION. MOST
> PEOPLE WOULD SEE IT AS A CHAIR ... THINGS
> EXIST BECAUSE PEOPLE PERCEIVE THEM TO
> EXIST, AND THEY'RE GIVEN THE DEFINITIONS
> ... I GUESS A MAJORITY OF PEOPLE AGREE ON
> DEFINITIONS, AND THAT'S HOW A DEFINITION
> IS.

However, he is not willing to say the majority could be wrong. His cohort, E.L. (22, F) points out that conventions serve an essential function: "That's the way we all view it, and that's the way we can all understand each other." V.F. adopts a position like W.W.'s, showing how truth can eventually come to dominate reality:

> YOU ALWAYS SEE THE APPEARANCE OF SOME-
> THING ... APPEARANCE MEANS THINGS. IT
> APPEARS DIFFERENTLY TO YOU THAN IT
> MIGHT APPEAR TO SOMEONE ELSE ... THE
> REALITY BEING BY MORE DEMOCRATIC VOTE
> ... THEY ARE ALL GOING TO SAY THAT THEIR
> SEEING REALITY IS THE ONLY MEASURE WE
> HAVE, IS BY CONSENSUS ... IF YOU ARE TAK-
> ING A VOTE, YOU ARE VOTING ON WHAT
> APPEARANCE IS THE MOST CORRECT REPRE-
> SENTATION OF REALITY. YOU ARE GUESSING
> WHICH REALITY IS REAL.

Each individual perceives a true aspect, and as W.W. says, "What you think is the most important as far as you're concerned." Nevertheless, the collectivist approach to truth works because it compounds different aspects additively. Knowledge for V.F. is like an accumulation of information:

EVERYONE PERCEIVES THINGS THROUGH DIF-
FERENT FILTERS. YOU NEED TO INTEGRATE
ALL THE FILTERS . . . BECAUSE YOU SEE MORE
AND MORE ASPECTS OF A DIFFERENT THING.
BUT THEN YOU'RE TALKING ABOUT A HUMAN
REALITY IF YOU INTEGRATE OVER ALL PEO-
PLE.

This corresponds to what Baldwin called "social meaning," the kind
of common knowledge in which each individual attributes to the
other the awareness that they share in a common knowing process.
The appearance of social meaning at Level Four is reflected in the
return of control to the social world, or to the authority of a truly
general acceptance. At Level Three, the real fell under the inner
subjective control of mental self (opinion) and the outer objective
control of body (fact). At Level Four, *self* and *reality* are mental or
physical substances behind appearance. They are organized essences
abstracted from experience by the process of social corroboration.
The uncorroborated is determined as systematic error contributed
by mind, while that which is commonly accepted is determined as
material reality.

Knowledge is both sensory and "supersensible." As we have
just seen, mind abstracts or induces a pattern from the units of
sensory information which different individual perspectives supply.
Knowledge is thus a compounding of experiences into an abstract
"total" experience, what W.W. called a "definition." It is as if a
generalized other existed to actually take this impartial and objective
perspective. The Mind of this generalized other is able to effect its
generalization through powers of association modelled on the cause-
effect relations of the material world.

V.F. (26, F)   SEEING IS A PIECE OF DATA AND KNOWING IS
A GENERALIZATION. "THIS CAR IS RED" AS
OPPOSED TO "ALL CARS ARE RED" . . . A gener-
alization? GENERALIZATIONS ARE FOR THE
PURPOSE OF PREDICTING. IT HAS NOTHING
TO DO WITH A PARTICULAR CAR. IT IS A SYS-
TEM OF ABSTRACTS WHICH MAKES A WORLD
VIEW.

Knowledge or understanding is therefore *supersensible* by virtue of
going beyond the information given to a predictive generalization. As
Hegel pointed out in his third stage of consciousness, both concepts
of *force* (generated by the physical world) and *law* (generated by the
mental–social world) introduce some general quality that goes beyond the sensible particulars to bind them into one whole. It is very
much in the spirit of this Hegelian stage that Baldwin talks of Mind

and Body as general substances uniting, respectively, the minds and the bodies of particular individuals.

The positivistic combination of the empiricist psychology of mind, the copy theory of knowledge, and the conventional theory of truth, creates an ambiguity in the notion of reality. On the one hand, it appears to be a "human reality," something defined by our knowledge of it, through an impartial quasiscientific rationality. On the other hand, it also seems to have some existence or purpose beyond that. Perhaps this is why V.F. said (above) about the reality of mind, "Maybe the mind is part of the brain we don't understand." The dualism of noumenal and phenomenal pervades the psychophysical dualism as well. There is a paradoxical feeling that the mental is something bigger or more real "above" the mundane physical reality, which is bound by certain earthly limits. E.L. says about truth, "When you get into big things, things aren't always one way or the other— mental things you can't always say black or white."

It is in following this path that we reach the Level Four understanding of *self*. In D.H. Lawrence's "The Rainbow," Ursula has doubts about the materialist philosophy of her physics professor:

> But the purpose, what was the purpose? Electricity had no soul, light and heat had no soul. Was she herself an impersonal force, or conjunction of forces, like one of these?

E.L. echoes the romantic sentiment when she says, "You can know every aspect of the chemical, whereas to me you just can't know every aspect of a person." What is this additional quality? Even though the mental is seen as different from the physical by virtue of being "outside law," it has to be defined in terms of its own internal regulation, its formal, systematic quality. V.F. says, "Type of thinking is probably the way a person uses or doesn't use logic, a type of planning, a way of running your life or not running it." An undergraduate puts it this way:

> B.C. (22, M)   THE WAY YOUR MIND PUTS THINGS IN A LOGICAL PROGRESSION—THOUGHT PATTERNS . . .
> I THINK THE SELF IS THE LIFE FORCE IN A LOGICAL PROGRESSION. Is that the same thing? WELL, NO. LIFE FORCE IS THE THING THAT MOTIVATES YOU, BUT THE LOGICAL PROGRESSION IS JUST THE INTELLECT, THE THOUGHT PROCESSES OF THE SELF.

For B.C., this inner self is quite separate from his corporeal self:

> I MEAN THE BODY FOR ME IS JUST AN APPEARANCE, IS JUST A SHADOW. IT'S THE LIVING FORCE INSIDE YOU KNOW, THE IDEAS THAT EMANATE, THAT ARE THE SELF.

In this sense, the self is soul, the noumenal essence or being of someone. An intellectual high school senior responds this way:

J.F. (18, M)   What is the self? I DON'T KNOW. THE SELF, YOU CAN DESCRIBE IT AS THE *SOUL* OF ONE, THE INNER THING THAT MAKES HIM GO . . . GIVING YOU A REASON FOR BEING.

By Level Four, the self has been differentiated from the mind as soul, a purer part of mentality, where purity is associated with formal, abstract, or logical intelligence. J.F. continues:

> IT IS SOMETHING MORE THAN THE MIND, IS ALL I CAN SAY. IT GOES DEEPER. SAY IT IS THE PSYCHE . . . THE MIND SEEMS TO BE STRAIGHT-FORWARD: A PERSON HAS TO HAVE DEPTH TO HIM . . . I THINK THERE IS A SOUL, MENTAL, AND PHYSICAL SELF . . . THE SOUL DOES SEEM TO BE SEPARATED FROM THE MENTAL AND PHYSICAL . . . THE SOUL IS COMPLETELY SEPARATE. IT IS SO MUCH HIGHER UP THAN ANY OF THEM, BECAUSE THE MIND CANNOT COMPREHEND THE SOUL . . . IF YOU BELIEVE IN GOD, IT IS CLOSER TO GOD . . . THEN EVERY THOUGHT THAT EVERY PERSON IN THE WORLD HAS, NO MATTER HOW MUCH OF A GENIUS HE IS, GOD IS ALWAYS HIGHER THAN HIM BECAUSE HE GIVES HIM THE GENIUS THOUGHTS.

In order to understand the conceptual function of "soul" as defining individuality, we also have to consider dialectically related conceptions of "plurality" at this level. We have already seen the way in which society and self are related in the epistemological function. Reality is defined by a social group, and the self's judgment contributes equally to this. But (in W.W.'s words), "What you think is the most important as far as you're concerned," and V.F. emphasizes the importance of "getting all the (individual) points" before you could "integrate" them, or "take all the different points, and find some picture of the whole." This is not a simple conformism, but a democratic conventionalism that gives some say to the individual. Objectivity is impartiality, made possible by the differentiation of the generic individual from its interpersonal context of roles. "If somebody is different, it is usually assumed that he is wrong, until he convinces other people," is the way we reach a "human reality," as V.F. called it. Thus epistemologically, Level Four dialectically reconciles the particular with the general, the individual with the system.

The notion of soul is likewise Janus-faced. The physical attributes of the soul yield a common "species-essence," defining person-hood, a fusion of individuals through what Norman O. Brown calls the "erotic sense of reality" (Brown, 1968, p. 82). Our high-school senior J.F. says of the body, "In some people it differs, but I also say it links you to the rest of them—it gives you an identity with man." Later J.F. sees a snag in this: "Because you are part of mankind, your thoughts are always related to someone else's thoughts." This calls for some segregation of you as self, as identity, as M.L. also notes:

M.L. (22, F)   ESPECIALLY IN TODAY'S WORLD, PEOPLE TEND TO THINK OF MANKIND AS BEING A MASS. MASS SOCIETY, MASS COMMUNICATIONS, MASS MEDIA. THERE HAS TO BE A PART FROM THAT HUGE MASS, THAT CAN BRING YOU ALONE WITH YOURSELF. TO BE ABLE TO DO THAT IS CONFIRMATION THAT THERE IS IN-DEED INDIVIDUALITY IN THE WORLD AND THAT THERE IS STILL A SELF.

For this reason, J.F. defines his self as "an individual in that society, a separate unit individual . . . the soul is the essence of identity in the self." W.W. says, "It's just that you're separate from everything else," and another undergraduate says, "The person must be a unique individual, despite his membership in a species of like beings." Even the logical, intellectual quality of spirit emphasizes its separateness, because logic is "entirely self-contained" (V.F.).

The self–society dialectic can be troublesome:

B.C. (22, M)   BECAUSE THE PROHIBITIONS OF THE SOCIETY PROBABLY ARISE OR DO ARISE FROM PARTS OF EVERYBODY ELSE'S SELF . . . AND HENCE THE ALTERNATIVES ARE EITHER LETTING YOURSELF BE SUBMITTED TO THAT, TO THOSE PROHIBITIONS, FLOWING ALONG WITH THE STREAM SO TO SPEAK, OR THE OTHER WAY—LIKE GOING AGAINST THE GRAIN.

B.C. sees Martin Luther as the archetypal self, refusing to be engulfed by tradition, in order to preserve his self: "You have to admire their standing up for and testifying for what they believe in, that's kind of—there I think the inner self, the soul, comes through." "Self-direction," or "self-monitoring" makes one autonomous *in spite of* external influences. It is a negative way of defining the self. For B.C., it is the ability to defy the norm by saying, "I will not, I cannot, and I will not." It is a resistance against "some external force trying to invade the self," a resistance to outer control which requires an internalized *self*-control. J.F., M.L., W.W., V.F., and B.C. (all in their early 20's), see self-control as central to consciousness and self. For B.C. something becomes part of your self. when you "integrate it into yourself" rather than "allowing yourself to be sold on something. . . . I think you have to convince yourself. You know, sit down and say, 'Well, of course. It's logical. Of course I believe it.' "

This brings us to the trancendent or reflective character of self at Level Four. Existence of self and consciousness of self are closely tied. If, as K.X. said above, knowledge is really control, then self-control is a form of self-knowledge. A second undergraduate expands on this theme:

M.L. (22, F)	I'M NOT SURE THERE IS MUCH CONTROL WITHIN THE SELF. THE MIND OR THE CONSCIOUS WILL TRY TO MAKE DECISIONS ABOUT THE SELF, BUT THE SELF BEING SO MANY PARTS IS UNGOVERNABLE BY ITSELF, AND IT MAY BE VERY DIFFICULT IF ONE HAS A VERY STRONG WILL. BUT THERE ARE SO MANY OTHER PARTS OF THE WAY ONE IS, AND UNCONSCIOUS THINGS THAT PEOPLE DO. THE SELF IS NOT ALWAYS CONSCIOUS OF ITSELF, OR OF ITS BEING, AND EVERYWHERE IT EXISTS, SO THAT YOU CAN'T HAVE THAT CONTROL. IF THE MIND IS NOT AWARE OF IT . . . THEN THERE IS NO WAY THAT IT CAN CONTROL IT.

Transcendence or reflection is not only implied in the notions of self-control, but also in (a) going against the grain; (b) J.F.'s idea that the soul is "so much higher up," and in his idea of God; (c) the inner self for M.L. having "the most direct control over your mind"; and (d) V.F.'s and B.C.'s description of the intellectual self ordering the thinking process. It is even implied in (e) the copy theory of knowledge (expounded by W.W.), since from that viewpoint, the internal image must be constructed and apprehended by something. All these characteristics form a new basis for distinguishing people as "spiritual" beings from other things. People are "on a different plane," and are "aware of the life force itself."

What we have on our hands at Level Four is a further differentiation of "I" and "me," such that for the first time there appears an existential component of self, its essential attribute, the *cogito*. "I think when you are observing yourself, you are doing one of the most, I will use the word *spiritual*, things you can ever do," is B.C.'s way of putting it. E.L. stresses the cogito in tackling the issue of personal identity:

E.L. (22, F)	Is your self always the same or does it change? I THINK PART OF IT IS ALWAYS THE SAME AND YOU KNOW THAT IT'S YOU. IT GOES THROUGH CYCLES OF CHANGE LIKE PUTTING OUT LEAVES. THERE'S STILL SOMETHING

> THAT'S YOU, THAT MIGHT BECOME MODIFIED, BUT YOU ALWAYS RECOGNIZE IT AS YOUR-SELF. What part stays the same? USUALLY I KNOW HOW I'M GOING TO REACT TO SOMETHING ... IT'S STILL ME. What is the way in which you know it is you? THE ONLY WAY I KNOW IS BECAUSE MY MIND IS MY SELF. YOU'RE ALWAYS THINKING, AND THAT'S HOW YOU KNOW YOU'RE THERE. It's the actual process of thinking? YES, I THINK SO.

Later on in the interview she says rather pithily, "Just the going on of oneself is a thinking, almost."

The cogito is the central core of certainty. The following illustrations are answers to the question, "How do you know you exist?"

E.L. (22, F)	I CAN'T EVER DENY, ER, I'D ALWAYS BE SURE OF MYSELF. I MIGHT NOT KNOW ABOUT ANYTHING ELSE, BUT I'D ALWAYS BE SURE OF MYSELF.
D.A. (18, F)	WE HAVE THE CAPABILITY OF ASKING IN THE FIRST PLACE "DO WE EXIST?" SO MAYBE IF WE CAN ASK THAT QUESTION, I CAN ASK IT, I CAN THINK ABOUT IT, SO MAYBE I AM.
P.L. (22, M)	BECAUSE I THINK. IF I DON'T EXIST, WHAT AM I? SO THEREFORE I HAVE TO EXIST, BECAUSE I AM SOMETHING ... IT IS NOT REALLY WHAT I BELIEVE, BUT IT COULD BOIL DOWN TO: EVERYTHING ELSE MIGHT BE FIGMENTS OF MY IMAGINATION, BUT I KNOW THAT I EXIST ... I AM AWARE OF MYSELF, SO I MUST EXIST.

This self-awareness often brings with it the notion of self as an empirical "self-concept." P.L. (22, M) said that the self is "what a person thinks of himself. How he thinks he handles things," while W.W. opined that "the self is what you are, what I think W.W. to be ... you know how you act in certain situations ... and you know what to expect of yourself." We saw just now a similar statement about the self from E.L.: "Usually I know how I'm going to react to something." This amounts to a *generalized self*, corresponding to the generalized other implied in the conventional view of knowledge discussed above. The reflection is the reflection of the "I" upon the "me," and the self-concept is just the observable "me." Reflection is like all knowledge: it is prediction and control of empirical regularities. Self-awareness is confounded with self-control. As in psychology (Broughton & Riegel, 1977), when the self is thought of only in its empirical aspect (what Baldwin calls the object-self), the "I" or subject-self becomes vestigial. This leaves the self as a self-concept without a self-conceiver. It is in later levels of development that this lost subjectivity must be replaced.

This self-observing force exerting inner control is given the characteristics usually ascribed by philosophers to "substance" (cf. Hegel, 1975; Cassirer, 1923; Frondizi, 1953): individuation (discreteness and independence), permanence, uniqueness, self-identity, personality, transcendence, and the possession of "attributes" through which it is manifested and from which it is inferred.

We have already seen some examples of individuation as an issue in defining identity in relation to society. Showing the intimate relation between this and many of the other characteristics of substance, M.L. says that the self is:

> THAT PARTICULAR PART OF THE PERSON THAT HAS THE MOST DIRECT INFLUENCE ON THEIR LIVES. A LOT OF PEOPLE THINK OF MANKIND AS ONE MASSIVE UNIVERSE, OR THE SELF AS BEING ONE HUGE MASS. BUT WHEN YOU START TALKING ABOUT WORLD SPIRITS, OR GOD AS A COLLECTIVE IDENTITY, YOUR SELF IS THAT PART THAT IS YOU, THAT HAS THE ARMS, LEGS, PHYSICAL ATTRIBUTES OF ONE'S SELF, THAT HAS THE MOST DIRECT CONTROL OVER YOUR MIND, AND YOUR PARTICULAR BODY. IT IS THAT PART THAT MAKES IT INDIVIDUAL.

Finally, the Level Three notion that the permanence and personal identity or sameness of the self is equivalent to the retaining of specific opinions, character traits or memories, is transcended at Level Four. Self-identity now resides in the *system* or structural relation of parts to whole. P.L., a geologist, says:

> THE BASIS OF THE WHOLE THING STAYS THE SAME ... Is it the same self? IT CAN BE THE SAME SELF, BUT IN A DIFFERENT FORM. LIKE METAMORPHOSIS OF SANDSTONE TO QUARTZITE. IT IS THE SAME MATERIAL, JUST IN A DIFFERENT FORM. The same material? THE SAME COMPOSITION.

Thus, the same kind of systematic interrelatedness that typifies mind body, and knowledge and reality at this level comes to characterize the internal structure of the self. At Level Four, as Baldwin suggested, the metaphysical problem underlying all categories is the relation of general to particular. The two poles of force (or control) and law (logic, form) provide the paradigm/concepts through which the parts are made into coherent wholes.

Level Five: "Subjective"

The theories of actuality are not content to accept the various modes of the actual which experience reveals; this would be too pluralistic. All actuality must be reduced to one type: it must be perceptual, or rational, or moral, or spiritual. So the actualist shifts his ground, proposing an ideal of unity for reality, and introducing a monistic postulate in order to overcome the dualisms and pluralisms of his own requirement of actuality. The great dualism of mind and matter is in this way overcome when the presupposition of mind is carried over as a postulate into the domain of matter, as in spiritualism and theism. Materialism, on the other hand, extends the sphere of matter, in the form of brain cells or chemical elements, in order to explain the reality of mind. Its presupposition is also converted into a monistic postulate. (Baldwin, 1915, p. 219)

In this next phase of philosophical development, as Baldwin describes, the grand classes of *mind* and *body* substance encounter disrespect.

L.R. (22, F)   Does the brain control the body? IT IS PRETTY MUCH LIKE WHICH CAME FIRST, THE CHICKEN OR THE EGG, WHICH IS MAYBE NOT SCIENTIFICALLY. THEY ARE BOTH SO INTERTWINED THAT YOU COULD NOT SAY ONE CONTROLLED THE OTHER ... THE MIND CONTROLS THE BODY LIKE IN PSYCHOSOMATIC ILLNESSES ... I BELIEVE IN A SENSE THAT EVERY DISEASE IS PSYCHOSOMATIC ... Is that the mind controlling the body? IT'S MORE A CASE OF THEM BEING HOPELESSLY INTERTWINED ... I WOULD HAVE BLAMED IT ON PLATO. THE EARLY PHILOSPHERS INVENTED THE DIVISION OF THE BODY AND THE SOUL.

L.R. is a modern-day instantiation of Ursula's physics professor, espousing a deterministic reductionism which Ursula, presumably at Level Four, had found counterintuitive. In Baldwin's words, L.R. "extends the sphere of matter in the form of brain cells or chemical elements, in order to explain the reality of mind":

What is the mind? THE MIND IS THE BRAIN, THE ACTUAL PHYSICAL BRAIN ... It's the same as the brain? YEAH. Any difference between mind and brain? NO ... MIND IS MATTER THAT KNOWS HOW TO DO TRICKY THINGS. IT IS SPECIAL KINDS OF CELLS OR SOMETHING, SPECIAL CHEMICALS.

D.O., also 22, said, "I guess there is no such thing as immaterial things." Paradoxically, there is a return to the psychophysics of Level

Two, where mind was equated with brain, reduced to a bodily organ:

L.R. (22, F)   What is the difference between mind and body?
THE DIFFERENCE BETWEEN APPLES AND
FRUIT ... MIND IS A PART, A SORT OF
CATEGORY OF THE BODY. IT IS ONE OF THE
PARTS OF THE BODY, LIKE FEET.

The difference of course is one of form rather than content. Whereas
Level Two had yet to actually differentiate mind from body, Level
Five is a "monistic postulate." This means that it is a self-conscious
reduction of mental to material, logically posterior and in response
to the development of a mind body dualism. Mind is a "category" of
the body. Only the inane activities of philosophers like Plato could
have given rise to the illusion of two separate existences.

The skepticism about there being a separate mental substance
extends to embrace the *self*:

L.R. (22, F)   What is the self? I THINK IT IS WRONG TO SAY
YOU HAVE A SELF. YOU ARE WHAT YOU SEE,
WHAT THE BODY CAN DO. SO I DON'T REALLY
BELIEVE IN THE SELF. IT'S A PHILOSOPHICAL
INVENTION SOMEBODY MADE UP TO SELL
DEODORANT.

Where Level Four romantically defended the speculative, philosophical principle of life and soul, L.R. undermines it:

Where does the person come from? THE PERSON
IS JUST THE PHYSICAL THING. NOTHING ME-
TAPHYSICAL. WHAT I MEAN IS THERE ISN'T
ANYTHING THAT GOES TO HEAVEN WHEN
YOU DIE. THERE ISN'T ANY DISEMBODIED LIFE
FORCE, LIKE THERE IS IN STAR TREK ... THE
MIND ROTS WHEN YOU DIE, JUST LIKE THE
BODY DOES.

However, we would overlook Baldwin's important insight were
we not to realize that mechanical materialism is simply the other
side of the coin from spiritualism or subjective idealism. Both have
in common the formal characteristic that they are monistic reactions
against an already comprehended dualism. The fact that they are
alternatives to each other is revealed not only through an analysis of
their logical interconnections, and mutual implication, but through
an empirical discovery of their cooccurrence in the same subject.

The breakdown of self as substance, perhaps underlying Erikson's *identity crisis*, is paradoxically built upon a heightened sense
of reflectivity. As Baldwin points out in describing the *reflective
dualism* of the "content" stage (Table 2), Mind and Body are not only

"hopelessly intertwined," but they are contents within a single domain of "Experience." Thus, on the idealist side of the coin, mind is "carried over ... into the domain of matter." Mind and body become identified with "mind-experience" and "body-experience," parts of yourself set over against the experiencer:

D.L. (22, F)   I'VE EXPERIENCED MY MIND A LOT ... What is the mind? IT'S JUST ALL THOSE THINGS THAT DRIVE YOU CRAZY FIVE MILLION TIMES A MINUTE. I DIDN'T EVEN KNOW WHAT THE EXPERIENCE OF THE MIND WAS ... THE EXPERIENCE OF THE MIND TELLS ME I AM SEPARATE FROM WHAT'S HAPPENING ... You talked about the mind, what is the body? FOR MYSELF, I EXPERIENCE THEM LINKED UP. EXPERIENCE I HAVE WITH THE BODY IS THE SAME AS THE EXPERIENCE I HAVE WITH MY MIND ... FOR ME EXPERIENCE OF MIND AND BODY IS A SIMILAR EXPERIENCE. DEFINITELY A PART OF ME, BUT NOT MY TRUE SELF.

Ever since Level Three, there has been an unavoidably social aspect to meaning. Level Five is no exception. However, with the introduction of the notion of experience, there enters a new complication: the self now exists chiefly in experience, but whose experience is it?

L.R. (22, F)   What makes up a person? IT'S A TANGLED WEB. A PERSON'S NATURE EXISTS MOSTLY IN THE MINDS OF PEOPLE WHO HE INTERACTS WITH. AND A PERSON'S CONCEPT OF HIS OWN NATURE EXISTS IN WHAT HE THINKS OTHERS THINK OF HIM.

D.O. (22, F)   What is the self? I OFTEN WONDER. I SAID THAT I THOUGHT THE SELF WAS WHAT YOU DID, YOUR ACTIONS, AND LITTLE THINGS LIKE WHAT YOU WEAR AND HOW YOU CARRY YOURSELF AND HOW YOU KNOW OTHER PEOPLE SEE YOU ... I THINK IF YOU'RE AWARE OF THE WAY OTHER PEOPLE SEE YOU, YOU CAN ESTIMATE YOURSELF AND SAY "IS THIS THE WAY I WANT PEOPLE TO SEE ME." Is the person-you-want-to-be-taken-as part of yourself? THAT *IS* YOUR SELF.

The problem introduced by the notion of experience is that it makes *reality* into an appearance to me. L.R. goes on to render a modified version of the *cogito*: I think I am, therefore I am what I think.

IT GETS PRETTY CONFUSING SOMETIMES WHEN YOU TRY TO KNOW YOURSELF. IT GETS INTO THINGS LIKE "AM I THIS, OR DO I *THINK* I AM THIS" ... AND I THINK THAT IS SORT OF THE SAME THING. Is there no way to tell if it's what we are or what we think we are? I HAVE DECIDED THAT IT IS RIDICULOUS TO WONDER ABOUT IT. BE-CAUSE IT IS A CASE OF SUBJECTIVE REALITY, AND WHAT YOU ARE IS THE SAME THING AS WHAT YOU THINK YOU ARE. THERE IS NO OTHER WAY.

Exists is equated with "exists for me":

T.L. (19, M) WHATEVER EXISTS FOR ME IS REAL. WHATEVER I EXPERIENCE. WHATEVER HAS AN EFFECT ON ME, MYSELF.

J.N. (18, M) struck terror into the heart of the interviewer by refusing to answer questions that had the word "real" in them. He explained that all experience was real, by definition, and none more real than any other. Pressed to respond, he said,

REALITY IS MY OWN BELIEF, IF I THINK SOME-ONE LIKES ME, THEN THAT'S REAL EVEN IF SO-CIETY SAYS IT ISN'T ... THERE'S NO ABSOLUTE TRUTH. IT'S AN EXPRESSION OF SELF, REVEAL-ING YOUR TRUTH, AN ELEMENT OF YOURSELF.

Cassirer (1923, p. 387) has succinctly described this form of "ancient skepticism.":

Among the skeptical "tropes" intended to show the uncertainty of sensuous and conceptual knowledge, the "trope" of $\pi \rho \acute{o} s \tau \iota$ stands in the first place. To know the object, our knowledge would, above all, have to be in a position to grasp it in its pure "in itself" and to separate it from all the determinations, which only belong to it relatively to us and other things. But this separation is impossible, not only actually, but in principle. For what is actually given to us only under certain definite conditions can never be made out logically as what it is in itself and under abstraction from precisely these conditions. In what we call the perception of a thing, we can never separate what belongs to the objective thing from what belongs to the subjective perception and contrast the two as independent factors.

In the words of L.R.,

THERE COULD BE AN UNSUBJECTIVE REALITY, AND THAT COULD BE WHAT THE MIND RE-FLECTS. BUT THAT UNSUBJECTIVE REALITY WOULD JUST BE ARBITRARY. IT WOULD NOT MATTER TO ANYONE BECAUSE NO ONE WOULD BE ABLE TO SEE IT. SO IN THAT SENSE IT COULD BE UNREAL ... IT SEEMS KIND OF ACADEMIC.

L.R. implicitly rejects the copy theory of knowledge articulated at Level Four, as indeed the good bishop Berkeley had done before her. With what could the copy be compared? Only another copy.

In this last excerpt from L.R., and in J.N.'s comments above, there is also a resistance to the social-conventional truth developed at Level Four. There is a return, albeit not without discomfort, to a more immediate definition of the real.

> A reaction tends to show itself, whenever speculation has reached its full maturity, toward the recognition of experiences of immediacy, experiences in which the dualisms and oppositions of actual and ideal, the presupposed and the postulated, have not been developed ... Hence appear various attempts to find an immediacy, whether of revelation or of intuition or of inspiration or of contemplation, in which a purer and fairer vision of the real emerges upon the gaze of man. (Baldwin, 1915, p. 220)

However, Level Five cannot attain a "purer and fairer" vision with which it is comfortable. The added reflectivity implicit in the emergence of the "free" abstract self and its experience is a curse in disguise. It is the curse of philosophy, of abstract and idealistic thought. For example, L.R. complains about the fruit of the tree of knowledge, and the paradise lost, in the following way.

> IT GETS INTO "I KNOW THAT YOU KNOW THAT I KNOW." OR PEOPLE WONDERING WHAT YOU EXPECT OF THEM. IT IS AN EXTRA STEP THAT COMPLICATES THINGS ... A PERSON SHOULD BE ABLE TO EXIST WITHOUT HAVING TO WORRY ABOUT EVERYTHING HE DOES FALLING ON TOP OF HIS HEAD. A PERSON SHOULD BE UNEXPOSED TO ADVERTISING. A PERSON SHOULD BE ALLOWED TO INSTINCTIVELY KNOW WHAT HAPPINESS IS, AND HENCE BE HAPPY. I THINK IT'S IMPOSSIBLE *NOW*.

Reflection implies comparison, comparison implies an ideal, and an awareness of difference, of falling short. The only solution within Level Five is to give up the contradictory dream of actual and ideal, of truth and the perfection it seems to imply, and withdraw into a thoroughgoing "deep subjectivity," to use Poole's apt phrase:

> D.L. (22, F)   PEOPLE ARE CONSTANTLY PILING THINGS ON TOP OF THEMSELVES. RATHER THAN ASKING THE QUESTION "WHAT AM I DOING HERE?", AFTER I'VE REALIZED WHO MY SOUL REALLY IS, THEN IN THAT CONSCIOUSNESS I CAN DO ALL THOSE THINGS. IT'S *PLAYING*, NOT REAL. YOU'RE SEEKING REALITY ... BUT IT ALWAYS CRACKS ... HUNG UP ON IMAGERY INSTEAD OF GOING INTO *EXPERIENCE* ... IT'S LIKE TRYING TO COVER OVER LOOKING AT WHAT'S YOUR LIFE. THEN MY BEING IN ITS TOTALITY IS AWARE, COMPLETELY HERE. THEN I CAN PLAY. THOSE THINGS DON'T HAVE THE SAME POWER BECAUSE I DON'T GIVE THEM THE POWER. I DON'T NEED THEM TO BE REAL ANY MORE. THEY'RE JUST THEMSELVES.

D.L. returns to consciousness. Consciousness is relation, relation is all things, and all things are conscious, or have selves. Objects of awareness, previously assumed to be different in nature from the mind aware of them, are now found to have a natural identity with consciousness. This stage Hegel (1967, pp 217–218) called *self-certainty*, his fourth level of selfconsciousness. The noumenon which we saw at the previous level has become completely submerged in the phenomenon. The insight to be conserved is that nothing is given in itself. However, thence leaps an inference that drives Level Five into a cul-de-sac, leading to the unwarranted conclusion that reality and impartiality are pretenses, and that there can be no objectivity. In freeing the self from both law and force, it is merely erected as a total law and a total force combined in one. Level Five shows great distaste for reifying, on the sides of both subjective and objective "controls." Nevertheless, in trying to reduce mind to matter or matter to experience, this kind of thinking presupposes a subtler and even more profound reification of both self and reality.

Level Six: "Rational"

As Cassirer (1923, p. 388) points out, there are two very different forms of skepticism. Ancient skepticism (e.g., Protagoras), despaired of reaching the absolute "things" because the world required those things to be put into relation with minds or perceivers for them to be known. *Reality* dissolved again into appearance. This despair however is only felt when there is a tacit clinging to the notion that there could have been essences or substances, and that they would have been the only objective realities possible, were objectivity possible at all. There *could* be an unsubjective reality, said L.R. above, but we just have no way of knowing, so in the end it makes no difference.

Modern skepticism (e.g., Hume) on the other hand can only set in when it is realized that nature consists of *laws*, and not of things. This position cannot allow the leap from the fact that nothing is given in itself but always in a relation, to the conclusion that there can be no objectivity, since it is precisely the job of these laws to account for the nature of the relations. While physical reality was "lawful" at Level Four, Level Six elaborates a reflective concept of law, which can then be applied to the mental realm as well as the physical one. This yields social sciences as legitimate rational pursuits in addition to the natural sciences. At Level Four, remember, a certain primitive positivism led to a tendency to exclusively define the real in terms of the sciences of strict causal determination: the natural or even physical sciences.

"We just have no way of knowing" was the desperate plea of

our Level Five romantic, L.R. Early in his life, Piaget saw the important parallel to the history of ideas:

> In the eighteenth century, the French Revolution, provoked by the advent of the sciences of man, is the point at which faith ceases to be enriched by science. As a result, the Romanticism of the nineteenth century is a return to the self and a rejection of science. Romanticism engenders, in its turn, positivism ... But positivism cannot prevail because it lacks a theory of knowledge. (Piaget, 1918; see Gruber & Voneche, 1977, p. 46)

At Level Six, "The subject ... is perforce a critic, an epistemologist, a reasoner about ideas and realities" (Baldwin, 1906, p. 266). In other words, the missing theory of knowledge is at last found. To use the felicitous phrase employed by another proponent of genetic logic, Lonergan (1957), individuals undergo an "intellectual conversion," by which they realize that their epistemic activity is not something apart from the known, but is itself constitutive of knowledge.

R.B. (26, M)   (TRUTH) ISN'T OBSERVABLE. YOU CAN'T GET TRUTH DIRECTLY FROM OBSERVATION. THAT'S RUN THROUGH WITH THE CATEGORIES OF YOUR OWN MIND ... How do you prove something true? YOU PROVE IT TRUE BY GIVING REASONS. AND THE REASONS THAT YOU GIVE ALSO REFLECT YOUR CATEGORIES ... What do you mean "run through with the categories of your own mind"? YOU CAN USE THE CATEGORIES THAT YOU HAVE TO SORT THE DATA COMING IN, TO UNDERSTAND, TO GIVE MEANING TO THOSE EXPERIENCES ... THAT'S THE PROCESS OF INTERPRETATION. THE CATEGORIES YOU HAVE AREN'T PURELY PERSONAL. YOU GAINED THEM THROUGH EXPERIENCE OF OTHERS' WRITING, AND OTHER MINDS. YOU ADOPT SOME FROM OUTSIDE AND DEVELOP SOME ON YOUR OWN. YOU USE WHATEVER WORKS.

It no longer suffices to make a radical split between *mind* and *reality* as at Levels Four and Five, fudging it first by making truth entirely objective (Four), and then making it entirely subjective (Five). The only resolution is to set up criteria distinguishing subjective and objective *within* experience. Subjectivity is seen as *presupposing* objective reality, rather than excluding it or swallowing it up. They become logically correlative. Criteria are set defining what is objective knowing and what is subjective. Another way of saying this is that the subjective world of thought is subdivided into rational and irrational. At Level Five, in the attempt to introduce the reality of experience which lay behind Mind and Body, all reality was mistakenly reduced to experience. At Level Six, a new reflectivity introduces a needed distinction between the psychological as actually existing, and the actual existence or nonexistence of the contents contemplated by the psyche. The control is returned to the force of legitimate argument and to the criteria of validity which hold within the appropriate sphere of thought.

> N.S. (26, F)   SUBJECTIVITY REFERS TO THAT ASPECT OF EXPERIENCE THAT A PERSON BRINGS TO EXPERIENCE. OBJECTIVITY IS WHEN IT MEETS THOSE CRITERIA WHICH WE HAVE ESTABLISHED FOR TRUTH IN THAT PARTICULAR AREA . . . WE GET THIS DISTINCTION OF SUBJECTIVE AND OBJECTIVE BECAUSE OF OUR EXPERIENCING OF EXPERIENCE.

As H.M., a very bright high school senior, says, within this world view objectivity is attained by submitting observations to the criteria of "logical processes." These are not only generally accepted, but are grounded in some way. They generate truly synnomic meanings. The criteria of rationality are thus coherence within the categorical system, and congruence with observation.

At the dualistic adolescent levels (Three and Four), external control was attributed to consensus arrived at interpersonally or by the social group. The *cogito* was confused with the *controlling* of things. At Level Five, there arose disenchantment with convention and with the loss of freedom entailed by control. This led to an attempt to return control to the individual in the shape of his or her object-self, experience. At Level Six the contradictions of this subjectivism and solipsism are avoided by returning control to an impersonal, rational system of synnomic meaning, which bears a regulating relationship to society and individual alike.

> Thus society is carried out of the pre-logical into the logical stage of thought, through the personal competence and insistence of individuals. Society is the disciplinary agent, the schoolmaster, to the individual's thought; but the pupil outgrows the social school. He learns that he and the society alike, of which he is a part, have to submit to the twists of another and impersonal system of controls: those of nature, given in perception; and those of logical consistency, given in the body of reasonable thinking. (Baldwin, 1915, p. 19)

Self is conceived of at Level Six for the first time epistemologically, as *knower*, or *judge*. Self is rational self-awareness, comprising a reflective perspective that critically interprets self and world alike. Where Level Five rejected self on the grounds that it was no substance, Level Six instead explicitly accepts what was implicit and presupposed before: that self is the self-determining function of experience, that which is necessary for experience, which constitutes it, and knows it to be *the self's* experience (not someone else's).

Instead of being just "me" (self-concept or others' concepts of me), self is also a transcendent "I," the actually existing center of organization, the conceiver of self and everything else.

> R.B. (26, M)   What is the self? WHOLE WAYS I SEE MYSELF, SEE WHAT I DO. MY OVERT ACTIONS. HOW I SENSE MYSELF, HOW I FEEL. ALTHOUGH I AM REACTING TO OBJECTIVE CONDITIONS (THE EXISTENCE OF OTHER THINGS AND PEOPLE IN THE OUTSIDE WORLD), THAT THE PERCEPTION OF IT IS MY OWN. THERE'S SOME KIND OF FILTERING PROCESS THAT'S FILTERING THOSE AND BRINGING THEM THROUGH TO ME . . . THE SELF IS MY WHOLE MEANS OF DEALING WITH MY OWN FEELINGS AND THE WORLD AS IT CONFRONTS ME . . . THE PART OF ME THAT SEES MYSELF IS CLOSER TO THE CORE OF WHAT MY SELF IS. THE ACTIONS THAT EMANATE FROM THE SELF COME BACK ON THE SELF, THEY ARE BOTH DETERMINED BY THE SELF, AND COME AROUND AND DETERMINE WHAT THE SELF IS AT THE NEXT POINT IN TIME.

M.F., a teacher of classical studies, says,

> IT IS THE THING THAT STRUCTURES YOUR BELIEFS, YOUR UNDERSTANDING OF WHAT YOU ARE AND WHAT THE WORLD IS, AND HOW THOSE TWO THINGS FIT TOGETHER . . . PERHAPS ONE'S PERCEPTION OF ONESELF INDEPENDENT OF THE THING BEING PERCEIVED.

M.F. stresses that the "self" is a metaphor, as is all conceptual knowledge. Its validity is defined by its usefulness to a particular culture. Much as the pragmatic notion of truth is seen here to extend to the concept of self, in the following response of M.F.'s to a question about friendship, we see also the intersubjective quality of truth extended to self-consciousness:

> I THINK BEING SENSITIVE AND AWARE OF WHAT CONSTITUTES ANOTHER PERSON'S SELF IS A CHANGE IN YOUR SELF, THEN I SUPPOSE THAT CHANGE OCCURS. THE GREEKS HAVE A WORD FOR IT—FILIA . . . PART OF IT IS SEEING YOURSELF IN THE OTHER PERSON—SEEING THAT PART OF THE OTHER PERSON'S SELF THAT IS AND COULD BE YOU, YOUR SELF. I THINK LOVE IN THAT WAY IS A WAY IN WHICH THINGS COME TOGETHER, AND A WAY IN WHICH YOU SEE THE UNITY OF THINGS RATHER THAN THEIR DISPARATENESS.

A point that Baldwin makes about the mature notion of subjectivity is that while subjectivity is singularity, it is a *general* or universal property of individuals, and does not imply that we are each unique cells walled off from each other. What binds us together at this level of the universal meaning of logical unity is our common function of shared self-awareness, realized as common, and as an ideal defining property of humanity (cf. Hegel's fifth stage of Reason, 1967, pp. 271–272). At this level, for the first time a set of explicit logical polarities becomes of central concern: unity–difference, general–particular, potential–actual, permanence–change, etc., because the notion of knowing as reason—a transformation of reality with an internal logical structure—has been distinguished from, and then has joined forces with, empirical fact.

> The logical type of reality appears when experimentation in its many forms serves to establish or to annul the true or false assumptions of the imagination; when the period of logical process proper—judgment, reasoning, implication—is ushered in. The germinal distinctions of control are hardened into the categories of existence and reality. The two substances, mind and body, are set up over against each other; the self retires into the citadel of subjectivity, distinct from all its thoughts; the ego-self becomes, both in thought and in action, the reflective and self-assertive individual. The judgment, with its synnomic force, holding all to the results of each, succeeds to the uncritical presumption of social custom and habit, and to the schematic assumption of the imagination. As on the functional side, there is a releasing of the faculty of thought, so on the side of content or reality, there is a crystallizing of the meaning of existence in the categories into which thought casts its objects. Thought, logical process in short, comes in to settle the questions of possibility and probability of the semblant imagination and to decide what is to be accepted as real. (Baldwin, 1915, pp. 27–28)

The logical mode emerges precisely because the substantive dualism did not succeed. The idea that all existing things could be sorted into either mind or body is contradicted by the testimony of our experience. Eventually, the very distinction between the two kinds of existence becomes an object of thought. Many other logical distinctions within reality are also made in the logical mode, such as singular–general, form–content, etc. These describe certain kinds of reality. Abstract and formal though they be, they are real distinctions or categories. Such logical meanings are presupposed in any system of thought, whether this be a particular theory, or a whole domain (the natural or social sciences, for example). In the logical mode, the necessary implicit role of such presuppositional meanings is realized.

> Existence is not the same as reality, except so far as we find it is, at any stage of knowledge, all that what we call reality is able at that stage to mean . . . Here it is in place to indicate the distinction of existence from reality . . . Reality as a meaning is inclusive of existence, but it is not in

all cases exhausted by it ... It is a meaning of more exclusive and invariable sort ... Assuming that whatever reality may later on come to mean, it is not now a meaning; the existence-markers exhaust the spheres of substantive meanings. This state of things issues at once ... to certain perplexities and embarrassments for the solution of which the mode of judgment or reflection is achieved. The progression into this mode brings the breaking up of the existence meaning into reality and existence meanings. The substances become fewer than the existences; the realities are logical meanings or presuppositions behind existence. All of which means that the two existences, mind and body, are as yet, in the substantive mode, unfinished meanings, needing to be taken up for revision by the individuations of the logical mode. (Baldwin, 1906, pp. 242–44)

Level Six displays a kind of *theoretical* self-consciousness. Level Five focused on the relatedness of Mind and Body to the self, and so construed them as experiences. Level Six can step back to a deeper presuppositional order *behind* those experiences, seeing it as a theoretical order. Thus the mental and physical can be referred to parallel spheres of laws or domains of knowledge. They are grasped methodologically, in relation to what is now an epistemological self.

N.S. (26, F)   MENTAL AND PHYSICAL ARE TWO DIFFERENT SYSTEMS OF DESCRIPTION DESCRIBING ME, OR MY BRAIN. EACH HAVE THEIR OWN LAWS. THEY ARE PARALLEL DESCRIPTIONS OF WHAT IS HAPPENING ... TWO DIFFERENT WAYS OF DESCRIBING WHAT'S GOING ON IN ME—NEURONS FIRING, OR THOUGHTS.

N.B. (26, M)   WE COME TO FIND OUT ABOUT THIS ONE THING IN TWO DIFFERENT WAYS ... ONE BY EXPERIENCING THEM, AND THE OTHER BY DOING PHYSIOLOGY. THE LAWS THAT APPLY TO MENTAL STATES ARE NOT THE SAME AS APPLY TO BRAIN STATES. YOU'RE CUTTING IT UP IN TWO DIFFERENT WAYS.

As Baldwin promised above, "speculation takes the form of an interpretation of this (mind–body) dualism itself ... a reflection upon the result of this former thinking." The kind of parallelism proposed within this interpretation (Baldwin, 1904) prevents the monistic reification that Level Five indulged in when it made mind epiphenomenal, or matter imaginary. While mind and brain are in some important ways still identified with each other, the mental is understood as an emergent level of organization in its own right. "Mental things have physical determinants–they're dependent on physiological processes," says R.B. "But they go beyond them—they have an existence that is more than truly physical." This already provides some self-understanding for a thinker like Baldwin, whose very construction of a genetic logic constitutes a form of resistance to the reductionism which aims to explain psychological development purely in terms of biological or physical laws.

No higher level than six was evident in the data from the study reported. Nevertheless, a few adults interviewed at a later point may represent something of an advance over Level Six. Their interviews have been excerpted and discussed elsewhere (Broughton, 1980a). These adults are individuals who clearly understand the rationalist and idealist positions which are central to Level Six, but who then go on to criticize those concepts. In particular, their critique focuses on the following ten weaknesses:

1. The overemphasis of reflective cognition as the form of rationality;
2. The corresponding failure to account for preflective and sensuous consciousness;
3. The difficulty in explaining the connection of theoretical to practical consciousness;
4. The assumption of an epistemological (subject–object) dualism;
5. The consequent difficulty in showing how ideas are to be connected to or validated in the material world;
6. The assumption that the single theoretical self is the primary subjective pole in the knowing process;
7. The resulting restriction of sociality to a "community of individuals";
8. The consequent failure to grasp the centrality of communication or collective action;
9. The failure to construe the activities of the human individual or collective as historical in nature;
10. The inability to conceptualize or explain processes of human alienation (by which false dualisms are created, and knowing or being are reified).

These dissatisfactions partially overlap with what Baldwin called the *embarrassments of thought*. Baldwin saw the remaining contradictions of the logical mode as deriving from its rigidly discursive, methodical character. In one volume (Baldwin, 1915), he suggested that this period might be succeeded by an "over-discursive" period which comprised a reaction against the logical mode.

The ten objections raised by our "critical" adult subjects correspond broadly to the criticisms which dialectical, materialist, and phenomenological thinkers have brought to bear on the Enlightenment traditions of rationalism and idealism. These criticisms have become familiar to the developmental psychologist via the parallel sociohistorical critiques of Piaget's theory (Broughton, 1979). If Baldwin is correct in assuming a correspondence between the history of ideas and the development of consciousness, we should not be surprised if the intellectual critiques of Enlightenment philosophy find a parallel in the further development of "natural" philosophical thought in individuals beyond Level Six. This speculative Level Seven would then bear a similar relationship to Level Six that Level

Five bore to Level Four. It would add a third and higher type of relativism or skepticism to the two which Cassirer describes. However, it remains unclear how Level Seven would be related to Baldwin's hyperlogical consciousness. The history of ideas has certainly not testified unequivocally in favor of Baldwin's provocative claim that the ultimate level of the development of consciousness is aesthetic-cum-contemplative.

Discussion

There are several general questions raised by this account of levels in the development of philosophical thinking. The issues that stand out have to do with (1) the status of the "structures" just described; (2) the relevance of the empirical findings to Baldwin's theory; and (3) the levels of phenomenological reflectivity addressed by Baldwin and me.

1. The Status of Levels of "Natural Philosophy"

The levels described here do not have the characteristics normally associated with structural stages. There is no clear separation of content or surface structure from formal infrastructure within levels, and there is no clear logical hierarchy between levels. Anyway, it is not possible to establish a structural stage sequence from cross-sectional data (Broughton, 1978b). It would be better to term them *ideal types*, quasilogical patterns of qualitatively related concepts (Broughton & Zahaykevich, 1980). It remains an open question whether philosophical concepts appear to have developmental levels of this particular kind because of some inherent or historically formed quality of philosophical thinking and discourse, or merely because of the particular methodology and conventions of description that I have employed.

2. Relevance of Findings to Baldwin's "Genetic Logic"

It must be admitted that this study of levels of philosophical conceptualization has been cast in the mold of Piaget's cognitive structuralism rather than taking the form of Baldwin's more complex and functional theory of genetic modes. Baldwin's preferences for describing the actual functional processes of thought, the social interactions in which it originates, and the subjectivity which it constitutes, have all been underemphasized in pursuing the methods of more recent developmental psychology. Nevertheless, many of

Baldwin's original concerns in his search for a genetic psychological grounding for philosophy have been retained by modern empirical psychologists of development, and to this extent attempts to align empirically derived structural sequences with Baldwin's series of modes are not total folly, as Wallwork demonstrates in Chap. 10.

We have seen considerable formal correspondence between Baldwin's sequence and ours, especially at the more general levels of analysis. Thus, a number of Baldwin's basic developmental speculations find confirmatory parallels in our empirical results:

1. The existence of a relatively autonomous course of development within theoretical reason;
2. The intimate interrelatedness of different philosophical categories within theoretical reason at each level;
3. The continuous dialectic of metaphysics and epistemology, emerging from an initial state of mutual undifferentiation;
4. The increasing reflectivity of each level of movement from "objective" world views to "dualistic," and finally to "subjective" ones;
5. The salience of mind–body categories in the overall process;
6. The complexity and difficulty of developing a conception of subjectivity;
7. The correlativity of subjectivity with objectivity;
8. The association between philosophic concepts and an understanding of the individual–society relationship.

In addition, some quite specific features of Baldwin's developmental sequence have received some confirmation in the empirical study:

1. The dominance of "the senses" and of "primary conversion" in early levels of consciousness;
2. The "personalized" nature of concepts in the early world views;
3. The concepts of inner and outer following upon the early levels;
4. The entry of "secondary conversion" as a way of clarifying the inner-outer distinction;
5. The distinction between immature and mature dualism;
6. The "embarrassing" ambiguity of the personal body in the dualistic phase;
7. The paradoxes and contradictions of psychophysical dualism;
8. The subsequent, and presumably dependent, emergence of epistemological dualism;
9. The late emergence and salience of the concepts of "experience" and "consciousness";
10. The variety of positions reflecting on the mind–body relation (parallelism, interactionism, epiphenomenalism etc.);
11. The difficulties engendered by the subject–object split;
12. The concern for formal synnomic criteria of judgment and truth in the penultimate phase of idealistic thought; and
13. The further "embarrassments" remaining within even fully developed systems of theoretical thought (e.g. the difficult relationship of judged fact to value).

Apropos of this last point, some incidental evidence was encountered that tended to support Baldwin's claim that the development of the theoretical interest only gradually disentangles itself from the moral interest, allowing a fuller integration of the two domains at later stages.

Passing from similarities to differences, we should note that several features of Baldwin's account resisted incorporation into the present empirical scheme: the distinction between sense and memory modes, the activities of play, imitation and experimentation, the notion of semblance, the emphasis upon meaning, and the pancalistic end-point of development.

On the other hand, the empirical scheme promises to add several considerations not treated extensively by Baldwin: the relation of concepts of mind and body to concepts of life (cf. Schecter, 1979), and to concepts of self, the ontological complexities of the "divided self," and the emergence of positivistic, relativistic, and solipsistic thought.

3. The Problem of "Levels of Reflectivity"

Another way of stating the overall differences between the results presented here and the theoretical concepts of Baldwin is that the former seem to bear on a more reflective level of consciousness than the latter. Baldwin's concern was more the *medium* of thought, ours the *categories* and *beliefs* comprising the structure of thinking. Baldwin was also interested in this "higher" level of reflectivity as evidenced in his citation of an excerpt from an interview where he asks a 16-year-old woman about truth (Baldwin 1908, p.367n). However, in general, Baldwin's focus is generally the phenomenology of thought, whereas ours has been its structure. And for this reason, Baldwin's stages or modes tend to apply to younger age ranges than those we have studied.[6] This may help to explain why some of the parallels drawn between the two schemes in this chapter were not always entirely perspicuous.

In conclusion, we can therefore say that in future research it would be good to attend more carefully to the distinctions of form from content, of objective from subjective, of structure from process, and of reflection from that which is reflected upon.

---

[6] Perhaps one could even go so far as to argue that all our levels of philosophy fall *within Baldwin's logical stage*, since the structural interview approach presupposes a capacity for reflective judgment. A more extended discussion of such issues is available on request from the author.

Please note that in Kohlberg's chapter below, he draws parallels in such a way that the mind/body split occurs in childhood rather than in adolescence. In this respect, Kohlberg's account is probably closer to Baldwin's than mine is.

REFERENCES

Bakan, M. Mind as life and form. In R. W. Rieber (Ed.), *Body and Mind*. New York: Academic Press, 1980.

Baldwin, J. M. *Dictionary of philosophy and psychology*. London: MacMillan, 1902.

Baldwin, J. M. Mind and body, from the genetic point of view. *Psychological Review*, 1903, *10*, 225–247.

Baldwin, J. M. Genetic progression of psychic objects. *Psychological Review*, 1904, *11*, 121–133.

Baldwin, J. M. Sketch of the history of psychology. *Psychological Review*, 1905a, *12* (2–3), 144–165.

Baldwin, J. M. *Elements of psychology*. London: MacMillan, 1905b.

Baldwin, J. M. *Thought and things (Vol. 1)*. London: Swan Sonnenschein, 1906.

Baldwin, J. M. *Thought and things (Vol. 2)*. London: Swan Sonnenschein, 1908.

Baldwin, J. M. *Thought and things (Vol. 3)*. London: Swan Sonnenschein, 1911.

Baldwin, J. M. *History of psychology: a sketch and an interpretation (2 vols.)*. New York: Putnam, 1913.

Baldwin, J. M. *Genetic theory of reality*. New York: Putnam, 1915.

Broughton, J. M. The development of conceptions of subject and object in adolescence and young adulthood. Unpublished doctoral dissertation, Harvard University, 1974.

Broughton, J. M. The development of concepts of self, mind, reality and knowledge. In W. Damon (Ed.), *Social cognition*. San Francisco: Jossey-Bass, 1978.(a)

Broughton, J.M. The cognitive-developmental approach to morality. *Journal of Moral Education*, 1978, *I*, (2), 81–96.(b)

Broughton, J.M. The limits of formal thought. In R. Mosher (Ed.) *Adolescents' development and education*. Berkeley: McCutchan Publishing Co., 1979.

Broughton, J. M. Genetic metaphysics: the developmental psychology of mind–body concepts. In R. W. Rieber (Ed.), *Body and Mind*. New York: Academic Press, 1980.

Broughton, J. M. The divided self in adolescence: Laing's "David." *Human Development*, 1981, *24*, 1, 13–32

Broughton, J. M. & Riegel, K. F. Developmental psychology and the self. *Annals of the New York Academy of Sciences*, 1977, *291*, 149–167.

Broughton, J. M. & Zahaykevich, M. K. Personality and ideology in ego development. In J. Gabel & V. Trinh van Thao (Eds.), *La dialectique dans les sciences sociales*. Paris: Anthropos, 1980.

Brown, N. O. *Love's body*. New York: Vintage, 1968.

Cassirer, E. *Substance and function*. Chicago: Open Court, 1923.

Cross, L. The development in childhood of reflective conceptions of knowledge and reality. Unpublished honors thesis, Harvard University, 1975.

Freeman-Moir, D. J. A sense of the general: the psychological epistemology of James Mark Baldwin. Unpublished doctoral dissertation, Harvard University, 1975.

Frondizi, R. *The nature of self*. Carbondale, Ill.: Southern Illinois Univ. Press, 1953.

Furth, H. Children's conceptions of social institutions: A Piagetian framework. *Human Development*, 1976, *19* (6), 351–374.

Gabel, J. *False consciousness*. London: Blackwell, 1975.

Glaser, B. G., & Strauss, A. L. *The discovery of grounded theory: strategies for qualitative research*. Chicago: Aldine, 1967.

Gruber, H. E., & Vonèche, J. J. *The essential Piaget*. New York: Basic Books, 1977.

Habermas, J. *Knowledge and human interest*. Boston: Beacon Press, 1971.

Hegel, G. W. F. *Phenomenology of mind*. London: Macmillan, 1967, (Reprint, 1910.)

Hegel, G. W. F. *Logic*. London: Oxford Univ. Press, 1975. (Reprint 1873.)

Husserl, E. *Formal and transcendental logic*. The Hague: Martinus Nijhoff, 1978.

Inhelder, B., & Piaget, J. *The growth of logical thinking from childhood to adolescence*. New York: Basic, 1958.

Inhelder, B., Sinclair, H. & Bovet, M. *Learning and the development of cognition*. Cambridge, Mass.: Harvard Univ. Press, 1974.

Kohlberg, L. Stages in conceptions of the physical and social world. Unpublished monograph, University of Chicago, 1963.

Kohlberg, L. Cognitive stages and preschool education. *Human Development*, 1966, *9*, 5–17.

Kohlberg, L. From is to ought: how to commit the naturalistic fallacy and get away with it in the study of moral development. In T. Mischel (Ed.), *Cognitive development and genetic epistemology*. New York: Academic Press, 1971.

Kohlberg, L., & Gilligan, C. The adolescent as philosopher: the discovery of the self in a post-conventional world. *Daedalus*, 1971, *100* (4), 1051–1086.

Laing, R. D. *The divided self*. London: Travistock Press, 1960.

Lonergan, B. J. F. *Insight*. New York: Philosophical Library, 1957.

✓ Perry, W. *Forms of intellectual and ethical development in the college years*. Cambridge, Mass.: Bureau of Study Counsel, Harvard University, 1968.

Piaget, J. La biologie et la guerre. *Feuille Centrale de la Société Suisse de Zofingue*, 1918, *58*, 374–380. Reprinted in H. E. Gruber & J. J. Vonèche, *The essential Piaget*. New York: Basic, 1977.

Piaget, J. *The child's construction of the world*. London: Littlefield Adams, 1929.

Ryle, G. *The concept of mind*. London: Hutchinson, 1949.

Schecter, B. Animism and metaphoric thinking in children. Unpublished doctoral dissertation, Teachers College, Columbia University, 1979.

Selman, R. L. The development of conceptions of interpersonal relations. Mimeo manual, Harvard/Judge Baker Research Project, 1974.

Winnicott, D. W. *The maturational processes and the facilitating environment*. New York: International Universities Press, 1965.

9

MORAL DEVELOPMENT

Lawrence Kohlberg
**Graduate School of Education,
Harvard University**

In 1954 I commenced a study of the development of moral judgment in childhood and adolescence (Kohlberg, 1958). The way I defined the problem to myself was "old-fashioned." It was the way it was defined at the turn of the century by McDougall, Dewey, Baldwin, G.H. Mead, and others. As stated by McDougall (1908),

> The fundamental problem of social psychology is the moralization of the individual by the society. This moralization proceeds through, first, the stage in which the operation of the instinctive impulses is modified by the influence of rewards and punishments; second, the stage in which conduct is controlled in the main by anticipation of social praise and blame; and third, the stage in which conduct is regulated by an ideal that enables man to act in a way that seems right to him, regardless of the praise or blame of his immediate environment.

Dewey (Dewey & Tufts, 1932) and McDougall both viewed the problem of moral development as a question of moving through levels: (1) the premoral or *preconventional* level of "behavior motivated by biological and social impulses with results for morals"; (2) the *conventional* level of behavior "in which the individual accepts without critical reflection the standards of his group"; and (3) the autonomous or *postconventional* level of behavior in which "conduct is guided by the individual thinking and judging for himself whether a principle is good, and not accepting the standard of his group without reflection."

It seemed reasonable to me that moral development passed through stages, but this in turn implied certain other assumptions

277

shared by turn-of-the century psychologists. These were (1) that there are culturally universal features of mature morality; (2) that these features involve reasoning and judgment; (3) that mature morality is more adequate or reasonable than immature morality; and (4) that mature morality involves autonomous, self-constructed, or self-chosen principles, rather than internalized cultural norms.

Since 1900, the psychological study of moral development had rejected these assumptions and hence seemed to me to offer little in posing and answering McDougall's (or my own) problem. More recent psychological research had focused upon studying antecedents of guilt (as projectively measured), antecedents of behavioral conformity to command or customs ("resistance to temptation"), antecedents of ratings of personality in terms of "virtues prized in America" (friendliness, honesty, self-control, etc.) or in terms of moral "knowledge" (endorsement of conventional moral beliefs). Such studies hardly addressed the problem of moral development as the development of some universal human capacity. Learning or psychoanalytical studies of what might cause a young Nazi to feel guilt or to conform to a rule to exterminate the non-Aryan hardly seemed to speak to the problem of moral development.

As I said at the time:

> In an attempt to arrive at a concept of the moral which is empirically observable and independent of the observer's values, most modern social scientists have ended up defining individual morality as behavioral conformity to the more common rules of the individual's culture. . . . Such a conception of individual morality necessarily eliminates any special theoretical significance which could be assigned to the question of how moral attitudes develop. Morality can no longer be viewed as a higher stage of development to be accounted for, as something which differentiates social man from social animal and the social adult from the social infant. For the dog and infant may "conform" to many rules of the culture, yet we do not view them as moral beings. When a view of the moral as simple behavioral conformity has been used in empirical studies of children by workers such as Turner and Hartshorne and May, no age increase in such moral traits as honesty and altruism has been found. . . . In addition this view eliminates any but a very minimal "moral" or social value from morality. Whatever be the reasons for which we admire and desire to encourage man's morality, that admiration and desire are not elicited by a simple conformity to cultural rules. Even the thoughtful though "culture bound" layman as well as the philosopher prizes conformity to rules only in terms of the aspects of morality he is apt to define as "having moral principles." Such aspects include selection and ordering of the rules, intelligent interpretation of them, and inner conformity to them in difficult situations rather than outer conformity in routine situations.
>
> Even if we add the concept of guilt to the concept of behavioral conformity, our conception of morality will not allow us to define

morality as it has been conceived by most social thinkers. Tendencies toward self punishment or selective inattentions associated with "instinctual" acts probably do not increase after the seventh or eighth year; they do not define a full developmental dimension. They obviously can be considered a social good even less than behavioral conformity.(Kohlberg, 1958, p. 2)

It seemed to me that an alternative approach needed to start with a careful study of the development of moral judgment:

An alternative approach to the observation and assessment of morality might be based on the characteristics of moral judgment, as these have been considered by philosophers.

The endeavors of moral philosophers in this direction may be seen as a clarification of the concept of the moral as it has been used generally by thoughtful men. The educated layman in Western cultures believes that a man is moral if he acts in accordance with his conscience—that is, if he acts in accordance with a previous judgement that such-and-such is right to do in this situation. An action, regardless of its consequence or its classification by the culture, is neither good nor bad unless it has been preceded by a judgement of right or wrong.

If we infer that no such judgement took place before an act, we say the actor did not know what he was doing and we make no moral evaluation of his act; if we infer that action was in accordance with such a judgement, we feel we must so far approve the character of the actor regardless of our own evaluation of the consequences or the class of the act.

The judgement of a person as morally good or bad is quite different from the judgement of an object or animal as good or bad. We tend to say that objects and animals are not moral agents because they do not have "free will," or because they do not "know right from wrong." We can state the meaning of this usage less metaphysically by saying that no object can be judged morally or can be said to be a moral agent unless its conduct can be itself guided or determined by its capacity for making moral judgements. . . .

We demand, however, that the judgement on which action is "based" fulfill certain conditions before we will consider it to be a moral judgement. If we can explicate a set of criteria which correspond to enlightened ordinary language usage of a concept of a moral judgement we may be in a position to begin psychological study of the moral in both a descriptive and normative sense. Working criteria do exist which many of us use every day in appraising our own judgements and those of others as moral. . . .

(a) Moral action is oriented to or preceded by a value judgement.

(b) Moral judgments are viewed by the judge as taking priority over other value judgments.

(c) Moral actions and judgements are associated with judgements of the self as good or bad.

(d) Moral judgements seem to be justified or based on reasons which are not limited to consequences of that particular act in that situation.

(e) Moral judgements tend toward a high degree of generality, universality, consistency and inclusiveness.

> (f) Moral judgements tend to be considered as objective by their makers, i.e., to be agreed to independently of differences of personality and interest.
>   The history of ethics may be viewed very largely as the effort to find some content, some principle, some line of argumentation which would logically justify, or show to be cognitively correct, judgements which are moral in the preceding sense. . . . Moral orientations then tend to be linked to moral principles and it is moral principles which give rise to concepts of moral rationality. (Kohlberg, 1958, p. 5)

When I turned to empirical psychological studies of moral judgement development in 1954, not much could be found except Piaget's (1965(1932)) landmark volume. Accordingly, I proposed a thesis which would apply and extend Piaget's moral judgment stages through adolescence and also examine the influence of various types of social experience on moral development. An example of such experience would be peer-group interaction, as Piaget's theory suggested.

A professor of mine had on his shelf a second-hand book by J.M. Baldwin entitled *Social and Ethical Interpretations of Mental Development*, which he loaned me. I was particularly interested in it since Piaget referred to the work in his volume on moral judgment. I found the book difficult, but exciting. However, since it relied on no empirical data, I did not know what to make of it.

After I had collected my data, I returned to the book, and its sequel, *Thought and Things*. Looking for something to improve upon Piaget's stages, my study indicated clear weaknesses in Piaget's account of his first two moral stages (the heteronomous and the autonomous), and Piaget provided few clues to defining what appeared to be higher or more mature modes of moral judgment we found in our older subjects. The attraction of Baldwin's account for me then was that (1) it defined moral stages in terms of the formal properties of moral judgment focused upon by moral philosophers; and (2) it captured ideas that my subjects seemed to be expressing, but which Piaget's account could not accommodate.

Only much later did I learn of the historical connection between Baldwin and Piaget. Baldwin was banished from American academia for violating the Victorian sexual mores of the time and settled in Paris just before World War I. There he was in weekly contact with Janet, who communicated something of his work to Piaget. As I read more deeply into Baldwin, I realized that Piaget had derived all the basic ideas with which he started in the twenties from Baldwin: assimilation, accommodation, schema, and the adualism, "egocentricity," or undifferentiated character of the child's mind. I saw, too, that Piaget's overall enterprise, the creation of a genetic epistemology and ethics which would use epistemology to pose problems for develop-

mental psychology and use developmental observation to help answer epistemological questions, had also been Baldwin's.

Incorporating Baldwin's conceptions with Dewey's three-level
scheme, I came up with the stages defined in Table 1. We need then
to outline Baldwin's theory of moral development as it has entered
into, and in part has been verified by, our research on moral stages
(Kohlberg, 1969, 1971, 1979).

Baldwin's Levels of Moral Development: Their Cognitive Side

There are two important aspects to Baldwin's theory of moral
development: the series of stage-by-stage *cognitive differentiations*
of subjective and objective (occurring in the domains of logic and
value), and the *affective activities* of willing and role-taking. In this
section, and the three following, we will deal with the cognitive side,
looking first at logical judgment and then at value judgment. After
that we will move to the affective side.

The development of logical cognition involves a successive set
of differentiations between the subjective and objective poles of
experience. In early childhood, the child is *adualistic*, failing to
differentiate the inner (the mental, the subjective), from the outer
(the material, the objective). The child then makes these successive
differentiations: first the inner/outer, then the mental/material, and
finally the subjective/objective (see Broughton's Chap. 8 and Moir's
Chap. 6). An example of these sequential differentiations arises from
studying the development of the child's conception of the dream
(Piaget, 1929; Kohlberg, 1969).

> The dream is a good example of an object or experience with which
> the child is familiar from an early age, but which is restructured in
> markedly different ways in later development. One of the general
> categories of experience is that of substantiality or reality. Any expe-
> rience must be defined as either subjective or objective. As the child's
> structuring of this category develops, his experience of the dream
> changes. According to Piaget, the young child thinks of the dream as a
> set of real events, rather than as a mental imagining. This represents
> the young child's "realism," his failure to differentiate the subjective
> appearance from objective reality components of his experience.
>
> Table 2 indicates the actual steps of development which are
> found in childrens' beliefs about dreams. The first step (achieved by
> about 4 years, 10 months by American middle-class children) is the
> recognition that dreams are not real events; the next step (achieved
> soon thereafter), that dreams cannot be seen by others. By age six,
> children are clearly aware that dreams take place inside them, and by
> seven, they are clearly aware that dreams are thoughts caused by
> themselves.

Table 1
Definition of Kohlberg Moral Stages

I. Preconventional level

At this level the child is responsive to cultural rules and labels of good and bad, right or wrong, but interprets these labels in terms of either the physical or the hedonistic consequences of action (punishment, reward, exchange of favors), or in terms of the physical power of those who enunciate the rules and labels. The level is divided into the following two stages.

Stage 1: *The punishment and obedience orientation.* The physical consequences of action determine its goodness or badness regardless of the human meaning or value of these consequences. Avoidance of punishment and unquestioning deference to power are valued in their own right, not in terms of respect for an underlying moral order supported by punishment and authority (the latter being Stage 4).

Stage 2: *The instrumental relativist orientation.* Right action consists of that which instrumentally satisfies one's own needs and occasionally the needs of others. Human relations are viewed in terms like those of the market place. Elements of fairness, of reciprocity, and of equal sharing are present, but they are always interpreted in a physical pragmatic way. Reciprocity is a matter of "you scratch my back and I'll scratch yours," not of loyalty, gratitude, or justice.

II. Conventional level

At this level, maintaining the expectations of the individual's family, group, or nation is perceived as valuable in its own right, regardless of immediate and obvious consequences. The attitude is not only one of conformity to personal expectations and social order, but of loyalty to it, of actively *maintaining,* supporting, and justifying the order, and of identifying with the persons or group involved in it. At this level, there are the following two stages:

Stage 3: *The interpersonal concordance or "good boy-nice girl" orientation.* Good behavior is that which pleases or helps others and is approved by them. There is much conformity to stereotypical images of what is majority or "natural" behavior. Behavior is frequently judged by intention; "he means well" becomes important for the first time. One learns approval by being "nice."

Stage 4. *The "law and order" orientation.* There is orientation toward authority, fixed rules, and the maintenance of the social order. Right behavior consists of doing one's duty, showing respect for authority, and maintaining the given social order for it's own sake.

III. Postconventional, autonomous, or principled level

At this level, there is a clear effort to define moral values and principles which have validity and application apart from the authority of the groups or persons holding these principles, and apart from the individual's own identification with these groups. This level again has two stages.

Stage 5: *The social-contract legalistic orientation,* generally with utilitarian overtones. Right action tends to be defined in terms of general individual rights, and standards which have been critically examined and agreed upon by the whole society. There is a clear awareness of the relativism of personal values and opinions and a corresponding emphasis upon procedural rules for reaching consensus. Aside from what is constitutionally and democratically agreed upon, the right is a matter of personal "values" and "opinion." The result is an emphasis upon the "legal point of view," but with an emphasis upon the possibility of changing law in terms of rational considerations of social utility (rather than freezing it in terms of Stage 4 "law and order"). Outside the legal realm, free agreement and contract is the binding element of obligation. This is the "official" morality of the American government and constitution.

Stage 6: *The universal ethical principle orientation.* Right is defined by the decision of conscience in accord with self-chosen *ethical principles* appealing to logical comprehensiveness, universality, and consistency. These principles are abstract and ethical (the Golden Rule, the categorical imperative); they are not concrete moral rules like the Ten Commandments. At heart, these are universal principles of *justice,* of the *reciprocity* and *equality* of human *rights,* and of respect for the dignity of human beings as *individual persons.*

Table 2
Sequence in Development of Dream Concept[a]

Step	Scale pattern types						
	0	1	2	3	4	5	6
1. *Not Real:* Recognizes that objects or actions in the dream are not real or are not really there in the room.	−	+	+	+	+	+	+
2. *Invisible:* Recognizes that other people cannot see his dream.	−	−	+	+	+	+	+
3. *Internal Origin:* Recognizes that the dream *comes from* inside him.	−	−	−	+	+	+	+
4. *Internal Location:* Recognizes that the dream *goes on* inside him.	−	−	−	−	+	+	+
5. *Immaterial:* Recognizes that the dream is not a material substance but is a thought.	−	−	−	−	−	+	+
6. *Self-caused:* Recognizes that dreams are not caused by God or other agencies but are caused by the self's thought processes.	−	−	−	−	−	−	+
Median age of American children in given pattern of stage (Range = 4–8)	4.6	4.1	5.0	5.4	6.4	6.5	7.1

[a]Number of American children fitting scale types = 72; not fitting = 18.

The concept of stages implies an invariant order or sequence of development. Cultural and environmental factors or innate capabilities may make one child or group of children reach a given step of development at a much earlier point of time than another child. All children, however, should still go through the same order of steps, regardless of environmental teaching or lack of teaching.

Table 2 shows a series of patterns of pluses or minuses called Guttman Scale types, suggesting that the steps we have mentioned form an invariant order or sequence in development. If there is an invariant order in development, then children who have passed a more difficult step in the sequence, indicated by a plus, should also have passed all the easier steps in the sequence and get pluses on all the easier items. This means that all children should fit one of the patterns on Table 2. For instance, all children who pass or get a plus on Step 3, recognizing the dream's internal origin, should also pass Step 2 and Step 1 [see results in Table 3] . . .

The culturally universal invariants of sequence found in the dream concept can be adequately understood through Baldwin's logical analysis. . . . The steps represent progressive differentiations of the subjective and objective which logically could not have a different order. The first step involves a differentiation of the *unreality* of the psychic event or dream image. The next step is the differentiation of the *internality* of the psychic event from the externality of the physical events. A still later step is the differentiation of the *immateriality* of the psychic event from the materiality of physical events. This sequence corresponds to the logical tree in Figure 1. (Kohlberg, 1969, pp. 356-359)

Differentiation of sign
and referent

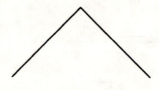

unreal-symbolic   real events
events

Differentiation of the outside-
shared from the inside-unshared

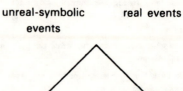

unreal inside-body   unreal outside-
events invisible   body events
to others   (pictures, movies)

Differentiation of the immaterial
from the material

internal mental   internal physical
events   events

FIG. 1   Successive differentiations in the development of the dream concept

Table 3
Percentage of Children of Each Internality Scale Type at Three Ages

Scale type	Age		
	4	5	7
0	63	31	19
1	8	14	11
2	0	6	5
3	5	23	41
4	16	17	23
5	8	7	2
Total	100	100	100
	(N = 31)	(N = 32)	(N = 32)

In adolescence the final differentiation is made, that between the subjective and objective. This distinction is closely linked to an awareness of possibilities and to an orientation to logical, as opposed to empirical criteria of truth. The *objective*, the outer world and shared beliefs about it, are seen now as the referents of subjective thoughts whose meaning can be called into question. The adolescent can be a solipsist: only thought or self exists or can be known. To establish a balanced relation between subjective and objective requires a new differentiation, that between the logical or rational and the irrational. This means the differentiation of universal and rational "logic"—scientific thought or method—from arbitrary subjective thought. Objectivity becomes a characteristic of a perspective or a method of thought rather than of things or of the products of thought (knowledge). Objectivity is identified with universalizability, with what could be concluded by inquirers from experiences based on general methods or rules of inference (see Broughton's Chap. 8)

Baldwin's stages of moral judgment (Table 4) are parallel steps in the differentiation of the subjective and objective in the area of ends or *values*, rather than in the area of facts or objects. With regard to valuation, Baldwin holds that primitive thought is first adualistic in that values are assumed to be *syntelic*. In other words, the child uncritically assumes that his value attitudes are shared by everyone, or that what is a value for one is a value for all. In the second place, according to Baldwin, primitive evaluation is adualistic in that it is *projective*, i.e., in that there is no differentiation between objective and physical properties of the object and the subjective and psychological values of the object. The adult ordinarily views the values of objects not as intrinsically located in the perceptual–physical attributes of the object, but as based upon some relation of the object to the satisfaction of some subjective state, desire, or ideal held by some person. Without a person valuing, or without a purpose or standard, an object or event is not conceived to have value. This adult dualism of subjective and objective in the value domain is expressed at the concrete level in the distinction between means and ends (and at a more abstract level in the distinction between value and fact). Instrumental evaluation, i.e., selection of an object or act in light of its value for a particular need, involves the ability to disregard various other values associated with the object, based upon its relation to other needs or persons irrelevant to the given end. Such instrumental abstraction depends upon the capacity to localize value as the subjective experience of a self, with the corresponding ability to see external things or acts as having purely objective physical-causal properties. Such instrumental thinking, implied by the notion of an opportunistic or expedient moral type, is impossible at the projective and syntelic level of evaluation.

Table 4
Baldwin's Ethical Stages

I. Objective or Adualistic Stage

1. Value is *syntelic.* Failure to localize or distinguish for whom a bad event is bad. The value of an event to another person is shared by the self without basis; or the evaluation of the event by the self is believed to be held by others without basis.

2. Value is *projective*. Failure to see the value of an event as a means to an end, on which its value is strictly contingent, or as an expression of a purpose which defines its value. Value of an act is dependent on its consequences and on irrelevant perceptual similarities to other valued acts. There is a general failure to differentiate good and right from other meanings of good and right.

3. Duty is perceived as based on *objective* or external necessity. Duty or right action is identified with that which the self "has to do" or is compelled to do by external forces, authority and sanctions.

II. Dualistic, Prudential, or Intellectual Stage

1. Value is *relativistic.* Judgments of right and good are relative to self-interest and judgments may be seen as conflicting where interests conflict.

2. Value is *instrumental* and based on need. The value of an object or act is based on its relation to an actual need or end involved in the particular situation.

3. Duty is perceived as a *hypothetical* imperative. Direction of action is not by compelling prescription or external pressure but is advisory and contingent on needs or motives of the actor.

III. Ethical or Ideal Stage

1. Value is public or *synnomic*. The moral value accorded by the self to the event is that which it is believed could be accorded to it by anyone. At the same time this value which the public could hold is a value based on the self's own legitimate perspective in the situation. The value is not the opinion poll value but the value which the self perceives when taking the role of "any rational man" in the society, or which we think society ought to take.

2. Value is ideal and objective. Events are valued not in terms of ideal desires which the self *does* have, but in terms of ideal desires which the self *should* have. It is felt that objects or events *should* be valued in certain ways, that value requires an effort of judgment and appreciation.

This first level of evaluation by the young child is reflected in a multiplicity of concrete characteristics. In the first place, projective valuing leads to a confusion of the perceptual or physical qualities of an act or object with its value, whether this value is instrumental (technical, economic, or egoistic) or moral. The moral and the instrumental goodness or badness of a person are not only confused with each other but with physical–perceptual qualities like clean–dirty, pretty–ugly, etc. The value of an act is judged in terms of its manifest physical consequences rather than in terms of its purpose or its conformity to standards. Physical similarity between two objects implies that both have similar moral value, so that value judgments are justified on grounds of value-irrelevant similarity. Thus a 4-year-old girl cried because she had been given a pair of sunglasses with a picture of the Disney dog, Goofy, on them and was laughed at by the other 4-year-old as "Goofy." She went on to say, "These glasses (her own) are God and these glasses (the other girl's) are Jesus, and God is better than Jesus." This set of evaluations in terms of value-irrelevant equations of labels is based on locating the value of a moral label in the label itself, as a sort of "thing" to be associated with the self rather than in viewing the label as expressing a subjective judgment of correspondence to a standard. The badness of the label "Goofy" lies in the label and the child shares its badness if the label is associated with her, regardless of any actual judgment of her action as "goofy." When the young child tells his teacher, "Make him stop calling me that," it is assumed that the mere physical naming is what is harmful rather than a valid mental judgment by the other.

It is evident, then, that projective modes of valuing are not concrete and physicalistic in the sense of the deliberate disregard of immaterial values implied in philosophies of hedonism or in the older child's chant that "Sticks and stones can hurt my bones, but names can never hurt me." Instead they represent a confusion between physical and moral values resulting in endowing physical values with quasimoral values and moral values with quasiphysical properties.

With regard to the judgment of persons, syntelic and projective confusions lead to the ascription of quasimoral worth to wealth, strength, attractiveness, or power. We may illustrate this confusion by the following interview response with Tommy (age 9) about whether it is right to steal a drug to save one's wife:

His wife was sick and if she did not get the drug quickly, she might die. Maybe his wife is an important person and runs a store and the man buys stuff from her and can't get it any other place. The police would probably blame the owner than he didn't save the wife. That would be like killing with a gun or knife.

Interviewer: Would it be all right to put the druggist in the electric chair for murder?

If she could be cured by the drug and they didn't give it to her, I think so, because she could be an important lady like Betsy Ross, she made the flag.

Interviewer: Is it better to save the life of one important person or a lot of unimportant people?

All the people that aren't important because one man just has one house, maybe a lot of furniture, but a whole bunch of people have an awful lot of furniture, and some of these poor people might have a lot of money and it doesn't look it.

Tommy defined the moral value of the woman's life, and the punitive reaction of the sociomoral order, as relative to the woman's importance. *Importance* is defined by a confused mixture of social visibility, social power, social function, and wealth. Eventually, the decision as to whether to save one important person or many unimportant persons is based on a quantitative assessment of furniture. Awarding moral value to furniture is *syntelic* in failing to differentiate what the community holds as a shared or moral value (the value of life) and what the individual holds as a private value (the desire for furniture). It is *projective* in treating the value of persons as tied to physical properties (wealth or furniture), or in treating the value of physical things as intrinsic rather than as a means to some subjective end.

A developmental shift from a syntelic and projective evaluation of social power to a purely instrumental one is indicated by two responses by Tommy—one at the time of the interview quoted above, and one a year later—to the question, "How much is the policeman respected by people?"

> Age 9: He's respected a lot. He directs traffic and when you're on the corner he blows the whistle and you're supposed to respect him and go. The policeman can do a lot. He can put you in jail.
> Age 10: He's not too important. The younger kids get taken by their mothers across the street, so they don't really need the policeman, and when they grow up they should know better themselves, so you don't really need a policeman.

At this second period, what Baldwin called the *intellectual* stage, Tommy has an instrumental mode of valuing life, as indicated in his response to a situation as to whether a doctor should heed the request of a woman dying of cancer and put her out of her pain.

> Well, if she wanted to, he could, but her husband probably wouldn't stand for it. . . . Like if a pet dies you can always get another one, but if this man married another woman, well he wouldn't have a wife just the same as the one he had.

The naïveté of Tommy's purely instrumental approach to value suggests the need for a third level of evaluation above his current second level, a third level termed by Baldwin the *ethical* or *ideal* stage of evaluation. The term *ethical level* is appropriate, because this level defines the content of the ethical field, e.g., "the primary subject of ethical investigation is all that is included under the notion of what is good or desirable for man; all that is reasonably chosen or sought by him, *not as a means to some ulterior end, but for itself*" (Sidgwick, 1931). In Baldwin's intellectual stage, the fact of desire or need is the end-point of value. In the ethical stage intrinsic values are defined, i.e. values or purposes which are *desirable* rather than simply *desired*. The term *ideal* implies a differentiation between the desires people *do* have and the desires they *should* have. At the *intellectual* stage one has an ideal self only in the sense of wishing to possess objects or traits which are means to satisfy given or nonideal needs or ends (e.g., wealth, strength, power, beauty, etc.). At the ethical stage, one has an ideal self in the sense of wishing to possess ethical, good or desirable motives or ends. The contrast between the two "stages" of response concerning ideal-self questions is indicated by the following responses:

Interviewer: Would you want to be a good son?

George, age 10: Sure, be good to your father and he'll be good to you.

Interviewer: Would you want to take after your father?

Phil, age 10: Well, it's nice but you really shouldn't take after somebody unless he's real good. If you act exactly like your father you get the habit of following these people. You should only take after people when they are really being good.

In other words, at the projective stage, value is not relative to a self; at the instrumental stage it is relative to a concrete actual physical self; at the ideal stage it is relative to an ideal and socially general self, i.e., a self which it is desirable that everyone have.

Expressed as the development of the means–end dichotomy, an ideal self means the ability to view desires as means. There is a search for some further end to which various desires are means, and in terms of which they may be evaluated. Put in terms of objects, there is the concept that various acts or objects *should* be desired, regardless of whether in fact they *are* desired; ethical values are more objective than instrumental values. This is not a return to the projective stage where objects have a quasiperceptual intrinsic value. At the ethical stage the intrinsic worth of the object is still the product of an act of value judgment by an observer; it is intrinsically "there" only in the sense that the *ideal observer* would judge it to be truly there. Some effort toward appreciation of the object is required, some process of judgment and experience by which the value of the object comes to be genuinely recognized—some further perspective of it to be gained. The actual value resides in the standard, and it is subsumption of the experience of the object under the standard which gives it value.

Ethical values are also more universal than instrumental values. In this sense the ethical stage has a parallel to the syntelic stage of believing the valued was shared and that the shared was valuable. However, at the ethical stage, values are said to be shared in the sense of being synnomic rather than syntelic. Ethical values are values which the individual believes everyone should hold, whether they do or not. Efforts to state ethical principles are efforts to state rules and values which every human being ought to accept, whether or not they do accept them. The sharedness of "synnomic" valuing or moral principles is similar to that involved in scientific judgment. The standard of truth of scientific observation and inference is the standard that anyone else could make the same observation and inference. In fact, scientists in their experiments observe something no one else has observed and often draw conclusions at variance with general or group belief. They assert the validity of their own personal belief on the grounds that anyone else would come to the same conclusions if they followed the same methods of observation and inference.

We have so far discussed Baldwin's stages as stages in apprehension of the desired or the good, but they have parallel meaning in the sphere of the required or the ought. Corresponding to the definition of ethics as the field of the intrinsic or the ideal good, is the definition of ethics by Kant (1949) and others as the field of intrinsic or unconditional duty, of the categorical as opposed to the hypothetical prescription of action. We quoted earlier an example of an instrumental-stage response treating a moral decision as a matter of hypothetical rather than categorical imperatives. According to Baldwin, the categorical imperative of the ethical stage must be distinguished not only from the hypothetical imperative of the instrumental stage but from the earliest sense of external compulsion or necessity characteristic of the projective or syntelic stage:

> First, there is the case in which the sanction is objective and unconditional, which we may call "objective necessity." "I am compelled to do this," or, "I must do this for you compel me," is its form. Second, the case of personal selection and decision within a whole of objective or possible social sanctioning, giving the "hypothetical imperative," "I should do this under certain conditions," or, "I should do this if I want this to happen," or "I am impelled by prudence, by my interests, to do this." This in turn passes over, third, into the "moral necessity" of ideal conformity: "I must do this because it is right," or, "I ought to do this." (Baldwin, 1911, pp. 139–140)

At the stage of objective necessity, the child would say, "I (or you) have to come inside because it's raining." At the hypothetical stage, he would say, "If I (or you) don't want to get wet, I'd (or you'd) better come inside." In the first case the child merely presents some usually compelling event; in the second stage, the child simply states a means–end relationship and makes action dependent on the existence of a natural motive in the self on the particular occasion.

In the third stage, a person makes assertions that an act should be done regardless of whether there is at the moment a corresponding need or outer press. This necessity is based on a line of reasoning, thought, and feeling, not on physical pressure. The *value* which does the reasoning does not defer to another self or aspect of the self to make the choice. There is, then, a certain necessity and impersonality about obligation both at the first and the third stage. At this third stage, this impersonality and disregard of the self's needs is that of the conscientious self[1]-oriented "only to duty." While the definition of duty may be highly personal and strongly focused on providing for the needs and feelings of others, the acting subject who follows such a definition of duty feels that as duty; it is distinct from his own feelings toward those needs. In contrast, at the first stage, it is not the action and conformity of the subject which is impersonal, it is the pattern or object conformed to which is impersonal and indifferent to needs. Outer authority or law may be seen as completely indifferent to the intention, needs, or welfare of anyone, but the self's reason for obeying authority is based completely on the personal need or fear of punishment.

An example of decision based on "objective necessity" rather than the categorical imperative is the response of Johnny (age 9) to the question, "What do you want to be?"

> Whatever my father orders me to do. He's my father and he works for the railroad. If he wants me to work for the railroad, I have to work for the railroad.

An example of movement from objective necessity to the "hypothetical necessity" of the instrumental level was given in Tommy's second set of responses. Or we may quote the reply of 10-year-old Danny to a situation concerning whether a boy should tell his father a confidence about a brother's misdeed. In reply, Danny said:

> In one way, it would be right to tell on his brother or his father might get mad at him and spank him. In another way, it would be right to keep quiet or his brother might beat him up.

In psychological language, we could say that each of Baldwin's stages carries with it a predominant attitude or "set." At the ethical stage, for example, there is a "moral set" of categorical obligation geared to an ideal self. To understand this moral set, we need to contrast it with two other sets, the preferential or *values* set (similar to Baldwin's instrumental level) and a *cognitive set* (similar to Baldwin's projective level).

A *values set* assumes that moral judgments or choices express the habits and feelings of the judger about the acts or objects in question. In the case of a choice between objects and acts, the one which is more strongly valued by the self is chosen. The basic datum of choice in such a view we might term neutrally a value. By a *value*

---

[1] It should be noted that Baldwin's ethical or ideal stage is formulated as a stage of the self, not simply as a stage in the conceptualization of moral rules.

is meant merely a definable class of objects or class of acts which has a valence, whether this valence be viewed as derived from a drive, a habit strength, or whatever.

Such a value can be defined both in terms of the individual and in terms of a group or subculture. Groups or subcultures would be expected to have different values or assign different modal preference strengths to various classes of acts and objects. Individual differences in values would be expected to be determined by the strength of the value in the child's subculture, and by the effectiveness of the training of the value in the child by relevant socializing agents.

Usually users of the values approach assume that a value is oriented to as desirable as well as desired, and is to some extent rationalized, generalized, and systematized. In ordinary use of the term "values," we imply an orientation intermediate between sheer factual desire and a moral orientation. If we say we value art, it means more than saying that we desire to look at or buy paintings, as we desire to eat, sleep or scratch ourselves. We feel that it is good that others, too, like art and that there are reasons for liking it which more or less form part of a system organizing our preference. On the other hand, we do not feel it is a duty to like art, and perhaps feel that our artistic activities have no claim to interfere with our duties.

Some of the subjects studied in my thesis seemed to respond to the moral choice situation in this way, i.e., in terms of choosing in terms of habitual feelings and attitudes without striving to get the morally right answer. These were subjects at Baldwin's instrumental level. An example would be this 16-year-old's response to the question about stealing a drug for one's wife.

> Yeah. If my wife was dying, I'd do the same thing too.
> (Is it his duty?)
> No, but if my wife was dying I would.
> (Would a good person do it?)
> What do you mean, good?
> (Trying to do right?)
> Well, I don't know. It depends on how much he likes his wife.

Another set that children took toward our material is not one of expressing values, but one of attempting to predict the culturally correct answer. This is a cognitive set, which we called the intellectual conformity or intellectual prediction set. Even in the case of choices of art works, such a set, rather than the expression of personal values, may dominate response. A *New York Times*'s advertisement portrays two paintings and asks, "Here are two paintings. If you were unexpectedly asked to judge these paintings, would you be able to express a well-reasoned opinion or would you be fearful of exposing ignorance? To remedy this situation, etc."

Indeed, material in our interviews indicates that the orientation of children at Baldwin's projective level to our problems was a cognitive or test-taking one. In its most naive form, this was indicated by the 65% of the 10-year-olds who, when asked, "Is there a right answer to these questions and who knows it?" replied that "You know the right answers because you have them in the book there behind the questions." In spite of initial explanations regarding research and the researcher's status, several asked if they were being graded. For such children, questions might be hard, not in the sense of implying difficult moral decisions, but in the sense that, as one boy says, "They don't get them right if they're not good thinkers, or if they are always worrying about stuff, or just play with things like I'm doing with the microphone now, and then they don't get their answers right."

Even though such a boy is oriented to "getting the right answer," he is very naïve as to what the right answer is in the moral sphere. We can contrast such a set toward the right with Baldwin's concept of an ideal self or a general moral set in decision-making. Such a moral set involves, on a higher level, both elements of the *values set* toward expressing the self's values and the *intellectual conformity set* toward adapting values to the appropriate expectations in the given situation. In its full sense, a moral set implies an orientation toward a right decision, a decision which an ideally good or wise person could make, though perhaps a decision which no individual could actually attain.

While there are cognitive and affectively neutral elements to a moral set and a directedness toward a right answer, the set is different from the intellectual prediction set. A moral set involves doing justice to felt values in the situation rather than the achievement of success in the display of ability regardless of such felt values. It involves consistency of one decision with decisions made in other situations, even at the cost of appearing externally in error. The solution must do justice to what the self believes and yet meet the situation. Thus the choice is difficult in the sense mentioned before, the difficulty of doing justice to all the values which the self believes are true and important, not the difficulty of guessing the right answer to a test item.

A *moral set* is cognitive in the sense of representing an effort to make a *rational decision*, rather than being cognitive in the sense of predicting an arbitrary external response, an external social reality, or being cognitive in the sense of ignoring affect or felt values in the situation. A rational moral decision implies ignoring personal non-moral (selfish) values or affects but does not imply ignoring personal moral values and affects, e.g., the sense of justice. The concept of a moral set toward decision-making is best exemplified in the concept of moral principles. As conceived by philosophers, moral principles are not rules prescribing or proscribing a certain act, e.g., the Ten Commandments, but are rules or methods of choosing between apparently legitimate alternatives, e.g., the categorical imperative or the utilitarian maxim. Essentially, however, principled persons do not consistently define the right by reference to a definite verbal formula or maxim at the principled level, unless they are concerned with ethics as an intellectual discipline. Rather, the right is defined as the decision an ideally moral or rational person or self would come to after thoroughly comprehending the particular situation or value-conflict.

Integration of Baldwin's Levels with the Stages of McDougall and Dewey: Six Moral Stages

We have described the distinctions in Baldwin's three moral levels as they slowly became meaningful in our clinical analysis of moral judgment data. The basic data to which we have been referring comprised responses to ten hypothetical moral dilemmas. The ten situations used were ones in which acts of obedience to legal–social rules or to the commands of authority conflicted with the human needs or welfare of other individuals. The child was asked to choose whether one should perform the obedience-serving act or the need-serving act, and was then asked a series of questions probing the thinking underlying their choices.

Our original subjects were a core group of 72 boys living in Chicago suburban areas. The boys were of three age groups: 10, 13, and 16. Half of each group consisted of popular boys (according to classroom sociometric tests), while half consisted of socially isolated boys. All the groups were comparable in I.Q. (An additional group of twenty-four 16-year-old lower-class delinquents was also interviewed at this time.)

In addition to Baldwin's distinctions, the distinctions between the Dewey–McDougall levels of (a) reinforcement and habit, (b) convention and concern for approval, and (c) reflective standards and self-judgment were equally evident in our data. We have preferred to call these levels preconventional, conventional, and postconventional. The term conventional means conforming to and upholding the rules and expectations of society or authority just because these are society's rules, expectations or conventions. The *preconventional* level is so-called because it has not yet come to really understand and uphold conventional or societal rules and authority. The *postconventional* level is so-called because it understands and basically accepts society's rules, but this acceptance and understanding is based on the prior formulation and acceptance of general moral principles or values underlying society's rules. These principles in some cases come into conflict with society's rules, in which case the *postconventional* individual judges by principle.

One way of understanding the three levels is to think of them as three different types of relationships between the *self* and *society's rules and expectations*. From this point of view, *Level A*, a preconventional person, is one for whom rules and social expectations are something external to the self; *Level B*, a *conventional* person, is one who has internalized the rules and expectations of others, especially authorities, and identifies the self with these rules; and *Level C*, a *postconventional* person, is one who has differentiated self from the rules and expectations of others and defines values in terms of self-chosen or internal principles. To illustrate intuitively these levels as they appeared in our interviews, we may cite three different responses to a dilemma regarding whether or not to tell one's father about a brother's disobedience after he has confided in you.

Here is Danny's response at Level A (preconventional), already quoted as representing Baldwin's instrumental stage. Rules and expectations are outside the self. The self's moral judgment predicts or describes them; *it does not identify with them.*

> In one way it would be right to tell because his father might beat him up. In another way it's wrong because his brother will beat him up if he tells.

Here is Andy's response to the dilemma at Level B (conventional). The self's moral judgment is *identified* with the rules and expectations formulated by others, especially authorities. It is not what others will do, but Andy's internal concern about the internal concerns or expectations of others which determines his judgments.

> He should think of his brother but it's more important to be a good son. Your father has done so much for you. I'd have a conscience if I didn't tell, more than to my brother, because my father couldn't trust me. My brother would understand, our father has done so much for him, too.

Here is Ken's response to the dilemma at Level C (postconventional). The self's moral judgment is differentiated from the rules and expectations of others. What others expect is one thing, what is right is another. What others expect may be identified with or may define the right, but there are grounds for such identification. The right is defined with reference to general principles such as "what is justified by trust," as opposed to specific rules (do's and don'ts) or specific role-expectations.

> Well, it's not really a matter of a brother and son decision, it's a matter of a right or wrong decision. Is the father right or is the son right? The father's act in the first place wasn't justified. Because of the original lack of good faith on the father's part, I don't think the brother has any obligation to tell. If the father's position had been justified, then I think Joe's lying would be unjustified. As it is, the brother has an obligation to keep quiet; his brother confided in him and trusted him.

In discussing these levels, McDougall stressed the differences between them in terms of the type of motive involved at each level:

> (1) The (preconventional) stage in which the operation of the instinctive impulses is modified by the influence of rewards and punishments, (2) the (conventional) stage in which conduct is controlled in the main by anticipation of social praise and blame, (3) the highest (postconventional) stage in which conduct is regulated by an ideal that enables a man to act in the way that seems to him right regardless of the praise or blame of his immediate social environment.

Danny, the preconventional, is concerned about punishment; Andy, the conventional, is concerned about approval; Ken, the postconventional, is concerned about "conscience," what is right to him regardless of his brother's or father's approval.

The McDougall–Dewey levels just outlined are described from the standpoint of the relation of the self to society. They do not clearly reflect the child's qualitative cognitive and epistemological growth. Our data suggested that Baldwin's three-level distinctions defined "stages" (or sublevels) in the basic series, preconventional, conventional, and postconventional (autonomous-ethical). The resulting stages are presented in Table 1.

Baldwin's notion of a movement from projective to instrumental valuing at the preconventional level is necessary to account for the fact that the earliest preconventional stage (Stage 1) is not an instinctual orientation to impulse gratification and reward and punishment, something closer to our and Baldwin's Stage-2 orientation. Baldwin's notion of an ideal-self stage is also necessary to clarify the fact that a conventional approval orientation is an orientation to ideals represented by significant others, not simply to approval and expectations as such. This orientation to ideals at the conventional (Stage 3) level was indicated by Billy's moral struggle about euthanasia quoted in the prior section.

Baldwin (as we discuss in detail later on) believes that the ideal self arises through identification with significant others, a notion corresponding to most conceptions of the conventional level as identificatory. Conventional morality requires some basis for choice where there is a conflict between the expectations of various role partners. This choice is made in terms of authority and affection linkages to the role partner, the two being fused in the parental relationship.

This attitude was naively expressed by Andy in his reply to the story about telling one's father about one's brother's lie:

> If my father finds out later, he won't trust me. My brother wouldn't either, but I wouldn't have a conscience that he (my brother) didn't.

Andy equates his "conscience" with avoidance of disapproval by authorities, but not by peers. Praise and blame are, of course, effective reinforcers even in the child's earliest years. In these early years, however, disapproval is but one of the many unpleasant external consequences of action that are to be avoided. In contrast, conventional adolescents attempt to make decisions and define what is good for themselves by anticipating possible disapproval in thought and imagination and by holding up approval as a final internal goal. This is not because of a hedonistic concern for approval, but because they cannot define the ideally right except in terms of judgment of an "ideal self" or of an authoritative or moral person related to the self.

> I try to do things for my parents; they've always done things for you. I try to do everything my mother says; I try to please her. Like she wants me to be a doctor and I want to, too, and she's helping me to get up there.

According to Baldwin, developing an *ideal self* involves a situation in which the child conforms, but does not see such conformity as enhancing his own impulses, or as due to his own weakness relative to the other who is enhancing himself. The child must come to see the denial of his own wishes as somehow self-enhancing.

The experience required, says Baldwin, is one in which the child perceives the parent as putting pressure on the child to conform to something outside the parent. Such an experience is not bipolar since the parent wants the child to be like himself vis-à-vis his attitude toward the rule. The parent's self is seen as simultaneously commanding and obeying. This initiating action and conforming are both seen as parts of the same self, a self-controlling self.

Such conformity to a third force might simply be perceived by the child as indicating that a third person dominates the parent as the parent dominates the child. However, the fact that such pressure to conform goes on in the absence of the third person or authority tends to give rise to the concept of a generally conforming self. In addition, the fact that the conformity is shared in the family or group gives rise to a sense of a common self which the child is to become.

Originally, such a general or ideal self is largely in the image of the parents. It is ideal to the child, it is what he is to become, but it is largely realized in the parents. This does not mean that there is no differentiation of parents from the rule; the parents are seen as obeying the rule. It does mean that the image of a good, conforming self which obeys the rules is in the parents' image.[2] Clearly this is the way in which Andy, the conventional subject just quoted, experiences morality.

Baldwin's account helps us also in defining the Dewey–Mac-Dougall *principled, reflective, autonomous,* or *postconventional* level. According to Baldwin, further development of the ideal self transforms it from a personal image into something more like abstract principles. By experience of conflict between models or "ideal values," the ideal self becomes a more abstract "conscience" oriented to abstract principles. The conventionally moral as "shared" becomes the universalizable, synnomic or "shareable," and the moral then becomes the "rational," that on which good men can ideally agree. Baldwin's emphasis on the level of autonomous or reflective morality as oriented to "shareability" and to "oughtness" or impersonality in obligation comes from the Kantian tradition in morality. It is necessary to supplement the McDougall–Dewey view of autonomous morality as simply reflective, critical, and rationally oriented to experiential ends.

In summary, our integration of the Baldwin and Dewey–Mc-Dougall levels allows us to:

1. Differentiate stages within the three major levels of moral development;
2. Relate moral judgment development to the child's cognitive and epistemological development;
3. Integrate the account of morality as the deontological principle of philosophic formalists like Kant with the moral levels of Dewey and McDougall defined in terms of a morality of approbation (rewards, approval, conscience) and of teleological reflection upon ends.

Similarities and Contrasts Between Baldwin's and Piaget's Levels of Moral Judgment

We have discussed our debt to Baldwin in the formulation of our moral stages. We need now to relate Baldwin's thinking to Piaget's, the primary starting point of our own thinking about moral

---

[2] It should be noted that Andy's "identification" with his father and mother is not an identifying with them as specific individuals, but as "good persons" to whom he is related. Identification is not with the mother or father as such, as it is in Freud's version of moral identification.

stages. In so doing, we shall explain not only the overlap between the stages of Baldwin and Piaget, but our reasons for rejecting Piaget's stage account where it diverges from Baldwin's.

According to both Baldwin and Piaget, the child must develop from a stage in which experience is adualistic. In terms of value judgment, there are two chief aspects of this adualism, aspects which may survive in various forms at fairly advanced ages. The first adualism involves the inability to differentiate between subject and object, or between ideas and the objects to which they refer. This Baldwin calls a projective attitude. The second adualism is the inability to differentiate the meaning of the object to the self from its meaning to others, the uncritical unconscious assumption that the self's attitudes toward the object are generally shared. This Baldwin calls a *syntelic* attitude.

Piaget, in adopting Baldwin's theories, labeled the first adualism, *primitive realism* and the second adualism, *egocentrism*. In his treatment of moral judgment, Piaget focuses on these attitudes as they relate to conceptions of the rules. Moral realism, according to Piaget, is the confusion between rules and things and the ascription of quasiphysical reality and force to rules. Moral egocentrism is the uncritical assumption that all rules, and also the self's perceptions of the rules, are universally shared.

According to Baldwin, as we have seen, the next level of instrumental thought is related to the localization of value experience in the self and the corresponding ability to see external things as pure means, which, in turn, is one phase of the discrimination by the subject of his own ideas from the objects or states to which they refer.

Like Baldwin, Piaget sees imitation and obedience as in themselves inadequate to establish an internalized morality, but unlike Baldwin, he sees a sense of conformity to moral rule as also inadequate to account for such a development. According to Piaget, the child feels a "heteronomous respect" toward his parents and elders, a respect composed of fear and love or admiration. This same respect is transferred to, or experienced toward, rules which acquire a sacred and unchangeable aspect. Such respect is heteronomous or unilateral because it does not imply a reciprocal right or wish to be respected by the authority. The authority's rights are not based on his duties, and any action or command of his may be viewed as right. Respect for the rule is also unilateral; it is not based on the function of the rule in serving individuals and their values.

Such heteronomous respect for the rules combines with the child's egocentrism to give the rules a fixed, external, quasiphysical cast. The child's egocentrism or inability to take the point of view of another prevents him from seeing the rule as serving a purpose for the selves who created it. There is a confusion of concept and thing, called *realism*, which leads to a perception of rules as fixed things outside of minds, and to a rigid, literal application of rules. One expression of this is a judgment of action by its actual consequences rather than according to its intentions. Another expression of the quasiphysical nature of rules is a belief in "immanent justice," or of natural events as punishing. In general, the heteronomous sense of justice is one insisting on inevitable and expiatory punishment.

Whereas Baldwin sees moral development largely in terms of increased depersonalization and social generalization of rules, Piaget sees such development as largely an increased relating of conformity to individual selves. Such development occurs in the transition of the child to the stage of mutual respect or autonomy. Mutual respect implies an attitude of reciprocal conformity and approval. In this stage, rules are seen as the product of agreement and cooperation. Respect for the rules is based on contract and on the group goals they serve, rather than on a belief in their intrinsic value. The sense of justice centers around the attitudes of equality and reciprocity themselves as manifested in contractual maintenance, exchange, and distributive equality. Punishment is oriented toward restitution to the victim rather than to retribution. The development of the attitude of mutual respect is largely dependent on interaction with age peers, according to Piaget. Even though adult authorities endeavor to be democratic, the natural prestige of the elders hinders a full development of reciprocal orientations.

Piaget does not develop a stage of the ideal in his book on moral judgment. However, parallel to Baldwin's account of the development of the subjective in adolescence, he describes the development of formal thought during adolescence, a development necessary for the formation of social ideals and principles. Whereas concrete operational thought performs operations upon object-images, formal thought uses operations upon other operations or upon verbal propositions. Accordingly, every logically possible combination or transformation of concepts can be worked out in hypothetico-deductive fashion. This means that empirically anticipated events are subordinated to logically possible events, so that empirical events are seen as merely cases of some more general formal system.

As a result, the adolescent becomes interested in ideas, attempts to systematize ideas, has his own opinions, and wants to evaluate and change society according to some ideal schema. These ideological trends are in turn related to his own planning of a long-range career. Without stressing the planning and systematizing of life and society, Piaget says that affect is for the first time felt for ideas and ideals rather than for the particular persons and events which represent them in the child's experience.

Respect and Obligation for Piaget and Baldwin

The basic difference between Piaget's and Baldwin's accounts of levels of moral judgment is that Baldwin believes that a sense of internal obligation or duty does not arise until a third "ideal" or "ethical" stage following an instrumental consequences stage. Furthermore, a sense of respect and a sense of duty arise hand in hand, rather than the concept of duty arising from respect. Piaget, in contrast, attributes a sense of duty or obligation to the first heteronomous or projective stage and derives it from an attitude of respect.

As Piaget indicates, the other side of an attitude of respect is an attitude of obligation. Obligation implies the side of the attitude which constrains us to do something, to make action conform to some requirement or model independent of the actor. Respect implies the side of the attitude directed toward a social object from which the requirements or models of action emanate. It implies an attitude that the object conformed to has some generalized value justifying such conformity.

According to Piaget, who follows Bovet, the attitude of respect in some sense precedes any regular obedience and imitation:

> Without respect, the rules would not be accepted and the rules would have no power to compel the mind. . . . It is a fact that the child in the presence of his parents has the spontaneous feeling of something greater than and superior to the self. This respect has its roots deep down in certain inborn feelings and is due to a sui generis mixture of fear and affection which develops as a function of the child's relation to his adult environment. (Piaget, 1965, pp. 377–379)

We may note as a problem that ambivalence, or fear and love, do not in themselves suffice to constitute an attitude of respect in the sense of "looking up to," a feeling of something greater than or better than the self. Thus they need not, as is claimed for respect, lead the young child "to attribute to his parents the moral and intellectual qualities which define his ideas of perfection."

That most young children feel both dependence and fear toward their parents we need not question. That the child is not only dependent but also rather uncritical in his assessment of what he and others can do also seems unquestionable. Whether there is in the very immature child any dynamic linkings between the two of the sort usually termed *idealization*, as Piaget thinks, is an open question.

We certainly may need and fear someone without idealizing him, though many adolescents and adults clearly do idealize.

The concept of respect essentially seems to refer to a tendency to believe that our attitude or actions of obedience, imitation, dependency or fear are (or should be) deserved by the object or person toward which they are directed. It implies that the person is, in some general sense, worthy of being given or shown conformity at some cost. It is obvious that it is possible for a child to obey or imitate without any attitude that the person he obeys or imitates needs to be worthy of such conformity beyond the fact that he can get it.

In contrast, the concept of respect for Baldwin implies an attitude toward a person as something *more* than a person, as representing something beyond what any individual self could be. To Baldwin, this is an *ideal self*. When the individual respects someone, it is not only because he can do this or that, but because there are an indefinite number of virtues and abilities which he also represents.

Baldwin defines three stages of development in terms of respect or dependence (see Wallwork's Chap. 10). At the earliest projective stage, there exists a physical dependence and a respect for superior force or for the control exerted by the parent. At this stage the intellectual interest of the child is in "who does what" in the physical and social world and an interpretation of the world in terms of quasihuman, quasiphysical forces.

In the next or "intellectual" stage, the child respects intelligence, the fact that the adult has purposes, predicts, and adjusts means to ends better than he does. At this stage the interest is in planning, and in finding a teleological purpose or design for everything. The child feels dependent in terms of his own inability to explain and design things and actions and feels admiring in terms of an interpretation of others as possessing more of what intellectual ability he feels he has.

At this stage the child sees no differences in basic self, no differences in purposes and motives between himself and the person he admires. He interprets the other's purposes in terms of his own general motives, in terms of a natural selfishness and he is not interested in purposes which cannot be interpreted in this way. Accordingly, at this point the attitude of respect does not imply any reluctance to get around the respected person.

The third or ethical stage of respect, Baldwin says, occurs when the child respects someone for being a better person or self, for being good, having good purposes and attitudes, for wanting and knowing how to conform to standards of conduct better than the self. The sense of inadequacy is more or less one of moral inadequacy and a need for guidance.

Such an attitude need not imply any utilitarian dependence on the person respected. However, it does imply that the respected person can judge the self in the same way that the self tries to judge itself.

Our thesis data suggested that Baldwin's characterization of the development of respect and obligation was closer to the mark than Piaget's. We first asked our children the meaning of the word respect. Our Stage-1 children gave answers of overt obedience; respect means, "Do what they say." Even after attempting to explicate the word in terms of "looking up to" or "thinking they are good," most of the children kept with this concept. Thus, if asked whether "you could do what the teacher said and still not respect her," many gave answers like, "Yes, if she told you to open the book to page 128, you could open the book but turn it to a different page."

With this concept of respect, Stage-1 children tend to think that people only respect persons to whom they are in direct relationship of subordination. Thus when asked whether people respect someone with a lot of money, they say that they would be respected by their servants, but not by others, or when asked about respect in a hierarchy, they say that one respects one's immediate superior in a hierarchy more than someone higher up, e.g., "I don't think civilians would respect the senator as much as the policeman because he only gives orders to the high officers like the judge or policeman." At the same time, however, we saw that Stage-1 children may respect a power figure projectively (or regardless of what need he is a means toward) and syntelically (in terms of vaguely shared attitudes).

Some Stage-1 children gave projective responses to property as well as to power, i.e., attributing some intrinsic value to the possession of property, which is fused with the authority and functional usefulness of the individual (Tommy's response to the value of life as based on furniture ownership in the Heinz dilemma).

Does this projective value of status imply an attitude of sacredness or respect? It does insofar as a child may be said to respect furniture, to which Tommy reduces status. Thus the "sacredness" for Tommy of furniture and its possessors does not seem to be because these represent or symbolize some vague being or order felt as greater than the self. There seems to be nothing "behind" the value of furniture as a respected object as there is for the moral respect postulated by Baldwin. While property is desired and protected by parents and other beings more powerful than the self, it is not respected as a symbol of them since they are subordinated to it.

In contrast, at the conventional level, at Stage 3, we find Baldwin's ethical respect in the sense that it is respect for the willingness and ability of the authority to fulfill his duty or responsibility. It implies that one respects someone who does something the self finds difficult and unpleasant, something the self does not want to do. For Type 3, one's evaluation of authority is intrinsic; it is because he does what one wouldn't like to do even though it is good.

The thinking of Stage 1, then, did not seem to indicate the primitive but pervasive motivation which Piaget called *heteronomous respect* linked to the adualisms. Thus, it was not seen as containing the basis for the development of Baldwin's ideal or ethical stage. This is particularly true if we follow Baldwin in interposing a prudential egoistic stage between primitive respect and moral respect.

Piaget hypothesizes an emotional attitude of heteronomous sacredness, respect, and obligation, which collaborates with and helps moral realism and a quasiphysical rigidity in perception of the social order. However, the only materials he uses to indicate the existence of the emotional attitude of unilateral respect are the cognitive naïvetés of the heteronomous child which they are designed to help explain. To indicate that rules are felt to be "sacred" and "untouchable," he shows that the child has a belief in the fact that they cannot be changed. To indicate an attitude of "awe" for parents, he indicates a child's belief in their unlimited age and knowledge.

However, such beliefs may be due to the child's having no need to limit the abilities of anyone for lack of any respect for the unlimited. Others may be seen as knowing all, but knowledge may not be seen as of tremendous difficulty or value. The father may be seen as no different than God, but the child may have no feeling of the divineness of God in any adult sense. The father may be seen as knowing all, but so may the self. Thus Piaget himself quotes remarks such as, "Then Daddy couldn't know everything either, nor me neither."

Primitive equations of a "higher" concept with a "lower" concept may always be read in two ways. If a child equates father or God with an animal, we may believe this to be a mystic or magical attribution of higher qualities to animals—or we may say that the child attributes animal-like qualities to the father or to God. If a child says a culprit should be punished with death, we may believe that this indicates that respect for the rules is so strong it demands that the ultimate value of life itself must be sacrificed—or we may believe that the child sets no high value on the concept of life.

In summary, our stage schema attempts to incorporate the "valid" elements of Piaget's heteronomous and autonomous stages in characterizing our first two stages. Some of the agreements and contrasts in interpretation involved are summarized in Table 5. As Table 5 indicates, our interpretation of the first two stages is closer to Baldwin's interpretation of his first two stages (cf. Table 3) than to Piaget's. When so interpreted, much of Piaget's characterization of moral judgment may be taken up into a schema which seems to meet the criteria of stages quite successfully.

Baldwin's Theory of Morality and Conscience as the Ideal Self

Our account of Baldwin's moral theory in the last four sections has so far stressed its formal or cognitive side, the side reflected in a series of subjective–objective differentiations in value judgment. Fundamentally, however, for Baldwin, moral experience is not cognitive, but a matter of (1) affective role taking or ejecting the self into others, and (2) of willing and of conflict of wills. Both these features are involved in Baldwin's notion of conscience as the *ideal self*.[3]

Baldwin engaged in a careful analysis of the phenomenology of science which for him discredited the most popular nonrational or noncognitive accounts of moral experience in his day. These were: (1) that morality was an expression of altruistic social instinct (Darwin); (2) that morality was internalized or overlearned cultural habit (Spencer, Bain); and (3) that morality was a matter of sympathy or empathy (Hume). Baldwin's analysis and criticisms of these theories of morality are equally valid today as critiques of ethological theories of morality as instinctive altruism, behavioristic theories of morality as habit, and social learning theories of morality as learned empathic response.

According to Baldwin, two features requisite for morality are a degree of consistency and a degree of altruism. Considering first altruism, we may ask if all social action is determined by a self or self-concept, how can any action be unselfish? Baldwin's answer is that moral action is determined by and enhances a general or ideal self, as described in our discussion of Baldwin's ideal stage. As opposed to moral action, premoral or amoral action is determined by a concept of the concrete self with its historically given needs, desires, and interests.

---

[3] The more formal, cognitive, or epistemological side of Baldwin's notion of the ideal self was picked up not only by myself in 1958, but also by van den Daele (1968). He proposed and empirically verified a logically oriented ordered sequence of stages of the ideal self. Each stage described a structurally more advanced and adequate conceptualization of the kind of ideal form envisioned for the self.

Table 5
**Piaget's Stages of Moral Development Compared with First Two
Kohlberg Stages**

Stage 1 (Heteronomous stage)

1. Value and conformity are *egocentric* or *syntelic* (Baldwin). (Manifested in absolutism of value or unawareness or moral perspectives.) Our interpretation similar to Piaget's.

2. Conformity is *realistic* or *projective* (Baldwin). Judgments of bad are made in terms of physical properties and consequences of action rather than in terms of the act's psychological intentions or functional appropriateness to some norm. Manifested in objective responsibility, in physicalistic definitions of lies, and in belief that punishment is a physically automatic response to deviance (immanent justice and expiative, rather than restitutive or reforming, punishment).

   Piaget: There is a confusion of rules and things. Rules are oriented to as fixed sacred things. Deviance is always wrong. Acts are evaluated in terms of the "letter of law," and in terms of consequences instead of intentions.

   Our interpretation: Objective responsibility is merely an expression of "projective" modes of value and a failure to differentiate moral good from other kinds of good. It does not imply an orientation to rules in the usual sense of a concept of a rule-orientation. We find Type 1 not oriented to rules as entities, but oriented to projectively bad acts and to obedience to persons, not rules.

3. Conformity is *heteronomous,* or based on unilateral respect or *objective necessity* (Baldwin), i.e., might makes right. Manifested in belief that obedience to adults or other power figures is right when it conflicts with other rules or welfare considerations, and in belief that punishment makes an act wrong necessarily.

   Piaget: Duty is based on a sense of heteronomous respect for adults transferred to their commands and rules. This respect, compounded of love and fear, leads to an overevaluation and sense of sacredness of authority and rules.

   Our interpretation: Adults must be seen representing something beyond themselves before they are "respected." While we find children of Type 1 oriented to obedience, we find little evidence that they respect authorities in any sense beyond recognizing that they are more powerful. Various kinds of response used by Piaget as indicating a sense of the "sacredness" of adults are interpreted as indicating cognitive naiveté, independent of emotional overevaluation. Often they indicate a lack of awareness of moral rule, against which the adult is to be measured rather than an idealization of the adult.

Baldwin says that the premoral self is not only concrete, it is bipolar and inconsistent. Premoral interaction involves an active, assertive, controlling self and a passive, submissive, imitative self. The child may be either as occasion arises. With a younger child, or a parent in a permissive mood, the child himself defines what is to be done and the other is merely an object to be manipulated, an agent in terms of which the action may be carried out. With an older person, or in a novel situation, the child expects to be an object in terms of which action determined by the other is carried out.

In either case the self determining the child's action is "selfish." The act of adjusting to, or obeying, another need not imply an experience of self-control and unselfishness since the self controlling

Table 5 (continued)
Stage 2 (Autonomous stage)

1. Value and conformity are relativistic.
2. Conformity and punitive justice are flexible and oriented to intentions and functional needs.

   Piaget: Rules are seen as the expression of understandable human purposes and as means to those purposes. Deviance may be justifiable in terms of an intent to conform to the "spirit" or purpose of the rule or in terms of a particular unusual situation. Acts are evaluated in terms of their intent.

   Our interpretation: Rules may be seen as merely instrumental acts, as commands based on the individual needs of authority. Deviance may be justified on the basis of an act being a means to a natural end. The end is not itself evaluated in terms of its worthiness for a moral self. Rules are seen as a basis for shared action but not as a basis of shared evaluation or judgment.

3. Conformity is autonomous or based on mutual respect. Manifested in sense of the need to conform to peer-expectations, in concern about distributive equality, in the importance of exchange or reciprocity, in the notion that peer vengeance is similar to authority's punishment, and in the notion that adult punishment is not the ultimate criterion of wrong but is only a painful consequence to be considered in decision-making.

   Piaget: Conformity is based on empathic identification with the needs of others, shared goals, maintenance of agreement and a concern for approval by those approved of by the self. Conformity as to the attitude of other equals.

   Our interpretation: These attitudes may be invoked as a basis of conformity without any really internalized conformity, shared goals, or concern for others. There may be no differentiation between "legitimate" and other needs of self and all may be hedonistically oriented. Needs of others empathized with is based on the degree to which the other comes within the boundaries of the self. Equality is not a norm but a fact. "I and my needs are as good as anyone else's." A seeking to maximize quantity of approval by direct instrumental techniques.

---

the child and demanding sacrifice of his wishes is not his own self. Though the child's action may be determined by the dominating self of the other, still that other self is conceived by the child in its own image as a basically impulsive or need-gratifying self (insofar as motives are assigned to it at all). The experience of unselfish obligation requires that the two selves or wills be identified or unified with one another, an integration which is not achieved by motives to imitate or obey in themselves.

According to Baldwin, the problem of the genesis of the moral self is not solved by the internalization of prescribed habits in the sense of the learning theorists or the associationists of Baldwin's day, as we stated in discussing the utilitarians. Even if the child accepts certain conforming habits or rules as part of himself, this does not guarantee the existence of a concept of a moral or altruistic self as determining action. It does not imply a difference between a child's feeling of self-assertion and dominance in carrying out a conforming habit and its feeling in carrying out a deviant or asocial one.

Considering the moral self as a consistent self, the inconsistency of the premoral child can also be defined in terms of the bipolarity of his self. When interacting with another person who appears stronger, who offers something to appreciate or imitate, the child is submissive and flexible. When interacting with a weaker or fully understandable or predictable person, the child appears dominating and inflexible, a kind of rigidity which does not imply real consistency. For Baldwin (1906), consistency of character requires a "social bond of union" for the child's various situational selves or roles (p. 40). Whereas altruism reflects the ideality of the self concept, consistency reflects its generality.

In order for the concept of a shared self which wants to be good and rule-conforming to arise, situations must arise in which the child conforms, but does not see such conformity as either enhancing his own impulses, or due to his own weakness relative to the other who is enhancing himself. The child must come to see the denial of his own wishes as somehow self-enhancing. Baldwin says the experience required is one in which the child perceives the parent as putting pressure on the child to conform to something outside the parent. Such an experience is not bipolar since the parent wants the child to be like himself vis-à-vis his attitude toward the rule. The parent's self is seen as simultaneously commanding (the child) and obeying (the rule). Thus initiating action and conforming are seen as both parts of the same self, a self-controlling self. This is a form of reciprocity, but a different form of reciprocity than that stressed by Piaget.

Such conformity to a third force might simply be perceived by the child as indicating that a third person dominates the parent as the parent dominates the child. However, the fact that such pressure to conform goes on in the absence of the third person or authority tends to give rise to the concept of a generally conforming self. In addition, the fact that the conformity is shared in the family or group gives rise to a sense of a common self which the child is to become.

Originally, such a general or ideal self is largely in the image of the parents. It is ideal to the child, it is what he is to become, but it is largely realized in his parents. This does not mean that there is no differentiation of parents from the rule; the parents are seen as obeying the rule. It does mean that the image of a good, conforming self which obeys the rules is in the parent's image.

Baldwin characterizes the determinant of moral action as a "self," rather than as rules or as situational consequences, in an effort to account for the introspective phenomena connoted by *conscience.* Rules enter into moral decisions, not as habits, but in terms of a general rule-obeying self which is not certain in its decisions.

The concept of conscience implies some thinking process in which the mind exerts a strong force on the rest of the self to follow its behests, but which the self identifies with. That is, the compulsion is obeyed out of the self's strength and disobeyed out of the self's weakness, unlike neurotic or impulsive compulsions. It implies choosing in the "line of greatest resistance" as William James put it.

Concepts of conscience and duty imply a rather subtle mingling of feelings of freedom and constraint in action. They imply that I feel compelled to perform an act, but that this compelling force exists within the self or personality. I am "compelled" to do right in opposition to the remainder of the self, as opposed to impulse, fear, or self interest. Thus, as opposed to the rest of the self, conscience is compelling. But, as opposed to outside forces, conscience is free. Just as it must override other forces within the self, it must override external forces. All this is implied in the phrase "ought to," as opposed to "want to" or "have to." When we reify the "ought," when we see it as having a psychic locus, we call it conscience.

The experience of conscience or of resistance to temptation, then, is not reducible to internalized habit nor to anticipation of guilt. Neither is it reducible to empathy or sympathy. Sympathetic concern for consequences enters into moral decision not as spontaneous impulse, but in terms of a self which is regularly concerned about others and their legitimate claims.

Baldwin uses the good old Victorian example of a decision as to whether or not to give a handout to a beggar. One cannot simply sympathize with the beggar and let his self or his wishes determine action. On the other hand, one cannot simply determine action by one's own natural self which would like to spend the money on its own purposes. Rather the decision is made by a self trying to do right, which attempts to anticipate what an ideal self, an all-wise, purely motivated self would choose or recommend in the situation. Such a self is general, it is to the actor's mind the same for both himself and the beggar. It is a process of thought and feeling which would justify both the beggar's asking and the actor's giving, or repudiate both. Though general, it is not simply a rule. In 99 cases out of 100, one might refuse beggars; yet the merit of the claim of the individual beggar must be examined if a moral choice is involved.

The concept of the ideal self, then, is invoked by Baldwin to account for what we earlier called a moral set, a set toward altruism and self-consistency, which is independent of settled attitudes of obedience to particular rules or sympathetic involvements with particular persons in particular situations. The need to postulate such a set appears most closely in the way in which thinking and choosing are directed in situations of moral conflict. Where particular rules and sympathies break down, the moral person has a moral set directing him to reach some morally integrated solution to which his moral self could assent.

We quoted Billy, age 13, in his response to a mercy-killing story involving a conflict between rules against murder on the one side and sympathy for suffering on the other.

> If I was a doctor, I just wouldn't like to kill people, but in a way he'd be doing her a favor. These are murder. I really don't know, but I can't see anybody being killed, . . . I don't think a person should be killed like an animal. It wouldn't be any compliment to that person, but then she wanted it. I'm trying to put myself in the shoes of the doctor and I don't think anyone can imagine the pain. If it were absolutely necessary, if they were sure she would die and she were out of her mind, they would do it in a painless way.

Billy cannot simply sympathize with the woman and let his sympathy determine his choice. Neither can he simply determine his action by a habitual self of natural reluctance to kill nor of conformity to definite prescribed rule. There is rather a struggle to decide rightly, to anticipate what an ideal self, an all-wise and ethical self, would choose. The appeal is to a general self, to a reorganizing perspective, which is the same for himself and for the doctor. Though general, it is neither simply a socially accepted rule of society nor a simple habit. The boy has perhaps never before questioned the habitual view or social rule that killing is wrong. It is not simply spontaneous sympathy, however, but his moral set, his ideal self, which requires the examination of the merit of the claim of the individual woman in the individual situation.

Billy's set is termed self by Baldwin, because it is a total point of view or perspective, an organized unity of attitudes, not a single concrete orientation to a single concrete rule. It is ideal because it represents a groping. It is not his concrete self, not the concrete self of another, such as his parent (though some preadolescent children say that to decide what is right they think of what their parent would think about it). It is this ideal nature of the ethical self that makes it altruistic.

We have stressed so far Baldwin's account of conscience as an ideal self, like the role-taking self at Billy's Stage-3 level, the ideal "good boy" stage. The higher development of the ideal self is described by Bradley (1872) as the morality of "my station and its duties."[4] Like Baldwin, Bradley recognizes, however, that the ideal self cannot be fully identified with society but develops beyond it.

The possibility of a postconventional sense of obligation is what leads Baldwin to reject the notion that the fundamental moral sentiment is respect for social rules and authority as Piaget and Durkheim believe. As Baldwin (1906) states it:

> As to the second form of universality—giving a rule on which all may act—this also does not alone exhaust the sort of sanction which ethical rules have. We can imagine a form of society built on the basis simply of a system of conventional social rules which each citizen is always to observe. This would be strictly a social sanction; the rules would be civil; they might be compulsory, but they need not be ethical. Such a society would lack just the one thing which we have found essential to human society considered as a progressive organization; the thing omitted by the traditional theories of human society which liken law to convention, and conformity to convenience and utility. This lack is just the principle of growth: the give-and-take of personal influence between the man and the group . . . in the individual it is what we mean by his ethical growth . . . And as in the individual . . . so in society also ethical sanctions supersede those of intelligence, convention and mob-suggestion . . . If we bring this finally under the question of rules, we reach a last possibility: *that in the ethical realm the individual may rule himself by rules which are in advance of those which society prescribes, and also exact them.* (pp. 559–567)

For Piaget, a postconventional principle is a purely intellectual construction, its affective source is still respect for other persons (heteronomous or mutual respect). For Baldwin, the germ of postconventionality lies in the origin of morality as social but ideal, and a progressive differentiation of the ideal from its embodiment in concrete persons.

In the end, the fundamental distinction between Baldwin's moral psychology and Piaget's is that Piaget's psychology has no self. Piaget starts with an ego knowing objects, but knowing them first egocentrically. Development is a progressive movement toward objectivity. In contrast, for Baldwin all experience is experience of a self, not just of a bodily and cognitive ego. This means first that central to the self is not cognition but will. Second, it means that from the start experience is *social* and reflective. The child's sense of self he derives from other selves and ejects back into them. The sense of self is a sense of will and capacity in the relation of self to others. The individual is fundamentally a potentially moral being, not because of social authority and rules (as Durkheim and Piaget

---

[4] Like Baldwin and Royce, Bradley derives his moral phenomenology from a neo-Hegelian position.

telos

thought) but because his ends, his will, his self is that of a shared social self.

Baldwin's Theory of the Development of the Social Self

In cognitive-developmental or "symbolic-interactional" theories of society, the primary meaning of the word *social* is the distinctively human structuring of action and thought by role-taking, by the tendency to react to the other as someone like the self, and by the tendency to react to the self's behavior in the role of the other (Mead, 1934; Baldwin, 1897). There are two subsidiary meanings of social, the first, that of affectional attachment, the second, that of imitation. Both human love and human identification, however, presuppose the more general sociality of symbolic communication and role-taking. Before one can love the other or can model his attitudes, one must take his role through communicative processes (Mead, 1934). The structure of society and morality is a structure of interaction between the self and other selves who are like the self, but who are not the self. The area of the conflicting claims of selves is the area of morality, or of moral conflict, and the modes of role-taking in such conflict situations represent the varying structures of moral judgment and choice defining our various stages. Role-taking itself represents a process extending beyond the sphere of morality or of conflicting claims. Moral role-taking itself may have many affective flavors, as our discussion of attitudes of empathy, guilt, disapproval, and respect suggested. Basically, however, all these forms imply a common structure of reciprocity between selves with expectations about one another.

Although basically cognitive, the processes responsible for social development are theoretically different from those responsible for development of physical concepts because they require role-taking. Since persons and institutions are "known" through role-taking, social-structural influences on social development may be best conceived in terms of variations in the kind and structure of role-taking. According to Baldwin, role-taking is a broader term than imitation. All role-taking has imitative components or roots. At the adult level, however, we do not overly imitate, we "role-take."

According to Baldwin, imitation is a basic functional tendency called *accommodation*. As stated by Baldwin (1906), "Reaction of the imitative type is the original form of mental accommodation to the environment" (p. 258). It is clear that imitation involves a cognitive copying process. There is a sense in which any cognition is a copy of a part of the environment, since an image or symbol has a relation of likeness to an environmental object or structure. In Baldwin's view, representation or imagery then implies a distinctive active copying tendency, since he believes all images and representations are forms of action, not passive redintegration of sensations (as introspective associationism and psychoanalysis claimed). Baldwin finds in imitation not only the origins of accommodative cognition but of self-control or will (see Freeman-Moir, Chap. 6).

Baldwin's view that the child's knowledge of society develops at first through imitation seems to be saying little more than the social-learning truism that the child's knowledge of society grows through the observational learning of the behavior of others (learning, which translated into performance, is termed *imitation*). The more distinctive feature of Baldwin's view is that such imitation provides the structure of the child's social relationships, i.e., of his self as it relates to other selves. In the social-learning view of imitation, it is a matter of little moment whether a response is learned by imitation or by reinforced trial and error since it functions in the same way one learned. In contrast, Baldwin argues that imitation is important because it determines the structure of the child's self-concept, and of his concepts of others, a structure, in turn, determining the use of the behavior pattern learned through imitation.

According to Baldwin,

> The growth of the individual's self-thought, upon which his social development depends, is secured all the way through by a twofold exercise of the imitative function. He reaches his subjective understanding of the social copy by imitation, and then he confirms his interpretations by another imitative act by which he ejectively leads his self-thought into the persons of others. (Baldwin, 1906, p. 527)

Baldwin's central claim (made also by Mead, 1934) is that the child's self-concept and his concept of other selves necessarily grow in one-to-one correspondence. The child cannot observationally learn the behavior pattern of another without putting it in the manifold of possible ways of acting open to the self. Once it becomes something the self might do, when others do it, they, too, are ascribed the subjective attitudes connected with the self's performance of the act.

As stated by Baldwin,

> What the person thinks of himself is a pole or terminus and the other pole is the thought he has of the other person, the "alter." What he calls himself now is in large measure an incorporation of elements that at another period he called another. Last year I thought of my friend, W., as someone with a skill on a bicycle. This year I have learned to

ride and have imitatively taken the elements formerly recognized in W's personality over to myself. All the things I hope to learn to become are, now, before I acquire them, possible elements of my thought of others.

But we should note that when I think of the other, I must construe him as a person in terms of what I think of myself, the only person whom I know in the intimate way called "subjective." My thought of my friend is not exhausted by the movements of bicycling, nor by any collection of such acts. Back of it all there is the attribution of the very fact of subjectivity which I have myself. I constantly enrich the actions which were at first his alone, and then became mine by imitation of him, with the meaning, the subjective value, my appropriation of them has enabled me to make. (Baldwin, 1897, pp. 13–18)

According to Baldwin, then, there are two intertwined mechanisms of society, of sharing. The first is imitation of the other, the second is *ejection* i.e., empathy or projection of one's own subjective feelings into the other. Imitation of the other not only leads to a changed self-concept (e.g., a self who rides the bicycle), but it leads to a changed concept of the other because the activity (bicycle-riding) has a new meaning after it is done by the self, and this meaning is read back as part of the other.

The basic starting point of any analysis of the growth of social knowledge, then, must be the fact that all social knowledge implies an act of sharing, of taking the viewpoint of another self or group of selves. This fact is paralleled on the active side by the fact that all social bonds, ties, or relationships involve components of sharing.

Two basic psychological mechanisms of sharing have been proposed by developmental theory, role-taking, and imitation. Baldwin (1897) and Mead (1934) engaged in extensive written debate as to the relative priority of the two mechanisms in social development. Baldwin viewed similarity of self and other as directly striven for through imitation, whereas Mead viewed it as the indirect result of role-taking involved in communicative acts. The child's attitude, he thought, became like that of the other because both respond alike to a common symbol or gesture. Because the child has responded in the past to the other's gesture, when he makes the gesture himself, he calls out in himself implicitly the response he calls out in the other. Mead further points out that much sociality, much mutual role-taking, occurs through cooperative interaction in which each individual's role is different, in which roles are complementary rather than similar. Nevertheless, the study of infancy indicates that similarity to others is directly striven for, and that such striving or imitation precedes, rather than follows, the development of linguistic communication. Accordingly, it seems to us that Mead's conceptions must be embedded in a broader developmental account of the self which includes early imitative behavior and the matrix of infant cognitive development out of which the self emerges.

Like Mead, Baldwin was struck by the fact that the younger child's social interaction is structured in terms of dyadic complementary roles, and that young children tend to play out both sides of these complementary roles as a mechanism of self-development. According to Baldwin, the basic unit of the self is a bipolar self–other relationship, with a resulting tendency to play out the role of the other, i.e., the child either has an imitative or an ejective attitude toward another person. When the child is imitating or learning from the other, his attitude is one of accommodation, i.e., his behavior is being structured by the structure of the behavior of the other. It is a matter of little import whether the child's action is structured by the other in the form of instruction or command. A modeling is taken as an implicit command, and an explicit command can always be modeled (i.e., "Do it this way," accompanied by a demonstration). In either case, the structure of the activity belongs to both parties, but it is being passed on from the active to the passive one. The central focus is upon a novel structure which the active agent has which the passive agent does not.

In contrast, the active or assimilative self is one which knows what it is doing and which ejects its own past attitudes into the other. Whether the child is active or passive, there is a focus upon an activity of one person with an attitude of accommodation to it in the other. The attitude of the child practicing something he has already learned through imitation or compliance, then, is always different than the attitude he held in the process of learning it. In learning an activity associated with the superior power or competence of the adult, the child's attitude is accommodatory and, in that sense, inconsistent with the prestigeful activity being learned. Accordingly, the child tends to turn around and practice the activity on, or before the eyes of, some other person whom he can impress, into whom he can eject the admiration of submissiveness he felt when learning the act.

The actual ejective phase of self-development appears first in the second year of life. At that age, the child seems to attribute feelings to others and to show things to, and communicate with, others. At the end of the second year, a "negativistic crisis" (Ausubel, 1957) typically occurs. This is a phase in which self and other are sharply differentiated and the difference between copying the self and copying (or obeying) the other are sharply distinguished. An example of the counter-imitation of this era is a 2½-year-old's consistent response of "not goodbye," when someone said "Goodbye" to him.[5]

Interestingly, however, it is just at this age of independence that the child acquires a need for an audience, a need reflected in "look at me" or attention-seeking behavior. Indeed, it is striking to notice that "look at me" behavior often is a phase of imitative acts at this developmental level. The father takes a big jump, the same 2½-year-old imitates, and then demands that the father look at him just as he looked at the father in imitating. Imitation immediately placed the child in the model's role, and led him to eject into the adult his own capacity for admiration.

Age-developmental studies suggest that look-at-me attention-seeking precedes the seeking of approval from others. It is clear that the child who shows off to the adult the act he has just learned from him will not seek the adult's approval. As the child matures, he recognizes that imitation of the act does not make him as competent as the model, and that performance of one competent act still leaves the adult a generally superior performer. As the child acquires a stable sense of the superiority of the older model, "look at me" after imitation becomes the request for approval (e.g. "Did I do it right?"). Baldwin's (1897) account, then, suggests that much of the need for approval is born from the fact that most of the child's accomplishments are imitative. Almost everything the young child strives to do or accomplish is something he sees another person do first and which he learns, in part, imitatively. The young child's accomplishments, his talking, walking, dressing himself, toileting, etc., are all activities that he sees others do and knows they can do. Because they are his models for activity, their approval of his performance counts.

The interpretation just advanced reverses the social-learning account of the relations between imitation and social approval. Gewirtz (1969) notes, like Baldwin, that almost every behavior which socialization requires is a behavior children see others do first. Accordingly, says Gewirtz, when a child is rewarded for a step in socialization, he is also being rewarded for imitating, and so a generalized habit of imitating is born. Baldwin reverses this relation, seeing the need for social reinforcement as arising from imitation.

Baldwin, then, proposes that the motivational basis of social reinforcement is to be found in the child's imitative tendencies, his

---

[5] This negativism about imitation and obedience is paralleled by a negativism about receiving help, the insistence on "doing it oneself." A typical expression was the same child's insistence that a coat be put back on him after it had been removed by a helpful adult, so he could take it off himself.

tendencies to engage in shared activities. The child's look-at-me behavior is not so much a search for adult response as it is a search for confirmation of social or imitative learning. Insofar as the desire for approval arises developmentally out of look-at-me behavior, it, too, is not a sign of some more concrete reward which the child seeks.

As we elaborate in a subsequent section, the child's dependence on social reinforcement is heaviest at the developmental stage where he is concerned with "doing things right" but has no clear, internal cognitive standards of what is right and so must rely on the approval of authorities to define "right" behavior. The child's initial desires to perform competently, to succeed, rest on intrinsic competence motivation. The infant struggles to master a task without the least concern for adult reward for performing the task, and without the least concern for the adult's judgment as to whether or not he is doing it right.

Social development up to age 6–7 is not a matter of internalizing extrinsic social reinforcement into intrinsic competence motivation; rather, it is a process of growing sensitivity to external social definers of standards of competence, and in that sense an increased sensitivity to extrinsic social reinforcement. This increased sensitivity, in turn, is the result of a growing sense of dependence upon having a social model of performance. The tendency to imitate, to seek a model of performance, itself rests primarily upon intrinsic competence motivation, upon the "need" to act or function. The child's fundamental motive in imitation is expressed in the familiar cry, "what can I do?" Relying on models to do something interesting and effective, he comes to feel increasingly that he must also rely on them to tell him how he is doing. In this view, competence motivation engenders imitation which engenders social dependency through an increased sense of discrepancy between the child's own activities and the norms embodied in the activities of his models.

In Baldwin's account, the development of the imitative process into social dependency (the need for approval), is also part of the development of imitation into *identification*, where identification is the combination of attachment, admiration, and desire for normative guidance which forms a focus of the child's attitude toward his parents. Identification as discussed by Baldwin is a constellation of attitudes similar to that termed *satellization* by Ausubel (1957). Ausubel distinguishes between an imitative *incorporatory* attitude and a *satellizing* attitude. An incorporative child is a general imitator, he is always ready and eager to imitate any interesting or prestigeful model, because such imitation is a primitive form of self-aggrandizement, of getting something the model has or sharing his prestige. In contrast, the satellizing child is loyal to his past modelings of his parents and to their expectations, and will pass up the opportunity to copy the new prestigeful response of the model.

The distinctions between an incorporatory and a satellizing attitude are suggested by the following examples:

> *Incorporatory.* Boy, age 4, to male adult interviewer: "You're twice as big so you have twice as much brains. I'm going to knock your brains out, and then they'll go in my brains and I'll be twice as smart."
>
> *Satellizing.* Boy, age 12, asked about his father: "I'd like to be like my father because I think of him as nice, and I was brought up by him, and learned the things he taught me so I could be a good boy, because he always taught me to be good."

Baldwin's Theory of Identification

Baldwin's conception of the development of the ideal self covers a broader canvas than moral development as usually conceived. As an example of the role of the ideal self in social relations, one might cite the state of "being in love" as conventionally (or romantically) defined. All psychological analyses of love, including the psychoanalytical, agree that it involves a relationship of identification (or sharing between selves) involving idealization of the other, and a sense of being governed by an unselfish or sacrificial concern for the love object. In other words, it involves a sense of sharing based on the ideal self, not the concrete self.

Baldwin, then, has elaborated a distinctive theory of identification, and linked it to a conception of the ideal self. Baldwin's theory of identification is closer to that propounded much later by Ausubel (1957) than that of subsequent psychoanalytic and neopsychoanalytic theorists.

This concept of *identification* implies the following (which distinguishes it from psychoanalytical views of identification):

1. Identification is viewed as a stage of more general imitative or social-sharing processes.
2. Accordingly, it is not uniquely dependent upon particular motives and ties only present in the early parent–child relationship.
3. Identifications are not totally fixed, irreversible, or "internalized." Identifications are "solutions" to developmental tasks which may change object or nature with new developmental tasks.

Baldwin's account distinguishes identification (generalized enduring modeling and perception of a portion of the self as shared with the parents) from imitation, but makes the distinction relative and one of developmental structure, rather than of dichotomous processes. In Baldwin's account, enduring tendencies to model are a component of a larger constellation of attitudes termed satellization by Ausubel. The constellation includes the following components:

1. Tendencies to imitate the parent or other model;
2. Emotional dependency and attachment to the parent;
3. Tendency to conform to the parent's normative expectations;
4. Perceived similarity to the parent;
5. Idealization of the parent or of his competence and virtue;
6. Vicarious self-esteem derived from the parent's competence or status;
7. Ability to derive self-esteem from the parent's approval and so to forego other sources of prestige or competence, with associated security of self-esteem, moderate level of aspiration, etc.

This constellation is believed to develop more or less gradually in the "latency" years (4–10) in most (but not all) "normal" children, and to wane or decline with the growth of independence in adolescence.

It is, of course, not necessary that the ideal self and identification be centered on the parents in Baldwin's theory, as it is in Freud's. Such centering, however, is natural because the child tends to assume (1) that he is to become or grow up to be like his parents, that his parents are models of his future self; (2) that parents are the source of pressure to conform to rules; and (3) that since, as members of a family, parent and child identify with one another's interests and characteristics, they have a common or general family self or identity.

What are some of the implications of Baldwin's theory of identification? We have investigated this question in the study of the development of children's attitudes toward their parents. Baldwin sketched a conception of identification in which imitation was one component of a cluster of attitudes of perceived similarity, dependency, attachment, approval-seeking, and moral conformity toward the parent. The sequence of development is quite different from that of psychoanalytic theory (as shown in Table 6).

The sequence described by Baldwin fits the available evidence

Table 6
The Development of Identification

Neopsychoanalytic	Baldwin
1. Child's dependency based on care-taking and affection.	1. Child's imitation of competent and interesting behavior of adult.
2. Imitation as a substitute for parental nurturance.	2. Desire for normative conformity, i.e., a sense of shared standards for behavior, desires to imitate.
3. Internal normative conformity in order to maintain self-approval based on 2.	3. Dependency, i.e., persistent sense of need for guidance and approval by the model.

on the development of the boy's orientation to the father from age 4–8 (Kohlberg, 1966). The development of the boy's attachment and identification with the father is of particular interest because it is the first strong attachment which cannot be explained in terms of the physical caretaking or social instinct theories so frequently introduced in discussions of the mother–child tie. The existence of the shift has been documented in studies using various measures which all show preschool boys as somewhat female-oriented in doll play and show a shift to male-oriented preference at about age 6. While all identification theories postulate such a mother–father shift for the boy, none provide a very adequate mechanism for it. It does not seem that the shift could be a result of the fact that the father actually becomes the primary nurturer and rewarder in these years while the mother ceases to be. On the other hand, the psychoanalytic account in terms of castration anxiety raises many difficulties in accounting for a positive shift in dependency.

The explanation of a developmental shift in the boy's orientation to his parents is straightforward. The child learns to sex-type himself and his activities during the second and third year. By the age of 3–4 the boy knows quite well he is a boy and prefers "boy things" to "girl things" simply because he likes himself and that which is familiar or similar to himself. Up to this point in his development, he has remained mother-oriented, however. Tending now to prefer masculine activities, he seeks a model for these activities. Thus he is led to select his father rather than his mother as a model. Imitation in turn leads to emotional dependency upon the father.

The existence of such a sequence was confirmed in a semilongitudinal study of boys, age 4–8 (Kohlberg & Zigler, 1967). Like other studies, this study indicated that there was a clear preference for appropriately sex-typed objects and activities by age 3, a clear preference for imitating the male figure by age 5, and a clear preference for orienting social dependency to the male at age 6. The age at which an individual child advanced through this sequence varied considerably. Regardless of the boy's speed in moving through the sequence, however, he moved through it in the same order, i.e., the tests mentioned defined a cumulative Guttman scale.

We have stressed the boy–father identification to establish the fact that the formation of human social bonds or attachments requires components of past shared-identity (similarity) and of the disposition to share and learn new behavior patterns (imitation). Baldwin's theory stresses that a social attachment bond is a relationship of sharing, communication, and cooperation (or reciprocity) between selves recognizing each other as other selves. In contrast, modern child psychological theories have denied that experience of, and desire for, sharing and communication between selves are the primary components of a human social bond. Their model of the child's attachment to others has been based on a model of an attachment to a physical object, or to a physical source of physical pleasure or pain. The physical-object concept of social attachment is equally basic to Freudian (1938) theory (cathexis of the physical body of the other), to reinforcement theory (presence and response of the other is associated with reinforcement), and to ethological social-instinct theory, (which implies that clinging responses are imprinted on the body of the mother as the baby chick is imprinted on a physical decoy).

If, in contrast to physical theories, one takes the desire for a social bond with another *social self* as the primary motive for attachment, then this desire derives from the same motivational sources as that involved in the child's own strivings for stimulation, for activity, mastery, and for self-esteem. Social motivation is motivation for shared stimulation, for shared activity, and shared competence and self-esteem. Social dependency implies dependency upon another person as a source for such activity, and for the self's competence or esteem. The basic nature of competence motivation, however, is the same whether self or the other is perceived as the primary agent producing the desired stimulation, activity, or competence, i.e., whether the goal is independence mastery, social mastery (dominance), or social dependence. The differences between the two are differences in the structures of the self–other relationships involved.

In our discussion of Baldwin's theory of the bipolar social self, we indicated the exact sense in which the same desire to master an activity or situation would at one time lead the child to imitative following, at another to dominating "showing off," at a third to independent "doing it myself." The polarity between active mastery and passive dependence is, then, not a polarity between two motives but a polarity of social-situational and self definition.

Human attachments, even in the first two years of life, reflect the fact that they are attachments to another self or center of consciousness and activity like the self. This fact of human attachment implies the following characteristics:

1. *Attachment involves similarity to the other.* Attachment is only to another person, not toward physical objects.
2. *Attachment involves love or altruism toward the other*, an attitude not felt toward bottles or cloth mothers. Altruism, of course, presupposes the "ejective" consciousness of the feelings and wishes of the other, i.e., empathy or sympathy.
3. *Attachment and altruism presuppose self-love.* The striving to satisfy another self presupposes the capacity or disposition to satisfy one's own

322 The Cognitive-Developmental Psychology of James Mark Baldwin

self. Common sense assumes that the self (as body and center of activity) is loved intrinsically, not instrumentally (i.e., not because the body or the body's activities are followed by reinforcement or drive reduction). It is this nucleus of self-love which is involved, also, in organizing attachment to others.

4. *Attachment presupposes the desire for esteem in the eyes of the other or for reciprocal attachment.* In other words, it presupposes self-esteem motivation and the need for social approval, again presupposing ejective consciousness.

To summarize, following Baldwin, a human social bond presupposes a relation to another self, a relation which involves various types of sharing and of identification between the self and the other.

Current Status of Baldwin's Theory

At the turn of the century, a group of neo-Hegelian American philosopher–psychologists, responding to James's Darwinian functionalism, elaborated what I have elsewhere termed the *cognitive-developmental theory* or approach. Of these thinkers, Dewey and Baldwin elaborated the most comprehensive theories of cognitive and social development. Dewey's theory (with its elaborations by Mead) represents the broadest framework for the study of human development; Baldwin's theory provides more surprising insights and more precision to the understanding of cognitive and social development. Baldwin's cognitive theory has been taken over and improved by Piaget, but his theory of social development remains a fundamental ground for cognitive-developmental psychology.

As for the development of the child's epistemology, discussed by Broughton, Baldwin's account of social development has led to a series of observations and findings in the mid-twentieth century which have not yet been absorbed by child psychology, which has accepted the cognitive-developmental approach only in the more restricted cognitive areas studied by Piaget. Baldwin took for himself a larger problem than Piaget's problem of the development of intelligence. Baldwin attempted to provide a unified account of all of mental development, the development of emotion, imagination, morality, religion, and the self. Werner and Cassirer attempted a similar project in the thirties, but their efforts were too formalistic to yield the concrete insights and stages emerging from Baldwin's theory. The study of aesthetic and religious development could benefit from Baldwin's theory as much as have my studies of the development of morality and identification. If modern psychology is to benefit from Baldwin's psychological theory, however, it must retain Baldwin's concern for the philosophical as well as the psychological problems of development.

The study of cognition by American child psychology failed to progress for two generations because of an inadequate epistemology, sometimes called logical positivism or behaviorism. The critical defect of this epistemology for child psychology was that it did not allow the psychologist to think about cognitive processes as involving knowledge. The critical category of the stimulus–response approach was learning, not knowing, where the concept of learning did not imply knowing.

To study cognition one must have some sort of concept of knowledge in terms of which children's development is observed. Piaget's fundamental contribution to developmental psychology, following Baldwin, has been to observe children's development in terms of the categories (space, time, causality, etc.) which philosophers have deemed central to knowing. The fact that the cognitive categories of the philosopher are central for understanding the behavior development of the child is so apparent, once pointed out, that one recognizes that it is only the peculiar epistemology of the positivistic behaviorist which could have obscured it.

In my own area, moral development, the epistemological blinders psychologists have worn have hidden from them the fact that the concept of morality is itself a philosophical (ethical) rather than a behavioral concept. One can be pluralistic as to philosophical concepts and arrive at the same research conclusions. Piaget need not have an ultimately correct concept of causality, as a philosophical category, to conduct valid research on the empirical development of causal concepts. Similarly, whether one starts from Kant, Mill, Ross, or Baldwin in defining morality, one gets similar research results. While philosophical concepts of morality differ from one another, their differences are minor compared with the differences between almost any philosophical concept of morality and such psychological concepts of morality as "conscience is a conditioned avoidance reaction to certain classes of acts or situations" (Eysenck, 1961), or "moral values are evaluations of action believed by members of a given society to be 'right' " (Berkowitz, 1964).

An adequate psychological explanation of cognition or of morality must include an explanation of the universality of these concepts throughout humanity, an explanation which cannot be purely psychological in the usual sense. The psychologist cannot study cognition or morality in an epistemologically neutral way, and I would argue that it is not epistemologically (mataethically) neutral to say, as Berkowitz has, that, "moral values are evaluations of action believed by members of a given society to be 'right' "—it is metaethically wrong.

If the psychological study of concepts presupposes an epistemological position, must not the results of psychological inquiry lead to both partial validation and partial correction of its initial epistemology? That insight into the *is* (the development of knowledge and morality), and insight into the *ought* (epistemological and moral norms and criteria) must have some relationship seemed obvious to philosophers and psychologists of fifty years ago such as Dewey, Mead, and Baldwin. One wonders whether it was anything but the desire of behaviorists, logical positivists, and analytic philosophers to set up "independent disciplines" or "games" of psychology and philosophy that made them think the psychologist–philosophers of fifty years ago were wrong.

REFERENCES

Ausubel, D. *Theory and problems of child development.* New York: Grune & Stratton, 1957.

Baldwin J. M. *Social and ethical interpretations in mental development.* New York: Macmillan, 1897 [4th edition, 1906].

Baldwin, J. M. *Thought and things (vol. 3).* London: Swan Sonnenschein, 1911.

Berkowitz, L. *Development of motives and values in a child.* New York: Basic Books, 1964.

Bradley, F. H. *Ethical studies.* London: Oxford Univ. Press, 1962 (1872).

Dewey, J. & Tufts J. H. *Ethics.* New York: Holt, 1932.

Eysenck H. J. *Handbook of abnormal psychology: An experimental approach.* New York: Basic Books, 1961.

Freud, S. *The basic writings of Sigmund Freud.* New York: Modern Library, 1938.

Gewirtz, J. L.. Mechanisms of social learning: some roles of early stimulation and behavior in early human development. In D.A. Goslin (Ed.), *Handbook of socialization theory and research.* Chicago: Rand McNally, 1969.

Kohlberg L. The development of modes of moral thinking and choice in the years ten to sixteen. Unpublished doctoral dissertation, University of Chicago, 1958.

Kohlberg, L. A cognitive-developmental analysis of children's sex-role concepts and attitudes. In E. Maccoby (Ed.) *The development of sex differences.* Stanford, Calif.: Stanford Univ. Press, 1966.

Kohlberg, L. Stage and sequence: The cognitive-developmental approach to socialization. In D.A. Goslin (Ed.), *Handbook of socialization theory and research.* Chicago: Rand McNally, 1969.

Kohlberg, L. From "is" to "ought": How to commit the naturalistic fallacy and get away with it in the study of moral development. In T. Mischel (Ed.) *Cognitive development and genetic epistemology.* New York: Academic Press, 1971.

Kohlberg, L. *The meaning and measurement of moral development.* Heinz Werner Lectures, Clark University Press, 1979.

Kohlberg, L. & Zigler E. The impact of cognitive maturity on sex-role attitudes in the years four to eight. *Genetic Psychology Monographs*, 1967, *75*, 89–165.

McDougall W. *An introduction to social psychology*. London: Methuen, 1908.

Mead, G. H. *Mind, self and society*. Chicago: Univ. of Chicago Press, 1934.

Piaget, J. *The child's conception of the world*. New York: Harcourt Brace, 1929.

Piaget, J. *The moral judgement of the child*. New York: Free Press of Glencoe, 1965 (1932).

Sidgwick, H. *Methods of ethics*. London: Macmillan, 1931 (1887).

van den Daele, L. A developmental study of the ego-ideal. *Genetic Psychology Monographs*, 1968, *78*, 191–265.

PART V

RELIGIOUS AND AESTHETIC DEVELOPMENT

Introduction

> (R)eligion and art, institutions of sen-
> timent in general, may be called
> "luxuries" of life. They do not seek
> justification in practical utility or di-
> rect advantage; they are the flower-
> ing of human feeling and aspiration
> in products peculiarly their own.
> They represent the social, and spring
> from it, and are thus an index and
> measure of social values and social
> attainments; but they go beyond the
> socially attained, and give new form
> and force to the demand of the indi-
> vidual for a full and complete per-
> sonal life.
>
> Baldwin, 1911a, pp. 142–143

As we have seen, scientific (or theoretical) and moral (or practical) reason, and their relationship, were of vital concern to Baldwin. These have indeed been the issues taken up most readily into contemporary cognitive-developmental psychology. In this modern psychology, the theoretical and the practical are interpreted exclusively as forms of reason, and therefore serve as the two pillars supporting the edifice of rationality.

However, Baldwin himself was much less a rationalist of this kind. For him, the scientific and the moral could not be the terminus of development, of education, or of social progress for that matter. Instead, they provide the ground for other modes of consciousness: the religious and (ultimately) the aesthetic. For Baldwin there is more than truth and duty. There is, above all, goodness and beauty, which alone are capable of completing our understanding of reality and the fulfillment of our human potential.

In both religious and aesthetic modes, the separation of theoretical and practical is overcome by transforming their boundaries. Religious consciousness links theory and practice in postulating a transcendent ideal that is nonetheless experienced as existing. Dealing with the dichotomy at a more radical level, aesthetic consciousness dissolves theory and practice into an immediate synthesis, an apprehension of reality as a whole that is not mediated by either ideas or norms.

By making religious sentiment and aesthetic feeling dependent upon personal growth, Baldwin's treatment carries two important implications. The first is that neither religious nor aesthetic sensibility is irrational. If they were, they could and surely would emerge independently of the prior intellectual and moral development of the individual. Second, by reserving for these two sensibilities the title of "highest mental processes," Baldwin stresses that man is naturally and ineradicably theistic and aesthetic, and that the progress of theoretical and practical reason can only be understood as the gradual realization of fundamentally transcendent interests. To transcend the interest in knowledge and value is to fulfill a demand arising naturally in the course of the development of the individual as a person.

Ernest Wallwork does us all a favor in bringing attention back to Baldwin's early (1897) and classic work on religious development. Baldwin himself abandoned serious study of religion as he developed the genetic theory of *pancalism* so that by the time of his autobiographical reflections (1926, 1930), he no longer deemed his ideas on the subject even worthy of mention. We might speculate that this reflected both his own biography, and history in general. His early conversion to the Presbyterian faith and his plans to enter the ministry soon wilted in the greater heat of his passion for philosophy and psychology. This makes sense in the context of the concessions that faith had to make to reason around the turn of the century. Baldwin's reconciliation was a psychoevolutionary theory that proposed religion as a natural and universal outgrowth of personal and social development, a development which nevertheless led just as naturally to theism in maturity. Darwin's discussions on religion had had the effect of undermining it as an epiphenomenon. Quite to the contrary, Baldwin established the religious spirit the more firmly by his naturalism. Nevertheless, his evolutionary/developmental approach took care not to imply that science *required* God to explain purpose in nature, and he thereby left room for an act of faith.

Like Kant, Baldwin saw religion as rational, but not exclusively intellectual. Like Kant, he rejected the purely logical or ontological arguments for the existence of God which took their roots in dogmatic theology. Rather, religion was to be understood in the light of psychological facts, both rational and emotional, a possibility opened up by Kant's constructivist philosophy. Again in the Kantian tradition, Baldwin refused to see religious experiences as truths uniquely revealed by certain institutions or as "special" miraculous phenomena to be experienced and interpreted by qualified experts. Instead, he argued that religious experience was part of common experience, as natural as, say, speech.

Up to a point, Baldwin also follows Kant in seeing transcendent religious ideas as *symbolic*. By this he means that they do not constitute knowledge in the sense of being interpretations of experienced objects. They are grounded in sociality and morality, particularly in the "practical imagination." This, unlike the theoretical imagination, is not instrumental to the discovery of knowledge, but to the appreciation and realization of the good. Religious ideas are "regulative principles" of the practical reason. They have validity, but only by virtue of principles of the subjective kind. In a sense, they are heuristics that assist reason in its task of unifying the known and the unknowable. Reason assumes Nature as an intelligible unity, adapted to our cognitive faculties' capacity for understanding, and therefore potentially knowable, if not already known.

The subjective, imaginative, and as–if quality of religious experience draws it away from facts toward *interest*, away from the sphere of the cognitive, and toward the realm of *sentiment*. The logic of the sentiments is affective, active, and social rather than merely cognitive or objective. As Wallwork recounts, the criteria defining religious experience are the sentiments of *dependence* and (especially) *mystery*. These sentiments develop in their function and logical organization in passing from an initial physical stage, to their final and ideal form in an ethical stage. Thus the existence of God is not defined through direct experience, but in these sentiments of reliance upon and reverence toward him, feelings which are fitting only for a divinely perfect being.

As Baldwin deviates from Kant in stressing the religious sentiments, he surpasses him in the degree to which he demonstrates the *social* nature of religious phenomena. Kant rationalized historical religion, ignoring the ways in which different religions had concretely existed. He also avoided analysis of religious practices, going so far as to argue their superfluousness. For him, true religion was reverence for God shown through obedience to the moral law, which he argued must be looked upon as though it were divine command. Following Hegel, Baldwin restored attention to the history of religions. In addition, responding to the social science of his time, Baldwin embraced in his system the myths and rituals of religious practice, while at the same time departing from Durkheim's and Levy-Bruhl's devotion to the primitive. However, he felt the exclusively sociological or anthropological perspective to be impoverished (Baldwin 1911a, Chap. 4) and pointed instead to the quasi*personal* form of the religious object. This, he argued, testified to the origin of religion in the individual's personal life. Still Kantian in holding that morality leads to religion rather than presupposing it, he nevertheless added an original social psychological twist. The divine object, he suggested, could only be formed by the psychic ejecting of the *ideal self* (see Kohlberg's Chap. 9). This in turn could only arise in the normal course of development of self-consciousness, a genetic movement carried forward by the social dialectic of self and other. This ideal object was not just psychologically imagined, but was actually experienced as an *existing personal presence*. The reality of the religious ideal limits its generalizability in a manner that differentiates it from the scientific ideal and the ideal ethical self. Thus while Kant held that the consciousness of divine presence was the pure consciousness of duty, Baldwin preferred to interpret it as the awareness of the ideal social partner—the supreme Companion and Aid, who assists and consoles all alike.

This approach, both personal and social, fits well with his elaboration of the role of imagination and the sentiments in religious experience. In the upper reaches of psychological development, he is concerned to transcend the rationalistic rule of formal law and principle. He struggles to restore *experience* to a central place in the psychic economy. Also, he strives to return the *control* of experience to the *self*, rather than subordinating it to

> the mere recognition of the several modes of the actual in which the self has to allow and accede to another control foreign to itself. (Baldwin, 1911b, p. 12)

Thus religiosity is differentiated from sociality: both proceed from the movement of the growth of self, but society calls the movement towards a practical adjustment, whereas religion calls it towards inner perfection, harmony and tranquillity (Baldwin, 1910, p. 100).

Wallwork shows why, in Baldwin's eyes, religion cannot be the terminus of development. As a mode of experience, religion juxtaposes theoretical and practical, and in the interpersonal self which it presupposes it can also reconcile public and private interests. Nevertheless, it cannot overcome the duality of thory and practice, nor that of subject and object. It also leaves unresolved the dichotomy which it created between finite and infinite personality. On this account, the religiousness of experience cannot be erected into a comprehensive and final system of thought.

This is where Michael Parson's chapter takes off. Self and absolute, subject and object, knowledge and will, which are separated one from the other in cognition, can only be reconciled in the experience of *aesthetic immediacy*. This is the heart of Baldwin's doctrine of pancalism. Aesthetic experience is an imaginative act that protests the partial nature of the specific modes of meaning. It fulfills all interests, rather than pursuing any specific one. It does so in allowing the semblance of one's own inner world to be felt in the aesthetic object (whether that be art or nature). This object accordingly becomes the subject as well as the object of contemplation, i.e., it is attributed the inner life with which the self identifies.

This is not an endorsement of blind mysticism. Pancalism does not promote the idea that development and fulfillment culminate in unintelligible feeling. Baldwin's position is, rather, a species of aesthetic idealism. In reaction against his friend Bergson, and in deference to Hegel's critique of intuitionism in the *Logic*, Baldwin stresses that aesthetic experience is a *reflective intuition*. It is a reasoned admiration. It is not a destruction of all limits in order that the subject may wallow in sublime oceanic bliss. *Au contraire*, it is a disinterested and idealizing mode of experience which always has some object, always makes a judgment, and always attributes an aesthetic quality to the object. In addition, this judgment is always in principle communicable and intends a universal validity—that the contemplated object is beautiful in a way fit for the satisfaction of all. It is the nature of such synthetic experience to move beyond specific aesthetic objects of contemplation to reality itself as a whole. Such synthetic experience includes the idea of God, but now seen as referring to that organic or spiritual whole within which self and world can finally be known.

Despite a few succinct statements (e.g., 1930, and 1926, vol. 2, Chap. 22). Baldwin's philosophical account of pancalism and the nature of aesthetic immediacy is difficult, and often obscure. While he emulates the achievement of Kant's *Critique of Judgment*, his exposition lacks the clarity of that classic. The role of aesthesis becomes more comprehensible when viewed from its psychological and developmental perspective, as Parsons's account demonstrates. While aesthetic experience emerges as the highest form of consciousness, it does not spring fully formed out of the head of ethics or religion. It too undergoes a stage by stage development, in parallel and interacting with the general development of the mind through prelogical, quasilogical, and logical phases (compare Freeman-Moir's, Lee's, and Broughton's chapters). It is the underlying theme of Baldwin's grand scheme that the license of fanciful imagination and play must be brought under the control of rational knowledge and reflective conduct before the imagination can at last give rise to *meaningful* aesthetic experience. Play and imitation provide vital links between aesthetic development and the genesis of knowledge and sociality. Parsons follows the phases of aesthetic development in relationship to four categories or concepts in the artistic domain: *immediacy, semblance, personalizing,* and *idealization.* Since these are categories and phases in the emergence of reflective *symbolism,* they presumably contribute in turn to religious development, which we have noted is centrally concerned with the symbolic and as–if meaning of objects of worship. Both beauty and religious transcendence accentuate the significance of sentiment, interest, and appreciation in contrast to knowledge, fact, and objectification. Along with this, they raise the important question of design and the role of authorship in nature and cosmos as much as in the work of art. (Here again, Baldwin introduces social psychology into the transcendent.) Perhaps these are some reasons for the traditional historical association of art and religion. However, the precise connections between religious and aesthetic development cannot be examined here, since Baldwin does not deal with them.

Both Wallwork and Parsons demonstrate in some detail the relevance of Baldwin's theories to modern empirical work in developmental psychology. Wallwork focuses on what is perhaps the leading contemporary theory of religious development, James Fowler's account of "stages in faith," Fowler, like Baldwin, has tried to articulate an ecumenical theory of the way in which religious belief and experience evolve. As for Baldwin, the development is a rational one, but does not exclude feeling, action, or sociality. The Baldwinian struggle between faith and reason is wrestled out again, in the arena of the contemporary secularized world. Wallwork points out many important convergences between Fowler's and Baldwin's interpretations, but also many important differences. The net result is an exposition and critique of both Fowler and Baldwin that provides a valuable theoretical and empirical overview for contemporary researchers and educators in psychology departments and divinity schools.

Parsons draws parallels between Baldwin's account of aesthetic categories and stages and his own empirical findings concerning the cognitive development of aesthetic judgment. Again, the parallels described are both remarkable and illuminating. As Fowler's stages of faith did in the religious domain, Parsons's stages make Baldwin's speculative psychology of art more concrete and specific.

In bringing together strong theory with careful interpretive work in empirical psychology, this section helps to indicate promising directions for future conceptualization and methodology in the developmental understanding of art and religion.

REFERENCES

Baldwin, J. M. *Social and ethical interpretations in mental development.* New York: MacMillan, 1897.

Baldwin, J. M. *Darwin and the humanities.* London: Allen & Unwin, 1910.

Baldwin, J. M. *The individual and society.* Boston: Gorham Press, 1911 (a)

Baldwin, J. M. *Thought and things (Vol.3).* London: Swan-Sonnenschein, 1911 (b)

Baldwin, J. M. *Between two wars (vol. 1 & 2).* Boston: Stratford, 1926.

Baldwin, J. M. James Mark Baldwin. In C. Murchison (Ed.) *The history of psychology in autobiography (Vol. 1).* New York: Russell & Russell, 1961 (1930).

10

RELIGIOUS DEVELOPMENT

Ernest Wallwork
Yale University

The scientific study of religion has "come a long way," to cite a recent advertisement, since the late nineteenth-century writers with whom Baldwin was familiar. Spencer, Müller, Wundt, and Tylor are seldom even mentioned today, much less seriously studied, although they were the prominent elder scholars against whom Baldwin and his academic peers did battle. Yet there have been surprisingly few major theoretical advances in the scientific study of religion beyond the contributions made by Baldwin's own generation of distinguished scholars, that is, by Durkheim, Weber, Freud, and Troeltsch. Recent social scientists of religion (e.g., Parsons, Erikson, Bellah, and Berger) have derived their leading ideas primarily by combining themes found in these turn-of-the-century figures.

The excitement of Baldwin's interpretation of religion is increased by the realization that he was working, in a different way, with many of the same strands of thought which helped launch Durkheim, Weber, and Freud. It is worth returning to Baldwin (but not to Müller and Tylor) for fresh theoretical stimulation, because he sought to reconcile the same philosophical and empirical currents of thought about religion as his better known contemporaries and he did so in such a way as to converge with them on several of the most influential of twentieth century perspectives. More significantly still, Baldwin forged a genuinely unique developmental approach to religion, which remains a largely untapped resource to the contemporary student of religion, with rich implications for both theory and empirical research. Unlike those Piagetian inspired studies that straightforwardly apply the development of cognition to the understanding of religious figures, stories, and parables (like R. Goldman's *Religious Thinking from Childhood to Adolescence*), Baldwin does not ignore the deeper psychological processes and motivations involved in religious faith. It is Baldwin's richer understanding of the self that most distinguishes his work from that of Piaget, and it is the full engagement of this self in religion that makes his theoretical paradigm in this area so suggestive.

Religion for Baldwin arises out of the same dynamic processes that encouraged Kohlberg to move beyond Piaget's study of moral judgment. Religion is a product not of cognition alone, but of dialectical growth of consciousness of personality in oneself and others. However, religion, more than morality, is viewed by Baldwin as involving nonrational motivations (which reach out toward Freud's far deeper understanding of unconscious processes), even though Baldwin himself had a deep antipathy to Freud's work (Baldwin, 1930/1961). Religion is also seen as always a social phenomenon, which both arises out of interpersonal interactions and depends upon collective symbols and rituals, as Durkheim's work, on which Baldwin relies, makes so very clear. Baldwin's theory thus stands as a potential bridge, albeit a very sketchy one, among the very different approaches to the study of religion of cognitive developmental theory, depth psychology, and sociology.

Basic Perspectives

It seems useful to begin by locating Baldwin's perspective in the broader intellectual movements that gave rise to twentieth-century scientific approaches to religion. One of the ways in which Baldwin stands out among his nineteenth-century predecessors and alongside Durkheim, Freud, and Weber—is his manner of joining the rationalist and nonrationalist traditions stemming from the Enlightenment. As Bellah (1970, Chap. 1) argues, modern-scientific study of religion is largely a joint product of these two traditions. This is the case because the scientific method is an offshoot of rationalism, whereas religion involves an irreducibly nonrational component. Until the turn of the century, these traditions were often in conflict, especially in the study of religion. Scientific rationalists, following Hume's *The Natural History of Religions*, were committed to explaining away religion as a crude science or primitive ethics resulting from cognitive immaturity and/or emotional distress (see Johnson & Wallwork, 1973, Chap. 1). Nonrationalists, like the romantics, reacted by rejecting the scientific approach altogether and concentrated instead upon the subjective meaning of religious experience.

As a scientist, Baldwin was strongly committed to empiricism and rationalism. But he disagreed with the typical scientific rationalist's dismissal of religion as a primitive science. Against the equation of religion with a theoretical system of any sort, Baldwin cited Schleiermacher in defense of his own claim that religion is grounded, not in cognition or even moral judgment, but in feelings. These feelings are not the product or a prescientific mentality or world view, but of the normal responses of human subjects to universally shared experiences. As such, religious feelings cannot be eradicated from human behavior, as rationalists have often supposed. Religion unlike science is not a theoretical system at all and its functions cannot be handled by one. Baldwin thus arrives, via a different route, at the conclusion of Durkheim's study of the sacred, Weber's work on charisma and Freud's analysis of myth, namely, that the nonrational element in religion must be given a central and irreducible place in an adequate account of human behavior.

Baldwin attempted a similar reconciliation of the related conflict between naturalism and idealism. His scientific orientation was linked to naturalism but Baldwin objected to the reductionism, not to mention, materialism, of the naturalistic tradition. He wanted to do justice to the inner world of consciousness, as described by idealists, but from a scientific perspective. The solution to this problem was to expand the concept of nature to include the growth of consciousness itself. For Baldwin, nature came to include virtually everything the idealists had been talking about. Idealists, in his view, were far more accurate than naturalists in describing the complex subject matter with which any science of religion has to deal. And so Baldwin did not hesitate to go to Kant, Hegel, and Schelling for much of his descriptive material, especially for accounts of the more developed stages of religious experience. Unfortunately, idealists had failed to provide anything approaching an adequate account of the way in which we come to be religious developmentally. The beginnings of such an account had been made by naturalists. But Baldwin believed their accounts suffered from a double error. First, naturalists reduced the qualitatively more advanced to primitive antecedents, and second, they tended to interpret the primitive essence of religion thus defined as a product of extraneous, even biological, motivations.

Against the first of these errors, Baldwin insisted that religion, like cognition and morality, passes through qualitatively more advanced developmental stages that cannot be reduced to their antecedents. The religious beliefs of children and simple societies, Baldwin admits, show a naive credulity, as Enlightenment critics like Hume had charged. But religious beginnings are simply not the same as endings, any more than an infant's first explorations of objects contain the core of his mature scientific thoughts. The developmental concept of qualitatively different stages enabled Baldwin to effectively undercut the typical Victorian quest for the primitive essence underlying all religions, a quest which, although it concentrated on the crude beliefs of aborigines, was often designed to debunk the foundations of modern Christianity and Judaism.

To say that the more developed is qualitatively different from its antecedents is not to deny the existence of common characteristics which enable one to identify each stage as a form of religion. This common ingredient in religious development is identified by Baldwin as a fundamental "interest" involving distinct emotional and conative motivations not found in other attitudes. However, the typical naturalist's reduction of this interest to another, more basic propensity, like economic self-interest or speculative curiosity, does not commend itself to him. The religious interest is a motivation *sui generis* (Baldwin, 1915, p. 87). Briefly, this interest is in an ideal self, as a source of nurture and object of devotion. A product of this interest, religion cannot be explained by economic interests (Marx and Engels, 1964) or mere speculative curiosity (Spencer, 1896 and Tylor, 1981). Religious motivations stand alongside theoretical, moral, and aesthetic interests as one of the irreducible, and, when properly understood, ubiquitous motivations of persons.

Antireductionism of this sort in other theories would tend to undermine the aim of scientific explanation. But part of the ingenuity of Baldwin's developmental approach is its ability to focus the perspective of scientific naturalism on the vicissitudes of the religious interest through stages without compromising the qualitatively distinct nature of subjectively felt experience.

Definitional Issues

Few issues are more important in the scientific study of religion than the way in which the phenomenon is defined. Unlike Max Weber, who argued that definitions of religion should be taken up, if at all, only at the end of scientific inquiry (Weber, 1963, p. 1), Baldwin realized the difficulty of beginning a study in the absence of clear criteria identifying the subject matter.

Baldwin approached the definitional task, as most scientists have, by critically evaluating received definitions. But he differed from many scientists in his day and ours by seriously attending to the analytical definitions of professional philosophers. For Baldwin realized what too many behavioral scientists have subsequently forgotten—namely that the concerns of philosophy and science overlap on the definitional problem. Philosophical accounts, he believed, provide superb descriptions of the mature or "developed religious sentiment" (Baldwin, 1901–05, vol. 2, p. 459). But they are often too sophisticated for earlier and simpler expressions of religiosity. The latter are captured by anthropological definitions, like those of Spencer and Tylor, but these bias the case against more sophisticated forms of religious faith by reducing their complexity to a primitive essence. The problem, as Baldwin saw it, is to avoid these extremes by disengaging "a permanent element, common to all the changes, by the presence of which these changes, no matter what their differences, can be called *religious*" (Baldwin, 1901–05, vol. 2, p. 453). The permanent form was to be isolated from its changing content in such a way as to avoid reducing the complex to the simple, the differentiated to the global.

Baldwin was initially attracted to definitions of religion based on subjective feelings. One reason for this attraction to the emotional side of religious experience was the difficulty Baldwin experienced in isolating the formal qualities of the various objects of religious sentiments, given the diversity of religious symbols and the different meanings associated with these symbols at various stages of psychosocial development and cultural evolution. Moreover, Baldwin was anxious to highlight the distinctiveness of religious faith against the intellectualist readings of Tylor, Müller, and Spencer. Against these definitions of cognitive belief, Baldwin cites the observation that " 'the word for true religion in the Lutheran language is Glaube, and the essence of Glaube is fühlen' " (Baldwin, 1901–05, vol. 2, p. 456).

What is common to primitive and advanced religious experience, Baldwin argues, is not a common idea, say of the deity, but certain emotional sentiments. An idea is religious if it calls forth certain distinguishing sentiments. By a *sentiment*, Baldwin means an enduring emotion, which, once formed, in large measure controls what we feel and what responses we make when a particular situation contains the object of our sentiment. The two sentiments which mark religion are: (1) the sense of dependence upon an object of worship, and (2) the sense of mystery toward that object.

Baldwin's description of *the sense of dependence* is partly derived from Schleiermacher, for whom dependence meant a receptivity affected by another (Schleiermacher, 1963, p. 12; Baldwin, 1906, p. 340; 1915, p. 88). Baldwin agrees with Schleiermacher that this is "a common element in all piety." But he does not go on to insist that dependence is "absolute," in Schleiermacher's sense, namely, that the feeling is one of having received one's existence from a "whence" beyond the empirical world. Rather, dependence refers to the subjective feeling of *trust* and *faith*. Sometimes faith and trust are understood primarily with Protestant orthodoxy as feelings of grace derived from the religious object's active presence. At other times, faith is interpreted, with evangelical groups, as feelings associated with a spontaneous, self-giving, or conscious act of the will. Baldwin refers in this connection to Paulsen, for whom trust meant an act of the will whereby the believer entrusts his or her life to the infinite (see Paulsen, 1930, I, 2.9; Baldwin, 1906, pp. 34–41). Baldwin apparently sought to combine feelings of receptivity with self-giving emotions under the single term, dependence, in order not to bias his case against some religious traditions by definition. Full religious dependence is a double movement involving receptivity toward the active care of another as well as active self-giving to the other in loyalty.

The *sense of mystery* is described in terms of reverence, awe, respect, and fear. Mystery includes the sense of wonder discussed by Spencer and Tylor, but wonder in their sense is said to be too specific and emotionally shallow to cover the vicissitudes of this feeling across the entire spectrum of development. Baldwin prefers Durkheim's broader and more emotionally powerful description of awe and respect. The religious object is experienced as *worthy of respect* (*auguste*), as shown in the distancing posture assumed by the worshiper. Baldwin differs from Durkheim, however, in associating with mystery the sense of the "not-yet," the "more-than-I," the "coming-into being" of that which is beyond comprehension. Mystery involved being conscious of a religious presence that has yet to be understood; it is the emotional sense of some superior being beyond current cognitive comprehension. In comparison with dependence, Baldwin is inclined to view the range of feelings associated with mystery as "the profounder element in religious emotion" (Baldwin, 1906, p.340).

The religious sentiments of dependence and mystery are always experienced, like any other sentiment, in relationship to particular objects. There are three very different senses, Baldwin is careful to point out, in which the term *object* is used in this connection: (1) the mere external symbol, emblem, or thing immediately before the eye of the worshiper; (2) the further meaning, significance, or content attributed to the symbol; and (3) the reality which the symbol and its meaning discloses, discovers, or reveals. Among these various, non-exclusive objects, the third, ultimate reality, is properly assigned by Baldwin to philosophy and theology. Of the other two, the first (external symbols), is said to be too diverse for inclusion in a general definition of religious experience:

> There is *no one form always assumed by the object of worship*, no single embodiment of deity common to all religions. The form of the object of worship is subordinate to the meaning given to it in the intention of the devotee. The actual object . . . varies from the crudest

physical and inanimate objects up to the highest abstractions of thought and the noblest creations of art. (Baldwin, 1909, p. 94)

If there are no common external symbols, there is a commonly understood object of religious experience in the second sense, namely in the meaning attributed to these symbols. Common to all religious experience is the sense of an objective presence or sacred object of devotion.

This objective presence is everywhere understood to be *personal* or *quasi personal*, that is, it always has for the worshiper the significance of an agency like himself. "However dead the mere thing of worship, the image, the fetish, the work of art, may be, it still means a center of behavior which may be taken to indicate an attitude on the part of the God toward the worshiper" (Baldwin 1909, p. 95). In fact, an object could not excite the religious sentiments of dependence and respect unless it were thought to possess at least some of the personal qualities with which these feelings are inextricably linked from early infancy.

The religious presence is like the self, yet it is also significantly different. In the first place, a religious being is always *superior* to the adherent. This is suggested by terms like holy, sacred, or divine. Second, the religious object is understood to be an *immaterial spirit*, presence, ghost, god, or God—"something behind the cloud, some one behind nature—the Great One who breaks law and works his will for his own, for ours, for a priest's, for a Redeemer's sake" (Baldwin 1901–05, vol. 2, p. 460). Third, the religious presence possesses something like a *personal will* and, presumably for this reason, can be approached and appealed to in the ways we deal with one another. For example, "the gods are propitiated to secure their favour and to mitigate or appease their wrath" (Baldwin, 1901–05, vol. 2, p. 461). Festivals, prayers, and sacrifices are all ways of seeking to favorably influence superior beings with dispositions and wills similar to our own. In Zenophanes' famous saying, all men's gods are in form like themselves.

This emphasis upon the personal characteristics of the religious object leads Baldwin to dispute the claim, which has become more widespread subsequently, that any ultimate world view is a religious one. Historically, Baldwin observes, all the great religions of the world have had personal gods. Buddhism is sometimes cited as an exception (e.g., by Durkheim), but Baldwin argues that Buddhism did not become a religion before its founder began to be deified. The limiting case beyond religion for Baldwin is marked by the absence of any trace of personality. A case in point is the speculative philosophical system in which all traits of personality have finally disappeared.

In the systems of speculative pantheism and high reflective mysticism personality no longer appears. These, however, can not make good the claim to be religious, since the sentiments they excite are no longer pure, and the active rites of religious practice become altogether irrelevant. One does not expect personal consideration from the "universal order," nor does one worship "pure reason" or "new thought." In passing from the religious state of mind to the theoretical and speculative, something is changed, the religious shading is lost. (Baldwin 1915, pp. 93-94)

This is not to deny that speculative systems and ideologies perform some of the functions traditionally met by religions. But these similarities of function do not make a system of thought religious, if the latter does not possess the distinguishing features and evoke the sentiments which universally mark phenomena as religious.

Baldwin's insistence on the personal characteristics of the religious object also results in a disagreement with Durkheim's influential discussion of the impersonal character of the sacred. Durkheim easily shows, argues Baldwin, that the external symbol— the flag or churinga— is an impersonal thing. But the French sociologist fails to support his claim that the religious meanings attributed to totems by Australian aborigines are devoid of personal connotations. In fact, Durkheim's own data suggest that even totemism is "not without the marks of animation or life, and that it is, in a crude sense but still positively, *quasi-personal for the consciousness of the devotee himself*" (Baldwin, 1915, p. 96).

Developmental Explanation

Turning from description to explanation, Baldwin's developmental theory deals with the subjective meanings attributed to external symbols. Religious meaning is viewed as no less a human construct that the simplest datum, which is also a product of mental activity. In keeping with his opposition to cognitivist interpretations of religion, which today would include Piagetian-inspired studies of religious stories, Baldwin insists that religious meaning is always the construct of the practical imagination. Cognition takes a secondary place to the primary and directive role of will and emotion in imaginatively positing the existence of religious objects. In the formation of religion, it is "the logic of emotion and interest" more than the logic of knowledge that predominates.

Religious apprehension via imaginative postulates of practical reason governed by affective interests differs from scientific knowledge, which is primarily in the service of theoretical interests. To be sure, the scientific method also makes use of practical imagination in postulating hypotheses which go far beyond what is actually known. But the goal of science is additional information about matters of fact; imaginative hypotheses ultimately yield to empirical verification. By contrast, the goal of practical imagination is some form of appreciation, satisfaction, realization or fulfillment (Baldwin, 1911, p. 12). Whereas the goal of science is objective knowledge, the ideal of practical imagination is some form of "worth" to human subjects. Such completion of the self in the realm of value is no less valid a mode of apprehending reality than science for Baldwin, because the rationalist's exclusive devotion to the true needs to be complemented by appreciation of the good and the beautiful. In the absence of ethical, aesthetic, and religious forms of appreciation, human beings would not only fail to apprehend reality adequately, we would also fall short of realizing the full potentialities of human nature.

What is imaginatively postulated in religion is a *worth* or *value*, which is Baldwin's way of speaking about what H.R. Niebuhr means by faith in "a center of value" and Tillich by an "ultimate concern" (see Niebuhr, 1960, pp. 100–13; Tillich, 1952). "The sacred thing is the center of worthful experiences," Baldwin states, in an unusually succinct formulation (Baldwin, 1915, p. 102). Anticipating Erikson's later discussion of religious identity, Baldwin observes that a "human being," if wholly deprived of the sense of unity with society and with the world, which is at the root of his reliance on his scheme of life, seems to perish like a plant deprived of warmth or nourishment" (Baldwin 1901–05, vol. 2, p. 456). All such "worths, presenting something to aim at, to live for, to desire, are ideals" (Baldwin, 1915, p. 102).

Because the object of religious devotion is an ideal, it cannot be directly experienced or proved; rather it must be imagined or anticipated. Built upon assimilated knowledge, the religious object, like any other ideal, always transcends the empirically known. But unlike other ideals, the religious is always a person or entity like a person. The religious object is a self like the worshiper, although being an ideal self, the deity also represents a further carrying out in the imagination of the meaning of selfhood or personality.

The genetic problem, as Baldwin saw it, is to explain how the meaning of selfhood or personality can take on ideal form such as to give rise to the specifically religious sentiments of dependence and mystery. The answer, in brief, is that the practical imagination, by means of what he calls *affective logic*—involving affective generalization, idealization, and ejection—constructs the deity out of the meaning and worth of personality at the various stages of development. The deity, being at least something like a person, is constructed out of what the adherent already understands and appreciates about the basic characteristics of personality, in himself and others. Comprehension of the religious object is a byproduct of the dialectical growth of self–other consciousness. The deity profits from the same give-and-take between an individual and his fellows whereby consciousness and moral worth of personality is gradually refined (Baldwin, 1901–05, vol. 2, p. 461).

Religious development represents a further outgrowth of the dialectical relationship of self and other that also issues in moralization. Because moral development establishes what is valuable about persons, moral change necessarily precedes religious change. For example, the child during the first moral stage considers persons as valuable primarily for their physical attributes, while, during the second stage, wisdom is the character trait that is most valued. Finally, ethical behavior properly so-called becomes the focus of appreciation. Religion is, as it were, added on to these moral stages, although not in a mechanical way, but as a further outgrowth of them. Moral change, Baldwin writes, is "the nerve-element in the development of the individual", (Baldwin, 1906, p. 450) and so it is in the development of religion also. Religion builds on moral development by postulating the actual existence of the ideal of personality constructed at each stage. Whereas the ethical ideal is understood to be nonexistent, the deity "is set up not as simply ideal, simply desirable and possible, but as actually existing" (Baldwin, 1915, p. 119). That is, the religious move beyond morality affirms the existence of one or more beings who fulfill the highest values, stripped of the imperfections of finitude.

Viewed developmentally, God (or the gods) is a product of the imagination spurred on by the human tendency (1) to *generalize* particular personality traits in terms of their emotional relevance; (2) to *idealize* the complete fulfilment of partial qualities; and (3) to *eject* the actual existence of that which is ideal. In *ejecting*, the self reads what it has come to understand and value about personality outward onto reality. The resulting product of the imagination is definitely not experienced as fictional by the believer. To the contrary, the distinguishing characteristic of religion, in comparison with morality, is the sincere conviction that the ideal actually exists. From the believer's standpoint, God is a personal presence evoking trust, dependence, respect, awe, even fear. To experience fully the actual presence of an ideal of personality in the form of a deity is normally to be completely overwhelmed.

So the voice of Jehovah commands, "Take off thy shoes from off thy feet, for the place whereon thou standest is holy ground." The creeds of theology, which ring of infinitude and juggle with synonyms of personality, are ... inadequate to express the religious ideal ...

Religious awe—a singular combination of fear, respect, and admiration—meets its object half-way. As perfect this object is admirable, as personal it commands respect, as powerful it is to be feared. But all of these attributes are coloured by the glamour of the ideal. It is not ordinary fear, but fear of one having endless power; not ordinary respect, but respect for the morally highest, the supremely excellent; not ordinary admiration, but acquiescence in eternal wisdom and contemplation of divine beauty. These feelings are fused in one sentiment, one interest, as in the object the attributes are fused in one ideal person, God. (Baldwin, 1915, pp. 104–105)

In the more advanced stages of religious development. this concrete anthropomorphism tends to disappear, but religion never loses its immediate, experiential basis. The heart of religion is the sense of the presence of the divine, without which creeds and proofs of the existence of God lack all cogency.

The believer's relationship to the deity is like that of an inferior to a superior person. With Freud, Baldwin recognizes that the earliest expressions of religion reflect the child's relationship with his parents. Rather than viewing these origins as evidence of the infantile, wish-fulfilling, and hence, illusory nature of religion, however, Baldwin tends to view the child–parent relationship as an appropriate paradigm by which the individual understands his or her relationship to the deity.

God is an actual presence, like that of the child's superior—father, mother, elder brother, counsellor, friend—all designations realised in actual religious creeds. These are not mere figures of speech, but aspects in which the actual presence is symbolised to this believer or that, in this emergency or that. (Baldwin, 1915, pp. 106–107)

The mature believer recognizes parental religious symbols for what they are, namely, inadequate human means of expressing the true nature of the relationship to the transcendent. All genuinely religious thought represents faith seeking understanding, for Baldwin as for Anselm. Without experience of the divine reality, religious symbols and thought are at best empty forms.

Because the religious person believes that the moral ideal actually exists as the deity, religious judgment combines practical with theoretical reason. Baldwin (1915) states this reconciliation in the following manner:

Now in the religious life, we find a singular union of these two great modes of development within the mind, the logical and the teleological, as we have called them respectively. The logical erects classes and establishes facts and truths, by its methods of proof; the teleological issues in affective interests and defines ends and values. Now, in the religious life we find the object, God, looked upon as *really existing, as if* established by processes of knowledge, while, at the same time, it is determined by the religious interest *as an ideal or end.* Religion claims to present both a system of truth and a system of personal and social values. God is *both fact and ideal*. (p. 108)

It is morality rather than logic, however, that takes the lead in the developmental process. Religion represents a further outcome, in the process of growth, beyond morality, because "the individual could not believe in a good deity unless he had conceived the good person" (Baldwin, 1906, p. 450).

Once religion has postulated the actual existence of the ideal of a given moral stage, it turns back on, and provides further support for, that stage. "The religious consciousness is, therefore, in its integrity both a cause and an effect. It is the effect of the ethical construction which has gone before, and which is embodied in the content of the accepted religious beliefs. But it is cause in respect to the complete acceptance and loyal pursuit of the ethical ideal . . ." (Baldwin, 1906, p. 452). Religious postulates have their own independent causal influence, because the sense of the presence of God engenders fitting attitudinal responses. The feeling of being inspired and helped by a deity in whom one trusts as well as the feeling or respect for divinely legitimated obligations are religious sentiments that rather obviously reinforce moral judgment and behavior. In Baldwin's more evocative language, "Through his personal communion the individual finds his forces renewed, his courage revived, his emotions purged, his aspirations directed, his visions of beauty and good clarified" (Baldwin, 1915, p. 106).

The two distinctively religious sentiments of dependence and mystery are explained by the processes which confer actuality on the products of practical imagination. Dependence, for example, is explained by means of *ejection*, whereby the self reads what it has come to understand and appreciate about personality outward onto another individual. Just as the self grows by projecting what it understands about itself onto other selves in interpersonal relationships, so , too, the religious self progresses by reading the divine Other in terms of what the believer understands about personality, in self and others. What is projected or ejected outward is an idealized self. But there are two different ways in which this idealization occurs which Baldwin does not always make clear. In the first place, the divine other is read as *complementing* the most strongly felt needs or interests of a given stage. If, as during the first years of life, the child is primarily concerned about obtaining physical and emotional care, the deity will be pictured as a gigantic, all-powerful caretaker. Later, when the child is primarily interested in obtaining knowledge about persons and things, the the deity will be pictured as a gigantic, all-powerful caretaker. Later, when the child is primarily interested in obtaining knowledge about persons and things, the deity becomes omniscient. In both cases, the deity is read as complementing the self's inability to satisfy pressing needs or interests. Dependence is the natural response of someone who relies upon a superior to complement his own inadequacies.

Religious dependence not only derives from ejecting an ideally complementary personality, it also derives from ejecting an idealized version of one's own assimilated abilities. The process here is similar to the way the self reads its assimilated self-concept into other persons. The deity is less a complement of felt inadequacies and more a perfect realization of developed achievements. The sense of dependence produced by this second ejective process results from falling short of an ideal that one at best partially realizes. The sense of incompleteness is similar to that held in relationship to the complementary ejects, but it derives from a different source, namely idealization of one's own capacities, and the result is often additional moral stimulation toward further perfection in the image of the deity.

In Baldwin's account of the stages of religious development, *complementary* dependence is stronger during the first stages, giving way to *ideal* dependence with the attainment of the ethical stage. The reason is that early portraits of the deity tend to be idealized ejections of parental figures, who complement the child's needs, whereas later images of the deity express ideal versions of the mature ethical self's own achievements. The processes out of which both ejects arise, however, are present from the beginning. "There are in every mind" from the beginning of childhood, Baldwin writes, "not only the two contrasted selves, facing each other [that give rise to the sense of the complementarity]; but also, in addition, a sense of the presence of a possible 'good self', a higher or ideal personality . . ." (Baldwin, 1909, p. 98). The latter, when ejected, clothes the divine Other with the raiments of self-perfection, giving rise to a sense of inadequacy in relation to an ethical ideal to which one looks for behavioral guidance.

Both the complementary eject and the idealized-self are part of the general religious tendency to seek complete and harmonious fulfilment of the self beyond the weaknesses and contradictions of finite existence. The one impulse or need that religion everywhere exhibits, Baldwin writes, is "that of setting up a Self, ideal in character, personal in form, as the goal of development and the end of striving" (Baldwin, 1909, p. 105). The complementary eject and the idealized eject are different aspects of this single religious drive for self-perfection, a drive which is never realized, but hovers before the believer's gaze, in the form of an idealized god-person. In relationship to this image, the believer inevitably feels dependent upon one who far exceeds his or her realized capacities.

The correlative sense of mystery is explained as a response to the process of accommodating oneself to that which has yet to be understood regarding the nature or will of the divine eject. In relationship to the divine, the believer spontaneously assumes the lifelong attitude of the accommodating self vis-à-vis unknown aspects of others, especially superior persons. There is an

> expectation of yet more manifestations from this highest of all persons—manifestations which he cannot anticipate nor cope with; which he must submit to when they come, learn of only when they have come, propitiate in the ways that please persons, and stand in awe of from first to last. This is also not at all a new mental movement; it also has been present as an essential *motif* of his progress from first to last . . . At each and every stage of his growth he has been able to make progress only as new elements of personal suggestion have presented themselves to him. So it would be quite wrong if we expected this attitude of expectation, accommodation; of readiness for the novel, the self-disturbing, the ill-understood; the lesson of arbitrary obedience—if we expected all this to stop suddenly, and not urge itself into the realm of the mysterious. Character has been all along to him the mysterious thing. The filling in of the mystery, sufficiently for his life-needs, has taken all his pains; but there is always the sphere of mystery still, from which are constantly emerging the unexpected attributes of personal character (Baldwin, 1906, pp. 339–40)

The emotions associated with mystery range from respect through reverence and awe to fear, but the common element is the sense of the presence of the unknown.

Religious Stages

The stages of religious development follow the three stages of socioethical growth: (1) the physical-spontaneous, (2) the intellectual, and (3) the ethical. Each stage is chiefly characterized by the dominant social interest for which it is named. Because a worth or value for Baldwin is always a function of an interest, the predominant motivation for social cooperation during a stage determines its characteristic ascription of worth to personality and, consequently, to the deity. In Baldwin's psychology, the self is essentially constituted by a set of interests which determine what is valuable to a person:

> It is the organization of interests which constitutes the established inner control process; and inner control is only another name for the progressive movement of what is felt as the subjective life or the self. The mass of subjective interests is no more and no less at any time than the subject or self. What the individual has in mind when he is

conscious of self, is the movement of processes which embody his interests. (Baldwin, 1911, p. 102)

The interests that determine what we value in another person, including the god-person, are neither innate nor invariably egotistic. Rather, social interests develop through qualitative transformations of the self in dialectical interaction with others. Each of the dominant social interests of later stages appears in some embryonic form early in childhood, but each interest has its time of ascendancy. The patterned growth of successive social interests in interaction with others yields "a genetic progression in the life of interests" (Baldwin, 1915, p. 14).

During the first, *physical–spontaneous stage*, the infant's dominant social interests are focused by the exigencies of physical existence and by spontaneous emotional attachments. Apprehension and interpretation of persons and events in the world are controlled by biological needs, together with spontaneous affections which tie the child instinctively to other human beings. The lines of demarcation within the infant's world are drawn by practical and emotional, not primarily cognitive, interests (Baldwin, 1915, p. 16). As a consequence of these pressing biological and affective interests, the first person to stand out from the undifferentiated world of the newborn is the chief caretaker. Among the numerous characteristics of the caretaking one, the infant's helplessness leads him or her to be primarily impressed by superior physical attributes (size, strength, power) and emotional succor. From these esteemed attributes, the infant makes quasideities out of the actual persons in the immediate environment.

The first indications of religious *dependence* are evident in the infant's "instinctive" or "spontaneous" trustfulness of the universe. Before the first distinction between persons and things occurs, the infant displays a global trust or *primitive credulity*, to use Bain's phrase, towards the entire environment (Baldwin, 1906, p. 343). This initial trustfulness is not religious dependence in the proper sense, because it is not directed toward persons, who have yet to be differentiated from things. Genuine religious dependence in the form of trust toward, and reliance upon, persons only really begins with the emergence of the caretaker from the initial haze of the newborn's universe. The caretaker's emergence is motivated by the child's intense concentration upon the one who relieves pain and satisfies desire (Baldwin, 1906, p. 344). In contrast with Freud's emphasis upon the role of the father in the genesis of religion out of infantile helplessness and Erikson's counterstress upon religious trust in the halo of the maternal presence, Baldwin insists that an infant may make a quasideity out of either parent or both. "The actual person whom he selects as the object of this primitive emotion of dependence depends upon the incidents of his rearing" (Baldwin, 1906, p. 343). What determines the direction of trusting dependence is not the sex of the parent for Baldwin, but successful fulfillment of the caretaking function. Dependence is experienced in relationship to the adult who generally satisfies the basic needs of the small child.

It is scarcely surprising, given the overwhelming needs of the human infant, that physical attributes should be conflated with goodness at the earliest stage of moral development. For the child whose world revolves around his own psychosomatic exigencies, the person who is the chief "relief agency" is genuinely good. The caretaker is the ideal personality, and this ideal is read in terms of those superior capacities that complement the infant's requirements. The child naturally develops a strong sense of dependence upon the deity-like parent who is his or her principal source of gratification, relief, and comfort. Somewhat later in the developmental process, the child's verbal responses to questions about the nature of God show that the first deity is constructed out of concrete experiences of actual dependence upon caretaking adults. God is always made in the image of parents. Insofar as parental attributes are ejected in idealized form, God, the deity, is "the great man, the powerful hero, the giant, the being most in likeness to the greater manifestations of physical nature, while yet personal" (Baldwin, 1906, p. 353). Similarly physical, fatherlike characteristics have recently been found by Goldman to typify the very young child's picture of God when praying (Goldman, 1968, pp. 88–90).

The first feelings of *mystery*, like those of dependence, appear when the caretaking person begins to stand out from the background of the newborn's undifferentiated world. In the formation of awe and mystery, it is the unpredictability, not the regularity, of caretakers that gains the infant's attention. Persons, in contrast with inanimate objects, strike the young child as dynamic, somewhat unreliable, and quite incomprehensible. By virtue of their self-willed activities, persons appear to be endowed with magical or mystical properties. A young boy, for example, who is helped by his father is continually mystified by the resources at the latter's command, resources that he has yet to understand through imitative behavior. As the growing child understands more through accommodation and reads more of what he understands into those about him through ejection, he also becomes increasingly aware of the complexity of others, and of his inability to fully anticipate their action (Baldwin, 1906, p. 358). The sense of mystery, rather than diminishing, tends to increase in intensity as the growing child's first discoveries widen awareness of that which is poorly understood.

The second, *intellectual stage* is ushered in by a transitional period of punishment, which breaks the child's preoccupation with relief from physical discomforts and satisfaction of affective needs. Punishment is a rude-awakening factor in the growth of intelligence, because it forces the child to concentrate upon verbal communications about the rules he or she is supposed to obey. Punishment for disobedience taxes the child's understanding of human affairs by introducing a new capriciousness on the part of significant others. The child is forced to think of the caretaker as an instructor, who inflicts pain, withholds love, and refuses aid. Relief is sought through intellectual comprehension of instructions. "The child comes to look upon the father or mother as the all-wise, the explainer of problems, the solver of riddles. His sense of dependence comes to be confidence in a higher intelligence than his, and this higher intelligence he places, of course, in the persons who relieve his uncertainties, who compel his obediences, who administer sanctions, who give explanations" (Baldwin, 1906, p. 346). Insofar as these traits are idealized and ejected onto a god, the deity becomes omniscient.

Building upon this initial sense of dependence on the higher intelligence of parents, the child passes through two distinct periods during the so-called questioning mania, which begins around age 3. The child's questioning begins with "What?" and, later, proceeds to "Why?" "Wa'dat, Wâdie?" ("What's that, Daddy?") was the typical cry of Baldwin's daughter, Helen, during the first of these periods. Her father describes it as the period during which the *causal tendency* is prominent, because the child tends to be satisfied with any answer that reveals the activity of a living agent. It is sufficient for the child to be told that a thing is what it is because a living person or animal made it that way. A table is " 'the thing that the carpenter makes'," the bread is " 'what the cook bakes'," the doll is " 'what I play with'," and so on (Baldwin, 1906, pp. 346–347). Satisfaction with these responses indicates development of the capacity to think of persons as agents, an ability which has its origins in the child's own sense of willing what he has done in play. The child's generalization, idealization, and ejection of agency onto a deity yields the religious sense of dependence upon the acts of an all-wise, arch-cause.

The second distinct period within the intellectual stage begins when the child becomes dissatisfied with explanations couched in terms of personal agency. In this later period, the child wants to know why the agent undertook the action. And this calls for an explanation in terms of design or teleology. The child realizes from watching and listening to adults that acts are generally means to self-chosen ends, and he experiences this himself in limited fields, such as play.

Generalizing this observation, the child seeks to explain every object in terms of its purpose.

With the emergence of the *teleological* from the causal period, dependence takes a far more intellectual turn. During the first (causal) period, dependence was primarily focused on the physical or personal power of another. Satisfactory answers to "what" questions ended with the personal agency of someone in the immediate environment. By contrast, "why" questions show the dependence of the growing child on properly intellectual explanations. It is no longer enough to tell the child that something is what it is, even though the answer implies the action of a living person or animal; he goes further and insists on the reason for the action (Baldwin, 1906, p. 349). The deity who is ejected during this period is, predictably, the arch-designer.

Because the intellectual stage begins with a concern about understanding parental instructions in order to avoid punishment, the child is concerned throughout both subperiods with anticipating the dictates of authority, securing favors, and avoiding punishments. But there is little of the properly ethical motivation in this behavior. Intelligence is used primarily for purposes of personal gratification or, to use Kohlberg's language for his Stage 2, instrumental hedonism. Hence, the child during this stage does not hesitate to deceive or to manipulate. As Baldwin observes, the child anticipates "reproof, and to avoid it covers his deed under a mask of innocence, or creates an actual device to avert punishment or to gain undeserved reward. He uses his little brother as a screen for his own sins, laying the blame for wrong-doing where it does not belong, claiming as his own actions which he did not perform, concealing his own thoughts and actions when it is to his advantage to do so" (Baldwin, 1906, pp. 349–350). Deception of this sort represents the negative side of dependence on superior authority.

The deities ejected during the second stage reflect this orientation and behavior toward authority figures just as clearly as they indicate the child's intellectual interest in the supreme cause(s) or designer(s). The gods, like the child's perception of parents at Stage 2, are jealous of their rights, gratified by praise, pleased with offerings, and given to pursuing their own interests and glory through human agents. When their interests are neglected or thwarted, deities, like aggrieved parents, pursue with "unerring vengeance" those who follow "after strange gods" (Baldwin, 1915, p. 106). A religious subject who is faced with a god of this sort tends to become preoccupied, for good reason, with acts of propitiation designed to secure divine favor or to appease divine wrath. At the same time, the religious actor attempts to get away with as much as possible, by using lies, tricks, vicarious sacrifices, and whatever other devices have proved effective in earlier social interactions (Baldwin, 1915, pp. 350–351).

It is quite possible, Baldwin notes in discussing these defensive manuevers, to define religion in such a way as to eliminate egoistical and unethical acts from the scope of properly religious behavior. But a stipulative definition of this sort arbitrarily excludes those primitive rites and ceremonies practiced by children and in simple societies which we ordinarily take to be religious acts, even though they are mainly self-interested. Ethically dubious and even unacceptable acts are fully religious for Baldwin, as long as they evidence the appropriate feelings of dependence upon a superior person or persons. The fact that religion makes use of moral beliefs does not mean that it always draws upon the best ethical judgments available.

The feeling of *mystery* during the second stage is also an outgrowth of "what" and "why" questions. The first real "reverence for personality" arises with the child's preoccupation with anthropocentric answers.

> The category of personality becomes in itself, as we have seen, a somewhat familiar resort of the child for explaining both the "what" and the "why" of events, and with the answer which leads him back to a living agency he tends to rest satisfied. This category of personality, therefore, in this period, seems to absorb and supersede both the other two categories—those of cause and design. The child's mysteries in the universe are largely *pooled in the one great mystery of personality;* and this in turn ceases to be the simple mystery of a terrifying outburst of force, or a blind agency of wisdom without counsel; it becomes the sort of agency of which the child himself seems to have an inkling in his own action. (Baldwin, 1906, p. 359)

The child cannot help finding persons the most interesting, instructive, and difficult-to-understand objects in his environment, especially as he moves into increasingly more complex social relationships beyond the family. He or she naturally develops an appreciation of the mysterious potentialities of personal agents, whose potentialities far exceed the assimilated habits of the accommodating self.

The child is particularly mystified by the ethical behavior of adults. He or she can readily understand selfish behavior, but not those actions which are frankly generous, thoughtful, and kind. The child is especially mystified by ethical discussions and controversies. It was apparently not unusual in the Victorian era for a young child to break into tears after listening to adults engage in earnest conversation about the right course of action. Baldwin interprets this behavior as a reaction to intellectual–moral bewilderment (Baldwin, 1906, p. 361). This sentiment, when projected onto the deity, becomes reverence for the mysteries of the deity's moral attributes.

The third, so-called *ethical stage* of religious development differs from the others in being more sharply differentiated from nonreligious phenomena. Baldwin marks this difference by referring to the earlier two stages as *quasi-religious*. To be sure, the earlier stages are genuinely religious insofar as they elicit emotions of dependence and mystery vis-à-vis superior beings. But during the first stage, the religious object is not clearly differentiated from actual persons, while the deity ejected during the second stage is often not morally superior to the egoistic subject (Baldwin, 1906, pp. 352–353). During the third stage, the object of dependence and respect becomes a morally good, even perfect, person. And because belief in the actual existence of this ideal distinguishes religion from morality, it is not until the third stage that religion in the proper sense of the term, comes into existence. It is only when religious faith is fully differentiated from ethics that its specific characteristics become clearly discernible. Baldwin here follows Schleiermacher and Hegel in assuming that the essence of religion is only realized at the end of the developmental process.

The ethical stage is characterized by a preoccupation with moral norms and values, together with correlative feelings of remorse, guilt, and repentance. A new appreciation of moral standards and an endeavor to act in accordance with them gradually subordinates earlier instinctive impulses and egoistical desires.

The ethical self has its rude beginnings in the experience of punishment during the intellectual stage. These experiences together with ongoing attempts to understand the mysteries of adult ethical behavior gradually prompt the child, toward the conclusion of the second stage, to limit impulsive and hedonistic behavior. In Baldwin's words, "the child finds himself stimulated constantly to deny his impulses, his desires, even his irregular sympathies, by conforming to the will of another" (Baldwin, 1906, p. 41). Through obedience, the child comes to realize that adult behavior is not capricious, as previously imagined, but highly regular. Other persons are viewed as possessing a consistency of character resulting from actions willed in accordance with a consistent set of reasonable moral standards.

Obedience to authority prepares the ground, but does not give rise to the ethical stage. For the latter to emerge, a new conception of personality must first arise. This new self represents a step beyond both the self of assimilated habits and the self of ever new accommodations. It involves viewing the self as obligated to a presence or *socius* beyond the self, an awareness which begins when parents and teachers are seen as acting in relationship to a family law or *socius* beyond themselves. At first, the child only dimly senses that his parents act reluctantly in the service of principles beyond their momentary impulses. This higher law stands in the same relationship to these authorities as their commands do to the child. Gradually, this presence is recognized for what it is, namely, public opinion as embodied in laws and mores and as explicated by teachers, parents, and other authority figures.

With recognition of the *socius*, the good person comes to be understood as one who obeys the moral law. Parents and teachers are now thought to be good not by virtue of their physical powers or intellectual abilities, but because of their acquiescence to common moral and legal standards. Only insofar as the child gets into the habit of acting obediently in imitation of them does he or she feel good.

The new self of moral obligation is neither the assimilated self of former habits nor the self of accommodations. It is not the former, because obligations often violate what one wants to do on the basis of acquired habits and private preferences; it is not the accommodating self acting out of sympathy, because moral obligation is based on impersonal, often external, social norms. The two selves of habit and accommodation have to be gently shoved aside to make room for properly ethical development. A new concept of the self has to appear, that of "*a dominating other self, a new alter*" (Baldwin, 1906, p. 52). This third self appears with internalization, through imitation of shared moral opinions. In this way, there is formed "the presence of something in him which represents his father, mother, or in general, *the lawgiving personality*" (Baldwin, 1906, p. 55). How this new sense of self differs from earlier self-understandings is illustrated by Baldwin's account of a boy tempted to steal an apple, when no one else is present. There is in him, first, the greedy, habitual self eyeing the apple. There is also the receptive, accommodating, imitative self mildly prompting him, out of respect for his father, to leave the apple alone. To these two aspects of the younger self, there is added, with the advent of the third stage, a new sense of oneself as obedient to moral standards regardless of egoistical desires and personal sympathies. When the child hesitates about what to do, instrumental hedonism is now balanced not by the faint imitation of the accommodating self, but by the sense of the new and better obedient self hovering before him. The child develops a consistent, self-legislating self of his own.

The growing child proceeds to do what persons always do with thoughts about themselves; he ejects the new self onto others in his social group. Others including younger siblings are expected to share the same sense of responsibility to the collective rules and values.

The religious sense of *dependence* fostered by these developments arises out of the sense of sinfulness which accompanies formation of conscience. Remorse, shame, and guilt produce an "ethical" sense of inadequacy in place of the physiological–affective helplessness of the first stage and the intellectual inferiority of the second. A change simultaneously occurs in what is needed by way of complementarity. The believer feels dependent upon divine forgiveness, redemption, moral acceptance, and favor. The emotional responses to forgiveness include assurance, peace, communion, and reliance upon the Higher-than-we (Baldwin, 1906, p. 352).

The divine eject upon whom the ethical believer feels dependent not only complements inadequacies; the deity also represents an idealization of the newly achieved moral capacities. In this ejective move, the divine "not-I" is read in terms of the believer's own moral personality or, at least, the ideal of character he is trying to approach. "There must be somewhere, feels the child, a self which answers to all the elements of the law ... whose presence in my thought makes my own self morally so incomplete" (Baldwin, 1906, p. 339). Dependence on the deity ejected in this way is experienced as reliance on an ideally good person for guidance and stimulation toward moral perfection.

As the ethical self continues to develop by taking the role of others and making moral judgments, so, too, does the ejective deity. A crucial aspect of growth within the ethical stage is development of the sense of being a companion, a *socius* who thinks not only of one's own interests, but those of all other selves as well. A continuing problem for every ethical individual is the frequent opposition between egoistic interests and those of others. The contradiction between mine and thine can be resolved only by either accepting currently sanctioned social norms or positing new principles which resolve the conflict fairly. This is the strictly ethical move. Alongside it, there also develops a sense of the possibility of a good self or ideal personality, whose decision would be, in all cases the proper and correct one, whatever the consequences for personal interests. This is the ideal or perfect self which, as supreme *socius*, is ejected at the highest reaches of religious development. Just as the highest ethical principles establish an ideal of harmonious practical relationships in social community, so, too, the "religious demand or postulate is that of a perfect self, a fully realized or complete person, in whom the opposition between private and public interests would be completely overcome" (Baldwin, 1909, p. 99). In the religious move beyond the ethical, the ideal is "made actual, brought into human life, and symbolised concretely in the religious emblem that stands for God" (Baldwin, 1915, p. 104). The deity is constituted by ejecting the self as ideal *socius*.

Once the believer has reached the ethical stage, nothing less than an ethically perfect *socius* will excite genuine worship. It is only when the deity adds to omnipotence and omniscience such ethical attributes as justice, righteousness, mercy, grace, and love that we properly speak of the *divine*. It is in relation to the divine that *dependence* is said to reach its highest and richest form.

The sense of *mystery* (reverence, awe, and respect) at the third stage is evoked by belief that the divine not only carries each moral ideal to its highest pitch of perfection, but also harmoniously realizes all ethical ideals, including the contrasting ideals of justice and mercy. *Reverence* is a response not simply to the ideal of excellence, however, but to its actual realization. The deepest source of mystery, derives from the fact that the intellect is continually baffled by the way in which the object of religious devotion transcends the ordinary antinomy between the ideal and the real. By definition, moral ideals are abstractions that do not exist. The religious adherent has no experiential knowledge of infinite justice, mercy, love, and grace, yet he or she must use finite categories to express them. The deity is also an individual, like other persons, yet his particularity is not subject to the limitations which are essential for knowing the identity of all other individuals. The intellect, baffled by these demands of religious development, is plunged by them into "the most profound sense of mystery" and the "most stirring religious experiences" (Baldwin, 1906, p. 364).

The three foregoing stages of religious development are paralleled by their opposites, namely, the religiously bad or evil. Just as good acts and states of affairs are subject to generalization and idealization, so, too, are those that are bad. Actualized through ejection, evil intentions and acts are made incarnate in demons, evil spirits, and devils, as the good is similarly personified by the deity. In contrast to the supremely good God is the arch-enemy, ideally bad, Satan, the *summum malum*. Although Baldwin does not work out a fully developed stage-by-stage theory of the religiously bad, he does make it clear that belief in the actual existence of the devil is abandoned by the final stage of religious development, where Satan is finally routed by the supremacy of the ideally Good.

Sociological Considerations

The preceding psychological account includes an important sociological dimension, insofar as the self develops through the give-and-take of social role relationships. The sense of personality, which is idealized and ejected as the deity, is formed through attempting to understand others by means of what one understands about oneself and, then, by reading the self again with the added knowledge derived from the attempt to understand those others. Baldwin went on to employ social role theory as a springboard for more extensive theoretical and empirical explorations into relatively stable, institutionalized religious beliefs and practices. Underlying this exploration was Baldwin's fundamental conviction that religion is ... always social—always an institution ..., embodying the results of social intercourse, and showing a certain unity of personal motive and practice among the individuals of a community" (Baldwin, 1909, pp. 92–93). To appreciate the modernity of this perspective, it is sufficient to contrast it with William James's polar contention that religion refers to "the feelings, acts, and experiences of individual men in their solitude, so far as they apprehend themselves to stand in relation to whatever they may consider the divine" (James, 1958, p. 42). Against James, Baldwin insisted that the psychologist cannot "rest content with an individualistic theory of religion—the view that religion springs up in the individual in the form of rational insight or private intuition—in the face of the conclusion drawn from comparative and anthropological study, to the effect that religion is, in its origin, always social—always an institution." (Baldwin, 1909, p. 92).

Society and the individual are viewed by Baldwin as mutually interdependent. Society, which is constituted in large part by shared beliefs and practices (Baldwin, 1906, p. 504), is made up of ideas that originate in the minds of others. But the individual is no less dependent upon society than society is dependent on the contributions of its members. For an individual to progress psychologically, he or she must be met at least halfway by ready-made cultural beliefs and practices. A religious institution is thus "always the embodiement of the actual *religious experience* of individuals of a certain [level of development] ..., while religious experience in turn is always a personal interpretation of an existing [institutional] religion" (Baldwin, 1909, p. 93). The institutionalized creeds, symbols, rites, and prescriptions studied by sociologists and anthropologists are nothing more than objective expressions of the subjective meanings discovered by the individual members of the society. At the same time, religious meaning is never solely the creation of a single individual taken in isolation from the sacred traditions of a group: "No man is religious by himself, nor does he choose his god, nor devise his offering, nor enjoy his blessing alone" (Baldwin, 1901–05, p. 460). Even the most idiosyncratic convictions and rituals are variations on the collective patterns. "Personal experience can never release itself from the bond . . . to culture which gives it its necessary environment and support" (Baldwin, 1909, p. 93).

Religious change is explained by Baldwin in terms of the dialectical relationship that exists between individuals and society. In accommodating to what collective symbols and rites have come to mean historically and assimilating them to a particular level of cognitive–ethical–religious development, the individul changes their original meaning. No individual passively internalizes all the received religious traditions of his group. Some members of society fail to achieve adequately the typical level of development prevailing in their culture, while others far exceed it. If an innovation deviates too radically from accepted ways of thought and action, collective sanctions are commonly invoked against the deviant in the name of sacred tradition. But, within limits, there is considerable latitude for individual differences and their cumulative collective results.

Religious institutions also change in response to the valid criticisms of perspicacious individuals and the creative innovations of those few who dare to move beyond conventional perspectives. Extending his model of individual growth to society, Baldwin contends that societies assimilate and accommodate to creative individuals, just as they do to it.

> The new thought is "projective" to society as long as it exists in the individual's mind only; it becomes "subjective" to society when society has generalized it and embodied it in some one of the institutions which are a part of her intimate organization; and then finally society makes it "ejective" by requiring, by all her pedagogical, civil, and other sanctions, that each individual, class, or subordinate group which claims a share in her corporate life, shall recognize it and live up to it. (Baldwin, 1906, p. 541)

Durkheim's emphasis upon the individual's dependence on society is thus joined with a Weberian and Eriksonian stress on the creative contribution of individuals to the social heritage.

Baldwin's unique combination of developmental psychology and sociology leads to some interesting views on the symbolic aspects of religion. Symbols are the central focus of collective religious devotion for Baldwin as for Durkheim and his sociological disciples. Objectively considered, the external objects that serve as the symbols around which intense religious sentiments cluster are quite ordinary things of little utilitarian value. "A fetish, a totem, a churinga, a charm, a relic, a locality, a sound, an eclipse, an idol, a picture, things animate and things inanimate, may and do serve as objects of religious or quasi-religious veneration" (Baldwin, 1915, p. 92). Clearly, then, it is not the particular emblem or external thing as such, but some further value or significance that stirs the religious sentiments. It is the "meaning or presence, the spirit, force, or god, which the emblem stands for or symbolises; this is, properly speaking, the 'religious object' " (Baldwin, 1915, p. 92, n. 1).

Thus far, Baldwin's analysis of symbols and their meaning follows Durkheim's (1912/1965) treatment in *The Elementary Forms of the Religious Life*, a book to which he is self-consciously indebted. Baldwin also follows Durkheim part of the way in suggesting that there is a sense in which a god of a group is an expression of its own internal spirit:

> The deity shows the growth of the normal social relations, and reflects their character, because he is the projected personal ideal of the group. While the deity must be thought of by these individuals as apart from them, since he is personal, yet he is the controlling spiritual presence, the voice, the oracle of the group, and may be approached through the proper mediation with rites and ceremonies. The tribal deity is in this important sense, then, the tribal spirit; he is conceived in terms of the tribal self. (Baldwin, 1909, pp. 101–102)

It does not follow however, that the group, *as it exists*, is the true object of religion, as Baldwin thought Durkheim was arguing. The existing social group is not what the religious ideal denotes nor what the national aspirations celebrate. To use Baldwin's example, Americans do not sing "My country, 'tis of thee, Thou land of liberty—Of thee I sing," to America *as it is*, but to America *as it should be*. The hymn is to liberty; America is the symbol. "The social ideal is symbolised by the group, just as the ideal self or god of the individual is symbolised in the concrete object of religious devotion" (Baldwin, 1915, p. 114). Contrary to Durkheim, society itself, not just its objective emblem (totem, flag) symbolizes the ideal.

In fairness to Durkheim, it should be noted that, by 1912 when *The Elementary Forms of the Religious Life* was written, society had come to refer more to shared collective ideas and ideals than to structural relationships. Durkheim also writes that objective symbols refer to shared collective ideals. But Durkheim does not say that society is a symbol of the ideal, because society for him includes ideals of what society *as it is* in terms of behavior should be. The disagreement between Durkheim and Baldwin is partly over the meaning of society. In Durkheim's more idealist reading, society includes ideals generated by current patterns of social interaction, whereas Baldwin's more naturalistic reading views society in terms of current behavior, institutions and the like. But Durkheim gives *symbols* a more naturalist reading, insofar as he claims that they refer to society *as it is*, as both a structural and cultural system.

Baldwin interprets *symbols* as always referring to meanings *beyond* any empirical entity.

Baldwin attempted to work out the main lines of religious evolution by sketching its most primitive and advanced societal forms. Levy-Bruhl's (1926) discredited notion of prelogical thought patterns among "primitives" is employed to explain the failure to distinguish subject and object in "mystic participation" and identification with the totem (Baldwin, 1915, p. 62). To Baldwin's credit, however, he cautioned against uncritically assuming that the adult primitive's thought patterns exactly follow those of modern children, and he called for objective testing of developmental hypotheses in the field (Baldwin, 1915, p. 55).

Far more interesting than these speculations about the primitive case is what Baldwin has to say about religion in the modern world. Baldwin appreciated the importance of secularization, but he was far from envisioning the collapse of religion into scientific positivism (Baldwin, 1915, p. 39). *Secularization* for Baldwin refers not to liberation from the religious world view altogether, but to the institutional emancipation from religion of other social structures and functions, e.g., politics, education, medicine, and the theater. Such structural–functional differentiation heralds not a collapse of religion, but its alteration. Especially since the Enlightenment, religion has become a more personal matter. The external, legalistic authority of early religion, with its concern with correct rites, formulas, and prescriptions, has given way to a gentler prodding of the inner life (Baldwin, 1915, p. 91). Growth in the autonomy of judgment, producing a true democracy of conscience, has refined the religious interest, but it has not lessened or impaired it (Baldwin, 1915, p. 111, n. 1).

Despite this gradual personalization of religion, Baldwin was not tempted to envisage its institutional demise in the isolated individualism of Thomas Paine's "my mind is my church" or Jefferson's "I am a sect myself." Religion for Baldwin is "everywhere essentially a *social phenomenon*" (Baldwin, 1909, p. 94). Unlike the intellectual and ethical stages of development, religion never passes completely into the phase of inner autonomy to which Baldwin applies the term *synnomic*. Religion remains *syndoxic*, that is, it is apprehended as the common possession of the group, of the self along with others. The individual does not pretend to be the author of shared teachings, rites, observances, prescriptions, and prohibitions. The religious ideal, unlike logic and morality, can never be universalized in a self-legislating judgment of synnomic force, because, "in its essence, it is always a first-hand experience, it requires the actual presence of the Other" (Baldwin, 1915, p. 122). And the existence of God is made actual by the symbols and rites of a community.

> Man cannot have a private religion; men must be religious together. They cannot be religious together without a tradition, a local home, a more or less elaborate ritual or body of procedure. (Baldwin, 1909, p. 105)

Through ritual, individuals are united noncognitively to the spiritual order. In short, religion is always "a social phenomenon depending on a sense of union or communion between a group of human beings and their god" (Baldwin, 1901–05, vol. 2, p. 455).

For Baldwin, secularization cannot mean the end of religion, because the religious interest is ubiquitous. Far from being an epiphenomenon or a mere useless artifact of culture, religion is an essential dimension of personal and social growth. The self cannot develop without constantly constructing and reconstructing an ideal personality, which it spontaneously ejects upon reality. The heathen who carves out an idol with his hands and the philosopher who writes a learned treatise both reveal the same human impulse: "that of setting up a Self, ideal in character, personal in form, as the goal of development and the end of striving" (Baldwin, 1909, p. 105). To eradicate religion would be to "mutilate personality" by deflecting the normal course of individual development. One might have wished, Baldwin continues, that humanity had developed otherwise, without religion or toward a future religionless state of affairs. This might have been possible *"had humanity itself been different"* (Baldwin, 1909, p. 106). But the normal process of self-consciousness issues in social and moral ideals which are ejected in the religious move beyond morality. Where this process is thwarted, it tends to find a "sublimated equivalent," like modern occultism and science fiction.

> The man who scoffs at a creed stands in awe before the mysteries of table-turning and spirit-rapping; and the sceptic in the matter of miracles, accepts faith cures, telepathic messages from the unseen world, second sight and other equally miraculous violations of the natural order. The religious spirit, in short, outlives its recurrent forms of embodiment, and the rejection of this religion or that, this ideal or that, is always in the interest of some other embodiment, in which the same spiritual movement hastens to clothe itself. (Baldwin, 1909, p. 106)

In other words, inner developmental requirements necessitate the formation of religious objects, even when "progress" undermines traditional symbols and myths.

In general, Baldwin sees society playing three distinct functions in the genesis and maintenance of religion. First, social relations provide the necessary role-taking opportunities for personal religious development. Second, groups provide the developing individual with traditional symbols, stories, and prescriptions, that is, with the contents used in religious imagination and reflection. Finally, groups play an important role in making actual the reality of religious ejects, as they make possible a vivid sense of communion with the deity.

Religious Contemplation of the Absolute Beyond Conventional Faith

Religion may be a natural outcome of the developmental process, but it does not follow that it is the final, synthesizing terminus of self-development that one might expect. It is not, because conventional faith is incapable of resolving the antinomy between practical imagination and theoretical reasoning. There is, however, a further religious movement through the experience of aesthetic immediacy whereby self-reconciliation does take place within a larger vision of the absolute. To understand this further religious movement, it is first necessary to explore the central antinomies of selfhood, together with the aesthetic mode of reconciling them, with which the ultimate form of religious apprehension is intertwined.

Superficially, religious faith would seem to overcome the antinomy between practical imagination and theoretical reasoning, because it both idealizes its object, like morality, and actualizes it by means of the intellect. But faith does not in fact overcome the opposition between the ideal and the actual. The god-postulate does not genuinely reconcile theoretical and practical interests, partly because the absence of proof scandalizes theoretical reason. The ideal of reason is a body of neutral truth, independent of the personal life and interests of the individual. But it is upon the latter that the religious postulate is based. Moreover, even if a rational proof of the existence of God could be convincingly formulated, such a proof would lose contact with the actuality of immediate religious experience by means of which alone God is known.

> God would then be, like rational identity and moral law, an empty form, the postulate of values in an abstract realm; a norm of reason, instead of the actual person found by the devotee to be a "very present help in trouble." The warmth of intimacy of personal religion would be lost to humanity. (Baldwin, 1915, p. 126)

The actuality of God depends upon deep emotional convictions which stand in dramatic tension with the proofs of reason.

In order to resolve this basic antinomy of the religious life, it is necessary to move to the aesthetic mode of experience. Aesthetic apprehension of reality occurs through feeling rather than by knowledge or action; it thereby escapes to some degree the controls of factual, social, and practical life. Unlike the intellect, which aims at the true, and the will, which is directed toward the good, the aesthetic mode terminates with immediate or direct enjoyment. The immediacy of the aesthetic is analogous to the infant's alogical mode of apprehension, before the mediation of ideas is established. But it occurs beyond the mediation of reality through ideas and ideals. It is, in brief, "a mode of function in which consciousness, in the very midst of its dualisms and mediations, seems to forget or to banish the distinctions and oppositions in its content, and to bring its forces into equilibrium in a mode of direct apprehension—to throw away its lenses and look directly into the face of reality" (Baldwin, 1915, p. 176).

The aesthetic mode interprets the object for what it is and stands for, not for what the ideals of either theoretical or practical reason would make of it. The ideals of theoretical and practical reason are mutually exclusive; each demands the negation of the ideal of the other or at least its subordination to its own fulfillment. But actual experience contravenes these claims. "The true object is also valuable, and the enjoyment of something does not exclude its being a fact of the external world" (Baldwin, 1915, p. 236). On this experiential basis, the aesthetic interest seeks the full and intrinsic meaning of objects, reading them as both true and good, in the larger image of the beautiful.

In the freedom of aesthetic imagination, the spontaneous human interest in intrinsic completeness and perfection comes into its own. Aesthetic imagination is like play in its free use of reality. Just as play in infancy frees the growing individual *for* logical thought, aesthetic imagination frees the adult *from* thought. But unlike infantile play, the aesthetic imagination does not deny or discard established truths. On the contrary, it takes the true and the good with utmost seriousness. At the same time, "the aesthetic ... sweeps beyond the truth set up by knowledge as complete and absolute, and also beyond the good set up by the will as full realisation of the self; and depicts the real, perfect in all its aspects, as present in the semblant object itself" (Baldwin, 1915, p. 235). The contradictions of ordinary life no longer appear or, rather, they are taken up into a larger vision. The aesthetic mode is the means whereby the thing-reality of external verification, which is the presupposition of knowledge and truth, and the self-reality of inner affirmation, which is the postulate of the practical and the worthful, "*can in the process of experience come together after having fallen apart in the develop-*

ment of cognition" (Baldwin, 1906-1911, vol. 3, p. 13). The protest of the aesthetic imagination is against the partiality of both the reality of logic and that of morality. Its own ideal of reality, by comparison, is one of completeness, reunion, and reconciliation. "Completeness of spatial form, of harmonious colouring, of rhythmic movement, of dramatic arrangement, of truthful relation, of moral quality, even of aesthetic proportion and relation, all merge in that ideal of ideals, the perfect work of art" (Baldwin, 1915, p. 244). In it, the union of the actual and the ideal is realized.

A particular work of art, while complete in itself, is also a sample and model of a larger synthesis, namely, reality as a whole. Every genuine work of art is an autonomous entity, complete in itself and thus satisfying to the interest of aesthetic contemplation. Still, the aesthetic interest cannot rest permanently upon any one work. It reaches through particular satisfactions toward increasingly greater completeness and perfection, until it rests in contemplation of reality as such. This experience has the form of a self, because there is in aesthetic contemplation a healing of the schism between subject and object, and a reassertion of the oneness of experience. In one sense, aesthetic experience involves an expression of personal taste; in it, I find my own inner world mirrored. Yet the reality contemplated is also thought to have the same significance for all competent observers. The individual reads himself into it, but not his uniqueness. What he reads into ultimate reality is what he shares in common with others. And he speaks not for himself alone, but for the community, indeed, for all persons; for the aesthetic consciousness in general, not for his private taste and judgment alone. The individual feels that he is the organ of a universal taste that works in him. The whole of reality is thus objective in the sense that it is independent of the individual; at the same time, it is a reflection of subjective tastes common to the self and others.

The whole of reality that is apprehended in this way is the absolute, in the sense in which this term is normally used by idealists. An unconditioned entity, the absolute does not depend in any way upon a principle or relation foreign to itself. The absolute is not internally unrelated or lacking in internal structure; far from it. But it is what it is and remains what it is without any dependence upon or interference from anything beyond itself. As the whole of reality, the absolute synthesizes the various valid meanings determined from the partial points of view from which persons apprehend particular aspects of existence—actual, ideal, good, true, beautiful, and other. These special features of reality are not invalidated or annihilated by the absolute. Rather, each survives and contributes, in its own way, to the essential content of the entire synthesis. Each is taken up into and reinstated, in its proper perspective and place, within the whole of reality as such.

To grasp the whole in this way is to realize that the idea of God refers, not to an object in the world of objects, but rather to "an organic or spiritual whole with reference to which alone both self and the world are knowable" (Baldwin, 1901–05, vol. 2, p. 457). God, from this perspective, is in Tillichian fashion more a symbolic "idea through which we know than an idea of an object of knowledge" (Baldwin, 1901–05, p. 257). It is on this rather profound, highly abstract, theological note that Baldwin's developmental psychology of religion converges.

Critical Assessment in View of Recent Research

It remains to assess Baldwin's interpretation of religion in light of recent research. Among contemporary investigators, James Fowler's empirical study of faith development is clearly the closest to Baldwin's enterprise, as well as one of the most promising new approaches to the scientific study of religion in some time. For over six years, Fowler has been boldly fiddling with a structural stage theory of faith development while classifying interviews with 300 persons from ages four to eighty. The sample includes Protestants, Catholics, Jews, atheists, agnostics, and Western Adherents of Eastern religions, representing a reasonable range of socio-economic classes, ethnic backgrounds, and educational levels. A select longitudinal sample is being followed at five-year intervals, and cross-cultural studies are projected. Because Fowler's theory has been in a state of considerable flux and a definitive statement has yet to appear, the present interpretation attempts to fix, for critical and comparative purposes, a theory which is continuing to develop, like the stages it attempts to study. I will use the relatively stable theory that appeared between 1974 and 1976, noting subsequent (mostly unpublished) modifications where appropriate.

Fowler's identification of his subject matter and basic theoretical approach are exceedingly close to Baldwin's work. His focus is not on cognitive belief, as explored by Goldman and other Piagetians, but on *faith*, defined as an affectional–dispositional way of construing the whole of reality or the "ultimate environment." Central to Fowler's theory is his conviction that faith can be understood through the method of structural developmental analysis. Faith-knowing is believed to constitute a structural unity that develops, by assimilation and accommodation, through discernible *stages*. Because each stage builds upon the immediately preceding one, the sequence of stages is *invariant*. A stage cannot be skipped. Each stage integrates earlier operations into more complex and inclusive structural wholes, making the stage sequence *hierarchical*. The sequence of stages is thought to be *universal*, following the usual structural developmental hypothesis, although the evidence for this claim has yet to be accumulated.

Fowler has arrived at this approach independently of Baldwin, by joining the Piagetian–Kohlbergian paradigm with insights from psychoanalysts (primarily Erik Erikson) and theologians (like H. R. Niebuhr, Paul Tillich, Wilfred Cantwell Smith, and Richard R. Niebuhr). Partly as a consequence of this different lineage, Fowler offers a richer and more differentiated account then Baldwin of the various dimensions of faith development. Table 1 describes Fowler's six stages in detail, moving from simple structures to those that are more complex. Fowler claims, as does Baldwin, that his stages mark growth in self-awareness. For this to be the case, transformation in the understanding of personality, in self and others, must take place, although Fowler nowhere draws attention to this Baldwinian perspective. His approach focuses not on "ideal personality ejects," but on five "variables," "aspects," or "windows on" faith. It is by means of these five variables (in the earlier formulation) or aspects (as they are now called) that Fowler identifies each stage. These aspects have been reformulated several times, but most lists include the following: (1) sources of authoritative insights; (2) modes of appropriation (i.e., the typical forms people use to represent coherence); (3) uses of symbols; (4) types of role-taking, especially with persons holding radically different world views; and (5) responses to prototypical challenges. Table 2 describes these five windows (or variables) that both crosscut all six stages and provide the apertures for their identification. Fowler's detailed analysis of these several dimensions make his theory far more complex than Baldwin's treatment of personality ejects. Yet Fowler's stages roughly parallel and confirm many of Baldwin's earlier intuitions. Table 3 brings out this parallelism, which becomes clearer when we examine more carefully how each stage is centrally described in the two theories, forgetting for a moment, the differences that separate these approaches.

At Stage 1, Baldwin and Fowler are both impressed with the child's use of caretaking adults as prime resources in populating a superior world. In Baldwin's description of the physical–spontaneous stage, the infant actually makes quasideities out of the adult(s) upon whom he or she is dependent. The superior characteristics that most attract the child's attention are emotional succor and physical size. At a somewhat more advanced period within this first stage, the physical attributes of parents are projected onto deitylike figures.

Table 1
Fowler's Stages of Faith Development

The Stages: A Brief Overview

In our effort to give a structural developmental account of faith we have identified *six stages*— moving from more simple and undifferentiated structures to those which are more complex and differentiated. Faith manifests growing self-awareness as you move through the stages. The ages given with each of these stages represent an average *minimal* age. Many persons attain them, if at all, at later chronological ages. Stage attainment varies from person to person and equilibrium of a stable sort may occur for different persons or groups at or in different stages.

Stage 1: Intuitive–projective faith

The imitative, fantasy-filled phase in which the child can be powerfully and permanently influenced by the examples, moods, actions and language of the visible faith of primal adults. (age 4)

Stage 2: Mythic–literal faith

The stage in which the person begins to take on for himself/herself the stories and beliefs and observances which symbolize belonging to his/her community. Attitudes are observed and adopted; beliefs are appropriated with literal interpretations, as are moral rules and attitudes. Symbols are one-dimensional and literal. Authority (parental) and example still count for more than those of peers. (6½–8)

Stage 3: Synthetic–conventional faith

The person's experience of the world is now extended beyond the family and primary social groups. There are a number of spheres or theaters of life: family, school or work, peers, leisure, friendship, and possibly a religious sphere. Faith must help provide a coherent and meaningful synthesis of that now more complex and diverse range of involvements. Coherence and meaning are certified, at this stage, by either the authority of properly designated persons in each sphere, or by the authority of consensus among "those who count." The person does not yet have to take on the burden of world-synthesis for himself/herself. (12–13)

Stage 4: Individuating–reflexive faith

The movement or break from Stage 3 to Stage 4 is particularly important for it is in this transition that the late adolescent or adult must begin to take seriously the burden of responsibility for his/her own commitments, lifestyle, beliefs, and attitudes. Where there is genuinely a transition to Stage 4 the person must face certain universal polar tensions which synthetic—conventional faith allows one to evade:

individuality v. belonging to community

subjectivity v. objectivity

self-fulfillment v. service to others

the relative v. the absolute

Often Stage 4 develops under the tutelage of ideologically powerful religions, charismatic leadership, or ideologies of other kinds. It often finds it necessary to collapse these polar tensions in one direction or the other. Stage 4 both brings and requires a qualitatively new and different kind of self-awareness and responsibility for one's choices and rejections. (18–19)

Table 1 (continued)

Stage 5: Paradoxical–consolidative faith

In Stage 4 the person is self-aware in making commitments and knows something of what is being *excluded* by the choices he/she makes. But for Stage 4, the ability to decide is grounded, in part at least, on the fact that one set of commitments is overvalued at the expense of necessarily viewing alternatives to it in a partial and limiting light.

Stage 5 represents an advance in the sense that it recognizes the integrity and truth in positions other than its own, and it affirms and lives out its own commitments and beliefs in such a way as to honor that which is true in the lives of others without denying the truth of its own. Stage 5 is ready for community of identification beyond tribal, racial, class or ideological boundaries. *To be genuine, it must know the cost of such community and be prepared to pay the cost.* A true Stage 5 requires time and testing and regard for those who are different and who oppose you which Stage 4 does not have. In a true Stage 5, *espoused values and beliefs are congruent with risk and action taken. (30–32)*

Stage 6: Universalizing faith

Stage 5's commitment to inclusive community remains paradoxical. To affirm others means to deny oneself. Defensiveness and egocentrism make the affirmation of others' truth difficult and threatening. One's own interests and investment in tribe, class, religion, nation, region, etc., still constitute biasing and distorting loyalties, which have to be struggled with and overcome continually.

Stage 6 (universalizing faith) *is rare.* At this stage what Christians and Jews call the Kingdom of God is a live, felt reality for the person of faith. Here one dwells *in* the world as a transforming presence, but is not *of* the world. The sense of the oneness of all persons is not a glib ideological belief but has become a permeative basis for decision and action. The paradox has gone out of being-for-others; at Stage 6, one is being most truly oneself. Stage 6s' participation in the Ultimate is direct and immediate. Their community is universal in inclusiveness. Such persons are ready for fellowship with persons at any of the other stages and from any other faith tradition. They seem instinctively to know how to relate to us affirmingly, never condescendingly, yet with pricks to our pretense and with genuine bread of life. (38–40)

Quoted with permission. From: Fowler, J. Stages in faith: the sturctural-development approach. In T.C. Hennessey (Ed.), Values and Moral Development. New York: Paulist Press, 1976.

Fowler avoids saying that the child at the first *intuitive–projective* stage actually makes deities out of parents, although he recognizes with Baldwin that the "child's dependence on and affectional ties with them makes them prime authorities or references in his/her construction of a meaningful world" (Fowler, 1976, p. 191). According to Fowler, adults serve more as models of faith in power(s) and authority(ies) that even the young child dimly apprehends beyond his elders. However, Fowler seems to be thinking of children at the second period in Baldwin's first stage, when some such dim apprehension occasions projections beyond adults to the wider environ-

Table 2
The Variables of Faith Development[a]

Variable A: Locus of authority

This variable focuses on the question "Who or what is the reference by which the person gains or validates reliable orientation toward the ultimate conditions of existence?" Overall, the developmental sequence in this variable is from external authority to internal; from authority inhering in other persons, to authority in custom, institution, and law, and on to authority based on one's own more critical experience, judgment, and loyalties.

Variable B: Criteria and modes of appropriation

This variable fixes on the implicit or explicit criteria employed by a person in weighing and appropriating insights, claims, or (his/her own) intuitions as regards faith orientation. Developmentally, these range from unconscious characteristics of bodily and instinctual rhythms, to felt but not self-aware affinities and dependencies, to more-or-less self-aware adherence to the implicit norms of one's most primary communities, and to criteria growing from one's increasingly individuated sense of identity, commitment and purpose.

Variable C: Symbolic and conceptual functioning

In this variable we see the development of cognitive capacities as they focus on the matters with which faith deals. This variable traces the precursors and development of self-critical awareness and the ability to utilize symbols and concepts in an increasingly self-conscious way. Terminally it characterizes a postcritical capacity to dwell-in but also to transcend religious symbols in a direct participation in Being.

Variable D: Role-taking and extensiveness of identification

In this variable the work of Piaget, Kohlberg, Flavell, and Selman on the development of role-taking has been supplemented by the work of Kegan and Fowler on construction of community. This variable focuses on the person's way of constructing the inner motivations, intentions and feelings of other persons. It begins with initial egocentrism. Then, developmentally it leads through mutual role-taking and eventually to the ability to take the role of other groups and of their world-views. This development is correlated with a gradual expansion in the inclusion of other persons and groups in one's reference community, and moves toward a meaningful sense of membership in a universal commonwealth of being.

Variable E: Prototypical challenges with which faith must deal

Informed by Erikson's work on the developmental crises of the healthy personality, this variable seeks to clarify the typical existential challenges we find correlated with each stage. Less structurally definable than the other variables, this one tries to show how structural gains are interrelated with the rise and eventual solution of existential challenges.

[a]Quoted, with permission, from Fowler (1976).

ment. The disjointedness and capriciousness of the world that the young child constructs is recognized by Fowler as well as by Baldwin. Fowler attributes this capriciousness to preoperational thought (Piaget), while Baldwin goes beyond its cognitive sources to identify the resulting arbitrariness of the world as a principal source of infantile doubt and mistrust.

Table 3
Parallels between Baldwin's and Fowler's Stage Accounts of
Religious Development

Baldwin's stages of religious development	Fowler's stages of faith development
Stage 1 Physical–spontaneous	Stage 1 Intuitive–projective
Stage 2 Intellectual	Stage 2 Mythic–literal
Stage 3a Ethical	Stage 3 Synthetic–conventional
Stage 3b "	Stage 4 Individuating–Reflexive
Stage 4 Aesthetic–religious immediacy	Stage 5 Paradoxical–consolidative
	Stage 6 Universalizing

Baldwin characterizes Stage 2 as intellectual, whereas Fowler designates it *mythic–literal faith*. Despite the very different connotations of these rubrics, they actually describe similar phenomena. Baldwin depicts the child at this stage as being primarily interested in explanations couched in mythic stories about the causal agency of personal or animal agents. In a similar vein, Fowler writes about the mythic world view of this stage:

> No longer does the person experience the world as potentially so capricious, arbitrary or mysterious as before. The person operates with a more dependable understanding of the dispositions, intentions, motives and expectations of others and of oneself. The orderliness or dependability of the (cognitively available) world makes possible a projection of order and intentionality onto a more cosmic theater. (Fowler, 1976, p. 195)

Fowler's unpacking of "intentionality" resonates with Baldwin's discussion of early Stage-2 explanations in terms of personal agency as well as later Stage-2 causal interpretations taking account of an agent's reasons for action.

The third stage for Baldwin as well as for Fowler is characterized by the substitution of conventional beliefs for the spontaneous constructions of earlier periods. For both psychologists, moral development from instrumental hedonism at Stage 2 to respect for conventional morality is associated with transformation to the third religious stage. With this development, Baldwin sees personal inadequacies taking the form of sinfulness before internalized conscience, thereby heightening the need for forgiveness from an ideally good deity. Fowler also notes how God, in theistic expressions of this stage, becomes "the bearer of the role of the 'collective other' who sums up the legitimate expectations and the individual loyalties of the significant others and groups in one's life" (Fowler, 1976, p. 197). Fowler does not discuss sinfulness, but he implies its source when he says that "faith ... functions to sustain ideal self-images and bonds of affiliation with those significant others ... whose expectations, examples and teachings provide orientation" (Fowler, 1976, p. 197). This sounds very much like Baldwin's description of Stage 3 imitation of ideally good charismatic figures.

Baldwin's second period within Stage 3 corresponds to Fowler's Stage 4, *individualizing-reflexive faith*. With further improvement of role-playing, Baldwin argues, conventional moral standards yield to self-legislated ethical principles that impartially take account of all persons affected by a decision. Although human egotism often interferes with consistent moral action in light of these standards, God personifies the highest imaginable moral ideals of character. While Fowler's Stage 4 is less content specific than this theistic description, he also stresses Baldwin's point regarding the new subjection of the conventional religious ethos to the self's own internal standards. "The reference point for validating explanations has shifted from assimilating them to a nurturing ethos (Stage 3) to measuring them and that ethos against one's own experience, values, and critical judgments" (Fowler, 1976, p. 198). Fowler also notes the ideological quality of Stage 4, its concern with inner consistency, integration, and comprehensiveness, features clearly exhibited by Baldwin's discussion of mature theism.

The final stage for Baldwin as for Fowler involves postconventional recognition of the partiality and limitation of traditional symbols, while achieving an immediacy of at-oneness beyond them. Baldwin speaks of a freedom from conventional beliefs made possible by aesthetic imagination. Fowler discusses how much the same liberating function is served by appreciating the beliefs of other groups. Baldwin's immediacy of aesthetic–religious apprehension is echoed in Fowler's discussion of how the Stage 6 subject "is directly and nonmediately aware of the ultimate contexts of life. Symbols and concepts play a secondary function, making communication possible, though inevitably distorting. Stage Six draws on insights and vision from many sources, valuing them as helpful, if partial, apprehensions of Truth" (Fowler, 1976, p. 202). And where Baldwin's religio-aesthetic type integrates the contradictions of ordinary life in a larger vision, so, too, Fowler's Stage 6 embraces "conflict and paradox ... as essential to the integrity of Being," while viewing them as unified in "the oneness of Being" (Fowler, 1976, p. 202). Fowler's highest stage no less than Baldwin's moves beyond paradox to the immediacy of postcritical at-oneness.

Despite these striking ways in which Fowler's work supports some of Baldwin's hypotheses, there are several crucial differences separating their underlying theories. It is to these differences that I now want to turn, with the aim of critiquing each by the other, and, in the process, demonstrating the superiority of some central Baldwinian perspectives.

The most obvious difference is clear from the foregoing comparison, namely, Baldwin's tendency to read theistic content into stages that start off being broadly defined in terms of dependency and mystery. Fowler is more self-conscious and consistent about adhering to the formalist strategy of Piaget and Kohlberg. His stages have the advantage of catching all forms of faith in the developmental net, rather than only a select few. But this is a relatively superficial contrast in comparison with the deeper philosophical and theoretical issues over which Baldwin and Fowler divide. Because these underlying disagreements occur within the same basic paradigm of structural stage analysis, they are particularly instructive, especially at a time when new investigations along developmental lines are being considered.

As we shall see, Baldwin offers alternative assumptions about the nature of faith, the role of nonrational factors in its genesis, and the dynamics of stage change. Where Fowler diverges from Baldwin on these issues, the results are by no means always improvements. True, Fowler offers a more finely tuned analysis of each stage and his research methodology is more sophisticated than Baldwin's. But these improvements do not mean that his most basic assumptions are superior. To the contrary, some of Baldwin's foundational perspectives seem more plausible than Fowler's. Baldwin's theory also fits more closely with the Piagetian–Kohlbergian tradition, from which Fowler deviates significantly, despite professions of loyalty. At the very least, Baldwin's alternative developmental theory highlights controversial features of Fowler's work, while offering valuable resources for reinterpreting some of his interview data.

Fowler focuses his research on *faith*, which is roughly equivalent to Baldwin's sense of dependence, with some of the connotations of mystery. Faith is said to lie at a deeper level in the self than mere belief. One aspect of faith is affective receptivity, "a trust in another, reliance upon another, a counting upon or dependence upon another" (Fowler, 1977, p. 3). The other side of faith involves an active going out-of-the-self in trust and loyalty to someone or some thing, like the commitment side of dependency. Fowler places relatively greater emphasis on this second, dynamic character of faith than Baldwin, who underscores receptivity. Fowler insists, for example, that faith be understood as a verb rather than a noun. *Faithing* is said to be the actual focus of his work.

Fowler characterizes faith in a number of ways. In the first place, faith is always a relational phenomenon; it is a *mode-of-being-in-relation*. That to which faith is directed is variously described as the *transcendent*, or, in less traditionally religious language, as those "sources of power and value which impinge on life in a manner not subject to personal control" (Fowler, 1976, p. 175). Faith is also said to be a way of *knowing*. It is the relational process whereby persons actively construct or construe the totality of the environment in which they live and act. As a way of knowing, faith ties together *affectivity* and *valuing* (the *passional*) with *cognition* (the *rational*). In faith, one emotionally experiences ultimate reality more than one cognitively understands it, although cognition is inevitably involved in a subordinate role. Faith "composes a felt sense of the world as having character, patterns, and unity" (Fowler, 1977, p. 1). In relating persons to the ultimate, faith becomes a central aspect of the self's *guidance system*. It shapes the responses and initiatives a person makes to most experiences, giving consistency to moral character.

Like Baldwin's sense of dependence and mystery, there are two different sets of emotions involved in faith. On the one hand, faith involves respect and admiration for superior forces and powers. On the other, it can also involve fear, awe, even dread. Fowler seems to think that Erikson's work implies that persons tend to develop global, unambivalent dispositions based on one or the other of these polar emotions, in contrast with Baldwin who believes, like Durkheim and Otto, that the holy always engenders doublesided feelings of admiration *and* fear. Fowler's emphasis on unambivalent dispositions appears to be a product of his definition of faith as "a personal piety or pervasive disposition that permeates and gives coherence to all of a person's strivings and responses" (Fowler, 1974c, p. 4). A unitary disposition seems to be required in order to play this integrative role, as the following comment indicates:

> In faith . . . [t]he total self is involved. It may be disposed negatively and hostilely, distrustfully and rebelliously; or, it may be disposed positively—with love, trust, and loyal responsibility. According to Whitehead, "Religion is the transition from God the Void to God the Enemy, and from God the Enemy to God the Companion" (Whitehead, 1960, p. 17). Faith, which often comes to expression in religion, may apprehend the transcendent and one's relation to it in terms either of the Void, the Enemy, or the Companion. (Fowler, 1976, p. 178)
> Enemy, or the Companion. (Fowler, 1976, p. 178)

Fowler not only neglects the doublesided emotions of trust and fear of the holy, there is nothing in his theoretical perspective to account for this doublesidedness that is so central to Baldwin's developmental explanation.

Like Baldwin and other structural developmentalists, Fowler uses primarily formal terms to describe religious faith in order to avoid arbitrarily ruling out non-Western beliefs. However, Fowler is considerably less specific than Baldwin about the nature of the transcendent to which faith directs the self, and herein lies a major problem concerning the focus of his study. Whereas Baldwin limits the object of the religious relationship to a superior being, with at least some vague traces of consciousness and agency, Fowler sees faith expressed toward an exceedingly wide range of objects and fantasies. Sometimes the only limitation on something being transcendent is that it is beyond the believer's personal control (Fowler, 1976, p. 175). Presumably, the laws of physics and biology would thus qualify as transcendent sources of power, although Fowler may intend to exclude such laws by the additional qualification that the sources of power be "more than the mundane" (Fowler, 1976, p. 175). Since Fowler includes secular ideologies as genuine forms of faith, however, it is not clear just how a communist's belief in dialectical materialism, for example, is beyond "the mundane." At other times, faith is said to be directed toward something taken to be "ultimate" in some sense, usually with the implication that the "total self" is devoted to it, as a supreme center of value. Whether ultimacy in a hierarchy of subjective values is sufficient without total psychic commitment, or vice versa, is also unclear. A nation, party, or god might be a supreme value without calling forth thoroughgoing psychic commitment, but Fowler does not appear to recognize this possibility any more than he wrestles with how an ultimate secular value—like a nation—is beyond the mundane.

Fowler's ambiguity regarding that to which faith relates the self derives from the conflicting goals he shares with Baldwin, but treats somewhat differently. On the one hand, Fowler, like Baldwin, wants to study religious faith, an aim which requires a description of the phenomenon that resonates with traditional religious views. On the other hand, again like Baldwin, Fowler wants to define faith broadly enough to include everyone, even professed atheists and agnostics, not to mention plain secularists, who simply do not care about religion enough to even bother professing agnosticism. Baldwin could satisfy these divergent goals without sacrificing clarity about the object of faith being a superior entity with at least some vague traits of personality, because he did not make strong claims about faith operating constantly or functioning to integrate the self or as the self's primary behavioral guidance system. He could see evidence of the persistence of religion in very occasional occult beliefs and practices on the part of persons who were normally nonbelievers. Because Fowler views faith as behaviorally significant loyalty to whatever is adopted as a supreme, integrative value, he cannot be very clear about its precise object, without eliminating significant segments of the population. In other words, Fowler's claim that everyone has faith (in the strong sense that he has in mind) requires him to be extremely vague about its specific direction or object, in contrast with Baldwin, who can be quite specific, because these sentiments can be faint, occasional, and behaviorally insignificant.

In lieu of describing what faith is, Fowler offers various *windows* or *apertures* as indirect means of getting at it. This idea is similar to Wilfred Cantwell Smith's notion that the function of a definition of faith is not to provide necessary and sufficient criteria for identifying the phenomenon, but, rather, to point to a highly personal and unique relationship. For Fowler, as for Smith, various external expressions of faith allow us to infer its inner personal quality (Smith, 1964, p. 168; Fowler, 1974, p. 4). The problem with this approach is that the reader is left with a confused sense of what these windows reveal. Each faith-stage is presented by discussing how the various lenses on it differ from previous or subsequent stages, but this indirect method often leaves one with a sense of mystery about the subject matter being observed. Recent changes in Fowler's treatment of these windows only exacerbate the definitional problem in his research. The five aspects depicted above in Table 2 have been altered (see Table 4 and Fig. 1), and the list has been expanded to include Piaget's cognitive stages and Kohlberg's moral stages. These additional windows, as well as Selman's role-taking stages, are treated as if they reveal as much about faith as "symbolic functioning" and "form of world coherence," although the latter appear to be more basic.[1] Further clarification is obviously needed on the relationship between these several apertures and faith itself.

At some point Fowler will have to relate his windows to a clear

---

[1] Leroy T. Howe makes a similar criticism of Fowler's scoring procedures in an unpublished paper that I recently received. He writes that "it is not wholly clear how we are to construe all of these seven aspects in reference to the one underlying structure which is called faith. On the one hand, Fowler appears to maintain that it is the coordinating of all seven which is constitutive of the structure. On the other hand, those aspects which draw specifically upon the work of Piaget, Selman, and Kohlberg play an ambiguous role in the scoring of the faith development interviews themselves. No score is to be assigned on the Piaget and Kohlberg aspects, and the Selman material undergoes some considerable modification before it is scored. It would seem to me, therefore, that the structure of faith might best be brought into view by reference to the aspects of forms of world coherence, bounds of social awareness, loci of authority, and modes of symbolic functioning, with the stage descriptions thereby generated simply correlated in passing with the stages of cognitive, moral, and role-taking development described by other writers . . . I find myself inclining very strongly in the direction of saying that, given Fowler's own definitions for the word 'faith,' the forms of world coherence and symbolic functioning most especially illuminate the structure as a whole" (Howe, p. 12).

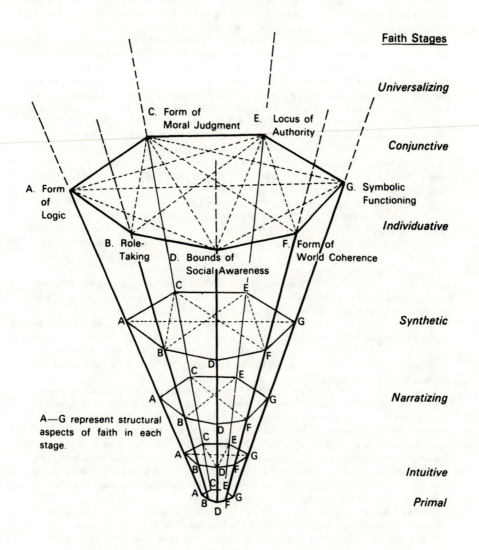

FIG. 1 Structure of Aspects at Stages of Faith Development (from Fowler (1977), with permission).

Table 4
The Revised List of Six Aspects in Fowler's Theory of Faith
Development[a]

Starting now with *Aspect A, the "Form of Logic,"* let us characterize briefly each of the elements indicated in Fig. 1. Our descriptions of the "Form of Logic" build upon Piaget's theory of cognitive stages. This aspect focuses upon the patterns of reasoning and judgement available to the developing person at each cognitive stage. For the equilibrated operational pattern of a given faith stage *fully* to emerge the correlated level of Piagetian cognitive operations must have been developed. Kohlberg and Selman (whose stage theories of perspective-taking and moral judgment are aspects C and B, respectively) claim that the Piaget cognitive levels are *necessary but not sufficient* for the correlated levels of perspective taking and moral judgment. Because of faith's qualification of the logic of rational certainty with a logic of conviction, however, it would be a mistake to assume that cognitive development, as Piaget understands it, always leads in faith stage transitions.[b] When examining accounts of the last three faith stages readers knowledgeable about Piaget's theory will find that we have identified substages in adulthood for Piaget's stage of formal operations. These stylistic variants or substages of formal operations we find to be necessary in order to describe stage-typical patterns in the employment of formal operations in the construction of and reflection upon comprehensive frames of meaning.

Aspect B, "Role-Taking," owes most to the previously mentioned research of Robert Selman on social perspective taking. In the faith stage theory we rely explicitly upon Selman's account of structural stages in perspective taking up to and through our stage 3. Beyond stage 3 we have found it possible and necessary to extend Selman's approach, applying it to persons' abilities to construct the perspectives of their own chosen groups or classes (stage 4), and then of groups, classes, or ideological and convictional traditions other than their own.

Aspect C, the "Form of Moral Judgment," represents an inclusion, with slight modifications based on our data, of Kohlberg's stages of moral reasoning. As will become apparent below there are significant parallels between moral judgment stages and faith stages.

Aspect D, "Grounds of Social Awareness," focuses on the extent of inclusiveness and accuracy of construal of the reference groups in relation to which persons ground their identity and define their moral responsibility. Parallel in some ways to role-taking, this aspect differs in that it attempts to account for the typical range of persons and groups "who count" in one's composition and maintenance of identity and of a meaningful world at each stage.

Aspect E, "Locus of Authority," centers on the patterns of constitutive-knowing and commitment by which persons, ideas, institutions, experiences, and processes of one's own judgment are invested with meaning-sanctioning authority. To whom or what does a person look for validation or legitimation of his or her most significant felt meanings? How is that "locus" constituted: how is it justified? With this aspect we are well into the elements of a logic of conviction. In the domain where the construction and worth of the self are at stake, trust in and loyalty to sources of authorization cannot be accounted for by a logic of rational certainty. In fact, trust in and loyalty to the logic of rational certainty as a comprehensive principle of authority is *itself* a faith position involving risk, judgment and conviction.

We have pointed out that faith reasons in "wholes." *Aspect F, "The Form of World Coherence,"* represents a focus on each stage's particular way of composing and holding a comprehensive sense of unified meanings. This aspect describes a sequence of stage-typical *genres* employed by persons to conceive or represent patterns of coherence in their ultimate environment. In the movement through its successive stages we see in this aspect, in a sensitive way, the reconciliation or integration of the two logics of rational certainty and of conviction.

Much work remains to be done with *Aspect G, "Symbolic Functioning."* It is in this aspect particularly that we must take account of the bihemispheric functioning of thought and imagination in faith. It is with reference to this aspect that that "regression in the service of faith development"

Table 4 (continued)

illumined by psychoanalytic investigators (Meissner, Erikson), and the integration of unconscious elements into consciousness described by Jungian students of faith and individuation (Cunningham, Edinger, Raduka) must be incorporated faithfully. In this aspect particularly, the dynamics of a logic of conviction must be seen as operative with powerful transforming potential for the orientation and functioning of the total psyche. Our present characterization of symbolic functioning at each stage is highly provisional. The theoretical and empirical engagement with this aspect at present constitutes one of the most vital yet difficult growing edges of this project.

[a]Quoted, with permission, from Fowler (1977).

[b]By extension of this point it can be seen why Kohlberg's claim that moral stage transition would "logically" occur prior to, and as a necessary condition for, faith stage transition is theoretically mistaken (see Kohlberg, 1974).

answer to the question, "what is faith?" It would be desirable if, in doing so, he would follow Baldwin's lead by relating his views to contemporary work in the philosophy of religion. Today, this means working with the special perspective of ordinary language philosophy. It is worth noting in this connection that at least some contemporary ordinary language philosophers are in agreement with Baldwin against Fowler that belief in a superior agent of some sort is a necessary criterion of religion. W.D. Hudson (1974), for instance, uses some of the same arguments as Baldwin in support of this position.

This is hardly the place to debate the merits of narrower definitions of religious faith versus broader ones. But there are some distinct advantages to Baldwin's narrower approach, despite the initial plausibility of Fowler's claim that everyone has an affectively laden orientation toward the larger environment in which they live. Baldwin's identification of religion with belief in a personlike deity seems incompatible with his additional claim that everyone is religious in this sense. However, it is worth recalling that impressive psychoanalytic evidence for transference supports Baldwin's supposition (i.e. we spontaneously project deep emotional experiences with significant others onto reality.) In this light, it seems more plausible to suppose with Baldwin and Freud that we all occasionally people the world with superior entities in this way than it is to believe that we integrate our lives around unambivalent dispositions toward ultimate values of some sort that behaviorally affect everything else that we do. Baldwin's greater specificity also makes it easier to identify the psychological factors that influence faith. If the deity is created by projecting our concept of personality, it becomes clearer precisely how Selman's role-taking stages and Kohlberg's moral stages are relevant. We also know that we need to look for psychological theories that account for our concepts of self and other, such as object-relations theory in psychoanalysis.

The narrower, more specific Baldwinian–Freudian notion of how we are all religious differs significantly from the kind of claim that Fowler wants to make about everyone having an affectively and practically significant ultimate value of some sort that is tied into a world view of some kind. The supposition that everyone has faith in this Fowlerian sense may too easily erase the very real differences between persons who have a picture of living in a world governed by a transcendent God and those who have no such perspective. Certainly, it is an important empirical issue that Fowler's broadly inclusive definition masks whether there are significant structural differences, and not just differences in beliefs, between religious adherents and nonadherents. It is possible, for example, that the lives of religious believers are more integrated around "ultimate sources of power, value and meaning" than the lives of those many secularists, who are not committed to movements like fascism and communism. The advantages of Fowler's inclusive stategy for comparing similarities between religionists and nonbelievers may be bought at the cost of ignoring significant differences that Baldwin's narrower definition of what it means to be religious would help isolate.

Baldwin and Fowler both emphasize the importance of the emotions in faith-knowing, but their place in the constitution of the psyche is not the same.[2] In Baldwin's model, the affections are part of "practical reason," which uses cognition in its imaginative construc-

---

[2] If faith is as deeply noncognitive as Baldwin and Fowler both suppose, designing an appropriate research strategy is bound to be difficult. Baldwin skirted this issue only by avoiding much firsthand empirical study. Fowler is at least grappling with research problems. But his reliance on single interviews lasting no more than 3 hours raises serious problems about the adequacy of his procedures, given what he takes faith to be. One wonders, for example, how verbal responses during such a short time-span can possibly reveal deeply noncognitive presuppositions and commitments. If faith is not to be confused with cognitive beliefs as Fowler himself so vigorously contends, why employ an interview technique that taps precisely these sorts of responses? Prima facie, these methods of eliciting deep emotional responses would appear to offer better windows on faith than the cognitive responses with which Fowler in fact works. Certainly, they are apt to reveal more about faith itself than the so-called windows that Fowler borrows from Piaget, Kohlberg, and Selman, namely, short-form tests identifying an interviewee's cognitive, moral, and role-taking stages. If faith is exhibited primarily by actual behavior, as its role as the self's primary "guidance system" suggests, Fowler's method would appear to offer little reliable information about the congruence between what interviewees say and what they do. Whatever is postulated on this score must be purely speculative on Fowler's part.

tions, while differing from theoretical reason in motivation and functioning. For Fowler, the emotions, or at least the central ones involved in faith, are placed, to use a spatial metaphor, not alongside theoretical reason, but *underneath* all psychic functions. In taking up this model, Fowler self-consciously sides with that theological tradition stemming from Augustine and including Luther in which *will* and *reason* are seen as serving the dominant affections or loves of a person. Faith does not result from consciousness and/or volition, but underlies them, motivating their use and direction.

From this vantage point, Piaget is turned on his head, with the argument that thinking and willing are always qualified by the specific affection that pervades the whole person–world polarity (Fowler, 1974c, p. 5). It is scarcely surprising, therefore, to find Fowler qualifying his claims about the congruence of his own structural-developmental work with that of Piaget. "I cannot adopt the Piagetian theoretical separation of cognition and affection, of reason and emotion, but rather have to account for their interpenetration in the dynamics of faith" (Fowler, 1978, p. 28). Positively, this implies a "sharp qualification of rationality by unconscious dynamics" (Fowler, 1978, p. 27). In a similar vein, Kohlberg's moral stages are said to rest not on rational reflection and role-taking alone, but on broader, noncognitive convictions and loyalties.

> Every principle of moral action serves some center or centers of value. Even the appeals to autonomy, rationality and universality as justifications for Stage Six morality are not made *prior* to faith. Rather they are expressions of faith—expressions of trust in and loyalty to the valued attributes of autonomy and rationality, and to the valued ideal of a universal commonwealth of being. (Fowler, 1976, p.209)

Apparently it did not occur to Fowler until recently that dissatisfaction with Piaget's (Kantian) dismissal of the affections as mere "motive-forces" does not require this drastic a remedy. Baldwin's middle position recognizes both the autonomy of theoretical reason from, and its occasional dominance over, affective dynamics for some purposes, as well as the decisive lead of the affections on other occasions. Baldwin's sharp distinction between theoretical and practical reason is admittedly dated, but it allows him to avoid choosing between overly cognitive and noncognitive images of the person. Recent support for this mediating position has come from ego psychologists who continue to recognize the significance of primary process, while acknowledging a relatively autonomous ego sphere. To his credit, Fowler hs recently modified the primacy granted the affections in his earlier writings. He now wants to expand Piaget's "truncated notion of cognition" in order to recognize that "there is no thought without feeling and no feeling without thought" (Fowler, 1977, pp. 9–10). The question remains, however, whether this new formulation will enable Fowler to do justice to the ways we construct our milieu by shuttling back and forth between cognitive operations and affective associations.

Whereas Baldwin takes self-integration as an ideal goal that is seldom achieved, Fowler begins with the premise that the self is already well integrated by faith commitments. Fowler rests his case largely on the evidence of depth-psychology (by which he means Erikson), but he ignores considerable clinical evidence of the self-divisions created by defense mechanisms and psychopathologies. Baldwin seems closer to ordinary experience and psychiatric findings in noting a frequent antinomy between theoretical beliefs and affective-intentional constructs. In fact, Fowler's own interview data reveal tensions between modern scientific theories and fantastic myths about Adam and Eve, Noah, and the like. Empirical doubts are thus raised about the harmony in world view that Fowler posits as an essential characteristic of faith, at each stage of development.

Baldwin and Fowler both write about the involvement of the *total self* in faith. But they mean something different by it. The act of faith for Baldwin draws upon all aspects of the self—emotions, reason, and volition—in a constructive movement of practical imagination. But this does not mean that the full capacities of the agent in any of these spheres are necessarily involved. Theoretical reason, for example, may form doubts about these imaginative constructs. The whole self is engaged only in the sense that all major aspects of the person are involved to some degree. Fowler sets forth the much stronger thesis that the act of faith actually unifies the self in its entirety, that is, there is no dimension of the self that stands back from the commitment. A disposition is consequently forged that reverberates throughout everything else that the person does. In the words of Richard R. Niebuhr, "Affective faith is an awakening, a suffering of a whole frame of mind that endows the individual with a resonance lying at the foundations of his existence. It qualifies all of his interaction with other men, with himself, and with his near and ultimate environment" (Niebuhr, 1972, p. 47; Fowler, 1974c, p. 5). If an underlying unification of the total self is Fowler's view, it would appear to be challenged by psychoanalytic and behaviorist evidence that a person may vacillate between trust and mistrust, hope and despair. A person may feel trusting and hopeful toward the universe in some situation (like the neutral context of an interview), while experiencing the world of other persons and institutions as hostile or malevolent on other specific occasions.

Fowler would presumably interpret such compartmentalized

responses as falling outside what he means by faith. But how, then, does faith, as a unifying experience of the total personality, deal with radically different "felt" experiences of the whole of reality in different situations? Is faith not present for those who experience the world in these ways? If not, Fowler's inclusion of all persons in his definitional net fails. If faith is present, how is the total self engaged? Fowler's assumption that faith is a unifying commitment reverberating throughout every aspect of the true believer's life appears to derive primarily from his own Protestant background. If Fowler wants to defend this point on psychological grounds, he will have to grapple with a number of recent psychological studies that seriously question the degree of intrapsychic consistency between affect, judgment, and behavior that he simply presupposes (see Bandura and Walters, 1963; Mischel, 1973; Mischel & Mischel, in Lickona, 1976, Chap. 5; and Rosenhan, Moore & Underwood, in Lickona, 1976, Chap. 13). According to these studies our ordinary assumptions about self-consistency may derive from defensive use of cognitive processes, such as selective perception and elimination of discrepancy (Festinger, 1957), to preserve a favorable self-image, when faced with contradictory thoughts, emotions, and actions. In short, the self-consistency that Fowler presupposes may be a self-serving illusion whereby the self identifies with selected experiences to the exclusion of others. It may be sufficient for Fowler's purposes that the self identifies itself as centered on ultimate values, despite such illusions, but, then, some further clarification of what is meant by the involvement of the total self is required (not to mention critical discussion of the self-concept).

The dynamics of stage change is the final major issue dividing Baldwin and Fowler. Baldwin, like Piaget and Kohlberg after him, is quite precise about the processes motivating stage changes. Moral transformations precede religious ones for Baldwin, because a god is always constructed in light of the believer's self-other concepts and moral convictions. Fowler is not only less specific about the dynamics motivating faith-stage changes, it is exceedingly difficult to ascertain what this theory is, given the presence of two contradictory positions in his writings. On the one hand, faith change is viewed as a consequence of changes in variables such as cognition, role-playing, morality, and participation in cultural symbols. Piaget's cognitive stages, for example, are said to be necessary, but not sufficient conditions, for correlative faith-stages (Fowler, 1978, p. 31). On the other hand, Fowler's notion that the affections of faith qualify and direct cognition and morality appears to imply that faith changes precede those in the variables, aspects, or apertures. Fowler argues in this vein against Kohlberg's updated version of Baldwin's argument that faith is a development following morality. "It is a mistake," he writes, "to assume that faith is or must be an *a posteriori* derivation of or justification for morality, the appeal to Kant notwithstanding. In fact, I would argue conversely, that . . . there is . . . always a faith framework or matrix encompassing and supporting the motive to be moral and the exercise of moral logic. This is the case, I hold, at *each* stage of development" (Fowler, 1976, p. 209). Fowler goes on to make a case for the primacy of loyalty to a center or centers of value in moral development, but he provides no hints about how faith itself develops, beyond occasional references to assimilation and accommodation. He thus avoids the centerpiece of any psychological theory by associating himself with structural developmentalism, but neglecting the mechanisms by which simple structures are transformed into increasingly more complex wholes.

The main reason for this surprising neglect of the specific dynamics of faith change derives, I suspect, from Fowler's desire to be a theologian as well as a psychologist. The theologian in him wants to see faith developing in relationship to the Transcendent itself, and not as a mere human construction, as Baldwin saw it, at least prior to the final aesthetic intuition where Baldwin too turns into a theologian. In Fowler's confessional words,

> I am convicted of the actuality, the *a priori* reality, of a transcendent source and center of being, value and power. I am convicted of the belief that human beings are ontically shaped for participation in and realization in their lives of this transcendent being, value and power. Further I am convicted that this source and center exerts, in manifold ways, an attraction, a valence, a drawing into itself of our hunger for excellence of being. (Fowler, 1974c, p. 10)

The stages of faith are thus a set of procedures by which people try to "apprehend" that which is genuinely transcendent. But there is a serious question whether Fowler's own faith does not finally undermine his psychological theory, in the sense that he shies away from discussing psychological dynamics that might threaten the genuineness of faith's intuitions.

It is rather awkward, after all, to hold that faith is a genuine apprehension of transcendent reality at the same time that one explains precisely how it arises developmentally. This problem does not arise for Piaget and Kohlberg, because cognition and morality do not exist as external realities to be apprehended. It is otherwise with faith. The *apprehending* that is done in Fowler's faith carries the sense of being grasped by something outside oneself, while also meaning the name for an act of a subject. And it is this state of being affected by the transcendent that the theologian in Fowler resists explaining, lest he explain it away. Baldwin was no less worried about reductionism, but he was willing to explain the early stages of religion on purely psychological grounds, partly, it would seem, because he saved up one big intuition for his final stage. But Fowler wants to affirm the genuineness of the relationship to the transcendent at each stage, perhaps to avoid the elitism associated with the kind of mysticism that Baldwin embraces. My worry is that Fowler's theological position will preclude thorough formulation of the psychological dynamics involved in faith construction. I take it that this is another reason why faith is defined so vaguely and explanation is limited to the several "windows" on it. Baldwin's more specific identification of his subject matter as a personality-eject enables him to advance explanations beyond the point at which Fowler appears to have stopped.

Baldwin's personal theology, however, also mars his work as a psychologist of religion. There can be little doubt, for example, that his final, intuitive-aesthetic stage is dictated more by his personal *Weltanschauung* than by formal criteria of development. And probably no aspect of Baldwin's theory of religion grates more sharply than his claim that achievement of this mystical stage is required for full human flourishing. Fowler's final stage is refreshingly ambiguous by comparison and less clearly identified with a particular philosophical-theological resolution. Nonetheless, Fowler also uses his stage theory, albeit in a different way, as an apology for traditional forms of faith. On those occasions when Fowler introjects very traditional terms for the object of faith (e.g., the transcendent and the ultimate), he implies that everyone is really trying—however unsuccessfully in the case of atheists, agnostics, and secularists—to relate themselves to the God of traditional religion. In other words, Fowler's theological convictions surface with terminological shifts that make the nonbeliever appear mistaken, whatever his stage.

On the whole, Baldwin's theory of religion even when compared with Fowler's recent bold extension of Kohlberg's work, remains enormously suggestive, despite its theological bias, somewhat archaic language, and quaint examples. His definition of religion remains plausible, and his stages appear to be far more accurate than one would have supposed. The general framework of Baldwin's theory of religion remains worthy of careful attention, particularly its focus on the problem of explaining personality ejects. Today, several different psychological and sociological theories are required to explain the formation and projection of self-other representations (e.g., Selman's role-taking theory, Kohlberg's moral stages, object-relations theory), but Baldwin's pioneering structural developmentalist approach provides some important clues as to how these diverse perspectives might be integrated. In most fields, the enduring value of innovative work of this sort qualifies a work for classical status, although, in Baldwin's case, unfortunately, we are only beginning to appreciate the profundity of his contributions.[3]

REFERENCES

Baldwin, J.M. (Ed.) *Dictionary of philosophy and psychology* (3 vols.) New York: Macmillan, 1901–1905.

Baldwin, J.M. Sketch of the history of psychology. *Psychological Review,* 1905, *12,* 144–65.

Baldwin, J.M. *Social and ethical interpretations in mental development: A study in social psychology,* 4th edn. New York: Macmillan Co., 1906.

Baldwin, J.M. *Darwin and the humanities.* Baltimore: Review Pub., 1909.

Baldwin, J.M. *Thought and things* (Vol. 3.) New York: Macmillan, 1911.

Baldwin, J.M. *Genetic theory of reality.* New York: G.P. Putnam's Sons, 1915.

Baldwin, J.M. James Mark Baldwin. In C. Murchison (Ed.), *The history of psychology in autobiography* (vol. 1). New York: Russell & Russell, 1961 (1930).

Bandura, A., & Walters, R.H. *Social learning and personality development.* New York: Holt, Rinehart, & Winston, 1963.

Bellah, R. *Beyond belief.* New York: Harper & Row, 1970.

Berger, P.L. *The sacred canopy.* Garden City, N.Y.: Doubleday, 1967.

Berger, P.L. & Luckmann, T. *The social construction of reality.* Garden City, N.Y.: Doubleday, 1966.

Durkheim, E. *The elementary forms of the religious life* [1912]. New York: Free Press, 1965.

Erikson, E. *Identity: Youth and crisis.* New York: Norton, 1968.

Erikson, E. *Young man Luther.* New York: Norton, 1958.

Erikson, E. *Gandhi's truth.* New York: Norton, 1969.

Festinger, L. *A theory of cognitive dissonance.* Stanford, Ca.: Stanford Univ. Press, 1957.

Fowler, J. *To see the kingdom: The theological vision of H. Richard* Niebuhr. Nashville, Tenn.: Abingdon Press, 1974a.

Fowler, J. Toward a developmental perspective on faith. *Religious Education,* 1974(b), *49,* 207–219.

Fowler, J. Faith, liberation, and human development: Three lectures. *The Foundation, 79.* Atlanta, Ga.: Gammon Theological Seminary, 1974(c).

Fowler, J. Faith development theory and the aims of religious socialization. Paper presented at the annual meeting of the Religious Research Association. Milwaukee, Wisconsin, October 24–26, 1975.

Fowler, J. Stages in faith: The structural-developmental approach. In T.C. Hennessy (Ed.), *Values and moral development.* New York: Paulist Press, 1976.

Fowler, J. Faith and the structuring of meaning. Paper presented at Section

---

[3] For further critical discussion of Fowler's (as well as my own) views on the relationship between morality and religion, see Wallwork (1980, pp. 269–297).

39 of the Convention of the American Psychological Assn. San Francisco, Calif., August 26, 1977.

Fowler, J. Mapping faith structures: A developmental overview. In J.W. Fowler & Sam Keen, *Life-maps: The human journey of faith.* Waco: Word Books, 1978.

Freud, S. *Totem and taboo* [1913]. New York: Random House, 1946.

Freud, S. *Future of an illusion* [1927]. Garden City, N.Y.: Doubleday, 1944.

Freud, S. *New introductory lectures* [1932]. New York: Norton, 1975.

Geertz, C. Religion as a cultural system. In M. Banton (Ed.), *Anthropological approaches to the study of religion.* London: Tavistock Press, 1966.

Giddings, F.H. The psychology of society. *Science, 9* (1899). 16.

Goldman, R. *Religious thinking from childhood to adolescence.* New York: Seabury Press, 1968.

Hartmann, H. *Ego psychology and the problem of adaptation.* New York: International Universities Press, 1958.

Hegel, G.W.F. *The phenomenology of spirit* (A.V. Miller, trans.) Oxford: Clarendon Press, 1977.

Howe, L.T. Conversion, growth, and stage sequences in faith development. Unpublished paper.

Hudson, W.D. *A philosophical approach to religion.* London: MacMillan, 1974.

Hume, D. *The natural history of religion.* Stanford: Stanford Univ. Press, 1956.

James, W. *Varieties of religious experience.* New York: New American Library, 1958.

Johnson, R., & Wallwork, E. *Critical issues in modern religion.* Englewood Cliffs, N.J.: Prentice-Hall, 1973.

Kant, I. *Religion within the limits of reason alone.* New York Harper & Row, 1960.

Kohlberg, L. Education, moral development and faith. *Journal of Moral Education,* 1974, *4,* 5–16.

Lévy-Bruhl, L. *How natives think.* New York: Knopf, 1926.

Lickona, T. (Ed.). *Moral development and behavior.* New York: Holt, Rinehart & Winston, 1976.

Marx, K. & Engels, F. *Karl Marx and Friedrich Engels on religion.* New York: Schocken Books, 1964.

Mischel, W. Toward a cognitive social learning reconceptualization of personality. *Psychological Review,* 1973, *80,* 252–283.

Niebuhr, H.R. *Radical monotheism and western culture.* New York: Harper & Brothers, 1960.

Niebuhr, R. R. *Experiential religion.* New York: Harper & Row, 1972.

Otto, R. *The idea of the holy.* London: Oxford Univ. Press, 1923.

Outka, G., & Reeder, J. (Eds.). *Religion and morality.* Garden City, N.Y.: Doubleday, 1973.

Paulsen, F. *Introduction to philosophy.* New York: Henry Holt, 1930.

Parsons, T. *The structure of social action.* Glencoe, Ill.: The Free Press, 1949.

Parsons, T. *Societies: Evolutionary and comparative perspectives.* Englewood Cliffs, N.J.: Prentice-Hall, 1966.

Quillian, W.F. *The moral theory of evolutionary naturalism.* New Haven, Conn.: Yale Univ. Press, 1945.

Ramsey, P. (Ed.). *Faith and ethics.* New York: Harper & Row, Torchbook, 1957.

Schleiermacher, F. *The christian faith* (Vol. 1). New York: Harper & Row, Torchbook, 1963.

Smith, W.C. *The meaning and end of religion.* New York: Mentor Books, 1964.

Spencer, H. *The principles of sociology.* New York: D. Appleton, 1896.

Tillich, P. *The courage to be.* New Haven, Conn.: Yale Univ. Press, 1952.

Tillich, P. *The dynamics of faith.* New York: Harper & Row, 1958.

Troeltsch, E. *The social teachings of the christian churches* (Vols. 1 & 2). New York: Harper & Row, 1960.

Tylor, Sir E.B. *Primitive cultures,* (Vols 1 & 2). London: J. Murray, 3rd ed., 1891.

Wallwork, E. *Durkheim: morality and milieu.* Cambridge, Mass.: Harvard Univ. Press, 1972.

Wallwork, E. Morality, religion and Kohlberg's theory. In B. Munsey (Ed.), *Moral development, moral education and Kohlberg.* Birmingham, Ala.: Religious Education Press, 1980.

Weber, M. The sociology of religion. Boston: Beacon Press, 1963.

Wundt, W. *Völkerpsychologie* (Vols. 1&2). Leipzig: W. Engelmann, 1900–09.

11

AESTHETIC DEVELOPMENT

Michael Parsons
University of Utah

The following essay aims to give an account of James Mark Baldwin's ideas concerning the aesthetic development of individuals. The topic plays an important part in Baldwin's psychology and his philosophy. No other cognitive-developmental psychologist has paid nearly as much attention to aesthetic experience as he did. One reason for this is the great scope of his ambition, which was to trace the development of mind in general, that is, of each of the modes of experience that characterizes a mature person's mentality. In his scheme, there were three major modes of experience: scientific, moral, and aesthetic. Among these three similarities and dissimilarities can be discerned.

One way to approach the subject of aesthetic experience is to consider it as a separate topic in its own right and to describe sequential stages of development within it. This is similar to what Piaget and Kohlberg have done with scientific and moral develpment. It is one of the approaches that Baldwin adopted, and I will give an account of his conclusions later in this essay. In addition, one can relate these stages of aesthetic development to stages in the development of the self, which for Baldwin is the central or organizing aspect of mental development as a whole. Baldwin established this relationship to stages of the self for the aesthetic as well as for the scientific and moral modes of experience, and in doing so he entwined the three strands together into one rope. This procedure again implies a parallelism between the three modes. While an account of the whole rope is well beyond the scope of the present essay, the relation between the stages of aesthetic development and those of the cognitive core will be described later.

However, Baldwin has another and grander way of relating these three modes together, one which stresses the noncorrespondences between them and which gives to aesthetic experience a peculiar significance in his scheme. It seems best to deal with this first, albeit in a sketchy way (since it is not the primary focus of this paper). This will provide some context for the development to be discussed later and will facilitate some initial remarks about Baldwin's conception of aesthetic experience. Then there will follow a brief discussion of both the nature of aesthetic experience and its role in Baldwin's psychology, lest questions of this sort become dragons at the mouth of the cave.

I

Pancalism

Baldwin's grandest way of relating the three major modes of experience consists in a doctrine which he labels *pancalism*, a characteristic neologism which forms the motto for his *magnum opus*, *Thought and Things*. Briefly, it is the doctrine that in aesthetic experience we have a better, i.e., more comprehensive, grasp of reality than we can have in either of the other two modes. This view puts him in the great tradition of German idealist aesthetics. It can be seen, for instance, as a restatement of the central view of Schiller's *Education of Man*, though the argument for it is more psychological and less metaphysical than is Schiller's. In a very general way, Baldwin might be said to rework the conclusions of idealist aesthetics from a genetic point of view.

The argument for pancalism requires a brief statement of Baldwin's general theory of the development of mind. In the first experience of a baby, there is no dualism, no sense of mind as against matter, of values as against facts, nor, more basically, of self as against not-self. Experience is all of one kind, unmediated, nonconceptual, only of objects taken as natural. Baldwin calls this beginning phase simply *adualistic*.

Very soon, however, dualisms begin to arise within experience; a world of meanings and ideas begins to be, side by side with the world of natural objects. The creation of this symbolic world, is, by and large, the work of imagination, which detaches images from the perception of natural objects and plays with them "experimentally." These two worlds are the beginning of dualism in human experience.

They are experienced as a question of control, a question as to whether the natural or the symbolic world is at any particular time in control of experience, i.e., determining its direction and character. The control of the symbolic world comes to be taken as *self*, contrasted with the control of the world of natural objects, the *not-self*. This self/not-self distinction has its own development in the individual, a development which is central to the whole development of mind, and which is discussed in detail elsewhere in this volume. The important point for our purpose is that the development of the self, and therefore, of the mind in general, requires the elaboration of dualisms. In effect, self creates itself by setting up the contrast with the not-self; mind needs a world of objects for its emergence. This is one of the great insights of the idealist tradition, though there it was usually treated as a matter of metaphysics and not of psychology.

A great deal of our experience is therefore dualistic, and both science and morality are outcomes of dualism. They both acknowledge the existence of the two worlds, the natural and the symbolic, and both are motivated by the need to resolve the tension between them. Science achieves this resolution by accepting as ultimate the control of the world of natural objects, morality, that of the world of ideas. Both resolutions are stable but partial, since they are achieved by exclusion. This exclusion is itself felt as a part of experience. The scientist can say, "This is the way the reality is." But he is aware that as a scientist, he can say nothing about how it *should* be, because, as a scientist he has already accepted the control of the natural world as arbiter of judgments of reality. The reverse is true of the moralist: he can say how the world should be, but is aware that saying so does not make it so, and that as a moralist he cannot determine how to make it so. Both, therefore, offer a grasp of reality, but one which is partial and in complementary ways. Hence, according to Baldwin, the long dispute in the history of philosophy as to which is most real, the world of natural objects or the world of ideas.

Baldwin asks: Is there a way to "overcome" the dualisms? That is, is there a mode of experience which is nondualistic, but which supercedes rather than precedes the stages of dualism? Is there a mode which is postdualistic in that it does not ignore, but rather profits from, the results of dualism and can use all the judgments which dualisms have made possible? His answer is that mature aesthetic experience does this. It can do this because an aesthetic object perfectly unites the two worlds; it is both a natural object made wholly significant, and an idea perfectly embodied in a natural object.

The perfection of this match is important. In dualistic experience the two worlds are matched, but never perfectly so. In science, some of the features of a natural object can be explained by theory. But there are always features that escape the theory, and the theory is never perfectly exemplified by the natural object, since the theory is general and the object is particular. In morality there is an ideal which can be partially embodied in the actual world but which always transcends it, because everything actual is subject to change and decay. An aesthetic object, in contrast, is a case of complete fusion of the two worlds; an object every aspect of which is significant, and an idea wholly embodied in some natural object. Both controls therefore are allowed full play. The self can find itself fully in an aesthetic object, while at the same time all the claims of the not-self are acknowledged. Therefore it allows, according to Baldwin, maximal satisfaction of the psychological motives which led in the first place to dualism, as well as of the specific aesthetic motive. Putting it another way, there is nothing an aesthetic object cannot include in its constitution; it can include any and all of the judgments of science and morality and put them to use as its own ingredients. It creates not by exclusion but by inclusion, and so is a more comprehensive apprehension of reality.

This, briefly, is Baldwin's argument for the doctrine of *pancalism*. It is worth noting that the idea of the perfect synthesis of natural and symbolic world is at the heart of the idealist tradition and is a traditional account of the aesthetic object. There is a similar notion, for example, in Dewey's *Art as Experience*, where what he calls an *experience* refers to the felt significance of experience perfectly expressed in some material object or sequence of events. Dewey says that human experience naturally strives toward that state. Since the precepts of pancalism have already been summarized in Wallwork's chapter, I shall say no more about the doctrine here, but a number of points can now be made about Baldwin's use of the concept of aesthetic experience.

The role of the concept of aesthetic experience

The primary concept in Baldwin's philosophy and psychology is not art nor work of art; it is *aesthetic experience.* In the same way, he studies moral *experience*, rather than individual acts of morality. This, or course, is not because he is a psychologist, but because he comes from an idealist background. He takes *experience* as the most encompassing fact of human life; and he distinguishes modes of experience from one another in terms of the peculiar qualities and interests that characterize them.

I will present Baldwin's definition of the qualities and interests that make experience aesthetic in a moment. Given this definition, or any such definition, one can thus derive the idea of *art*: anything that is an object of interest in aesthetic experience is an aesthetic object, and anything that is made deliberately to serve as an aesthetic object is a work of art. Many things can be aesthetic objects: mountains, driftwood, urinals, and so on. The complete list would include symphonies, dances, paintings, poems. The chief difference is that the latter things are likely to be more satisfactory as aesthetic objects because they are created for the purpose.

The focus on aesthetic experience is of great importance in facilitating the construction of a scheme of aesthetic development. One of its virtues is its unifying and simplifying power. There are, after all, many different arts and art media. The differences among them are very striking and obvious; what they have in common is not. In fact, it was not until the eighteenth century that music, literature, and painting were commonly grouped together as arts and distinguished from crafts and other activities. To the eye of common sense, the most important thing about an art form is the character of the medium, and most studies of children's aesthetic abilities or developmental histories have dealt with their abilities to work in a particular medium. They rarely speak of things aesthetic at all; instead, they concentrate on abilities in individual art forms. This common-sense, nontheoretical approach usually obtains results which are dubiously relevant to aesthetic concerns. (See, for example, Golomb, 1974; Moore, 1973; Gardner et al., 1972, 1975; Botvin & Sutton-Smith, 1977; Kellogg, 1969; Lowenfeld & Brittain, 1970; and DiLeo, 1970.) Even those psychologists who have thought about questions of generalizing across media (e.g. Werner & Kaplan, 1963) have thought in nonaesthetic terms, such as the generalization of the concept of a diagonal (Olson, 1970).

In contrast, Baldwin's view is that the various arts have in common the aim of producing aesthetic experience. Hence, that notion is a key organizer to get at both what is important about the arts and what is important about chidren's development in the area. Without it, one might well find stages of the development of something, but it is unlikely to have much to do with what makes art art or to generalize across the arts. We may study, for instance, the development of the ability to draw five fingers on each hand when drawing people, the ability to mix and match colors, to recognize styles, to remember tunes, or to think of many uses for a house brick. None of these abilities have centrally to do with anything aesthetic. Baldwin, as far as I know, is unique among psychologists, until very recently, in choosing to define his unit of investigation as aesthetic experience.

The concept generalizes across another set of distinctions in the same way. There are a number of different roles in connection with the arts: artist, audience member, and critic, to name a few. The differences between these roles are also very striking at first glance. They appear to consist in quite different activities, and many psychologists have assumed that they therefore call for quite different abilities. It has, for example, been argued that only the abilities of the art critic can be expected to show a cognitive-developmental character, but not those of the artist or the audience member (Gardner, 1973). This is because criticism alone seems to require "formal–operational" skills (e.g., the comparison and the relation of particulars to abstract principles). Also, many studies have dealt with children's creative abilities in different art forms, albeit studies conducted without reference to their appreciation (e.g., the strong tradition of studying the development of children's drawings in Werner & Kaplan, 1963, DiLeo, 1970, and Olson, 1970).

Baldwin's view, however—and it is part of the idealist tradition—is that these roles (artist, audience, critic) have in common what is most significant about them: they are all concerned with a particular aesthetic experience. Nor is their relationship to this experience relevantly very different. The artist as s/he creates a work must constantly look at it and respond to it, i.e., engage in the activity we would attribute to an audience member. The audience member, on the other hand, must recreate for himself the significance of the work and its parts as he perceives it, in a mental activity essentially similar (if a little more guided) to that of the artist. The critic must do the same thing; he must, perhaps, engage in the experience more fully, allowing it to come to a point of articulation and judgment. What is aesthetic about the experience, however, is what all three have in common: the act of experiencing the character and qualities of the aesthetic object.

A further benefit of the notion of aesthetic experience is that it enables one to consider responding and judging together, not as incompatible activities or as unrelated. Instead, they are both a part of experience. Aesthetic experience begins with perception, includes feeling, and moves toward explicit judgment. Nor are these different activities, but rather they are interpenetrating phases of the same activity. Judgment is already inherent in perception and in feeling; feeling is implied by judgment; and so on. For example, one sees an object as sad or lonely, as strident or exultant; this involves perception, feeling, and judgment. The same remark would be true of moral experience: to feel guilty is implicitly to judge one's act as morally wrong, and so on. It seems to follow that it would be best not to study the development of judgment alone, since stages of judgment would also be stages of something broader (i.e., experience). This interpenetration of judgment and experience is perhaps most obvious in the case of aesthetics; but it is equally true of moral or scientific experience. In Baldwin's scheme, the units of study are scientific experience, moral experience, and aesthetic experience. All three are parallel in that they comprehend both the judgmental and the feeling sides of mental life, both cognitive and affective. This is a basic strength of cognitive-developmental psychology, and it seems to derive from this use of the notion of experience.

The Objectivity of Aesthetic Judgments

The question whether, and in what sense, aesthetic judgments can be objective is a familiar enough topic of discussion. From what has already been said, it is clear that Baldwin believes that they are objective in just the same way judgments in science and morality are objective. This is implied in the view that aesthetic experience offers a grasp of reality: if objectivity in some sense were not possible, the grasp of reality would necessarily be illusory. It seems worth explaining briefly how Baldwin thinks this process works and why it is important for psychologists.

The elements of an aesthetic object are both sensory and ideational, but they constitute a whole because they are organized. To say they are *organized* is to say they relate to each other in a way that "fits". This fittingness of the elements with each other produces a strong sense of the unity of the object and is called *form*. The internal relations of the elements of the aesthetic object are seen as complete: everything is there that is fit, and nothing that is not. The obverse of this is a sense of isolation, or unrelatedness, to things external to the object. Because the internal relations are complete, there is no need to relate the object to the surrounding circumstances. It is isolated, detached, from its surroundings, and we can attend to it by itself, for itself. In this detachment of the object from its circumstances, Baldwin believes, control passes from the external to the internal. *Internal* here has two simultaneous senses: internal to the object and internal to the person experiencing it.

On the one hand, experience is directed by the internal relations of the elements of the object, as they are actually perceived to be. These relations are taken as given, as facts which must be acknowledged. What fits or doesn't fit is not determined by whimsy, or desire, anymore than in scientific or moral judgments. Aesthetic judgments are based on the facts about the aesthetic object. There are tests and standards to eliminate idiosyncrasy in determining what is factual and relevant, just as there are in science and morality. These tests amount to an appeal to what is phenomenally objective in perception, i.e., to whatever appears as a property of the object when closely attended to. Admittedly, such tests are rather nontechnical and may not settle close cases. But there certainly are many clear cases: for example, Picasso's *Guernica* is not, factually speaking, a happy work, nor is the fact that it is worth one million dollars relevant to its aesthetic character. So we may say that, phenomenally, *control* of the aesthetic experience lies in the character of the object.

On the other hand, the control is also, and simultaneously, in the person. The person creates the object (whether s/he is artist, perceiver, or critic) because *the sense* of fittingness and unfittingness must come from within the person, must be, as Baldwin many times puts it, "read into" the object from the inner life of the perceiver. He thinks this is obviously true, as we shall see, of any feelings "read into" the object, as well as of the form found within it. This reading in, however, is not done consciously, nor is it susceptible of deliberate control. The point is that form, in a successful aesthetic object, is both what *ought* to be (i.e., what would be most fitting) and what *is* (i.e., the factual fittingness in the object). Hence the control is dual, which is why the experience is completed by inclusion and not exclusion of any possible considerations.

Psychologically, no doubt there is an interplay in that the mind picks up suggestions from the work, develops them, and tests them out on the work again. Phenomenally, the work is experienced as suggesting or demanding some responses, refusing others. Fittingness is found in the work, and it establishes what is to be relevant. Hence, object judgments are just as possible in aesthetics as in logic or morality. The expressive character of a work of art is experienced as a character of the object, and not of the self; and therefore is experienced as being there for anyone who looks. A judgment that a poem is joyous, for example, is a judgment that everyone would find it to be joyous, *if* they read it in the right circumstances, and *if* they had the abilities to understand it and to perceive it objectively.

The qualifications in this last sentence are important. The experience is that the joyousness is there for anyone to find; it does not matter whether anyone else actually finds it. That is, the judgment is not that others *do* agree, only that they *would* agree, *if*, etc. Aesthetic judgments are again parallel to other kinds. A scientist announcing a new theory does not suppose that others do agree with him, but that they would agree with him, *if* they had the relevant evidence, the proper understanding, and followed the appropriate logic, etc. In this sense, his judgment is objective even though he continues to be a lonely voice in a scientific dispute; it is not merely a personal preference because no one else agrees with it. Baldwin's word for this character of judgments is *synnomic* and the idea is obviously important. In the attempt to explain the growth of cognition from a Darwinist point of view, Baldwin necessarily stresses its social character. Human mentality is essentially social in that it requires interaction with others for it to be. Also, scientific, moral, and aesthetic judgments are necessarily social, because they must pass through a consensual stage in which correctness is understood as consisting in the consensus of one's society. This is necessary if one is ever to understand one's own interpretations as correctible and having any general authority. To speak this far of human sociality, however, is to speak only of how the individual comes to think like his fellows, to adopt the common view. It does not explain how society's views are themselves correctible, nor how collective mental progress and creativity are possible; and it leaves one at the mercy of various forms of relativism in all areas. Baldwin, who unlike Durkheim was determined to avoid relativism, takes the next step to be of great importance: the emergence of the ability to criticize society's views on one's own authority. This authority is not the authority of one's own idiosyncrasies (as it is before the consensual stage), but the authority of the individual's own judgment of the facts and their relations, asserted, if necessary, in spite of society's disagreement. Such a judgment is necessarily *synnomic*, or objective in the sense explained.

Baldwin, then, defends the objectivity of aesthetic judgments. It seems to me that this view is necessary if one is to have a cognitive-developmental psychology of aesthetic experience. For we are not dealing here with the development of an isolated concept, such as art or form, as the term cognitive development might suggest. We are dealing, rather, with the development of a fundamental mode of experience which, like science and morality, is essentially normative in character. A number of concepts will develop as constituent parts of this mode of experience, but it is its normative character that is its core, because this is what gives it distinctness as a "mode of experience." If it were not distinct in this way, it would not have a distinct course of development, but would instead be a part of moral or scientific, or some other, development. By *normative character* I mean that objective judgments are possible, and that various aspects of experience have inescapably a relevance or irrelevance in the making of those judgments. The same is true of Kohlberg's work on moral judgments. It is not just that the concept of rights, for example, develops; it is also that the relevance to moral judgments of the concept of rights develops. This is what makes the development of that concept a constituent part of moral development. This point saves us from a proliferation of distinct cognitive developmental schemes, each detailing the development of a concept, and enables us to select the core developmental structures for attention. Baldwin thinks there are three such core structures: the scientific, moral, and aesthetic. We may wish to add more; but it seems that any plausible addition must be synnomic in character.

II

The Nature of Aesthetic Experience

In this section I will describe Baldwin's account of aesthetic experience. This is necessary before discussing the different developmental levels of that experience.

It is perhaps helpful to note at the beginning that Baldwin's account of aesthetic experience (in contrast at times with his terminology) is not an idiosyncratic one. It is compatible, for example with that of Monroe Beardsley, in his *Aesthetics* (1958). No doubt this is, in part, true because of the abstract level at which he moves. But the point is important, since otherwise it would be unlikely that his account of the development of the aesthetic would be of much interest to us. In general, his account stresses, as any naturalistic theory must do, the connections between aesthetic and ordinary experience, the one being, in general, a heightening or intensification of certain features of the other.

There are four interrelated notions Baldwin uses to characterize aesthetic experience: these are *immediacy, semblance, personalization,* and *idealization.*

Immediacy

What does it mean to say aesthetic experience is *immediate*? It is perhaps easiest to define immediacy in terms of its opposite. *Mediation* occurs in experience when one thing refers (or points) to some other thing. Signs and symbols stand for some other thing, for example, and are said to mediate their meanings. Experience of a meaning via a symbol is then said to be mediate. In a purposeful experience, means often are experienced as pointing to their end. Logical deduction is also highly mediated, since each step is experienced as leading to the next. Discursive judgments in general are also mediated, since they can all be reduced to the form "A is B," in which one idea leads to another. An example may help. Consider the judgment, "trees are a renewable resource." To begin, one reads the word "trees" and thinks of the objects, trees. One does not normally attend closely to the word, to its size, for example, or its blackness on the page. One gives it sufficient attention only to recognize it and be directed to its meaning. The same is true of "renewable resource." In addition, the sentence as a whole states a judgment of the form "A is

B"; in reading it we move from the first idea to the second. We make the transition, but do not attend closely to it, to the particular way it is done. Rather we attend only sufficiently to recognize the word "are" as a transition. For these reasons a normal reading of the sentence is a highly mediate experience.

This condition is the opposite of the aesthetic, where full attention is given to what is actually presented. One attends to the presented object and its qualities for their own sake and not to something beyond it. Attention is absorbed by the object, not its abstracted significance, by the present, not the future, by the means, not the end. It is undivided and nondiscursive, i.e., does not "run" from the actual to something else pointed to, and is, in short, immediate.

There are several kinds of immediate experience, as Baldwin points out. There is the immediacy of naïve sense experience, such as a baby may be presumed to have before he has a symbolic world. There is the immediacy of mysticism and of the contemplation of simple and distinct ideas, which formed the cornerstone of Cartesian philosophy. The methods of phenomenology may be thought of as aiming at immediacy in the contemplation of intentional objects of all kinds. Also there is the immediacy of aesthetic experience in its several stages of development.

Semblance

Semblance is Baldwin's word for a feature widely acknowledged as a basic characteristic of aesthetic experience. It corresponds, for instance, to what Susanne Langer (1953) means by the *virtual* character of aesthetic objects. It is the concern for the appearance rather than the reality of objects, the interest in how things look, or seem to be, rather than in what they actually are. For the sake of clarity I will mention a few simple examples of the *semblant:* a car may look fast, whether or not it is; a wall may look solid, though in fact it is about to crumble; a singer's voice may appear to be effortless, though it is not; a two-dimensional surface may appear to be three-dimensional. All these are cases of the semblant in its most general sense. They are not the only kind of case, because mental objects also can be semblantly apprehended, e.g., the idea of a square, the concept of justice, a logical connection. There are again connections here with phenomenology and hermeneutics, which were also being created contemporaneously with Baldwin. Aesthetic experience is not the only kind of semblant experience, just as it is not the only kind of immediate experience.

Buy my examples relate only to potential aesthetic objects, and I shall discuss only that case.

Baldwin's view requires that, in principle, anything can be an aesthetic object, provided only that it is capable of being apprehended through the senses. This is necessary because, as we have seen, an aesthetic object represents a perfect fusion of the world of the senses and the world of meanings. All material objects are potential aesthetic objects, as are sounds and patterns of movement. Words are perhaps a limiting case, because they may seem hardly to exist without their conventional meanings. But they are, after all, perceptible by sense, sounded, or "heard internally"; they are combined sounds and meanings, and so can become aesthetic objects. This accounts for the problems of translation in literature, for poems and novels are made of words and not of meanings. Collingwood (1938) has an interesting corollary of this point, which is that each of the arts has its origin in a specialization of body movement. This is as true of painting and drawing—specialization of hand and arm movement—as it is of speech, dance, or music. The reason is that the movements of one's own body, while certainly physical, are also the first things naturally experienced as meaningful. They are in everyone's experience at the heart of the fusion of the natural and the symbolic, the "place where two worlds meet," and are from the beginning involved in the creation of meanings. One can say then, with Collingwood, that movement is the mother of the arts. A body that did not have the power of movement at will could not have aesthetic experience, because it could not overcome the dualism of nature and meaning. Nor, presumably, could it create the dualism in the first place.

To repeat, aesthetic objects must consist in sensory materials as well as in meanings. The point is worth stressing because many idealists have seemed to deny it or ignore it; and this is at times true of Baldwin. It is also widely thought to be true of Croce and Collingwood. Baldwin sometimes speaks as if ideas alone can become aesthetic objects. Ideas certainly can be organized in different ways, and their organization is often described as harmonious, elegant, or in other ways aesthetic. We have probably all heard the claim that mathematical proofs can be beautiful. Baldwin makes this claim and says it also of the organization of a person's life, that, for example, "the development of character by the observance of moral rules is as beautiful as the progress of a musical composition" (Baldwin, 1911, p. 203).[1]

This kind of talk was common in Baldwin's time, but later

---

[1] All subsequent quotations from Baldwin are from *Thought and Things* (vol. 3).

writers and artists have not been sympathetic with it. The twentieth century has come to regard aesthetic objects as necessarily organizations of a sensory medium; meanings are important constituents of works of art, but they must be incorporated somehow in particular pieces of sensory material. Philosophers and artists since Baldwin's time have given much attention to the character and possibilities of organization in different sensory materials. This topic was first approached scientifically by Fechner, whose work Baldwin mentions but clearly regards as of subordinate significance. The necessity of the sensory medium, however, as we have seen, is actually required by Baldwin's own larger views, and his occasional lapses should not obscure this truth.

Semblant objects include a wider range than *aesthetic* objects, the latter being that subset of the former which is capable of being apprehended through the senses. We may then say that there is both a positive and a negative character to the attention that focuses on such objects.

On the negative side, there is what is *not* of concern, or at the center of attention, what is "bracketed." There is no attention to anything beyond the appearance. For instance, it is enough that the car *looks* fast. If one goes on to ask whether it really is fast, one's concern is no longer aesthetic but practical. The question of reality is not raised nor is it rejected as irrelevant. As Collingwood says, imagination is indifferent to, or prior to, the distinction between reality and unreality. Baldwin speaks of this negative aspect as revealing the freedom of the imagination. One is not limited to reality, as one may be in other modes. In imaginative modes one can go *beyond* it (in the sense of ignoring the facts of the matter or the practical consequences), in favor of make-believe, or as-if. The control of experience, as he puts it, passes from the external object to the self, *Semblance* reveals "the psychic tendency to consider the object as detached from the external and thus as under inner or subjective control." A simple example of this freedom is from children's play, in which a chair may easily become a horse or a space ship. More generally, this means that semblance is not re-semblance. Art, for example, is not photography (though Baldwin allows that photography can be art). Where a work of art depicts something, one's interest (if it is to be aesthetic) is not in whether it is a faithful depiction of an original. One attends to the depiction, not to the original, nor to the accuracy of the reference of the depiction to the original. Otherwise it is not a case of semblant (nor, it will be noted, of immediate) experience.

On the positive side of the description of semblance, we may say that the semblant object claims attention. It is true that one may be more—and less—fully attentive in the semblant mode itself; Baldwin makes rather a point of the inattentiveness of children's play. But in aesthetic experience, attention is fully given to the semblant object, and hence that experience is in a sense fully guided by it. However, this does not deny a more sophisticated form of the freedom and inner control just spoken of. For the semblant object is in turn created by the attention which it "claims." Attention is given only to appearance, and the object is constituted only as appearance; hence it is neither a scientific nor a practical object. Each observer must freshly create the semblant object as such for himself.

Another way to say this is to say that the observer must interpret the object *as if* it were something. An appearance must be the appearance of something, not of nothing: something must appear as if actual, that is to say, it must be an intelligible or meaningful appearance. Baldwin says: "all art . . . must mean something, must, that is, present, render or depict things, situations, events, relations, which are so far possibly real as to be understandable" (p. 158). Baldwin in any case believes that there cannot be sense-data that are wholly uninterpreted, that have no significance at all; for something to appear at all requires that it be at least minimally meaningful. Hence the idea of a "mere ink-blot" in the following sentence is to be taken as a limiting case engendered by logic, rather than as descriptive of possible experience: "The absolutely grotesque and unintelligible—the mere ink-blot, or the mere noisy crash—loses interest, whether in play or art" (p. 159).

It follows that works of art, though they must present the appearance of something, may nevertheless be what we call abstract or nonobjective. Actual blots and crashes are not ruled out, only "mere" blots and crashes. For example, an ink-blot that is pregnant with emotion is semblant, since it has the appearance of emotion. And, of course, it would be hard to find an inkblot that does not carry some suggestion of emotion. Emotions can, after all, be "presented, rendered or depicted"; and this is a fact of great importance for aesthetic experience. Its importance is such that Baldwin created for it the separate category he called "personalizing."

Personalizing

Personalizing is best regarded as a subset of the semblant. It refers to the finding in semblant objects of qualities which can be described only in terms having to do with human feeling—cases, in other words, where the semblant appearance is an appearance of feeling.

I will give some simple examples which parallel the set given in the discussion of semblance: a tree may *look* lonely, or defiant; a piece of music may *sound* sad or brooding; an inkblot may *appear* serene or joyous. The examples are similar to the first set in that they describe appearances; but they differ in that the appearances are described in terms normally used only of human feeling.

It is commonly thought that terms of this kind enable us to say what is most important about works of art. At the least, we may say, if we were not impelled to say things of this sort, art would be of considerably less interest to us than it is. It would not be heroic, or tragic, or sentimental, or emotionally involving in any way. A stronger view would be that we would have no category of the aesthetic at all. Baldwin evidently is inclined toward this stronger view; i.e., that the aesthetic necessarily has somehow to do with the presentation of human feeling. We can contrast wine-tasting: it is not an aesthetic affair on this view, although it is a matter of immediacy and of the semblant. The reason is that wine cannot sensibly be said to be sad or brooding, lonely or defiant, or describe in terms normally used of human feeling.

It may seem on second thought that it is not sensible to say that a tree looks lonely or defiant, that it is puzzling in a way that it is not puzzling to say that it looks solid. How, it might be asked, can a tree be lonely? Here one must remember that what is at issue is not the tree as a scientific object but as an *appearance*—the tree reconstituted as an aesthetic object. Loneliness is ascribed to the tree as appearance, but not to the tree as scientific object. The assertion is that the tree *looks* lonely, but not that it *is* lonely. In the same way, we mean the tree *looks* solid, not that it *is* solid, as long as we remain in the semblant mode. In both cases, we have descriptions of the way the tree looks, not of how it is. We do in fact say things of this sort all the time; such speech communicates perfectly well in normal use and does not puzzle us. The puzzle arises only on second thought, not on first. Criticism of the arts is full of such statements and they seem to be irreplaceable; that is, there seems to be no other way to say what we mean when we say that the tree looks lonely. In Baldwin's view these facts are of the greatest importance in defining the aesthetic. This makes his view a part of the expressionist view of art, according to which the essence of the aesthetic is that it expresses emotion. There has been a great deal of discussion within that tradition of just how art expresses emotion, and of what *expresses* means, and in fairness, no widely accepted answer exists.[2] It is important to see,

---

[2] The classic discussions are in Collingwood's *The Principles of Art* (1938), and Langer's *Feeling and Form* (1953). A useful summary and discussion of the question is in Beardsley's *Aesthetics* (1958).

therefore, that such questions do not have to do with whether it is true that the tree looks lonely, but with how that comes about. They are not a challenge to the fact, but rather a request for an explanation of the fact.

Characteristically, Baldwin has an explanation, and it resides in a psychological theory. It is helpful, therefore, to see that this theory, purporting to explain the expressive character of the aesthetic, is not directly involved in his description of the aesthetic as expressive, nor is it the same as his theory of the development of aesthetic experience. It is a subsidiary element within the whole, though undoubtedly an important one. His explanation depends on a theory current at his time, often known as the theory of *Einfühlung*. The root idea is this: as we attend to a work of art (visual, musical, verbal) and trace out the patterns—the risings and fallings, the stresses, conflicts, and resolutions—our body unconsciously reproduces the physical and nervous equivalents. This then gives rise to the feelings and emotions that would be felt if one were oneself going through the actions involved. Baldwin's own general account is summarized thus:

> A fruitful character of the semblant object . . . is that called in the later German literature of aesthetics, *Einfühlung* . . . It is the making of any object into a thing of semblance or "inner imitation," with the added character that such an object has a greater or less degree of subjective control attributed to it. There is a certain *feeling-into* the given object (Einfühlung) of the subject's own personal feeling: an attribution to it of the inner movement which its construction requires. (p. 166)

Baldwin was familiar with several versions of this theory, and was not quite satisfied with any. This is made clear in a footnote to the above passage, in which he says: "The great confusion that reigns in the German literature on the topic makes it seem desirable to postpone the final choice of an equivalent (for *Einfühlung*) until the concept itself is better defined" (p. 167). His own summary and use of the theory remains always at a rather general and common-sense level. He frequently speaks simply of feeling that has been "read into," "felt into" or "transferred to" an object. His use of the words "personalizing," "personification," and "identification" are similarly derived from a common-sense vocabulary. Indeed, he often seems to regard such phrases as self-justifying, as if they are simply a restatement of the facts of expression, rather than as an explanation of them. The theory of *Einfühlung* has not retained much popularity since Baldwin's time because it has remained ineradicably vague, in just this way. It does not remove much of the puzzlement surrounding the claim that "the tree looks lonely," to say that it is because the sense of loneliness has been "read into" (etc.) the tree by the observer.

John Broughton has made the interesting suggestion that, for Baldwin, the capacity for *Einfühlung* derives from the original absence in the baby of the distinction between self and other. In the adualistic stage, there are feelings in the world, but they are not experienced as located clearly either in the self or in the not-self, since this distinction is not yet securely established. Instead, they are experienced simply as being in the one world which is all there is. This early experience is retained as a capacity through later stages, and results in both *Einfühlung* (the apprehension of feeling in objects) and as what we now call *empathy* (apprehension of feeling in other persons).

Idealization

The fourth major concept Baldwin uses to characterize the aesthetic is *idealization*. The most basic sense of this notion is organization or form. Aesthetic objects are complexly organized objects, wherein each part is somehow related to each other part and also to the whole. These relations are determined by whatever seems to be fitting (i.e., there is a relationship between any two parts whenever they seem to "fit" each other in some way). The *fit* constitutes the relationships; without fittingness there would be no forms to be apprehended. There are various kinds of *fittingness* which constitute various kinds of forms. There is, for example, the fittingness with which a premise fits a logical deduction, and that with which a particular act fits a particular moral character. I have already discussed the kind of fittingness appropriate to aesthetic objects; it is that with which sensory materials fit each other.

Experience normally is of partial forms. It is neither chaotic nor perfectly shaped. It is a matter of some elements fitting together in various ways, with other elements not being as fitting, or not fitting at all. These partial forms in experience often seem to call for their completion, to suggest something not actual. To follow these suggestions and supply the completion of "a bit of organization once begun" is to organize the data, or to *idealize* them. It is a going-beyond the factual to something felt as more fulfilling and is again a function of the freedom of the imagination. It is a deep motive of mind, to be found in all areas of experience. A well-known example is the case of perception itself. In vision, for example, there is a tendency to organize sense-data into simple shapes, a tendency which Gestalt psychologists have amply illustrated since Baldwin wrote. Baldwin himself did a number of studies of visual organization, which no doubt influenced his thinking.

Fittingness is in this way a product of mind, something read into objects by the imagination. Nevertheless, it is not, in Baldwin's view, purely subjective. I have already discussed the sense in which judgments of fittingness are for Baldwin objective, or synnomic. The form is found, at least as a suggestion, in the object, and objects cannot be made to fit together simply by wishing, for they are experienced as accepting some forms and refusing others. The completion which fulfills the partial form of a given object is determined, or at least guided, by the given object and its partial form.

Idealization in this sense is a requisite for aesthetic experience, in Baldwin's view. He says: "Art always has its symbolic meaning, which proceeds by the further development of the motives present in the content or material. It is part of the intent of the imagination that the organization shall go forward to its consummation" (p. 205). To this is appended a footnote: "Accordingly, when we say that the lover idealizes his lady in finding her beautiful, we give the true and sufficient explanation."

Science and morality also require idealization. They both go beyond the recognition of the partial forms of normal experience to the construction of something further, and this something is nevertheless suggested by and corrected in light of the data. Science constructs hypotheses to organize belief; morality constructs practical ideals to guide our conduct. Hence science, morality, art, are alike in requiring idealization. They differ in that they hold different ends in view, namely, truth, goodness, beauty. These three words represent different kinds of completions, or organizations. Truth, as established by science, is an organization of hypotheses and evidence; goodness is an organization of means and ends. Beauty comes from the organization of sensory appearances. It will be clear from what has already been said that this does not preclude an organization in terms of "logical or sentimental meanings," as Baldwin would say, so long as this organization takes place in a sensory medium. In the painting of our lonely tree, for example, loneliness might be said to be the organizing principle, though what it organizes is the paint. Idealization in aesthetics, means that a sensory medium is so organized as to become expressive in just this way.

Of course, there are different sensory media to be organized, and there will therefore be different specific kinds of organization. As I have said, a lot of work has been done since Baldwin exploring the nature of these various possibilities (e.g. Prall, 1967). Baldwin himself is not much interested in this question; he regards it as an empirical question exactly what kind of organization a particular medium lends itself to. He says:

The general requirement that any content, in order to become aesthetic, must be fit to be taken up in the grasps of imagination as a detached and relatively complete semblant whole, does not determine at all the actual groups of contents in this mode of experience or that, which do find themselves most fit. Each of the great types of aesthetic experience represented by what is called a "fine art"—pictorial, plastic, dramatic, literary, musical, etc.—should be experimentally investigated, and the rules of construction of the peculiar material . . . thus made out. There will thus arise a true science of aesthetics, in the sense suggested by one of the first advocates of experiment in this field, Fechner. . . . (p. 204)

However, in a general way, and before the science is done, he can indicate what kinds of organization are aesthetic, because "certain requirements have become historical in aesthetic theory: variety in unity, harmony, balance, symmetry, proportion, consistency, rhythm, movement within limits . . ." (p. 203). These are the kinds of formal arrangements that have in the past generally been found pleasing, and on which expressive qualities are based.

III

The Development of Aesthetic Experience

In Part II, I briefly described Baldwin's conception of aesthetic experience. To recapitulate, he describes aesthetic experience as experience which is immediate (i.e., finds significance in presented objects rather than in something more remote), semblant (i.e., attends to sensory appearances without further questions about reality), personalized (i.e., finds appearances expressive of feelings), and idealized (i.e., completes the formal tendencies inherent in appearances). In this section I consider Baldwin's conception of the development of aesthetic experience.

According to Baldwin there are three great levels of aesthetic development, which are related to the movements occurring in the development of mind in general. This latter development is discussed elsewhere in this book, and I can give only the briefest summary here. However, this summary, and the chart which follows, may serve the reader as a kind of map of the rest of my discussion.

There are three major levels of mental development in general, the *prelogical*, the *quasilogical*, and the *logical*. These are related to the three levels of aesthetic development, thought not in terms of a precise correspondence. The first level is adualistic in the sense already described, where the dualism between the self and the not-self, and hence other dualisms, have not yet arisen. The child at this level is limited to perceptual and memory images, and aesthetic experience is not yet possible. This is because semblant experience is not yet possible, because the child cannot disregard the actual in order to attend to the semblant. Dualism (and the quasilogical level of mind in general) begins precisely with this ability. It consists in the ability to separate meanings and objects, and to impose one on the other consciously (but not reflectively). The general name for this ability is imagination, according to Baldwin, and the activity he calls make-believe, or *play*. It represents the first assertion of the self as against the world of not-self, and its action tends to be whimsical and arbitrary. A child may pretend a stick is at one moment a witch and at the next a horse; in this he is not significantly guided by the actual character of the stick. For this reason, though play is the first form of semblant experience, Baldwin is not willing to call it aesthetic experience, strictly speaking. One reason for this is that it is the seed, not only of aesthetic experience, but also of moral and scientific experience. Nevertheless, I include play in my exposition that follows.

The next level of aesthetic experience is also quasilogical, and occurs as the child begins to pay more attention to the object and to conceive its inner life in terms guided more closely by its form. Baldwin's name for this activity, as we have seen, is *idealization*, and it results in *spontaneous aesthetic experience*.

The last level of aesthetic experience is made possible by the capacity for *reflection*. Reflection itself is made possible by the interpretation of the self as the subject of experience, and everything else as not-self. This greatly sophisticates the mental life that has previously occurred; for example, it makes self-critical and synnomic judgments possible in all modes of experience. Hence the onset of the capacity for reflection makes possible both the general logical level of mental life, and the specific level named *reflective aesthetic experience*. These two levels are therefore contemporary as capacities in the life of an individual. Baldwin, however, because he is most concerned with the argument for *pancalism*, does not speak of them in this manner but says instead that where the general mental level is logical, the aesthetic level is postlogical. One reason for this is presumably that logical experience is mediate, and aesthetic experience immediate, and the phrase *logical aesthetic experience* would not make sense. But this cannot be all, since the use of the word "reflective" in both cases instead of "logical" would make the relation clearer. In fact, Baldwin is here, in my judgment, being misled by his system-building ambitions. Therefore, in both the chart and the exposition that follows, I have ignored the implications of the phrase *postlogical* and speak of *reflective aesthetic experience* as parallel with the level of logical mental life in general.

The three levels of aesthetic experience can be discussed in terms of three of the four characteristics already described: personalization, idealization, and immediacy. All of them are equally cases of semblance. The following, therefore, is a graphic representation of semblance. Table 1, therefore, is a graphic representation of their relationships.

columns, or its rows. I have chosen to use the columns, and will deal first with the levels of personalization, then of idealization, and, finally, of immediacy.

Table 1
Relationship between the Levels of Aesthetic Experience and the Levels of Mental Development

General Level of Mental Development	General Level of Aesthetic Development	Levels of Personalization	Levels of Idealization	Levels of Immediacy
Prelogical	None	———	———	Naive
Quasilogical	Play	Identification	———	Naive
	Spontaneous aesthetic experience	Identification	Various forms recognized but not distinguished	Naive
Logical (and postlogical)	Reflective aesthetic experience	Reflective identification	Forms of science and morality used "semblantly"	Transforming results of judgments into immediate apprehensions

Levels of Personalization: Play and Spontaneous Aesthetic Experience

Young children commonly read feelings into objects. For example, they personify dolls, tin soldiers, tools, clouds, and so on. As Baldwin says, in one of his rare examples: "A stick of wood becomes a soldier, and a lamppost a priest!" (p. 160). Baldwin in fact calls the form of personalizing at this level *personification*. This is an ordinary word for what we (including adults) do at times; but it should be clear that what Baldwin intends here is not a reflective or even a self-conscious process. He thinks that children at the earliest level have just begun to construct a conception of the not-self, and of other persons, of the location of feelings, emotions, and other human attributes. On the one hand, when children personify objects in play, they do know what they are doing in the sense that they are aware of the animate/inanimate distinction and are not making mistakes. On the other hand, they do not have a clear sense of the interior life of other persons, and the mentality or feeling attributed to objects in play is arbitrary, discontinuous and stereotyped.

Baldwin distinguishes this from a second form of personalizing, which he calls *identification*. Identification requires a more developed conception of the interiority of others. To personify, one ascribes some form of life to the object; to identify, one imagines a mental life for the object and checks it out against one's own possible experience. Baldwin puts it thus: "in the one, we sympathize with the object as a person, and do imitatively what it seems to do; in the other, we take it up into our own life and carry its impulse forward in our own" (p. 173). The point seems to be that the second is more articulated and more emotionally involved than the first. To personify a broomstick, one treats it as alive; that is, as any form of life with any personality, however unlikely. To identify with it one tries to imagine what that personality is more exactly, and tries out, as it were, its imagined feeling structure in one's own experience. To tell how it feels, i.e., to know what personality it is, one imaginatively adopts its gestures as one's own, and imagines how one would feel in that situation. Then one reads back into the broomstick the imagined feelings as its own. There is in this process a kind of double, or reciprocal, control of experience. One's construction of the personalized object is guided by one's own feeling; at the same time one's own feeling is guided by the appearance of the object. Each provides a sort of check, or test, of the other. Hence, the process is not arbitrary, it is "serious." As Baldwin says: "The first departures from the purity of the play consciousness . . . seem to be those which modify the freedom of the personal motive and with it reduce the arbitrariness of the selected content . . ." (p. 168).

It is not clear, whether in this distinction between personifying and identifying, Baldwin is constructing technical terms and definitions (is he clear enough for that?) or elucidating ordinary language (is he too schematic for that?). Nevertheless, he seems to be describing familiar enough phenomena. It may be helpful to give a simple example of what Baldwin has in mind. Children of elementary school age do seem to identify with figures in stories, films, and TV shows. That is to say they experience (imaginatively) the hero's triumphs, his dangers as their dangers, and so on. They share vicariously his feelings, that is those feelings that appear to originate in his situation and belong to him. But these feelings, at the same time, are actually felt only by the readers, and, if we like to say so, are "read in" by them. Normally in this process the child remains aware of the distinction between reality and art, i.e., that what is happening is fictional and that the experience involved is not actually his, but only vicariously his. He remains aware of this, although he seems unable to be reflective about the awareness. Reflectiveness, which brings with it much greater articulation and control, comes only with the third level of aesthetic development. Very young children, however, do not seem to identify in this way with fictional characters. Their reactions are not based so closely on the situations or characters in the fictions, but appear to be a good deal more arbitrary. They respond often to particular details, their attention caught in what appear to be idiosyncratic ways, guided more by whim, chance association, or memory images than by attention to the fiction as such. Another way to say this is to say that memory images often seem as important at this stage as presented visual or verbal images. A consequence is that the awareness is not clearly maintained that the emotions involved are not actually, but only vicariously, his.

There is a well-known phenomenon in response to fictions, much discussed in the aesthetics of the theater and sometimes called a *loss of distance*, in which the maintenance of this awareness is at issue. It is where, with strongly emotional and especially threatening material, we somehow respond emotionally as if no longer to fictions, but as if to reality; fear felt on behalf of the hero is suddenly felt as if on behalf of oneself, and so on. Young children can seem genuinely frightened, for example, at a routine TV crime show. Aestheticians have sometimes written as if this kind of case is not uncommon among adults and have conjured up images of yokels who clamber onto the stage to save the heroine in distress. This is portrayed then as in some way a mistake or a lack of sophistication. Baldwin's interpretation makes the adult cases implausible, but the young children's cases not so much. His scheme allows us to interpret what is involved as a regression back beyond the first stage of personalization, to the point where one does not distinguish whose feelings are at issue. Loss of distance, in other words, may be a matter of cognitive development, having to do with the grasp of a very basic distinction between the self and the not-self. It is something that cannot happen when one is operating at the first or the second level of the development of personalization.

The question arises when we talk about identifying with fictional characters how far this is similar to empathizing with actual people. The similarities appear to be strong, and the fact is relevant to the topic of the pedagogical uses of art, especially of literature. It should be noticed that Baldwin's account of the process of identifying with aesthetic objects (i.e., imagining what feeling it has by adopting its gestures, then reading the results back into the object) is very similar to his account of the process of empathizing with people, which is discussed in Kohlberg's chapter in this book. In fact, it seems to be a more general form of the same ability. Now a developed capacity to empathize with others is important in moral experience, both because a knowledge of the feelings of others is necessary for moral judgments, and, more importantly, because the developing capacity for taking the perspective of others is thought to be requisite for the developing capacity for moral judgment. Therefore, one important question suggested by Baldwin's account is whether empathetic abilities can be fostered best or first through art. It is plausible that one's abilities to experience vicariously the feelings of others (actual or fictional) can be more finely guided and stimulated by a good novelist than by the less carefully structured interactions of social life. Many people have been convinced of the moral effects of great literature. Here is an interpretation of that conviction, which, if correct, would add exposure to approriate works of art to the instruments of the moral-development educators.

Comparison with some empirical data

Before passing on to a discussion of the third level of personalization, I would like to illustrate the nature of the first two levels with some examples drawn from research done by myself and colleagues. This requires a brief explanation of the nature of our research and its general results. I will try to say no more than is necessary for the purposes of illustration.

For some time we have been discussing a number of paintings with children and analyzing their opinions and judgments about the paintings (Parsons et al., 1979). From the data thus collected we have identified four levels of aesthetic experience that are distinguishable with high measures of interjudge reliability. This research was not based on Baldwin's work, which we did not know at the time we began, but was rather modeled as a parallel to Kohlberg's work with moral judgments. It is less general, less theoretical, and more empirical than Baldwin's work. I should add that our descriptions of levels must be regarded as tentative, since they are based not on longitudinal data, but on a cross-sectional study of 136 school students from first through twelve grades. There is certainly a good deal more research to be done before they can be taken as firmly established; some of this is continuing. Nevertheless, it may be of some interest to ask how the two schemes match.

The following chart briefly summarizes those of our results that coincide best with Baldwin's notion of personalizing, and compares our four levels of this with his three. I will call on some of the detail summarized in this chart to illustrate Baldwin's levels. As I do this, I

Table 2
Comparison of Baldwin's Levels of Personalization with Relevant
Parts of Parsons' Conclusions

	Baldwin	Parsons	Level
Play *(personification)*	Personifies object without close attention to its actual character; basis of feeling is arbitrary.	No distinction between subjective and objective bases for feeling; idiosyncratic associations with details of the work.	1
Spontaneous aesthetic experience *(identification)*	Identifies with object, feeling is felt personally, but awareness maintained that it is vicarious. Cannot clearly distinguish moral from aesthetic in response.	Identifies with a main character in work; responds in terms of heroes and villains; sentimental range of feeling: rejects ugly, ironic, intense, ambiguous, tragic.	2
Reflective aesthetic experience (reflective identification)	Aware of purpose of art as expressive; is reflective in seeking for emotional significance of object; clear about the "semblant" character of the moral and scientific content of a work.	Emphasis on expressiveness of art; tendency to identify with artist's feelings or to focus on own immediate affect; relates theme, form and feeling together as projecting a total attitude, but still rejects the ugly and the tragic.	3
		Discussion of artist, background, relevant only as guide to what is there; emphasis still on expressive character; but accepts the expression of any kind of feeling, including ugly, painful, tragic.	4

think it will emerge that there is a remarkably close fit; i.e., that the data, collected and organized originally without reference to Baldwin's scheme, nevertheless seem to support it. The major exception to this is that Baldwin omits our third level, which contains the possibility of a relativist view of aesthetic judgments. Another way to say this is to say that he does not distinguish between our third and fourth levels but coalesces the two into his third and last. We found the distinction between our third and fourth levels significant in large part because of the relativist issue; I will return to a discussion of Baldwin and relativism shortly.

I return to the illustration of the character of Baldwin's first two levels of personalization. We asked questions about the feelings of characters in the paintings, of the child, of the artist and of the painting considered as a whole. Baldwin's first stage of personification does not clearly appear in our transcripts, because we did not record conversations with children younger than first grade. However, we did assume it was a stage in which the feelings aroused by the paintings were very much as already described: governed by associations, memories, highly idiosyncratic, not always apparently relevant to the painting, and not firmly located in either self or in the painting. I will give an example, from a discussion with a 5½-year-old boy of a reproduction of Currier and Ives' "Preparing for Market," a rather detailed scene of farm life. He volunteered that he liked the painting very much, and when asked why, he said it was because it reminded him of his cowboy hat. There are no cowboy hats in the picture and no cowboys. It seemed that he was reminded of his hat by the horse in the picture, and that what he was reminded of was quite as relevant and important a part of the experience as what he actually saw. And in the context it seemed clear that he did not distinguish between what he thought of and what he saw; these were not two elements of the experience for him. The pleasure of thinking about the hat was all one with the pleasure of seeing the painting, because the thinking was all one with the seeing.

We have many examples of Baldwin's second stage, identification. We found children at this stage tend to focus on particular characters in the painting one at a time and attribute feelings to them. In so doing they are guided principally by the general subject matter rather than by the particular expressiveness of the painting. This distinction is not as difficult to make as it might seem. In explaining their interpretations, children at this level did not refer to the way the painting was done (to the gestures of persons or objects, to the use of color for expressiveness, etc.); they referred instead to what the painting was about. That is to say, they tend to use stereotypes about how people feel, and to assume that others have motives and responses similar to what their own would be. For example, a child's response might run thus: This is about a circus; people enjoy watching circuses; the feeling is one of enjoyment. Our research in general substantiated the view that children of this age are dominated by subject matter, i.e., what the painting is about, rather than how it is done. And the most important point seems to be this: if asked how the painting makes them feel, they usually described a feeling already attributed to a character in the painting, and did not distinguish their own feeling as different or problematic. Two simple examples:

Q. What kind of feeling would you say is in this painting?
A. Hatred.
Q. Why's that?
A. Because they are fighting.

Q. Is that the main feeling or are there other feelings?
A. I think that's the only one.
Q. What feeling do you get when you look at this painting?
A. The feeling of hatred, like out to kill.   (Girl, 4th grade)

*   *   *

Q. What kind of feeling would you say is in this painting?
A. People are having fun.
Q. What feeling do you get when you look at this painting?
A. Like the people in the background are enjoying the show, and the food
   that they are eating.   (Girl, 4th grade)

Levels of Personalization: Reflective Aesthetic Experience

According to Baldwin, the third level of mental development is marked by the capacity for reflection. When the self is understood as the subject of experience, and experience as its object, then experience itself becomes available for scrutiny and analysis. One can describe, distinguish, ponder, question, different aspects of experience. This makes possible greater clarity about the kinds and motives of experience, and the nature of different kinds of judgments. It also brings greater awareness of the limitations and possible biases in judgments.

The advent of reflectivity is of great importance in all areas of development, and not least in connection with aesthetic experience. Baldwin's discussion of how it affects personalization is short but pithy:

> There is an identification of the self with the aesthetic object in all enjoyment of art; and so far from finding this process losing force when the elements of the self become more refined and reflective, we find, on the contrary, a new willingness to go with the thing and submit to the illusion of unity with it. The intent to identify the self with the movements suggested by the work of art becomes a more or less conscious part of the aesthetic effect. We seek for analogies from life and mind to justify what we feel, and for symbols to make concrete the meaning of inner control taken over from the thing . . . (p. 191)

The ability to reflect on experience brings a new understanding of the purpose and nature of art. Most of the adolescent and many of the preadolescent students in our research were clear about the expressive nature of art. They had come to see it as a matter either of "expressing feelings," or as "conveying messages," in either case having meanings which would be hard to put into words. And, as Baldwin says, the new understanding was in general welcomed and the expressiveness of art explored. Art for many of our adolescent subjects was primarily a matter of exploring oneself, by finding out what range of feelings appealed to one, and what kinds of emotion were possible. Getting this expressive function clearer meant also getting clearer what art is not: abandoning the view, for instance, that it is a matter of representing actual appearances faithfully. Most of the "rules" guiding judgment previously are discarded, often very gradually; a wider range of subject matter is acceptable. Some of these points I return to under the topic of idealization, for the two topics cannot always be kept quite separate.

We also identified three features of response at this level that perhaps can be seen as corollaries of Baldwin's central point, i.e., the new awareness of the expressive nature of art. The first is a greater awareness of complexity and varying nuances of feeling, along with an increased tolerance of, even a seeking for, ambiguity of feeling in both self and painting. The exact character of one's emotive response to a painting often was of great interest, and there was acknowledgement of the possibility of different responses of different individuals to the same work. This rests on an awareness of the distinction between one's own feeling and that of characters in the painting, which was missing at the previous level.

The second corollary is an awareness of the importance of the medium, style, and composition of the work, in addition to that of the subject matter per se. There is an awareness that the same subject may express different sets of feelings, depending on the particular way it is treated, and the treatment therefore requires more attention. Another way of putting this is to say that for the first time there is an ability to distinguish the appeal of the matter represented from the appeal of the representation. This allows one to say that the choice of a beautiful subject, e.g., a beautiful woman, does not guarantee a beautiful painting, and, vice versa, that an unappealing subject might nevertheless be used in an appealing painting.

The third point is an awareness that the artist had choices in the creation of the painting, because s/he was not simply capturing the appearances of some object. His/her conceptions, feelings, or intentions therefore become of some interest, and many of our adolescent subjects fastened on this as a way of discussing the painting in general. For some, the artist's intentions were used as a criterion for deciding the significance of a painting or the rightness of different interpretations.

These points are taken from the results of our research, but are suggested by Baldwin's brief remarks. A great deal more detail could be offered, but I will content myself with one example that illustrates what I have said. It is from a discussion of Picasso's "Guernica" with a 16-year-old boy.

Q. What kinds of feeling are there in the painting?
A. Well, there's like panic and pain, a lot of confusion. You can see it, in this painting, like you have to use your imagination, and I guess that's good. I don't know, though, I think myself I like pictures that are lifelike, that you can—but this is good though, I can see that. You have to use your imagination to see feelings.
Q. What do you mean by lifelike?
A. Well, I like things that look like a tree and things that look like a person . . .
Q. Do you think this would be better if it were more realistic?
A. Well, not necessarily. Like, not for this type of painting. Well, in this painting what's important is, he gets his idea across and you understand what's going on, like the pain and the suffering and everything that goes along with a bombing. He doesn't need to have everything drawn out perfect and identical to what the real thing looks like.
Q. You'd say there are strong feelings in the painting?
A. Yeah. I imagine that,—well, it seems like the artist knew what he was painting about. He was actually, like, in a bombing, or his family or close friends of his got killed in a bombing . . .
Q. How would you rate the painting?
A. Well, yeah, I like it. I imagine it's—well, it's not so important how I feel about it because I'm sure that artist was really happy with his work. And, well, it makes you think.
Q. Why isn't it important how you feel about it?
A. Well, it's just that when an artist is painting a picture, he should just mostly be doing it just because he likes to; it's just like an outlet, like he wants to get it out of his system. And when you look at it you have to think and use your imagination. It gets you to thinking about how it's like. It's like everybody can see this picture and they can see different things in it. Not like in a nature scene that's painted perfectly—in this everyone sees it differently and they can think of their own experiences and it lets the person use their own imagination . . .

I think it can be seen that the reference to the artist's feelings or intentions can easily lead one into a kind of relativism. One could say, for instance, that if the artist got his feelings "out of his system" it is a good work of art, or if he got his message across, or carried out his intentions. Usually our subjects (as in the' preceding extract) would go on to conclude that their own response was, therefore, irrelevant, because at best only the artist could tell whether this criterion had been met. There is in the philosophy of criticism a famous discussion of the issues, whether the artist's intentions are relevant to either interpretation or evaluation of works of art, and whether they are accessible to anyone but the artist (Wimsatt & Beardsley, 1946; see also Beardsley, 1958). A summary of the discussion would be too long here, but it seems that the artist's feelings or intentions can be relevant only if they are somehow determinable *via* the work of art, and not only *via* private knowledge. The important point here, I think, is that, for adolescents, to discuss the artist's intentions is to be tempted (at least) to relativist views.

An alternative route to relativism, which is simply the obverse of the above, and which we also observed, is to assert that only the viewer's response is relevant. If there are two interpretations or judgments, then both are equally valid, each for the respective viewers. Our research convinces us that relativism of these naive sorts is unquestionably a temptation, and often an actuality, at this level.

The topic is important because the possibility of relativism with respect to aesthetic judgments does not arise in Baldwin's discussion. He is philosophically against all forms of relativism and emotivism, and, as I have pointed out, regards aesthetic judgments as synnomic or objective in character. He thinks, as we do, that at the last level, there is an appeal in support of judgments to the publicly available features of the object, i.e., to whatever is apprehended as open for any one to see, *if* they are in the right circumstances, etc. It is not that one's own experience of the object is discounted as evidence at this level; quite the contrary, for it is the only final arbiter of judgments (the same is true of science and morality). It is rather that the distinction is finally clear within experience itself between those elements that are idiosyncratic (personal associations, memories) and those that are relevant responses to actual features of the objects. These actual features include, of course, such things as the appearance of loneliness of the tree or of panic and pain in Picasso's "Guernica."

We did not get data clearly belonging to this last level in our research, both because we did not interview persons beyond 12th grade and because at that time our questions did not attain the precision necessary to be sure of the distinctions. There is a sense, in any case, in which the mapping of this last level is the traditional concern of the philosophy of criticism, since one would expect critics to have mostly attained maturity of aesthetic experience. We rely, therefore at least temporarily, on the results of such work as Beardsley's (1958).

The parallel with Kohlberg's account of the development of moral judgment is striking in connection with this topic of relativism. There is in both a level at which people use rules for judgment, and a point at which they move beyond them. In confronting the inadequacy of the rules, they confront also the possibility of relativism, which sometimes does and sometimes does not become overtly articulated. Nevertheless, there is a final movement beyond this to a recognition of some kind of principle, in our case, to the principle that evidence relates to features of the work which anyone could see, *if*, etc. Baldwin's account, to repeat, collapses these two levels into one.

Levels of Idealization: Play and Spontaneous Aesthetic Experience

The first level, called *play* by Baldwin, is controlled as much by association as by perception, attention is not (according to him) characterized by idealization, because it is not clearly focused on the appearance of the object, and hence there is no sense of form emerging from that appearance. Play is arbitrary, disjointed, idiosyncratic. As Baldwin says: "Any old thing will do to play with, and any old purpose may be played out upon it" (p. 171). Furthermore, "in play the situation may be developed and extended *ad libitum* as long as the impulse to play continues. The dramatization may run out in this direction or that, knowing no limitation or rule, and seeming to have no ideal, no growing form" (p. 201).

Because it is not idealized, Baldwin chose not to regard play as a stage of aesthetic experience at all. He chose to call it a precursor, but not an early form, of aesthetic experience. This is an intelligible decision in light of what has been said, but it seems to me an unfortunate one. Any developmental scheme must raise the question: At what point does experience become aesthetic, or moral, etc.? This question is largely a question of choice rather than of fact, because it is really the question: At what point shall we choose to call experience aesthetic, moral, etc? And it seems to me that, given any scheme of continuities and discontinuities such as we find in Baldwin or Kohlberg, it is better, because more generous, to choose not to say the young child is unaesthetic or nonmoral. I would rather say that from the beginning, though in a limited way, the child is a citizen of the realm of aesthetics, in that objects do have from the beginning an appeal by virtue of their appearances.

The beginning of idealization transforms play into *spontaneous aesthetic experience*, according to Baldwin. It brings principles of relevance, tests that can be made, the possibility of making judgments. Spontaneous aesthetic experience is more serious, because there is a sense of fittingness, and the freedom of caprice disappears.

The consequence is that the first effects of idealization are described by Baldwin largely as restraints. Play, in its movement from reality, creates freedom from reality; idealization brings it back for testing. That is to say, the meaning created by the imagination is now referred back to the natural world. This is another way of saying there is a closer attention to the character of actual objects. This "experimental meaning" is the origin of scientific experiment and moral concern, as well as of aesthetic judgment. It follows that idealization is possible only when the individual has reached a dualistic stage in his/her general cognitive development (i.e., has achieved some version of the distinction between self and not-self) because it entails this ability to test ideas, i.e., to compare some symbolic or imaginative creation with the natural world. Baldwin does not discuss just which version of dualistic experience is necessary, except, of course, that the individual has not yet achieved the "reflective" distinction between subject and object. Hence, the stage of spontaneous aesthetic experience must be understood to span a rather long period.

In his discussion of the restraints that the "testing" of idealization brings with it, Baldwin does not deal with the organization of the sensory medium as such; i.e., with what might be called formal aesthetic concerns, such as symmetry, balance, contrast, etc. This is also true of his discussion of the reflective level of idealization, and I will discuss the point in that connection. Meantime, what he does focus on are the tests of truth and morality, which he asserts are both present in aesthetic experience. They are not actually employed, but are experienced as if employed, as semblant tests. There is, he says, "when play gives place to art, the assumption of the common verification, as if it were secured." The full passage reads:

> I may play as I please, only my whim setting limits to my freedom; I may see hob-goblins in my tobacco smoke, and ask you to play with me that they are there. But I cannot . . . call anything I please beautiful. To do so, we must distinguish the shapes of hob-goblins, and reach some sort of agreement as to their beauty. This agreement is not that reached . . . through experimental tests . . . but the semblance of such testing is present. I must at least be willing to appeal to you, suggesting, if not requiring, that you agree with me in the result of my idealization . . . there is, when play gives place to art, the assumption of common verification, as if it were secured. (p. 171)

I shall try to illustrate what he means. As a brief summary, I give a comparison chart of levels of idealization, similar to that of personalizing.

First, I will speak of the test of *truth*. Together with the tendency for children at this level to focus on subject matter, and to ignore the medium and its peculiarities, goes a growing demand for realistic presentation, at least in American culture. Increasingly in the elementary school years, paintings are judged in terms of how well they represent the appearance of objects in the world, i.e., how realistic or accurate they are in presenting their subject matter. This is a kind of truth test, i.e., truth with respect to the facts of appearances; and requires the ability to make an implicit comparison of the painting with its subject in reality. It demonstrates, too, a degree of decentering, i.e., an increased ability to consider the appearance of paintings and objects as others would see them.

Our research is full of examples of this, and we were able to distinguish two sublevels. First a child will ask that things "look

Table 3
**Comparison of Baldwin's Levels of Idealization with Relevant
Parts of Parsons' Conclusions**

	Baldwin	**Parsons**
Play	No idealization; response is whimsical and idiosyncratic; no possibility of judgment.	The appeal of the art object is located in an egocentrically close self-object relation— i.e., that of liking it ("my favorite"). Hence there is no distinction between liking and judging. No distinction between subject and "treatment"; art not clearly distinguished from other objects; little sense of form, unity or theme.
Spontaneous aesthetic experience (idealization)	Possibility of objective judgment through us of tests of truth and morality. "Semblant" character tf tests not brought to reflection.	Appeal is conceived as the satisfaction of (often unarticulated) rules such as: it is skillfully made, it required hard work, it is well arranged it is realistic, it is appropriate aesthetic subject; conventional view of what subjects are suitable for art; little sense of character of medium.
Reflective aesthetic experience (reflective idealization)	Reflective awareness of "semblant" character of tests allows dropping inappropriate rules, such as realism.	Criteria determined in terms either of artist's intentions or of viewer's feelings; possibility of relativism: values originality, strong feeling (distinguishes aesthetic from moral judgments); aware of alternative styles and formal approaches; speaks of genres, kinds; aware of medium and its character; distinguishes appeal of subject matter from beauty of treatment; relates parts to whole, and style and form to theme.
		Judgment based on qualities of the work that are in principle public and are based on perceptual or intentional aspects of it; criteria formulated in terms of work itself, open to revision through discussion and trial; strong emphasis on form and complex qualities; subject matter related to this; any subject could be suitable for art, depending on treatment.

real," or as they are "supposed to," that they are readily identifiable and comprehended, and that they do not defy what everyone knows to be the case. We called this *schematic realism*. It changes slowly into the next substage, which we called *photographic realism*. In this latter the test is more precise: that what is represented be the visual appearance of objects, rather than just what everyone knows about them. This can be illustrated from discussions of Picasso's "Weeping Woman." The younger children objected to the placement of two eyes on one side of the face, and the fact that the eyes looked like "boats." Yet they did not object to the hands, which, though considerably contorted, have five fingers, and on each a fingernail. Some would count the fingers to make sure (the first one counted wrong):

Q. Is this the way you'd expect a painting of a weeping woman to be painted?
A. No.
Q. Why not?
A. When someone cries that's not how he looks. The other eye is supposed to be over here, not there.
Q. What do you think the artist should have done differently?
A. Put the eye over here, put another finger on that hand. (Boy, 2nd grade)

Q. What about the eyes?
A. They're weird and they shouldn't both be on the same side.
Q. What about the hands?
A. They're okay.
Q. Do you think the artist should have done them any differently?
A. No, they're okay.   (Boy, 2nd grade)

Older students began to object to the hands as well. Although the hands had five fingers and fingernails, they weren't enough like "real" hands (i.e., weren't photographically correct):

Q. What about the hands?
A. They're weird.
Q. Is there anything he should have done differently?
A. Made the hands look like real hands.
   (Girl, 6th grade)

Q. What about how he made the hands?
A. The fingers are weird cause they don't go like a real hand. (Girl, 6th grade)

These criteria of realism are retained at more articulate levels (in discussing) Bellow's "Firpo and Dempsey":

Q. Would you say that you like this painting or you don't like this painting?
A. I like this one a lot because I like boxing, and I like the way they made these guys, showing their muscles so it looks real.
Q. Would you say that this is a good painting or it's not a good painting?

A. Yeah, because their faces, they look real. They've got shading in them
    and he knows how to draw faces and bodies well.   (Girl, 7th grade)

Similarly, the chief criterion of color becomes its appropriateness. Earlier, children like colorfulness for its own sake, choose
bright, strong colors, and think, in effect, the more colors the better.
However, in this quasilogical stage, *realism* of color becomes more
important. To the question, "What makes these colors good?" typical
responses are:

Cause there's dogs that color and dresses that color.

Cause when you look at a real person like that you think that's what it
would look like.

Well, you know, it's just like if it wasn't a painting it would really look
like that.

Similarly, the conception of artistic ability, what it takes to paint
a good painting, covers such items as manual skill, perseverance in
getting it right, patience, hard work. Time is also frequently mentioned. It is assumed that the harder a painting is to do, the better it
is. This amounts to admiration for craftsmanship, which has often
been thought to be the beginning of aesthetic appreciation.

Q. Why would this painting be hard?
A. They'd have to try really hard to get the drawing right and it might take
    a month to draw one thing.   (Girl, 4th grade)

Q. What does it take to paint a painting like this?
A. It takes time and you really have to work at it.   (Boy, 2nd grade)

Q. Which do you think would be the hardest painting to paint?
A. The first (Renoir) because it would be hard to get the colors in it and it
    has a lot of details.   (Girl, 6th grade)

Q. Would the Renoir be harder or easier than the Klee?
A. Harder because it has more things in it and it's real. (Boy, 5th grade)

These cases illustrate Baldwin's contention that during the stage
of spontaneous aesthetic experience judgments about truth are an
integral part of the response. They are, however, used only semblantly. Judgments are made about representations as if they were
reality, but the child remains quite aware that they are not reality.
The spontaneous aesthetic experience is not a delusion, or illusion. It
is always experience of something "as if," and although the child
focuses on the object represented and not on the medium, he remains
aware that it is a representation. A good illustration is the fact that
most children have no difficulties with fantasy, such as is found in TV
animation or in comic book heroes and monsters. There is often a
curious mixture of the demand for realism with the acceptance of the
fantastic that I do not know how to describe in general. For example,
I have discussed with children how realistically the comic-book

figure *Hulk* is drawn, and found no demur over his wildly unrealistic characteristics. Baldwin himself speaks of "hobgoblins," about which nevertheless agreement can be sought.

On the other hand, although there is a sure awareness of the semblant character of these tests, the awareness is not a reflective but a spontaneous one. This means that the criteria being applied (e.g., realistic appearance) do not seem to be reflectively chosen; there is no thought that they need to be justified, but are taken as obvious. Moreover, though the judgment is taken to be one that others would agree with—and hence is "objective"—it is not considered so much a matter of individual judgment as of common acceptance. There is frequently felt to be no need to give reasons, because both the facts and the criteria can be taken for granted. Also, the kinds of criteria for different kinds of judgments are not distinguished. For example, scientific illustrations are judged in the same way that art drawings are judged. The scientific, the moral, and the aesthetic are not clearly distinguished as concerns, and so aesthetic judgments will be based on a mixture, or confusion, of different kinds of reasons. Getting clear about these differences requires raising them to reflection, and therefore, waits until the next level of aesthetic experience.

These remarks apply also to the other kind of test incorporated into spontaneous aesthetic experience—the practical or moral. The moral opinions of the child at this level are often the basis of judgments made within aesthetic experience, and constitute restrictions on what can be accepted aesthetically. This is most obvious in connection with narrative in literature and film. There is a demand for "goodies and baddies", i.e., a clear delineation between the heroes and the villains in moral terms. Moral ambiguity, especially on the part of the hero, is not well received. In addition, the demands for stereotyping go beyond the moral into a penumbra of personal attractiveness, from which the moral is not distinguished. Thus children's narrative heroes are usually good-looking, or strong, or unusually brave, or clever in some way, often in combination. The chief alternative to this is where the hero is a colorless character, designed largely for easy identification on the part of the reader; a good example would be Jim in *Treasure Island*.

These points, with respect to moral judgments, can also be illustrated from our research on children's responses to paintings. Again, we found two substages of what Baldwin has in mind. In the first, the child takes it for granted that paintings should be about pleasant and interesting things, and should avoid unpleasantness of all kinds. Concepts of pleasantness and unpleasantness are highly stereotyped. For example:

Q. Is this a good thing to paint a painting about?
A. Not that good.
Q. What do you think artists should paint about?
A. The ocean and trees and pretty things.   (Boy, 2nd grade)

Q. Is this the kind of thing you'd expect an artist to paint about?
A. No, cause I sometimes look at sad paintings and I get tears in my eyes, and I just want things to come out all right. I don't like sad things.
Q. Is it good to paint about things that are sad?
A. No, I like paintings to be nice and not about sad things. (Boy, 3rd grade)

At the second substage, the range of subject thought suitable expands to include sad, nostalgic, and unpleasant matters. However, violent, cruel, or tragic themes are still rejected. For example:

Q. Is this a good thing to paint about, a girl and a dog?
A. Yeah.
Q. Why?
A. Cause, I like animals.
Q. It's good to paint about animals?
A. Yeah.
Q. What if this were a sad painting about an animal, like a dog was hurt or something bad had happened to him? Would that be a good thing to paint about?
A. Yeah, cause it would show that dogs get hurt—it would show that animals get hurt.
Q. What if it were about something mean, like someone being mean to an animal?
A. I wouldn't like that.
Q. Would that be a good thing to paint about?
A. I don't think so.   (Boy, 5th grade)

Q. Is boxing the kind of subject that you would expect people to paint about?
A. No, because it's portraying violence and I don't think many people like that.   (Girl, 10th grade)

Q. Is this the kind of thing you'd expect an artist to paint about?
A. Sort of, but not this way, because people don't like to look at it. This is a sad picture, they look at it, not as something to relate to but they look at the parts all mangled, and people don't want to look at that. When parts of the body are missing people don't like to keep that in their mind. Most war pictures are painted about people who have just been shot and are laying on the ground, but this painting has people all in different pieces and it's not how most war paintings would be painted.
                                                             (Boy, 10th grade)

Levels of Idealization: Reflective Aesthetic Judgment

As we have already seen, the last level begins when the individual understands the self as the subject of its experience, and experience thereby becomes the object about which the subject can reflect. Previously one had been able to think about things and problems; now one can think about experience itself, and the concepts, feelings, and judgments which are part of it. Hence, one can become more aware of the differences between kinds of judgments, and the criteria that are relevant to them. One main result of this reflectivity is a release from the restrictions that the previous level imposed.

At the spontaneous level, judgments of truth and moral worth were incorporated into aesthetic judgments unreflectively, and the effect was restrictive. For example, elementary school children constructed a number of rules for judgment, including the rule of realism and rejected art works that did not conform. Similarly, they rejected certain subject matters on moral grounds. The new awareness of kinds of judgments means that these restrictions can be dropped where they are irrelevant, and there can be much more flexibility about criteria of excellence.

To illustrate, in our research we found a level where the demand for realism was dropped, except in cases where a painting seemed to require it. Otherwise, there was acceptance of various degrees of abstraction and distortion. There was a much greater awareness of a variety of styles of painting, of intentions of the artist, and of possible responses of the viewer. It was not that the idea of a "test for truth" was dropped; it was rather that the validity of multiple possible sets of criteria was acknowledged, and the question often became how to determine which set of criteria to apply. Some responses to Picasso's "Guernica" that seem to illustrate this development are:

Q. Would this be a better painting if it were more realistic?
A. I think it is better the way it is, abstract, or even more so, in a way. This relates to the total confusion of the situation.   (Boy, 12th grade)

Q. Would this be a better painting if it were more realistic?
A. No, I don't think so. If he's trying to show his feelings and if this is what his feelings are then this is the way the painting should be.
(Girl, 10th grade)

Q. Would this be a better painting if it were more realistic?
A. I don't think so, because photographs will capture action but I think the artist tried to go inside of the action, and I think a simple photograph or reproducing it on a painting just reduces the effect of what this tries to do.   (Boy, 12th grade)

The same thing is true of judgments of moral worth. They are dropped from aesthetic experience where they are inappropriate. Where they are not, they are understood as semblant judgments and apprehended as qualities of the work itself. Several of our older subjects, for example, responded to the felt quality of moral outrage at modern war in Picasso's "Guernica," though they did not always express this well. Their comments certainly contrast with the earlier rejection of the painting because its subject was unpleasant:

Q. Do you like this painting?
A. I like it because wars are sometimes necessary. I think there are other ways to solve things, I think since I was born I can remember war going on with one country or another and it is a fact and I would buy it because it represents it and the people.   (Girl, 12th grade)

Q, Is war the kind of subject that you would expect people to paint about?
A. I think war is a real life situation, war is one of the largest events in history. When they write about history books, one of the main things is war, which tells a lot about the whole world situation. It's not necessarily a good topic but one that many artists would be concerned with. (Boy, 12th grade)

Q. Is this the kind of thing you'd expect an artist to paint about?
Q. Yeah, for someone who has lived through an experience. I wouldn't expect someone who has read about it, but for someone who was in the town and for him to come out and to paint something like this, I wouldn't think him off his rocker because in an abstract way it's captured all the feelings and expressions and things that went on in that time. (Boy, 11th grade)

Another way of describing this change is to say that, because the nature of scientific and moral judgments is clearer, these judgments can be more easily distinguished from aesthetic judgments. Art comes to be seen as having its own purposes and concerns. This is no longer information giving nor edification, but the expression of emotion. Hence a much wider emotional range is acceptable. Various kinds of doubts and insufficiencies are allowed in one's heroes, and tragedy is possible. Similarly, there is greater openness to the art of other cultures and traditions, since one no longer confuses appreciating a work with an acceptance of whatever doctrines or attitudes it contains, as actually true or worthwhile.

One rather obvious omission in Baldwin's discussion of this level must be mentioned: the greater interest in the art form itself, understood as a sensory medium that can be worked with. Baldwin, as we have seen, stresses the ideational and feelingful aspects of organization in aesthetic objects, and the clarity regarding them that reflection brings. But the most basic and obvious sense of organization in the arts refers to the *medium*, the physical stuff the object is made from. In this connection too, we found a change. The medium is no longer "transparent," to be looked through in search of the subject matter. It is now understood as the proper focus of attention. A painting of a cabbage can be as significant as that of a king, and the difference is understood to be largely in the treatment of the medium. There is more interest in purely sensory matters; for example, colors are no longer stereotyped under their class names as reds, blues, browns, and so on. Textures are attended to; questions of arrangement are raised and alternative possibilities pondered. There is awareness of different styles, and a style comes to be seen as itself an achievement. There is a fascination with the question of what can be done with various media and an interest in experimenting with techniques. The result is greater attention to the actual individual character of the particular surface of the aesthetic object, and this change would loom large in a purely descriptive account of this last level.

The reason that Baldwin ignores this aspect of idealization is presumably that his interest, in *Thought and Things* and in *Genetic Theory of Reality*, is primarily to argue the case for pancalism. Hence he spends his time discussing the "logical and sentimental" judgments that get incorporated into the organization of aesthetic objects. But there is nothing in his discussion that prohibits the addition of this part of the development of idealization.

Levels of Immediacy

There may still be a question, however, regarding the notion of immediacy, which the reader will remember is Baldwin's fourth and last defining characteristic of the aesthetic. *How* can logical and practical judgments be incorporated into aesthetic experience? Judgments, Baldwin has said, are necessarily affairs of mediation; the aesthetic is necessarily immediate. Is there a contradiction here? Putting it another way, when the self-consciously judgmental level of reflection is reached, why is aesthetic experience not left behind, as a sort of primitive version of mentality? The answer is that just as one can, in any situation, move from immediate experience to mediated, so one can return from mediated experience to immediate. The return, however, is richer than the departure, because it can incorporate the judgments achieved in the second phase. The phenomenon is neither mysterious nor unusual. To give an oversimplified example suppose one parks at night in an empty parking lot behind a rundown hotel in the middle of Denver, as I did recently. One might be struck by the emptiness, the strange light, the silence. This is an initial, relatively unreflected upon, immediate experience. Then one looks around and makes some judgments: there are few cars, although it is a parking lot; the insufficient electric lighting creates the strange light; the character of a lot like this is determined by the economic conditions of poverty. These are discursive mediated propositions that make connections and lead attention from one item to another. Then one can move back to an immediate apprehension of the parking lot at night, to savor again its peculiar quality: its strong sense of loneliness, of being an alien, inhospitable terrain. This quality is again *had* immediately, without intervention of judgments, but this time more richly because of the context of judgments. The judgments can be retained not as discursive items of information, but as ingredient in the qualities appearing. The light *looks like* poor electric lighting; the area *looks* poor and socially deteriorated. Then these are no longer only items one knows but qualities one sees.

The example is a commonplace one, meant to make the point that this sort of thing happens all the time. Dewey called it the *funding* of immediate experience. The difficulty with the example is not so much its triviality, as that it seems to suggest that there is an initial immediate experience which is unfunded. This is never true, just because it is happening all the time. Even our simplest perceptions include a funding by previous judgments; for example, a stone looks heavy because we have experienced heavy objects before. We could say experience is never logically immediate, though it often is so phenomenally.

Baldwin is concerned with this feature of experience, because of his interest in the role of scientific and moral judgments in the reflective stage of aesthetic experience. He concludes that aesthetic experience can ingest judgments of all kinds to its own benefit and without losing its immediacy. Two kinds of art that could be used to illustrate his point are science fiction and religious poetry. In science fiction it is important that the situations be convincing; although they are explicitly not in the real world, they must at least seem to be in a possible world. Many kinds of overt calculation and judgment may go into writing such a novel, or reading it; they will be relevant to an appreciation where they can fund experience. That is to say, they will be helpful where they produce an immediate sense that the situation is scientifically possible. Scientific judgments then work to enhance the aesthetic object. It follows that the theories and calculations in such a novel do not have to be scientifically sound; they have only to appear to be so.

The same holds true of religious poetry. It may help aesthetically to make judgments concerning the poet's actual devoutness, or his religious orthodoxy; but it helps only if these judgments fund subsequent experience of the poem such that they make the poetry appear more devout. But, since it is only the appearance of devoutness that matters, such inquiries are not strictly necessary; the actual devoutness of the poet is not an aesthetic concern. Nor does the reader have to share the religious convictions of the poet in order to enjoy the poetry, as some have thought. For, to repeat, the actual truth or worth of the feelings expressed are not at issue, although the poem makes it appear so.

Another way—Baldwin's way—of saying this is to say that the judgment of scientific possibility, or of religious devoutness, as with the earlier judgments in the Denver car park, are taken semblantly, that is, as appearances. For anything that is immediate is necessarily semblant, and vice versa.

In terms of levels of immediacy, then, we may say that all levels of aesthetic experience are immediate. But at the reflective level, it is richer because it is *funded* with more judgments, and those judgments are themselves more articulated and differentiated. It is also clearer, because the results of reflection are retained without destroying the immediacy. With this account of the richness and clarity of immediacy at the reflective level, we come full circle to Baldwin's notion of pancalism, because, of course, it is just these characters that lead him to claim for aesthetic experience the most comprehensive grasp of reality.

IV

Let us close with a few words summarizing the main achievements of Baldwin's work in the area of aesthetic development and its chief limitations.

First, and most importantly, he manages to conceive in a relevant and fruitful way a general scheme for the aesthetic development of the individual. He does this by focusing on aesthetic experience, which his knowledge of the philosophical tradition in aesthetics enables him to construe appropriately. This focus allows him to pick out for attention the developmental thread that most matters in connection with the arts, i.e., what is aesthetic. In so doing it brings together the creative, appreciative, and judgmental activities, and also generalizes across the various art forms. The selection of this focus is of fundamental importance in his work, and it seems that its significance has not been fully digested by the cognitive developmental movement since his time. The fact that no one since his time has come up with a usable alternative cognitive developmental scheme in the area of the arts and the aesthetic is a witness to this. In short, Baldwin helps us conceive a way to fill an obvious lacuna in the scope of cognitive-developmental theories.

A second achievement is the way in which his notions of

aesthetic development are integrated into his general theory of the development of mind. The stages through which he believes the aesthetic experience of an individual passes are derived from both his observations of individuals (though he did not collect data systematically) and deduction from his general theory. Specifically, they are deduced from the levels of the development of the understanding of self, first the adualistic level, then the dualistic but not reflective level, lastly the dualistic and reflective level. There are not currently many candidates for the role of a theory which can integrate or relate together the various strands of cognitive development. Baldwin's success in establishing a relationship between stages of aesthetic experience and stages in the understanding of self lends further plausibility to the claim of his general theory to be integrative in a fashion much to be desired.

The third achievement is that Baldwin's account contains a fair amount of detail as to the character of the particular stages, and that what he says is not inconsistent with the data that have been collected since his time. One could even say that these data, such as they are, support his more general formulations. Beyond this, and perhaps more importantly, his work is detailed enough to serve as a guide to further empirical investigation. On the basis of his work, various specific hypotheses concerning the experience of particular arts could be derived and subjected to empirical test. This derivation would no doubt require some imagination on the part of the researcher if it is to be specific enough, but Baldwin's work abounds with suggestions. It could well serve as a springboard for further empirical work pursuing the aesthetic development of individuals, and it is to be hoped that it will do so.

As for the major limitations, three have been mentioned. The first is rather general and has to do with the brevity and difficulty of Baldwin's presentation. His writing is often tortuous and it is not always easy to figure out his intentions. He mixes technical and ordinary language without warning. Moreover, he does not take care to clarify concepts and does not use examples. Finally, his vocabulary is often very abstract; and he is allusive. His manner of writing makes it somewhat difficult for psychologists to use his ideas easily.

A second point is not unrelated. Baldwin has many different concerns in mind as he writes, and his attempt to discuss a number of different kinds of relationships as he goes results in a complex organization. Nowhere does he present as a separate story his account of the development of aesthetic experience, though it would seem very desirable to do so. In his work, this story is related to at least three other concerns: the parallels with scientific and moral development, the connections with the development of the self, and the argument for pancalism. This latter is the dominant purpose of *Thought and Things* and *Genetic Theory of Reality* as explained at the beginning of this discussion. The topic is unquestionably important, but, whatever its merits, its presence is not helpful to psychologists interested in the lesser question concerning the development of aesthetic experience.

Last, there are at least two omissions in Baldwin's account which a more empirically oriented approach reveals. Baldwin does not discuss the points at which the character and qualities of the medium itself become significant in aesthetic experience, and the growing importance of formal arrangements of the elements of the medium. This is such an important aspect of mature aesthetic experience that its developmental history cannot reasonably be ignored. The other omission is of relativism with respect to aesthetic judgments. Relativism is more common in connection with aesthetic than with moral judgments, and there are probably psychological (as well as cultural) reasons for this, having to do with the dominant role of feelings as reasons for judgments. I agree with Baldwin that it is not the end-point of development (otherwise, I have argued, we could not properly speak of cognitive development in this connection). But it seems too common and too important to be ignored in a developmental account.

Of course, these deficiencies are minor compared with the achievements. The omissions mentioned are probably due to Baldwin's concern with the argument for pancalism and this concern illustrates what seems to be his dominant and most fruitful characteristics, when compared with contemporary psychology: the enormous reach of his ambition, the wide range of his knowledge and concerns, and the constant interplay between psychological and philosophical considerations in his work. It seems as if these characteristics were necessary if a theory of aesthetic development was to be initiated, and a revival of them on the contemporary scene would be welcome.

REFERENCES

Baldwin, J.M. *Thought and things* (Vol. 3) London: Swan Sonnenschein, 1911.

Beardsley, M. *Aesthetics: Problems in the philosophy of criticism.* New York: Harcourt, Brace & World, 1958.

Botvin, G., & Sutton-Smith, B. The development of structural complexity in children's fantasy narratives. *Developmental Psychology*, 1977, *13*, 4, 377–388.

Collingwood, R.G. *The principles of art.* Oxford: Clarendon Press, 1938.

DiLeo, J.H. *Young children and their drawings.* New York: Brunner-Mazel, 1970.

Gardner, H. Style sensitivity in children. *Human Development,* 1972, *15,* 325–338.

Gardner, H. *The arts and human development.* New York: Wiley, 1973.

Gardner, H., Kircher, M., Winner, E., & Perkins, D. Children's metaphoric productions and preferences. *Journal of Child Language,* 1975, *2,* 1, 125–141.

Golomb, C. *Young children's sculpture and drawing.* Cambridge, Mass.: Harvard Univ. Press, 1974.

Kellogg, R. *Analyzing children's art.* Palo Alto, Calif.: National Press Books, 1969.

Langer, S. *Feeling and form.* New York: Scribner, 1953.

Lowenfeld, V., & Brittain, W.L. *Creative and mental growth.* New York: MacMillan, 1970.

Moore, B. A description of children's verbal responses to works of art in selected grades, one through twelve. *Studies in Art Education,* 1973, *14,* 3, 27–34.

Olson, D. *Cognitive development.* New York: Academic Press, 1970.

Parsons, M., Johnston, M., & Durham, R. A cognitive developmental approach to aesthetic experience. In R. Mosher (Ed.), *Adolescents' development and education.* Berkeley: McCutchan, 1979.

Prall, D.W. *Aesthetic judgment and aesthetic analysis.* New York: Appollo, 1967.

Werner, H., & Kaplan, B. *Symbol formation.* New York: Wiley, 1963.

Wimsatt, W.K., & Beardsley, M.C. The intentional fallacy. *Sewanee Review,* 1946, *54,* 468–488.

GLOSSARY OF
KEY TERMS

**Together with their Definitions, as Employed in
Genetic Logic; Accompanied by Illustrations and
Instances[1]**

affective: happening in consciousness but not referring to an object.

agenetic: not genetic (q.v.): not involving real growth or change. Ill.: mechanical action, such as the action and reaction of billiard balls.

aggregate: having the commonness (q.v.) of being entertained by different minds, apart from their consciousness of agreement: common meaning held in common.

autonomic: self-controlled, self-directed; subject to no authority or law foreign to itself. E.g.: the aesthetic interest, as accepting no external interference or control.

autotelic: having no end or purpose beyond or outside itself; not instrumental (q.v.). E.g.: "play for play's sake," "art for art's sake."

coefficient: the mark or character which differentiates one mental object from all others. E.g.: "memory coefficient," "coefficient of externality."

common: in some way involving entertainment by more than one mind. Cf., community. Ill.: public opinion is common.

community: (1) the property attaching to judgments and propositions (a), of being accepted by different persons in common ("community by whom"), and (b), of holding good for all persons in common whether accepted by them or not ("community for whom"); (2) the commonness of the acceptance (a) accorded to and (b) due to judgments and

---

[1] From Baldwin's *Genetic Theory of Reality* (1915), supplemented with some earlier terms from his *Elements of Psychology* (2nd edn., 1905). The reader may compare the definitions due to different writers, given in Baldwin's *Dictionary of Philosophy and Psychology* (1901–1905).

propositions. E.g.: (1) the force or import of a proposition as being (a) aggregate (q.v.), and (b) synnomic (q.v.); (2) any agreement in belief, whether (a) actual or (b) appropriate.

con-aggregate: pertaining to that which is held in common as being common; i.e., pertaining to an aggregate (q.v.) of syndoxic (q.v.) meanings of knowledge. Ill.: your and my common understanding of public opinion is con-aggregate.

content: that part of an entire meaning (q.v. sense 1) which is recognitive (q.v.). E.g.: the diamond ring as a recognized object (content), apart from its value, its use for adornment, etc. (intent, q.v.).

contrast-meaning: one of the terms of a contrast, which, together with the contrasted term, makes a whole single meaning (q.v.).

control: the limiting, directing, regulative (as against the constitutive) factor in the determination of anything. Ill.: the determination of a physical object has the external control afforded by sensations of resistance; that of ends, goods, objects of desire, has the inner control of appetite, interest, etc.

conversion: (1) the process of turning a mental object or state into another which it represents or stands for; (2) the resulting testing and confirmation of the former. Cases: my memory image of a house is converted into a percept when I revisit the actual house (primary conversion); it is converted into your memory or perception when I accept your report to confirm or revise my own (secondary or social conversion); it is converted into judgmental or other psychical terms when I reflect upon, criticize, or otherwise assimilate it to the body of my experience (tertiary or psychical conversion).

datum: that which is given without cooperation or process on the part of the mind. E.g.: a mental object considered as stripped of all meaning (q.v., sense *determination*: the formation of something, mental or physical, by all the factors which enter into it. E.g.: the (mental) plan of this book as conceived; or the book as a (physical) result.

dualism: a distinction between two contrasted classes, interpreted as two sorts of existence or reality. Cf., contrast-meaning. E.g.: the dualisms of "mind and body," "self and not-self," "subjective and objective."

eject (and *ejective*): another person's mind apprehended in terms of one's own.

empirical: belonging to, or derived from, the observation of events themselves; derived from experience.

form: that which sets a limit to a contort; that which is filled.

genetic: belonging to an origin or birth; showing real growth or change. E.g.: genetic series, genetic progression (q.v.).

immediate: present to consciousness without mediation (q.v.). Instance: bookkeeping as furthering the ends of business.

immediacy: the condition of being immediate (q.v.). Cases: (1) primitive immediacy: that of supposed simple sensation or pure feeling; (2) transcendent immediacy: that in which processes of mediation are fulfilled or completed. Cf., intuition; (3) synthetic immediacy: that in which the motives of different mediations are synthesized and reconciled, as in aesthetic contemplation, considered as uniting the true and the good.

individuation: the mental process of finding or treating something as a single thing. Ill.: the tree, perceived as a whole, including its leaves and the single leaf, taken as a separate thing, are in turn individuated.

inner: pertaining or belonging to the individual's consciousness. Instances: inner process, inner control, etc.

instrumental: serving as means (q.v.) or instrument to something else. Instance: knowledge used for practical ends (in the theory of instrumentalism, all knowledge is instrumental in this sense.)

intent: that part of an entire meaning (q.v.) which is selective (q.v.) over and above that part which is recognitive (q.v.). Ill.: a diamond ring has the intent of personal adornment besides its content (qv.) as a recognitive object.

intersubjective: subsisting between individual minds. Instance: social intercourse.

intuition: (1) the content of immediate apprehension; (2) the content of the higher immediacy (q.v. case 2) of fulfilled or completed process.

meaning: (1) any mental object with all its signification; (2) the signification (only) which attaches to a mental object, content, or datum (see these terms). Cf., intent. E.g., as in the phrases: (sense 1) "that idol is my meaning—what *I* mean," and (sense 2) "the idol means God—what *it* means."

means: that which serves as instrument, tool, or medium to something else. Cf., mediation. E.g.: money, the means of trade; bribery, the political means; "the end justifies the means."

mediation: the relation by which one mental content (object, idea, etc.) serves as medium or means to the presence or determination of another. Cf., conversion. Cases: the memory-image of a house mediates the perception of the actual house (cognitive mediation); the plan to take a walk mediates the excursion (active or practical mediation); the "middle term" of a syllogism mediates the conclusion (logical mediation, also cognitive in character); the intention to commit murder mediates the making of the bomb which in turn mediates the actual murder (voluntary mediation, also practical in character).

mode: any phase of existence, considered as being *sui generis*. Cases: in psychology, the (psychic) modes of self-consciousness, volition, thought; in objective science, the modes of vitality or life, consciousness or mind, community or social intercourse; in genetic theory, the (genetic) modes or stages of a genetic progression (q.v.).

motor: stimulating, or contributing to, movement.

object (mental): whatever the mind can or does apprehend, attend to, or think about. Ill.: in saying "I see the dog" and "I am thinking of nothing," I make "dog" and "nothing" equally my mental object.

objective: belonging to things considered as *objects* of consciousness.

ontological: pertaining to reality considered as independent of or as owing nothing to our apprehension; that is, as existing per se. Ill.: the "ontological point of view" assumes or posits such a reality.

pancalism: the theory according to which the aesthetic mode of being real, apprehended in the contemplation of the beautiful, is all-comprehensive and absolute. Ill.: in the contemplation and full enjoyment of an object as beautiful, what we realize includes all the aspects under which the object may be found really existent and of real value; as such, it is unrelated (not relative) to anything outside of itself.

postulation: the suggestion of something for acceptance, made without adequate grounds in fact or convincing logical proof. Ill.: the existence of the moral ideal may be postulated.

presumption (of reality): (1) the primitive and uncritical attitude of acceptance; (2) that which is so accepted. E.g.: the savage's credulity, the child's acceptance of the reality of persons and things. Synonym: reality-feeling.

presupposition: the admitted but unstated ground upon which something rests. Ill.: the statement "the sun will rise tomorrow" has the presupposition of the continued existence of the solar system.

practical: having reference to practice, utility, or value. E.g.: the practical interest and the practical life as contrasted with the theoretical.

pragmatelic: tending to or seeking practical ends. E.g.: the motives of gain, pleasure, utility, in contrast with those of knowledge.

pragmatic: pertaining to that which is practical in its relatively remote and objective consequences. E.g.: knowledge considered as leading to or issuing in practical results. Hence the theory which gives such an account of knowledge is called pragmatism.

private: peculiar to or possessed by one individual only. E.g.: dreams, immediate states of feeling.

progression: a genetic movement or process involving a series of stages or terms called genetic modes, which are qualitatively *sui generis*. Cf., mode. E.g.: the progression of self-consciousness, that of feeling.

project (and *projective*): a mental object at a stage of apprehension earlier than that at which the dualism of inner and outer is reached. Ill.: both physical objects and persons, as present to the infant's apprehension.

psychic (*-al*): belonging to the one person's immediate conscious process. Cf., psychological. Ill.: the psychic "point of view" is that of one's simple awareness of his own psychical or mental events.

psychological: belonging to the mind as made object of observation. Cf., psychic. Cases: (1) the observation or interpretation of one mind by another; (2) reflection upon one's own mental processes as if they were those of another; both represent the "psychological point of view."

psychonomic: pertaining to influences, forces, and conditions which limit, hem in, interfere with, or otherwise serve to control (q.v.) the mental. Instance: brain processes considered in relation to the mind.

public: having the commonness of being recognized by different minds as current or social. Cf., social meaning, under social. Instances: public opinion—that which is recognized by the individual as the common thought of the group; public meaning (e.g., the self)—that thought (e.g., of the self) which is common to all, and of which all recognize the common or social character.

reality-feeling: the primitive undisturbed sense of reality.

recognitive: (1) subject to recognition; hence, (2) belonging to the cognitive rather than to the conative or affective functions. Cf., meaning, sense (1). E.g.: of (1) a memory image subject to recognition; of (2) a statement of fact as embodying knowledge.

schema: a determination of mental content, by the imagination, as a proposal or suggestion. E.g.: "make-believe," semblant (q.v.) objects generally, as set up by the imagination.

schematize: to set up a schema (q.v.) of the imagination. E.g.: to suggest something playfully, or as an artistic combination, or as a proposed logical relation.

selective: (1) due to or determined by processes of preference, interest, choice; hence (2) belonging to the affective and active rather than to the cognitive functions. Cf., meaning. Ill.: (1) anything desired is a selective meaning; (2) interest is a selective function.

semblance: the character by reason of which an object is semblant (q.v.). Ill.: play has the semblance of reality.

semblant: set up consciously in the imagination as if real. E.g.: the "as-if" situations of play and art.

social: pertaining, referring, or belonging to two or more minds which sustain relations to one another. Instances: social intercourse—typified by the "speaker and hearer" relation; social meaning—common knowledge, in the sense of syndoxic (q.v.), recognized by all as common property; social situation—the body of relationships subsisting in a group.

socius: (1) the individual's thought of self as involving others; (2) the single self or person considered as involving others in the conditions of his thought. Ill.: the impossibility of having strictly private thought reveals the socius.

subjective: belonging to the subject, i.e., to consciousness itself.

syndoxic: having the commonness (q.v.) of being entertained by the thinker as common to himself and others.

synnomic: having the commonness (q.v.) of binding force upon all, in the mind of each. E.g.: truths and duties, held by one person to be equally true and binding for all.

syntelic: having the commonness attaching to ends or purposes entertained in common by different minds. Ill.: the common intention of different men to get rich.

teleological: (1) pertaining to which is intentional, volitional, end-seekng; hence (2) pertaining to that which develops by some inner impulse or motive, as if it were end-seeking. Ill.: (1) teleological process: such as the development of an interest; teleological meaning: such as an end held in view, or a system of such ends; (2) vital processes—in appearance tending to an end.

theoretical: having reference to knowledge, truth, or science. E.g.: the theoretical interest and life, in contrast with the practical (q.v.).

trans-subjective: apart from or foreign to all mental processes of apprehension, both individual and social. Cf. ontological. E.g.: the reference of knowledge to its object, as being isolated from all apprehension.

BIBLIOGRAPHY OF MATERIALS BY AND ABOUT JAMES MARK BALDWIN

A. Books by Baldwin

Handbook of psychology (2 vols.). New York: H. Holt, 1889–91. (Reprinted by A.M.S. Press, New York, 1976).

Elements of psychology. New York: H. Holt, 1893.

Mental development in the child and the race. New York: Macmillan, 1895. 3rd ed. 1906. (Reprinted by Darby Books, Darby, Pa., n.d.; and A.M. Kelley, Fairfield, N.J., 1966).

Social and ethical interpretations in mental development. New York and London: Macmillan, 1897. 5th ed. 1913. (Reprinted by Arno Press, New York, 1973; and Scholarly Reprints, New York, 1976).

The story of the mind. New York: Appleton, 1898. (Reprinted by A.M.S. Press, New York, 1976; and Scholarly Reprints, New York, 1976).

Development and evolution. New York: Macmillan, 1902. (Reprinted by A.M.S. Press, New York, 1976).

Fragments in philosophy and science. New York: Scribner, 1902. (Reprinted by A.M.S. Press, New York, 1976).

Dictionary of philosophy and psychology (3 vols. in 4; ed. by Baldwin). New York: Macmillan; 1901–1905. (Reprinted by Peter Smith, Gloucester, Mass., 1960).

Thought and Things or Genetic Logic (3 vols.). London: Swan Sonnenschein & Co., 1906–11. (Reprinted by Arno Press, New York, 1974; by A.M.S. Press, New York, 1976; and by Scholarly Reprints, New York, 1976).

Darwin and the humanities. Baltimore, Md.: Review Publ. Co., 1909. (Reprinted by A.M.S. Press, New York, 1976).

The individual and society, or psychology and sociology. Boston; R. Badger, The Gorham Press, 1911. (Reprinted by Arno Press, New York, 1973; and by A.M.S. Press, New York, 1976).

History of psychology (2 vols.). London: Watts, 1913. (Reprinted by A.M.S. Press, New York, 1976).

Genetic theory of reality. New York: Putnam, 1915. (Reprinted by Arno Press, New York, 1974; and by A.M.S. Press, New York, 1976).

The superstate and the eternal values. (Herbert Spencer Lecture). Oxford, 1916.

France and the war. New York: Appleton, 1916. (First published in *Sociological Review*, April, 1915, *8*, 65–80).

American neutrality, its cause and cure. New York: Putnam, 1916.

Paroles de guerre d'un Americain. Paris: Alcan, 1919. (Reprinted in *Between Two Wars*, Vol. 2).

Le mediat et l'immediat (E. Philippi, trans.). Paris: Alcan, 1921.

Between two wars, 1861–1921 (2 vols.). Boston: Stratford, 1926. (Reprinted by A.M.S. Press, New York, 1976).

B. Articles by Baldwin

[Trans.] German psychology of today. [Trans. from the 2nd French ed. of T.A. Ribot's *Psychologie Allemande contemporaire*]. New York: Charles Scribner's Sons, 1886.

Contemporary philosophy in France. *New Princeton Review,* 1887, *3* (1) 137–144. (In *Fragments in philosophy and science,* 359–371 [slightly altered].)

Postulates of physiological psychology. *Presbyterian Review,* 1887, *8,* 427–441. (In *Fragments in philosophy and science,* 139–158 [slightly altered].)

Review of *Elements of physiological psychology,* by G.T. Ladd (New York: Charles Scribner's, 1887). *Presbyterian Review,* 1887, *8* (32), 763–767.

Dream excitation. *Science,* 1888, 300, 216.

Review of *A study of religion, its sources and contents,* by J. Martineau (New York: Macmillan). *Presbyterian Review,* 1888, *9* (35), 507–509.

The idealism of Spinoza. *Presbyterian Review,* January, 1889, *10* (37), 65–76. (Also in *Fragments in philosophy and science,* 24–41 [slightly altered].)

Dr. Maudsley on the double brain. *Mind,* 1889, *14* (56), 545–550.

Review of *Principles of empirical or inductive logic,* by John Venn (New York: Macmillan). *Presbyterian and Reformed Review,* 1890, *1* (1), 168–170.

Recent discussions on materialism. *Presbyterian and Reformed Review,* 1890, *1* (3), 357–372. (Also in *Fragments in philosophy and science,* 42–61 [slightly altered].)

Origin of right or left-handedness. *Science,* 1890, *16* (408), 302–303.

Right-handedness and effort. *Science,* 1890, *16* (408), 302–303.

Psychology at the University of Toronto. *American Journal of Psychology,* 1890, *3* (2), 285–286.

Infant psychology. *Science,* 1890, *16,* (412), 351–353.

Review of *Witnesses to Christ: The Baldwin lectures,* by W. Clark (University of Michigan, 1887). *Presbyterian and Reformed Review,* 1891, *2* (5), 160–161.

Letter to the editor, *American Journal of Psychology,* 1891, *3* (4), 593.

Review of *James's Principles of psychology* (New York: H. Holt, 1890). *Educational Review,* 1891, *1* (4), 357–371. (Also in *Fragments in philosophy and science,* 371–389.)

Suggestion in infancy. *Science,* 1891, *17* (421), 113–117.

443

Review of *Introduction to philosophy*, by G.T. Ladd (New York: Charles Scribner's, 1891). *Presbyterian and Reformed Review*, 1891, *2* (7), 539-540.

Review of *Elements of logic*, by E. Constance Jones (New York: Scribner & Welford, 1891). *Presbyterian and Reformed Review*, 1891, *2* (7), 549-550.

The coefficient of external reality. *Mind*, 1891, *16*, 389-392. (Also in *Fragments in philosophy and science*, 232-238 [revised]).

Suggestion and will. Paper presented before the Second International Congress of Psychology, 1892. In *Proceedings of the International Congress of Experimental Psychology, Second Session*, London: Williams & Northgate, 1892, 49-56. Abstracted in: The origin of volition in childhood. *Science*, 1892, *20* (51), 286-287. (Also in *Fragments in philosophy and science*, 159-167 [slightly altered]).

Infants' movements. *Science*, 1892, *19* (466), 15-16.

Experiments on color-vision. *Mind*, 1892, *1* (1), 156-159. (Summaries of current French researches).

How does the concept arise from the precept? *Public School Journal*, 1892, *11* (6), 293-294.

The Psychological Laboratory in the University of Toronto. *Science*. 1892, *19*, 143-144.

Tracery imitation. *Nature*, 1892, *47* (1207), 149-150.

Among the psychologists of Paris. *Nation*, 1892, *55* (1413), 68.

With Bernheim at Nancy. *Nation*, 1892, *55* (1415), 101-103.

The International Congress of Experimental Psychology. *Nation*, 1892, *55* (1419), 182-184.

Feeling, belief, and judgment. *Mind*, 1892, *1*, 403-408. (Also in *Fragments in philosophy and science*, 239-247 [slightly altered]).

Action and volition. *American Journal of Psychology*, 1892, *5* (2), 272-277. (Summaries of current German and British researches).

The American Psychological Association. *Nation*, 1893, *56* (1437), 25.

New method in child psychology. *Science*, 1893, *21* (533), 213-214.

Review of Goldschneider, *Zur Physiologie und Pathologie der Handschrift*. *American Journal of Psychology*, 1893, *5* (3), 420-422.

Distance and color perception by infants. *Science*, 1893, *21* (534), 231-232.

Internal speech and song. *Philosophical Review*, 1893, *2*, 385-407.

J. Charcot and P. Janet: Abstracts of their papers. *American Journal of Psychology*, 1893, *5* (4), 549.

Review of articles by G.S. Fullerton and J. McK. Cattell. *American Journal of Psychology*, 1893, *5* (4), 549-550.

The Columbian Exposition. *Nation*, 1893, *57* (1478), 303-304.

Color perception: A correction. *Science*, 1893, *22* (544), 10.

Psychology. In *Johnson's Universal Cyclopaedia*, New York: A.J. Johnson & Co., 1893-1895, Vol. 6, 835-840, and 1897, 835-840.

Imitation: A chapter in the natural history of consciousness. *Mind*, 1894, *3* (9) 26-55. (Also in *Fragments in philosophy and science*, 168-209 [slightly altered]).

Review of books by G. Compayre and F. Tracy. *Psychological Review*, 1894, *1*, 182-184.

Philosophy: Its relation to life and education. *Presbyterian and Reformed Review*, 1894, *5* (17), 36-48. (Also in *Fragments in philosophy and science*, 1-23 [slightly altered]).

Personality-suggestion. *Psychological Review*, 1894, *1* (3), 274-279.

The origin of right-handedness. *Popular Science Monthly*, 1894, 44 (5), 606–615.

Psychology past and present. *Psychological Review*, 1894, 1 (4), 363–391. (Also in *Fragments in philosophy and science*, 77–137 [slightly altered]).

Review of F. Queyrat, *L'imagination et ses variétés chez l'enfant* (Paris: Alcan, 1893). *Psychological Review*, 1894, 1 (4), 428.

Review of C. van Norden, *The psychic factor* (New York: Appleton, 1894). *Psychological Review*, 1894, 1 (5), 534–535.

Review of W. Wallace, *Hegel's philosophy of mind* (Oxford: Clarendon Press, 1894). *Psychological Review*, 1894, 1 (5), 536–537.

The origin of emotional expression. *Psychological Review*, 1894, 1 (6), 610–623. (Also in *Fragments in philosophy and science*, 120–138 [slightly altered]).

Review of recent literature on the personal and social sense. *Psychological Review*, 1894, 1 (6), 646–652.

Bashfulness in children. Educational Review, 1894, 7 (5), 433–441.

(Ed.), Studies from the Princeton laboratory. *Psychological Review*, 1895, 2, 236–239.

(With W.J. Shaw). Memory for square size. *Psychological Review*, 1895, 2, 236–239.

The effect of size-contrast upon judgements of position in the retinal field. *Psychological Review*, 1895, 2, 244–258.

(With W.J. Shaw). Types of reaction. *Psychological Review*, 1895, 2, 259–273. (Also in *Fragments in philosophy and psychology*, 287–302 [slightly altered]).

The social sense. *Science*, 1895, 1, 236–237.

(With J.McK. Cattell). Consciousness and evolution. *Science*, 1895, 2, 219–223.

Differences in children, from the teacher's point of view. I, II. *Inland Educator*, 1895, 1, 6–11, 269–273.

Professor Watson on reality and time. *Psychological Review*, 1895, 2, 490–494.

The cosmic and the moral. *International Journal of Ethics*, 1895, 6, 93–97.

The origin of a "thing" and its nature. *Psychological Review*, 1895, 2, 551–573. (Also in *Princeton Contributions to Psychology*, 1896, 1, 105–127.)

Consciousness and evolution. Princeton Contributions to Psychology 1895–96, 1, 145–153.

Genetic studies. I, II. *Princeton Contributions to Psychology*, 1896, 1, 145–182.

The genius and his environment. *Popular Science Monthly*, 1896, 49, 312–320, 522–534.

Two scientific congresses. *Popular Science Monthly*, 1896, 50, 196–200.

Heredity and instinct. *Science* 1896, 3, 438–441, 558–561.

Physical and social heredity. *American Naturalist*, 1896, 30, 422–430.

A new factor in evolution. *American Naturalist*, 1896, 30, 441–451, 536–553.

(With W. Mills, F.A. Lucas, H.W. Elliott, C.L. Morgan, G.C. Buchanan). Instinct. *Science*, 1896, 3, 355, 409, 441, 482, 597, 669, 780, 900; 4, 728.

On criticisms of organic selection. *Science*, 1896, 4, 724–727.

The "type-theory" of reaction. *Mind*, 1896, 5, 81–90.

Review of recent literature on feeling. *Psychological Review*, 1896, 3, 211–218.

(With G.T. Ladd). Consciousness and evolution, *Psychological Review*, 1896, 3, 296–308.

Differences in pupils from the teacher's point of view. III, IV. *Inland Educator*, 1896, 2, 126–129, 232–235.

Introduction. In J.D. Sterrett, *The power of thought*. New York: Scribner's Sons, 1896.

Mr. Spencer's psychology. *American Naturalist*, 1897, *31*, 553–557.

(With L. Farrand and J.McK. Cattell). Notes on reaction types. *Psychological Review*, 1897, *4*, 297–299.

Determinate evolution. *Psychological Review*, 1897, *4*, 393–401. Also in *Princeton Contributions to Psychology*, 1897, *2*, 90–98.

Organic selection. *Nature*, 1897, *55*, 558. Also in *Science*, 1897, *5*, 634–636. German: Organische Selektion. *Biol. Centralbl.*, 1897, *17*, 385–387.

The psychology of social organization. *Psychological Review*, 1897, *4*, 482–515.

The genesis of social "interests." *Monist*, 1897, *7*, 340–357.

Determinate variation and organic selection. *Science*, 1897, *6*, 770–773.

Invention vs. imitation in children. *Inland Educator*, 1897, *5*, 58–62.

The genesis of the ethical self. *Philosophical Review*, 1897, *6*, 225–241.

President's address on selective thinking. *Princeton Contributions to Psychology*, 1897–1898, *2*, 145–154.

Preface to K. Groos, *The play of animals*. New York: Appleton, 1898.

On selective thinking. *Psychological Review*, 1898, *5*, 1–25. Also in *Princeton Contributions to Psychology*, 1898, *2*, 145–168.

(With F.W. Hutton & H.S. Williams). Isolation and selection. *Science*, 1898, *7*, 570–571, 637–640.

Language study. *Science*, 1898, *8*, 94–96.

(With J. Jastro and J.McK. Cattell). Physical and mental tests, *Psychological Review*, 1898, *5*, 172–178.

Social interpretations, *Psychological Review*, 1898, *5*, 213–217.

Child study. *Psychological Review*, 1898, *5*, 218–220.

Recent work in the Princeton psychological laboratory. *Scientific American, Supplement*, 1898, *45*, 18693–18696.

Recent biology. *Psychological Review*, 1898, *5*, 213–217.

Social Interpretations: A reply to Professor Dewey. *Philosophical Review*, 1898, *7*, 621–630.

(With J.McK. Cattell). The schedule for psychology of the International Catalogue. *Science*, 1899, *10*, 297–298.

Heredity and variation. *Nature*, 1899, 60, 591.

The social and the extra-social. *American Journal of Sociology*, 1899, *4*, 649–655.

The Royal Society Catalogue and psychology. *Nature*, 1900, *61*, 226–227.

Hemianopsia in migraine. *Science*, 1900, *11*, 713–714.

Psychology. *Universal Cyclopedia* (Vol. 9) New York, 1900. Pp. 363–391.

A scheme for classification for psychology. *Psychological Review*, 1901, *8*, 60–63.

Historical and educational report on psychology. In *Chicago World's Columbian Exposition, 1893, Report of the Committee on Awards, Special reports upon special subjects or groups (vol. 1)* Washington, D.C.: Gov. Printing Office, 1901, 357–404.

Preface to K. Groos, *The play of man* (E.L. Baldwin, trans.). New York: Appleton, 1901. Pp. ix + 412.

Notes on social psychology and other things. *Psychological Review*, 1902, *9*, 57–68, 185.

Dr. Bosanquet on "imitation." *Psychological Review*, 1902, *9* 597–603. Also in *Princeton Contributions to Psychology*, 1903, *3*, 45–52.

Mind and body from the genetic point of view. *Princeton Contributions to Psychology*, 1903, *3*, 21–43. Also in *Psychological Review*, 1903, *10*, 225–247.

Research in psychology: report to the Carnegie Institution of Washington. *Princeton Contributions to Psychology*, 1903, *4*, 1–34.

Dr. Bosanquet on imitation and selective thinking. *Psychological Review*, 1903, *10*, 51–63. Also in *Princeton Contributions to Psychology*, 1903, *3*, 53–67.

(With B. Bosanquet). Imitation and selective thinking. *Psychological Review*, 1903, *10*, 404–416. Also in *Princeton Contributions to Psychology*, 1904, *4*, 33–47.

The limits of pragmatism. *Psychological Review*, 1904, *11*, 30–60. Also in *Princeton Contributions to Psychology*, 1904, *4*, 33–47.

The genetic progression of psychic objects. *Psychological Review*, 1904, *11*, 216–221.

Sketch of the history of psychology. *Psychological Review*, 1905, *12*, 144–165.

Thought and language, *Psychological Review*, 1906, *13*, 181–204.

Introduction to experimental logic. *Psychological Review*, 1906, *13*, 388–395.

The history of psychology. In *Congress of Arts and Sciences*, 5, Boston: Houghton-Mifflin, 1906.

On truth. *Psychological Review* 1907, *14*, 264–287.

Comment on Prof. Moore's paper "Experience, habit, and attention." *Psychological Review*, 1907, *14*, 297–298.

Logical community and the difference of discernibles. *Psychological Review*, 1907, *14*, 395–402.

Genetic logic and theory of reality ("real logic"). *Psychological Bulletin*, 1908, *5*, 351–354.

Knowledge and imagination. *Psychological Review*, 1908, *15*, 181–196.

Motor processes and mental unity. *Journal of Philosophical Psychology*, 1909, *6*, 182–185.

The influence of Darwin on theory of knowledge and philosophy. *Psychological Review*, 1909, *16*, 207–218. (Reprinted in *Comparative Psychology*, *vol. 4: Darwinism*. Washington, D.C.: University Publications of America, 1977).

The springs of art. *Philosophical Review*, 1909, *18*, 281–298.

La memoire affective et l'art. *Revue Philosophique*, 1909, *67*, 449–460.

Discussion: Darwinism and logic: a reply to Professor Creighton. *Psychological Review*, 1909, *16*, 431–436. [Reprinted in *Thought and Things*, vol. 3, app. B].

La logique de l'action. *Revue de metaphysique et de morale*, 1910, *18*, 441–457, 776–794.

The basis of social solidarity. *American Journal of Sociology*, 1910, *15*, 817–831.

Psychology and philosophy. *American Yearbook*, 1910, *27*, 641–650. [Summarized in *Thought and Things*, vol. 3, app. C.]

La logique et la pratique. *Revue de metaphysique et de morale*, 1911, *19*, 211–236.

The religious interest. *Sociological Review*, 1913, *11*, 306–329.

French and American ideals. *Sociological Review*, 1913, *6*, 2, 97–116.

The development of animal psychology. *IXe Congress International de Zoologie*, 1914, 528–535.

Deferred imitation in West-African gray parrots. *IXe Congress International de Zoologie*, 1914, 536–537.

France and the war. *Sociological Review*, 1915, *8*, 65–80.

L'aboutissement de la médiation logique: l'intuition. *Revue de metaphysique et de morale*, 1922, *29*, 393–410.

James Mark Baldwin. In C. Murchison (Ed.), *The history of psychology in autobiography, vol. 1.* Worcester, Mass.: Clark Univ. Press, 1930; London, England: Oxford Univ. Press, 1930. (Reprinted by Russell & Russell, New York, 1961.)

C. Books and Articles Dealing with Baldwin's Work

Ormond, A.T. Review of Baldwin's *Handbook of psychology, vol. 1. Presbyterian and Reformed Review*, 1891, *2*, 543–544.

Bolton, T.L. Review of "Mental development in the child and the race." *American Journal of Psychology* 1895–1896, *7*, 142–145.

Nichols, H. Professor Baldwin's "New factor in evolution." *American Naturalist*, 1896, *30*, 697–710.

Höffding, H. Report to the Danish Academy. *Bulletin of the Royal Academy of Science and Letters of Denmark*, 1897, 7–17. (Reprinted in *Philosophical Review*, 1897.)

Dewey, J. Review of "Social and ethical interpretations." *Philosophical Review*, 1898, *7*, 398–409.

Dewey, J. Reply to Baldwin. *Philosophical Review*, 1898, *7*, 629–630.

Dewey J. "Social and ethical interpretations in mental development." *New World*, 1898, *7*, 504–522.

Tufts, J.H. Baldwin's "Social and ethical interpretations." *Psychological Review*, 1898, *5*, 313–321.

Havard, H., *Revue de metaphysique et morale*. 1899 (January).

Caldwell, W. "Social and ethical interpretations of mental development." 1899, *5*, 182–192.

Giddings, F.H. The psychology of society. *Science*, 1899, *9*, 16.

Abbott, A.H. Experimental psychology and the Laboratory in Toronto. *University of Toronto Monthly*, 1900, *1*, 85–89.

Elwood, C.A. The theory of imitation in social psychology. *American Journal of Sociology*, 1901, *6*, 721–741.

Ball, S. Current sociology. *Mind*, 1902, *10*, 145–171.

Bosanquet, B. & Grosse, E. Kunstwissenschaftliche Studien. *Mind*, 1901, *10*, 399–402.

Yerkes, R.M. Review of "Development and evolution." *American Naturalist*, 1903, *37*, 348–356.

Russell J.E. Review of "Thought and things." *Journal of Philosophy, Psychology and Scientific Methods*, 1906, *3*, 712–714.

Moore, A. "Thought and Things": Review. *Psychological Bulletin* 1907, *4*, 81–88.

Ellwood, C.A. *Sociology in its psychological aspects*. New York: Appleton, 1912.

Bristol, L.M. *Social adaptation*. Cambridge, Mass.: Harvard Univ. Press, 1915, 192–199, 304–312.

Brett, G.S. *A history of psychology*. New York: Macmillan, 1912–1921, *3*, 296–298.

Barnes, H.E. Some contributions of American psychology to modern social and political theory. *Sociological Review*, 1921, *13*, 204–227.

Giddings, F.H. *Studies in the theory of human society.* New York: Macmillan, 1922, 161–167.

Bogardus, E.S. *A history of social thought.* Los Angeles: Univ. of Southern California Press, 1922, 368–388.

Davies, A.E. The influence of biology on the development of modern psychology in America. *Psychological Review,* 1923, *30,* 164–171.

Piaget, J. Étude critique: "L'experience humaine et la causalité physique" de L. Brunschvicg. *Journal de Psychologie,* 1924, *21* (6), 586–607 (see especially 598–601).

Karpf, F.B. *American social psychology.* New York: McGraw-Hill, 1932, 269–291.

Obituary: James M. Baldwin, psychologist, dies. *New York Times,* 6, Nov. 9, 1934, p. 21.

Piaget, J., *The moral judgement of the child.* New York: Harcourt, 1932, 269–291.

Urban, W.M. James Mark Baldwin. *Psychological Review,* 1935, *42,* 303–306.

Ellwood, C.A. The social philosophy of James Mark Baldwin. *Journal of Social Philosophy,* 1936, *2,* 55–68.

Chavez, E.L. *3 Conferencias (sobre) la vida y la obra de 3 profesores ilustres de la Universidad Nacional de Mexico.* Mexico: Ediciones de la Universidad, 1937, 3–28.

Holmes, E.C. *Social philosophy and the social mind: A study of the genetic methods of J.M. Baldwin, G.H. Mead, and J.E. Boodin.* New York (privately printed), 1942, 5–21.

Jandy, E.C. *Charles Horton Cooley—His life and his social theory.* New York: Dryden Press, 1942, 98–102.

Sewny, V.D. The social theory of James Mark Baldwin. New York: King's Crown Press, 1945.

Simpson, G.G. The "Baldwin Effect." *Evolution,* 1953, *7,* 115–127.

White, F.N., & Smith, H.M. Some basic concepts pertaining to the "Baldwin Effect." *Turtox News,* 1956, *34,* 51–58.

Kohlberg, L. The development of modes of moral thinking and choice. Unpublished doctoral dissertation, University of Chicago, 1958.

Mayr, E., Behavior and systematics. In A. Roe & G.G. Simpson (Eds.), *Behavior and evolution.* New Haven: Yale Univ. Press, 1958.

Noble, D.W. *The paradox of progressive thought* [Chap. 4: James Mark Baldwin: the social psychology of the natural man]. Minneapolis: Univ. of Minnesota Press, 1958.

Martindale, D. *The nature and types of sociological theory.* Boston: Houghton-Mifflin, 1960, 313–317.

Dunn, L.C. "The American naturalist in American biology. *American Naturalist,* 1966, *100,* 481–492.

Becker, E. *The structure of evil.* New York: Free Press, 1968 (especially Chap. 6).

Kohlberg, L. Early education: a cognitive-developmental view. *Child Development,* 1968, *39,* 1013–1062.

Petras, J. Psychological antecedents of sociological theory in America: William James and James Mark Baldwin. *Journal of the History of the Behavioral Sciences,* 1968, *4,* 134–141.

Wilson, R.J. *In quest of community: Social philosophy in the United States, 1860-1920.* [Chap. 3: James Mark Baldwin: Conservator of moral community]. New York: John Wiley and Sons, 1968.

Kohlberg, L. Stage and sequence: The cognitive-developmental approach to moralization. In D. Goslin (Ed.), *Handbook of socialization theory and research.* Chicago: Rand McNally, 1969.

Krantz, D.L. The Baldwin-Titchener controversy. In D.L. Krantz (Ed.), *Schools of psychology,* New York: Appleton Century Crofts, 1969.

Braestrup, F.W. The evolutionary significance of learning. *Videnskabelige Meddelelser Dansk Naturhistorisk Forening,* 1971, *134,* 89–102.

Böhme, G. Der Streit zwischen Baldwin und Titchener über einfache Reaktionen. Unpublished manuscript, Max Planck Institut, Starnberg, Germany, 1973.

Mueller, R.H. The American era of James Mark Baldwin (1893–1903). Paper presented at the 81st Annual Meeting of the American Psychological Association, Montreal, August, 1973.

Broughton, J.M. The development of natural epistemology in the years 10–26. Unpublished doctoral dissertation, Harvard University, 1974.

Lysaght, T. Far worse than weeds: The philosophical and literary development of George Herbert, as interpreted according to the psychological theory of James Mark Baldwin. Unpublished honors thesis, Harvard University, 1974.

Mueller, R.H. The American era of James Mark Baldwin (1893–1903). Unpublished doctoral dissertation, University of New Hampshire, 1974.

Freeman-Moir, D.J. A sense of the general: The psychological epistemology of James Mark Baldwin. Unpublished doctoral dissertation, Harvard University, 1975.

Selman, R.L. Level of social perspective taking and the development of empathy in children: Speculations from a social-cognitive viewpoint. *Journal of Moral Education,* 1975, *5,* (1), 35–43.

Mueller, R.H. A chapter in the history of the relationship between psychology and sociology in America: James Mark Baldwin. *Journal of the History of Behavioral Sciences,* 1976, *12,* 240–253.

Phillips, S. Psychological antecedents to Piagetian concepts. *Psychologia,* 1977, *20,* 1–14.

Ross, B.M., & Kerst, S.M. Developmental memory theories: Baldwin and Piaget. In H.W. Reese and L. Lipsitt (Eds.), *Advances in child development and behavior (vol. 11).* New York: Academic Press, 1977.

Woodward, W.R. Lotze, the self, and American psychology. *Annals of the New York Academy of Sciences,* 1977, *291,* 168–177.

Cahan, E. The comparative historical fates of James Mark Baldwin and Jean Piaget. Unpublished honors thesis, Harvard/Radcliffe Colleges, 1978.

Piaget, J. *Behavior and Evolution.* New York: Pantheon, 1978.

Russell, J., *The acquisition of knowledge.* New York: St. Martin's Press, 1978.

Woodward, W.R. William James' psychology of will: Its revolutionary impact on American psychology. Paper presented at Annual Meeting of Cheiron, the International Society for the History of the Behavioral and Social Sciences, Wellesley, Mass., June, 1978.

Pauly, P.J. Psychology at Hopkins: Its rise and fall and rise and fall and . . . *Johns Hopkins Magazine,* 1979, *30* (6), 36–41.

Russell, J. The status of genetic epistemology. *Journal of the Theory of Social Behavior,* 1979, *9,* 14–26.

Wetmore, K. The early career of James Mark Baldwin. Unpublished manuscript, Peabody Museum, Harvard University, 1979.

Cairns, R.B. Developmental theory before Piaget: The remarkable contributions of James Mark Baldwin. *Contemporary Psychology,* 1980, *25* (6), 438–440.

Hoff, T. The appointment of James Mark Baldwin to the University of Toronto in 1889. Unpublished dissertation, Carleton University, Ottawa, Canada, 1980.

Rieber, R.W. Wundt and the Americans. In R.W. Rieber (Ed.), *Wilhelm Wundt: The making of an experimental psychology*. New York: Columbia Univ. Press, 1980.

Russell, J. Baldwin, Hegel and the dialectic of personal growth. Paper presented at Annual Conference of the British Psychological Society, Aberdeen, Scotland, March 1980.

Broughton, J.M. The genetic psychology of James Mark Baldwin. *American Psychologist*, 1981, *36*(4), 396–407.

Cairns, R.B. Self reflections. *Merrill-Palmer Quarterly*, in press.

NAME INDEX

Page numbers in *italics* indicate where complete references are listed, and 'n' indicates footnote.

A

Allport, F., 3
Anker, P., 62n, *79*
Arendt, H., 211, *217*
Ashby, W. R., 88, *96*
Ausubel, D., 315, 317-319, *324*

B

Bain, A., 124, 131-135, 145, 147, *167*, 305
Bakan, M., 227, *275*
Bales, R. F., 216, *218*
Bandura, A., 383, *386*
Bateson, W., 56-58
Beardsley, M. C., 398, 403n, 417, 418, *432*, *433*
Becker, E., 213, *217*
Bellah, R., 335, 336, *386*
Bentham, J., 125n
Berger, P. L., 335, *386*
Bergson, H., 41, 81, 331
Berkowitz, L., 323, *324*
Berlin, I., 3
Bertalanffy, L., *78*, 118-119, *121*
Bever, T., 69, *78*
Blachowicz, J. A., 119, 120, *121*
Boring, E. G., 42, *44*, 89, *96*
Bosanquet, B., 38
Botkin, P. T., *209*
Botvin, G., 393, *432*
Bovet, M., 231, *276*, 301

C

Cahan, E., 4, *8*
Campbell, D. T., 4, 7, 49, 88, 94, *96*, *97*, 98, 99, 101, 103, 106, 107, 109, 111-120, *121*
Carnap, R., *209*
Carpenter, W. B., 18, *44*
Cassirer, E., 259, 263, 265, 272, *275*, 322
Cattell, R. B., 3, *8*, 13n, 14n, 38
Chomsky, N., 5, 69, 70, 71, *78*
Claparède, E., 41, 42
Colby, A., *209*, *217*
Collingwood, R. G., 166, 400, 401, 403n, *432*
Condillac, É. B. de, 23
Cooley, G. H., 87, 213

Bower, T. G. R., 69, *78*
Boyd, D., 215n, *217*
Bradley, F. H., 310-311, *324*
Braestrup, F. W., 33n, 35n, 44
Brentano, F., 125
Brittain, W. L., 393, *433*
Broughton, J. M., 5n, 6, *8*, 213-216, *217*, 219, 230, 232, 241n, 247, 258, 271, 272, *275*, 281, 285, 322, 332, 405
Brown, N. O., 256, *275*
Bruner, J., 5
Brunschvicg, L., 81
Bryan, W.L., 13n
Buck-Morss, S., 5n, *8*
Buffon, G. de, 89

451

SUBJECT INDEX

CPSIA information can be obtained at www.ICGtesting.com
Printed in the USA
LVOW040847240113

317010LV00006B/62/P